Nuffield Co-ordinated

TEACHERS' GUIDE

Published for the Nuffield–Chelsea Curriculum Trust
by Longman Group UK Limited

General Editors,
Nuffield Co-ordinated Sciences
Geoffrey Dorling
Andrew Hunt
Grace Monger

Authors of this book
Geoffrey Dorling
Andrew Hunt
Neil R. Ingram
Grace Monger

Practical evaluators
Mark Ellse
Roger Norris

Consultative Committee,
Nuffield Co-ordinated Sciences
Malcolm Frazer, Chairman
P.J. Black
A.M. Dempsey
Geoffrey Dorling
Andrew Hunt
Neil R. Ingram
W.J. Kirkham
John Lewis
Grace Monger
Elizabeth Passmore
K. Pinder
Beta Schofield

The Nuffield–Chelsea Curriculum Trust acknowledge their debt to the many contributors to earlier Nuffield Schemes.

Contributors and advisers, Biology
D.R.B. Barrett
Barbara Case
Elizabeth Fenwick
Peter Openshaw
J. Parkyn
John Peters
Pamela Rivaz
Tim Turvey
Graham Walters
John Wray

Contributors and advisers, Chemistry
David Barlex
T.P. Borrows
Tim Brosnan
A.M. Dempsey
John Groves
Roland Jackson
Roger Norris
Pamela Rivaz
Lindsay Taylor
A.S. Travis

Contributors and advisers, Physics
Mark Ellse
Alan Boyle
Iain Hall
Philip Poole
Pamela Rivaz
David Tawney
E.J. Wenham

Longman Group UK Limited
Longman House, Burnt Mill, Harlow, Essex CM20 2JE, England and
Associated Companies throughout the World.

First published 1988
Copyright © The Nuffield-Chelsea Curriculum Trust 1988

Illustrations by Hardlines
Cover illustration by Plus 2 Design

Filmset in Times Roman
Printed in Great Britain
by Butler & Tanner Ltd., Frome and London

ISBN 0 582 04250 X

Contents

Physics 273

Foreword

The publication of Nuffield Co-ordinated Sciences marks an important step in the work of the Nuffield-Chelsea Curriculum Trust. Since the publication of Revised Nuffield Biology, Revised Nuffield Chemistry, Revised Nuffield Physics and the Nuffield Science 13 to 16 integrated science modules (the Nuffield courses now being used by schools for 13- to 16-year olds) significant changes have taken place in the demands of society – and the examination boards and groups – on the work of teachers and pupils in the science classroom.

First, the GCSE has given explicit expression to the growing wish among scientists and science educators that children of all ages should be taught (and, ultimately, examined) about the processes and skills of science as well as about the knowledge content. It has also given official endorsement to the need to teach children that the work of science is done in the context of our society: of technology, of industry and of our environment. Secondly, the Secretary of State's policy statement "Science 5–16" has set down the requirement for schools to provide courses of broad, balanced science for all pupils in 20 per cent of curriculum time. That policy commands broad support – most importantly from the Association for Science Education, the Secondary Science Curriculum Review and the Royal Society. Thirdly, the Secondary Examinations Council has published its National Criteria for syllabuses entitled "The sciences: double award" leading to double certificates in science.

The Trust has welcomed all these developments, in the belief that many of the underlying aims correspond with the aims consistently pursued in Nuffield science materials over twenty years: to teach young people the reality of science through enquiry, experimentation and investigation as much as by the transmission and testing of unchallengeable facts or formulae.

The responses to what society and examiners now require have been various. In this course the Trust is offering a way forward for the large number of science teachers who would like to carry the best elements of the three separate sciences over into a course which closely links the ideas of all three; which can provide for the whole range of pupils in the 20 per cent of time available; and which can satisfy the GCSE criteria for the double award in the sciences.

The Trust is conscious of its debt to many groups and individuals for their advice, support and devoted work. First, to the General Editors of the project, Geoffrey Dorling, Andrew Hunt, and Grace Monger, who wove a multitude of strands into intellectual cohesion, and themselves wrote the final drafts of most of the material. Then to those whose thought and guidance helped to create the project: the Consultative Committee, with its energetic and enthusiastic Chairman, Professor Malcolm Frazer, and its expert members embracing the Inspectorate, the Secondary Examinations Council, the Secondary Science Curriculum Review, educators and scientists from the Universities, science advisers and, most important, science teachers; the many teachers whose response to a questionnaire helped determine the direction and content of the course; and to Professor Paul Black, the Trust's academic adviser.

I am happy to record our thanks, also, to the many teachers and educators who wrote draft material for the course. Among them I record a special debt to Tim Turvey, who did much additional work on some of the worksheets, and to Dr Neil Ingram for invaluable work in preparing our draft GCSE examination syllabus submission.

New though this course is, it has nevertheless drawn on many of the pioneering ideas of its Nuffield precursors, and I am happy to record our debt to all those who created our earlier courses.

Finally, and with great pleasure, I must thank all those in the Trust's office who have worked to let the materials see the light of day in worthy form – William Anderson and his successor as Publications Manager Dieter Pevsner, with Catherine Blackie, Sarah Codrington, Sheila Corr, Philip Ellaway, Frank Kitson, Carl Newell, Deborah Williams and Mary de Zouche – and, finally, Andrew Ransom and his colleagues at Longman, who have sustained the project with a warmth of commitment and support far beyond the norm.

K.W. Keohane
Chairman, The Nuffield-Chelsea Curriculum Trust

General introduction

GENERAL INTRODUCTION

Chapter 1   About Nuffield Co-ordinated Sciences

Intentions and strategy

Nuffield Co-ordinated Sciences has been developed and written in response to a number of new challenges to science teachers in secondary schools.

These challenges are embodied in the DES publication *Science 5–16: A statement of policy*. The statement suggests that pupils should spend one-fifth of their time in school studying science and that they should receive, in that time, a scientific education that is both broad and balanced.

The old forms of separate-science teaching are not ideally suited to this new aim, since one-fifth of curriculum time allows children to learn only two of the three sciences, and this can hardly be said to pass the "broad and balanced" test.

One solution is the integrated science approach – as in the Nuffield Science 13 to 16 modular scheme already in use in many schools.

Nuffield Co-ordinated Sciences is a new and different solution, for the many teachers who believe that there is great merit in preserving the separate identities of biology, chemistry and physics. The difference lies in limiting the knowledge content of each subject so that all the topics will fit into the available time. In addition, the three strands – of biology, chemistry and physics – are linked and interrelated throughout the publications as described in Chapter 2 of this *Guide*.

There is now wide support for the principles that science courses should draw extensively on the everyday experience of the pupils and that all courses should achieve a balance between the acquisition of knowledge and the development of scientific skills and processes.

We have responded to these expectations in a number of ways. We have tried to ensure that all the material will have immediate significance to pupils, both in terms of its intrinsic interest and by being manifestly connected to the real, everyday world. We have seen to it that the science is presented in a context – within a practical problem, for example, or in relation to a real-life activity.

We have studied the findings of the Assessment of Performance Unit (APU) and have adopted their categories of performance as a basis for making sure that the course includes a balanced coverage of a range of practical skills.

The Nuffield context

The authors of the course acknowledge their double debt to existing Nuffield courses. They have drawn on them for teaching ideas. They have also relied heavily on the experience of teachers who have taught the courses to evaluate the draft materials and judge their appropriateness as part of a scheme of science for all.

Nuffield Co-ordinated Sciences has been deliberately designed as a distinct alternative to Nuffield Science 13 to 16 to give schools a choice. Nuffield Co-ordinated Sciences concentrates on Biology, Physics and Chemistry while Nuffield Science 13 to 16 incorporates a wider range of sciences. The two courses overlap and we have used the "Further information" section in the later chapters of this *Guide* to point out those parts of Nuffield Science 13 to 16 which might be useful in the context of Nuffield Co-ordinated Sciences.

We started by developing a programme for years 4 and 5 in secondary schools to make the examination course available as soon as possible. By the time that this *Guide* is published we will have made substantial progress towards extending the scheme to cover year 3. The year 3 publications will make it possible either to continue with an integrated approach from years 1 and 2, or to embark on co-ordinated sciences in preparation for year 4. The publications will consist of a single book for the pupils together with a set of copyright-waived worksheets.

Nuffield science courses

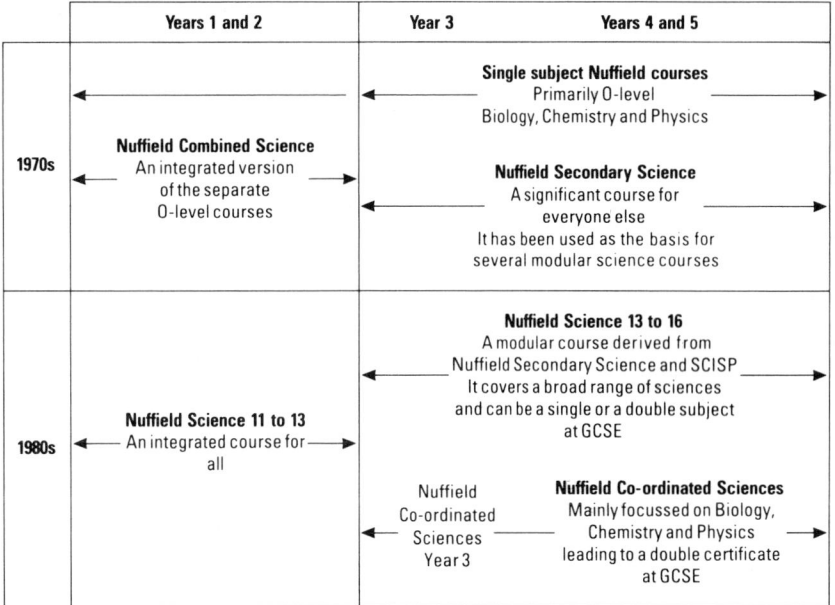

	Years 1 and 2	Year 3	Years 4 and 5
1970s	**Nuffield Combined Science** An integrated version of the separate O-level courses		**Single subject Nuffield courses** Primarily O-level Biology, Chemistry and Physics **Nuffield Secondary Science** A significant course for everyone else It has been used as the basis for several modular science courses
1980s	**Nuffield Science 11 to 13** An integrated course for all	Nuffield Co-ordinated Sciences Year 3	**Nuffield Science 13 to 16** A modular course derived from Nuffield Secondary Science and SCISP It covers a broad range of sciences and can be a single or a double subject at GCSE **Nuffield Co-ordinated Sciences** Mainly focussed on Biology, Chemistry and Physics leading to a double certificate at GCSE

Significance

We have been influenced by the "significance test" which was used to select topics for study in the Nuffield Secondary Science course. The authors of that course believed that the science studied should:

- have immediate significance for the pupils in terms of its intrinsic interest
- be concerned with the real adult world.

The second aspect of significance can carry science beyond its usual boundaries. In the real world science does not exist in isolation from society, and social and moral problems can arise in the course of any scientific study.

Significance is also stressed by giving emphasis to the pupils' own experimental work, the spirit being one of investigating problems which are seen as real by them.

Teaching science in terms of significance means that we must be continually aware of the everyday lives of our pupils and the activities they are involved in, whether it be sport, shopping, running the home, repairing cars, watching television, or whatever happens to be the latest fashion. We must continually relate what is happening in the laboratory to real life situations.

We have also tried to emphasize the relevance of the topics included in the course by giving attention to the applications and issues involved in the interaction of science and technology with society. We have been influenced by the Science and Technology in Society (SATIS) project of the Association for Science Education and have incorporated a number of SATIS units into our scheme.

Contexts

The syllabus for Nuffield Co-ordinated Sciences emphasizes the importance we attach to making the course seem significant to the pupils. Each topic is placed in context. Some of the contexts relate to the individual person; others are social, historical, environmental and industrial.

One of the advantages of a co-ordinated sciences course is that the contexts can be chosen to suit the subject, so long as a balance is maintained over the course as a whole.

GENERAL INTRODUCTION

The work of famous scientists

We have tried to encourage pupils to reflect on the nature of science and the status of scientific ideas. We believe that pupils should meet the idea that scientific theories are not immutable but that they are subject to change. In Chapter **P**10, for example, pupils are asked to evaluate two alternative theories.

We have tried to cater for pupils who in the past may have dropped science subjects at the earliest opportunity but who will now find themselves taking a core science course. We hope that by putting some of the science in its historical context we will help pupils to see that science has human and cultural aspects which they can relate to their other interests. The work of men and women scientists and technologists is described in each of the three books.

Science and industry

We have tried to respond to the demand that schools should put across more positive images of industry and commerce. Traditional descriptions of industrial processes in textbooks have generally been impersonal and lacking in intellectual challenge. They make it seem as if all the problems involved in carrying out a process have been solved by working out the scientific principles involved.

A number of industrial processes feature in the Chemistry part of the course. As far as possible these accounts illustrate the types of jobs which people do, their responsibilities and the problems they have to tackle. They also illustrate the need for team work and the way in which people of different disciplines work together to solve technical problems. We received much help from a number of companies in preparing up-to-date accounts of these topics.

Environmental science

Figure 4 (on page 12) shows that there is a strong theme of environmental science running through the course. Environmental topics provide opportunities for pupils to discuss problems for which there is no definite right answer. We have been concerned that such debates should be based on scientific knowledge and understanding of the issues.

Earth science does not feature as a separate subject in Nuffield Co-ordinated Sciences but we have tried to incorporate a number of important earth-science themes into the programme.

Differentiation

We have set out to devise a double subject science course which can be interpreted appropriately with the whole GCSE ability range. This has to mean that there is more material in the texts and in the worksheets than any one girl or boy can be expected to undertake. Parts of the texts will seem too advanced for some while other parts will seem too simple for others. We have indicated our approach to differentiation under the heading "Suggested routes" in the later chapters of this *Guide*. In Chemistry and Biology, the more difficult route is shown on the righthand side of the flow diagrams; the easier route is on the left. In Physics, all pupils follow the unlabelled route; where differentiation is intended, alternative routes are labelled "faster" and "slower".

The sections headed "Purposes" also help to indicate how we have built in differentiation in terms of the knowledge and understanding required if pupils are to gain the top GCSE grades.

We have kept in mind these words from the DES Policy Statement:

"The science which is provided for lower-attaining pupils in years 4 and 5 should not be different in kind from that provided for average and more able pupils; it should however be differentiated in treatment."

There can be no substitute for the imaginative teacher who can interpret a course to his or her pupils. We recognize that some boys and girls will need considerable guidance when working from the pupils' texts. The details of our strategies for differentiation in Biology, Chemistry and Physics are discussed in more detail in later chapters of this *Guide* (see pages 23, 159 and 275).

Strategies

Figure 1 (on page 7) shows the main topics in each of the three books. In Biology and Chemistry the topics and chapters are published in an order which might be adopted as a teaching sequence. In Physics the content is arranged in such a way that each topic is revisited a number of times during the course.

We believe that learning from the written word should be an important feature of a science course. We have been influenced by the Schools Council Publication *Reading for learning in the sciences* by Florence Davies and Terry Greene (Oliver and Boyd, 1984). This book explains that in science books there are various types of text which pupils have to learn to deal with. Pupils need support and direction from teachers so that they can become effective readers. Active reading can be a group exercise which helps pupils to increase their success in learning from science texts.

We hope that our use of "commentary text" will help pupils to understand the purpose of what they are being expected to do. Commentary text is included to make pupils aware of the links between the sciences; it gives hints about the ways in which the various sections of the books should be tackled; and it gives some indication of the levels of differentiation.

In an attempt to develop the range of skills and processes which help to make up science, the pupils are often asked, in the pupils' books, to undertake a variety of tasks. There is clearly not time for a pupil to practise the full range of skills in any one topic. The choice of skill or process developed in a particular context has been based on the experience of the teachers who advised the editors during the writing of the material.

The pupils' books include two types of questions. One type is designed to set up a dialogue between the authors and the pupils. These questions have to be thought about while reading the text. The other type of question is intended as an accompaniment to the text. Questions of the second kind do not have to be looked at during a first reading.

Instructions for practical activities are not given in the main text. We hope that this makes it easier to adapt the course to the needs and interests of the pupils.

Interdisciplinary inquiries

We hope that teachers will want to include interdisciplinary activities as a feature of the Nuffield Co-ordinated Sciences programme. These may be of two kinds:

- case studies which give pupils an awareness of the importance of interdisciplinary approaches to tackling technological problems;
- practical investigations which require pupils to draw on their knowledge and skills to tackle a problem which cuts across the boundaries of the separate sciences.

Case studies

The SATIS publications include units which illustrate an interdisciplinary approach to technological problems. Pupils working on these units will have to draw on their knowledge of more than one science. Examples include:

110 "Hilltop – an agricultural problem"
204 "Using radioactivity"
304 and 305 "A medicine to control Bilharzia – parts 1 and 2"
404 "How would you survive?"
506 "Materials for life – new parts for old"
508 "Risks"
802 "Hypothermia"
805 "The search for the magic bullet"
906 "IT in greenhouses"
1004 "Lavender"

Interdisciplinary investigations

The course provides opportunities for pupils to plan and carry out their own investigations. The publications include suggestions but these are not mandatory, so we hope that in time teachers will find examples of problems to investigate which help to illustrate the fact that many real problems are interdisciplinary.

Timing

There are many different patterns for school timetables. So we have decided to give our timings in 35 to 40 minute periods assuming that there are 8 periods in a 40 period week for double-subject science in years 4 and 5. This represents 20 per cent of curriculum time as recommended in the DES Policy Statement *Science 5–16*.

We have tried to ensure that the course can be taught in about 51 weeks over two years. This allows for field trips, school exams and other events which disrupt the normal timetable.

Our timings are based on 3×135 periods for covering the basic course in the three sciences. In addition, time will be needed for such things as end of topic tests, and revision.

We think that teachers have a right to expect that a published scheme is workable. In an attempt to ensure this we have included detailed teaching routes for each chapter broken down into single, or double, period units. These are not meant to be followed slavishly, but they will give a sense of the relative emphasis to be given to each part of the course.

Science departments will have to translate the timings into a form appropriate to the school timetable. They will also have to find a way of dividing the available time between the three subjects. We imagine that in many schools the course will be taught by three teachers, but this is not the only possible plan. It could be taught by two, or even by one science teacher in certain circumstances.

We expect that in most schools there will be well over 51 weeks for the course so there is some allowance for the fact that it always takes longer to tackle a course than the authors expect. However, we hope that even so there will be time for extra investigations including interdisciplinary inquiries.

Chapter 2   Co-ordination issues

Introduction

Co-ordination of the content and development of the separate sciences is the feature that distinguishes this course from independent, self-supporting courses in Biology, Chemistry and Physics on the one hand and Integrated Science courses on the other.

There are two aspects to co-ordination. First it is a process that has taken place in devising and writing the course. Secondly it is an essential process that takes place within a Science Department teaching this course.

Co-ordination within the course

Co-ordination in the planning and writing of the course has taken place in three ways. First there is co-ordination of content – what is developed in one science is taken up in another. Secondly, there is a co-ordination of ideas. Ideas that are common to two or more sciences are developed according to a common policy. An obvious example of a concept common to all the sciences is that of energy. The way that has been treated is detailed below. Lastly, there is a co-ordination of strategy. All three sciences are presented to the pupil in a similar way.

Co-ordination of content

Figure 1 shows suggested pathways through the work of all three sciences, laid

Sequence of topics

Biology	Chemistry	Physics
• What's what?	• Petrochemicals	• Introduction
• Many forms of life		• Building bridges successfully
• Light means life	• Chemicals from plants	• Cooking food quickly
	• Chemicals and rocks	• Motion
• How do animals feed?		
• The gut as a food processor		• Controlling motion
• Diet and good health	• Materials and structures	• Machines and engines
• The breath of life		
		• Keeping yourself warm
• Transport round the organism	• Glasses and ceramics	• Ideas in physics
• Keeping going	• Metals and alloys	
• Skeletons and muscles	• Polymers	• Using electricity
• Detecting changes	• Foams, emulsions, sols and gels	• Energy and electricity
• Keeping things under control	• Keeping clean	• Fibre optics and noise
• Making sense of an environment		• Making waves
• The webs of life	• Dyes and dyeing	• Making use of waves
• Salts and cycles		• Crashes and bangs
• Staying alive	• Chemicals in the medicine cupboard	
• Farms, factories and the environment	• Fuels and fires	• Rising and falling
• To destroy or to conserve?		• Making use of electricity
• Living things multiply	• Batteries	• Radioactivity
• People are different	• Soil	
		• Energy where it is needed
• Growing up	• Fertilizers	• Waste not, want not?
• Handing on to the next generation	• The Periodic Table	• Making pictures with electricity
• Changing with time	• Atoms and bonding	• Control
		• Communication

Figure 1

out side by side. The spacing between each topic is proportional to the suggested time allowance. In this way it can be seen how the content of one science is related in time to the content of another. There are two aspects to this.

First, it shows up some helpful concurrent links that can be made between the sciences. It can be seen, for example, that work on chemicals from plants, in Chemistry, starts just after corresponding work on photosynthesis in Biology. At a time when the work in Physics is concerned with the flow of electric currents, work in Chemistry is concerned with more general properties of metals. Human influence on the environment is explored in Biology at the same time that radioactivity (with its obvious social implications) is being studied in Physics.

Secondly it shows the extent to which each of the sciences can be relied upon to provide background to any particular topic. Examples of the way in which any one science takes up ideas already developed in another are given on page 14. Other examples that can be picked out are the work on cells and batteries in Chapter **C**14 of the Chemistry book, which assumes an acquaintance with work on energy and electricity covered in Chapter **P**17 of the Physics book. In a similar way, the work on temperature control in an organism, which is a part of Chapter **B**12 of the Biology book, relies on some previous understanding of the relationship between evaporation and energy transfer which is developed in Chapter **P**2 of the Physics book. The study of digestion in Chapter **B**5 makes more sense in the light of work on carbohydrate molecules in Chapter **C**3; while the investigation of fertilizers in Chapter **C**16 assumes that the nitrogen cycle has been introduced in Chapter **B**15.

When devising alternative pathways through the material, schools will need to bear in mind the way the development of some major ideas has been co-ordinated across the sciences. This means that in some instances it is essential to ensure certain priorities – as for example in ensuring that introductory work on energy in Physics precedes the development of ideas about energy in Biology and Chemistry. These important priorities are made clear in the charts on pages 10–12, which show the development of ideas about energy, particles and the environment in all three sciences. It is also possible to construct alternative pathways so that the work taught by any one teacher includes material from more than one pupils' book. For example, some schools may prefer to teach work found in the Physics chapter "Radioactivity" alongside material from the Chemistry book. In this way, particular teacher-expertise can be used to best advantage.

There is a third way in which the contents of the three sciences are linked to each other and to other areas of study. These are links of cross-reference and application. Examples from a range of sciences can often be used to illustrate particular scientific ideas (see page 14). It is not essential in such cases that the cross-reference is already familiar to pupils when first introduced. For example, the work on chemicals from plants in Chapter **C**2 of the Chemistry book looks forward to the use that will be made of this in future work in Biology, such as in the study of digestion. Work on optical fibres in Physics (Chapter **P**13) reminds pupils of earlier work on glass in Chemistry (Chapter **C**6) but does not explicitly use ideas from that chapter.

Cross-references of this sort are numerous and have been treated specially in the pupils' books by the use of a commentary text. This text is set apart from the normal text of the book and provides, for the pupil, a parallel commentary on the work. Amongst other things this commentary text tells pupils where, in their other science books, they may find related material.

Finally, co-ordination of content can take place in carrying out interdisciplinary problems and investigations. It is hoped that all pupils will have an opportunity to do some of these. There are at least two ways in which the present material can be used to encourage interdisciplinary studies. In the first place, closely linked topics such as Chapter **P**12 "Waste not, want not?" and

Chapter C13 "Fuels and fires" can be taught as an integrated unit of work. Secondly, several of the worksheets will be seen to involve ideas from more than one science – for example Worksheet **P3B** "Using radioactivity" and Worksheet **B9A** "Investigating respiration".

Co-ordination of concepts and ideas

A common policy has been adopted in the development of any idea that occurs in more than one science. In this chapter, there follows an account of the policies adopted towards the most important of these common ideas. These are the concept of energy, the meaning of the word "particle", and the impact of science on the environment.

Energy

The approach to energy has been influenced by a number of recent publications, in particular by Nuffield Science 11 to 13. The following points made by many of the authors of these publications have been taken up in Nuffield Co-ordinated Sciences:

There is often a confusion in pupils' minds over the scientists' "book-keeping" view of the conservation of energy and the everyday idea that energy is somehow being used up.

Accepting that processes of change usually involve the transfer of energy, the idea of an "energy cost" involved in bringing about a desired change is introduced prior to any consideration of energy conservation.

Eventually, energy cost and energy conservation are reconciled by recognizing that the dispersal of energy in the surroundings results in it being impossible to utilize this energy fully again. This is compared with the "loss" of material resources by their wide dispersal.

The idea that energy is transformed when it is transferred leads pupils to think that the energy associated with different things (chemicals, electricity, motion, hotness) is essentially different. This tends to make energy seem a material substance, rather than a quality ("having energy") of a system which, like temperature for example, can change according to the circumstances.

Consequently, the idea of energy transformation and reference to "forms of energy" has been, as far as possible, excluded from Nuffield Co-ordinated Sciences. Two special names have been retained however. These are kinetic energy and internal energy. The first is too well embedded in the language of science for it to be easy to exclude it; the second is given limited use when it is necessary to refer to energy stored internally in a body (as the kinetic and potential energy of its atoms and molecules).

There is confusion in the use of the word "heat" both to refer to a particular manifestation of energy in relation to the temperature of a body, and as a mode of energy transfer when two bodies of unequal temperature are in thermal contact.

We have therefore decided not to use the word "heat" as a description of a "form of energy". Instead, the word "heat" is only used to describe a process by which energy is transferred from a hot body to a cold one. This means that the word "heat" is only used in the verbal sense of "to heat" and "heating". Consequently, the energy transfer required to raise the temperature of one kilogram of a substance by 1 °C is described as the "specific heating capacity" of the substance.

The approach to energy adopted by Nuffield Co-ordinated Sciences can be summarized as follows:

- When things happen, energy is usually transferred.
- If energy is involved in a change, it will be transferred and re-arranged, but the total amount stays the same.

- We become aware of energy only when it is transferred and there are two important processes of energy transfer: work and heat.
  Heat is the name of a process whereby internal energy is transferred from a hotter to a cooler body.
  Work is the name of a process whereby energy is transferred when a force moves its point of application.
- Many changes involve energy being transferred to the surroundings. But the temperature rise which results is often so small that the energy appears to have vanished.

Figure 2 shows the way ideas about energy are inter-related in the three sciences.

Energy: co-ordination

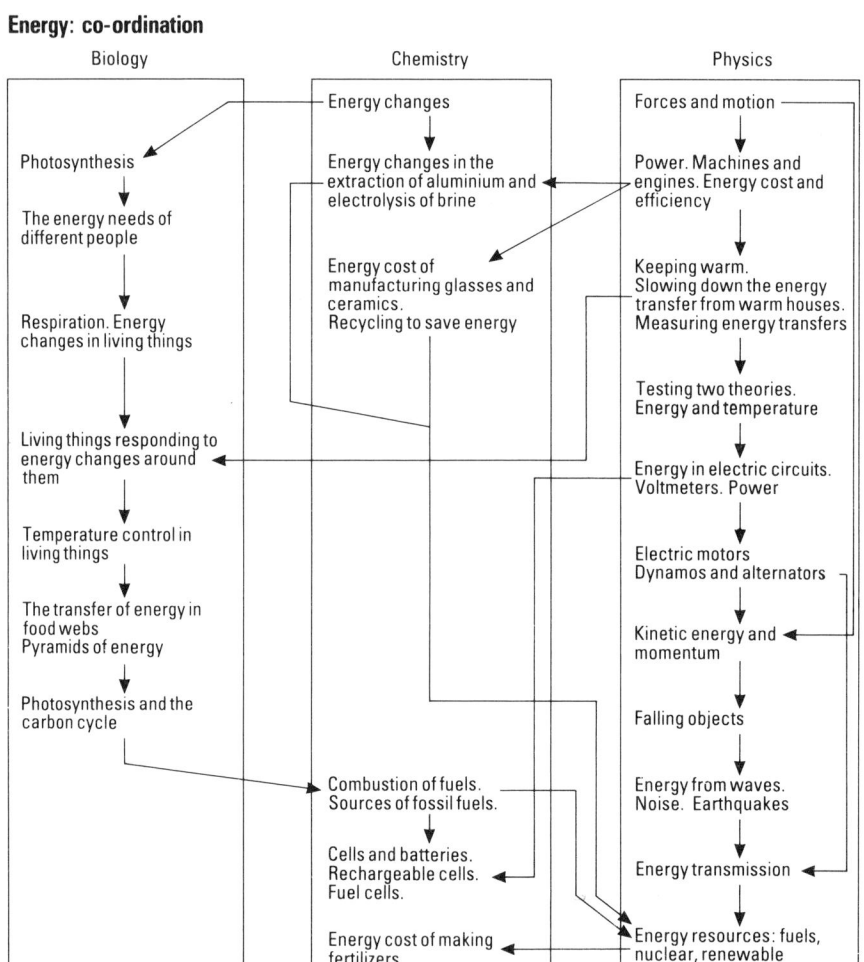

Figure 2

Particles

It is common to use the word "particle" in Physics as a general term for atom, molecule or ion since in many cases, such as when developing ideas of the kinetic theory, it is inconvenient and unnecessary to draw any distinction between these different entities. In Chemistry, on the other hand, it is essential to distinguish between atoms, molecules and ions. The distinction is an important one, as for example when comparing the strong forces within molecules with the much weaker forces between molecules.

The word "particles" is also used in all three sciences to mean "small specks of matter". It is used in this way when talking of colloidal particles, dust or smoke particles.

There seemed no way of avoiding the use of these terms in any of the ways listed above. However in the Physics book, some trouble has been taken to point out to pupils that the word "particle", used in conjunction with the theory of the structure of matter, means the same thing as "atom" or "molecule" or "ion" and that it is used when distinction between these things is not important. This is reinforced from time to time by using the correct particulate term, either in brackets or on its own, particularly when a specific substance is referred to.

Elsewhere, the use of the term "particle" is generally substantiated by a reference to its precise meaning in the context in which it is being used.

Figure 3 shows the way the ideas about particles are taken up in all three sciences. Not surprisingly, the concept is central to work in Chemistry.

Particles: co-ordination

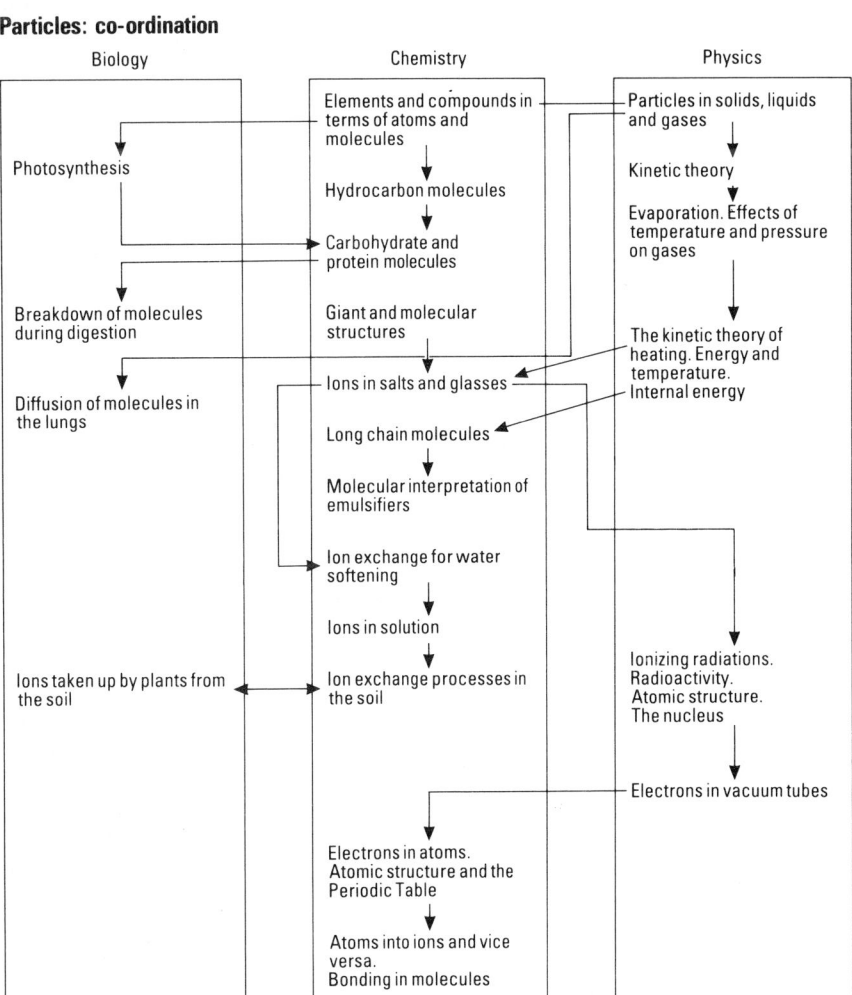

Figure 3

Environment

All three sciences show a common concern for the impact of the applications of science on the environment and for the impact of the environment on other things. Work in chemistry includes several topics from the earth sciences – for example, rocks and minerals, and weathering. It considers the impact of the environment on materials, in corrosion, and the possible pollution of the environment when considering, for example, fertilizers.

Biology includes work on the environmental factors which affect living organisms and concerns itself with matters of conservation. In Physics, the impact of things as different as noise, earthquakes and the possible effects of nuclear power are all considered at some point in the course.

Figure 4 shows the way we have incorporated environmental considerations into the course.

Environment: co-ordination

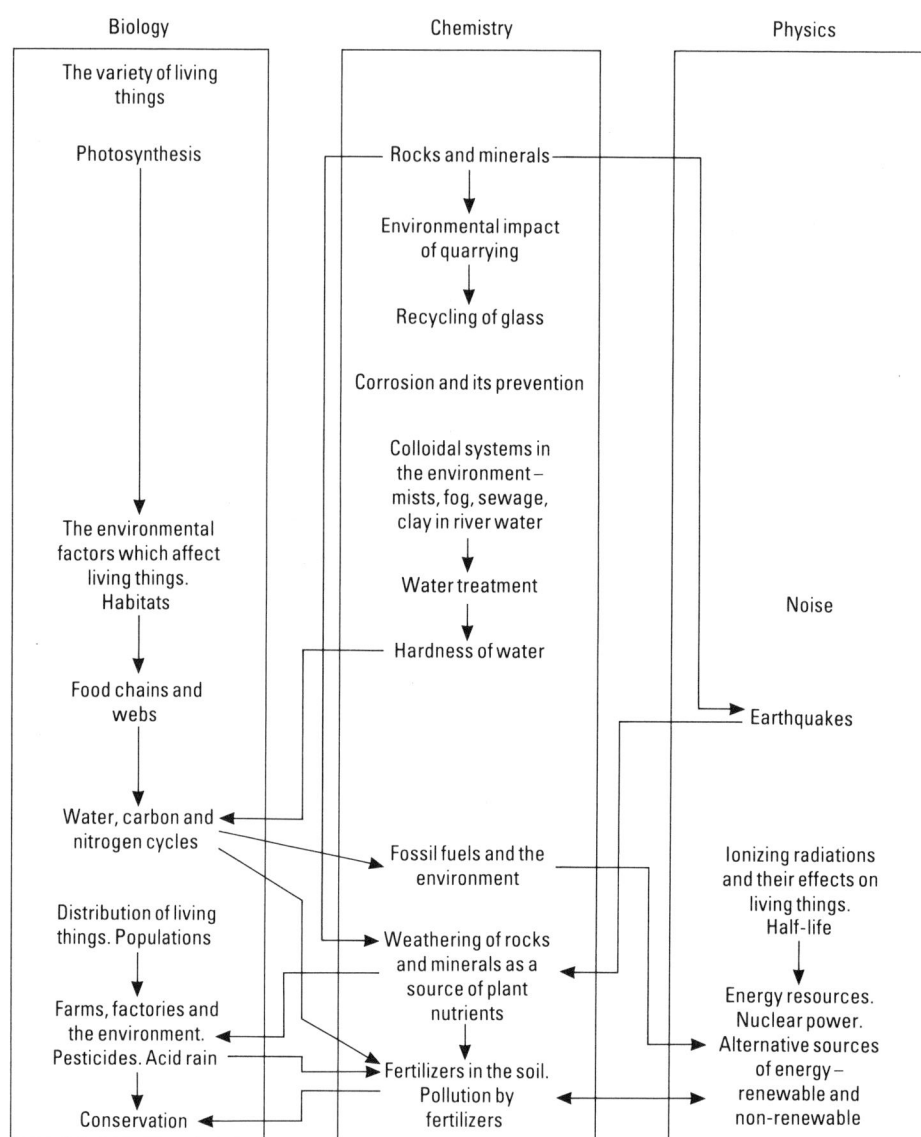

Figure 4

Units and conventions

We have adopted a common policy in the use of units and other conventional notation. In general this has meant following the policy laid down by the ASE in their booklet *Signs, symbols and units*.

However there are one or two points of policy adopted by the course which would not clearly follow from a reference to the ASE's publication.

Units for volume

We have adopted the litre (symbol, L) and the millilitre (symbol, ml) as the units for volume measure where no obvious shape is indicated. This decision has been taken because the litre is a familiar everyday unit of volume. Medicines are dispensed in 5-ml spoons while paints are sold in litres. For solids and one or two other cases where the use of the litre would be anomalous, the unit adopted is the cm^3 or the m^3 as appropriate. This again is in line with everyday practice (wood for example is measured in m^3).

As a consequence of the decision to use the litre as the basic unit for volume, the symbol L is not used for anything else.

Negative indices

Negative indices are not used in any of the books. In the case of units, the solidus (/) is used instead. In order to avoid using the solidus twice for acceleration the convention has been adopted of giving units as, for instance, metres/second every second.

Safety symbols

The conventional safety symbols used in Chemistry have been adopted.

Chemical names

The ASE book about chemical nomenclature (1985) emphasizes that the names recommended are appropriate for students taking the more advanced chemistry courses. The authors of the book stress that the names used should be appropriate to the level of understanding of the student and they invite teachers to adjust the complexity of systematic names to the maturity and knowledge of the student.

We have studied these recommendations and decided not to require a knowledge of chemical nomenclature in Nuffield Co-ordinated Sciences. We have used trivial and systematic names but this information is not required for examination purposes.

We have tried to avoid creating barriers which will prevent pupils seeing the connections between school science and their everyday experience. However this does not lead to consistency when farmers still talk about "muriate of potash" while some supermarkets list a hexacyanoferrate(III) salt among the ingredients of table salt.

As a rule, systematic names have been used for the simpler inorganic and organic chemicals. Everyday names have been used for polymers and biological molecules.

Co-ordination of strategy

The work of all three sciences has been devised in relation to an agreed set of skills and processes which are detailed in Chapter 3 of this *Guide*. The relationship between the work of each of the sciences and the skills and processes they reflect are highlighted in the pupils' books and also in the relevant sections of the teachers' guide.

The presentation of the material is common to each of the sciences. Each book provides pupils with an account which he or she can read in parallel with the work in class. It also gives the pupils questions to answer and directs them to other activities. Each subject presents class activities in the form of worksheets, and we have thus removed all the instructions for experimental work from the text itself. Each text has placed "relevance" and "social impact" at the forefront of its presentation, developing the scientific ideas as they are needed. These common modes of presentation should give some overall unity to the work.

There are worksheets in all the sciences which provide opportunities for the planning and carrying out of investigations. To help this work, each science carries a worksheet, numbered "0", which can be used to help in the planning of investigatory work.

GENERAL INTRODUCTION

Co-ordination within the science department

It is necessary when teaching this course to be aware of both the content and order of presentation of the work in all three sciences. In writing the course, duplication of work has, as far as possible, been avoided. So essential preliminary work to the development of an idea in one science may well have taken place in another. An example of this is the work on energy in Chapter **B**14 of the Biology book and Chapter **C**13 of the Chemistry book. Both of these pieces of work assume that the pupil is already familiar with earlier work on energy covered by Chapters **P**8 to **P**10 in the Physics book.

Similarly, Chapter **C**18 of the Chemistry book, which deals with atoms and bonding, assumes that pupils have already met ideas about atomic structure and electrons, covered in Chapters **P**3 and **P**19 of the Physics book.

A sample pathway through the contents of the three books, given in figure 1, takes note of this need for co-ordination in the teaching order. Other pathways are possible, but all will have to be aware of the extent to which ideas developed in one science depend on ideas developed in another.

Awareness of the content of all the sciences allows co-ordination to take place in another way. Examples from all the sciences can be used to illustrate the development of ideas in any one particular science. Instances of this will be found in the pupils' books. The use of catalysts and their importance in industry is discussed in Chemistry. This can be related to the study of enzymes in Biology. In Chapter **B**3 the factors which affect photosynthesis are discussed, and this experience can be used as an introduction to the study of reaction rates in Chapter **C**15 of the Chemistry course. The processes of breaking down and building up molecules are vital in digestion and growth. These biological examples help to illustrate the chemistry of polymers and the smaller molecules from which they are made. Finally an example from Physics: in Chapter **P**1, increasing stiffness by making materials into tubes is discussed. This is related, amongst other things, to the structure of plant stems. Teachers will be able to think of many more examples, all of which will help pupils to establish essential links between the sciences.

Cross-links of this sort are not confined to the three sciences. Many examples will be found where links are established between the immediate scientific ideas being studied and work in earth sciences, geography, home economics, technology, and so on. Work on rocks and minerals in Chemistry relate to studies in the earth sciences such as the rock cycle and the geological timescale, as does work on earthquakes in Physics. There are many links with home economics: the properties of fibres (Chapter **C**8), foams and emulsions (Chapter **C**9), dry cleaning and washing (Chapter **C**10), dyes (Chapter **C**11), fire hazards and flameproofing (Chapter **C**13) are all part of the Chemistry course. In Biology, work on food, diet and health have similar links with home economics. Physics looks at pressure cookers and microwave ovens. Work in Biology also links with physical education through topics such as oxygen uptake and muscle contraction; and with geography in the study of the impact of human activity on land use and the environment. Physics makes a number of links with technology in areas such as engines and electronics.

Chapter 3   Skills and processes

Developing skills and the understanding of processes

The DES Policy Statement *Science 5–16* says:

> "The objectives of broad science cannot be determined solely in terms of listing items of syllabus content: full weight must be given to the development of scientific skills and processes as well as to knowledge and understanding."

This statement is paralleled by the philosophy which has underpinned Nuffield courses for the past twenty years. The following quotation is taken from the original *Introduction and guide* to Nuffield Chemistry:

> "Our chief concern will be to encourage pupils to be scientific about a problem. This means that they must have mental and manipulative skill in the exploration of a situation which, though familiar to us, is new to them. In all new situations one gropes and fumbles and is likely to make mistakes. This, however, is the exercise by which judgement develops. A pupil must have graded opportunities to be right or wrong, and must be guided and encouraged to become better at finding out whether or not he or she is right. This is time-consuming at first but only time-wasting in the context of having to cover a traditional syllabus: properly organized, it brings considerable benefits later on .... We have to learn to judge when to keep silent leaving the pupil to puzzle out the problem, and when to give encouragement and advice. That the pupil should see the point of experimental work is of the greatest importance .... The pupil must learn that it is proper to have an opinion or an idea about anything observed, but cannot begin to think scientifically without checking whether the idea fits the observed experimental facts."

Nuffield Co-ordinated Sciences has similarly tried to give as much emphasis to the development of scientific skills and the understanding of processes as it has to knowledge and understanding of ideas. Having said that, it is important not to underestimate the latter. Processes and skills cannot be exercised without some knowledge and some ideas upon which to exercise them. However it does not follow that all that knowledge and all those ideas upon which the acquisition of skills and process may be based have to be learned and remembered.

- In this course, pupils will find some ideas that are so important that they should be learned and remembered. Often these ideas are developed as part of a practical investigation. An example of this is the exploration of the way forces act on an electric current in a magnetic field (Worksheet **P18B**) which is fundamental to understanding how electric motors work.
- At other times, pupils are given an investigation to do whose outcome (as a piece of "knowledge and understanding") is not important to the course as a whole. Here they can exercise their developing skills in science without any feeling that there is an essential "right answer" to be obtained. The suggested investigations into wrapping films, methods of corrosion protection, descalers and flameproofing agents provide opportunities to plan and carry out investigations in contexts where pupils can use science skills without having to master difficult concepts at the same time.
- Sometimes, the development of some important skill or process is aided by a more extended piece of science, where short-term understanding of an idea is required. But here again, the pupil is not expected to retain a long-term understanding of these ideas (for recall in an examination). An example is the study of alum and the alum industry in Chapter **C4** of the Chemistry course.

Here is an interesting story about how alum used to be made from rock, seaweed and urine. The pupils have the opportunity to plan and carry out an experiment to see if they can make some alum from shale by a more modern process. At the same time they can use ideas about elements and compounds to give a simple explanation of the changes they observe. So there are planning and manipulative skills as well as opportunities to apply theory. In the end they are not expected to recall the chemical, historical and industrial details for examination purposes.

Because skills and processes cannot be developed without some "science" on which to build them, a distinction has to be drawn between the content of the pupils' books and the "syllabus" content which defines precisely the knowledge and ideas that pupils are expected to retain from the course.

The skills and processes developed in Nuffield Co-ordinated Sciences

There is considerable agreement between many major curriculum developments in science about which are the skills and processes most important to science. These have been encapsulated in broad terms in the National Criteria for the sciences. In this project, we have decided to adopt the broad headings of skills

Main categories	Sub-categories (from National Criteria)
1. Graphical and symbolic	• extract from information presented in diagrammatic, symbolic, graphical, numerical or verbal form, data relevant to a particular context; • translate information from one form to another.
2. Use of apparatus and measuring instruments	• follow instructions accurately for the conduct of experiments; • handle apparatus and materials effectively; • work with due regard for safety.
3. Observation	• observe, measure and record accurately and systematically.
4. Interpretation and application .	• use data, recognize patterns in such data, formulate hypotheses and draw conclusions; • explain familiar facts, observations and phenomena in terms of scientific laws, theories and models; • suggest scientific explanations of unfamiliar facts, observations and phenomena; • recognize that the pursuit of science is subject to practical constraints and theoretical limitations.
5. Planning and carrying out investigations	• select or formulate propositions amenable to experimental test; • devise procedures and select apparatus and materials suitable for checking the validity of data, conclusions, generalizations, hypotheses and predictions; • carry out investigations; • recognize and explain variability and unreliability in experimental measurements; • evaluate critically the design of experiments, experimental observations and other data, and draw conclusions.
6. Problem solving	• apply scientific ideas, formulæ and methods to solve qualitative problems; • make decisions based on examination of evidence and arguments; • explain everyday and technological applications of science, and evaluate associated personal, social, economic and environmental implications.
7. Communication	• communicate logically and concisely.

Figure 5

and processes laid down by the Assessment of Performance Unit, and we have interpreted these in the light of the National Criteria. This list, defined by the APU as "categories of science performance", is shown in figure 5.

To the APU list we have added:

6 Problem solving
7 Communication.

Learning to use skills and processes in science

The extent to which these skills and processes are used in the development of the course content is itemized in the detailed notes on each of the sciences. However, simply experiencing the use of these skills and processes will not necessarily mean that pupils acquire an understanding of the part they play in the scientific process. For this to happen, pupils will not only need to use these skills but also to **know** that they have used the skills. The use of pupil profiles in the assessment of practical work will enable pupils to evaluate how well their skills are developing, and will help them to realize when the same skills appear in the different sciences. It is very important that they appreciate that the skills and processes they use are not simply related to particular experiments or ideas, but apply generally to all science. They will need, for example, to appreciate that straight-line graphs are not simply a way of presenting Hooke's Law for springs, but are a generally applicable process that demonstrates proportionality between two quantities. Similarly, the process of classification is equally applicable to living things in Biology and to the Periodic Table in Chemistry. The use of models is another general idea that is used in all three sciences.

There are several ways in which pupils can learn the generalities of the scientific process at the same time as they apply skills and processes to particular investigations:

a The most able pupils will certainly make their own generalizations from the repeated application of the same skills and processes to different problems in science.

b Pupils will benefit from being reminded verbally of previous uses of the same process or skill when it is used for a particular investigation.

c The commentary text in the pupils' books sometimes points out to the pupil that a skill or process used in a new piece of work has already been used elsewhere (either in this science, or another). For example, in Chemistry, pupils are introduced to a key to use to determine the structure of substances (Chapter **C5**). The associated commentary text says:

> "This section shows you how to test a substance in the laboratory to decide on its structure. Alternatively you can look up the properties in a set of data tables. To help you, the section includes a key. You can find other examples of keys in Chapter **B1** of your Biology book."

d The use of some of the more important processes is flagged in the margin of the pupils' book where they are used, either in the development of the content or in questions.

The use of graphical and symbolic representation is self-evident in its use. Similarly no attention is drawn to the use of communication skills, since their universality is apparent. The remainder of the main categories of science skills and processes have been flagged, however. This is done by the codes shown in figure 6.

M — MEASURE   I — INTERPRET   A — APPLY   P — PLAN   O — OBSERVE

Figure 6

Experimental work

Developing skills in science and acquiring an understanding of processes is intimately bound up with experimental work. This is one reason why, in science courses, pupils spend much time doing experimental work. But this is not the only reason.

There are three main purposes for the laboratory activities.

● To give pupils first-hand experience of phenomena.

Some of the experiments are included to help pupils to understand concepts. The activities in the laboratory are planned to give them experience of the problems which the theory has been developed to solve.

● To teach practical skills.

The pupils must acquire some practical skills if they are to carry out scientific investigations and solve problems. The work of the APU has shown that it is not enough to assume that these skills will be acquired incidentally as the pupils engage in practical science.

Pupils need to be instructed in the skills. They must have practice and they must be made aware of the skills which they are expected to master. However, we think it important that the mastery of manipulative skills should not become an end in itself. Wherever possible, the practical activities, which are included mainly as an exercise to develop skills, can also be seen to have a purpose in the context of the topic being studied. What we have tried to avoid is trying to teach skills at the same time as trying to help the pupils to understand new concepts.

● To provide opportunities for pupils to plan and carry out scientific investigations.

The experiments which are designed to help pupils to understand new concepts have to be carefully designed and organized by the teacher if they are to be successful. This is guided discovery. Such experiments are important but they do not give pupils the experience of being a problem-solving scientist. It is unlikely that the pupils will feel that the experiments belong to them. They also tend to encourage the belief that experiments have "one right answer".

We want pupils to have the chance to plan and carry out investigations into practical problems which seem to have significance in the world outside school. Such problems may well be more technological than theoretical.

In this context we are concerned with the following kinds of practical problem solving. Examples of the four types are given on pages 24, 161, and 276–8.

Type I: laboratory investigations designed and carried out by the pupils using equipment supplied.
Type II: laboratory investigations designed and carried out by the pupils using equipment selected by themselves.
Type III: the design of a piece of equipment, or other artefact, to perform a particular task.
Type IV: investigations outside the laboratory including field work.

There is little doubt that if practical problem-solving activities go well they can do a great deal to motivate pupils and give them confidence in the use of process skills. It is equally certain that if they go badly the situation can be very frustrating and nerve-wracking for teacher and pupils alike. Two of the keys to success are forethought and realistic planning.

The needs of able pupils

Finally, we return to the DES Policy Statement referred to earlier. In section 79, it says:

"The demands on the able pupils should be extended so that they are challenged not by the task of accumulating ever greater stores of scientific knowledge but by the application of principles to the real world, by the opportunity to investigate and solve problems, and by the necessity of bringing scientific method to bear on assignments where the answer cannot be predicted in advance."

This statement summarizes the way in which Nuffield Co-ordinated Sciences has itself dealt with the needs of more able pupils. Several examples will be found throughout the course where pupils who have managed to cope quickly with the core material are asked to undertake some investigation which extends the course, but whose results are not built upon in the remainder of it. Examples of such investigations can be found in all three sciences. In Physics, for example, work on force and motion in Chapter P5 is largely concerned with establishing that unbalanced forces are needed to change motion. The relationship between the unbalanced force and the mass and acceleration of the moving body (Newton II) are not an essential part of the course. However able pupils may cope easily with this material. For them, Worksheet P5D suggests how they may try to establish a link between the size of the force and the mass and acceleration of the body and thus lay down foundations for more advanced work later. In Chemistry, an example will be found in Chapter C12 in the analysis of aspirin tablets. This is an extension to the course, in which pupils use skills already acquired by doing simpler experiments to investigate antacid tablets.

Similarly, to take an example from Biology, Chapter B7 deals with breathing and respiration. For more able pupils, Worksheet B7A sets the problem of using hydrogencarbonate indicator to investigate how plants and animals in a closed community affect the environment around them. This investigation draws together what pupils have learned about both respiration and photosynthesis and applies it to a new situation.

Chapter 4   Assessment

Nuffield Co-ordinated Sciences leads to a General Certificate of Secondary Education in the Sciences. The award will be a double certificate, as defined by the "National Criteria for the Sciences: Double Award". The aims of the course and the form of the assessment meet these National Criteria, which are published elsewhere.

Candidates will receive two grades on the basis of their performance. Grades are awarded on a thirteen-point scale, ranging from AA to GG. It is planned that a candidate who just fails to achieve grade GG may be awarded a single grade of G. Schools should consult the syllabus document published by the examinations group for detailed guidance on the operation of the grading scheme.

Part of the assessment will be made internally by the course teachers and part externally by means of written examinations. It is an explicit aim of the Co-ordinated Sciences course to emphasize the development of candidates' scientific skills as they undertake the process of scientific inquiry, and this aim will be reflected in both the internal assessment and the written papers.

The internally assessed component will account for 30 per cent of the total marks awarded, and it will assess both practical skills and non-practical skills. The assessment should be co-ordinated across the three sciences in order to avoid unnecessary duplication. Once a candidate has demonstrated competence in a skill in one subject area, it should not be necessary to test that skill further in the other sciences before awarding an assessment mark.

Practical skills will be assessed from written work produced independently by candidates under supervision by their teacher, and from observation of candidates' practical work done in the presence of the teacher. The assessment scheme will suggest specific objectives which schools can use to assess the level of achievement of each candidate, rather than assessing how much assistance a candidate requires to complete a particular task. These objectives will be based upon the categories of assessment proposed by the Assessment of Performance Unit, which are used throughout the course and in this *Guide*.

One advantage of an internal assessment model which uses specific objectives based on achievement is that it can be used to monitor a candidate's developing skills throughout the course. This can be of benefit to pupil and teacher alike, and it is a feature of the internal assessment scheme that it can be operated in this way, with each candidate's achievements at the end of the course providing the basis of the assessment mark. Candidates' work will be moderated within schools and between schools, and teachers will be required to collect representative samples of work for the purpose of moderation.

Non-practical skills will be similarly assessed using specific objectives based on achievement, and will test the ability to communicate logically and concisely.

Detailed guidance on the operation of the internal assessment scheme will be found in a teachers' handbook to be published by the examinations group and, later, in a short book on the assessment of Nuffield Co-ordinated Sciences to be produced by the Nuffield–Chelsea Curriculum Trust.

The external written examination will test understanding and knowledge of scientific ideas and processes, and the ability to use scientific skills. There will be three papers, each containing questions from the three science disciplines, balanced in accordance with the "National Criteria for the Sciences: Double Award". In addition, there will be some interdisciplinary questions drawing together ideas from different subject areas of the course.

Papers 1 and 2 (70 per cent) will be taken by all candidates, and the marks awarded will grade candidates in the range from G to CC. Both papers will consist of a mixture of structured and short answer questions, designed to test understanding of scientific ideas that are of direct relevance to the everyday world; and both will emphasize scientific skills and process as well as knowledge.

Paper 3 is an optional paper for candidates attempting the grades BC to AA. It will be a mixture of structured and free response questions, with no choice, and will contribute 70 per cent of the marks for these higher grades. The remaining 30 per cent of these marks will come from the internal assessment.

It is important that candidates be entered for Paper 3 if the school is confident that they are capable of attaining the higher grades BC to AA. A candidate cannot be awarded a higher grade on the result of Papers 1 and 2 alone. But neither will a candidate's CC grade be pulled down by a bad result on Paper 3.

BIOLOGY

Introduction to Biology

The Biology course aims to introduce the biological principles which will help pupils to explain many of the phenomena they will observe in the natural world. It also will help them towards a greater understanding of the functioning of their own bodies and their behaviour and should encourage a responsible attitude towards all organisms and the environment in which they live.

The course content is divided into four themes:

The variety of organisms   Living organisms and their environment
The processes of life   The continuity of life

The topics are presented in this order to allow time for some ideas to be introduced in Chemistry or Physics. It is also necessary, in some cases, for purposes of co-ordination. For example, it is helpful if pupils have gained some knowledge of the molecular structure of carbohydrates from Chapter **C**3 "Chemicals from plants" before they study photosynthesis in Chapter **B**3.

It also makes sense to leave the more difficult ideas encountered in genetics and evolution until the end of the course where a more mature attitude will be of benefit.

But there has to be some flexibility, as another factor which always has to be taken into account in biology courses is the seasonal nature of some topics. This is particularly true of ecological work, which needs to be carried out at a time of year when the weather conditions are likely to be favourable.

Each theme is developed in an order that forms a logical sequence but there are alternatives, both in the order in which the chapters can be used and in the order within chapters.

Significance

Revised Nuffield Biology has been an important influence in the development of these materials and teachers familiar with that scheme will be aware of the similarities.

This new course is also concerned with acquiring an understanding of biological principles and with applying the knowledge gained, but more emphasis has been given to the development of skills.

Observation has always had an important role in biology. We have now given more attention to the next stage, which involves recognizing patterns. The collection and interpretation of data have also been important skills and there are still many opportunities for pupils to collect data for themselves although we have provided information collected by other people also. The data are of the kind that pupils would not find it easy to collect. Using knowledge to solve problems is a skill which is encouraged, especially where it concerns environmental issues and the consequences of the actions of humans.

Understanding the way organisms function is a major theme. We have included a consideration of human sexuality in the chapters which deal with the way organisms reproduce. This topic is developed in a responsible and sensitive way which goes beyond the presentation of the facts to deal with personal aspects of sexual behaviour in the context of care and concern for other people. Other themes are concerned with understanding how organisms react with each other and with their environment, how information is passed on from one generation to the next and the changes in organisms, including humans, which take place over a long period of time.

Throughout this course it is possible to choose between a practical approach or a more theoretical one – whichever is best suited to the needs of pupils.

Differentiation

In Nuffield Co-ordinated Sciences the biological topics are introduced with a familiar phenomenon or with a practical activity as a starting point. This is designed as a worthwhile exercise for all pupils.

Most of the material in the chapters of the pupils' book is suitable for all pupils but there are some concepts which only those aiming for the higher GCSE grades need to understand. For example, all pupils should know that sex hormones are produced by the ovaries and testes but only those aiming for higher grades need to know of the co-ordinating role of the hypothalamus and pituitary gland. All pupils should be able to recognize the different trophic levels in a food web but it is only necessary for some to understand that the flow of energy through an ecosystem limits the number of trophic levels. Differentiation has also been introduced into the questions asked in the pupils' book and while there is no reason why all pupils should not attempt all the questions, most teachers will want to choose questions at an appropriate level to suit the individual needs of their pupils.

Differentiation has been allowed for in the worksheets too. All of the worksheets are suitable for most pupils to use. It is the level of analysis and interpretation of results which allows for differentiated treatments. Teachers may need to give guidance but pupils will often make their own decisions about the depth of interpretation of results.

Experimental work

Experimental work is an integral part of a chapter. It has three main purposes.

● To give pupils firsthand experience of phenomena.

Examples of this include the experiments related to Chapter **B**3, in which pupils can see for themselves many of the phenomena associated with photosynthesis. These include the absorption of light by chlorophyll and the presence of starch in a green leaf. The experimental work associated with Chapters **B**13 to 18 also illustrates this aim in the different context of fieldwork.

● To teach practical skills.

In Biology the pupils need a number of practical skills. These include the use of accurate measuring instruments also needed in Chemistry and Physics, for timing and for determining volume, mass, length and temperature. Pupils are expected to use instruments in a biological context to measure, for example, the size and growth of organisms or the rate of water loss from leaves. Another skill, always underestimated by pupils, is how to use a microscope correctly.

● To provide opportunities for pupils to plan and do scientific investigations.

One of the most important aspects of planning biological investigations is making sure that an appropriate control is included whenever necessary. Pupils are often asked to suggest a suitable control for an experiment and the inclusion of a control is an essential component of many of the experiments they are asked to design.

Chapter 3 of the general introduction lists four types of practical problem solving used in this course. They can all be seen in the Biology part of the course.

Type I: Laboratory investigations designed and carried out by the pupils using equipment supplied

There are many examples, particularly in Chapters **B**3 to **B**12, in which the investigations or experiments are set out in a structured way with instructions for the pupils to follow. It may be appropriate for some pupils to plan their own way of carrying out these investigations whilst others may need to use the worksheets provided. Pupils should always be encouraged to try out their own ideas and some worksheets may be used to provide the guidelines only.

Type II: Laboratory investigations designed and carried out by the pupils using equipment selected by themselves

Some of these are extensions to worksheets while others are suggested in the pupils' book. There may also be individual pupils who wish to develop their own way of investigating a particular problem and this should always be encouraged where facilities allow.

Type III: The design of a piece of equipment, or other artefact, for a particular task

Worksheet **B**17A is an example; it asks the pupils to design a biogas generator.

Type IV: Investigations outside the laboratory, including fieldwork

Most of the investigations involving work outside the laboratory are associated with Chapters **B**13 to **B**18. Ecological fieldwork is a very enjoyable part of any Biology course but it needs a lot of planning and is somewhat dependent on the weather for its success. There are other opportunities, when surveys are suggested, such as Worksheet **B**7H "Starting, stopping and carrying on ...".

Worksheets

In the Biology part of the course many of the worksheets are not concerned with work of a strictly experimental nature. This applies to the worksheets associated with the first two chapters. Here observation is the skill which is important. Identifying organisms is a necessary part of a biologist's training and the use of a key to identify a selection of common birds is a useful practical exercise although it is not experimental in nature. It also gives useful practice in making decisions and following instructions.

Other examples are the worksheets which give guidance for investigating the structure of a joint (Worksheet **B**10B) and those dealing with the structure of other organs such as the heart (Worksheet **B**8D) and lungs (Worksheet **B**7D).

As well as worksheets which give instructions and guidance on carrying out practical work, there are those which give descriptions of experiments performed by other people and provide data collected by others. These are a very valuable way of saving time and of giving pupils access to data which it would be difficult for them to collect for themselves. The emphasis is usually on the interpretation and analysis of the data provided.

The worksheets concerned with giving instructions for carrying out practical work will undoubtedly be modified as a result of their use with classes. This should be seen as a normal and essential part of their function.

Safety

Safe conduct in laboratories is of vital importance. In biology many of the necessary precautions apply to the handling of living organisms. Teachers must make themselves familiar with the regulations which apply to schools and keep themselves up to date in this area. Some of the hazards are removed now that the use of blood and saliva is no longer allowed in schools. Warnings should always be given when using flammable chemicals and it is important that instruments used for dissection are sharp as much more harm is done with blunt ones. Hazard signs appear on the worksheets whenever the pupils need to be reminded to take particular care.

Topic B1 The variety of organisms

Chapter B1 What's what?

Purposes

Knowledge and understanding

At the end of this chapter all pupils should:

1 appreciate why organisms are classified into groups

2 recognize the binomial system of naming organisms, and know the binomial names for two different organisms

3 appreciate the idea of organisms belonging to different species.

Processes and problem solving

Graphical and symbolic representation
Worksheet **B1B** asks pupils to interpret a pie chart of the different numbers of species in the animal kingdom.

Using apparatus and measuring instruments
Microscopes are used to observe the structure of organisms in Worksheet **B1A**.

Observation
Worksheet **B1A** enables pupils to observe similarities and differences between living organisms, and then to use these diagnostic characteristics to sort them into groups.
  Careful observation is necessary when using the identification key in Worksheet **B1C**.

Timing

4 periods.

Suggested routes

The flow diagram in figure **B1** overleaf outlines two possible routes through this chapter. They are not, of course, the only way through the material.
  Section **B1.1**, which emphasizes the importance of observation, is supplemented by opportunities to observe common organisms closely, in Worksheet **B1A**. It is not necessary to complete both parts of this worksheet, but sufficient time should be devoted to the exercise for pupils to get a chance to observe closely and report their findings.
  Section **B1.2** and Worksheet **B1B** are simple exercises that emphasize how many different species of animal there are in the world and how long they live for. In the flow diagram they are given as a simpler alternative to section **B1.3**, although they could also make an appropriate homework exercise as a prelude to **B1.3**.

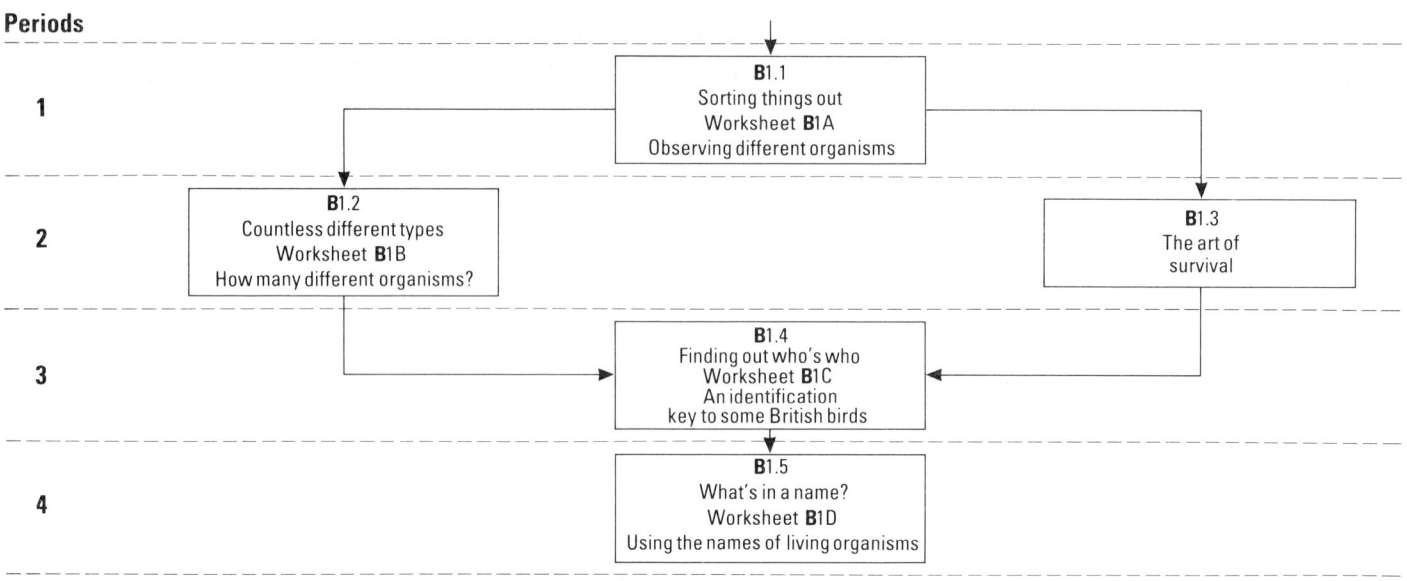

Figure **B**1

Section **B**1.3 is a moderately difficult exercise, and one that is perhaps best suited to the more theoretically inclined groups, although it can be supplemented by vivid video material (see "Supplementary material").

Worksheet **B**1D, which complements the introduction to the naming of organisms in section **B**1.5, should be completed by all pupils.

Opportunities for co-ordination

The classification of organisms into their appropriate groups may be compared with the classification of chemical elements in the Periodic Table, introduced in Chapter **C**1 "The elements of chemistry". In Chapter **C**12 "Chemicals in the medicine cupboard", certain chemicals are classified as drugs, analgesics or antacids.

Chapter **C**8 "Polymers" provides a link with Worksheet **B**1C in its use of an identification key.

Notes and answers

B1.1   Sorting things out

It is an interesting feature of human behaviour that people are good at sorting different objects into groups on the basis of their similarities and differences. This section introduces the idea that characteristics which show variation can be used to classify a number of objects into different groups. From the outset, the criterion of a successful classification is one that is useful to the classifier.

Worksheet **B**1A contains two simple observation exercises, but it is not necessary to complete both parts unless there is plenty of time. The first part of this worksheet requires pupils to sort woodlice into various groups. It is relatively easy to distinguish the different types of woodlice, but much more difficult to describe exactly why the organisms have been so arranged. It is important that the pupils be encouraged to describe the similarities and differences between the groups in a table or a short written account; they need not be put off by the fact that they do not know what the different parts of the anatomy of the woodlice are called, or the correct names of the different types of woodlouse themselves. Indeed, pupils might even be encouraged to make up their own names for the parts of the anatomy and the species.

Part 2 of Worksheet **B**1A involves the comparison of a number of photosynthetic protists from a pond, and provides an opportunity to make accurate observations and draw simple diagrams.

The section ends by describing a species in terms of discrete breeding groups, which may or may not show structural or behavioural differences. This should be covered by all groups.

B1.2   Countless different types

Worksheet **B**1B involves interpreting a pie-chart for the total number of species of animal in the world. (The estimates provided are conservative ones.) Pupils like record-breakers, and the organisms featured at the end of the worksheet are considered to be some of the oldest of their type in the world. It is worth pointing out that, just as very few humans live to 120 years of age, so very few of these organisms actually survive to the ages stated.

B1.3   The art of survival

It is interesting to note that some plants are able to survive for very much longer than animals. In the absence of competition, and because of its indeterminate growth, the creosote bush has been growing in the Mojave desert for at least 10 000 years.

This section is designed to show that the creosote bush is able to extract moisture from its inhospitable habitat, and will carry on growing indefinitely in the absence of competing species. This can form a prelude to work in the chapters on ecology (especially Chapter **B**13). Details of useful video material are given in this chapter under "Supplementary material".

Organisms survive because they have special features. Different species show different features. Without these, the organisms would not be able to survive inhospitable conditions.

Answers to selected questions

3 This plant germinated at a time when the last glaciers were disappearing from Britain, and when Neolithic culture was beginning to become established in the Middle East. This single plant is as old as our civilization.

5 The plant must have a minimum water loss, extract sufficient water from the soil, capture any moisture condensing from mists and avoid excessive grazing by desert herbivores.

6 Few plants will be able to compete with it for moisture or light, and relatively few herbivores will be able to tolerate such extreme conditions.

7 The creosote bush consists of a large number of creeping stems which gradually spread outwards in a ring across the desert. As it does this, the older stems tend to die away, leaving a circle of ground in the centre of the plant. In the absence of competition, the circle grows larger and larger – the oldest is 25 m across. Although the individual stems in the rings are not, themselves, very old, the single organism has managed to survive for many thousands of years.

8 Growth in animals is determinate, stopping when a maximum size is reached.

9 Ephemeral plants germinate, grow, flower, set seed and die within a few days. Their seeds are very resistant to high temperatures, and can survive for many years in dry, hot sand. It is a feature of such plants that they produce copious numbers of seeds.

10 Shortage of food and moisture, temperature regulation and predation.

B1.4   Finding out who's who

The use of keys to identify organisms is an important skill, and one which pupils should acquire in these lessons. One aim of this section is to familiarize pupils with common garden birds that can be seen almost everywhere. If teachers can show pupils how to use keys whilst generating some interest in local birds, then the aims of this section will certainly have been met.

The key, presented in Worksheet **B**1C, should be used in two ways. It is essential that pupils be given the chance to use the key to identify the photographs of the birds in the pupils' book. Identification keys that are robust enough to identify birds in the field are difficult to produce, and are not easy to use. By concentrating initially on the photographs, pupils should become familiar with the mechanics of the key, as well as with the shapes and colours of the birds themselves. (Details of useful video material are given under "Supplementary material".)

Pupils should now be encouraged to try to identify some of the birds in the locality. It will rapidly become clear that the species included in this key are only a few of those that can be seen. Any pupils who become interested in this activity will need more comprehensive field guides to help them; many of these are available quite cheaply.

Answer to selected question

12 The birds in the key that have different male and female forms are the blackbird, chaffinch and house sparrow.

B1.5   What's in a name?

All scientists recognize the need for a standard system of naming organisms. The system adopted is the one proposed by Linnaeus. Worksheet **B**1D provides an opportunity to establish the rules for naming organisms.

Practical work

Worksheet B1A   Observing different organisms

REQUIREMENTS

Each group of pupils will need:
Containers suitable for the organisms, such as beakers
Coverslips
Forceps
Light microscope with low and high power objective lenses
Microscope slides
Paintbrush, small thin
Pencils, sharp
Rulers
Tray, large plastic, covered with white paper

Access to:
Photosynthetic protists, several different species (for example, *Spirogyra, Cladophora, Euglena, Chlamydomonas*)
Woodlice, a collection, preferably containing several different species

The procedure is detailed on the worksheet. Pupils are asked to try to use their own descriptions of the similarities and differences between the specimens.

Worksheet B1B   How many different organisms?

REQUIREMENTS

Each group of pupils will need:
Photographs in figure 1.7 of the pupils' book

The procedure is detailed on the worksheet.

Answer to selected worksheet question

The ages quoted in *The Guinness book of records*, 1986 (see "Further information") are:

Human	120 years
Tortoise	152 years
Lobster	50 years
Ocean quahog (mollusc)	220 years
Buprestid beetle	47 years
Andean condor	72 years
Boa constrictor	40 years
Tarantula	28 years
Sturgeon	82 years
Salamander	55 years

Worksheet B1C   An identification key to some British birds

REQUIREMENTS

Each group of pupils will need:
Photographs in figure 1.11 of the pupils' book
A videotape of British garden birds may be of value (see "Supplementary material" for details)

The procedure is detailed on the worksheet. Pupils should identify the birds in the photographs and a (carefully chosen) selection from the videotape, if used. They can then be encouraged to observe birds in their own locality.

Worksheet B1D   Using the names of living organisms

REQUIREMENTS

Each group of pupils will need:
Normal writing materials

The procedure is detailed on the worksheet.

Further information

Further information about garden birds can be obtained from the Royal Society for the Protection of Birds, based at The Lodge, Sandy, Bedfordshire, SG19 2DL. The society provides free information packs for teachers, and organizes a Young Ornithologists Club.

The Guinness book of records 32nd edition, Guinness Superlatives Ltd, 1986.

Supplementary material

Section **B**1.3 "The art of survival" can be graphically illustrated by a sequence in programme 6 of "The Living Planet" by David Attenborough. The entire series of programmes is available on four tapes, with teachers' notes, from BBC Enterprises (Education and Training), Woodlands, 80 Wood Lane, London, W12 0TT.

The BBC has produced a video called "The BBC Videobook of British Garden Birds", which features many garden birds (including all of those in the identification key in Worksheet **B**1C). It is obtainable from BBC Enterprises (Education and Training), Woodlands, 80 Wood Lane, London, W12 0TT.

Chapter B2   Many forms of life

Purposes

Knowledge and understanding

At the end of this chapter all pupils should:

1 be aware of the diverse nature of the different groups of organisms within the animal and plant kingdoms.

Processes and problem solving

Using apparatus and measuring instruments
A microscope is used to observe the structure of organisms in Worksheet **B2D**, and a hand lens may be helpful in Worksheet **B2C**.

Observation
Worksheet **B2B** asks pupils to observe a range of organisms from each of the five kingdoms, concentrating on the characteristics which have been used to place each organism in its particular kingdom.
    Pupils may observe the diversity of species in the animal kingdom, using Worksheet **B2C**.
    Worksheet **B2D** provides an opportunity to observe the diversity of photosynthetic organisms.

Planning and carrying out investigations
Part of Worksheet **B2D** involves designing an experiment to show what fir cones do in different atmospheres.

Timing

5 periods.

Suggested routes

Figure **B2** shows a possible route through the material. It is envisaged that as much time as possible should be allowed for pupils to observe the variety of forms within the animal and plant kingdoms.
    Worksheet **B2A**, which develops the idea of the different levels of organization within the Linnean hierarchy, follows on from Worksheet **B1D** and might make a homework exercise if teachers prefer to spend class time completing the other exercises.
    Parts of Worksheet **B2D** are quite difficult, and could be omitted if time or circumstances so demand.

Opportunities for co-ordination

This chapter provides opportunities for co-ordination with the classification of chemicals in Chapters **C1** "The elements of chemistry" and **C8** "Polymers". There are also links with Chapter **C15** "Soil".

Notes and answers

B2.1   The kingdoms of the Earth

In this book a five kingdom classification has been adopted, although the controversial nature of this system could be emphasized to more able groups. (It is hoped that teachers who prefer other models will accept that the most important aim of this section is briefly to give the pupils a "feel" for each of the major groups. The simplest way to do this is to give all the groups "kingdom status".)

Periods

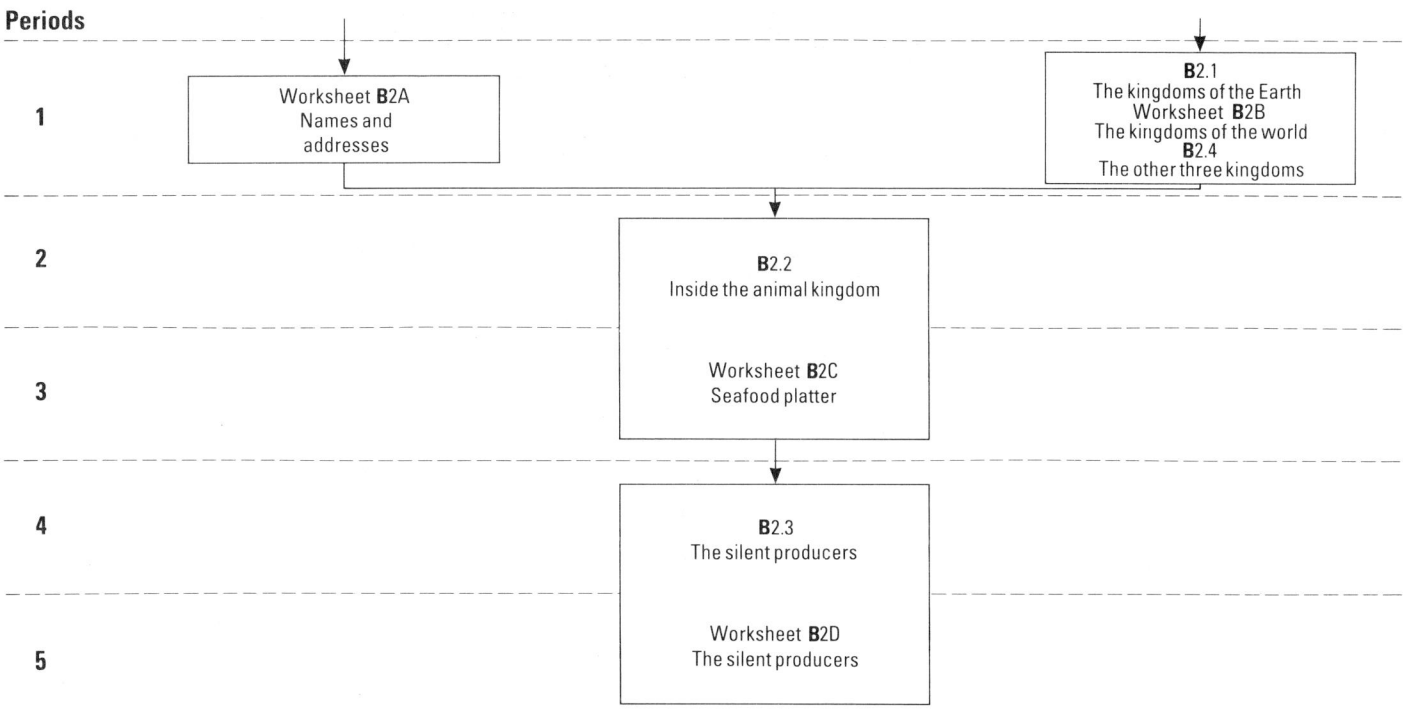

Figure **B**2

The classification recognizes five kingdoms: animals, Monera (including bacteria), protists (including heterotrophic and autotrophic unicells and their immediate multicellular descendants, algae), plants and fungi. The classification is, in essence, that outlined in Barnes, 1983 (see "Further information"). Worksheet **B**2B makes the point that some people do not think viruses are living organisms, and that those who do feel that viruses ought to be in a separate kingdom of their own (making six kingdoms).

Using photographs in the pupils' book and the descriptions in Worksheet **B**2B, pupils are asked to which kingdom various organisms belong. Two photographs (figures 2.1d and 2.1h) are viruses. It would be possible to use these photographs as a summary, and to present other living or preserved material in the classroom. These organisms need to be chosen carefully, as some material will be needed for the next section.

Answer to selected question

The photographs of the organisms featured in the pupils' book are:
a Carp, *Carassius*, animal
b Field mushroom, *Agaricus campestris*, fungus
c *Peranema*, protist
d Influenza virus
e *Mucor hiemalis*, fungus
f *Amoeba*, protist
g *Cephalanthera*, plant
h *Herpes*, virus
i *Actinia equina*, animal
j *Treponema* bacterium, Monera
k Coconut palm, plant
l *Streptococcus* bacterium, Monera.

B2.2   Inside the animal kingdom

The aim of the next two sections is to allow the pupil to develop an awareness of the diversity of animals and plants. A detailed understanding of the differences between the groups is not required; the emphasis should be on providing an enjoyable glimpse of the living world, rather than a surfeit of taxonomic detail. Section **B2.2** leads into Worksheet **B2C** – a study of the animals that we eat as "seafood".

Answers to selected questions

4 Centipedes have one pair of legs on each body segment, whilst millipedes have two pairs.

10a The method of reproduction and the shelled egg are reptilian characteristics.
b and **c** Homoiothermy is associated with birds and mammals. This animal's temperature is around 30 °C (lower than other mammals), although it is subject to wide fluctuations.
b Webbed feet and a bill are characteristic of birds.
c Fur, an external ear and milk production are uniquely mammalian characteristics. The mother platypus lacks nipples, and milk is produced from enlarged sweat glands and oozes over the fur of the abdomen. That this animal is a primitive mammal is beyond dispute.

11 Whilst the embryos are developing inside the uterus, no additional eggs can ripen in the ovaries. Once the young embryos are inside the pouch, the normal reproductive cycle can recommence. Marsupial animals can thus increase the number of young raised in any season.

13 As ungulates are often hunted by swiftly moving carnivores, their likelihood of survival is increased if the offspring can run as soon as they are born.

B2.3   The silent producers

This section considers plants, but it is important to remember that autotrophic protists are also producers, and form the basis of the food chains that will be encountered in Chapter **B14**. The brief treatment in the pupils' book is augmented by the examination of photosynthetic protists in Worksheet **B2D**. Parts of this worksheet are quite difficult, and could be omitted if time or circumstances so demand. There is a potential overlap between the specimens used in Part 2 of Worksheet **B1A** and those used in Worksheet **B2D**. Material should be chosen with care, so that pupils are not forced to examine the same examples twice. They can, of course, be asked to recall what they viewed earlier.

  Worksheet **B2D** also contains an experimental design exercise (in the section on conifers) that could be developed as an assessment activity. Pupils will need to obtain several cones of similar size, and place them in damp and dry atmospheres. They will also need to devise some method of measuring how "open" the cones are (for instance, by measuring any change in width).

B2.4   The other three kingdoms

This brief section develops ideas about bacteria, fungi and protists. It is suitable for use as a homework exercise.

Answers to selected questions

15 The role of fungi as agents of decomposition needs to be mentioned here. Cycles of matter are covered in Chapter **B15**.

16 Bread, alcohol and soy sauce need fungi.

17 The protists, such as *Euglena*. (Viruses too if they are considered to be organisms.)

Practical work

Worksheet B2A Names and addresses

REQUIREMENTS

Each group of pupils will need:
Writing materials

The procedure is detailed on the worksheet.

Worksheet B2B The kingdoms of the world

REQUIREMENTS

Each group of pupils will need:
Photographs in figure 2.1 of the pupils' book

The procedure is detailed on the worksheet.

Worksheet B2C Seafood platter

REQUIREMENTS

Each group of pupils will need:
Specimens of crab, lobster, prawns, shrimps, cockles, whelks and mussels
or
Photographs in figures 2.2, 1.7b, 2.12 and 2.13 of the pupils' book
Sea water, if living specimens are collected

Dishes
Forceps
Hand lens

The procedure is detailed on the worksheet.

Worksheet B2D The silent producers

REQUIREMENTS

Each group of pupils will need:
Ferns (*e.g. Dryopteris*)
Mosses or liverworts, showing sporangia (*e.g. Mnium, Funaria, Marchantia*)
Photosynthetic protists, unicellular **and** multicellular (*e.g. Euglena, Chlamydomonas, Spirogyra, Cladophora, Fucus, Laminaria*)
Maize, barley (both monocotyledons), broad bean and pea seeds (dicotyledons), washed in 1 % sodium hypochlorite solution and soaked overnight in distilled water
Maize, barley, broad bean and pea seedlings grown in Knop's solution (see *Note*)
Cones, male **and** female, of different ages, from a conifer (*e.g.* Scots pine)

Cement, polystyrene, or clear nail varnish
Coverslips
Drawing paper
Microscope slides
Microscope with high and low power objective lenses
Paper, white
Pencils

Note:
Culture the seedlings in gas jars lined with blotting-paper. The specimens used should be large enough to see expanded leaves and roots. (Revised Nuffield Biology *Teachers' guide 2* Chapter 13 gives experimental details.)

The procedure is detailed on the worksheet.

Answers to selected worksheet questions

2 Osmosis and the permeable nature of the cell wall are covered in Chapter **B**10, and need not be discussed in any detail here, where it is sufficient to observe that water and minerals will have to enter the organism across the cell wall. The question is useful because it introduces the idea of transfer of materials between an organism and its environment.

7 This is a difficult question. Many small leaves will have a greater total surface area than one large sheet of tissue.

13 There are two sorts of cones. The male cones produce a large amount of pollen that is carried by the wind to the female cones. The female cones contain the ovules and eggs. If an egg is fertilized, its ovule develops into a seed, and the female cone will eventually contain ripe seeds.

Further information

Barnes, R.S.K. *A synoptic classification of living organisms* Blackwell Scientific Publications, 1984.

Supplementary material

BBC videotape material, "Life on Earth" in particular, can be used to illustrate many of the organisms considered here. Interested teachers should contact BBC Enterprises (Education and Training), Woodlands, 80 Wood Lane, London, W12 0TT.

Topic B2

The processes of life

Chapter B3   Light means life

Purposes

Knowledge and understanding

At the end of this chapter all pupils should:

1 understand the significance of photosynthesis

2 understand the importance of chlorophyll as a light-absorbing molecule

3 understand the requirements for photosynthesis, the nature of the products formed and the effects of altering the conditions on the rate of photosynthesis

4 appreciate those structures in a leaf that enable photosynthesis to occur effectively.

In addition, those pupils aiming for higher grades should:

5 appreciate the variety of factors that limit the rate of photosynthesis, and ways of overcoming the limitations.

Processes and problem solving

Graphical and symbolic representation
Worksheet **B3H** asks pupils to plot graphs that relate the rate of photosynthesis to light intensity, light wavelength and carbon dioxide concentration.

Using apparatus and measuring instruments
Worksheet **B3A** uses the technique of paper chromatography to investigate plant pigments.

Worksheet **B3B** develops the technique for investigating the presence of starch in leaves, which can then be used as a matter of routine to determine whether photosynthesis has occurred (for example in Worksheet **B3D**).

The use of hydrogencarbonate indicator to investigate carbon dioxide production and consumption by leaves in darkness and in light can be introduced either as a class exercise or as a demonstration, when using Worksheet **B3C**.

Worksheets **B3E** and **B3F** both make use of microscopes to examine leaf structure.

Observation
The absorption of red and blue light by chlorophyll can be observed as part of a demonstration in section **B3.1**.

Worksheets **B3E** and **B3F** are concerned with the external and internal structure of leaves.

Interpretation and application

Pupils should use their knowledge of leaf structure to interpret the path of a carbon dioxide molecule through a leaf, from the air to the chloroplast.

In addition, those pupils aiming for higher grades might:

1 interpret the effect of decreasing light intensity or of varying carbon dioxide concentration on the rate of photosynthesis in a water plant, using data collected as part of Worksheet **B**3H or section **B**3.6

2 interpret how environmental factors limit photosynthesis, using data presented in section **B**3.6.

Planning and carrying out investigations

Worksheet **B**3B invites pupils to design controlled experiments to show that light, carbon dioxide and chlorophyll are needed for starch production. The requirement for carbon dioxide can also be investigated, using Worksheet **B**3D. (See also question 8 in section **B**3.2.)

Problem solving

The apparatus for measuring the production of oxygen by a water plant can be developed in order to study the effects of light intensity, light wavelength, temperature and carbon dioxide concentration on photosynthesis. Worksheet **B**3H sets the context for this problem-solving activity.

Timing

7 periods.

Suggested routes

There is a variety of routes through this material; the most appropriate pathway will depend upon the time allocated for practical work. Two possible routes are shown in figure **B**3; the righthand one is largely theoretical, and the lefthand one largely experimental. These routes should be regarded as just two of many possibilities.

Note that many of the practical investigations in this chapter need some degree of preparation a few days beforehand.

Opportunities for co-ordination

Much of the work in the Chemistry and Physics pupils' books is relevant to this chapter. For instance, the work on carbohydrate chemistry in Chapter **C**3 "Chemicals from plants" provides the chemical background necessary for an understanding of photosynthesis, and factors affecting the rates of chemical and biochemical reactions are discussed in Chapter **C**15 "Soil".

Chapter **P**8 "Machines and engines" introduces the concepts of power, energy and efficiency, which are developed further in Chapter **P**12 "Waste not, want not?"; these are important to a consideration of photosynthesis as a process by which plants trap energy from the sun. Chapter **P**3 "Radioactivity" discusses the carbon content of living plants and its relevance to radiocarbon dating, while Chapter **P**15 "Making use of waves" considers light as part of the electromagnetic spectrum, and is therefore co-ordinated with the selective absorption of colours from white light by chlorophyll.

Notes and answers

B3.1 A leafy world

The aims of this section are to explain why leaves look green, and to introduce chlorophyll as a remarkable molecule which "harvests" light energy. It would be possible to set up a demonstration of the light-absorbing properties of a solution of chlorophyll, using a design developed by the pupils as a result of discussion of question 5. Worksheet **B**3A separates the coloured pigments in leaves, using paper chromatography.

Periods

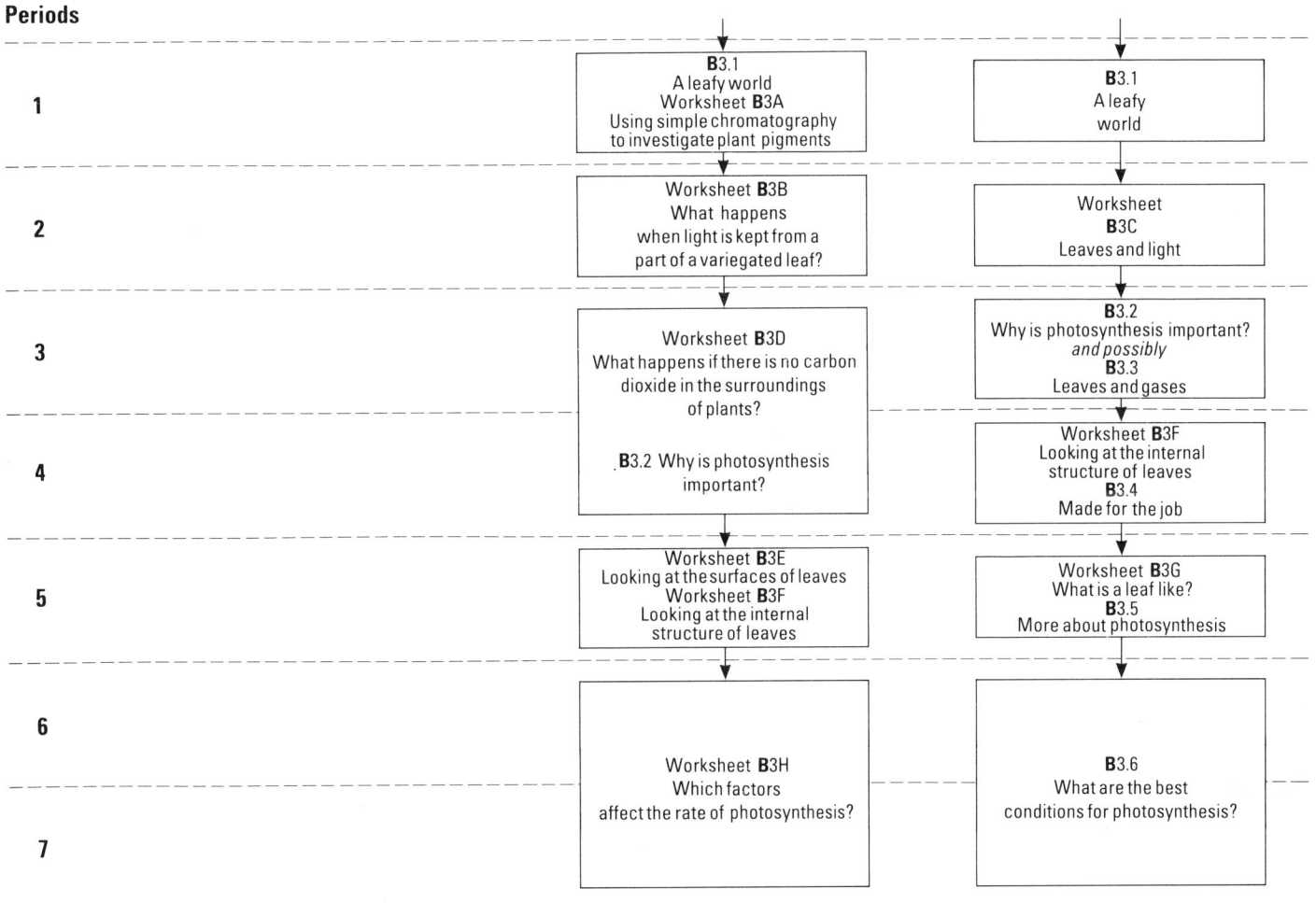

1	**B3.1** A leafy world Worksheet **B3A** Using simple chromatography to investigate plant pigments	**B3.1** A leafy world
2	Worksheet **B3B** What happens when light is kept from a part of a variegated leaf?	Worksheet **B3C** Leaves and light
3	Worksheet **B3D** What happens if there is no carbon dioxide in the surroundings of plants?	**B3.2** Why is photosynthesis important? *and possibly* **B3.3** Leaves and gases
4	**B3.2** Why is photosynthesis important?	Worksheet **B3F** Looking at the internal structure of leaves **B3.4** Made for the job
5	Worksheet **B3E** Looking at the surfaces of leaves Worksheet **B3F** Looking at the internal structure of leaves	Worksheet **B3G** What is a leaf like? **B3.5** More about photosynthesis
6	Worksheet **B3H** Which factors affect the rate of photosynthesis?	**B3.6** What are the best conditions for photosynthesis?
7		

Figure **B3**

Answers to selected questions

2 Some colours (red, blue, indigo, violet) disappear almost entirely whilst others (orange, yellow, green) are practically unaltered.

3 The pupils might well suggest that the missing colours have been absorbed by the chlorophyll solution.

4 Some pupils may need a little help to reason that if chlorophyll absorbs the red and blue light, then most of the light that passes through the leaf (*i.e.* is transmitted) is green light, so the leaves look green when looked at from underneath.

5 An arrangement such as the one in figure **B4** overleaf should be suggested.

B3.2   Why is photosynthesis important?

This section provides an important opportunity for pupils to design controlled experiments to investigate the factors that control the rate of photosynthesis. Worksheet **B3B** introduces the basic experimental techniques that can be adapted to test a variety of hypotheses, while Worksheet **B3C** provides experimental data for analysis by those who are not able to design and perform their own experiments. It is important, however, that **all** pupils are familiar with the technique of testing leaves for starch (see Worksheet **B3B**), and can perform it safely and as a matter of routine. This section stresses the significance of

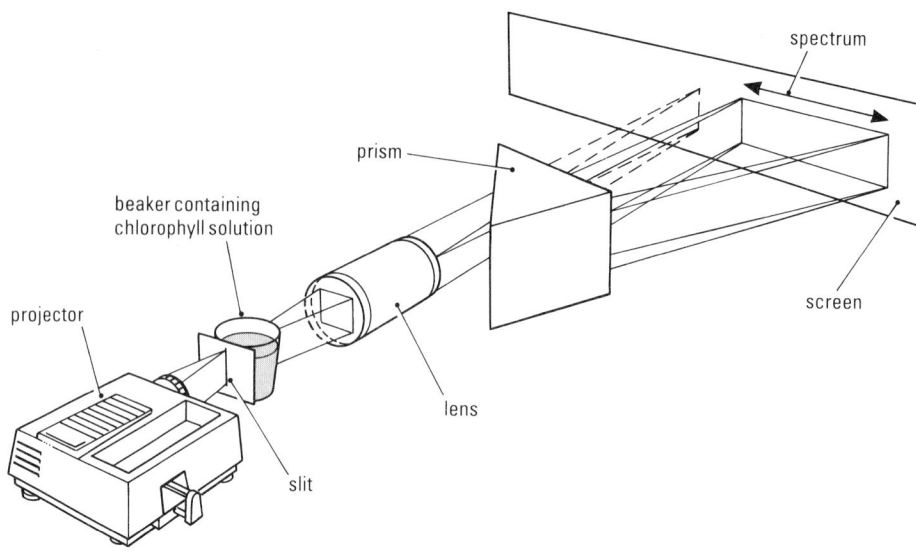

Figure **B4**

photosynthesis as the source of energy both for plants and for the animals that depend upon plants for food; the basis for all food production is the process of photosynthesis.

Answers to selected questions

7 Sugar cane is the obvious example of a plant that makes only sugar, and wheat is likely to be suggested as a plant which makes starch as well.

8 The need to use identical containers and materials for the plants should be stressed. Sodium hydroxide pellets absorb carbon dioxide gas. Black paper or aluminium foil can create dark conditions for the plants. (Note that both illuminated and dark plants should be kept at the same distance from a light source, so as to maintain approximately equal temperatures.)

B3.3 Leaves and gases

Photosynthesis plays a crucial role in maintaining the delicate balance of carbon dioxide and oxygen in the atmosphere. The numbers used in this section are designed to let pupils appreciate the importance of photosynthesis. They are **not** meant to be memorized!

Worksheet **B**3D investigates the importance of carbon dioxide in the surroundings of plants.

B3.4 Made for the job

Leaves can be visualized as "factories" for photosynthesis. The structure of a leaf is of major significance in allowing this process to occur efficiently. This section, combined with Worksheets **B**3E, **B**3F or **B**3G, should reveal how the structure of a leaf is closely related to its function. At the end of the section, pupils should appreciate which structures in a leaf enable photosynthesis to occur effectively. These include:

1 A large surface area, which ensures the absorption of as much light as possible and a large surface across which gases can be absorbed.
2 Transparent cells on the outer surfaces of the leaf, through which light can be transmitted.

3 Holes (stomata) in the surface of the leaf, which allow carbon dioxide and oxygen to diffuse in and out. In most plants stomata open in the daytime and close at night, and a mechanism by which the size of the pore is regulated must exist.

4 The presence of chlorophyll in the upper surface of a leaf, where the light will be most intense.

5 Spaces between the cells in the leaf, which allow movement of gases between the leaf cells and the air.

6 A well developed water supply in the veins which carry water to the leaf cells from the roots, and a transport system which removes the food products away from the leaf.

Other general points which could be mentioned are:

7 Ideally, a leaf has a very thin structure, with the result that no cell is too far from the surface.

8 The leaves grow, bend and turn to form a leaf mosaic, which means they do not overshadow each other.

B3.5   More about photosynthesis

This section is a difficult one, in which pupils should relate the consumption of carbon dioxide to glucose production. It should also become clear that the oxygen given out by a plant during photosynthesis comes from water (which is split into hydrogen and oxygen), and not from carbon dioxide. It is the hydrogen released from the water molecule that reduces the carbon dioxide to glucose. It is intended that the pupils should become familiar with the idea of chemical reactions occurring in and around the chloroplast, rather than have a detailed understanding of the different stages of the photosynthetic reactions.

Answer to selected question

9 It will help pupils to refer to figure 3.6 when answering this question. The molecule of carbon dioxide enters the leaf through a stoma and passes into an airspace. From here, it diffuses through the cell wall and cell membrane of a mesophyll cell and into a chloroplast, where it is reduced to glucose.

B3.6   What are the best conditions for photosynthesis?

By this stage, pupils should be familiar with the requirements for photosynthesis. It is reasonable to ask whether the rate of photosynthesis can be increased indefinitely by increasing the concentrations of the various "raw materials". This leads to a consideration of the idea of limiting factors in the process of photosynthesis (and also their relevance to agriculture and horticulture). The relationship between the rate of photosynthesis and such factors as light intensity, wavelength and carbon dioxide concentration can be investigated using Worksheet **B3H**.

Answers to selected questions

10 Light, an appropriate concentration of carbon dioxide, temperature and the availability of water all affect photosynthesis.

11 The light intensity is highest when the lamp is nearest to the water plant; therefore the rate of photosynthesis is directly proportional to the light intensity.

13 Much of the output of light from that bulb is at the red end of the spectrum. As red light is absorbed by green plants, the bulb could be useful. The results of

Worksheet **B3H** will confirm, for instance, that the rate of photosynthesis is faster in red light than in green light.

14 Some factor, other than light, must be limiting the rate of photosynthesis; it is most likely to be the concentration of carbon dioxide in the atmosphere.

15 In this case a different limiting factor is operating – possibly light.

16a It is most likely to be light.
b It is not likely to be temperature or light; it is most likely to be carbon dioxide.
c In these conditions it is not likely to be temperature or carbon dioxide; light is the most likely limiting factor.

Practical work

Worksheet B3A   Using simple chromatography to investigate plant pigments

REQUIREMENTS

Each group of pupils will need:
Leaves, fresh green (*e.g.* busy lizzie, grass, nettle, spinach or bamboo)
Leaves, variegated or red (*e.g.* copper beech, *Coleus*)

Propanone (acetone), 40 cm^3

Beaker, 250 cm^3
Boiling-tube
Bung, split
Capillary tube, fine, or hypodermic needle
Filter paper
Funnel
Glass wool
Pencils
Pestle and mortar
Scissors

Access to:
Receptacle for waste solvent

The procedure is detailed on the worksheet.

Worksheet B3B   What happens when light is kept from a part of a variegated leaf?

REQUIREMENTS

Each group of pupils will need:
Leaves, a selection from the following: variegated leaves (*e.g. Pelargonium, Coleus*), green leaves (*e.g.* privet, lime, busy lizzie) which have been in the light, green leaves which have been kept in the dark for 48 hours, green leaves which have been kept without carbon dioxide for 48 hours

Ethanol
Iodine in potassium iodide solution

Beaker, 250 cm^3, to serve as water bath
Boiling-tube in which to heat ethanol
Bunsen burner
Cork and pins *or* aluminium foil *or* black paper and paper clips, to cover areas of leaves
Dropping pipette
Forceps, blunt
Gauze
Glasses, protective
Petri dish or white porcelain dish
Tripod stand

If leaf discs are used:
Cork borer
Wooden board or white tile

Access to:
Receptacle to receive used ethanol containing chlorophyll
Water

Notes:
Leaves with thick cuticles or very hairy surfaces are not suitable because the reagents do not penetrate the leaf.

The ethanol should be used with care, since it ignites readily; all Bunsen burners should be turned off before it is used.

Leaf discs may be mounted on slides for examination under a microscope. They are more transparent if mounted in 50 per cent glycerol, thus making the distribution of starch easier to observe.

The worksheet can be developed in a number of ways. Variegated leaves such as *Pelargonium* or *Coleus* can be used to show that the distribution of chlorophyll is linked to starch synthesis. The importance of light for photosynthesis can be investigated by testing leaves from a number of plants that have been kept in the dark for at least 48 hours before the practical, and the role of carbon dioxide can be studied by using leaves that have been kept without carbon dioxide (by enclosing them in a conical flask containing soda lime) for 48 hours before the experiment starts.

Worksheet B3C   Leaves and light

REQUIREMENTS

Access to:
The pupils' book

This worksheet consists of descriptions of three investigations, with results for the pupils to interpret. The investigations could be set up as demonstrations in order to help pupils visualize what is happening (see "Demonstration experiments").

Worksheet B3D   What happens if there is no carbon dioxide in the surroundings of plants?

REQUIREMENTS

Each group of pupils will need:
Potted plants (such as *Pelargonium*) which have been kept in the dark for 48 hours

Ethanol
Iodine in potassium iodide solution
Sodium hydroxide pellets wrapped in a muslin bag

Beaker to serve as water bath
Boiling-tube in which to heat ethanol
Bungs, split rubber
Bunsen burner
Clamps to support conical flasks
Conical flasks or boiling-tubes in which to enclose selected leaves
Cottonwool
Dropping pipette
Forceps, blunt
Gauze
Glasses, protective
Lamp
Petri dish or white porcelain dish
Scissors
Tripod stand

This worksheet utilizes the technique developed in Worksheet **B3B**.

Worksheet B3E Looking at the surfaces of leaves

REQUIREMENTS

Each group of pupils will need:
Leaves (such as privet, ivy-leaved toadflax, lilac, busy lizzie)

Beaker in which to boil water
Bunsen burner
Coverslips
Forceps, blunt
Gauze
Microscope with high power ($\times 40$) objective lens
Microscope slides
Nail varnish, clear, or clear adhesive
Tripod stand

The procedure is detailed on the worksheet.

Worksheet B3F Looking at the internal structure of leaves

REQUIREMENTS

Each group of pupils will need:
Prepared slides of leaf sections
Microscope with low and high power objective lenses

The procedure is detailed on the worksheet.

Worksheet B3G What is a leaf like?

REQUIREMENTS

Access to:
The pupils' book

The procedure is detailed on the worksheet.

Worksheet B3H Which factors affect the rate of photosynthesis?

REQUIREMENTS

Each group of pupils will need:
Elodea, free of dirt and filamentous algae

Sodium hydrogencarbonate

Beaker or flask to hold water for filling syringe
Bench lamp fitted with 60 W bulb
Capillary tubing, narrow bore, 30 cm length
Clamp
Graph paper
Means of shielding apparatus from other light sources
Retort stand
Rubber tubing, short length
Rulers
Scissors or razor blade
Stopclock
Syringe, plastic, 20 cm^3

If wavelength is investigated:
Other light sources and filters

This worksheet can be developed in a variety of ways to suit the ingenuity and ability of the pupils concerned. It would be possible to set each group a different problem to solve, asking them to report back at the end of the practical session.

Demonstration experiments

The investigations described in Worksheet **B**3C can be performed as demonstrations, before the pupils analyse the data provided in the worksheet. The additional apparatus required is listed below.

Investigation 2

REQUIREMENTS

Leaves, freshly picked, such as privet or busy lizzie

Hydrogencarbonate indicator solution, previously equilibrated with atmospheric air
Water, distilled

Aluminium foil or black polythene
Aquarium tank, transparent plastic
Forceps, blunt
Light source (must be powerful)
Rubber bands
Stopclock
Syringe, 2 cm³
Test-tubes with rubber bungs, 3
Test-tube holder, consisting of spring clips attached to a piece of wood longer than the width of the aquarium
Thermometer

Investigation 3

REQUIREMENTS

Elodea, free of dirt and filamentous algae

Potassium hydroxide solution, concentrated
Potassium pyrogallate solution

Beaker, large tall, 500 cm³ minimum
Capillary analysis tube, J-shaped, with greased adjustment screw held firm by rubber tubing
Funnel, glass, with short stem
Light source, strong
Paper towels
Plasticine
Rulers
Test-tube
Trough, bowl or sink of water at room temperature

Further information

SATIS unit 201 "Energy from Biomass", which develops the ecological aspects of photosynthesis, could bridge this chapter and Chapter **B**14, where the theme of food webs is developed.

Note
SATIS ("Science and Technology in Society") is a series published by The Association for Science Education, 1986.

Chapter B4 How do animals feed?

Purposes

Knowledge and understanding

At the end of this chapter all pupils should:

1 understand why animals need to feed

2 know the internal structure of a human tooth and how the different types of teeth are used when feeding

3 understand the role of the bacteria forming acids in the mouth, leading to tooth decay

4 appreciate the differences between carnivorous, herbivorous and omnivorous modes of feeding; appreciate that these differences are reflected both in dentition and in the relative amounts of food needed to keep animals alive.

Processes and problem solving

Using apparatus and measuring instruments
Worksheet **B**4C uses disclosing tablets to study the distribution of plaque on teeth.

The effectiveness of toothpastes in killing bacteria can be investigated in Worksheet **B4F**.

Observation
Worksheet **B4B** provides opportunities for observing the variety of human teeth and the differences between the dentition of herbivores and carnivores.

Interpretation and application
Worksheet **B4A** allows data to be interpreted that relate the amount of food eaten by an animal to its nutritional quality.
   Worksheet **B4B** and section **B4.2** ask pupils to interpret the relationship between the dentition of carnivores and herbivores and their ways of feeding.
   Worksheet **B4D** allows data from surveys of dental health to be interpreted.
   Part of Worksheet **B4E** involves interpreting data that relate the incidence of dental caries to the fluoride content of the public water supply.

Planning and carrying out investigations
Dental hygiene surveys can be planned, using Worksheet **B4D**. Pupils can also find out which are the most popular sweets in their class.

Timing   5 periods.

Suggested routes   Figure **B5** presents two possible pathways through the material, differing in the emphasis given to the type of practical work performed on toothpastes. Teachers who would prefer to spend longer on human dentition could omit section **B4.1** and complete both Worksheets **B4E** and **B4F**.

Periods

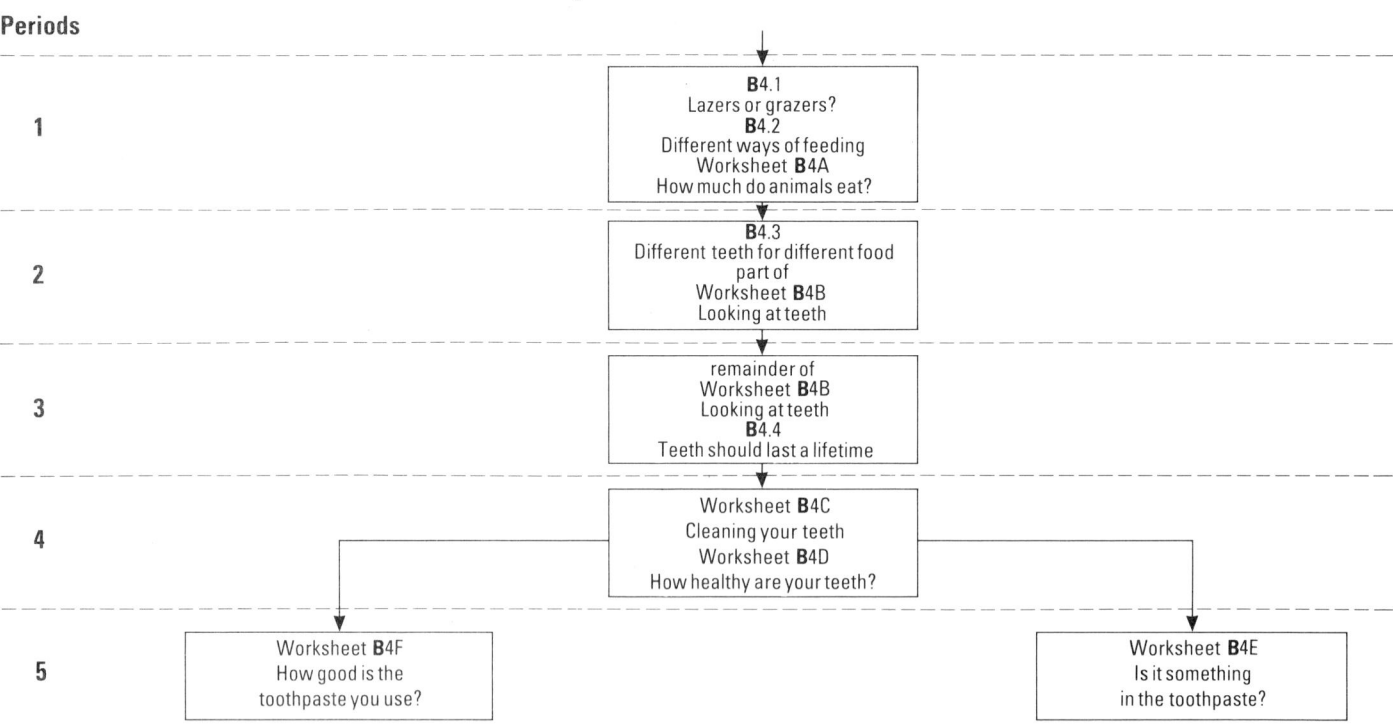

Figure **B5**

Sections **B4.5** and **B4.6** might form the basis of a homework exercise.

Opportunities for co-ordination

Fluoride and the water supply are also considered in Chapter **C10** "Keeping clean".

The evaluation of toothpaste may be co-ordinated with Chapter **C12** "Chemicals in the medicine cupboard".

Notes and answers

B4.1   Lazers or grazers?

The aim of this section is to introduce the idea that the type of food that is eaten (meat or vegetation) has consequences on the life-style of the animals concerned. This theme runs throughout this chapter and the next, since the type of food also affects the dentition and the digestive systems of the consumers.

Answers to selected questions

1 "Hunting or grazing" is an acceptable generalization.

2 The lions must get sufficient energy and nutrients from their food to enable them to feed only intermittently.

B4.2   Different ways of feeding

This section should be completed in conjunction with Worksheet **B4A**, which gives data on the amount of food eaten by tigers and elephants. It provides an interesting development of questions 1 and 2 in the previous section, and is a suitable exercise for homework. The photographs of animals feeding in figure 4.2 can be supplemented with appropriate video sequences (see "Supplementary material" section).

Answer to selected question

3 Herbivores: panda, elephant, slug.
Carnivores: praying mantis, ladybird, owl, hyena, vulture, lion.

B4.3   Different teeth for different food

This section should be completed in conjunction with Worksheet **B4B**. This allows differences between the dentition of herbivores and carnivores to be investigated, and the theme of human dentition, which will be developed in the subsequent sections of this chapter, is also introduced.

Answers to selected questions

6 Sheep lack upper incisors and canines.

7 Canines, and the upper premolars and lower molars called carnassial teeth. These teeth are for tearing and cutting flesh.

8 The cheek teeth of a plant-eater have a series of grooves and enamel ridges running across them. The ridges of the teeth in the upper jaw fit into the grooves in the teeth in the lower jaw. Similarly, the ridges in the teeth of the lower jaw fit into the grooves in the teeth of the upper jaw. When these animals eat, they move their jaws from side to side, and the teeth scrape against each other, grinding any food caught between them into small pieces.

The cheek teeth of a meat-eater fit tightly together when the jaw closes. This enables them to crush hard materials such as bone.

9 The mammals will have similar types of teeth to ours, although there will be some variation in size, number and shape.

B4.4 Teeth should last a lifetime

The idea of dental hygiene is developed in sections **B4.4** and **B4.5**. This section develops understanding of the causes of tooth decay – and the reasons why it can be so painful! The remaining parts of Worksheet **B4B** can now be completed. The accumulation of plaque can be revealed by disclosing tablets, using the method in Worksheet **B4C**.

B4.5 Prevention is better than cure

This section concentrates on dental hygiene. It should be supplemented by Worksheet **B4D**, a survey of dental health, the results of which can be compared with national figures for the 1960s and 1980s. Analysing the amount and type of sweets eaten by pupils in the class can lead to interesting discussions on diet and health, which can lead into Chapter **B6** "Diet and good health". The effectiveness of different toothpastes in killing bacteria can be investigated, using Worksheet **B4F**, and the effectiveness of fluoride can be considered, using Worksheet **B4E**. (Question 1 on this worksheet might make a suitable homework exercise.)

Answer to selected question

10 Regular cleaning to remove plaque, neutralization of the mouth contents after eating sweet or acidic food and reducing the amount of sugar kept in the mouth for long periods (chewing and swallowing sweets is better than sucking them).

B4.6 Different guts for different diets

This section resumes the theme of the first two sections, and serves as an introduction to the next chapter. It points out that mammalian plant-eaters and meat-eaters differ not only in their dentition, but also in their digestive systems.

Answer to selected question

11 A ruminant herbivore has an enlarged section of its digestive system, which contains the micro-organisms that break down the plant fibres. This is not the case with carnivores.

Practical work

Worksheet B4A   How much do animals eat?

REQUIREMENTS

Each group of pupils will need:
Pens

The procedure is detailed on the worksheet.

Worksheet B4B   Looking at teeth

REQUIREMENTS

Each group of pupils will need:
Skulls of rabbit, sheep, dog, cat (at least 1 herbivore and 1 carnivore)

Dental mirror
Drawing paper

Notes:
Skulls can be bought from dealers, or with a little patience can be prepared at school. If fur, skin and flesh are removed and the skull then heated in a pressure cooker, it becomes an easy matter to scrape it perfectly clean. It should then be scrubbed with a stiff paste of calcium chloride before being bleached with hydrogen peroxide. Take care that the bones do not become brittle and that fixed joints do not separate. Teeth should be glued into their sockets.

Very interesting results will be obtained if pupils can compare the teeth of older friends and relatives with their own. Modern alkaline toothpastes and fluoridation of drinking water, together with a greater knowledge of and interest in personal hygiene, have caused pupils to have better teeth than their parents. This will be revealed most clearly if the age at which the older generation lost their teeth can be determined.

The worksheet asks pupils to work out dental formulae for a herbivore, a carnivore and an omnivore. Details of the formulae should not be memorized. Typical examples are:

		Incisor	Canine	Premolar	Molar
Human	upper:	2	1 ·	2	3
	lower:	2	1	2	3
Rabbit	upper:	2	0	3	3
	lower:	1	0	2	3
Dog	upper:	3	1	4	2
	lower:	3	1	4	3

Note that these figures are for one half of the mouth, and need to be doubled in order to calculate the total number of teeth.

Worksheet B4C   Cleaning your teeth

REQUIREMENTS

Each group of pupils will need:
Disclosing tablets (1 per pupil)
Water, drinking, in a cup or beaker

Toothbrush (brought from home by each pupil)
Toothpaste

Access to:
Sink or bowl

This lesson can be developed in a number of ways. For example, brushes of differing hardness or different toothpastes could be used, or one different style of brushing could be employed. Similarly, an investigation could be made into the recent diet of the children, and an attempt made to relate this to the amount of plaque.

Teeth can often be obtained from a dentist, and at this stage a series of experiments could be carried out. For instance, the hardness of teeth could be compared with that of other materials such as bone or rock by using a file, or the effects of acids, soft drinks etc. could be investigated by standing teeth in them for a number of days or weeks.

Worksheet B4D   How healthy are your teeth?

REQUIREMENTS

Each group of pupils will need:
Pencils
Writing paper

The procedure is detailed on the worksheet.

Worksheet B4E   Is it something in the toothpaste?

REQUIREMENTS

Each group of pupils will need:
Pencils
Writing paper

The procedure is detailed on the worksheet.

Worksheet B4F   How good is the toothpaste you use?

REQUIREMENTS

Each group of pupils will need:
Petri dish, sterile, plated with sterile blood agar base and seeded with a suspension of
    Bacillus subtilis, with four wells cut in it

Chinagraph pencil
Forceps, blunt
Rulers
Tape, adhesive

Access to:
Discs impregnated with *Bacillus subtilis*
McCartney bottles
Nutrient broth No. 2
Toothpaste, 4 brands

Notes:
The bacterial cultures and agar plates must be prepared in advance.

To prepare the Petri dishes of blood agar base, tablets or powder should be bought from dealers and made up as directed (various preparations are now available). The material is made up in tubes, closed with cottonwool or loose fitting aluminium caps, and sterilized in a pressure cooker for 20 minutes. After the pressure has been released, the agar preparation (now liquid) is poured into sterile plastic Petri dishes (also obtained from dealers). The lids of the dishes should only be lifted enough to allow the agar to be poured, and then replaced. The agar will solidify as it cools.

The *Bacillus subtilis* suspension is prepared by adding the bacteria (possibly bought as an impregnated disc) to $10 \, cm^3$ sterile nutrient broth No. 2 in a McCartney bottle. This amount will be enough to flood two plates. The disc should be handled with sterile forceps, and the screw cap replaced on the McCartney bottle.

The culture is incubated at about 25 °C for 24 hours. Agitate from time to time to prevent clumps of bacteria forming, and shake thoroughly just before use.

Using a sterile pipette, flood an agar plate with $5 \, cm^3$ of the broth culture. Allow the liquid to run over the whole surface by tilting the plate. Allow the plate to dry before starting the experiment.

Now cut four wells for the toothpaste, or allow the students to add the toothpaste to discs of filter paper and place them on the surface of the agar.

Remember to sterilize **all** apparatus and materials used in this experiment. Ensure that the plates are sealed with adhesive tape after the students have added the toothpaste. **Do not allow them to open the dishes again.**

Incubate the dishes for two days at 25 °C (37 °C is no longer recommended for school use) and allow the pupils to see the results in a later lesson. (Growth can be slowed down by keeping the plates in a refrigerator once good results are apparent.)

Sterilize all dishes and dispose of them with care.

Further information

Two SATIS units could provide useful background material to this chapter. They are units 606 "The Tristan da Cunha dental surveys" and 401 "Fluoridation of water supplies".

Supplementary material

Video sequences of herbivores and carnivores feeding can be found in programme 11 of the BBC series "Life on Earth". Write to BBC Enterprises (Education and Training), Woodlands, 80 Wood Lane, London, W12 0TT.

Chapter B5   The gut as a food processor

Purposes

Knowledge and understanding

At the end of this chapter all pupils should:

1 appreciate that the gut is a coiled tube and is the site of digestion and absorption; different parts of the tube operate most efficiently at different pH values

2 understand the roles of longitudinal and circular muscles in peristalsis

3 appreciate that digestion is brought about by enzymes, acting as biological catalysts

4 know that the villi of the small intestine are the sites of absorption of the soluble products of digestion.

In addition, those pupils aiming for higher grades should:

5 understand how the rate of an enzyme reaction can be affected by temperature and pH

6 appreciate that enzymes are proteins

7 appreciate that small, soluble products of digestion are needed because the walls of the gut are selectively permeable.

Processes and problem solving

Graphical and symbolic representation
In Worksheet **B**5C pupils are asked to plot a graph of the heights of a healthy child and one with coeliac disease.

Using apparatus and measuring instruments
Experiments showing the action of amylase and protease can be performed, using Worksheets **B**5A and **B**5B.

Observation
Pupils may observe how X-rays are used to study the gut, in section **B**5.1.

Interpretation and application
Section **B**5.3 asks pupils to interpret a graph of experimental data illustrating the properties of enzymes.
   Worksheet **B**5C presents data showing the effects of the absence of villi on the growth of a child.

Planning and carrying out investigations
Section **B**5.2 and Worksheet **B**5A ask pupils to design simple investigations to illustrate the effects of various factors on amylase (such as pH, temperature, cigarette smoke).

Timing

5 periods.

Suggested routes

Figure **B**6 presents two possible approaches to teaching the materials in this chapter. Where the approaches differ, the righthand line indicates a more theoretical approach, whilst the lefthand line indicates an investigative route.

Periods

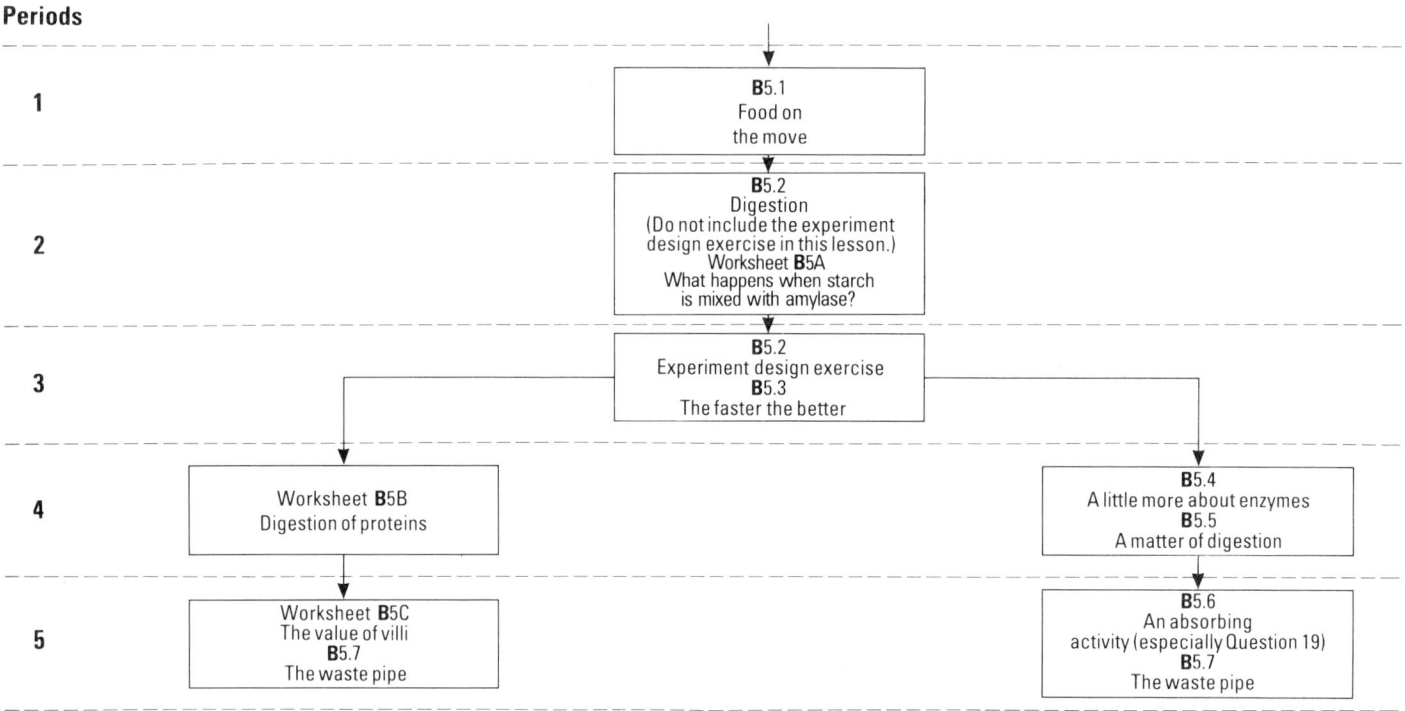

1	**B**5.1 Food on the move
2	**B**5.2 Digestion (Do not include the experiment design exercise in this lesson.) Worksheet **B**5A What happens when starch is mixed with amylase?
3	**B**5.2 Experiment design exercise **B**5.3 The faster the better

| 4 | Worksheet **B**5B
Digestion of proteins | **B**5.4
A little more about enzymes
B5.5
A matter of digestion |
| 5 | Worksheet **B**5C
The value of villi
B5.7
The waste pipe | **B**5.6
An absorbing
activity (especially Question 19)
B5.7
The waste pipe |

Figure **B**6

Opportunities for co-ordination

Several chapters in the Chemistry pupils' book are relevant to the work on digestion and enzymes in this chapter. For instance, enzyme function is closely related to its protein structure; the chemistry of protein and carbohydrate molecules is covered in Chapter **C**3 "Chemicals from plants". The pH of regions of the gut is important for their enzymes to function efficiently; pH is discussed in Chapter **C**12 "Chemicals in the medicine cupboard" and ions are introduced in Chapter **C**5 "Materials and structures". Enzymes are also found to be useful in household and industrial situations (see Chapter **C**10 "Keeping clean").

The membranes of the intestine are selectively permeable; the separation of large and small molecules using such membranes is covered in Chapter **C**3 "Chemicals from plants". The emulsification of fats by bile salts is also dealt with in Chapter **C**9 "Foams, emulsions, sols and gels".

Notes and answers

B5.1   Food on the move

This section begins by getting pupils to think about what happens to food once it is in their mouths. The mechanical breakdown by teeth (and cutlery) is described briefly; pupils should appreciate that small pieces of food are easier to swallow than large. The cream cracker exercise in question 11 is designed to show that the food must also be moist.

After completing section **B**5.3 on enzymes it would be possible to refer back to **B**5.1 in order to develop the idea of smaller pieces of food offering a greater surface area for enzymes to work on. At this point, more able pupils could be asked to design an experiment to test this.

The role of muscles in squeezing food along the gut (peristalsis) can be a difficult idea to understand, but it is hoped that the variety of approaches mentioned in the text will help to overcome any difficulties. A useful model (which is easy to make and which can be passed around the class) is a length of flexible pipe with a ball-bearing inside to act as a bolus of food. A piece of Bunsen burner pipe will do – it works better if the inside has been lubricated with oil. Pupils can squeeze the ball-bearing along the tube to simulate peristalsis, in which the circular muscles contract behind the bolus and the wave of contraction spreads down the tube. This is analogous to the finger squeezing the rubber pipe and moving down the length of the pipe.

Answers to selected questions

2 Height × width × depth.

6 The gut contents are not normally opaque to X-rays.

B5.2   Digestion

This section aims to establish that digestion is essential if food molecules are to get from the gut into the bloodstream. The food molecules need to be small enough to pass through the gut membranes. A useful analogy to explain the need to produce small molecules can be made with reference to soccer supporters: if the soccer supporters (glucose molecules) hold hands (chemical bonds) to form a long chain (starch molecule), they cannot get through the gaps in the perimeter fence (cell membrane). However, if their hand grips were to be broken (digestion), the fence would no longer be a barrier.

Worksheets **B**5A and **B**5B allow pupils to investigate digestion. Opportunities also exist to design experiments that test certain hypotheses about amylase. The experimental design exercises could be set for homework, although the pupils should be given the opportunity to carry out their own experiments in class. Re-evaluation of experimental designs in the light of experience is a valuable way of developing expertise in this area.

B5.3   The faster the better

This section aims to establish the nature of the substance found in saliva which helps with digestion. The term enzyme is used for the first time, and some of the general properties of these essential protein molecules are introduced. More able pupils will be able to link the information in this section to their findings in the investigations of the previous section.

Answers to selected questions

12 pH 7.0.

13 At high temperatures enzyme molecules are permanently altered. They are said to be denatured. At low temperatures molecules have less kinetic energy, so it is less likely for an enzyme molecule to make contact with a substrate molecule. Pupils could be asked to design an experiment to show that enzyme molecules are not denatured by low temperatures.

B5.4   A little more about enzymes

This section aims to show that enzymes are found in living organisms other than humans. It is also important to establish that enzymes can control the synthesis of large molecules from smaller ones.

B5.5   A matter of digestion

Pupils are expected to appreciate that the gut is not just a simple pipe, but has specialized regions in which particular tasks are carried out. In this section pupils are introduced to the events taking place in the stomach. Worksheet **B5B** allows them to investigate the effect of protease on egg white.

Answers to selected questions

15 Approximately pH 2.

16 It will reduce its activity because a pH of 2 is far from the optimum pH at which salivary amylase is most active.

17 It will neutralize the acid and provide the optimum pH for the pancreatic enzymes – about pH 8.

18 It will increase the surface area of the fat for the lipase enzyme to work on, thereby helping to speed up the breakdown of the fat into fatty acids and glycerol. It is important that pupils do not think that it is bile which converts fats into fatty acids and glycerol.

B5.6   An absorbing activity

This section continues the theme that the gut has specialized regions along its length. A portion of the gut devoted principally to the absorption of digested food products is one essential area. In question 19 pupils are asked to suggest the features such a portion may have. This can lead into a consideration of Worksheet **B5C**, which compares the growth of a child lacking villi with that of a comparable healthy child.

Answer to selected question

19 The region would need to be long enough to provide a large surface area for absorption. Pupils will need help to appreciate that the surface area can be, and is, increased by the presence of millions of tiny projections called villi. An opportunity to see microscope slides of transverse sections through the small intestine may be of some use at this stage.

B5.7   The waste pipe

The large intestine is the final specialized part of the gut to which pupils are introduced.

Answers to selected questions

20 They absorb water.

22 X = stomach; Y = duodenum; Z = ileum.

Practical work

Worksheet B5A   What happens when starch is mixed with amylase?

REQUIREMENTS

Each group of pupils will need:
1 % amylase solution
Benedict's solution
Iodine in potassium iodide solution
1 % starch suspension
Water, distilled

Bunsen burner
Dropping pipette
Glasses, protective
Spotting tile
Stopclock
Syringe, 20 cm³
Test-tubes and rack

Access to:
Amylase solution through which cigarette
    smoke has been bubbled
Sink
Sodium chloride
Water baths at various temperatures (*e.g.*
    25 °C and 35 °C)

Notes:
Check that the syringe plungers move
freely and allow pupils to practise
delivering single drops from a syringe.
    The requirements for the experimental
design exercise have been written in the
Access to list. Cigarette smoke can be
bubbled through an amylase solution,
using a U-tube attached to a filter pump.
One end of the U-tube is attached to the
pump, and the other end to a cigarette.
The suction from the pump is sufficient to
draw the smoke through the amylase
solution. This can be done as a
demonstration. Keep the windows open!

The starch is largely converted into maltose; the action of amylase serves to
illustrate the process of digestion.

Worksheet B5B   Digestion of proteins

REQUIREMENTS

Each group of pupils will need:
Egg white suspension, 10 cm³
10 % protease solution, 5 cm³

Glasses, protective
Stopclock
Syringes, 5 cm³, 2
Test-tubes, 2, and holder

Access to:
Dilute hydrochloric acid
Dropping pipette
Water bath at 37 °C

The procedure is detailed on the worksheet.

Worksheet B5C   The value of villi

REQUIREMENTS

Each group of pupils will need:
Graph paper
Pencils
Rulers

The procedure is detailed on the worksheet.

Answers to selected worksheet questions

2 Between 4 and 9 years old.

3 The normal boy grew 20 cm in this 3-year period, the coeliac boy only 10 cm.
Yearly rates of growth are therefore 6.67 cm and 3.33 cm respectively. Rates
calculated from the graph will, of course, depend upon its accuracy.

4 The normal boy grew twice as fast.

5 Almost all the commonly observed clinical features of coeliac disease arise as a consequence of poor absorption of food. They include loss of body mass, diarrhoea, muscle weakness, skin abnormalities, anaemia and, in children, a failure to grow.

6 He must be given a gluten-free diet for the rest of his life.

It is worth noting that certain brands of baby food advertise that they lack gluten. Pupils could be asked to look out for such brands and to bring the labels into school. A discussion of the various other substances besides gluten which are left out of baby food would provide a link with Chapter **B4**, which deals with diet.

Further information

The industrial applications of enzymes (for instance, in washing powders, malting, cheese making and immobilized enzymes) are covered in SATIS unit 710 "What is Biotechnology?".

Chapter B6   Diet and good health

Purposes

Knowledge and understanding

At the end of this chapter all pupils should:

1 understand that a balanced diet contains sufficient energy to maintain life, and that the energy requirements of a person vary with age and activity

2 understand why fibre and vitamins are needed for health; realize the unhealthy effects of eating too much fat and salt.

In addition, those pupils aiming for higher grades should:

3 know that the thyroid gland controls the metabolic rate.

Processes and problem solving

Graphical and symbolic representation
Bar charts showing data about energy requirements are plotted in Worksheet **B6B**.

Interpretation and application
Pupils analyse diets in Worksheet **B6A**.
   Worksheet **B6B** includes an analysis of the energy requirements of different people.

Problem solving
Worksheet **B6B** and several questions in the pupils' book are concerned with planning balanced diets.

Timing

3 periods.

Suggested routes

Figure **B7** indicates two possible approaches to allocating three periods to this chapter. The major difference between them is the time devoted to a consideration of the patterns of healthy diets. Section **B6.4** could be developed alongside Worksheet **B6B** or included in the work on balanced diets in Worksheet **B6A**. It is important to realize that overweight, underweight or anorexic pupils could be made to feel very embarassed by an insensitive presentation of this material.

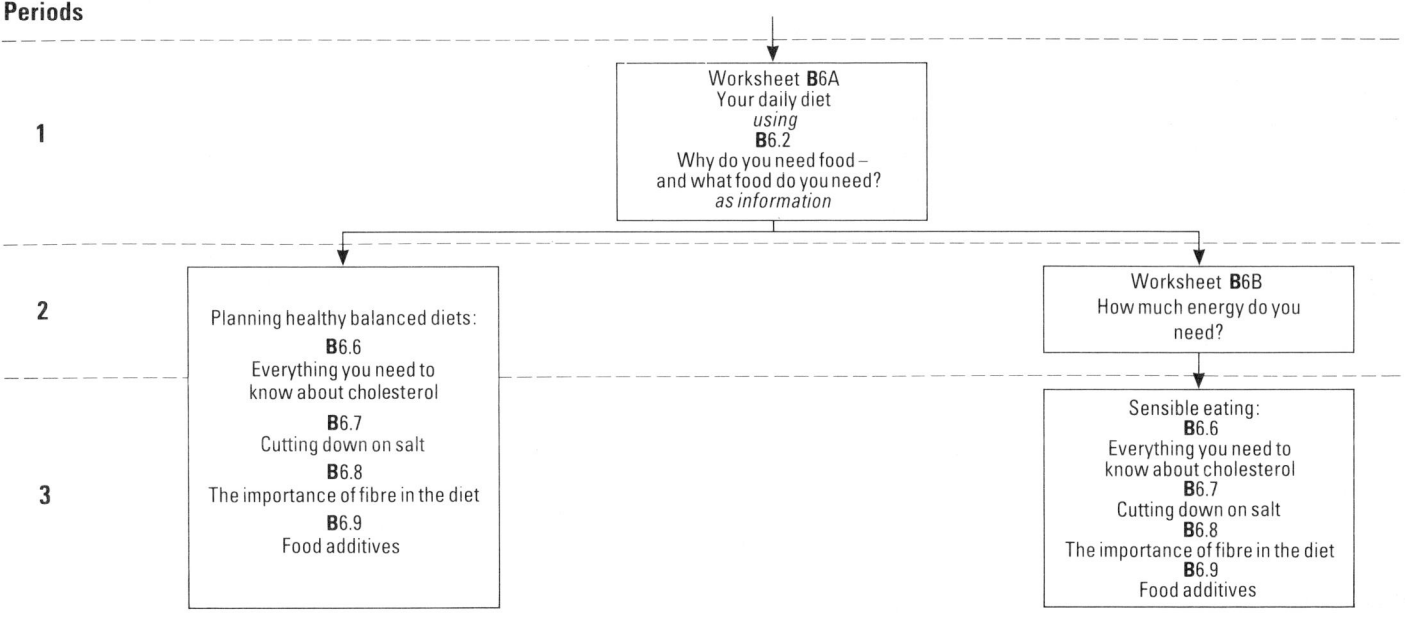

Figure **B**7

Opportunities for co-ordination

Chapters **C**3 "Chemicals from plants" and **C**8 "Polymers" provide the chemical background necessary for an understanding of proteins and carbohydrates as polymers, while Chapter **C**18 "Atoms and bonding" will help pupils to understand the breaking of chemical bonds in digestion. Chapter **C**9 "Foams, emulsions, sols and gels" discusses colloids and the emulsifying properties of some food additives.

A useful comparison to make is that between food and fuel, which may be supported by Chapter **C**13 "Fuels and fires".

Notes and answers

B6.1 What would you like for supper tonight?

This section allows pupils to begin to think about what they eat and why. It may be developed by using Worksheet **B**6A.

B6.2 Why do you need food – and what food do you need?

Sensible patterns of eating could include meat, but need not. The emphasis in this section, and indeed in the whole chapter, is that pupils should think carefully about what they eat and develop balanced diets that suit them.

Answers to selected questions

2 Cereal grains, seeds (such as beans or pulses) and nuts are all sources of protein.

3 Some vegetarian diets are probably healthier than diets rich in animal fats and low in fibre. Nonetheless, both vegetarian and meat diets need to be carefully planned.

B6.3 Getting the energy balance right

Worksheet **B6B** develops the idea that a balanced diet contains the right daily intake of energy. The number of kilojoules of energy needed each day will vary with the individual's age, health and activity.

Answer to selected question

4a Fat acts as an insulator against heat loss in cold climates.
b Protein is required for repairing damaged or worn body tissues.
c Women can lose a lot of blood during their menstrual periods, and may suffer from anaemia as a result. Additional iron makes up for what is lost in this way.
d Glucose can be readily absorbed into the body, and is immediately available for respiration in muscle cells. It can be thought of as an additional source of energy.
e Pregnant women require additional food in order to nourish the developing embryo. A strict vegan diet may not provide enough food or the correct minerals, particularly calcium and iron, for the embryo, as dairy products and meat are not eaten.

B6.4 Too fat or too thin?

Pupils often worry about their physical appearance, and this section needs to be taught with sensitivity. It makes the point that deposition of fat usually results from a surplus intake of energy and too little exercise. Anorexia is a topic that needs especially gentle handling, since its origins are psychological.

Answers to selected questions

7 Fat people are more prone to heart disease, high blood pressure and diabetes than people of normal mass.

10 Strong contenders should include biscuits, pies, fish and chips, and sweets. Of more relevance is the idea that in moderation these foods are not "bad". Taken together, or eaten to excess with the exclusion of other foods, they can form an unbalanced diet.

B6.5 Controlling your appetite

Fortunately, most of us are able to eat sufficient food to avoid the dreadful consequences of protein deficiency. Two-thirds of the world are not so fortunate. Pupils with an inclination (or a need) to diet should be warned of the potential dangers of excess dieting. All pupils ought to become aware of the dietary problems that face far too much of the world's population.

B6.6 Everything you need to know about cholesterol

This section provides useful guidance on the dangers of excess cholesterol and fats in the diet.

Answers to selected questions

13a The risk increases by about one quarter.
b It more than doubles.

14 Trim the fat off the lamb, use shortcrust instead of flaky pastry, eliminate (or reduce) ice cream and cream, perhaps replace the sweet course with cheese and biscuits and try reduced fat cheese (*e.g.* low fat cheddar).

B6.7   Cutting down on salt

This section continues the examination of diet by considering salt.

Answer to selected question

16 Certainly do not add it to the food that is on the table. Avoid excess convenience foods.

B6.8   The importance of fibre in the diet

Fibre is an important element in our diet. Fibre levels can easily be raised by eating wholemeal bread instead of white bread.

Answer to selected question

17 About 6 slices of wholemeal bread, 10 slices of wheatmeal bread and 18 slices of white bread.

B6.9   Food additives

It is important that pupils realize that not **all** substances with an "E" number are harmful. Indeed some, like ascorbic acid (vitamin C, E300) are positively beneficial. Even so, certain additives can cause reactions in some people.

Practical work

Worksheet B6A   Your daily diet

REQUIREMENTS

Each group of pupils will need:
Variety of food labels giving nutritional information

Access to:
Nutritional information, especially concerning size of regular portions

One approach to the analysis of diet is described on the worksheet. There are many ways in which this analysis can be developed. Pupils should be encouraged to bring in labels from tins and packets of food, which give many details of minerals, vitamins, fibre, salt, sugar, preservatives and colouring matter. Charts, tables and other forms of display could be prepared. Pupils may need help in estimating how much of each food they eat at each meal. From this they can work out their daily intake of energy and food substances into the body.

Worksheet B6B   How much energy do you need?

REQUIREMENTS

Each group of pupils will need:
Graph paper
Pencils

This exercise could be used as a basis for a class discussion on the energy requirements of different people. It is also suitable for use as a homework exercise.

Further information

There are a number of SATIS units that could provide background information for this chapter. They include units 703 "Vegetarianism", 102 "Food from Fungus", 108 "Fibre in your Diet", 404 "How would you Survive?" (a study of malnutrition), 104 "What's in our Food? – a look at food labels" and 208 "The Price of Food".

Chapter B7   The breath of life

Purposes

Knowledge and understanding

At the end of this chapter all pupils should:

1 understand how movements of the intercostal muscles and diaphragm bring about inhalation and exhalation through changes in pressure in the thorax; appreciate the antagonistic nature of the intercostal muscles

2 understand how the structure of the alveoli and blood capillaries allows gas exchange to take place

3 recognize the importance of diffusion in gas exchange across the alveolar walls.

In addition, those pupils aiming for higher grades should:

4 understand the significance of the pleural membranes and the pleural fluid in breathing

5 understand the role of goblet cells and phagocytes in keeping the lungs free from infection

6 appreciate that small animals with large ratios of surface area:volume are able to use diffusion as a method of gas exchange.

Processes and problem solving

Graphical and symbolic representation
Worksheet **B**7B uses a parallelogram model to illustrate the movements of the ribcage. Worksheet **B**7C uses a syringe model to illustrate the action of the pleural membranes.

Pupils can plot graphs relating the ratio of surface area:volume of an organism to its size, using Worksheet **B**7E.

Using apparatus and measuring instruments
Hydrogencarbonate indicator is used to detect changes between inhaled and exhaled air; pupils should understand the advantages of this method over the limewater method, using section **B**7.2.

Worksheet **B**7F asks pupils to measure the effects of exercise on the rate of breathing.

Observation
Worksheet **B**7D provides an opportunity to observe the structure of the mammalian thorax.

Pupils can use Worksheet **B**7G to observe the particulate nature of cigarette smoke, and then predict its effect on lungs.

Interpretation and application
Section **B**7.4 asks pupils to analyse the differences between inhaled and exhaled air, and to relate the tabulated data to the movement of gases across the alveolar membranes.

Section **B**7.6 helps pupils to see that health considerations may underly modern trends in smoking.

Planning and carrying out investigations
In Worksheet **B**7F pupils plan experiments to see if mental activity can alter the breathing rate. Worksheet **B**7H helps pupils to plan and carry out a survey into why people smoke and why some people continue to smoke.

Problem solving

Questions 2 to 4 involve calculating the changes in the composition of air when it is drawn into the lungs.

Using Worksheet **B**7E, pupils should appreciate the consequences that an organism's ratio of surface area:volume may have on its method of gaseous exchange.

Timing   9 periods.

Suggested routes   Figure **B**8 presents two approaches to this material. It is possible that the righthand route would be more suited to those wishing to achieve higher grades.

Periods

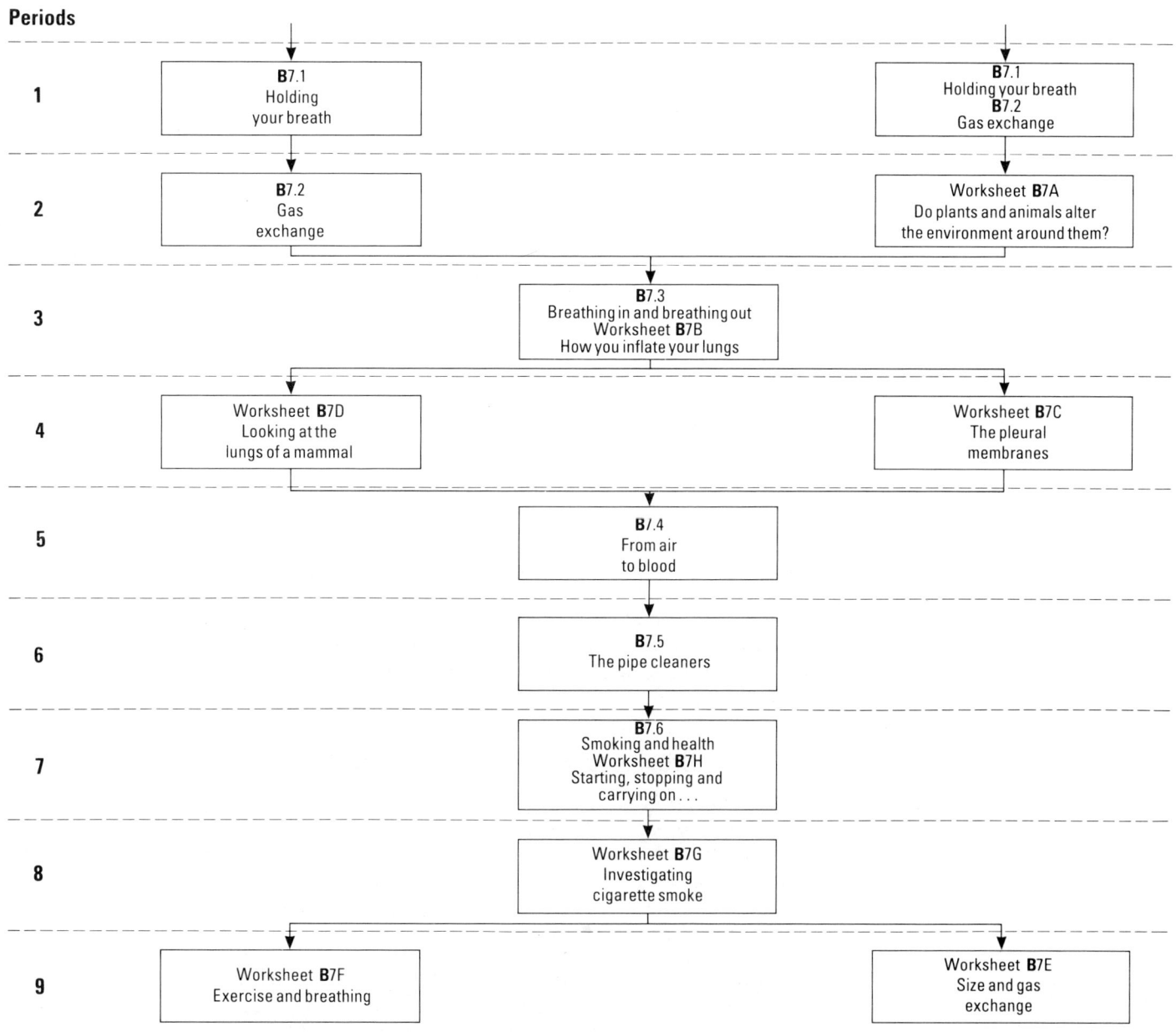

Figure **B**8

Opportunities for co-ordination

Chapter **P2** "Cooking food quickly" deals with particles in motion and the kinetic theory of matter, while the molecular attractions between liquids and gases are described in Chapter **C18** "Atoms and bonding". These chapters therefore lay the foundation for understanding the movement of gases across the alveoli.

Notes and answers

B7.1   Holding your breath

Most pupils will have tried to hold their breath for as long as possible at some time in their life, and no doubt they will have competed with each other to see who could last out the longest. This common experience serves as a useful introduction to breathing.

Pupils will be amazed at the breath-holding ability of Robert Foster. In fact, he did hyperventilate with oxygen for 30 minutes before his attempt. This information has been omitted because otherwise pupils may try to hyperventilate before they next dive into a swimming pool, unaware of the danger they are subjecting themselves to. It must be left to the discretion of the individual teacher whether to teach pupils about hyperventilation or not.

This is an important section that develops the idea that the composition of air is modified by being drawn into the lungs. The data enable simple calculations to be made.

Answer to selected question

2 Changes in the percentage of each gas are:
nitrogen $+0.49\%$
oxygen -4.56%
carbon dioxide $+4.07\%$.
Note that exhaled air also contains higher levels of water vapour.

B7.2   Gas exchange

The apparatus in figure 7.4 in the pupils' book can be easily assembled and used for a demonstration. Interpreting the exchange of gases in this situation is relatively straightforward. Although limewater is a specific test for carbon dioxide, hydrogencarbonate indicator is more sensitive to slight changes in its concentration.

Worksheet **B7A** provides an additional experiment that is more complex. The interpretation of the changes in the levels of carbon dioxide in the community can form a challenging exercise for practically minded groups. Less able groups can either attempt it when Chapter **B9** has been completed, or be guided through it now.

B7.3   Breathing in and breathing out

The models in Worksheets **B7B** and **B7C** provide a useful way of visualizing the changes in the thorax during inhalation and exhalation. When using these models it is important to emphasize the ways in which they are like the actual thorax, and the ways in which they are unlike the thorax. The relationship between pressure and volume can be developed from Chapter **P2** in the Physics pupils' book.

B7.4   From air to blood

It is important that pupils realize that the lung is not like a large bag filled with air, but has a more complex structure. They can examine the actual structure of the lungs, using Worksheet **B**7D. The X-ray photograph in figure 7.6 in the pupils' book begins the process of revealing the internal structure. Looking at actual X-ray photographs interests pupils, and hospitals will often respond favourably to a request for a suitable supply – particularly if you live near enough to make a personal visit.

The lung histology shown in figure 7.9 continues the examination of the internal structure. Prepared microscope slides should be used to supplement the photographs in the pupils' book.

The idea of the diffusion of gases into and out of the blood is developed from a consideration of experimental data. There are opportunities to expand on this theme, using the approach adopted in Chapter C18 of the Chemistry pupils' book – that of there being weak attractions between molecules in liquids and gases.

Answer to selected question

14 Although it is not possible to see that alveolar membranes are permeable to gases or that they have a moist surface, it **is** possible to see that their walls are thin and that they provide a large surface area over which gas exchange can occur. Pupils should be encouraged to recognize the features that help to make an effective gas exchange surface, and to see that other organisms have surfaces which meet the same criteria.

B7.5   The pipe cleaners

This section is important because it considers aspects of human health in relation to lung structure and function. The subsequent section develops the theme further.

B7.6   Smoking and health

A graphic demonstration of the nature of cigarette smoke can be undertaken, using Worksheet **B**7G. The harmful effect of cigarette smoke on the health of individuals is discussed in this section. Smoking also affects athletic performance, although this is often not recognized by those athletes who are also smokers! Worksheet **B**7F develops the idea that exercise affects the breathing rate. The corollary of this is that if smoking reduces the efficiency of the lungs, then smokers must find exercise more strenuous than comparable non-smokers.

This important section is further supplemented by Worksheet **B**7H, which asks pupils to conduct a survey into why some people smoke and why some people continue to smoke.

Practical work

Worksheet B7A   Do plants and animals alter the environment around them?

REQUIREMENTS

Each group of pupils will need:
Elodea, free of dirt and filamentous algae,
    about 5 cm long
Water animals, such as water snail or
    Gammarus

Hydrogencarbonate indicator solution
Water, distilled

Box or cupboard, light-proof
Chinagraph pencil
Clingfilm as covering material for tubes
or
Fitted caps, thin rubber
Light source
Rubber bands to fix Clingfilm, 8
Silver sand, well washed
Specimen tubes, 11 flat-bottomed,
    7 cm × 2.5 cm; 3 of these should have
    stoppers
Syringe and needle, 2 cm³ (or larger)

Notes:
This experiment should run for 12 hours
so it may be convenient to set it up
beforehand. Allow the students to inject
the indicator solution, observe the colour
changes and discuss their meaning.

Freshly prepared indicator solution
should be used. Useful comparisons can
be made if three tubes are prepared
beforehand to show the colour of the
indicator when in equilibrium with
atmospheric air (normal levels of carbon
dioxide), with exhaled air (increased levels
of carbon dioxide) and with air containing
no carbon dioxide. This can be done as
follows:
1 Stoppered specimen tube with indicator
solution, to show colour in contact with
normal air.
2 Stoppered specimen tube with indicator
solution, which was breathed into before
the stopper was inserted.
3 Specimen tube with indicator solution,
above which some granules of soda lime
are held in place in a piece of muslin
wedged in position by the stopper. (This
should be set up some hours in advance.)

The indicator solution in each of these
demonstration tubes should be diluted so
that the concentration corresponds to that
produced when 2 cm³ of indicator solution
are injected into each of the experimental
tubes.

A full interpretation of the changes in the levels of carbon dioxide in the tubes will
possibly elude all but the most able until Chapter **B9** is covered, since it is
necessary to establish that animals and plants respire (and thus produce carbon
dioxide) all of the time, but plants also photosynthesize in the light, and take in
carbon dioxide. In bright light, the rate of photosynthesis of plants exceeds the
rate of respiration of both plants and animals, so the levels of carbon dioxide in
the tubes actually fall, as shown by the purple colour of the hydrogencarbonate
indicator.

Worksheet B7B   How you inflate your lungs

REQUIREMENTS

Access to:
Parallelogram model of human ribcage

The ribcage model can be used to illustrate the movement of the intercostal
muscles. Note that the two sets of muscles are antagonistic, and that contraction
of one set pulls the other set back to its original length.

In figure **B9** the band between P and Q represents the external intercostal
muscles, which cause the ribs to move upwards and outwards. A band stretched
between R and S would represent the internal intercostal muscles, which cause the
ribs to move downwards and inwards.

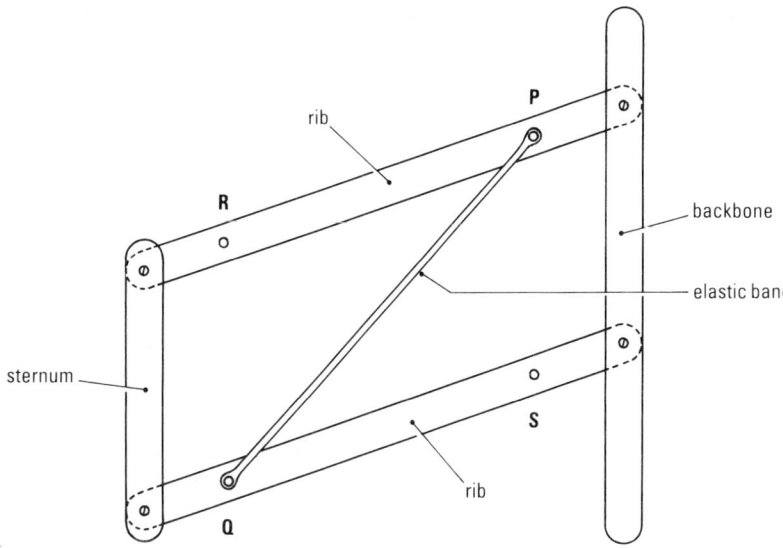

Figure **B**9

Worksheet B7C   The pleural membranes

REQUIREMENTS

Each group of pupils will need:
Water

Microscope slides, 2
Pipette
Syringe model of human thorax
Wood, strips

Access to:
Glue to hold wooden strips in position

Note:
The syringe model can be assembled as in figure **B**10. A finger over the hole in the syringe casing will enable the pressure in the barrel of the syringe to change when the plunger is moved. The plunger simulates the human diaphragm, and the syringe barrel represents the thorax. Note that the balloon almost fills the syringe, as do the lungs in the thorax.

The procedure is detailed on the worksheet.

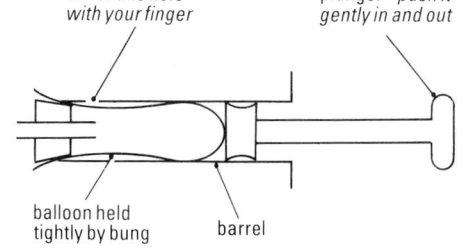

Figure **B**10

Worksheet B7D   Looking at the lungs of a mammal

REQUIREMENTS

Each group of pupils will need:
"Pluck" of sheep or pig

Beaker of water
Forceps, blunt
Hand lens
Scalpel
Scissors
Seeker

A "pluck" consists of lungs, heart, trachea, larynx and parts of the diaphragm; it can normally be obtained from a local butcher, and can be kept for a day or two in a refrigerator. Make sure the butcher does not leave the liver attached, as it is not needed in this worksheet and can raise the price of the "pluck" considerably. A "pluck" always arouses a great deal of interest and can be used to train the pupils' powers of observation, as the tissues vary greatly in texture and colour. Encourage pupils to discuss their observations and record the information in as much detail as possible.

Answers to selected worksheet questions

3 Lung tissue floats if it contains air; it sinks if it has been taken from an animal that has drowned, because water has entered the tissue. It also sinks if it is from a baby born dead, because air has never entered it.

5 The atria must pump blood only as far as the ventricles. They collapse on death.

6 Arteries have thicker walls than veins, and therefore appear less red. They contract on death and appear smaller than veins.

9 The cartilage in the trachea prevents it from collapsing. Note that the rings are incomplete where the oesophagus runs alongside the trachea.

11 The glandular tissue near the larynx is the thyroid gland. Its function is to produce the hormone thyroxine, which is important in the control of growth, development and the body's metabolism.

Worksheet B7E   Size and gas exchange

REQUIREMENTS

Each group of pupils will need:
Graph paper
Pencils

Access to:
Wooden blocks to simulate organisms

The concept of the ratio of surface area:volume is a difficult one; the use of wooden building blocks is a good way of helping the pupils to visualize it. The pupils should be allowed to build the model "animals" from the building blocks if they wish to.

Answers to selected worksheet questions

1 *Cubus major.*

2 If the linear dimensions of each "cell" are 1 cm, then the shortest distance will be 0.5 cm for *Cubus minor* and 1 cm for *Cubus major.*

3 6 cm² for *Cubus minor* and 24 cm² for *Cubus major.*

4 6 cm² for *Cubus minor* and 3 cm² for *Cubus major.*

Pupils ought to appreciate that larger animals have less surface area per cell available for gas exchange than smaller animals. An increase in available surface area is clearly of benefit to large animals – hence the discussion about size.

Worksheet B7F   Exercise and breathing

REQUIREMENTS

Each group of pupils will need:
Stopwatch

This simple activity is best done in pairs. Pupils should sit quietly and still for about two minutes at the start of the lesson in order to establish a resting breathing rate. This is a good Friday afternoon activity!

Worksheet B7H   Starting, stopping and carrying on...

The procedure is detailed on the worksheet.

Worksheet B7G Investigating cigarette smoke

REQUIREMENTS

Each group of pupils will need:
Universal Indicator solution

Chinagraph pencil
Cigarettes, 2
Clamps, 2, with stands and boss heads
Conical flasks, 2, with rubber bungs, each
  fitted with 2 bent glass tubes
Cottonwool
Dish for collecting ash from burning
  cigarette

Filter pump
Matches
Rubber tubing, short lengths
"T" piece, glass
Tubes, hard glass, 2, with bungs, fitted
  with tubes shaped to act as cigarette
  holders

In this experiment it is worth comparing high and low tar cigarettes. The acid nature of cigarette smoke can be investigated by bubbling it through Universal Indicator solution.

Demonstration experiments

The apparatus for detecting increased levels of carbon dioxide in human exhaled air, featured in section **B**7.2, would make an excellent demonstration. (This is affectionately called the "suck–blow" apparatus.)

Worksheet **B**7D will probably be performed as a demonstration.

Further information

Barrett, D.R.B., "Pleural membranes: a simple model", *J.Biol.Educ.*, **18** (1), 15, 1984.

Bell, G.H., Emslie–Smith, D. and Paterson, C.R. *Textbook of physiology* 10th edition, Churchill–Livingstone, 1980. (Earlier editions entitled *Textbook of physiology and biochemistry*.)

Beckett, B.S. *Biology: a modern introduction for G.C.S.E.* Oxford University Press, 1986.

The Guinness Book of Records 32nd edition, Guinness Superlatives Ltd, 1986.

Head, J.J. *A student's collection of electron micrographs* Edward Arnold, 1976.

Royal College of Physicians of London *Health or smoking?* Pitman, 1983. (Follow-up report to *Smoking OR health* Pitman, 1977.)

Chapter B8 Transport round the organism

Purposes

Knowledge and understanding

At the end of this chapter all pupils should:

1 know that xylem transports water and mineral salts through a plant, as well as providing internal support; phloem cells transport the products of photosynthesis away from the leaves; xylem cells are dead, and phloem cells are living

2 know that red blood cells carry oxygen around the body; white blood cells prevent infection establishing itself; platelets and several plasma proteins are involved in blood clotting

3 understand that the heart acts as two muscular pumps side by side: one side receives deoxygenated blood from the body, sending it to the lungs, and the other receives oxygenated blood from the lungs, sending it to the body

4 understand that arteries carry blood away from the heart and veins carry blood towards the heart; capillaries link arteries and veins and are the sites of exchange of materials with the tissues.

In addition, those pupils aiming for higher grades should:

5 appreciate the roles of phagocytes and antibodies in destroying invading micro-organisms.

Processes and problem solving

Graphical and symbolic representation
The making of models in question 11 shows that the concave shape of a red blood cell increases its surface area.

A bar chart is plotted to show how changes in the environment affect the rate of transpiration from a plant in a potometer, using data provided in Worksheet **B**8B.

Using apparatus and measuring instruments
Pupils can use potometers to investigate the uptake of water into a cut shoot of a plant, following instructions given in Worksheet **B**8A.

Those pupils aiming for higher grades might also carry out investigations to compare the diffusion and mass flow methods of moving molecules, using Worksheet **B**8C.

Observation
Figure 8.10 in the pupils' book shows how the colour of haemoglobin changes with its oxygen content.

Pupils can examine the structure of the mammalian heart, following the dissection instructions in Worksheet **B**8D.

In Worksheet **B**8E, the movement of dye through a celery stalk is investigated.

Interpretation and application
Section **B**8.2 asks pupils to interpret data from the use of radioactive tracers or aphid sap analysis in order to study the distribution of photosynthetic products in a flowering plant.

Pupils can interpret data from potometer experiments relating transpiration to the conditions around the leaves, using Worksheet **B**8B.

Planning and carrying out investigations
Question 31 asks pupils to design an investigation to find the effect of exercise on heart rate.

Pupils can devise investigations into the effect of environmental changes on the uptake of water by a plant stem, as an extension of Worksheet **B**8A.

Problem solving
Section **B**8.4 includes calculations of the number of red blood cells in the human body.

Those pupils aiming for higher grades might estimate the relative efficiency of blood and water in carrying dissolved oxygen, using information given in the same section.

Timing   10 periods.

Suggested routes   Figure **B**11 presents possible routes through the material in this chapter. The path on the right is an investigative approach; the centre route uses the same approach, but more theoretically. The lefthand route emphasizes the practical applications of the topic.

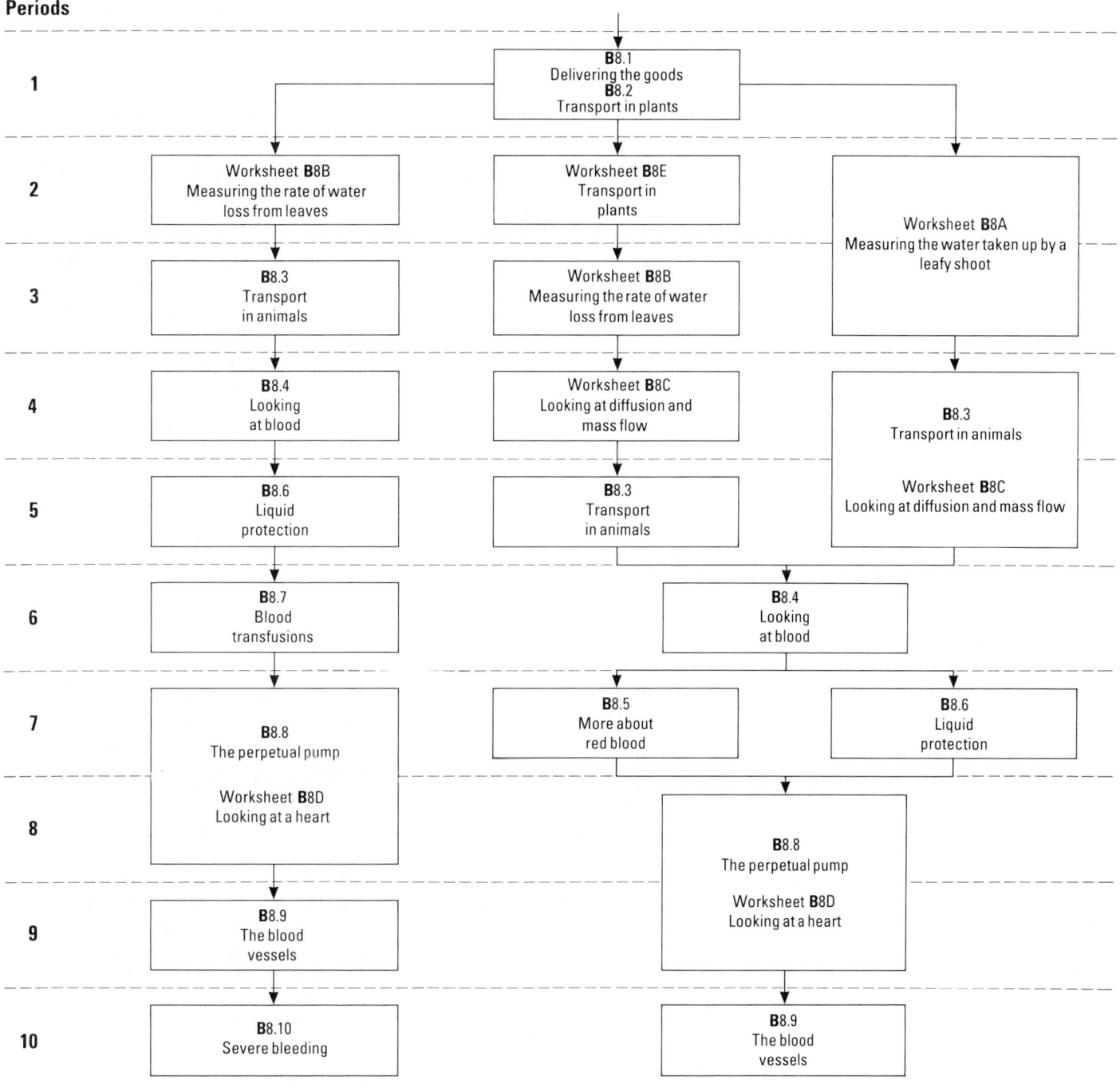

Figure **B**11

Opportunities for co-ordination

The pulse is considered in section **B8**.8 as an indicator of the heart rate; Chapter **P14** "Making waves" compares wave pulses with the human pulse. The work on blood plasma, which acts as a colloidal system, may be co-ordinated with Chapter **C9** "Foams, emulsions, sols and gels".

The technique of labelling carbon dioxide molecules with radioactive isotopes is used in studying the distribution of the products of photosynthesis around a plant. Chapters **C18** "Atoms and bonding", **P3** "Radioactivity" and **P12** "Waste not, want not?" are relevant. Chapter **C3** "Chemicals from plants" provides background information for the work on transport in plants in this chapter.

Notes and answers

B8.1   Delivering the goods

This section aims to introduce the idea that a transport system is essential in large organisms in order to service all the cells adequately. Some of the consequences of a "faulty transport system" are considered later in the chapter.

B8.2   Transport in plants

This section introduces the idea that an effective transport system is also essential to land plants. The use of radioactive tracers to investigate the distribution of photosynthetic products around the plant can be introduced, developing ideas from Chapter **B3**. Alternatively, the role of aphids as "phloem-sap extractors" can be discussed. Both are techniques that have been exploited to show that the products of photosynthesis (primarily carbohydrates, but also indirect products such as amino acids) travel through the living cells of the phloem.

Worksheet **B8E** enables pupils to investigate the movement of dye in a plant with a translucent stem (such as *Impatiens* or celery). More able candidates could be asked how they could use the technique to investigate the rate of water movement in the xylem. Alternatively, the investigation could be performed as a demonstration, or pupils could be asked to interpret figure 8.6 in the pupils' book.

The bubble potometer is a useful piece of apparatus for measuring the uptake of water into a plant stem. This is the same as the amount of water lost through transpiration, provided that the plant cells are turgid during the experiment. Although the apparatus is useful, it is also temperamental, and teachers might like to provide some of their pupils with working sets of apparatus if they are unable to assemble it for themselves. Worksheet **B8A** allows either option to be followed. For those teachers preferring to do this exercise as a demonstration, Worksheet **B8B** provides experimental data for analysis by the pupils.

Answer to selected question

3 In addition to sugars, the liquid in the phloem also contains low concentrations of amino acids, which are required by the aphids. In order to get adequate amounts of amino acids, the aphids have to ingest large volumes of sap. As a result, they produce vast quantities of sugary exudate, called honey-dew, which can make the leaves of a tree feel quite sticky, particularly at the height of summer. Ants are attracted to the honey-dew.

B8.3   Transport in animals

Worksheet **B7E** developed the idea that large organisms have ratios of surface area:volume that are too small to enable them to obtain sufficient oxygen by diffusion across the surface of their bodies. An internal transport system is a logical consequence of having a specialized region of gaseous exchange that is remote from most of the cells. It is interesting to note that whilst movement into and out of the capillaries is by diffusion, the transport around the body is by mass flow. Diffusion will be discussed further in Chapter **C**18 "Atoms and bonding", whilst Worksheet **B**8C allows pupils to compare the rates of diffusion and mass flow experimentally.

B8.4 Looking at blood

The red blood cell has a biconcave shape, which increases its surface area by comparison with a sphere of the same volume. Simple models can illustrate this concept. The remainder of the section aims to develop an awareness of the huge numbers of red blood cells in the body. More able pupils could compare the oxygen-carrying capacity of equal volumes of water and blood.

Answers to selected questions

13 $(5\,000\,000) \times (5 \times 1\,000\,000) = 2.5 \times 10^{13}$ red blood cells.

14 Blood is 63 times better.

B8.5 More about red blood cells

This section discusses anaemia, the effect of high altitude, "doping" and carbon monoxide poisoning, all of which can be understood through a knowledge of the role of red blood cells in the body.

Answers to selected questions

18 The response ensures that the cells of the body receive sufficient oxygen.

19 The team should arrive with enough time to spare for the increase in the number of red blood cells in the body to take place before the main tournament.

B8.6 Liquid protection

This section develops the theme of the body's defence against injury and cuts. The ideas are complex, but important. They need to be explained carefully.

B8.7 Blood transfusions

This section introduces an important topic with which all pupils need to be familiar, although a detailed analysis of blood groups in terms of surface antigens and antibodies is probably beyond the scope of all but the most able. The section will need to be taught carefully.

B8.8 The perpetual pump

The heart should be considered simply as a twin pump that allows blood to circulate between the lungs and the body. Worksheet **B**8D allows the internal structure of the heart to be investigated.

Britain has an appalling record for problems associated with heart disease. For this reason the text includes some information to help to educate pupils in this important area. This could be linked with the work on diet in Chapter **B**6. It could also provide an opportunity to discuss ethical problems. For example, with limited funds available to the National Health Service it is very difficult for decisions to be made about where the money should be allocated – to heart surgery and transplants, or to other essential operations.

The section ends with an exercise in measuring the pulse rate. Most people know that it can be used to measure the heart rate; the exact relationship between the contraction of the heart and the pulse rate need not be evaluated. Data concerning the pulse rate before and after exercise can be collected and analysed graphically. The **increase** in heart rate can be calculated for each pupil and related to fitness. The time taken to return to the normal pulse rate is also related to fitness.

B8.9   The blood vessels

It is hoped that pupils will be able to link the description of the blood vessels in the text to the transverse sections in figure 8.19. The terms artery, vein and capillary will need to be explained carefully in terms of whether they carry blood to or from the heart. The use of microscope or photographic slides could help to make pupils more aware of the differences between these blood vessels.

B8.10   Severe bleeding

It is important that pupils are aware of what happens when people bleed profusely. This section provides valuable information on how to deal with such a situation.

Practical work

Worksheet B8A   Measuring the water taken up by a leafy shoot

REQUIREMENTS

Each group of pupils will need:
Leafy shoot, with stem just wide enough to fit PVC tubing

Absorbent paper
Beaker, 250 cm^3
Bung with hole wide enough to take shoot
Capillary tubing, about 15 cm long, with a 90° bend
Flask, 250 cm^3, with side arm
PVC tubing, short length
Retort stands with bosses and clamps, 2
Scale, such as Scalafix or a piece of graph paper, attached to one length of capillary tubing
Scalpel or one-sided razor blade
Sink or large bowl of water in which shoot can be inserted into PVC
Stopclock
Syringe, 10 cm^3, and needle

Access to:
Bench lamps
Electric fan
Polythene hoods

Notes:
The choice of shoot is very important if this investigation is to succeed. A young woody shoot that is not easily crushed is ideal.

The success of this investigation also depends on air not collecting below the cut end of the shoot; the end of the shoot should be placed in water immediately after it has been cut. Care should be taken when setting up any equipment under water – a good fit is required and it is helpful to trim the end of the shoot with an oblique cut.

This is a very adaptable piece of apparatus. Once it has been set up, results are obtained with ease and the apparatus can be transported to different conditions. Readings can be obtained for long periods and it is light, cheap and easy to use. It is a great improvement on conventional potometers.

Worksheet B8B   Measuring the rate of water loss from leaves

REQUIREMENTS

Each group of pupils will need:
Graph paper
Pencils

Pupils are required to interpret data obtained from investigations with potometers. A complete interpretation would include a consideration of the diffusion of water vapour molecules from open stomata, and the effect of the atmosphere around the stomata.

Worksheet B8C   Looking at diffusion and mass flow

Part 1: Method A

REQUIREMENTS

Each group of pupils will need:
Agar jelly, cubes with sides 2 cm long, 2
    (allow pupils to cut their own cubes –
    see *Notes*)
Potassium manganate(VII) solution,
    150 cm^3

Beakers, 2
Filter paper or blotting-paper
Rulers
Glasses, protective
Scalpel or one-sided razor blade
White tile

Access to:
Water for washing cubes

Part 1: Method B

REQUIREMENTS

Each group of pupils will need:
Cubes of agar jelly in which eosin has
    been incorporated, with sides 2 cm long, 2
    (allow pupils to cut their own cubes – see
    Notes)
Hydrochloric acid, dilute

Filter paper or blotting-paper
Glasses, protective
Rulers
Scalpel or one-sided razor blade
Test-tubes, 3
Test-tube rack
White tile

Notes:
Agar is most easily prepared by purchasing tablets, adding water as directed and heating
in a pressure cooker. The liquid is then poured into a Petri dish and allowed to set.
Larger blocks can be prepared by pouring the liquid to greater depths in other dishes or
beakers. Eosin can be added before the agar and water are heated in the pressure cooker.
    The agar for both methods should be prepared to a depth of 2 cm, so that pupils can
cut their own cubes.

Part 2

REQUIREMENTS

Each group of pupils will need:
Bungs, 4
Chinagraph pencil
Clamps, stands and boss heads, 2
Cottonwool
Dropping pipettes, 2
Forceps
Glass rod, at least 20 cm long
Glass tubes, 20 mm diameter and 30 cm
    long, 2
Glasses, protective
Litmus paper, red
Rulers
Scissors
Stopclock

Access to:
Ammonia solution, 2M
Ammonia solution, 9M
Water

Part 3

REQUIREMENTS

Each group of pupils will need:
Chinagraph pencil
Cottonwool
Dropping pipettes, 2
Forceps
Glass rod
Glass tube, 20 mm diameter and 30 cm
    long
Glasses, protective
Litmus paper, red
Retort clamp, stand and boss head
Rulers
Scissors
Stopclock

Access to:
Ammonia solution, 2M
Ammonia solution, 9M
Water

Notes:
These notes apply to Parts 2 and 3 of this worksheet.
    Prepare 9M ammonia solution by diluting 0.880 ammonia solution with an equal
volume of water. 2M ammonia solution can be prepared by diluting 11 cm^3 of 0.880
ammonia solution with 89 cm^3 water. Each group of pupils requires about 4 cm^3 of each
solution. It is important to warn them to use strong ammonia solution with care, and to
supervise its use. Ventilate the room well.
    It is useful to prepare a blue colour standard with which the litmus paper can be
compared before the timed change has been judged to have taken place.

Worksheet B8D   Looking at a heart

REQUIREMENTS

Each group of pupils will need:
Heart

Dish or tray
Forceps, blunt
Means of taking measurements
Scalpel
Scissors
Seeker

Access to:
Bag for waste material

Notes:
Frozen hearts can be used, but such material bought from the butcher often lacks the main blood vessels and even part of the aorta. It is worth explaining requirements well in advance to butchers, as they are often willing to provide complete hearts if given time to collect them.

Worksheet B8E   Transport in plants

REQUIREMENTS

Each group of pupils will need:
Leafy shoots, transparent, 2 (*e.g.* groundsel, celery, flowering spinach), which have been in a weak dye solution for about 2 hours before the lesson

Water

Coverslip
Hand lens
Light microscope
Light source
Microscope slide
Razor blade
Rulers
Scalpel, blunt

The procedure is detailed on the worksheet.

Demonstration experiments

Worksheets **B8A**, **B8C** and **B8E** could be performed as demonstrations.

Further information

Bell, G.H., Emslie–Smith, D. and Paterson, C.R. *Textbook of Physiology* 10th edition, Churchill–Livingstone, 1980. (Earlier editions entitled *Textbook of physiology and biochemistry*.)

Heart Research Series. 16 booklets published by the British Heart Foundation, 102 Gloucester Place, London, W1H 4DH. Available from health clinics at no charge.

Bulletins of the Institute of Medical Ethics – published monthly, by I.M.E. Publications, 151 Great Portland Street, London, W1N 5PB.

Revised Nuffield Biology *Teachers' guide 2* and *Text 2 Living things in action* Longman, 1975.

Richardson, M., Studies in Biology No.10 *Translocation in Plants* 2nd edition, Edward Arnold, 1975.

Selkurt, E.E. *Physiology* 5th edition, Little, Brown & Company, Boston, 1984.

Simpkins, J. and Williams, J.I. *Advanced Biology* Bell & Hyman, 1984.

Chapter B9   Keeping going

Purposes

Knowledge and understanding

At the end of this chapter all pupils should:

1 know that aerobic respiration takes place inside cells and that it involves the transfer of energy from glucose, using oxygen and producing carbon dioxide; some energy may be transferred to the environment as heat

2 appreciate that when energy is transferred organisms are able to carry out processes such as movement, growth or the active transport of substances against concentration gradients

3 know that respiration can occur without oxygen; when yeast respires anaerobically the process is called fermentation and the end product is ethanol, while in animals lactic acid is produced.

In addition, those pupils aiming for higher grades should:

4 appreciate that respiration is controlled by many enzymes

5 know that metabolism is the term that describes all of the chemical reactions that occur within an organism

6 know that the rate at which an organism consumes oxygen may be used to estimate its metabolic rate.

Processes and problem solving

Graphical and symbolic representation
Pupils can plot a graph of data concerning the uptake of sulphate ions into the roots of a plant in aerobic and anaerobic conditions, using Worksheet **B9B**.

Section **B9.5** asks pupils to plot a graph relating the rate of fermentation of yeast to temperature.

Using apparatus and measuring instruments
Figure 9.7 in the pupils' book gives a recipe for making ginger beer, in order to illustrate fermentation.

Worksheet **B9C** is concerned with investigations into anaerobic respiration in yeast.

Observation
Recording the results of the investigations in Worksheet **B9C** forms a useful exercise in observation for the pupils.

Interpretation and application
Worksheet **B9A** provides an opportunity for pupils to interpret a graph of the change in dry mass of germinating broad bean seeds.

Pupils can consider the significance of anaerobic and aerobic respiration in hunting animals and in athletic races, using section **B9.6**.

In addition, those pupils aiming for higher grades might:

1 Relate the metabolic rate of an organism to its body size (see question 19 in the pupils' book).

2 Appreciate how radioactive tracers can be used to show that the radioactive carbon atoms in the carbon dioxide breathed out by rats were derived from glucose molecules that originally came from food (see Investigation 2, Worksheet **B**9A).

Planning and carrying out investigations
Worksheet **B**9C asks pupils to design experiments to test one of two hypotheses: either that respiration in yeast causes a rise in temperature, or that yeast produces carbon dioxide faster at higher temperatures than it does at lower temperatures.

In addition, those pupils aiming for higher grades might design an experiment to measure how much oxygen an organism consumes (see question 20 in the pupils' book).

Problem solving
Pupils are asked to design suitable controls and suggest improvements to experimental designs for several investigations into respiration in Worksheet **B**9A.

Timing

5 periods.

Suggested routes

Figure **B**12 presents two possible routes through this material. The righthand route is based around investigative work, whilst the lefthand one is more theoretical.

Periods

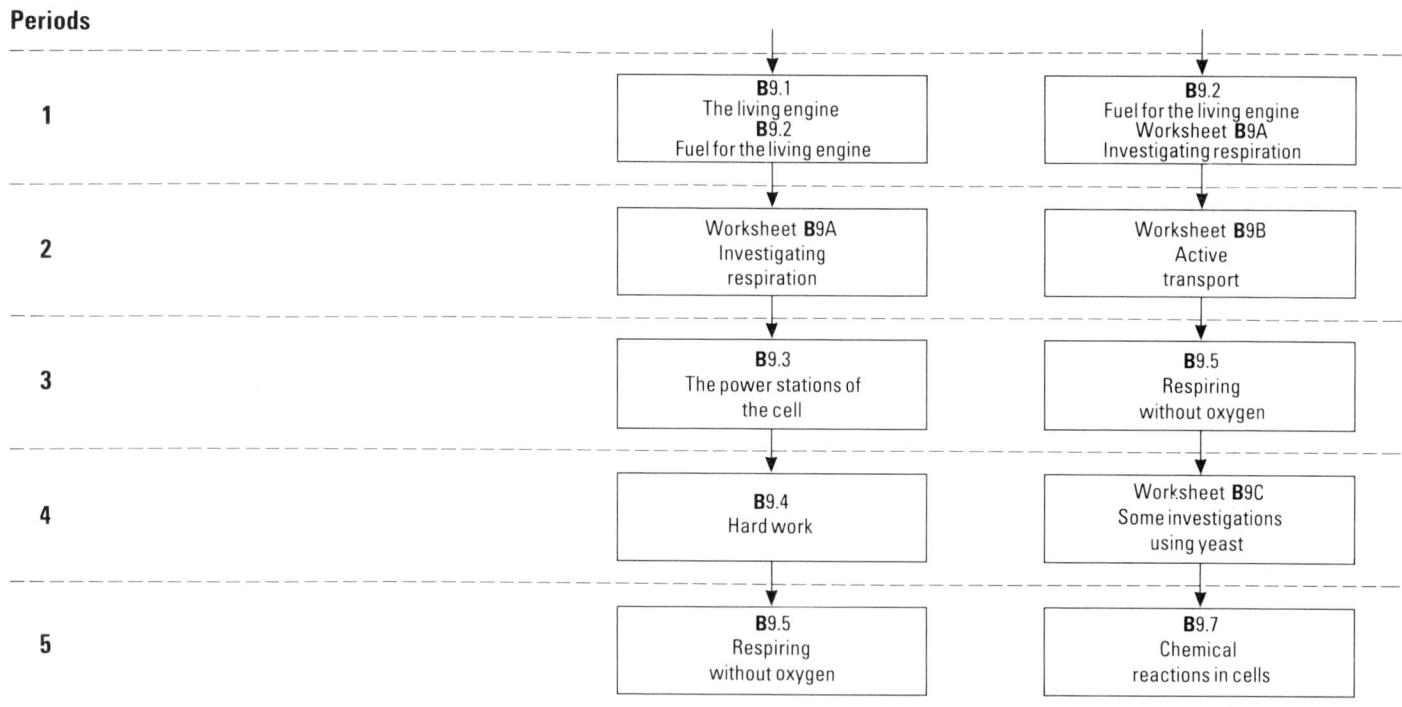

Figure **B**12

Opportunities for co-ordination

Section **B**9.3 compares respiration in living cells with combustion in an engine; Chapter **P**8 "Machines and engines" also uses the idea of the human body as an engine, and deals with energy transfer. The energy requirements of various activities are listed in Chapter **P**12 "Waste not, want not?", which also discusses the efficiency of the human "engine" and the fact that engines need fuel. Worksheet **C**13D (in Chapter **C**13 "Fuels and fires") measures the energy transferred when a fuel is burned. The transfer of energy from carbohydrate molecules to the cell may be co-ordinated with work in Chapter **P**10 "Ideas in physics – energy and change in temperature".

Investigation 2 in Worksheet **B**9A describes how radioactive tracers may be used to show that the carbon atoms in carbon dioxide exhaled by rats are derived from glucose in their food; this may be supported by Chapter **P**3 "Radioactivity" and the work on isotopes in Chapter **C**18 "Atoms and bonding".

Notes and answers

B9.1 The living engine

This section compares the human body with a mechanical engine. The analogy is a useful one and can be developed further. Both need a source of energy, require oxygen and produce waste gases. In both cases the energy transferred from the "fuel" can be harnessed to do "useful" work. But the analogy cannot be pushed too far, as the next section shows.

B9.2 Fuel for the living engine

This section aims to show how the transfer of energy inside cells differs from simple combustion. The term "respiration" is introduced, and the ideas are developed in Worksheet **B**9A. The experiments outlined in this worksheet can be demonstrated before the pupils complete the worksheet.

B9.3 The power stations of the cell

This section illustrates the importance of enzymes in controlling the transfer of energy from food molecules. The electronmicrographs should lead pupils to realize that mitochondria are the important organelles where respiration occurs. The presence of larger numbers of mitochondria in a cell which requires a lot of energy by comparison with one which requires less could provide the necessary link.

B9.4 Hard work

This section develops the idea that organisms transfer energy from food for useful purposes. Worksheet **B**9B asks pupils to interpret data on the uptake of ions into plant roots.

B9.5 Respiring without oxygen

It is important that pupils realize that respiration can occur in the absence of oxygen. Commercially, this forms the basis of the brewing and baking industries. The importance of anaerobic respiration in yeast can be studied experimentally, using Worksheet **B**9C.

The data in figure 9.5 in the pupils' book provide an opportunity for pupils to practise their graph-plotting skills. The shape of the graph should remind them of the typical shape obtained for the rate of enzyme controlled processes at different temperatures. This should indicate that anaerobic respiration also uses enzymes to help to make energy available.

Pupils can try to make their own ginger beer; some, of course, may already be well versed in the art of brewing beer at home. If there is an experienced brewer or winemaker in the class, he or she might be happy to describe the process in front of friends. Opportunities to develop a child's self-confidence when speaking to large groups ought not to be missed.

The section ends with a demonstration of anaerobic respiration in the muscles of the pupils' arms, which can be used to introduce the next section.

B9.6 Speed *versus* stamina

This section makes the comparison between aerobic and anaerobic respiration, using examples that pupils may find intriguing.

The cheetah is superb at running fast. The flexible spine enables the animal to achieve an enormous stride, and the small leg muscles are light and can contract quickly. However, the supply of energy to the muscles has to be so great during the fast chase that aerobic respiration is inadequate and anaerobic respiration is inevitably called upon to supply energy. It does not take long for the level of lactic acid to reach its peak; when this happens the cheetah has to drop out of the race.

The data in figure 9.11 indicate that for human athletes the proportion of energy being supplied by anaerobic respiration falls as the race gets longer. The questions which follow serve to emphasize that it is not the distance of the race which is important but the speed with which it is run. In a good long distance athlete the level of lactic acid rises slowly and, ideally, will not reach a peak until the moment he or she crosses the finishing line.

Answer to selected question

12 Because the first half of the race has been run too fast, too much energy has had to be obtained from anaerobic respiration. The rate of lactic acid build-up which results is sufficient to impair the functioning of the athlete's muscles and forces retirement from the race.

B9.7 Chemical reactions in cells

Metabolism is not an easy concept for pupils to grasp. This section aims to indicate what the word means and to illustrate the process by introducing it in terms of the chemical reactions occurring in respiration.

Question 20 provides an opportunity for pupils to design an experiment to investigate the oxygen consumption in a named living organism. A suitable apparatus is shown below.

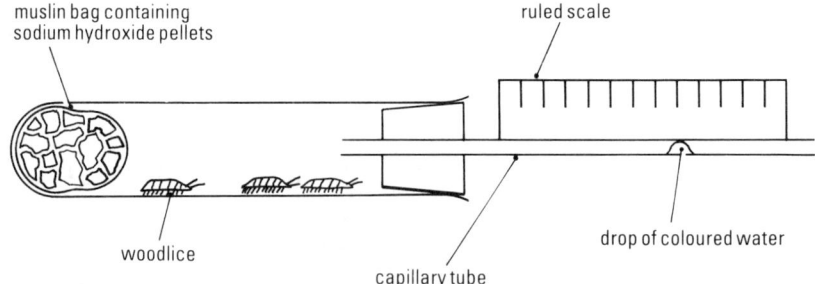

Figure **B**13
Suitable apparatus to investigate the rate of oxygen consumption in woodlice. The control should consist of the same apparatus without the woodlice.

A successful experimental design should include:

1 Setting up the experiment and the control at the same air temperature.

2 Taking accurate measurements of the time taken for the water to move a known distance.

3 Subtracting any distance travelled by the water in the control tube from the readings taken for the water in the experimental tube, in order to obtain an accurate value for oxygen consumption.

4 Expressing the oxygen consumption in sensible units such as mm/minute. If the diameter of the bore of the tube is known the results could be expressed in mm^3/minute. Some pupils may even suggest that mm^3/minute/g would be sensible units to use.

It would be possible to extend this procedure to enable pupils to investigate the factors that affect the **rate** of oxygen consumption (*i.e.* size, activity or environment). This would link quite well with the statements in question 19.

Answer to selected question

19 From the list of statements it is hoped that pupils will be able to suggest that the factors which influence metabolism are body mass (see parts **a**, **d** and **e**), activity (**b**, **d**) and environment (**c**, **d**).

Practical work

Worksheet B9A   Investigating respiration

REQUIREMENTS

Each group of pupils will need:
Writing materials

The procedure is detailed on the worksheet.

Answers to selected worksheet questions

2 Put seedlings into an incubator set at 95 °C for 24 hours, then find their mass. Repeat this process until a constant reading for mass is obtained.

3 The dry mass would have increased with time because the seedlings would have been able to photosynthesize.

8 The carbon atoms in the glucose eaten by the rats become the carbon atoms in the carbon dioxide they exhale. For this to happen the glucose molecule must have been changed inside the rat.

9 First, to provide a constant temperature near the optimum for the enzymes in the cells of the organism, and secondly, to ensure that the readings are taken at the same temperature and thus avoid any fluctuations in the gas volumes collected.

Worksheet B9B   Active transport

REQUIREMENTS

Each group of pupils will need:
Graph paper
Pencils

The procedure is detailed on the worksheet. There is some differentiation of questions on this worksheet; teachers may find that some pupils need assistance when attempting the more demanding problems. The rate of uptake of sulphate ions is faster in aerobic conditions, which suggests that the presence of oxygen improves the ability of the seedlings to take up sulphate ions. As oxygen is used in respiration, the process by which energy is made available, it is reasonable to suggest that the data support the hypothesis that mineral uptake by plants is an active process. However, the data for anaerobic conditions suggest that in this experiment diffusion can account for the uptake of some of the sulphate ions.

Worksheet B9C   Some investigations using yeast

REQUIREMENTS

Each group of pupils will need:

10 % glucose solution, previously boiled to remove oxygen, cooled and with fresh yeast suspension added, 10 cm³ (see *Notes*)

Yeast, fresh, suspended in water (for control)

10 % glucose solution, previously boiled to remove oxygen, no yeast added (for control)

0.03 % diazine green (Janus Green B) solution, 4 drops

Hydrogencarbonate indicator solution, previously aspirated with atmospheric air

Paraffin, liquid, 5 cm³

Bungs fitted with delivery tubing, 2

Specimen tubes, 2

Test-tubes, 10 cm³, 2

Test-tube rack

Notes:

The mixture of glucose and yeast needs to be prepared before the lesson. The 10 % glucose solution should be boiled to remove oxygen from the water and then cooled before adding the yeast suspension. Fresh yeast is preferable to dried yeast.

The experiment requires about 10 cm³ of the yeast and glucose mixture, which can be prepared by adding 12 g of fresh yeast to 150 cm³ of 10 % glucose solution. Stir the mixture thoroughly to obtain a uniformly cloudy suspension of cells. If dried yeast is used, add 6 g per 150 cm³ of 10 % glucose solution and stir the suspension very thoroughly for several minutes to make sure the cells are fully hydrated. Dried yeast takes time to become active, and the mixture should be prepared at least an hour before the lesson starts. Fresh yeast normally gives results within 30 minutes of being set up.

Some pupils can set up a control with glucose solution and no yeast, others a control with yeast suspended in water.

This experiment needs to run for at least two hours, with the temperature being recorded every 20–30 minutes.

The pupils can then design investigations to test certain hypotheses about respiration in yeast. The two hypotheses mentioned in the worksheet are not the only ones that could be tested. Pupils could be encouraged to formulate their own hypotheses, and then design experiments to test them.

Demonstration experiments

The experiments outlined in Worksheets **B9A** and **B9B** could be performed as demonstration experiments.

Further information

There are several useful references that provide background material for this chapter. These are:

Brock Fenton, M. *Just bats* University of Toronto Press, 1983.

Hawkey, R. *Sport science* Hodder & Stoughton, 1981.

Newsholme, E.A. and Leech, T. *The runner: energy and endurance* Fitness Books, 1983.

Revised Nuffield Biology *Teachers' guide 2* and *Text 2 Living things in action* Longman, 1975.

Simpkins, J. and Williams, J.I. *Advanced biology* Bell & Hyman, 1984.

Watson, A.W. *Physical fitness and athletic performance: a guide for students and coaches* Longman, 1983.

Whitfield, P. *The hunters* Simon & Schuster, 1978.

In addition, SATIS unit 603 "The Heart Pacemaker" could be of interest.

Chapter B10   Skeletons and muscles

Purposes

Knowledge and understanding

At the end of this chapter all pupils should:

1 realize the importance of lignin in supporting woody plants and of water in supporting non-woody plants

2 appreciate the principles of support in animals

3 know that a joint occurs where two or more bones meet, and that cartilage and synovial fluid reduce friction between the bones

4 realize that muscles bring about movement at a joint; muscles can only contract, and are stretched back to their original length by the action of antagonistic muscles.

In addition, those pupils aiming for higher grades should:

5 realize that the cellulose wall of a plant cell prevents it from bursting when it is placed in distilled water, as the uptake of water stops when the plant cell is turgid; animal cells placed in water will eventually burst

6 appreciate that the skeletons of swimming animals push against the water in order to move, and that they are supported by the water to some extent.

Processes and problem solving

Graphical and symbolic representation
Investigation 2 of Worksheet **B**10A presents a challenging exercise for the pupils, in which they are asked to plot a graph of the **percentage** change in mass of some potato cylinders against the strength of the sucrose solution in which the cylinders have been immersed.

In Worksheet **B**10C, the pupils make Plasticine models of different shapes in order to investigate the effect that streamlining has on the speed of movement through water.

Using apparatus and measuring instruments
Section **B**10.1 describes how staining techniques may be used to test for lignin in the stems of flowering plants.

Worksheet **B**10A asks pupils to assess the effects of turgidity on different plant tissues.

Observation
Pupils may observe the differences in stem structure between land and aquatic flowering plants, using figures 10.3, 10.4 and 10.6 in section **B**10.1 of the pupils' book.

Figure 10.12 in the pupils' book shows a section through the hollow bone of a bird, with its strengthening cross-struts.

Pupils may observe the different types of joints in the body, using section **B**10.3.

Section **B**10.4 and the instructions given in question 25 allow pupils to observe the action of the antagonistic flexors and extensors when the arm is bent.

Part 5 of Worksheet **B**10A asks pupils to use microscopes to examine onion cells after they have been immersed in sugar solutions of different concentrations.

The relationship between antagonistic muscles and a synovial joint in the trotter of a pig can be observed, using Worksheet **B**10B.

Interpretation and application
Section **B**10.2 asks pupils to interpret graphical data showing that long legs are unable to support animals with large body masses, and to interpret how the arrangement of a giraffe's legs helps to support its body mass.

Planning and carrying out investigations
Worksheet **B**10C helps pupils to assess the best shape for an animal which moves through water.

Timing

5 periods.

Suggested routes

Figure **B**14 presents a flow diagram showing two possible routes through this material. The righthand route is more investigative and slightly more demanding than the lefthand route.

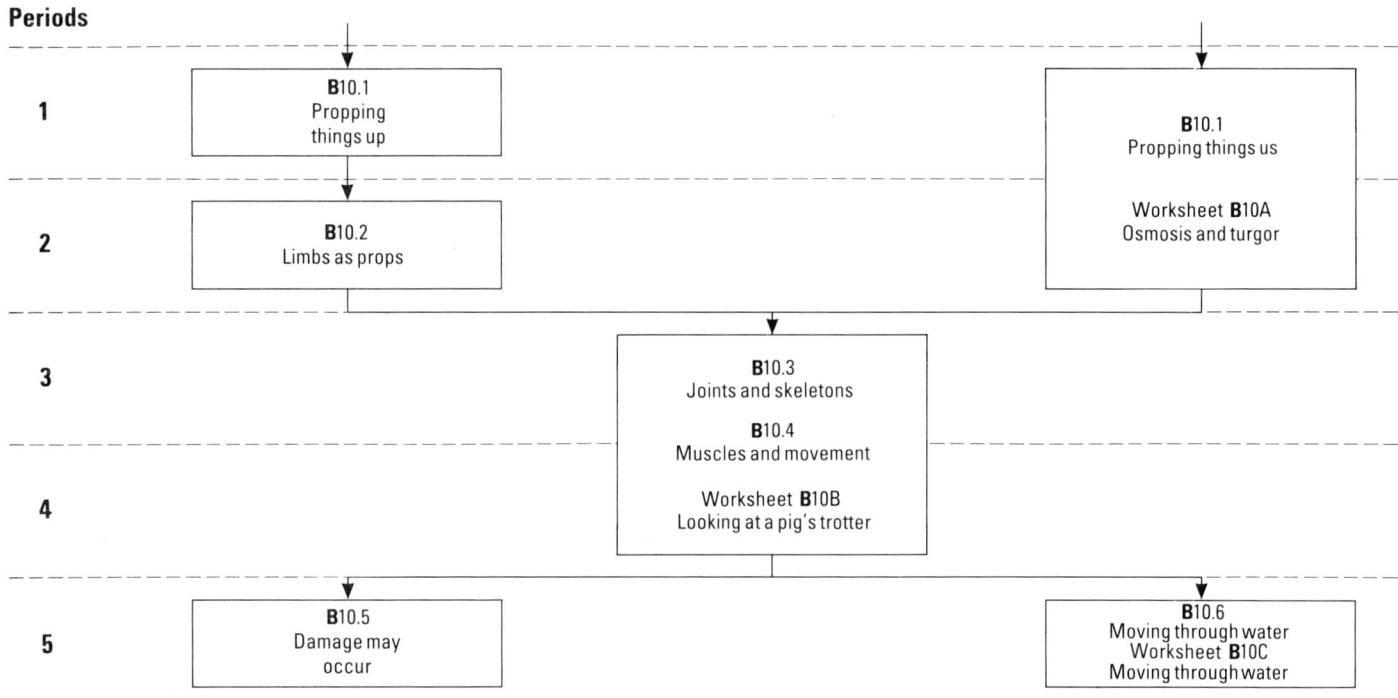

Periods

1 — **B10.1** Propping things up | **B10.1** Propping things us

2 — **B10.2** Limbs as props | Worksheet **B10A** Osmosis and turgor

3 — **B10.3** Joints and skeletons / **B10.4** Muscles and movement

4 — Worksheet **B10B** Looking at a pig's trotter

5 — **B10.5** Damage may occur | **B10.6** Moving through water / Worksheet **B10C** Moving through water

Figure **B**14

Opportunities for co-ordination

The movement of bones in a synovial joint depends upon there being little friction between the surfaces of the bones. Friction is covered in Chapter **P**5 "Controlling motion", which will also help pupils to understand why the streamlined shape of a fish reduces the effects of friction and drag in the water. The idea of the skeleton supporting the body mass of an animal (or the stem supporting a plant) can be co-ordinated with Chapter **P**1 "Building bridges successfully", where the strength of solids is considered. The treatment of the structure of muscle could be co-ordinated with Chapter **C**3 "Chemicals from plants", which covers protein chemistry.

Notes and answers

B10.1   Propping things up

This section examines the variety of methods used by plants for support, in particular the roles of water and wood in terrestrial plants and of water in aquatic plants. Osmosis is introduced in order to show the significance of turgid

Cubus minimonopodium

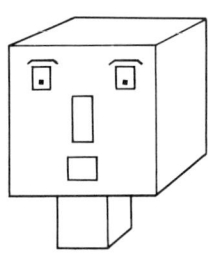

Cubus medimonopodium

Cubus maximonopodium

Figure **B**15

cells in supporting plant structures. Worksheet **B**10A consists of simple investigations into the significance of osmosis in relation to plant turgor.

Answers to selected questions

2 Lignin is found in the xylem. The columns of xylem cells are gathered into (vascular) bundles, which are **usually** arranged around the edge of the stem.

7 Water moves into the cells by osmosis. Eventually the cells become turgid and press against each other; their very stiffness provides the support for the plant stem.

B10.2   Limbs as props

There are many examples in biology of a particular structure being linked to a particular function. This section begins by getting pupils to think about the structure and function of a variety of limbs.

The main emphasis here is to establish that as animals get bigger they have legs which are much shorter and much thicker than would be expected if proportions were being maintained.

Answers to selected questions

8 There are several possible suggestions that pupils could make. Increased contact between the body and the ground will increase friction and will thus make movement a more energy-demanding activity. In addition, it may be more difficult to see prey if you are the predator, or to see predators if you are the prey.

10 The plotted line is not straight and suggests that bigger animals have shorter legs than might be expected.

For more able pupils, a quantitative approach could be adopted to show that bigger animals have thicker legs than might be expected. This approach uses cubes as model "animals", shown in figure **B**15. Data and questions follow.

In this series of models each animal has only been given one leg – hence the "pretend" names of *Cubus minimonopodium*, *Cubus medimonopodium* and *Cubus maximonopodium*. To simplify matters, each leg is also square-shaped.

C. medimonopodium is bigger than *C. minimonopodium*, each of the sides of its body being twice as long. In addition, the width of each of the sides of the leg of *C. medimonopodium* is twice the width of the leg of *C. minimonopodium*. Similarly, the linear dimensions of *C. maximonopodium* are twice those of *C. medimonopodium*.

Each cube represents the body of the "animal" which has to be supported by a single leg. The mass of the body is in proportion to its volume. The volume of a cube is calculated as the (length of one side)^3.

It is the cross-sectional area of the leg – rather than the length – which is important in supporting the animal; this is equal to the (width of one side)^2.

In order to make things easy, we can say that the mass of *C. minimonopodium* equals 1 mass unit, and the cross-sectional area of its leg equals 1 area unit.

The pupils should attempt the following problems:

A Use the information in the preceding paragraphs to complete this table.

Name of model "animal"	Length of body	Mass of body	Cross-sectional area of leg
C. minimonopodium	1	1	1
C. medimonopodium	2		
C. maximonopodium	4		

Imagine that *C. minimonopodium* is a stable animal that does not fall down. This means that its body is adequately supported by its leg. We can calculate the pressure that is acting on the leg as the mass of the body divided by the area of the leg that is in contact with the body. For *C. minimonopodium* the pressure is equal to 1 unit. This represents the maximum pressure that the leg can withstand.

B Calculate the pressure acting on the leg of *C. medimonopodium* and *C. maximonopodium*. Explain why each of these animals will not be stable on its leg.

If these two animals are to become stable, the pressure acting on the single leg must not exceed 1 pressure unit.

C What must the cross-sectional area of the legs of *C. medimonopodium* and *C. maximonopodium* be if these "animals" are to be stable?

D Use these data to explain why large animals have proportionately thicker legs than small animals.

Answers to selected questions on the model "animals"

A The body masses and cross-sectional areas are calculated as the cube and square, respectively, of each of the figures in the "Length of body" column.

B The pressure acting on the leg of *C. medimonopodium* equals 2 units, whilst the pressure on the leg of *C. maximonopodium* is 4 units. In both cases the pressure exceeds the maximum of 1 unit.

C In order to achieve stability, the cross-sectional area of the leg of *C. medimonopodium* must increase by a factor of two, from 4 area units to 8 area units. Similarly, the cross-sectional area of the leg of *C. maximonopodium* must increase by a factor of four, from 16 area units to 64 area units. The larger the body of the "animal", the thicker the leg must become.

B10.3   Joints and skeletons

This section is mainly concerned with joints. It would be helpful if a skeleton (or suitable joints – obtained from a butcher) were available to be looked at. See Worksheet **B10B**.

The synovial joint is dealt with in greatest detail, but pupils may know something about the other types mentioned if they are familiar with the "soft spot" in the skull of newborn babies or have heard about slipped discs.

Answer to selected question

15 The synovial fluid and cartilage reduce friction, the ligaments hold the bones together, the capsule holds the synovial fluid in place and the cartilage acts as a shock absorber.

B10.4   Muscles and movement

This section aims to explain the relationship between muscles and skeletons that enables movement to occur. Three types of skeleton are discussed – endoskeletons, exoskeletons and hydrostatic skeletons. Worksheet **B10B** deals with the examination of a pig's trotter; it can be used here (as recommended in the pupil's book) or in conjunction with the previous section. The flow diagram in figure **B14** combines the previous section and this section into a double lesson; the teacher should insert the worksheet exercise at the most appropriate moment.

Pupils can use themselves as examples of animals with an endoskeleton. It would be helpful if they could have access to living specimens of animals which have either of the other two types of skeleton.

Answer to selected question

14 It is an advantage for humans (and for tree-dwelling primates) to have long arms, but the extra operating distance is gained at the expense of operating force.

B10.5   Damage may occur

Pupils who are interested in sport are often aware of the injuries that can occur to their muscles, joints and bones. An appreciation of the vulnerability of joints and muscles is very necessary in this age of increased interest in sport and leisure.

Answer to selected question

27 There are many answers to this question. They include:

Age – this affects the strength and resilience of the tissues. Muscle strength starts to decline at 30 to 40 years of age, elasticity in tendons and ligaments from the age of 30, and the strength of bone starts to decrease after the age of 50. Inactivity accelerates these natural degenerative changes, whilst exercise tends to delay them.

Personality – temperament and maturity may make an athlete more or less likely to take risks.

Experience – more inexperienced athletes suffer more injuries.

Level of training – too much or too little will increase the likelihood of injury.

Insufficient warm-up period – this makes muscle and tendon injuries more likely.

Poor technique – when jogging on hard surfaces, for example, this may injure knee joints.

Poor general health and diet, or lack of rest and sleep.

The wrong equipment, particularly shoes and protective clothing. Joggers, for example, need shoes which give adequate support and which have a sole thick enough to provide shock absorption on hard surfaces.

B10.6   Moving through water

Animals have all sorts of special features which help them to move in their particular environment. This section aims to show the value of a streamlined shape for moving through water. This shape is not confined to aquatic animals; one has only to look at the shape of birds and some fast-running mammals such as the cheetah to appreciate this. The advantage of looking at aquatic animals is that it is easy for pupils to carry out an investigation in the laboratory which will test their ideas about the best body shape for moving through a particular medium. This is the purpose of Worksheet **B**10C, a practical exercise which is suitable for the assessment of several practical skills.

The theme could be developed by considering the idea that it is no use having a suitable shape for moving through water unless the shape is propelled through the water. The QE2 would not move if the propeller failed to turn. This begs the question, "What propels a fish?". The answer, of course, lies in the arrangement of the muscles of the tail; if a dead specimen is available, pupils could examine this arrangement. Like all muscles involved with movement, these are found in antagonistic pairs. Pupils may also be able to appreciate just how much of the total mass of a fish is devoted to muscle – essential for making progress through the comparatively viscous medium of water.

Some pupils may wonder why fish have fins. They appear to be a nuisance for moving forwards at speed because they provide a greater surface area in contact with the water, and so produce greater drag. Observation of living specimens will help pupils to appreciate the importance of fins.

Practical work

Worksheet B10A   Osmosis and turgor

Part 1

REQUIREMENTS

Each group of pupils will need:
Potato, raw

Sucrose solution, 2.0 mol/dm^3, 10 cm^3
Water, distilled, 10 cm^3

Balance for measuring mass (accurate)
Chinagraph pencil or marker pen
Cork borer or scalpel or one-sided razor
  blade
Filter paper
Rulers
Test-tube rack
Test-tubes with rubber bungs, 3
Tile, for cutting potato on

Part 2

REQUIREMENTS

Each group of pupils will need:
Potato, raw

Sucrose solution, 2.0 mol/dm^3, 35 cm^3
Water, distilled, 35 cm^3

Balance
Chinagraph pencil or marker pen
Cork borer or scalpel or one-sided razor
  blade
Filter paper
Pipette, graduated, 10 cm^3, or syringe
Rulers
Test-tube rack
Test-tubes with rubber bungs, 6
Tile

Part 4

REQUIREMENTS

Each group of pupils will need:
Dandelion, inflorescence stalk

Sodium chloride 10 % solution, 10 cm^3
Water, distilled, 10 cm^3

Chinagraph pencil
Forceps, blunt
Scalpel or one-sided razor blade
Tile
Watch-glasses, 2

Part 5

REQUIREMENTS

Each group of pupils will need:
Onion, raw

Sucrose solution, 2.0 mol/dm^3, 20 cm^3
Water, distilled, 20 cm^3

Bulb pipette
Chinagraph pencil or marker pen
Filter paper, 3 strips, about 2 cm × 5 cm
Forceps, blunt
Microscope
Microscope slides, 3, with coverslips
Paint brush, small, or glass rod
Pipette, graduated, 10 cm^3, or syringe
Scalpel or one-sided razor blade
Scissors
Test-tube rack
Test-tubes, 3
Tile

Teachers might like to arrange these practicals in a "circus", and to allow pupils to report their findings to the rest of the group. Alternatively, one or two experiments could be completed. Parts 1 and 5, for example, are easy to perform and informative; they can even be performed concurrently. If time is a problem, then the apparatus could be set up beforehand, but this is, for several reasons, a less satisfactory way of completing the worksheet.

  If time is available, Part 2 is certainly worth attempting as it gives valuable experience in making a series of dilutions and gives accurate results. Remember, however, that the potato tissue should stand in the sugar solution for one hour (45 minutes would be an acceptable minimum). Results are not satisfactory if the material is left overnight, although they may be acceptable if the test-tubes are kept in the refrigerator.

Worksheet B10B   Looking at a pig's trotter

REQUIREMENTS

Each group of pupils will need:
Pig's trotter

Dissecting dish
Forceps
Scalpel
Scissors

Pig's trotters are easily obtained from a butcher. They can be stored frozen, but allow plenty of time for them to thaw out before attempting the dissection.
   These cuts require some force, and pupils should be advised to take care. The dissection may be done as a demonstration by the teacher.

Worksheet B10C   Moving through water

REQUIREMENTS

Each group of pupils will need:

Balance	Stopclock
Bowl for tube to stand in	Tube, glass or clear plastic, at least 1 m
Chinagraph pencil	long, 2 cm diameter, fitted with a rubber
Lead shot	bung at the lower end
Plasticine	*or*
Retort stand and clamp, with extra load	Measuring cylinder, very large
on base	Wallpaper paste, about a 3 % solution

This experiment provides a good opportunity to discuss the processing and presentation of results. The pupils will find that the fish shape drops more quickly than a cube or sphere, and should conclude that the streamlined shape decreases drag.

Demonstration experiments

The dissection in Worksheet B10B and certain experiments in Worksheet B10A could be performed as demonstrations.

Further information

Barrett, D.R.B., "Body size and temperature: an extended approach", *J. Biol. Educ.*, **17** (1), 7–8, 1983.

Bell, G.H., Emslie-Smith, D. and Paterson, C.R. *Textbook of physiology* 10th edition, Churchill Livingstone, 1980. (Earlier editions entitled *Textbook of physiology and biochemistry*.)

Hardy, R.N., Studies in Biology No. 35 *Temperature and animal life* 2nd edition, Edward Arnold, 1979.

Revised Nuffield Biology *Teachers' guide 2* and *Text 2 Living things in action* Longman, 1975.

Selkurt, E.E. *Physiology* 5th edition, Little, Brown & Company, Boston, 1984.

Soper, R. and Tyrell Smith, S., *Modern biology for first examinations* Macmillan Education, 1979.

Also relevant are SATIS units 707 "Artificial Limbs", 503 "Paying for National Health" (contains information on hip replacement operations) and 509 "Homoeopathy – an alternative kind of medicine".

Chapter **B11**   **Detecting changes**

Purposes

Knowledge and understanding

At the end of this chapter all pupils should appreciate the following three principles:

1 there are certain external factors, called stimuli, which are detected by organisms and to which they respond

2 the responses of organisms to stimuli may increase their chances of survival

3 the receptor converts the stimulus into a form that can initiate a response by the effector.

These principles should be developed with reference to **one** of the following examples:

- The growth responses of plants to light and gravity.

- The responses of invertebrate animals to light.

- The responses of humans to visual stimuli.

- The responses of humans to aural stimuli.

- The responses of humans to tactile stimuli.

Processes and problem solving

Using apparatus and measuring instruments
Worksheet **B**11B allows an examination of the internal and external structures of the eye to be carried out by the pupils.

Observation
Figure 11.1 in section **B**11.1 of the pupils' book shows the effects of etiolation in mustard seedlings.
   Pupils may observe axon fibres in a nerve, using figures 11.19 and 11.20 in the pupils' book; they may also observe the optic nerve (and other structures) of a mammal's eye, using Worksheet **B**11B.
   The Braille and Moon alphabets may be examined, using Worksheet **B**11C.

Interpretation and application
Pupils should try to interpret the results of their investigations into the phototropic and gravitropic responses of shoots, using Worksheet **B**11A. These responses imply that auxins are present.
   Section **B**11.3 in the pupils' book asks them to interpret the effects of daylight on the activity of woodlice and other invertebrates.
   Figure 11.15 in the pupils' book shows the results of an investigation into the variation in sound frequencies detected by young people. Pupils are asked to analyse these data.

Planning and carrying out investigations
In Worksheet **B**11C, the pupils design experiments to show how good our sense of touch is for getting information from the environment.

Timing

5 periods.

Suggested routes

At the start of this chapter several principles were established. Teachers should aim to teach these principles with reference to one of the examples developed in the chapter. It contains far more material than can be completed in 5 periods. Teachers therefore need to be selective. This strategy allows teachers to develop the principles in a heuristic way if they wish.

Figure **B**16 presents the material in the form of a table. Teachers should select material for five periods that will allow the principles to be taught in a coherent manner. It is suggested that one "double period activity" and three "single period activities" are chosen.

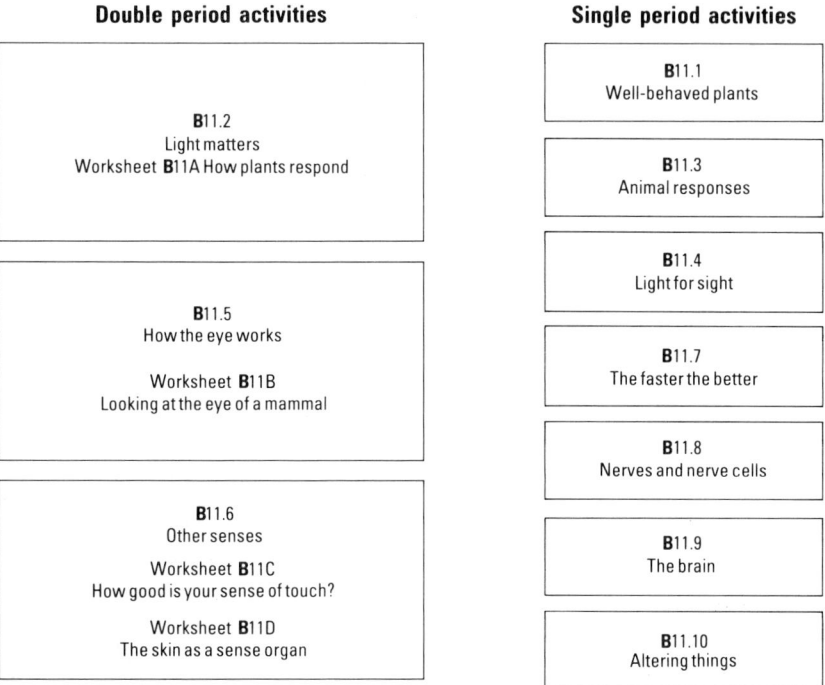

Double period activities

> **B**11.2
> Light matters
> Worksheet **B**11A How plants respond

> **B**11.5
> How the eye works
>
> Worksheet **B**11B
> Looking at the eye of a mammal

> **B**11.6
> Other senses
>
> Worksheet **B**11C
> How good is your sense of touch?
>
> Worksheet **B**11D
> The skin as a sense organ

Single period activities

> **B**11.1
> Well-behaved plants

> **B**11.3
> Animal responses

> **B**11.4
> Light for sight

> **B**11.7
> The faster the better

> **B**11.8
> Nerves and nerve cells

> **B**11.9
> The brain

> **B**11.10
> Altering things

Figure **B**16

Some combinations of "single period activities" could make interesting themes:

- **B**11.8 and **B**11.9 develop ideas about human nerve cells and the human brain.
- **B**11.3 and **B**11.4 develop ideas about how animals respond to light.
- **B**11.7 and **B**11.8 develop ideas about nervous reflexes.

Some teachers may wish to allocate more time to this chapter in order to cover section **B**11.10 (which deals with drugs and alcohol education), depending upon the health education policy of the school.

Opportunities for co-ordination

Some knowledge of the properties of light and sound is essential for an understanding of our senses of sight and hearing. Chapter **P**13 "Fibre optics and noise" contains much relevant information. Chapter **P**15 "Making use of waves" is also useful, as it covers colour, colour vision, wavelength and the behaviour of sound waves, and will help pupils to consider sense organs as transducers.

There are several opportunities for co-ordination with Chapter **P**21 "Communication"; interesting parallels may be drawn between the human nervous system (see section **B**11.7) and national or international communications systems, while section **B**11.8 describes a nerve as a "living communication cable" and likens it to a complex telephone cable comprised of many individual wires.

The study of drug abuse may be co-ordinated with work in Chapter **C**12 "Chemicals in the medicine cupboard".

Notes and answers

B11.1 Well-behaved plants

This section introduces pupils to the idea that the growth response of plants towards light is an example of behaviour (defined in the pupils' book as the responses that organisms make to stimuli) and that it has survival value. The section presents the important concept of:

STIMULUS → RECEPTOR → (MESSAGE) → EFFECTOR → RESPONSE

This is the main theme running through all of the examples in this chapter.

Answer to selected question

4 The hairs are the receptors and the hinge mechanism is the effector.

B11.2 Light matters

Having established that plants respond to light in a way which favours their survival, we still need to know how the response is achieved. Following the principles underlying this chapter, we need to discover how the receptor cells in the plant convert the stimulus into a form that can initiate the growth response by the effector. This section examines the idea by referring to simple experiments; it can be supplemented by Worksheet **B11A**.

B11.3 Animal responses

The data in figure 11.5 in the pupils' book were obtained by 14-year-old pupils, using pitfall traps. Explaining data such as these presents a challenge to the pupils, because a number of variables may be involved in addition to light. Animals at night may be less visible to predators and less prone to dehydration and they may find their prey more abundant at night. Pupils should be encouraged to develop hypotheses to explain the responses of invertebrates to light in terms of the principles of this chapter. If time permits, they could also plan and carry out investigations to test their hypotheses.

B11.4 Light for sight

This brief section introduces one of the most important receptor organs we possess – the eye. The structure and functioning of the eye are examined in later sections; the importance of having two eyes is investigated here.

Pupils enjoy working out their sight capacity. If class data are collected, the results could provide an opportunity to show the variation that is found whenever a characteristic is measured in a sample of humans. From the range of values obtained, an average can be calculated. This can be taken as the representative value.

B11.5 How the eye works

This section relates the structure of the eye to its function, and should be completed with Worksheet **B11B**. The emphasis should be to show how the eye converts electromagnetic radiation into nerve impulses that can cause the central nervous system to initiate a response. Sufficient factual detail should be included to allow these principles to be developed, but care should be taken to avoid overloading pupils with too much incidental detail.

B11.6   Other senses

This section includes material on the ear, the skin and the tongue. The aim is to develop the principles outlined at the start of this chapter. Teachers should select certain parts of this section, depending on which examples they have chosen. Worksheets B11C and B11D could be used at this point.

B11.7   The faster the better

This brief section deals very simply with reflexes, stressing their survival value to the organism. A distinction between cranial reflexes and spinal reflexes is not made in the text, but it could be mentioned that the reflex pathways which do pass through the brain do not pass through those higher centres of the brain that are involved in the making of conscious decisions.

B11.8   Nerves and nerve cells

This section develops the previous one with a consideration of the structure of nerves. These should be considered as a means of transporting the "message" to and from the co-ordinating centre of the body.

To get some idea of just how many nerve cells there are in the human body, pupils could be asked to work out how long it would take them to finish counting 28 billion cells if it took one second to count each one – taking into account rounding-up of numbers, the answer is about 887 800 years!

Answer to selected question

27 The fatty material acts as an insulator around the nerve, preventing the impulse from "leaking away" from it.

B11.9   The brain

A brief consideration of the brain completes the material on the ways in which humans detect and respond to changes in their environment. The emphasis is on aspects that are directly relevant to the pupils. A detailed consideration of the role of each part of the brain is beyond the scope of this course.

Answers to selected questions

32 Meningitis is a serious disease because the inflamed meninges membranes can affect the functioning of the brain. The symptoms include fever, severe headache, photophobia, vomiting and stiffness in the back and neck. Later symptoms include drowsiness and convulsions. The bacterial form of the disease needs to be treated immediately with antibiotics if permanent damage to the brain is to be avoided. The viral form is not susceptible to antibiotics and is much less easy to treat.

33 A loss of consciousness or confusion leading to a loss of memory for events before and after the injury. Recovery is often accompanied by nausea or vomiting.

34 Blood can build up inside the cranium and compress the brain. The symptoms of this are muscular twitches, convulsions or epileptic-type fits. Breathing is noisy, the pulse is slow and the pupils of the eyes may dilate (this occurs to different extents in different people). The body temperature may rise. Later symptoms are a reduction in the level of alertness and passing into a coma.

B11.10   Altering things

The significance of this section will depend upon the health education programme of the school. The importance of the idea that **all** of the drugs mentioned in figure 11.22 of the pupils' book are dangerous cannot be overstressed. None of these substances is safe, since they can all lead to dependence of one type or another.

It is worth pointing out that a carefully controlled prescription of barbiturates and benzodiazepines (*e.g.* Valium) can prove to be beneficial to some people for a short time. Longterm use is harmful since it leads to dependence. These drugs do not solve people's problems; they may, at best, increase their ability to withstand pressure and solve their problems for themselves.

The dangers of alcohol are becoming increasingly apparent, as are moves towards making it less socially acceptable to drink too much.

Answers to selected questions

38 Pleasure, curiosity, social anxiety, rebelliousness – it's a good way of being anti-authority – relief from worry or depression, fear of missing out or losing face, boredom, attention seeking and search for self-knowledge. (The last is not usually a reason within this age group, though it might be a motive for the few older teenagers who experiment with hallucinogenic drugs.)

39 Drugs which have been found to be addictive are used as little as possible. Amphetamines used to be quite widely used, for example as appetite suppressants, but now they are hardly ever prescribed. When drugs such as tranquillizers or sleeping pills are really necessary, they should be prescribed only for as short a time as possible – just to help the person over a bad patch.

Obviously there are cases when a drug's medical value outweighs the disadvantages of addiction – patients suffering from a painful terminal illness, for example, will be given morphine (heroin).

41 A larger person has a greater volume of body fluids than a smaller person. Therefore, if they both drink the same amount, the alcohol will be less concentrated in the blood of the larger person and will have less effect. Women, as a general rule, are smaller than men and have smaller volumes of body fluids. They are therefore more easily affected by alcohol.

Practical work

Worksheet B11A   How plants respond

REQUIREMENTS

Each group of pupils will need:
Pea seeds, germinated, 42

Compost, seed

Box, black on the inside, light-proof, with a hole at one end
Pots, 7.0 cm, 7

Access to:
Light source
Water

Peas give excellent results; they germinate readily and in many ways are easier to use than the traditional oats. The seeds should be soaked in water for at least 24 hours before setting up the experiment. Ten days should be allowed (at 20 °C) for results to appear.

Because the plants are hardy, a number of experiments can be set up. This worksheet gives a few ideas and then invites students to devise their own series of experiments.

Worksheet B11B   Looking at the eye of a mammal

REQUIREMENTS

Each group of pupils will need:
Eye of sheep or ox, fresh

Dish
Forceps
Hand lens
Scalpel, sharp
Scissors, dissecting
Tile
Tissue paper, thin, 2 cm²

Access to:
Hot and cold water
Soap
Towel

A great deal can be learned by studying the external features of the eye; frequently pupils fail to do this in detail because they rush to make the internal examination. Pupils who feel unable (or unwilling) to perform this dissection should be allowed to complete suitable alternative work (such as using books to find out the answers to the worksheet questions).

Eyes can usually be obtained from a butcher, who will require notice in advance in order to assemble a number for class use. The lens and internal surfaces will certainly be in better condition in fresh eyes, which will need to be obtained from an abattoir. Frozen material can, however, be used; if it is frozen solid it can be sawn in various planes with a fretsaw. Eyes that have been frozen may take 12 hours to thaw out fully.

If too much pressure is used to make an initial cut the aqueous humour sometimes squirts out, to the distress of more sensitive pupils. It may help to avoid this if the teacher makes the initial incision with a sharp scalpel blade.

Pupils should be encouraged to observe carefully and to think about the structures that they see. This dissection could form the basis of an assessment exercise.

Worksheet B11C   How good is your sense of touch?

Part 1

REQUIREMENTS

Each group of pupils will need:
Blindfold
Maze
Stopclock

Part 2

REQUIREMENTS

Each group of pupils will need:
Blindfold
Metal sheet, thin, with raised and
    depressed patterns of dots

Part 3

REQUIREMENTS

Each group of pupils will need:
Samples of Braille and Moon alphabets

Notes:
Each maze should be at least 30 cm × 30 cm (larger if possible). A maze consists of strips of card about 3 mm wide glued onto a thick base – either cardboard or plywood.

The metal sheets should be about 20 cm × 20 cm, and have series of metal dots punched into them with a centre punch. Each pattern should consist of six dots, but the spacing between the dots and the patterns themselves should vary both on a single sheet and between sheets. Some patterns can be made with raised dots, others can be made with depressed dots.

Braille texts may be obtained from The Royal National Institute for the Blind, 224 Great Portland Street, London W1N 6AA. Moon texts may be obtained from The Royal National Institute for the Blind, Moon Branch, Holmesdale Road, Reigate, Surrey. Drawings of the two styles of text are shown in the diagrams on the worksheet; these can be examined if it proves to be difficult to obtain actual samples of the texts.

Worksheet B11D   The skin as a sense organ

REQUIREMENTS

Each group of pupils will need:
Blindfold
Cork or expanded polystyrene, small pieces
Hairpins, wire, 2
Rulers

The procedure is detailed on the worksheet. It is important that the tips remain the measured distance apart; this can be achieved by pushing them through small pieces of cork or expanded polystrene.

Demonstration experiments

Parts of Worksheet **B**11A could be performed as demonstrations, where they could be developed to include the use of a klinostat to study gravitropisms.

Demonstration material of etiolated plants could accompany section **B**11.1 or Worksheet **B**11A.

Further information

Two SATIS units are relevant to this chapter. They are: unit 209 "Spectacles and contact lenses" and unit 406 "Blindness".

Supplementary material

Braille and Moon texts can be obtained from the addresses given in the notes for Worksheet **B**11C.

Chapter B12   Keeping things under control

Purposes

Knowledge and understanding

At the end of this chapter all pupils should:

1 understand the significance of sweating as a method of cooling the body and shivering as a mechanism for generating heat

2 appreciate how mammals and reptiles regulate their body temperatures

3 know that the kidneys remove excess water and waste products (such as urea) from the blood plasma.

Processes and problem solving

Graphical and symbolic representation
Opportunities for the graphical representation of data come in Worksheet **B**12A, where pupils plot a bar graph of the body temperatures of people, and in Worksheet **B**12B, where they display the results of an investigation into heat loss.

Using apparatus and measuring instruments
The heat loss from objects of different sizes is measured, using Worksheet **B**12B.
Pupils measure pulse rates before and after exercise, using Worksheet **B**12E.

Interpretation and application
Figure 12.5 in section **B**12.2 is a graph showing the daily variation in the body temperatures of a lizard and a cat in terms of their behaviour; interpreting this graph should help pupils to appreciate how reptiles and mammals regulate their body temperatures.

In section **B**12.3, pupils are asked to interpret data showing the changes in blood sugar levels over a 12-hour period.

Question 25 in section **B**12.4 asks for an interpretation of data on the intake and output of water in a human.

Worksheet **B**12B is concerned with relating heat loss to body size.

In Worksheet **B**12C, pupils interpret the effects of water and strong saline solution on red blood cells.

Worksheet **B**12D is a demanding exercise that involves analysing the composition of plasma, filtered fluid and urine to show the effects of filtration and reabsorption by the nephron.

Planning and carrying out investigations

Section **B**12.2 describes how cobalt chloride paper may be used to study sweat production. Pupils are then asked to design experiments to investigate the distribution of sweat glands over the body, the effectiveness of antiperspirants and the rate of sweat production before and after exercise.

Problem solving

Part 2 of Worksheet **B**12B involves calculating ratios of surface area:volume and the energy transferred from each beaker during the investigation.

Timing

5 periods.

Suggested routes

Figure **B**17 overleaf shows a number of possible routes through the material in this chapter. The two major sections that should be covered by all pupils are **B**12.2 and **B**12.4.

Two periods have been allocated for section **B**12.2. Teachers can choose which parts of the section they emphasize. Some time could be spent, for example, on the planning exercise investigating the effectiveness of antiperspirants. Alternatively, the relationship between body temperature and behaviour could be emphasized. This section could be extended into three periods, if desired.

It will be clear from the flow diagram that there is a choice of practical work that can accompany section **B**12.4. Worksheet **B**12C shows the effects of different concentrations of water on blood cells, and emphasizes the importance of controlling levels of water in the body fluids. Worksheet **B**12D is more demanding; it is concerned with the homeostatic role of the kidney.

There is a considerable degree of flexibility in the choice of material for the final period allocated to this chapter. Teachers might like to develop the work on temperature regulation (using Worksheet **B**12A or the more demanding Worksheet **B**12B). Alternatively, the function of the kidney might be considered, with section **B**12.5. Two new examples of homeostatic control might be introduced: blood sugar regulation (section **B**12.3) or a firsthand look at varying pulse rates (Worksheet **B**12E). The choice will depend upon the interests and enthusiasms of the group, and how well the principles of the chapter have been received.

Opportunities for co-ordination

Homeostasis is concerned with regulating the internal environment of the body. An interesting link between biology and physics may be made by comparing control in organisms with control in electronics, referring to Chapter **P**20, which relates the behaviour of control circuits to changes in their inputs. It is important, however, to **contrast** this method of control with the negative feedback mechanisms described in this Biology chapter.

Chapter **P**2 "Cooking food quickly" covers the kinetic theory of matter – essential for an understanding of evaporation and cooling with respect to body temperature (see section **P**2.3). This may be co-ordinated with the work on

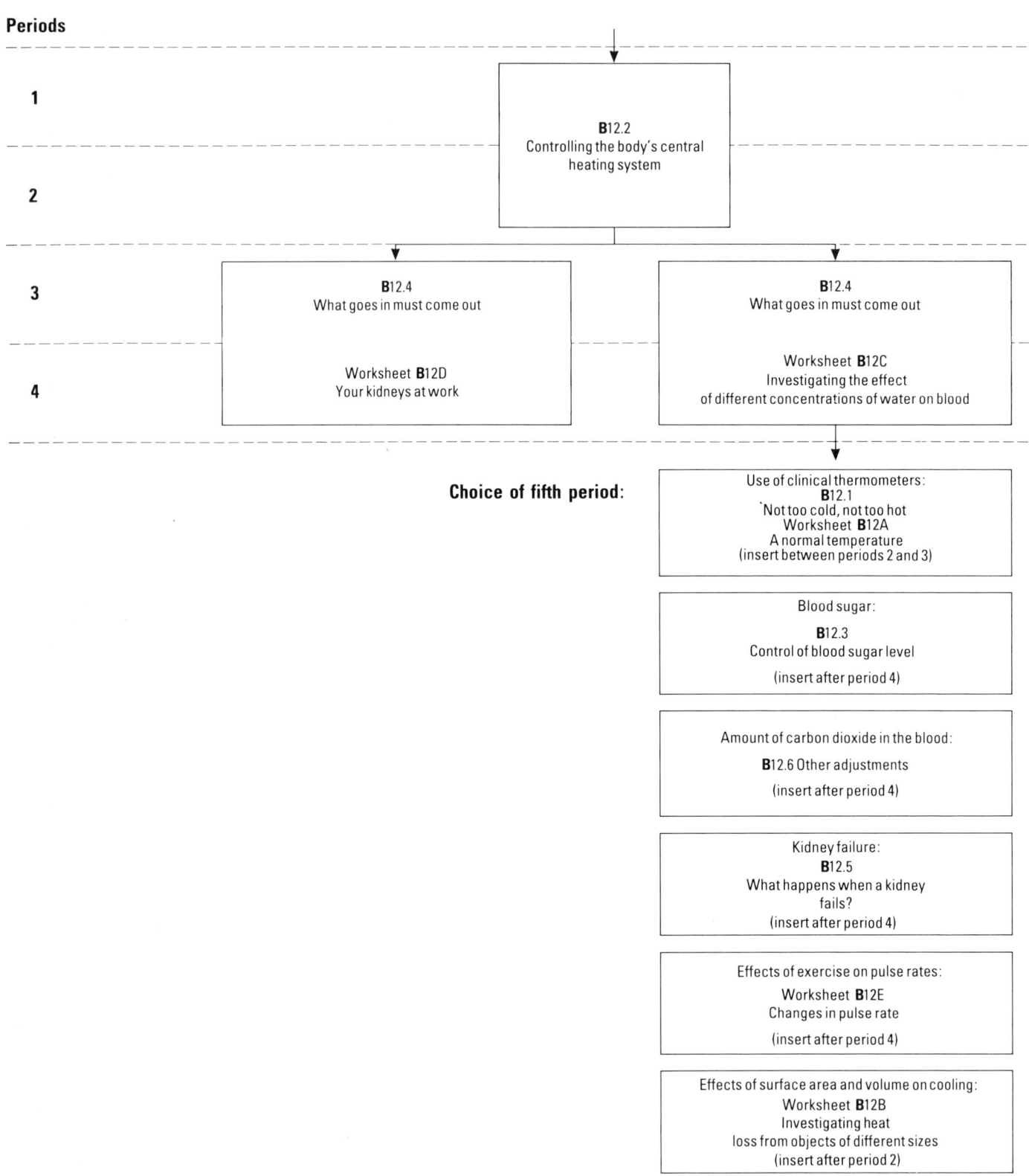

Figure **B**17

sweating (in section **B**12.2) – a process that involves the transfer of energy from the body to the air.

Section **C**3.2 in the Chemistry pupils' book describes the use of Visking tubing (a selectively permeable membrane) to separate large and small molecules. Kidney machines use a similar material for dialysis (see section **B**12.5). The importance of this process to the working of the body is emphasized in section C9.2 "How can we recognize a colloid?".

Notes and answers

B12.1   Not too cold, not too hot

Homeostasis is a vital process for maintaining life in organisms. This section introduces the idea by referring to various circumstances which can affect body temperature and indicating the responses needed to keep it constant. It can be completed alongside Worksheet **B12A**. Alternatively, the worksheet can be completed as part of the next section.

B12.2   Controlling the body's central heating system

This section aims to explain the mechanisms involved in controlling the responses needed to keep body temperature constant. In particular, the text makes a brief reference to those parts of the skin that are involved. Worksheet **B12B** may also be completed as part of this section.

The investigations using cobalt chloride paper are fun to do, and teachers might like to spend time developing these ideas. Adhesive tape can be used to stick squares of the moisture-indicating paper to the skin, but delicate areas should not be used for the investigations, as peeling off the tape could be painful! Sticking plaster is a useful alternative, but some people have an allergic response to it.

Clearly, the investigations in the text are qualitative in nature, and so it may be necessary to establish some method of comparing degrees of moisture output. Squares of dry absorbent material can be weighed and then stuck to the skin. Reweighing after an appropriate amount of time will reveal just how much water has been released from the skin. A very sensitive balance is needed, but the results do lend themselves to further study.

The section continues with a consideration of how sweating cools the body and of the role of the hypothalamus in keeping the temperature of the body constant. Behavioural methods of regulating body temperature are also discussed.

Answers to selected questions

15a By keeping its mouth open the crocodile is able to cool its body, which is being warmed by the sun. Being warm means that its muscles are able to contract quickly in order to attack prey. Presumably, if the crocodile were to spend time in the water its body would be cooler, but this would reduce its ability to move quickly. In addition, depending on how deep the water is, it may have to expend energy to keep afloat. Being warm on the river bank may also help it to speed up the digestion of food in its gut. Some pupils may suggest that having an open mouth makes it easier for birds to clean the crocodile's teeth.

b The muscles that a butterfly uses to vibrate its wings will generate heat, which will raise the body temperature until it is ideal for the flight muscles to work at peak efficiency.

c The lizards can only be active at the coolest parts of the day. In the heat of the midday sun the temperature of their bodies would soon rise to an intolerable level, and so they retreat into the shade.

B12.3   Control of blood sugar level

This section introduces the control of glucose levels as a homeostatic mechanism, and, through a brief consideration of diabetes, looks at the role of insulin within this mechanism. The section ends with a brief account of the production of insulin through modern techniques of genetic engineering.

Answers to selected questions

17 and **18** Each peak in the level of glucose in the blood occurs soon after a meal. These peak levels are not permanent, and they soon fall to a constant level which is greater than zero.

21 Diabetics feel weak because insufficient sugar is available in the blood. They may lose body mass because their fat reserves will need to be broken down to supply sugar. The lack of an immediate source of energy such as sugar will make them feel tired and weak.

22 A large volume of urine is produced because a lot of water is used to remove the excess sugar from the body. (Traces of sugar in their urine also make diabetics prone to urinary infections.)

24 Someone who has become very heavy will need more energy just to move the increased body mass around. Such a person will therefore need more insulin too, and the pancreas may not be able to provide the extra. There is the additional factor that people get fat because they overeat – and they tend to eat large amounts of the starchy and sugary foods which produce the greatest rise in blood sugar. Again, the pancreas might have produced enough insulin to keep pace with a normal diet, but not with overeating.

B12.4   What goes in must come out

The kidney is considered in this section as a filtration unit. Details of the structure and function of the nephrons are not required. This section can be completed with Worksheet **B**12C, which emphasizes that the amount of water inside the body needs to be regulated if damage to cells is to be avoided. The kidney plays a major role in the maintenance of a constant water level in the body. Worksheet **B**12D examines the functioning of the kidneys more fully.

B12.5   What happens when a kidney fails?

This section gives a brief account of the two alternative methods of treatment – dialysis or a kidney transplant – open to someone who suffers kidney failure.

B12.6   Other adjustments

This section considers a further example of homeostasis: the effect of increased levels of carbon dioxide on the breathing rate. It can be supplemented by Worksheet **B**12E.

Practical work

Worksheet B12A   A normal temperature

REQUIREMENTS

Each group of pupils will need:
Graph paper
Pencils
Rulers

The procedure is detailed on the worksheet.

By comparing the average value of the small sample of boys with the national average, it is hoped that pupils will begin to appreciate the effect that sample size can have on the validity of any representative value quoted.

It is probably desirable for pupils to gain experience of using a clinical thermometer, since this is a very useful skill to acquire. The correct use of a clinical thermometer should be demonstrated before the pupils try for themselves.

Worksheet B12B Investigating heat loss from objects of different sizes

REQUIREMENTS

Each group of pupils will need:
Water, cold

Beakers, 3, of volumes 100 cm³, 250 cm³,
    500 cm³; tea towels
Graph paper
Measuring cylinder
Rulers
Stands, 3
Stopclock
Thermometer

Access to:
Source of very hot water (as near boiling as possible)

It is necessary to have a source of very hot water and a safe method of transporting it around the laboratory. A secondhand tea urn has proved to be a useful acquisition for this purpose (as well as for school fêtes!). Pupils carry the water in beakers shielded with tea towels. Care should be taken to ensure that the beakers of hot water are stable on their stands.

The calculations in the second part of this worksheet are complex and may not be appropriate for all pupils. They should illustrate the relationship between the heat loss of a body and its surface area and volume. Although the temperature falls most quickly in the smallest beaker, more energy is actually transferred per unit time from the largest beaker.

It is important that pupils appreciate the analogy that can be drawn between this example and the case of animals. Some pupils will need to be helped to understand this.

Worksheet B12C Investigating the effect of different concentrations of water on blood

This worksheet describes a simple experiment and gives results for interpretation by the pupils. The procedure for their analysis is detailed on the worksheet. Alternatively, the pupils could perform the experiment for themselves, using the requirements outlined on the worksheet.

Worksheet B12D Your kidneys at work

The procedure is detailed on the worksheet.

Worksheet B12E Changes in pulse rate

REQUIREMENTS

Each group of pupils will need:
Chair or stool
Graph paper
Pencils
Stopclock

The procedure is detailed on the worksheet. The results are best recorded as a graph of pulse rate against time, with the exercise period clearly marked in.

Pupils may be very interested to find out whether the physical fitness of members of the class has any relationship to the results. A "scoring method" can be devised after discussion with the class. For example, an average figure can be found for students:

a sitting
b standing
c after exercise.

Each student could be given 15 points and have points deducted for figures above the mean. For example, when sitting, 1 point may be deducted for a pulse over 78 beats per minute, 2 points deducted if over 84 beats, 3 points deducted if over 96 beats (taking 78 beats per minute as the mean).

Fitness can also be judged by allowing points for regular training, membership of teams, cycling to school, walking and so on. No doubt the pupils will be familiar with this type of assessment, as it is sometimes used in magazines and on television.

Further information

Two SATIS units are concerned with the problems of artificial kidneys: units 302 "Living with kidney failure" and 503 "Paying for National Health".

SATIS unit 309 is concerned with microbes making insulin ("Microbes Make Human Insulin"), whilst unit 710 is entitled "What is biotechnology?".

Topic B3

Living organisms and their environment

Chapter B13 Making sense of an environment

Purposes

Knowledge and understanding

At the end of this chapter all pupils should:

1 know that an ecosystem is a habitat and a community considered together

2 be aware that organisms may respond to regular changes in their environment by behaving in characteristic ways

3 understand that organisms may compete with each other for a resource that is in short supply.

In addition, those pupils aiming for higher grades should:

4 understand that successful organisms will take the place of unsuccessful ones in a habitat, and eventually a stable climax community may become established.

Processes and problem solving

Using apparatus and measuring instruments
In Worksheet **B**13B, pupils measure the annual growth of trees and relate it to the weather.
   In Worksheet **B**13D, pupils measure the carbon dioxide production by sun and shade leaves.
   Worksheet **B**13E enables pupils to study the effects of inhibitory chemicals produced by plants on the growth of seedlings, and asks them to analyse the soil around a mature tree for inhibitory chemicals.

Observation
Much of this chapter is concerned with observing the habitats of different organisms.
   In Worksheet **B**13A, pupils gain experience of observing organisms within communities, by looking at a laboratory aquarium.
   As part of Worksheet **B**13D, pupils may observe the growth of competing plants around the bases of mature trees.

Interpretation and application
Pupils use the information given in section **B**13.1 to interpret which environmental factors are important for the survival of limpets.
   Section **B**13.3 asks pupils to interpret the significance of migration in birds and of seasonal reproduction in certain animals.
   Using figure 13.10 in section **B**13.4, pupils should interpret the effects of competition on the reproduction of mustard seeds.

In Worksheet **B**13D, pupils are expected to use the information about the physical features of certain plants to explain how these features are advantageous to the survival of the plants.

Planning and carrying out investigations
Worksheet **B**13C asks pupils to plan an investigation to show how blowfly larvae react to light.
    Worksheet **B**13D gives guidelines for planning an investigation to compare the compensation periods of sun and shade plants.

Timing

8 periods.

Suggested routes

Figure **B**18 presents a flow diagram for the materials in this chapter. Where two different worksheets appear in the same column, they may be regarded as alternatives. Needless to say, this is not the only possible route through the chapter, and teachers should feel able to use the materials in the way that seems most suitable to them.

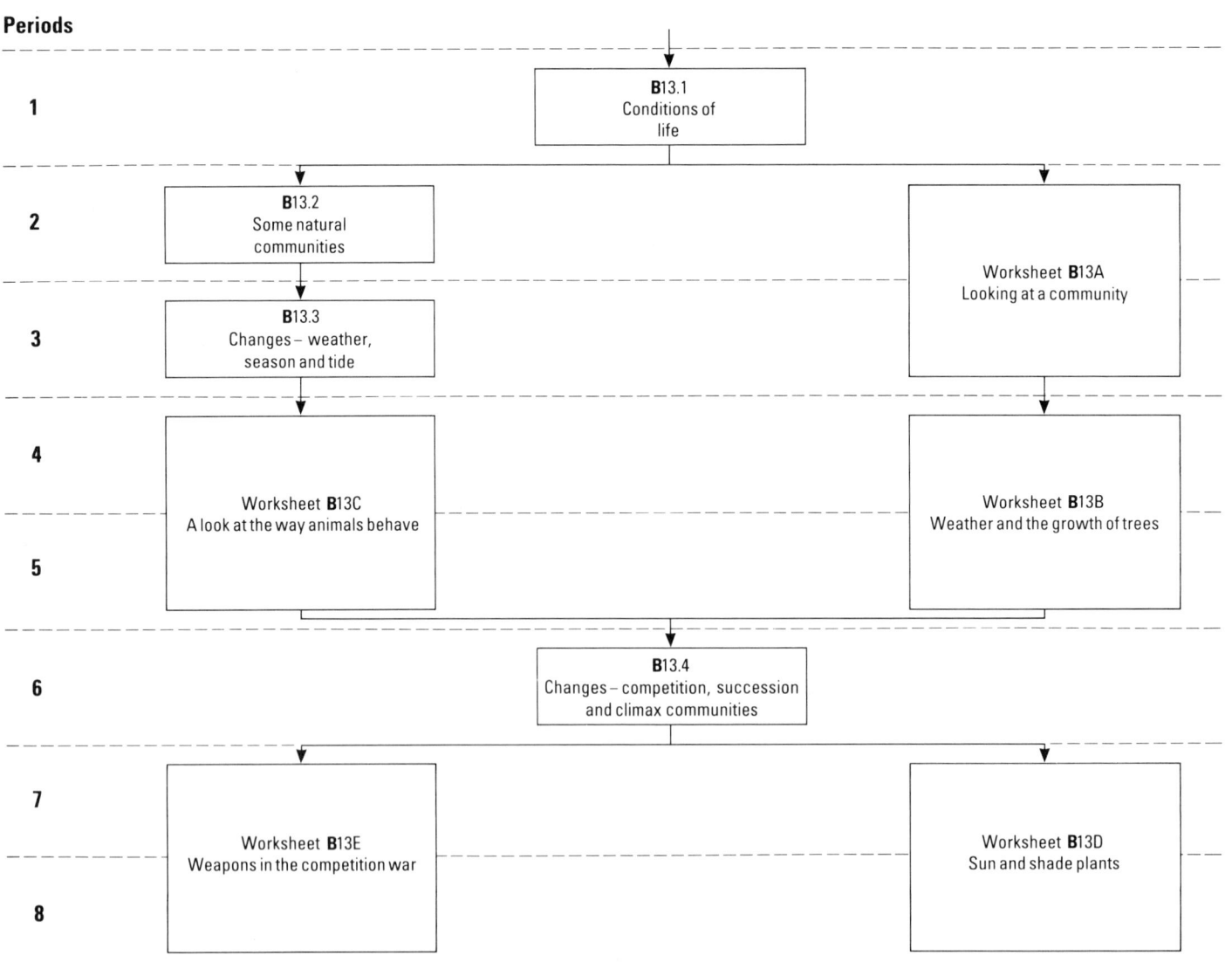

Figure **B**18

Time needs to be allocated for the practical work to be completed satisfactorily. To some extent, however, this will depend upon two factors that are difficult to take into account: the nature of the class and snags that may arise in the course of the experiments. The practical work forms an important part of this chapter; teachers should select only those worksheets that they feel can be covered most satisfactorily in the time available. A worksheet that takes longer than expected should not be curtailed. Rather, the time spent on the material in the pupils' book should be reduced to compensate.

The list under "Knowledge and understanding" for this chapter consists of a number of generalized principles that can be developed with reference to a wide variety of examples.

Opportunities for co-ordination

Although this chapter presents few direct links with the Chemistry and Physics books, an interesting reference to Chapter **P21** "Communication" could be made.

Notes and answers

B13.1 Conditions of life

Humans are introduced first, as examples of familiar organisms, with the intention of showing that we are atypical animals because of our considerable ability to manipulate our environment, thus escaping from the environmental constraints that control or limit most other species.

The limpet is used as an example of a contrasting organism, fully constrained by its environment. Pupils are asked to decide which environmental factors determine where the limpet can live. There is every opportunity here to encourage them to use this approach for other organisms – the photographs in figure 13.4 of the pupils' book could be used as some of many examples. The pupils may need some guidance here, since it could be difficult to define the environmental influences and constraints on, for example, very mobile animals. It is relatively easy to explain why limpets must live below high tide level, but not so easy to understand why blackbirds will be found in habitats on the edges of woodland rather than in dense woodland.

Answer to selected question

4 Descriptions of the habitats of the organisms mentioned here would be more meaningful if some idea were conveyed of any major environmental influences: these might either be apparent from the photographs or be appreciated by the pupils already. Most will be familiar with the earthworm, and should appreciate the cool, damp nature of its habitat.

B13.2 Some natural communities

This section develops the important concepts of habitats, communities and ecosystems. It can be supplemented by Worksheet **B13A**.

Answer to selected question

8a and **b** The coral reef and tropical rain forest are "rich" communities because temperatures are high and there is no shortage of water. Coral reefs are at or near the water surface, so light does not become a limiting factor.

The deep ocean floor is often "poor" because of total darkness, so all food chains rely on the arrival of dead remains falling from the surface. It is also cold, and communities found in cold environments tend to have fewer species than those in warmer environments. Pupils could be encouraged to speculate about why this should be so.

The hot desert is a comparatively "poor" community because water is a limiting factor. Also, temperature variation can be extreme, both daily and seasonally, producing further potential stress for organisms.

B13.3   Changes – weather, season and tide

It is important that pupils realize that most organisms have to survive in their environment as they find it – there is usually no "escape", as there often is for humans. However, figure 13.7 in the pupils' book provides examples of behaviour patterns fitted to regularly changing environments, and some pupils may see some of these (such as migrating birds) as examples of "escape" from an organism's present environment. There is scope here for pupils to contribute their own examples.

The passage entitled "Changing the body clock" may well provide a forum for pupils to relate their own experiences of, for example, waking at the same time each day, and how the time of waking can be altered – possibly when relaxing on holiday. The hidden effects of "jet-lag" on the decisions that businessmen and politicians make after insufficient periods of adjustment could provide another area for discussion.

Pupils can also carry out practical work related to this section, using Worksheets **B**13B and **B**13C.

Answers to selected questions

9 Bird migration is more concerned with the availability of food than with the higher temperatures further south.

10 Reproducing in spring means that delicate, unprotected young are not subjected to the rigours of winter weather, and are allowed a long growing season before the first winter. Conditions for growth are probably at their best during summer, with, for example, high light intensities and high temperatures. Food may also be far more readily available.

11 Tidal currents and light intensity will vary over 24 hours. Light intensity will also vary seasonally, as will water temperature. The availability of food is more likely to change during a year than during 24 hours.

B13.4   Changes – competition, succession and climax communities

This section discusses the idea of competition, and then studies the effect that it has on the composition of species within a community. Worksheets **B**13D and **B**13E may be used with this section.

The main point to emphasize is that limited resources will cause competition between individuals, resulting in stress. The fittest individuals will be at an advantage – this has obvious links with the chapter on evolution (**B**23). The unequal competition between different species leads to succession until a climax community is established.

Practical work

Worksheet B13A   Looking at a community

REQUIREMENTS

Access to:
Aquarium, containing a variety of organisms
Keys or reference material for identification

One of the major problems with this exercise is providing enough aquaria for the class to study. If the laboratories have demonstration aquaria that are already established, these would be appropriate for study.

An alternative (and very effective) approach is to set up a tank of mineral nutrient solution (such as Knop's culture) in an open place, and allow organisms to colonize it. Six to eight weeks is sufficient time to establish a viable community of microscopic organisms. Pupils can take samples from the tank, using small beakers, and search for organisms, using microscopes. They will need help when trying to identify the organisms, which is probably best given in the form of keys and diagrams.

A third approach to the problem is to set up several miniature "aquaria" in beakers. In order to reduce stress, the number of fish in the beakers should be limited to one. Ideally, pond water should be used for setting up the "aquaria", although tap water can be used if it has been allowed to stand in the open air for at least one day.

Worksheet B13B   Weather and the growth of trees

REQUIREMENTS

Each group of pupils will need:
Clinical thermometer
Graph paper
Pencils
Rulers

Access to:
A number of reasonably long twigs (at least 10 cm in length) from chestnut tree or other
    tree with clear terminal bud scars
Local weather data for the last 10 years

It will be necessary to obtain local weather data for the last ten years or so. A local weather station, a keen amateur or a local newspaper office may be able to help. It is particularly important to establish whether the springs and summers were "good", "bad" or "indifferent": rainfall, amount of sunshine and temperature are all important factors.

The material used for this worksheet should be shared and all class results collected before they are analysed.

Worksheet B13C   A look at the way animals behave

REQUIREMENTS

Each group of pupils will need:
Blowfly larvae

Water, iced

Bench lamp
Dish covered with plastic film
Graph paper
Pencils
Stopclock
Thermometer
Tub, plastic, sealed
Water bath or tin can

Access to:
A blacked-out laboratory

The procedure is detailed on the worksheet. Blowfly larvae can be kept for some days in a refrigerator.

Worksheet B13D   Sun and shade plants

Part 1

REQUIREMENTS

Each group of pupils will need:
Graph paper
Quadrat, 0.25 m²
Pencils
Rulers

Access to:
Tape measure
Trees in or near school grounds (*e.g.* in a park)

Part 2

REQUIREMENTS

Each group of pupils will need:
Leaves of sun and shade plants, *e.g.* dandelion and dog's mercury

Hydrogencarbonate indicator

Container, large glass, with tight sealing lid and glass well
or:
Boiling-tubes with bungs, 3
Pins to fasten plants in tubes, 2

The procedure is detailed on the worksheet. Part 2 of the worksheet must be performed in the late spring (*i.e.* mid-April onwards), when the plant material is available.

Worksheet B13E   Weapons in the competition war

Part 1

REQUIREMENTS

Each group of pupils will need:
Nicotiana seeds soaked overnight (about 50)

Plant material: garlic clove, leaves of rue, rosemary, basil, potato

Petri dish, sterile, with lid, containing potato dextrose agar

Cork borer, sterile
Rulers
Scalpels or knives, 3
Tile

Access to:
Ethanol to sterilize cork borer
Incubator at 26 °C

Part 2

REQUIREMENTS

Each group of pupils will need:
Cress or grass seeds, 100

Graph paper
Pencils
Plastic cups, 3
Rulers
Spoons, dessert, 3

Access to:
Soil from different places under a tree (the pupils should collect this themselves)
Tape measure
Water

The procedure is detailed on the worksheet. It might be worth trying different combinations of plants and seeds in Part 1.

The aim of Part 2 of the worksheet is to demonstrate that competition between a tree and colonizing plants can be reduced by chemicals produced by the roots of the tree. These chemicals inhibit the growth of seedlings.

Demonstration experiments

The experiment showing competition amongst mustard seedlings, featured in figure 13.10 in the pupils' book, could be demonstrated. It is very easy to perform and could be shown with many plant species. One disadvantage is the longterm nature of the experiment; fast-growing plants (such as mustard or mung beans) are therefore preferable, and the different stages of competition could be shown by staggering the time of seed-sowing. The experiment could be developed by measuring the surface area of leaves, internode distance, numbers of flowers or seeds, and dry masses.

Further information

Further information relevant to the worksheets can be obtained from the following sources:

Worksheet B13A:
Leadley Brown, A., Nuffield Advanced Biological Science *A key to pond organisms* Longman, 1970.

Worksheet B13B:
Chandler, T.J. and Gregory, S. (eds.) *The climate of the British Isles* Longman, 1976.

McKelvie, A.D., "A School survey of the flowering time of broom in the north of Scotland", *J. Biol. Educ.*, **4** (4), 227–233, 1970.

Lowry, W.P. "The climate of cities", *Scient. Am.*, August 1967.

Worksheet B13D:
Brown, G.D. and Creedy, J. *Experimental biology manual* Heinemann Educational, 1970.

Chapter B14   The webs of life

Purposes

Knowledge and understanding

At the end of this chapter all pupils should:

1 realize that a food chain is a component of a food web

2 understand the role of producers and consumers in a food web; recognize primary, secondary and tertiary trophic levels of consumers

3 understand the significance of the shapes of pyramids of numbers, of biomass and of energy.

In addition, those pupils aiming for higher grades should:

4 realize that the flow of energy through an ecosystem limits the number of trophic levels in a food chain, and that the energy available to the higher trophic levels limits the number of individuals in those levels.

Processes and problem solving

Using apparatus and measuring instruments
The energy of food substances can be estimated by following the procedure given in Worksheet **B14C**.

Observation
After looking at the parasite in figure 14.9 (section **B14.2**), pupils should try to work out which features may be characteristic of ectoparasites.

   Worksheet **B14B** guides pupils in observing holly leaves for evidence of parasitic insects.

Interpretation and application
Using information about the feeding relationships between organisms given in section **B14.1**, pupils are asked to work out various food chains.

   Questions 10 and 11 in section **B14.2** are concerned with interpreting maps showing the distribution of human parasites in the world in relation to the nutrition or income of the inhabitants.

In section **B**14.4, pupils are asked to interpret pyramids of numbers and biomass.

Worksheet **B**14A is concerned with interpreting the interrelationships between organisms in a food chain and in a food web.

Planning and carrying out investigations
Worksheet **B**14A will help pupils to design and perform an investigation of organisms in a food web.

Timing

3 periods.

Suggested routes

Figure **B**19 is a flow diagram showing a number of possible routes through this chapter. The time allocation is short, but it is important that enough material is included to illustrate the principles of the chapter, and that these principles are covered adequately. A detailed study of a habitat (Worksheet **B**14A, part 1) is time consuming; it could form the basis for an interdisciplinary study in some of the time that has been allocated for that work.

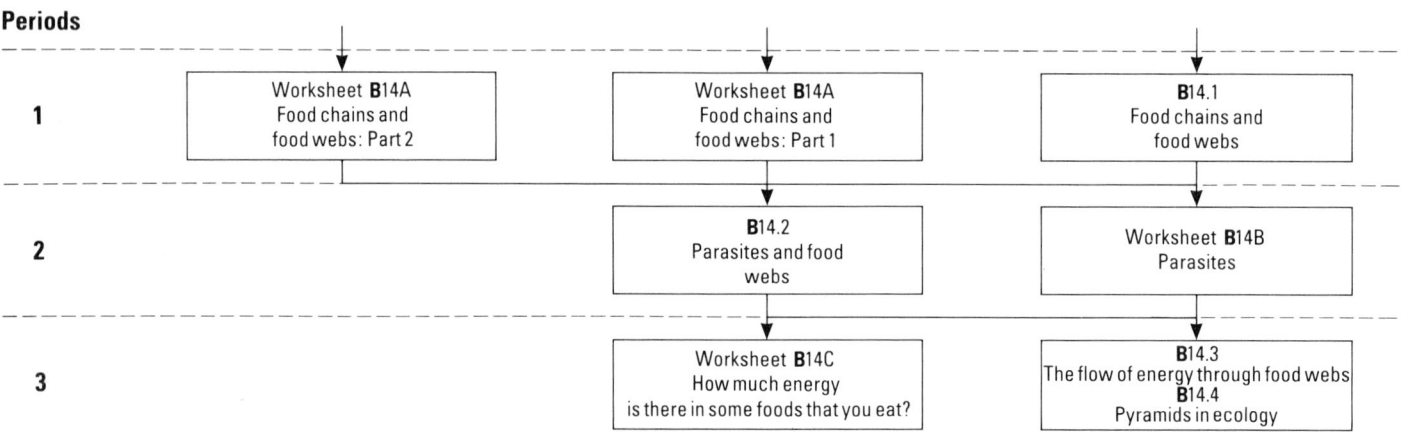

Figure **B**19

Teachers who wish to emphasize practical work should use the worksheets to develop the principles of this chapter, using parts of the pupils' material to support the practical work wherever appropriate.

One suggestion, not included on the flow diagram, is to use sections **B**14.3 and **B**14.4 and Worksheet **B**14C, and to omit the section on parasites (**B**14.2).

Opportunities for co-ordination

The transfer of energy is an important consideration when discussing food chains and food webs. Chapter **P**10 "Ideas in physics" contains background information on energy which may help pupils to understand energy transfer in the context of food chains.

Notes and answers

B14.1 Food chains and food webs

This section introduces food chains, taking as an example the food that humans eat. There are, of course, innumerable examples that could be given, but initially it may be preferable to use examples of food chains that include humans, so pupils can appreciate the concept in relation to their own food. It is important that they have a clear understanding of why the arrows indicating a transfer should always point from the consumed to the consumer – otherwise, they will often provide illogical arguments as to why the arrows "should" point in the reverse direction.

Worksheet **B**14A can help pupils to study feeding relationships within aquaria. While it is quite easy to set up simple food chains in such tanks, care should be exercised in the choice of organisms to be included. There should be no unnecessary suffering when secondary consumers feed, and it is inadvisable to include a higher level of consumer. (Teachers might like to use some of the ideas in section **B**14.1 of the pupils' book as background information if Worksheet **B**14A is to be used as an alternative to this section.)

Pupils are expected to work out food chains for themselves, either by observing organisms or from given data. Section **B**14.1 provides a series of guidelines applicable to any habitat for which the food web is to be worked out. It would be useful for pupils to have considered them before carrying out any field work.

Whilst it is necessary to have an approximate identification of an organism, there comes a point where it is not worth while trying to identify an organism any more accurately. Most vertebrates encountered and included in a food web can probably be identified according to genus or even species. In some cases dicotyledonous plants might be identified according to species, but it is almost certainly more economical of time and effort to be content with "speedwell", "dandelion", "bramble", etc. Teachers should use their own discretion here.

Invertebrates are difficult to identify because there are so many species, most of which try the skills even of professional taxonomists. Furthermore, there are often no common English names for them. This is not to say that there should be no attempt at their identification; working with a key, it should be possible to identify earthworms, slugs, snails, harvestmen, spiders, springtails, dragon flies, plant bugs and aphids, grasshoppers, earwigs, beetles, true flies, butterflies and moths, bees, wasps and ants.

Many pupils, of course, will recognize some or even most of these without recourse to an identification key. Only a few will recognize all of the organisms, however, and all should be encouraged to "try their hand" at working through a key.

Answers to selected questions

5 A source book will be of obvious benefit when finding information about the ancestors of domestic pets and their original or natural diets.

If the animal concerned is herbivorous, then there may be little value in exhaustive research to discover which plant species might be expected to form the whole (or part) of the diet, and simply "plants" could be entered at the bottom of the food chain.

Cats and dogs will be the most commonly kept carnivorous pets. Dogs are thought to have originated from the wolf, an extremely successful animal that in former times ranged throughout Europe, Asia and North America. Many different animals could reasonably have been included in their diet, and therefore in the food chain, although the food favoured by wolves appears to be various species of deer.

The domestic cat is thought to have originated in the Middle East and North Africa. There are now well-established feral populations of cats, and it would perhaps be easier for pupils to consider which small animals might be available for these feral cats, around farms or on derelict urban sites.

7 Crop plants and farm livestock would be the most useful foods to establish in the Moon base. Some pupils might suggest that the best crops would be those with a high yield, fast growth rates and low susceptibility to disease. Livestock introduces an extra link in the food chain, reducing the yield available to the human population. Pupils will understand this better after section **B**12.3, but there is no harm in introducing the idea now.

Pests and carnivores would be unwelcome additions to the Moon base food web.

B14.2   Parasites and food webs

This section uses the idea that although parasites are part of a food web, they differ from predators because they (usually) do not kill their host. Worksheet **B**14B provides an opportunity to look at one such example.

The maps in figure 14.8 in the pupils' book relate the distribution of human parasitic diseases to poverty and poor nutrition. Without being categorical about cause and effect, pupils should be able to make some suggestions that link the maps, bearing in mind the proviso about parasites just mentioned. They may need guidance to show how reduced poverty and increased food intake can decrease the incidence of disease – once again there is scope for discussion.

This section and its associated worksheet (**B**14B) describe some parasitic features, which are presented as special characteristics for survival in difficult habitats. Several aspects of life cycles that illustrate this are mentioned, although no one parasite is treated exhaustively and no complete life cycles are included.

B14.3   The flow of energy through food webs

The comparison of an oak woodland with a high moorland community is included to illustrate that, ultimately, more energy is stored and is therefore available in the "rich" woodland. This is not because more energy arrives there – if both are at the same latitude, then the moorland community will actually receive more radiant energy per unit surface area, because less is lost through atmospheric absorption at higher altitudes. The difference in the quantity of stored energy in each habitat is more closely related to ease of survival – lower temperatures, severe winter weather and high evaporative water loss make the moorland generally a more difficult place to survive in.

Although pupils might not realize it, there is a temporal element in this comparison, as the stored energy needs time to accumulate – more species growing to a greater size and covering more of the surface of the ground will, over a period of time, store more energy. More habitats develop as the community develops, so that ultimately the woodland community is richer than the moorland one.

B14.4   Pyramids in ecology

This section introduces the idea of pyramids of numbers, biomass and energy. Some indication of a pyramid of numbers might be possible from a consideration of organisms in a pond or mineral nutrient tank (see Worksheet **B**14A). When the producers are small, the pyramid of numbers has a broad base. However, the example of the English oak woodland shows that the pyramids can easily be "inverted".

Pyramids of biomass are generally preferable to pyramids of numbers because the relative sizes of each organism are taken into account. However, it is less easy to collect the data. To do this properly, organisms have to be collected from a unit area or volume of the habitat and dried before weighing. Obviously, this entails killing all the organisms, and there are ethical reasons why this should not be done when teaching ecology at this level.

There are two alternative methods that could be tried by teachers who wish to explore this topic experimentally: either to use data already available, or to use fresh (live) masses of the animals and dry masses of the plants.

Teachers must use their discretion here – an area of the school grounds used for ecological study will probably not harbour rarities, so there may be no objection to collecting all the plant material from a few sample areas for drying and weighing. However, this cannot be assumed if a habitat outside the school premises is being studied. If the dry masses of producers but fresh masses of consumers are used, pupils should be aware that this will produce an over-estimate of the consumer biomass. They should also appreciate that only a proportion of consumers from their sample area will have been collected. There is plenty of scope here for discussing the validity of results and for reaching conclusions from limited data.

Answers to selected questions

19 The producers in the river were unicellular photosynthetic protists, diatoms and flagellates.

20 If a scale of 1:100 000 is chosen, the maximum width of the diagram is 15 cm. Some pupils may note that it is not possible to draw the one tertiary consumer to scale.

Practical work

Worksheet B14A   Food chains and food webs

REQUIREMENTS

Each group of pupils will need:
Containers for the organisms
Sampling equipment appropriate to the habitat studied

Access to:
Appropriate keys and resources on the habitat studied

This investigation is divided into two parts. Teachers should select the part that is best suited to the needs of their pupils and to the time and resources available. The first part can be treated as an extension of Worksheet **B**13A or as an opportunity to explore a local habitat. The use of natural habitats for this purpose needs to be considered carefully, since it is improper for pupils to remove organisms from their natural surroundings for further study. The mineral nutrient tank discussed in the notes on Worksheet **B**13A in this *Guide* would also be highly suitable for this exercise.
   The second part of the worksheet is theoretical, and involves interpreting the interrelationships between organisms in a food web. It becomes clear from this exercise that a food chain is a simplification and that a food web is more realistic.

Worksheet B14B   Parasites

REQUIREMENTS

Each group of pupils will need:
Bench lamp, covered except for small aperture for light
Hand lens
Mounted needle

Access to:
Holly leaves, some of which are mined

The holly leaf miner appears to be far more common in towns than in the countryside, possibly because urban areas are warmer and have fewer frosty days. There is considerable variation between bushes in the amount of damage done by the miner, the frequency of its occurrence and the time taken for it to emerge.

Worksheet B14C   How much energy is there in some foods that you eat?

REQUIREMENTS

Each group of pupils will need:
Peanuts, unroasted

Water, 100 cm³

Balance, accurate
Boiling-tube
Burner
Measuring cylinder, 100 cm³
Mounted needle
Retort stand and clamp
Thermometer, stirring

Note:
It might be convenient to weigh the peanuts before the practical starts; they can then be provided in small Petri dishes with a note of the mass of each nut. A peanut should contain around 25 kJ/g of energy. If carefully performed, this experiment is about 50 % accurate.

The worksheet asks pupils to identify the major sources of error of the apparatus, to suggest improvements and to evaluate other designs of calorimeters.

Further information

ABAL (Advanced Biology Alternative Learning Project) Unit 9 *Ecology* Cambridge University Press, 1985. (This may be useful for Worksheet B14B.)

Several SATIS units are relevant to this chapter: unit 402 "DDT and malaria", units 304/5 "A medicine to control bilharzia" and unit 201 "Energy from biomass".

Chapter B15   Salts and cycles

Purposes

Knowledge and understanding

At the end of this chapter all pupils should:

1 know that plants need a balanced mineral intake for healthy growth, including trace elements

2 realize the importance of decomposer food chains in recycling nutrients

3 know how the carbon and water cycles are essential to life.

In addition, those pupils aiming for higher grades should:

4 be aware of the ways in which nitrogen can become available to organisms, including biological nitrogen fixation.

Processes and problem solving

Graphical and symbolic representation
Pupils plot graphs showing the growth of *Lemna* in different solutions lacking certain mineral ions, using Worksheet B15A.
   Part of Worksheet B15B involves plotting a graph showing the changes that occur in the height of a compost heap over a period of time.

Using apparatus and measuring instruments
Worksheet B15C introduces pupils to the use of Tullgren funnels to investigate the decomposers that may be found in leaf litter.
   Pupils may investigate the formation of root nodules in legumes, using Worksheet B15D.

Observation

The investigation in Part 2 of Worksheet **B15B** enables pupils to observe the longterm decomposition of different samples of leaf material by organisms in the soil.

Interpretation and application

After reading section **B15.1**, pupils should apply their understanding of mineral nutrition in plants to the need for fertilizers by plant crops.

In section **B15.2** pupils interpret photographs of decomposer organisms, to develop an understanding of decomposer food chains. Worksheet **B15B** asks them to put together part of a food web comprised of the organisms inside a decomposing compost heap.

Much of the second half of this chapter is concerned with interpreting the significance of chemical cycles for life on this planet.

It is important that pupils understand the significance of the nitrogen cycle in ecosystems, which is discussed in section **B15.4**.

Planning and carrying out investigations

Part of Worksheet **B15A** involves investigating the effects of mineral ion deficiency on the growth of *Lemna*.

Pupils may investigate the changes that occur inside a compost heap, using Worksheet **B15B**.

Problem solving

In Worksheet **B15C**, pupils are asked first to sort out the organisms they have collected from leaf litter into different feeding groups (primary and secondary consumers), and then to draw a pyramid of biomass for the food chain.

Timing

6 periods.

Suggested routes

Figure **B20** overleaf is a flow diagram showing suggested routes through this chapter. It is worth mentioning at this point that the worksheets require a certain amount of advanced preparation, and that the results take several weeks to develop. Time will need to be allocated in later weeks for regular reviews of these investigations. They are interesting and valuable, and it is worth making the effort to return to them periodically.

In suggesting a route for this chapter we have assumed that the investigation into mineral nutrition in plants will have been set up as a demonstration. Section **B15.3**, the water cycle, could be set as a homework exercise.

Opportunities for co-ordination

This chapter assumes that pupils are familiar with the nature of mineral ions; relevant chapters in the Chemistry pupils' book are **C5** "Materials and structures", which introduces ions, and **C18** "Atoms and bonding", which deals with atomic structure.

The significance of water both as a biological solvent and as a renewable resource is discussed in this chapter. This may be co-ordinated with work in Chapter **C10** "Keeping clean" (see especially section **C10.3** on the water cycle). There are also links with Chapter **C15** "Soil", which emphasizes the importance of soil for plant life. For example, section **C15.4** gives the chemical reasons why the distribution of wild plants is affected by the nature of the soil (see **B15.1**).

Section **B15.4**, which deals with the natural nitrogen cycle, may be supported by a knowledge of the chemical aspects of the nitrogen cycle, as given in section **C16.3** – a brief summary of the Haber process for the fixing of nitrogen on an industrial scale.

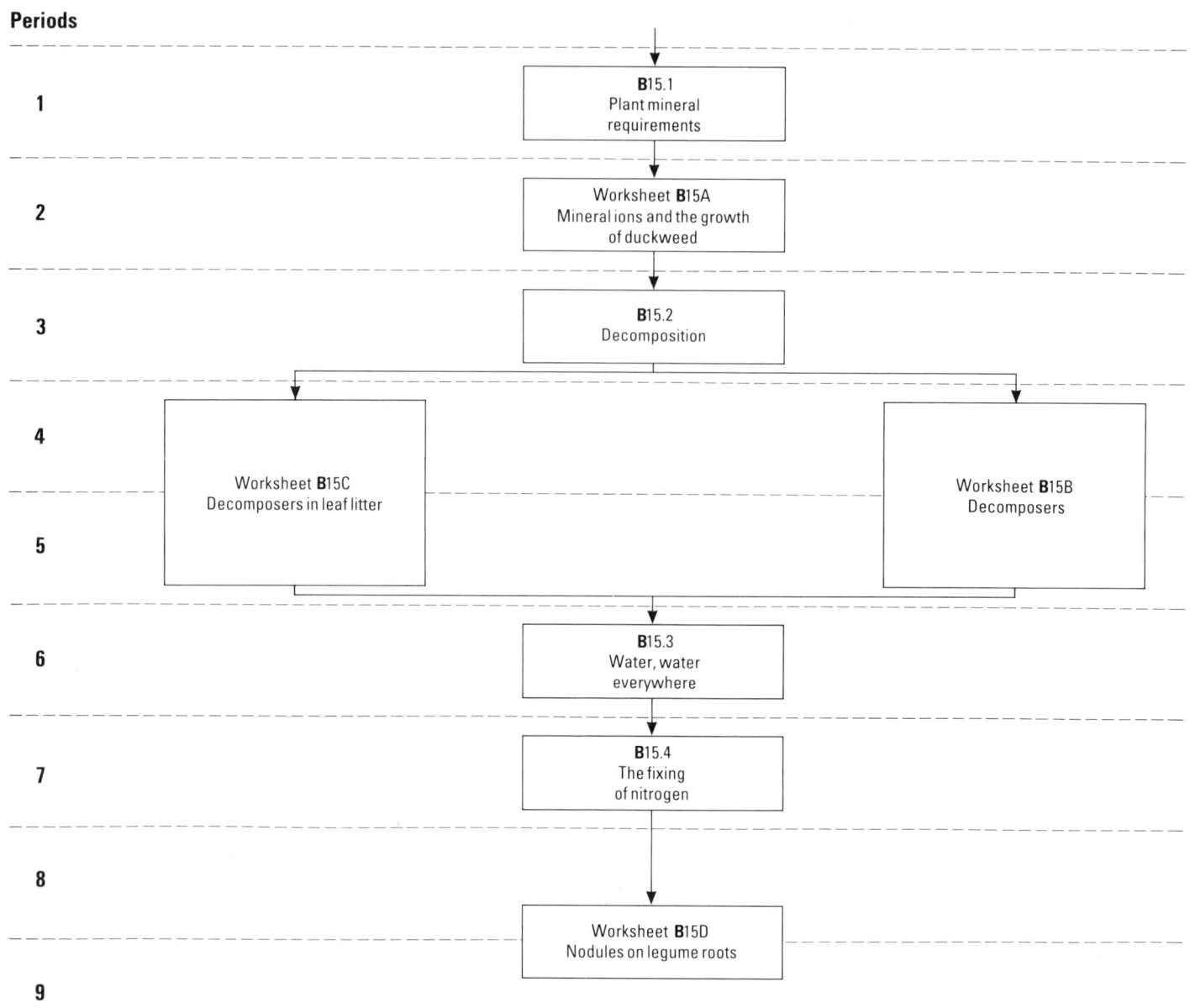

Periods

1 — B15.1 Plant mineral requirements

2 — Worksheet B15A Mineral ions and the growth of duckweed

3 — B15.2 Decomposition

4 — Worksheet B15C Decomposers in leaf litter / Worksheet B15B Decomposers

5

6 — B15.3 Water, water everywhere

7 — B15.4 The fixing of nitrogen

8

9 — Worksheet B15D Nodules on legume roots

Figure **B**20

Notes and answers

B15.1 Plant mineral requirements

This section outlines the mineral requirements of plants. It emphasizes the functions of ions in plants rather than the effects of ion deficiencies. Worksheet **B**15A develops this theme experimentally.

Answers to selected questions

1 Water.

7 The high levels of salt in the water would cause the plant roots to lose water by osmosis, and the plants would wilt and eventually die.

B15.2   Decomposition

Worksheets **B**15B and **B**15C are simple investigations into decomposition.
Worksheet **B**15B should be regarded as an extended study, to be carried out over
several weeks. It is important that the work on decomposition is linked to the
ideas of food chains and pyramids of biomass etc. developed in the previous
chapter.

Answer to selected question

9 This does not contradict the conclusion that the energy source of all food
chains is sunlight, since decomposer food chains start with the arrival of **dead**
material into the habitat. When alive, this material formed parts of food chains
which were dependent on sunlight. Without photosynthesis, there could be no
food chains, and consequently no decomposer food chains.

B15.3   Water, water everywhere

The idea of the cycling of materials is an important one. This section gives an
opportunity to establish the idea with an example that pupils find reasonably
accessible. The more complex nitrogen cycle is covered in the next section.

Answer to selected question

18 The cycle depends upon water being either a liquid or a vapour, depending
upon the circumstances. On Venus, water would be unlikely to condense to form
a liquid, and on Mars it is likely to be permanently frozen.

B15.4   The fixing of nitrogen

Worksheet **B**15D allows pupils to investigate root nodule formation in legumes.
An appreciation of the various ways in which nitrogen can be fixed is needed
only by those hoping to achieve higher grades.
   In previous work on plant nutrient requirements, pupils will have been
introduced to the ideas that plants need nitrate ions and that ions (including
nitrates) are released back into water or the soil during decomposition. The
energy released by lightning and its role in the formation of nitrates are now
discussed, and figures showing the significance of this source are given. One
estimate gives the frequency of thunder storms as 1800 at any one moment over
the entire Earth's surface.
   The treatment of nitrogen fixation is conventional, but relates it to agriculture
and the cost of fertilizer.

Answers to selected questions

17 Production could fall in natural habitats for a number of reasons. Natural
catastrophes such as eruptions, floods, droughts etc. will all slow production or
abruptly terminate it, but this may actually stimulate an increase in production
later on. For example, abnormal flooding may drown an entire habitat, but
when the flood water has subsided, the silt deposition with additional nutrients
may encourage more rapid plant growth than before.
   Reduced temperature always reduces production rates, as does reduced light
intensity caused by dust emissions, which in turn could be caused by natural or
human activities. All these examples give further opportunities for class
discussion.

21 The advantages of using human waste are that it would provide a source of mineral salts, an organic component to the soil and a solution to the problem of disposal; it has a low cost, involving collection and field distribution only.

The main disadvantage is the risk of disease transmission. In some societies the risk is high, and the costs to the society caused by such diseases may balance, and will probably offset, the advantages of sustained food production.

Practical work

Worksheet B15A   Mineral ions and the growth of duckweed

REQUIREMENTS

Each group of pupils will need:
Duckweed (*Lemna*), 20 healthy plants similar in size, colour and number of leaves

25 cm³ of each of the following solutions:
    complete mineral nutrient solution
    complete solution lacking nitrogen
    complete solution lacking magnesium
    complete solution lacking iron

Containers, plastic or glass, 4 (*e.g.* crystallizing dishes), with loose covers
Graph paper
Pencils

Access to:
Marker pen
Good light source

The procedure is detailed on the worksheet. Tablets containing balanced mineral salts can be obtained from biological suppliers.

Worksheet B15B   Decomposers

Part 1

REQUIREMENTS

Each group of pupils will need:
Graph paper
Pencils
Rulers

Access to:
A compost heap that will be undisturbed for several months
Tullgren funnel apparatus (see diagram on Worksheet **B**15C)
Key to identify organisms

Part 2

REQUIREMENTS

Each group of pupils will need:
Cork borer
Graph paper
Markers, 3 (to mark position of mesh bags on soil surface)
Mesh, nylon, 3 samples (*e.g.* tights, net curtain, plastic mesh of about 1 cm width)
Nylon string
Wooden block

Access to:
Flat leaves from one plant species (*e.g.* alder, apple, ash, beech, oak)
Soil in which to bury mesh bags

This practical ought to be performed only by those teachers and pupils who are able to work with a sustained interest for at least a term, since the changes occur slowly.

Worksheet B15C   Decomposers in leaf litter

REQUIREMENTS

Each group of pupils will need:
Leaf litter

Ethanol, 10 %

Collecting dish
Graph paper
Pencils
Trays for leaf litter and collected organisms
Tullgren funnel apparatus (see diagram on worksheet)

Access to:
Weighing balance

The procedure is detailed on the worksheet.

Worksheet B15D   Nodules on legume roots

REQUIREMENTS

Each group of pupils will need:
Pea or bean seeds, 4 per pot

Pots

Access to:
Running water
Various soil samples (*e.g.* vermiculite, sterile sand, sterile organic potting compost, garden soil rich in nitrates, garden soil in which beans have been growing, sterilized garden soil in which beans have been grown)

Note:
The legume seeds must be soaked in distilled water for 24 hours before germination.

The number of seeds needed depends upon the number of different soil types that are available. Vermiculite should be free from nitrates, and can act as a control. This experiment should run for several weeks in order to get good root growth before the plants are examined for nodules.

Further information

The importance of artificial fertilizers is considered in two SATIS units: unit 505 "Making fertilizers" and unit 207 "The story of Fritz Haber". Unit 201 "Energy from biomass" considers the conflict between adequate food production and soil fertility.

Chapter B16   Staying alive

Purposes

Knowledge and understanding

At the end of this chapter all pupils should:

1 appreciate the variety of methods of seed dispersal by plants

2 be aware of the variety of ways in which animals can colonize a habitat

3 appreciate the variety of factors that could account for the uneven distribution of organisms in a locality

4 understand that local populations of organisms can be of variable size

In addition, those pupils aiming for higher grades should:

5 recognize the need for factors limiting the growth of populations

6 understand the role of predators in regulating population size.

Processes and problem solving

Graphical and symbolic representation
In Worksheet **B**16D, pupils are asked to plot graphs of the distribution of *Pleurococcus* on trees.

Using apparatus and measuring instruments
Worksheet **B**16C uses choice chambers to study the habitat preferences of woodlice and gammarids.

Worksheet **B**16D is concerned with studying the distribution of *Pleurococcus* on trees, using quadrat techniques.

Observation
Pupils may observe the range of structural features developed by plants for the dispersal of seeds, using figures 16.5 to 16.11 in the pupils' book.

Worksheet **B**16B helps pupils to observe the range of organisms growing on pavements, paths and walls.

Interpretation and application
Pupils should interpret the significance of patterns of seed distribution and of the habitat preferences of barnacles, using section **B**16.2.

Question 14 in the same section (**B**16.2) is concerned with comparing the powers of dispersal of bats and humans during their colonization of New Zealand.

In section **B**16.3, pupils are asked to interpret the factors that control the distribution of a variety of organisms, including humans.

Using section **B**16.4, pupils should try to interpret changes in the population sizes of lemmings and to interpret data on the effect of predation on the population of deer on the Kaibab Plateau.

Planning and carrying out investigations
Question 28 in the section on populations (**B**16.4) asks pupils to suggest variables that should be controlled in an investigation of the changes in two populations of guppies.

Those pupils aiming for higher grades might design an experiment to investigate whether barnacle larvae detect low concentrations of chemicals in the water that surrounds them (see question 11 in section **B**16.2).

Worksheet **B**16A helps pupils to design an experiment to investigate the conditions needed for seed germination.

In Worksheet **B**16C, pupils are asked to devise methods of offering a "choice" of habitats to woodlice.

Timing

8 periods.

Suggested routes

This chapter contains a variety of materials that can be adapted to meet the requirements of a wide range of pupils. Figure **B**21 shows a few of the possible routes through the chapter. It is important that sufficient time is devoted to the practicals that are undertaken, and that appropriate worksheets are selected.

Periods

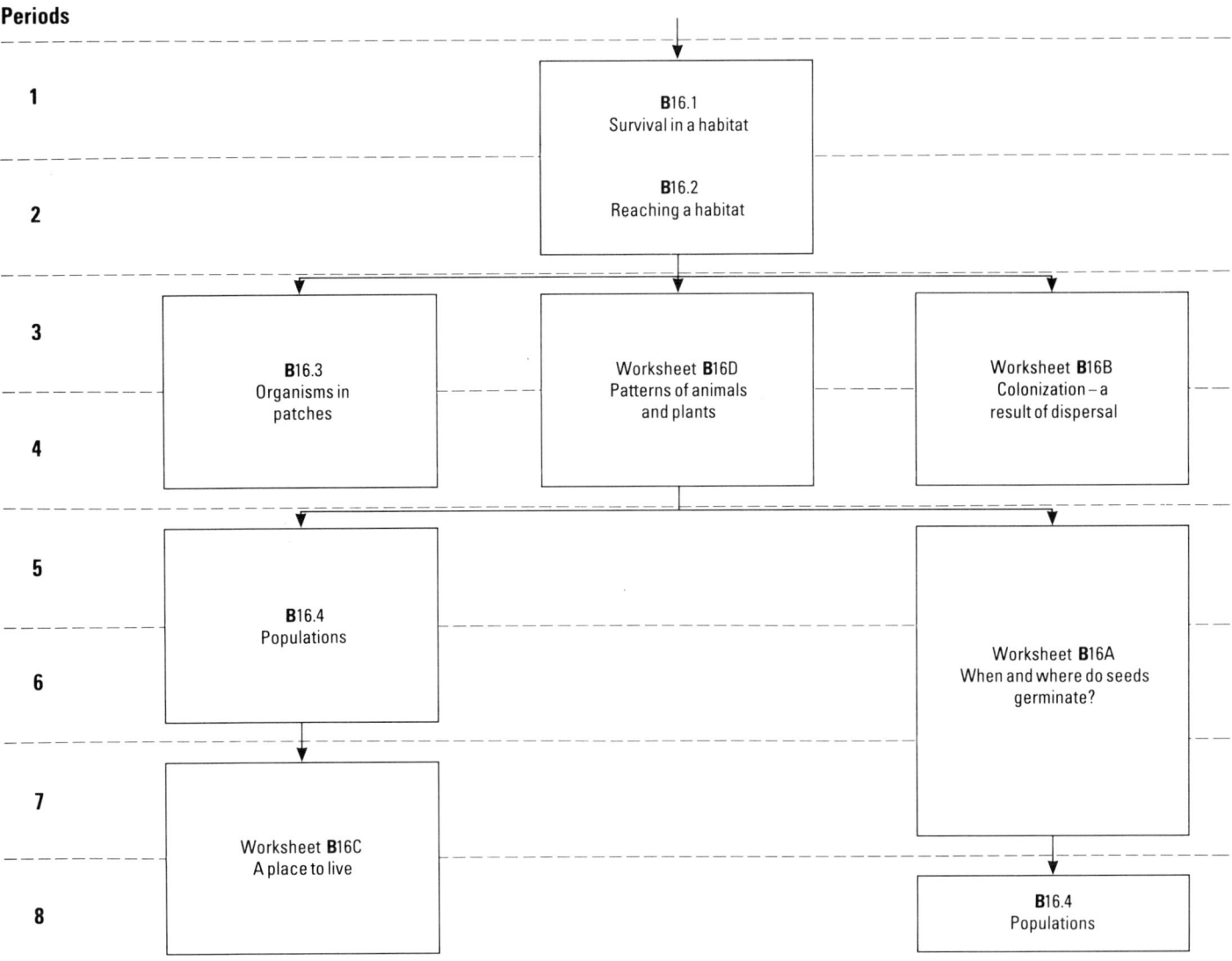

Figure **B**21

Notes and answers

B16.1   Survival in a habitat

In some ways the start of this chapter recalls Chapter **B**13, in that a range of environmental factors is encountered in both. Here the emphasis is on the availability of certain habitats for colonization, provided that the organisms can survive the environmental conditions.

B16.2   Reaching a habitat

This section forms the major part of this chapter, and should be developed with reference to a variety of examples. Pupils are not expected to remember the details of each example, but should appreciate how the different features and methods enable organisms to be dispersed. Worksheet **B**16A includes simple experiments on germinating seeds, and provides an opportunity for pupils to design their own experiments. Worksheets **B**16B and **B**16C are investigations into colonization and habitat preference.

The wide dispersal of sea snails shown in figure 16.13 in the pupils' book is remarkable, and is related to the very long duration of larval life. Most sea snail and other marine larvae travel much shorter distances, although with a planktonic life lasting three or four weeks considerable distances may still be covered. Unlike dispersing seeds, dispersing animals have some ability to avoid unfavourable habitats.

Answers to selected questions

11 This is a difficult exercise. Fresh sea water should be collected from an area that is some distance from the nearest barnacle colony, to ensure that it is free from barnacle secretions. The barnacle secretions could be collected by surrounding adult barnacles with fresh sea water. This water could then be transferred to a clean tank, into which barnacle larvae are added. The larvae should be able to settle on the sides of the tank. The control experiment should consist of an identical tank, containing the same number of larvae from the same sample, surrounded by an equal volume of the sea water sample which has **not** been exposed to adult barnacles. Both tanks should be kept in identical conditions and aerated. After a time, the number of barnacles that have settled in each tank should be compared.

14 All of the organisms could be dispersed, since they all reached the islands. We cannot say anything about the relative powers of dispersal of bats and humans, since we do not know when the first bats or the first humans arrived on the islands. We do know, however, that the bats (and humans) were able to disperse themselves more effectively than most other mammals, since they were the only ones that the Maoris found.

16 Sea plantain seeds are probably dispersed by car tyres. The plant has a distinctly maritime distribution, but it extends inland along trunk roads. Its natural distribution is related to the sea salt spray that finds its way into coastal habitats. The practice of salting the roads in winter to prevent ice formation creates an additional habitat for this plant along the grass verges.

B16.3   Organisms in patches

The factors that control the distribution of certain organisms are often hard to discover. Worksheet **B**16D guides pupils in the study of one organism, the protist *Pleurococcus*, whose distribution is reasonably simple to evaluate. Examples are also given in the pupils' book in such a way that the pupils should be able to think about what factors might cause the uneven distribution of the organisms.

B16.4   Populations

This section takes the guppy as a model to show that population sizes are controlled. It is possible to demonstrate this practically, although it is not recommended as it is hard to avoid placing the animals under stress. Population changes in natural environments are also considered.

Answer to selected question

29 The reason for the decline in the overcrowded laboratory population is probably limited resources, particularly food and space. A large number of offspring are produced in the understocked tank, many of which survive, leading to an increase in numbers.

Practical work

Worksheet B16A   When and where do seeds germinate?

REQUIREMENTS

Each group of pupils will need:
Cress seeds

(The pupils should provide their own apparatus lists)

Although this exercise in experimental design works well, it can be demanding in terms of technician time, since each group of pupils requests the apparatus it requires. Obviously the pupils will need to hand in their requirements well before the lesson is due to start – the design problem needs to be set in the lesson before the practical is due to begin.

One way of limiting the pressure on the technicians is to give the pupils a list of apparatus from which they select the pieces they want. In this way, the worksheet can be tackled in a double lesson, but time will need to be allocated later to review the results of the experiment. This worksheet is suitable for assessment purposes.

The exercise is useful because it teaches pupils about the need to vary just one factor at a time, keeping all the others constant. There is a number of factors that the pupils could choose to study; it is profitable for one or more groups to investigate the inhibitory effects of freshly squeezed orange or apple juice on seed germination.

Worksheet B16B   Colonization – a result of dispersal

REQUIREMENTS

Access to:
Books identifying plants, lichens and protists
Tarmac or concrete paths
Walls (*e.g.* old brick, cement, shady or sunny, etc.)

The success of this practical hinges on the pupils being able to recognize the types of organism that they encounter on walls and paths. It is not necessary for them to identify the organisms accurately. It will be sufficient to recognize them as lichens, mosses, protists, flowering plants, etc. Lichens form a group that has been deliberately omitted from Chapter **B**2 of the pupils' book because they cross the boundaries of two of the groups that are defined in that chapter. Lichens are made by an association between a photosynthetic protist and a fungus.

Worksheet B16C   A place to live

Part 1

REQUIREMENTS

Each group of pupils will need:
Gammarids, 5
Water weed, rotting

Dish, large
Sand or gravel
Silt or mud
Stones, large

Access to:
River or spring water

Part 2

REQUIREMENTS

Each group of pupils will need:
Woodlice, 10

Choice chamber (see *Note*)

Access to:
Drying agent (*e.g.* calcium chloride)
Water

Note:
Commercial choice chambers are obtainable from biological suppliers. Alternative models can be made following the design of figure 20, page 31, Revised Nuffield Biology *Text 3* (Longman, 1975), although teachers might prefer to use muslin or nylon mesh instead of zinc sheets.

Pupils should attempt only one of these investigations, unless teachers can set up both at the same time, in which case the pupils can observe both parts of the worksheet.

The first part of the worksheet provides an alternative to choice chamber work with woodlice, although it is dependent on there being an available source of fresh running water from which the organisms can be sampled.

Worksheet B16D   Patterns of animals and plants

REQUIREMENTS

Each group of pupils will need:
Clipboard
Graph paper
Paper
Pencils
Quadrat, 10 cm² (made from stiff cardboard or thin wood)
String, marked at 10 cm intervals

Access to:
Trees close to the school grounds

The procedure is detailed on the worksheet. It is important that pupils are shown exactly what *Pleurococcus* looks like before they attempt to study its density on the tree trunk. Much of the success of this exercise depends upon the pupils' ability to estimate sensibly the percentage of bark covered by the protist.

Further information

Dowdeswell, W.H. *Practical animal ecology* Methuen, 1969.
This is an extremely useful source of sampling techniques (such as how to investigate the distribution of organisms in a field).

Slingsby, D. and Cook, C. *Practical ecology* Macmillan, 1986.

Bülow-Olsen, A., Penguin Nature Guide: *Plant communities* Penguin, 1978.
Many pupils find this an attractive and informative guide.

Chapter B17   Farms, factories and the environment

Purposes

Knowledge and understanding

At the end of this chapter all pupils should:

1 recognize the need to control agricultural pests

2 be aware of the advantages and disadvantages of industrial pesticides, including the development of natural resistance by the pests

3 realize that the introduction of a new factor into an environment can have complex longterm consequences, using **one** of the following examples: the effect of surplus fertilizer on lakes and streams, acid rain or biological control.

Processes and problem solving

Observation
Part 1 of Worksheet **B**17B is concerned with observing the effects of acidity on the behaviour of *Gammarus*.

Interpretation and application

Section **B**17.2 discusses the effects of monoculture on the natural habitats of organisms.

After reading section **B**17.3, pupils should be aware of the effects of modern farming practices on agricultural pests. Question 12 asks them to evaluate the characteristics of an effective pesticide.

In section **B**17.6, pupils interpret the effects of industrial pollution on the distribution of the estuarine snail, *Hydrobia ulvae*. The same section asks them to consider the pressures on estuaries, generated by the conflicting needs for industrial expansion and conservation.

Planning and carrying out investigations

Worksheet **B**17B tests hypotheses concerning the effects of acid rain on soil samples.

Problem solving

In Worksheet **B**17A, pupils are set the problem of building a methane (biogas) generator.

Question 14 in section **B**17.4 asks pupils to decide what factors are important when considering the introducton of a biological control system into a natural community.

Timing

5 periods.

Suggested routes

The principal aim of this chapter is to illustrate the complexity of natural ecosystems, by showing what happens when their balance is disturbed by the actions of humans. The text provides a variety of examples to illustrate this idea. Teachers should select only those that they feel can be easily covered by their classes in the time available. Figure **B**22 shows two possible routes.

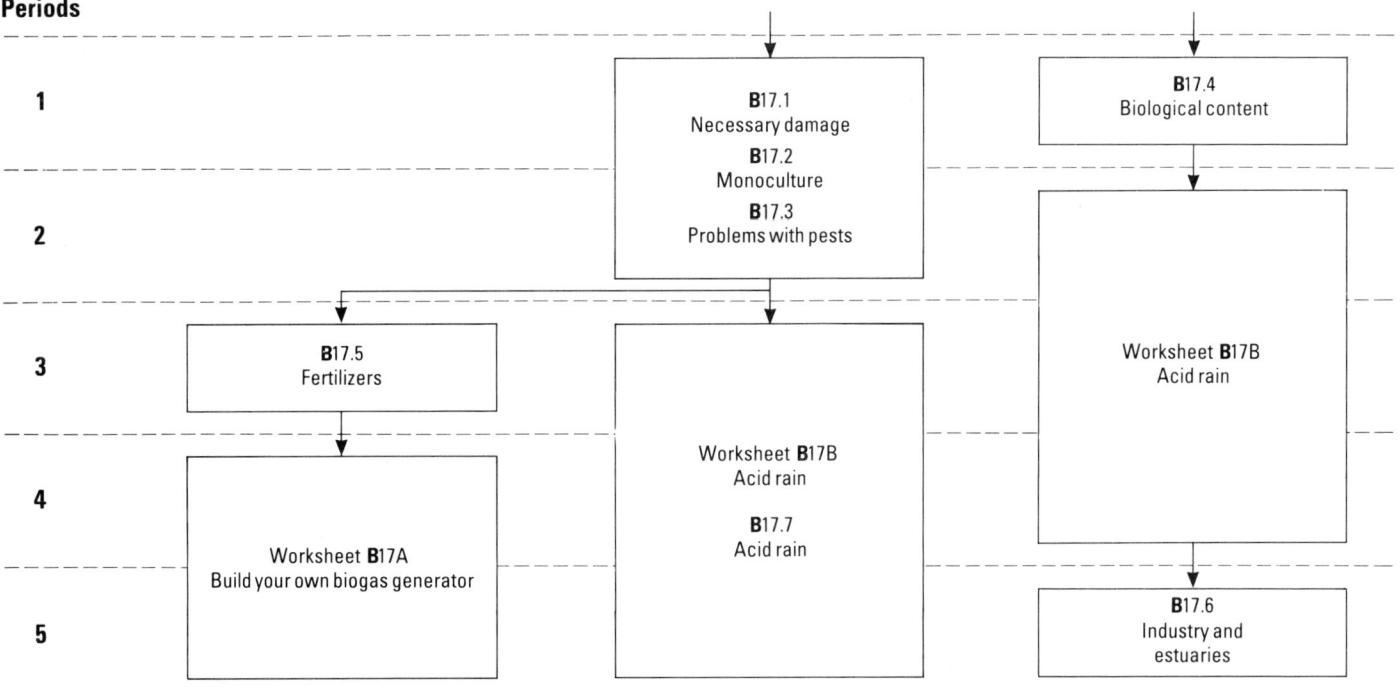

Figure **B**22

Opportunities for co-ordination

The importance of chemical pesticides in modern agriculture and their impact on the environment may be co-ordinated with work in Chapter **C16** "Fertilizers". The effects of waste from quarrying and industry can be linked with Chapter **C6** "Glass and ceramics". Chapter **C4** "Chemicals and rocks" is especially relevant to the work on acid rain in this chapter.

Notes and answers

B17.1   Necessary damage?

The chapter begins by pointing out that it is impossible for people to exist **without** changing the environment. "Damage" is often simply a question of scale, and while undesirable effects can be minimized, it may be impossible to eliminate them entirely. The chapter addresses the problems of environmental despoliation, including both large-scale problems and more localized problems, of which pupils may well have firsthand experience. The material included is not prescriptive – there are other large-scale problems which are not included. Alternatively, teachers may prefer to use examples of local damage. There is an opportunity here for pupils to investigate such problems using other published material. For example, several marine oil pollution incidents have now been documented, various initiatives concerning acid rain are under way and the Chernobyl nuclear disaster is well documented.

B17.2   Monoculture

Monoculture involves growing plants which are identical in as many respects as possible. Invariably they have similar flowering or ripening times and final heights. This makes cultivating and harvesting the crop easier, since it allows machines to be used more effectively.

B17.3   Problems with pests

The increased use of monoculture means that the problem of pests is more acute. Various ways of dealing with this problem are evaluated critically in this section. The use of pesticides places severe natural selection pressures on the insect population. It is not surprising, therefore, that insect populations become resistant to the pesticides. This example of natural selection can be mentioned when evolution is considered, in Chapter **B23**.

Answer to selected question

5 To encourage survival of natural wildlife that would not be able to flourish in the artificial environment of a monoculture field.

B17.4   Biological control

Biological control is an interesting attempt to reduce the incidence of pests without using chemicals. The danger of this method is that it is easy to underestimate the complexity of the interactions within a community; there may be serious and unforeseen consequences. A general discussion may develop from question 14.

B17.5   Fertilizers

The use of fertilizers has become an essential part of modern farming practice. The consequences of surplus fertilizer for streams and ponds are considered in this section, which provides another example of the complex interactions that occur when additional factors are introduced into an ecosystem. The technique of using compost and waste materials for generating methane is now exploited in some developing countries. (Worksheet **B**17A gives some guidance for pupils to try to develop some "alternative technology" for themselves.)

The clearing of forests for agriculture is a practice that always occurs when a country is developing. The global consequences of these activities are only now being considered seriously.

B17.6   Industry and estuaries

The pressure for industry to exploit estuarine sites, with their good communications, ample water supplies and low population densities, is balanced here against the need to preserve these habitats. The tension between these two competing needs is all too real and the issues are fought out in many public enquiries. The aim of this section is to help pupils to appreciate both sides of the situation. It could provide an opportunity for a class debate or a role-playing exercise.

B17.7   Acid rain

Acid rain is, and probably will remain, a major source of pollution, destroying plants and disfiguring buildings. Worksheet **B**17B guides pupils on how to test a number of hypotheses concerning acid rain.

Practical work

Worksheet B17A   Build your own biogas generator

REQUIREMENTS

Each group of pupils will need:
Apparatus selected by the pupils after consultation with the teacher

Access to:
Water bath at 30 °C
Sample of compost or manure
Water
Petroleum jelly

This is an interesting exercise that could stimulate pupils into considering the technological aspects of a topic that is becoming increasingly important. Methane gas produced in this way is being used commercially in some places to heat kilns and other industrial furnaces. In rural India, generated methane is being used to provide a source of heat, a practice that is beginning to overcome the problem of the lack of wood for heating.

Classes undertaking this exercise must be given ample time to design and discuss their pieces of apparatus before they give their apparatus lists to the technicians. Wherever possible, pupils should be encouraged to bring suitable containers from home.

Figure **B**23 overleaf shows a possible design for a biogas generator.

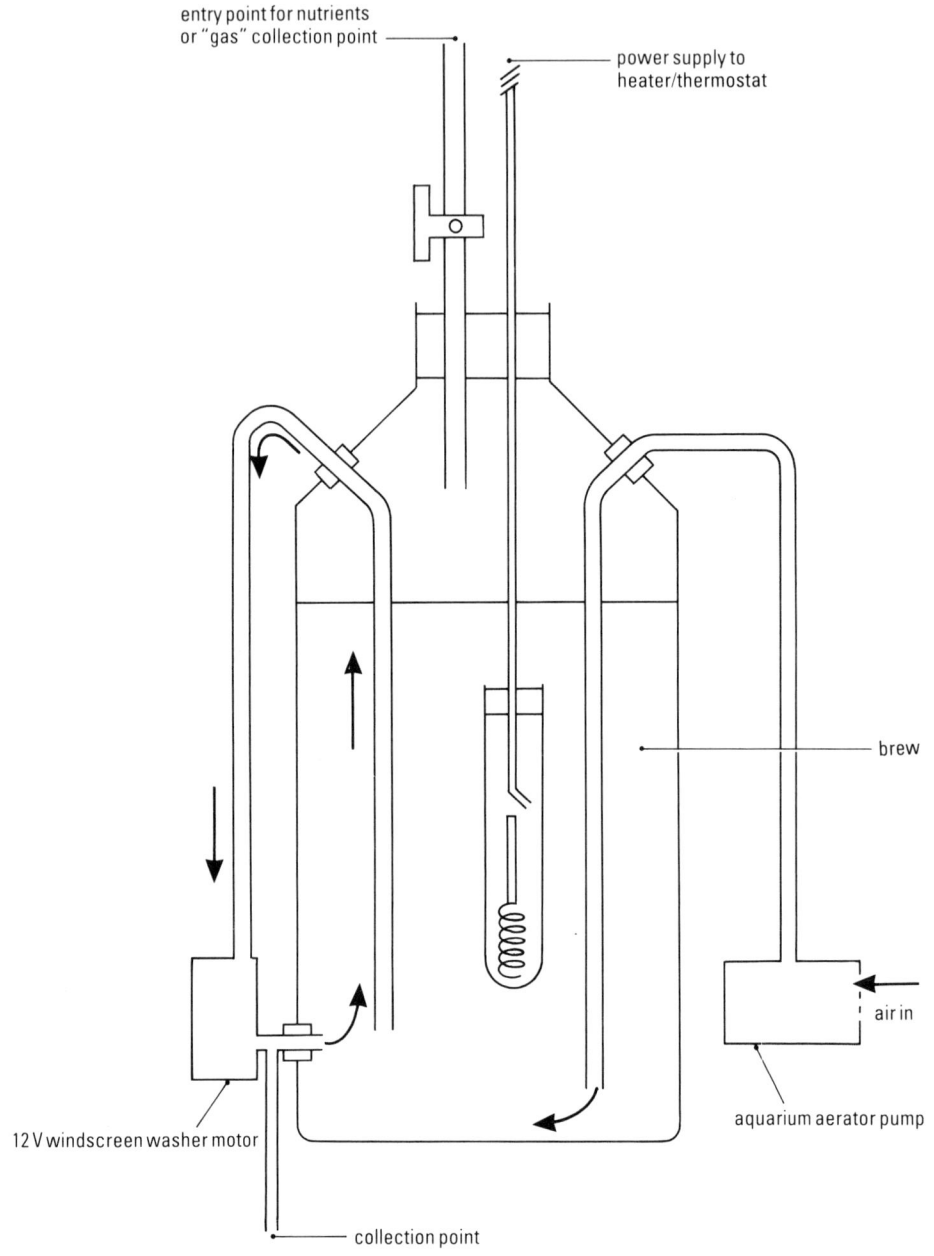

Figure **B**23

Worksheet B17B   Acid rain

Part 1

REQUIREMENTS

Each group of pupils will need:
Gammarids, 10
Pond weeds
Pond water which has been adjusted to pH 4, pH 5 and pH 6

Beakers, 3
Jar, large, or small tank
Marker pen
pH paper
Stones, several, small
Stopwatch

Part 2

REQUIREMENTS

Each group of pupils will need:
Soil samples (*e.g.* acidic, basic, neutral)

Container in which to collect water dripping through soil
Marker pen
Measuring cylinder, 250 cm³
Retort stand and clamp
Universal Indicator paper
Yogurt pots with holes in the bottom

Access to:
Ash from burnt wood
Distilled water acidified to different pH values
Rainwater

Notes:
The acidified water should be made up in advance. All pond water should be equally aerated before the first part of the practical begins.

The second part of the practical allows pupils to develop and test their own hypotheses about the effects of acid rain on soil. Different samples of soil can be made by adding peat, humus, lime or clay to a standard soil.

Further information

SATIS unit 301 "Air pollution – where does it come from?" includes a consideration of acid rain. Patterns of land usage, including monoculture, are covered in unit 409 "Dam problems". Units 210 "The pesticide problem" and 402 "DDT and malaria" consider pesticides, while the importance of artificial fertilizers is discussed in unit 505 "Making fertilizers".

Chapter B18   To destroy or to conserve?

Purposes

Knowledge and understanding

At the end of this chapter all pupils should:

1 recognize that the extinction of a species will have an effect on the remaining species in a community

2 know that conservation of habitats requires active management, and understand how one habitat is conserved.

In addition, those pupils aiming for higher grades should:

3 appreciate that some habitats should not be allowed to develop climax vegetation, if this will destroy rare species.

Processes and problem solving

Observation
Pupils may observe the different species in a locality, as part of Worksheet B18A.

Interpretation and application
In section **B**18.2, the conservation of Epping forest is considered.

Pupils should interpret the effects of the extinction of an organism on the remaining organisms in the community, using sections **B**18.1 and **B**18.2.

Planning and carrying out investigations
Worksheet **B**18A allows pupils to suggest ways in which an area could be conserved.

Problem solving
Question 13 in section **B**18.3 is a role-playing exercise which will help pupils to understand the problems faced by developing countries in exploiting their resources.

Timing   5 periods.

Suggested routes   Figure **B**24 shows two possible routes through this chapter; the righthand route is more investigative, including the only worksheet for this chapter, while the lefthand route gives a more theoretical approach.

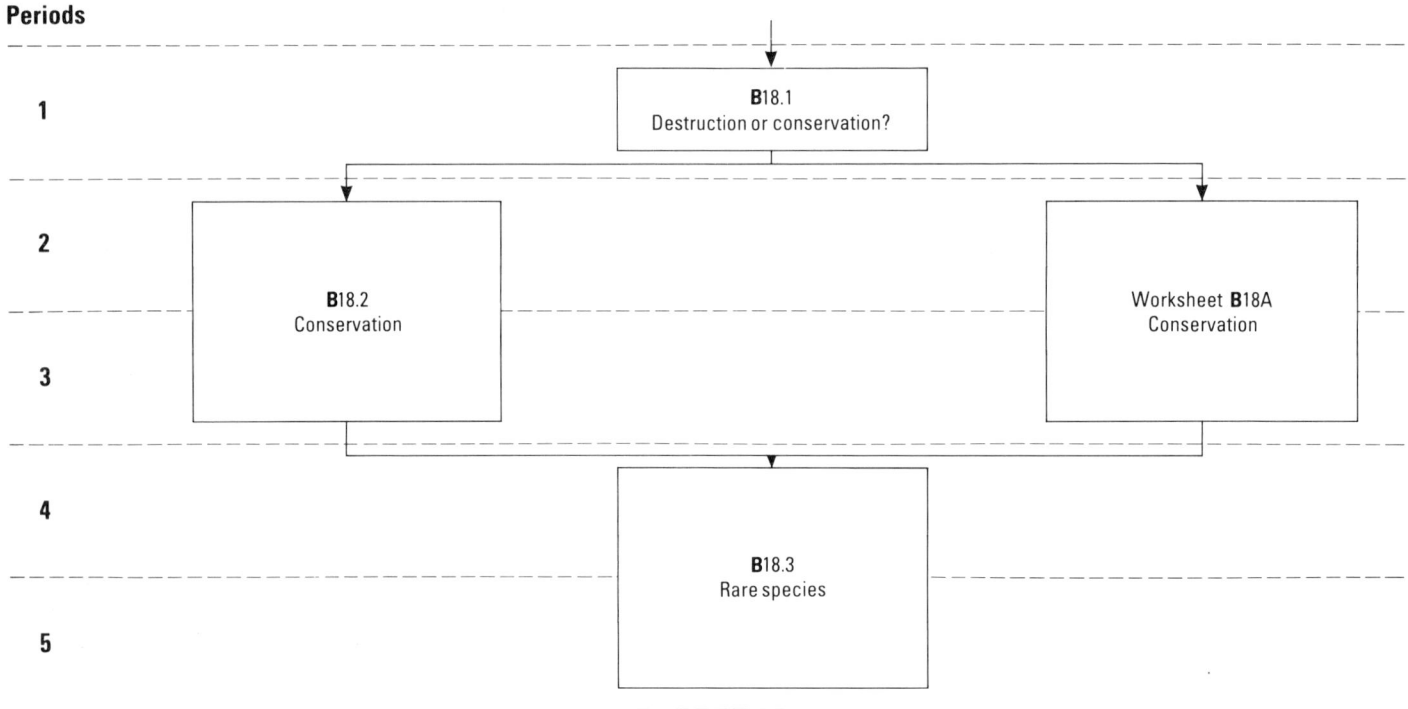

Figure **B**24

Opportunities for co-ordination   Chapter **C**4 "Chemicals and rocks", which deals with certain aspects of mining and quarrying, may provide useful background material for this chapter.

Notes and answers

B18.1   Destruction or conservation?

This section describes a variety of ways in which humans have altered the environment. Pupils should be encouraged to predict the longterm effects of these changes on the composition of the habitat.

Answer to selected question

3 Amenities (car parks, lavatories, etc.) need to be built. Erosion of soil can occur through trampling, wild plants may be picked and shy animals may be disturbed.

B18.2   Conservation

This section develops the case study of Epping forest as an example of successful conservation. It could be related to similar examples in your area. The principal aim of this section is to show that conservation involves active management of the area. Worksheet **B18A** could be used to replace some or all of the material.

B18.3   Rare species

Pupils are often interested in rare species, and television has brought an awareness of the problems into our homes. It is easy to become angry about the destruction of habitats in developing countries without realizing the pressures that are on the leaders of those countries. Question 13 allows pupils to think about the wider implications of such development, and could be used as a basis for a debate between the "developers" and the "conservators".

Practical work

Worksheet B18A   Conservation

REQUIREMENTS

Access to:
Compass
Identification keys
Large-scale Ordnance Survey map of the area
Measuring tape

The amount of time that is devoted to this exercise depends upon the inclination of the pupils or the teacher. A small group of committed pupils could successfully devote all five lessons to this exercise and produce some worthwhile results at the end. For others, two lessons might be sufficient. It is important that the area under consideration is not too large. Assistance should be provided whenever appropriate.

Within a working group, pupils should be given various responsibilities and be encouraged to report back to the rest of the group. This could form the basis for an assessment of a number of skills.

Supplementary material

A number of overseas aid agencies have simulation games which are helpful in understanding the delicately balanced economies of many villages in developing countries; such games have great educational value. They can be bought from the Oxfam Education Department, 274 Banbury Road, Oxford OX2 7DZ, or from TEAR, 100 Church Road, Teddington, Middlesex TW11 8QE.

Topic B4

The continuity of life

Chapter B19   Living things multiply

Knowledge and understanding

At the end of this chapter all pupils should:

1 know that asexual reproduction produces offspring that are identical to the parent

2 realize that sexual reproduction involves the fusion of a mobile male gamete (for instance, a sperm) with a stationary female gamete (for instance, an egg)

3 recognize the reproductive parts of a flower

4 understand the differences, in flowering plants, between pollination and fertilization and the differences between self-pollination and cross-pollination

5 understand what happens when a sperm fertilizes an egg.

In addition, those pupils aiming for higher grades should:

6 realize the importance of the differences between internal and external fertilization in animals

7 understand the significance of courtship

8 understand why oestrus is important in the reproduction of many mammals.

Processes and problem solving

Graphical and symbolic representation
In Worksheet **B**19D, pupils are asked to plot a scattergraph of data comparing the gestation periods of some members of the cat family.

Using apparatus and measuring instruments
Worksheet **B**19C provides an opportunity to use an eyepiece graticule when observing pollen grains growing.

Observation
Section **B**19.4 asks pupils to decide from photographs whether certain flowers are wind- or insect-pollinated and Worksheet **B**19A helps them to investigate further the similarities and differences between the two kinds of flowers. Section **B**19.4 also asks them to observe photographs of mating animals and decide which forms of behaviour result in internal fertilization.

Pupils may observe the growth of pollen, using Worksheet **B**19C.

Interpretation and application

In section **B**19.2 pupils are asked to decide from the evidence of photographs whether certain organisms reproduce asexually, sexually or by both methods. Section **B**19.3 asks them to explain the advantages of sexual and asexual methods of reproduction in plant breeding. In section **B**19.4 they may evaluate the significance of internal fertilization for land vertebrates.

Worksheet **B**19B asks pupils to interpret the significance of the daily pollen count.

Timing   6 periods.

Suggested routes   Figure **B**25 suggests one pathway through the materials in this chapter. It has been chosen so as to give emphasis to the practicals involving the reproduction of flowering plants. The work need not be so weighted, of course, and some teachers might prefer to stress animal reproduction, provided that items 3 and 4 of the list under "Knowledge and understanding" are covered adequately. However, human reproduction should not be considered here, as it is dealt with in the next chapter.

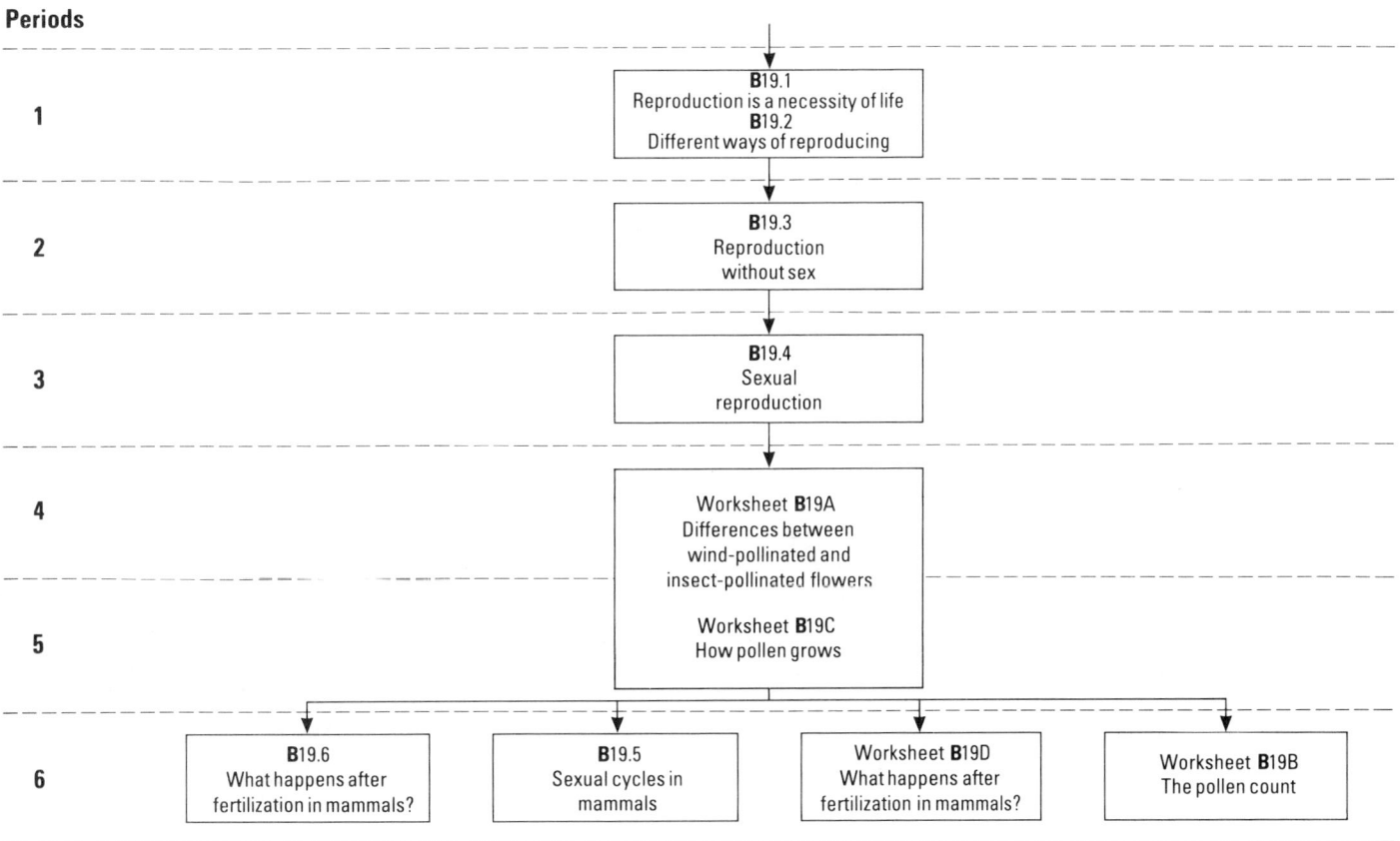

Figure **B**25

Notes and answers

B19.1   Reproduction is a necessity of life

This section introduces the idea that reproduction is a feature of all living organisms. It is a prelude to the next section.

B19.2   Different ways of reproducing

This important section presents a number of major ideas, in particular, the difference between sexual and asexual reproduction. The terms "female gametes" and "male gametes" are introduced.

Answer to selected question

1 The mature sycamore reproduces sexually. Yeast reproduces sexually and asexually. In figure 19.3 in the pupils' book *Saxifraga* has reproduced asexually, although it can reproduce sexually using flowers. *Hydra* can also reproduce sexually and asexually. Swans reproduce sexually, as do all birds and mammals.

B19.3   Reproduction without sex

This section deals with asexual reproduction, briefly in the case of animals, and at greater length in that of plants.

Answers to selected questions

2 Apples are produced by grafting stems on to superior root stocks. Budding is often used for roses.

3 Asexual reproduction enables a plant to produce a large number of (genetically) identical "offspring". This can result in the rapid colonization of an area in which the plant is established. Sexual reproduction results in (genetically) dissimilar offspring and serves to increase the ability of the plant to colonize areas with different or unstable environments.

B19.4   Sexual reproduction

This section begins by considering fertilization in flowering plants, both by self- and cross-pollination. Pupils may investigate the differences between wind- and insect-pollinated flowers, using Worksheet **B**19A, and how a pollen tube grows, using Worksheet **B**19C. The study of the pollen count in Worksheet **B**19B can also be done at this stage.

The section then studies sexual reproduction in animals (apart from human reproduction, which is dealt with in the next chapter). Pupils consider internal and external reproduction and what happens when an egg is fertilized.

Answers to selected questions

4 The wind-pollinated flowers are **a** (rye grass), **c** (nettle), **d** (hazel) and **f** (silver birch); the insect-pollinated flowers are **b** (apple) and **e** (crocus).

9 Not all of the eggs are fertilized, although the eggs release chemicals which attract sperms. Furthermore, the number of sea urchins that survive long enough to reproduce is limited by the resources of the environment.

15 Both reptiles and birds lay eggs with hard shells, so fertilization must occur before these are laid.

B19.5   Sexual cycles in mammals

The menstrual cycle is covered in the next chapter, but this short section prefaces it by considering the breeding season in a variety of mammals. The term "oestrus" is introduced.

Answer to selected question

17 This is less wasteful of sperm; females have enough time to wean the young born from a previous mating, before the next reproductive cycle begins.

B19.6   What happens as a result of fertilization?

The pattern of development of the human embryo is covered in detail in the chapters that follow. This short section introduces the idea that other animals may have different patterns of development. Worksheet **B**19D compares the lengths of the gestation periods of several mammals.

Practical work

Worksheet B19A   Differences between wind-pollinated and insect-pollinated flowers

REQUIREMENTS

Each group of pupils will need:
Specimens of insect- and wind-pollinated flowers such as those shown in figure 19.8 in the pupils' book, as available

The procedure is detailed on the worksheet.

Worksheet B19B   The pollen count

Information to be studied is given in the worksheet.

Worksheet B19C   How pollen grows

Part 1

REQUIREMENTS

Each group of pupils will need:
Drawing paper
Hand lens
Microscope slide
Microscope
Pencils

Access to:
Specimens of insect- and wind-pollinated flowers
or
Garden, school grounds or pot plants for collection of specimens

The procedure is detailed on the worksheet.

Part 2

REQUIREMENTS

Each group of pupils will need:
Flowers of busy lizzie or other insect-pollinated plants
Flowers of wind-pollinated plants

Culture solution, 2 cm^3 (15 % sucrose solution, 0.01 g boric acid, 0.01 g yeast)

Absorbent paper
Clock
Eyepiece graticule
Petri dish and lid

Worksheet B19D   What happens after fertilization in mammals?

REQUIREMENTS

Each group of pupils will need:
Graph paper
Pencils
Photographs in figure 19.24 of the pupils' book

Instructions will be found on the worksheet.

Further information

Hunt, P. Francis *Discovering botany* Longman, 1979.

Chapter B20   People are different

Purposes

Knowledge and understanding

At the end of this chapter all pupils should:

1 realize that the timing of puberty varies from person to person

2 know that adolescence is controlled by hormones produced by the testes or the ovaries; that the male sex hormone is testosterone, while the female sex hormones are oestrogen and progesterone

3 know what the main reproductive organs of men and women are and how they are arranged

4 understand the changes in the human ovary and uterus throughout the menstrual cycle and the significance of menstruation at the end of the cycle

5 know the origin of identical and non-identical twins

6 understand the biological aspects of human sexual intercourse, ejaculation, fertilization and implantation

7 be aware of the protection given to the embryo by the amniotic sac

8 understand the role of the placenta in transporting materials to and from the foetus

9 understand the process of human birth.

In addition, those pupils aiming for higher grades should:

10 realize the role of the hypothalamus and pituitary gland in humans in co-ordinating the activities of the endocrine glands to produce the sex hormones.

Processes and problem solving

Graphical and symbolic representation
Worksheet **B20A** will enable pupils to plot graphs of the variation, in certain characteristics, between members of the class. In Worksheet **B20B**, pupils may plot line graphs of the growth of a human embryo. Worksheet **B20C** analyses the growth of the human population in various parts of the world and asks pupils to interpret and predict from the figures.

Using apparatus and measuring instruments
Worksheet **B20A** invites pupils to measure variation in certain characteristics of size and mass.

Observation
In section **B20.2**, pupils observe the appearance of an "average" boy or girl of their own age. Section **B20.4** asks them to observe the sex ratio in families.

Interpretation and application
In section **B20.1**, pupils may interpret the growth curves of adolescent boys and girls. In this section, they are also asked to interpret the changes that occur during menstruation. Section **B20.2** asks them to explain some of the differences between the male and female reproductive systems. In section **B20.3** they may assess some of the health risks during pregnancy.

Timing
5 periods.

Suggested routes
This chapter places the facts of human reproduction in a context that is relevant to adolescent boys and girls. Opportunity is given for the social and emotional consequences of human sexuality to be discussed sensitively. For example, advice on hygiene during menstruation, on hetero- and homosexual feelings or on the dangers of engaging in sexual intercourse at an early age can be given in ways appropriate to the pupils concerned. The teacher may also stress the dangers of smoking, drinking and taking drugs in pregnancy. Among the other aims of the work the teacher may wish to help pupils to understand the effectiveness of contraceptives and to be aware of the major sexually transmitted diseases (including AIDS).

It is clear, however, that schools will have different opinions on how much of this material they should include in the pupils' science lessons. Indeed, schools with well developed Personal and Social Education programmes may prefer to omit much of the information in this chapter.

The requirements for this part of the course listed under "Knowledge and understanding" stress the biological aspects of human reproduction. These should be taught to all, irrespective of where the pupils learn about the social and emotional aspects of sexuality.

Figure **B26** overleaf presents a flow diagram of three possible routes through the material. The righthand route is one where all of the health aspects are taught, in addition to the biological principles outlined under "Knowledge and understanding". The middle and lefthand schemes place less emphasis on the emotional and social aspects of the topic, and draw on worksheets to amplify certain aspects.

Opportunities for co-ordination
Section **B20.3** discusses the need for a pregnant woman not to drink alcohol or to take any but essential drugs or medicines. This work may be co-ordinated with Chapter **C12** "Chemicals in the medicine cupboard".

Notes and answers

B20.1   What is it that makes sex different for us?

This section introduces a central idea of this chapter, that human sexuality has functions in our society other than the purely biological aim of reproduction.

B20.2   Sexual development

Since adolescents are often uncomfortably aware of the physical changes that are happening to them, this section begins by showing that there is great variation in the rate at which boys and girls mature. There is also great variation in the appearance of people's bodies. This theme is developed further in Worksheet **B20A**.

Next, the hormonal changes that accompany adolescence are discussed and the menstrual cycle is then considered in more detail. It is shown to be a hormone-controlled sequence that prepares an egg for fertilization, and then prepares the uterus to receive it if it is fertilized. Pupils learn that if fertilization does not occur the cycle ends with the period of menstruation.

The reproductive systems of the male and female are considered next.

The section now turns to the problems of coming to terms with sexual feelings. This can be a difficult area, and teachers should use the material here sensitively.

An account of sexual intercourse is included in this section.

Periods

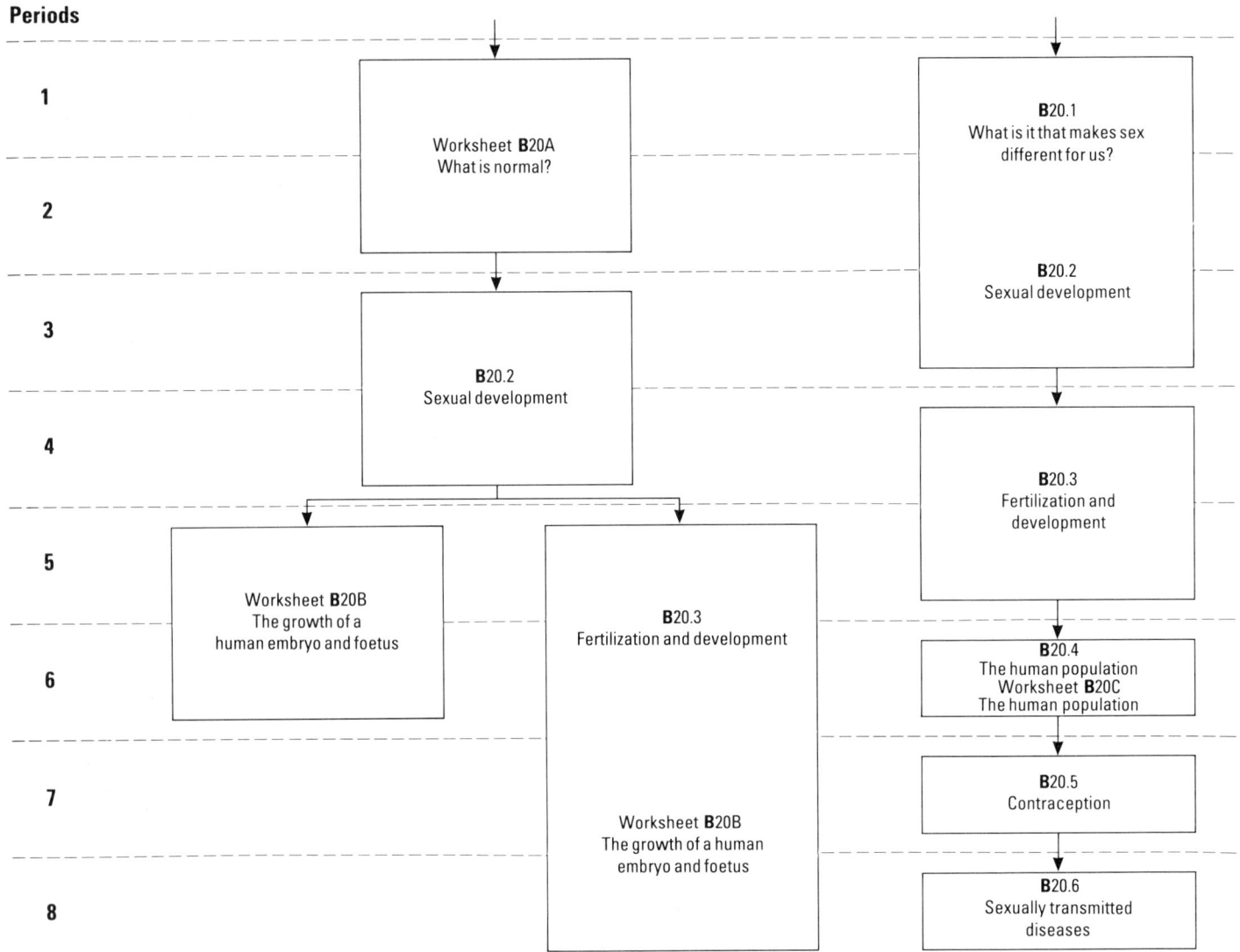

Figure **B**26

B20.3   Fertilization and development

The section begins with the moment of fertilization. It shows how this leads to the implantation of the fertilized egg in the uterus. It then considers the development of the embryo, the function of the placenta and the growth of the foetus. It closes with an account of the birth of a baby. Spontaneous abortion is also discussed.

Worksheet **B**20B asks pupils to interpret the growth pattern of the foetus.

Answer to selected question

19 From about day 9 to day 16 of her cycle. This assumes, of course, that the woman ovulates at the mid-point of her cycle. In many women, especially younger ones, this may not be the case, and the variation in the time of ovulation can be critical. Pupils need to understand that they run a risk of pregnancy whenever they have unprotected intercourse. Obviously, this risk is greater at some times than others.

B20.4   The human population

This section contains an exercise in sampling variation. Most of us know families which consist of several boys or several girls. When averages are taken over a whole neighbourhood, however, the ratio of sexes becomes more nearly equal.

Worksheet **B20C** is relevant. This allows pupils to analyse the growth of various human populations. It echoes the issues raised in Chapter **B**18, where the economic problems of developing nations were set in an ecological context.

B20.5   Contraception

This section describes the mechanics of a variety of contraceptive devices. No attempt is made to discuss the moral or ethical aspects of contraception, and teachers may wish to decide for themselves whether to do this.

B20.6   Sexually transmitted diseases

Sexually transmitted diseases, including AIDS, are treated briefly. Teachers may like to supplement the material with pamphlets which may be obtained from the Health Education Authority.

Answer to selected question

30 Promiscuous people or even those who have the occasional casual sexual encounter are at risk from these diseases. At the time of writing, the AIDS (HIV) virus is at low levels in the heterosexual population, although it is becoming increasingly prevalent in the homosexual community and among those who share hypodermic needles. This pattern could easily change as the AIDS virus becomes established in the heterosexual population. The contraceptive sheath offers some protection against all STDs, including AIDS, but it cannot confer absolute protection. In the light of these trends, it is becoming necessary to be much more thoughtful about our sexual behaviour.

Practical work

Worksheet B20A   What is normal?

REQUIREMENTS

Each group of pupils will need:
Graph paper
Pencils
Rulers

Access to:
0.9 % saline solution
Drinking cups
Scale for measuring height
Scales, bathroom, measuring in kg
Tape measure, in cm
Watch or clock

The procedure is detailed on the worksheet. It is important that pupils taste the salt solution from clean cups.

Worksheet B20B   The growth of a human embryo and foetus

REQUIREMENTS

Each group of pupils will need:
Graph paper
Pencils
Rulers

The procedure is detailed on the worksheet.

Worksheet B20C   The human population

REQUIREMENTS

Each group of pupils will need:
Graph paper
Pencils
Rulers

The procedure is detailed on the worksheet.

Further information

Health Education Authority *Pregnancy book* Health Education Authority,
78 New Oxford Street, London WC1A 1AH, 1984.

Supplementary material

The Health Education Authority's pamphlets on family planning and on sexually
related diseases.

Chapter B21   Growing up

Purposes

Knowledge and understanding

At the end of this chapter all pupils should:

1 understand that organisms develop

2 recognize the methods used to measure the growth of organisms

3 know that growth means an increase in living material

4 know some of the ways of telling the age of an organism

5 know that tumours are caused by uncontrolled cell divisions; some are benign,
others are malignant

6 recognize the principal stages in the development of a human from childhood,
to maturity, to old age

7 understand what is entailed in parental care in human families

8 know something about changes in life expectancy.

In addition, those pupils aiming for higher grades should:

9 appreciate the role of auxins in the growth of plants

10 understand the role of thyroid hormone in controlling metamorphosis.

Processes and problem solving

Graphical and symbolic representation
In section **B**21.2, pupils are asked to plot a graph of the relative length of the
human head and that of the rest of the body, at different ages.
   Section **B**21.4 asks them to plot graphs of the growth of a normal child and
that of a child with growth hormone deficiency.

Using apparatus and measuring instruments
As part of the work of section **B**21.2, pupils may measure the growth of humans.

Interpretation and application
In section **B**21.1, pupils may interpret growth patterns in barley seedlings. In

B21.6, they are asked to interpret data to determine the ages at which children acquire different skills. **B21.7** asks them to think what parental care means and to understand its social and biological value. This section also asks pupils to consider some data about life expectancy.

Worksheet **B21A** asks pupils to interpret data on the registrations of incidence of cancer in England and Wales in 1982

Planning and carrying out investigations
In section **B21.1**, pupils are asked to plan methods of measuring the growth of organisms.

Timing   5 periods.

Suggested routes   Figure **B27** presents a flow diagram for the materials in this chapter.

Periods

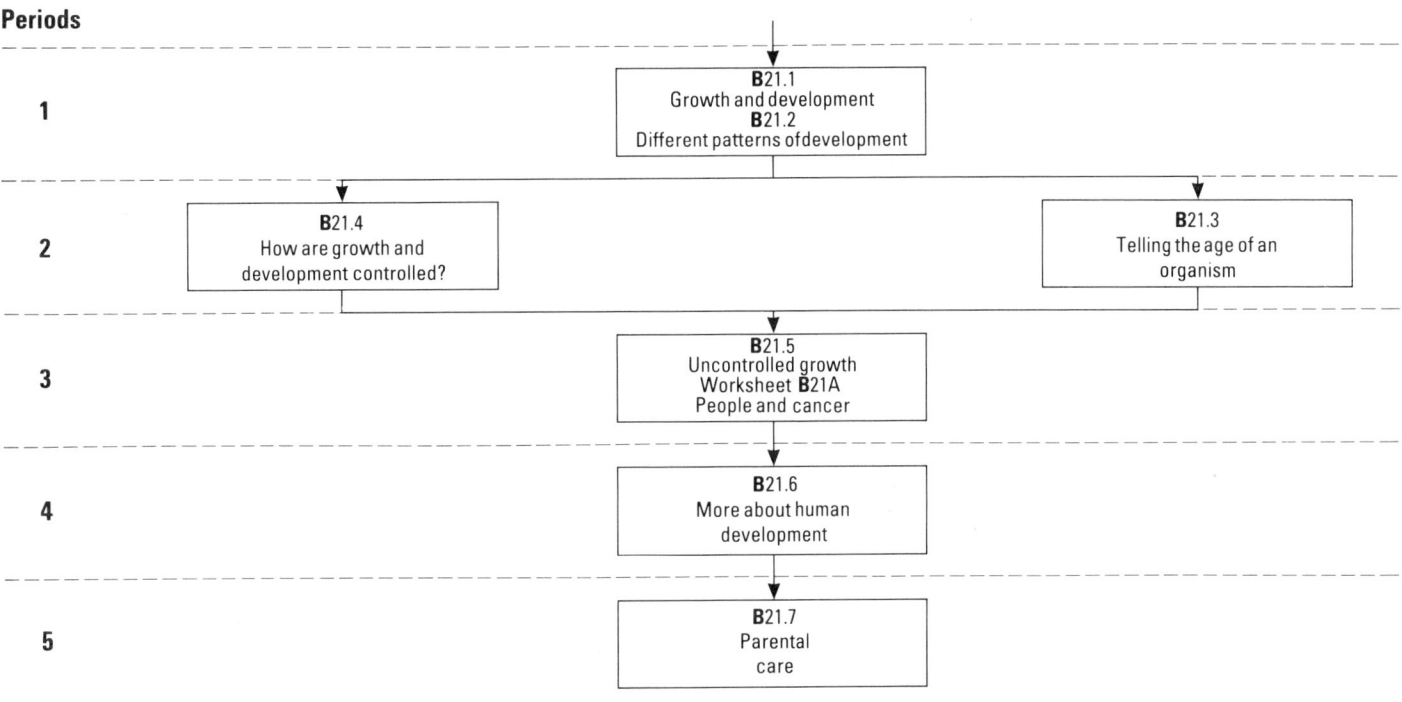

Figure **B27**

Opportunities for co-ordination   Section **B21.5** and Worksheet **B21A** consider cancer and its treatment and the work may be co-ordinated with the study of chemotherapy in Chapter **C12** in the Chemistry book "Chemicals in the medicine cupboard".

Notes and answers   ## B21.1   Growth and development

Growth is defined as a series of changes that can be observed and measured. Pupils are given the opportunity to try find ways of measuring the growth of different organisms.

Answer to selected question

2 Length and mass for the animals; height and girth of stem for the sycamore tree and seedling.

B21.2 Different patterns of development

This section studies the growth of the human body from birth to adulthood and provides a good opportunity for the assessment of measuring and interpreting skills.

B21.3 Telling the age of an organism

This section concentrates on ways of telling the ages of fishes, and can be linked with the exercise on the ages of organisms in Chapter **B2**.

Answer to selected question

9 The herring was eight years old.

B21.4 How are growth and development controlled?

This section contains some important, if rather complex, ideas that may be more suited to those aiming for higher grades. Questions 10, 11 and 12 could make homework exercises.

B21.5 Uncontrolled growth

This section aims at considering the biological aspects of cancer in a helpful way and so, for example, to help pupils to understand the important difference between benign and malignant tumours. Worksheet **B21A** provides additional information that may be of value.

B21.6 More about human development

Pupils are shown that the development of babies into children, and children into adults, involves acquiring a large number of skills; parents can help their children to gain these.

B21.7 Parental care

This section develops the idea of parental care raised in the previous one, by considering the roles of mother and father. It stresses that a child needs love as well as protection and suggests that men can "mother" children as well as women. The material ought to stimulate lively debate, since everyone has an opinion about parents! The section ends by considering maturity and old age.

Practical work

Worksheet B21A People and cancer

REQUIREMENTS

Each group of pupils will need:
Pencils
Rulers
Graph paper

The procedure is detailed on the worksheet.

Further information

Health Education Authority *Pregnancy book* Health Education Authority, 78 New Oxford Street, London WC1A 1AH, 1984.

Chapter B22   Handing on to the next generation

Purposes

Knowledge and understanding

At the end of this chapter all pupils should:

1 appreciate that the variation shown by organisms is partly inherited and partly results from environmental influences

2 know that chromosomes are found in the nucleus, that genes are carried on chromosomes and that genes are "instructions" for inherited characteristics

3 appreciate that gametes contain half as many chromosomes as the other cells of the body contain

4 know that cloning produces offspring identical to the parent

5 know that the "sex chromosomes" are "XX" in a female, "XY" in a male, and that an "X" or a "Y" chromosome is carried in the sperm nucleus

6 understand that alleles are different forms of the same gene

7 understand that cells do not develop normally if they contain abnormal numbers of chromosomes or if the chromosomes are damaged

8 understand how the offspring of a cross can be predicted from a knowledge of the genes of the parents

9 realize that such predictions are used in genetic counselling.

In addition, those pupils aiming for higher grades should:

10 understand the terms dominant, recessive, homozygote, heterozygote, F1 and F2 generations, mutation.

Processes and problem solving

Graphical and symbolic representation
Worksheet **B22B** involves plotting histograms and bar graphs of the variation in characteristics shown by organisms. Worksheet **B22C** is a genetical simulation exercise, using plastic beads to represent gametes, alleles and genotypes.

Using apparatus and measuring instruments
Pupils may measure variation in physical characteristics, using Worksheet **B22B**, and in the growth of seeds that have been exposed to different amounts of radiation, using Worksheet **B22E**.

Observation
Pupils are asked to observe the variation in plants in Worksheet **B22A**, in humans, insects and a number of plants in Worksheet **B22B** and in irradiated seeds in Worksheet **B22E**.

Interpretation and application
Section **B22.1** asks pupils to interpret data about characteristics of separated identical twins. Section **B22.2** asks them to distinguish between the effects of environment and heredity in data about plants and about people. Section **B22.4** discusses the application of cloning in plant cultivation, especially that of oil palms. In sections **B22.6** and **B22.7**, pupils use genetical analysis to predict the outcome of crosses between organisms and interpret various family trees. Section **B22.7** also asks them to interpret the significance of mutations and in section

B22.8 they are helped to recognize the needs of parents for counselling if they are likely to produce children suffering from inherited diseases.

Worksheet **B**22A helps pupils to interpret variation in certain plants.

Planning and carrying out investigations

Pupils are asked to plan the layout and measurements in the investigation in Worksheet **B**22E and to suggest how to improve its design.

Timing

8 periods.

Suggested routes

Figure **B**28 presents flow diagrams for the materials in this chapter. The righthand and middle pathways are alternative routes emphasizing practical work, while the lefthand route is more theoretical. The schemes differ in the amount of time allocated to section **B**22.6, which contains ideas that pupils may find difficult. Pupils should not begin this section until they understand sections **B**22.3 and **B**22.5. It is possible to allocate more time to **B**22.6 (as the righthand route and one alternative path through the lefthand route illustrate) but this will, of course, be at the expense of other material.

The lefthand route is probably more suited to fast-working groups.

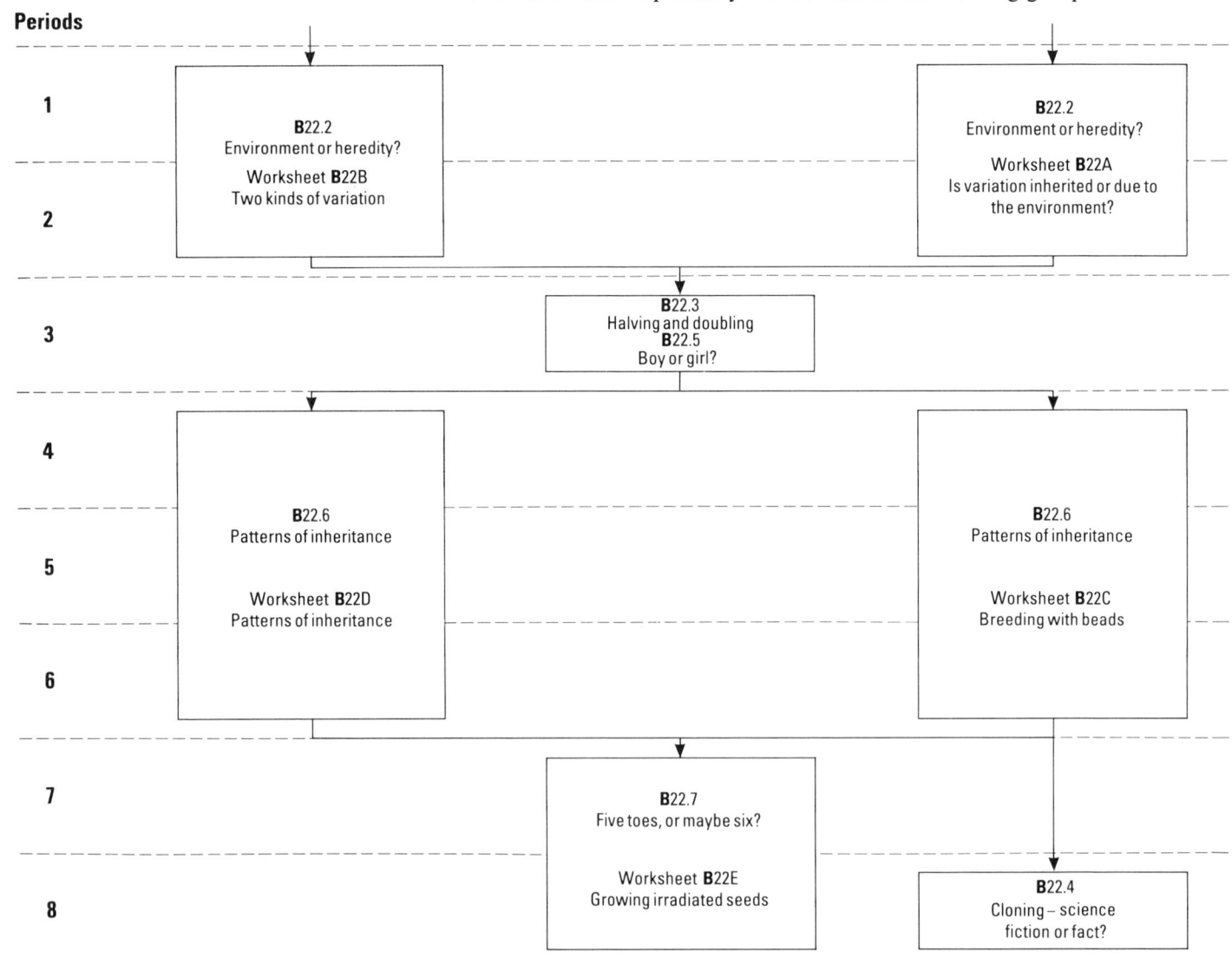

Figure **B**28

Opportunities for co-ordination

Section **B22.7** and Worksheet **B22E** discuss mutations and mutagenic agents. The topic might be co-ordinated with the work on radioactivity in Chapters **C18** "Atoms and bonding" and **P3** "Radioactivity" and with the work on X-rays in Chapter **C5** "Materials and structures".

Notes and answers

The main object is to introduce the principles of genetics. Wherever possible, examples from human genetics are used as these usually seem most relevant. However, it is important to stress that patterns of inheritance are similar in all organisms. Otherwise, little could be learned from human genetics alone.

B22.1   Alike or not alike?

The chapter opens by picking up a theme that appeared in Chapter **B20**, that of the natural variation in characteristics found in organisms. This should encourage discussion about the causes of variation, so that from the beginning pupils realize the importance of interaction between heredity and environment.

Answers to selected questions

4 Height remains the same; differences in head length are slightly greater in twins brought up together but are probably not significant.

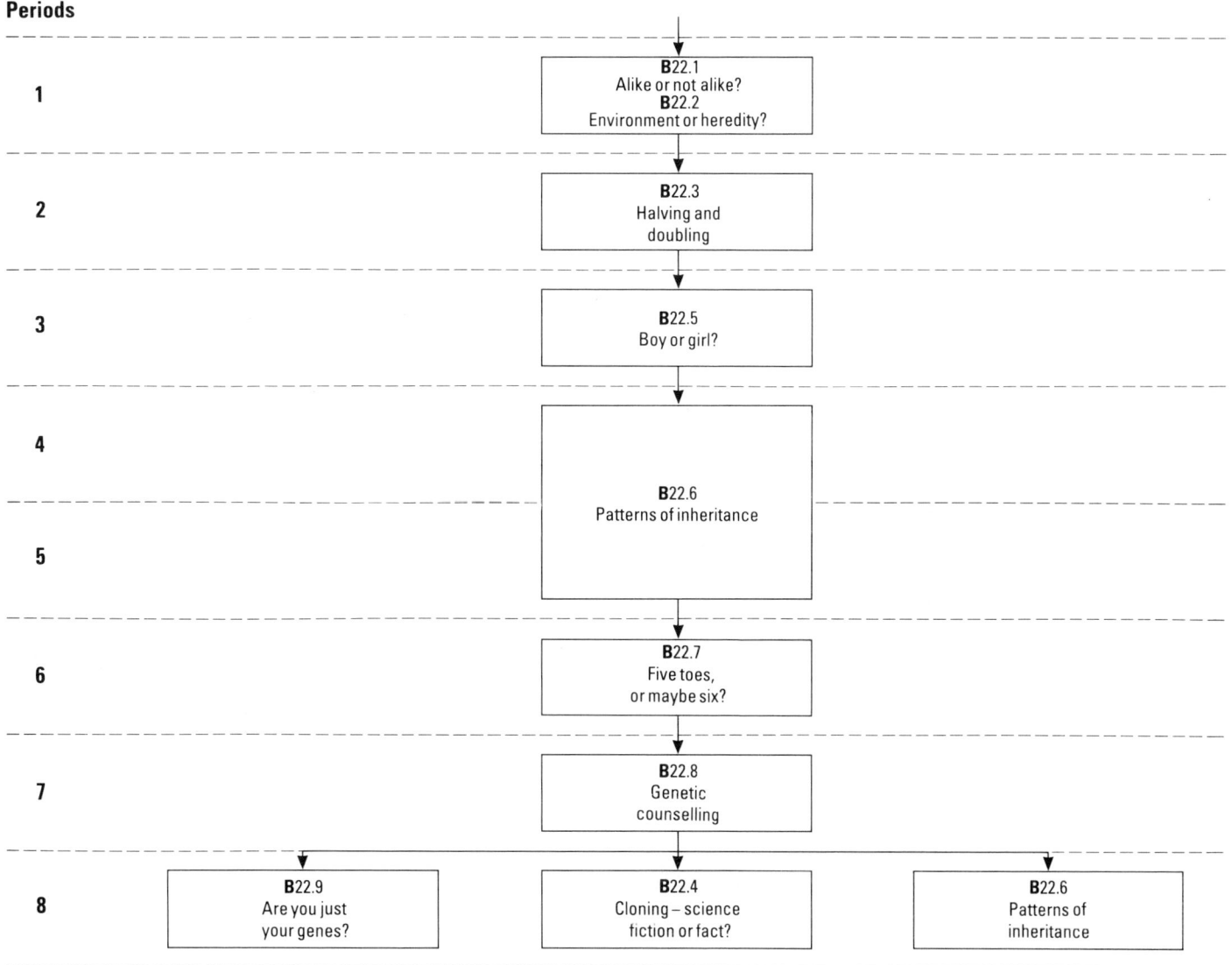

Figure **B**28 continued

5 Average differences in mass are greater and appear to be influenced by the environment. (However, some recent work suggests that mass, too, may be genetically determined to a greater extent than is generally accepted.)

B22.2 Environment or heredity?

This section introduces the idea of "nature and nurture", and can be completed alongside Worksheets **B22A** and **B22B**, in which pupils investigate variation in seeds and discontinuous and continuous variation.

The biology of the passage entitled "Why do people look like their parents?" is straightforward but it is a sensible precaution to find out in advance if there are any adopted children in the class. If so, it may be helpful to qualify the word "parent". For example, there are the "natural parents" who provide the sperm and the egg, and "real parents" who provide love, home and family; the two may not always be the same.

A thoughtful pupil might query why structures described as "long threads" actually appear in the photographs in the pupils' book as an "X" shape (the two chromatids and the centromere).

Teachers may think it appropriate to remind pupils of what they read about DNA in the Introduction to their Biology book (page 3).

Answer to selected question

7 A few of the characteristics listed are due only to heredity (*e.g.* blood groups), but most are strongly influenced by environment as well. There are links here with section **B22.9** "Are you just your genes?". Discussion might need careful handling if there is teenage antagonism towards parents, school and the local environment.

B22.3 Halving and doubling

This section introduces the idea that all human cells have the same number of chromosomes except for the gametes, which each have half of the total.

The stages of mitosis and meiosis are not dealt with in this course, though pupils should be aware of the importance of the nucleus to the functioning of the cell.

In this chapter, the importance of a constant number of chromosomes and accurately matching pairs is mentioned. The sterility of interspecific crosses (such as the mule) can be explained simply by saying that because the two sets of chromosomes do not match up properly, the single chromosomes cannot be shared out evenly to make eggs or sperms.

B22.4 Cloning – science fiction or fact?

Since cloning produces genetically identical offspring, this section will allow pupils to contrast it with the production of variable offspring provided by the sexual method. It will also introduce them to tissue culture, an application of the principles of cloning which is becoming more and more important commercially.

It may be appropriate at this point to teach the pupils to distinguish between the terms "gene" and "allele". These terms are not defined until section **B22.6**, although the term allele is introduced here, in passing.

The difficulties of cloning animals are stressed.

Answers to selected questions

9 There are various examples: bulbs, corms, runners, layering, grafting, cuttings

(sugar cane) and stem tubers (potato) are some of them. To many pupils it may be necessary to explain that a "seed potato" is not a seed at all. This question should reinforce the work on asexual reproduction in Chapter B19.

11 Cloning is quicker than seed production.

B22.5   Boy or girl?

This section shows how the difference in the chromosomes of the "23rd pair" determines the sex of a human being. These are the sex chromosomes. The female has XX and the male XY.

B22.6   Patterns of inheritance

All alleles are genes, but not all genes are alleles, since alleles are alternative forms of a particular gene. At GCSE level, where only monohybrid crosses are involved, the term allele can be used without any real confusion, since we only ever refer to a single **gene**. The words homozygote and heterozygote are used in the pupils' book text, but not genome. Genotype (see also Worksheet **B22C**) and phenotype are defined. Genetics is notorious for needing, even at elementary level, a whole new vocabulary in order to express ideas easily. Too many new words are daunting, but once the "language" has been learned pupils often enjoy being able to sound knowledgeable.

It is not envisaged that all teachers will use all of the material in this section with all of their classes. Enough should be done to give the pupils an understanding of how the offspring of a cross can be predicted by knowing the alleles of the parents. It may be helpful to do Worksheets **B22C**, in which pupils use coloured beads as models in breeding investigations, and **B22D**, in which they examine the pattern of inheritance in seedlings.

Teachers will probably find that the material which is most readily understood is the family tree of hair colour (figure 22.15 in the pupils' book), which is deliberately simplified to consider only red and brown hair.

Most classes will contain at least one pupil with a family tree including red hair. If the pupil is willing, this may be used to illustrate patterns of inheritance more effectively than those in the text.

Any work on pupils' own family trees needs to be approached with caution and must always be a voluntary exercise. It is helpful to have a few family trees for the use of pupils who do not have one of their own. Pupils may not know very much about their own families, or may be unwilling to expose private family matters. Also, there may well be adoptions and illegitimacies unknown to the pupils themselves, which they might unwittingly make public. Any oddities which seem to point in this direction can usually be explained away by saying that inheritance patterns are really more complicated than those used in class. It is as well to be aware of possible pitfalls beforehand.

The sections on blood groups and red–green colour blindness are probably only appropriate for those who can grasp the patterns and probabilities fairly quickly. Some pupils could become confused between inheritance patterns and the antigen–antibody reactions in blood transfusions. Those who can cope will probably enjoy the challenge of working out possible combinations of the three alleles of the ABO blood groups. Alleles A and B show co-dominance, and O is recessive to both A and B.

Answers to selected questions

19 Two, one allele from each parent.

20 Each sister has one allele for brown hair, and may or may not carry a recessive allele for red hair.

21 The boy must have inherited the allele from his mother's mother (= maternal grandmother).

22 Each of the boy's parents carries a hidden recessive allele for red hair.

23 You might expect some of the father's relations to have red hair, since a number of them must carry the hidden recessive.

In this particular family, only one of the boy's great-great-uncles on his father's side is known to have had red hair. This illustrates clearly how a recessive character can remain hidden for many generations, rather than just "skip a generation" as is often the case.

The first experiments in genetics

24 This is the familiar "back cross to recessive parent".

Parents   Tt   × tt
Gametes   T *or* t   t *or* t

There will be equal numbers of both tall and dwarf plants.

25 This cross is in effect the same as the original cross; the offspring are all tall. As a general point it should be stressed that it is only when there are large numbers of offspring that one can be sure that the dominant parent does not carry the hidden recessive gene. This is particularly relevant when dealing with animals that have small litters.

26 For a recessive character to show, there must be two recessive alleles present. If the alleles are similar then the organism is homozygous for that particular character.

27 Half of the F2 plants will be heterozygous.

Human blood groups and inheritance

28 Since O is recessive to both the alleles A and B, the person must carry the alleles OO.

29 One parent must belong to blood group A and one to group B. In addition, each must carry a hidden O allele: *i.e.* the parents must be AO and BO.

Sex-linked inheritance

30 The allele for colour blindness is recessive. It will show when the allele is present on both of the X chromosomes of the female. This is unlikely to happen since it would usually require a colour blind male to mate with a carrier female. Only one allele for colour blindness is needed for it to show in a male, and can be produced when a carrier female with normal colour vision mates with a normal male.

31 Margaret's daughters must all carry an allele for colour blindness, inherited from their father. They have normal sight as they have all inherited an allele for normal sight from their mother.

32 James inherits his normal sight from his mother. He does not inherit an X chromosome from his father.

33 Richard and Jonathan both inherit their colour blindness from their mothers.

34 Yes; whether or not she has inherited the allele for colour blindness depends on which of the two X chromosomes happened to be in the egg. She cannot know unless she has children. If she carries the recessive allele she has an even chance of producing a colour blind son.

B22.7   Five toes, or maybe six?

Most mutations do not improve the fitness of an organism. At best they may have neglible effects, but many will be harmful. Recessive genes which are harmful may be tolerated by an organism, provided that the other allele functions normally. A few mutations may, however, improve the fitness of an organism, particularly in an unstable changing environment. The theory of evolution rests upon this premise.

If irradiated barley is grown, the effects of radiation on the percentages of germination and survival past the seedling stage are very obvious. Sometimes mutations such as lack of chlorophyll can be seen. Worksheet **B22E** illustrates this point graphically. If the remaining healthy plants are grown and compared with the same number of control plants there is little difference between them, and the dry mass of the irradiated plants may even be greater than that of the control. So some plants may escape with no harmful mutations, while others might even show some improvement. Much effort has been spent in trying to use mutations to improve the yield of crop plants. There have been some successes, but they are few and far between.

Answers to selected questions

36 The parents, the grandfathers and the mother or father of the grandfathers must have carried the recessive allele.

37 The albino children will inevitably hand on the allele if they themselves produce offspring. Any of their normal brothers and sisters and aunts and uncles might pass on the allele for albinism.

B22.8   Genetic counselling

The counselling of people who are known to carry harmful alleles is becoming more and more important in Britain. It is said that most of us carry at least one harmful recessive allele. Provided we do not marry someone with the same identical allele (and, provided a husband and wife are not related genetically, the chances of this are normally low), then there will be no problems. Some harmful alleles are found more often than others in the population, however, and occasionally two normal "carriers" marry. Genetic counselling can tell these parents what chance they have of producing a child unaffected by the disease.

Cystic fibrosis is given as an example because the gene is relatively common in the population of north-west Europe, affecting about one child in 2000.

If a gene frequency of 1 in 25 is assumed, then there is a 1 in 625 chance of carriers marrying. With a 1 in 4 chance of the recessive appearing, this would mean one affected child in every 2500 members of the population as a whole. As yet, affected individuals rarely live beyond young adulthood but diagnosis and treatment improve their chances of survival. Work on the identification of carriers (at St Mary's Hospital, London) is well advanced, and can at least mean that a mother of one child already affected need not have another. Useful literature on this condition may be obtained from the Cystic Fibrosis Research Trust, 5 Blyth Road, Bromley, Kent BR1 3AS (telephone 01–464 7211).

Answers to selected questions
An inherited disease

38 Because of the sticky mucus resulting from cystic fibrosis, the cleaning mechanism of the lung does not work properly and food in the gut cannot be digested. Enteric-coated pancreatic enzymes are taken to help digestion, especially of fats.

40 There is a 1 in 4 chance that an affected child will be born.

41 3 in 4 children will be normal.

42 2 out of every 3 normal children will be carriers.

43 There is a 1 in 4 chance that the gene will not be passed on at all.

Dominant mutant alleles

44 1 in 2 children will have 6 fingers if the person is heterozygous.

45 Not if the allele is dominant.

B22.9   Are you just your genes?

It is important not to leave a study of genetics with a fatalistic attitude to life, particularly when it is realized that genes influence so many of our personal characteristics. Genes and the environment interact when producing a characteristic. You could (in theory, anyway) have a set of genes that could predispose you to become a brilliant pianist. But if you never sat at a piano you would never find this out! This is the message of this final section.

Practical work

Worksheet B22A   Is variation inherited or due to the environment?

REQUIREMENTS

Each group of pupils will need:
White or yellow (chlorophyll-deficient) strains of tobacco, tomato or barley seeds

Compost, damp

Petri dish with circle of moist filter paper in base, if tobacco seeds are being used
Pots, small (1 for each seed type)

The procedure is detailed on the worksheet.

Worksheet B22B   Two kinds of variation

REQUIREMENTS

Each group of pupils will need:
Graph paper
Pencils
Rulers
Stopclock
Tape measure

Access to:
A variety of specimens showing measurable variation for obvious characteristics, for example:
    stick insects
    woodlice
    pods of peas or beans
    branch of pine needles
    holly leaves
    bluebell flower spike
Sensitive weighing balance

The procedure is detailed on the worksheet.

Note:
The examples given in the worksheet are only a few of those that could be selected. Teachers could choose their own examples, avoiding overlap with Worksheet **B**22A.

Worksheet B22C   Breeding with beads

REQUIREMENTS

Each group of pupils will need:
Beads, plastic "poppet", in 2 contrasting colours; 200 of each colour

Beakers for the beads, 3
Marker pen or chalk

The procedure is detailed on the worksheet.

Note:
This simulation exercise works well, provided that the pupils fully appreciate what the beads and the beakers symbolize. It is important that the concepts of genes and alleles are explained carefully, since this is a fertile area for confusion.

Worksheet B22D   Patterns of inheritance

REQUIREMENTS

Each group of pupils will need:
Tomato seeds: parents and F1 generation of crosses involving variation in stem colour and leaf shape caused by single major genes

Compost, damp

Labels
Seed tray
Top of plastic or glass, for seed tray
Thermometer

The procedure is detailed on the worksheet.

Note:
Biological suppliers produce material that illustrates genetic variation, although it is expensive. This practical might make a suitable demonstration, particularly as the differences observed ought to be immediately obvious. If possible, parents and F1 and F2 generations should be sown. This experiment could be combined with Worksheet **B22A**.

Worksheet B22E   Growing irradiated seeds

REQUIREMENTS

Each group of pupils will need:
Seeds, irradiated at several different doses

Compost, damp

Filter paper for each dish
Petri dishes (one for each radiation dosage)
Distilled water
Ruler
Seed tray
Water, distilled

The procedure is detailed on the worksheet. This practical would also be suitable as a demonstration.

Demonstration experiments   Worksheets **B22D** and **B22E** are suitable for demonstration purposes.

Further information   Cohen, N. *Discovering genetics* Longman, 1979.

Gonick, L. and Wheelis, M. *The cartoon guide to genetics* Barnes & Noble Books, 1983.

Supplementary material

Publications of the Cystic Fibrosis Research Trust, Department PD130, Alexandra House, 5 Blyth Road, Bromley, Kent BR1 3RS. (01–464 7211.)

Chapter B23　Changing with time

Purposes

Knowledge and understanding

At the end of this chapter all pupils should:

1 have some idea of the age of the Earth

2 know the four observations that form the basis of the theory of evolution

3 understand how natural selection can operate in populations

4 appreciate that the natural variation that exists between organisms has arisen through mutations.

In addition, those pupils aiming for higher grades should:

5 realize that variation that is environmentally induced cannot be passed on to the next generation through genes

6 appreciate that fossils can show how much or how little an organism has changed.

Processes and problem solving

Graphical and symbolic representation
In section **B**23.2 pupils use the models of a drawing of a clock and an imaginary walk in time to help them to understand the age of the Earth. In Worksheet **B**23B they may carry out a simulation exercise to investigate the usefulness of camouflage to animals; they are asked to plot a graph of their results.

Using apparatus and measuring instruments
In Worksheet **B**23A, pupils may find the mass of the hard roe of a herring when estimating the number of eggs in it.

Observation
In section **B**23.8, pupils may observe variation in the frequencies of the forms of *Cepaea*. Section **B**23.9 asks them to decide from photographs what differences there are between fossil and present day forms of some similar species.
　Worksheet **B**23C asks them to use diagrams to compare the forelimbs of certain vertebrates. In Worksheet **B**23D they may also use diagrams to compare evolutionary changes in some bones of primates.

Interpretation and application
In section **B**23.2, pupils are asked to interpret the age of the Earth and the organisms on it. Section **B**23.7 gives practice in understanding the struggle for existence that usually accompanies the production of large numbers of offspring by many organisms. In section **B**23.8, pupils may interpret data, from a variety of organisms, which suggest that natural selection has operated to produce evolutionary change.
　Using Worksheet **B**23C, pupils may interpret the pattern of bones found in the forelimbs of vertebrates. Worksheet **B**23D asks them to interpret the evolutionary changes in the bones of primates.

Planning and carrying out investigations
Worksheet **B**23B asks pupils to carry out, repeat against a different background and record a simulation exercise to investigate the effectiveness of camouflage to animals.

Timing

5 periods.

Suggested routes

Figure **B**29 presents two possible routes through this material. Clearly there are many more. The routes differ in their emphasis on natural selection, which is at the heart of this chapter. At the very least pupils should understand how excessive reproduction and limited resources can lead to competition, which will eventually lead to genetic changes within the population. The righthand route emphasizes this. The lefthand route gives a more academic treatment of evolution, and will be appropriate for certain groups and teachers. Once again, material should be selected to suit the circumstances within the school.

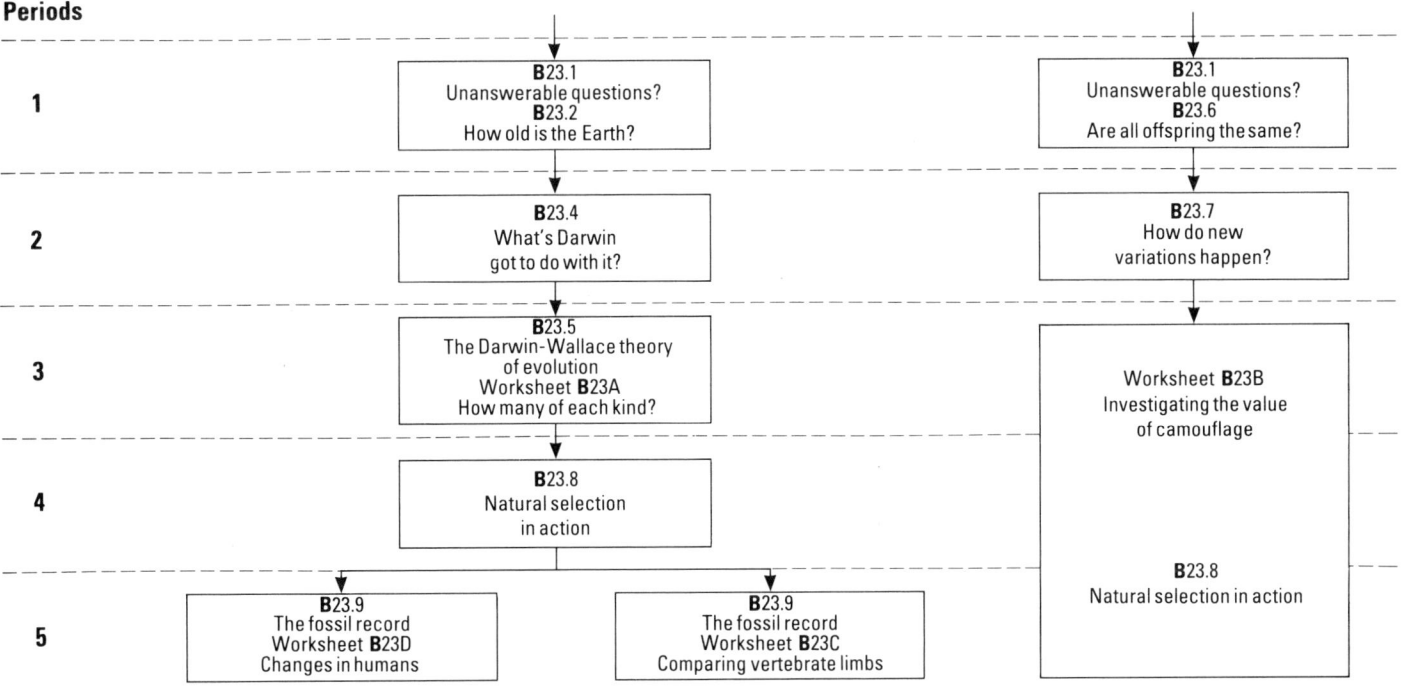

Figure **B**29

Opportunities for co-ordination

The work on the geological time scale in section **B**23.2 may be co-ordinated with the study of the formation of rocks in Chapter **C**4 "Chemicals and rocks" in the Chemistry pupils' book. The study of fossils in section **B**23.9 may be co-ordinated with the work on fossil fuels in the same Chemistry chapter.

Notes and answers

There are three parts to this chapter. The first deals in the main with the age of the Earth and when life began, and it develops the Darwin–Wallace theory of evolution by natural selection, using examples of the evidence on which it is based. The second part is much more relevant to everyday life in the present and shows how natural selection is happening all the time and is often influenced by humans. The last part introduces pupils to fossil evidence for evolution, emphasizing the way in which *Homo sapiens* has changed in a relatively short time.

B23.1   Unanswerable questions?

Neither scientific theories nor creation myths can ever **prove** how the universe began, nor how life developed, however much one may hope that one or other of them will. It is important to encourage pupils to look critically and objectively at scientific evidence and to keep an open mind. This is an area where strong (and often conflicting) religious beliefs may be encountered and must be respected. Science cannot hold all the answers to the questions which we may ask.

B23.2   How old is the Earth?

If pupils are to have any understanding of life history it is important to help them to understand the enormous length of geological time. As well as the clock face, a model with a scale of 1 mm for each year is quite useful. A time chart on this scale could be made as a long strip of graph paper stretching right round the laboratory, or along a school passage. Similarly, but with a change in scale to 1 mm = 1000 years, it would be possible to go right back to the creation of the Earth – this would come to 4 km, round and round the playing fields. There are opportunities for joint work with history and geography/geology, as well as the co-ordination with Chemistry Chapter C4, just mentioned.

Answers to selected questions

1, 2, 3 In the clock diagram in figure 23.2 in the pupils' book, bacteria are shown to have existed for about three-quarters of Earth history, but most other living things for only a quarter of the time (about 1200 million years).

4 The distance involved in the journey back to the Cretaceous period (about 70 million years), would be 70 m.

5 The oldest rocks in Britain are about 3000 million years old and our journey would be 3 km.

B23.3   What evidence is there of change?

Answer to selected question

6 In the past 2 million years, a number of the larger mammals found as fossil remains have become extinct.

B23.4   What's Darwin got to do with it?

Short biographies of Darwin and Wallace are included to give a historical and human background. So many accounts make the men look old and venerable, but they started off as young adventurers. Darwin's theory has had such a far-reaching effect on the way we think about evolution that it is difficult to imagine the way in which ordinary people thought in a pre-Darwinian world.

B23.5   The Darwin–Wallace theory of evolution

The evidence on which Darwin and Wallace based their theory is given here and illustrated by examples which should be relevant to pupils at all levels. The difficulties come in relating natural selection, which we can see happening today, to the evolution, not only of closely related species, but of very different forms of the same species.

The most important concept to get across to pupils is natural selection, for which there is plenty of evidence. This is summarized as four observations ("facts") upon which the theory is built. The theory is based on what has been happening in populations in recent times. It is an assumption (albeit a logical one) that these processes began a long time ago and led to the formation of the groups that we see today.

Fossil evidence shows that organisms in the past were both different from and similar to organisms which are alive today. This scientific evidence (and other evidence, based, for example, on adaptive radiation and geographical distribution) leads to theories about what may have happened in the past.

Even with the vast length of time that was available, evolution by a series of small changes alone might not have been possible. Modern theories such as that of punctuated equilibrium provide alternative explanations.

Practical work on the numbers of offspring produced by different organisms, based on Worksheet **B23A**, can be performed at this point.

Answer to selected question

7 Somewhere around a maximum of 400 eggs.

B23.6 Are all offspring the same?

Pupils should see that sexual reproduction results in organisms that show variation for characteristics. Variation is studied in populations of *Drosophila*. Ultimately (as the next section emphasizes), genetic variation arises from mutations. These occur in laboratory populations of *Drosophila*, but are less obvious in wild populations. The reasons for this are discussed.

Variation also occurs in human populations. Blood groups are an example of this. When doing work on blood groups it is important to make clear the difference between individuals and populations. With very few exceptions, a population will contain at least some individuals with each blood group.

It is important that pupils realize that only gene mutations can be inherited and that variation caused by the environment cannot be passed on to the next generation.

Answers to selected questions

8, 9 82 fruit flies have 38 bristles, which is the most common number occurring in 16 % of the sample.

10 The range is from 30–48 bristles.

11 Any mutant form which – perhaps as a result of its wing shape – is less well able to fly will probably leave fewer descendants, since the ability to find food, find a mate and spread to new habitats will all be affected. Differences in colour and pattern might make the fly more or less visible to predators. In laboratory conditions new mutant forms will be easily recognized and can be maintained, but in the wild they may disappear.

12 The proportions of the different blood groups in gypsy populations make it seem probable that they came originally from India.

13 Blood group "O" is most common in the British Isles and is higher in Celtic groups than in the English.

B23.7 How do new variations happen?

This work is really a reinforcement of the section on mutations in Chapter **B22**. It is a useful opportunity to make sure that it has been properly understood. There are many examples of domesticated animals (such as pigeons and dogs) where mutant forms would have little chance of survival in the wild.

Because most populations remain stable the enormous potential of most organisms for reproduction is not really appreciated. Only when colonizing do organisms begin to realize this potential, and then only for a short time.

How does the environment affect organisms? This is the crucial question, for it is the environment, acting on populations which are competing for limited resources, that generates the pressure of natural selection that will lead to evolutionary change. This leads into the next section.

Answers to selected questions

16 With variegated plants, if only half the leaf area is green the plant has only half the normal amount of photosynthetic tissue and so would be at a disadvantage in competition with fully green plants in the wild. Competition for light and space is removed in cultivation. Overgrown and neglected gardens provide many examples of competition and of the survival of only the most successful individuals.

17 If all the seeds germinated at once there would be more competition and even fewer would survive. If conditions soon after the time of germination are unfavourable, all the seedlings will die. With dormancy and staggered germination, there is more chance of at least some offspring growing to maturity, however bad the conditions. In commercial packeted seed a tendency towards delayed germination is undesirable and this characteristic has largely been bred out of crop plants.

B23.8   Natural selection in action

Several examples of natural selection are given in this section; it can be completed with Worksheet **B23B** which pupils may find entertaining. Teachers should select from this section the examples that suit their needs, but should realize that their examples may be more complex than those that appear here.

Antibiotic resistance in bacteria is a timely, but rather chilling, example of natural selection that affects humans. There are now numerous examples of the development of resistant forms of bacteria. A useful point to make here is the importance of finishing the whole course of pills or bottle of medicine, even if the person feels better and has apparently recovered, and never giving any doses of a medicine to someone for whom it has not been prescribed.

Answers to selected questions

22 There tend to be more yellow, banded snails in grassland habitats. Yellow snails are better camouflaged when the grass has grown in the spring. Brown and pink forms tend to predominate in woodland areas.

28 You would expect the number of S alleles in the populations where sickle cell anaemia occurs to decrease.

29 HbAA and HbSS.

30 Because only one of the alleles passes into an egg or a sperm when cells divide to form gametes, the parents could be any of the following: HbAA and HbSS; both could be HbAS; or one could be HbAA and the other HbAS; or one could be HbSS and the other HbAS.

31 The results in figure 23.22 of the pupils' book suggest that the presence of sickle cells prevents a person from being affected by malaria.

32a Natural selection removes the A allele because people with AA are susceptible to malaria and may die.
b Natural selection removes the S allele because people with SS have sickle cell anaemia and may die.

33 A and S are kept in the population because people who are AS are apparently immune to malaria and yet do not suffer from sickle cell anaemia.

34 The balance depends on the presence of malaria in an area, which means AS individuals tend to increase in proportion to AA or SS.

23.9   The fossil record

Almost any fossil can provide the focus for a lesson on this topic – the object itself is much more stimulating than a photograph. For each example, it should be possible to establish its age (give or take a few million years), the environment in which it lived and obvious similarities and differences between the fossil and its closest living relatives. Studying the past history of living things on our planet is a form of historical ecology. Pupils who have done work on ecology should have little difficulty in imagining the habitats in which the fossil animals or plants lived and how large scale environmental changes might have led to their extinction. However, it is important for them to realize that the reconstruction can only be as accurate as the information provided by the evidence, which is often scanty. Worksheet **B23C** allows pupils to think about the homology of the vertebrate limbs, which can supplement the inadequate evidence of the fossil record.

Dinosaurs never seem to lose their appeal and carboniferous forests are probably familiar from work on fuels. Ammonite fossils are widespread and interesting because they are not like any present day molluscs. The horseshoe crab (*Limulus polyphemus*) is sometimes inaccurately referred to as a king crab, which is a different organism. Horseshoe crabs are not really crabs at all, but a form of marine arthropod with no close living relatives. The strong similarity between modern horseshoe crabs and their fossil ancestors may be due to an unusually stable environment and to the absence of competition from any organisms better able to survive.

The final passage on the evolution of humans can be completed with Worksheet **B23D**. The old misconception that "men are descended from monkeys" can be corrected here. The change in the hand, with the larger thumb set at a wider angle to the fingers, has made the precision grip possible. This would not be of much use without the ability to walk easily on two legs, which leaves the hands free, leading the way to the production of specialized tools.

The larger brain has made possible the development of those characteristics which we regard as specifically human.

Speech is possibly one of the most important human attributes, leading to the transmission of culture and tradition from one generation to the next. Humans have rites surrounding death and other events of their existence; they also have the capacity for rational thought and moral and aesthetic values.

At a more obvious and practical level the use of fire and the production of tools for future use (not just for the present moment) are specifically human characteristics.

While scientists agree that selection, natural and artificial, is taking place in species which are present in the world today there is still considerable debate about the processes by which species evolved, and whether or not a supernatural Being is the ultimate explanation. The consequences of human influence on the selection of organisms, for good or ill, is much more important than discussion about what else might or might not have happened in the past. With most groups it is probably better to spend more time on natural selection and less on evolution.

Practical work

Worksheet B23A   How many of each kind?

REQUIREMENTS

Each group of pupils will need:
Groundsel plant, or other example, with fruits and flowers
Mould on bread (possibly *Mucor*)
Hard herring roe

Balance
Coverslip
Dish
Microscope
Microscope slide (with counting cell if possible)
Needle, mounted
Scissors

Notes:
The organisms suggested for practical work are easily obtainable, but many others are suitable. These include butterfly eggs on cabbages, snail eggs in ponds and many annual or biennial weeds and garden plants.

Pupils will be amazed to find the number of seeds in, for example, a tomato; they can then make an estimate of the number of fruits produced by one plant. This quantitative approach is an important aspect of biology and should be introduced whenever the opportunity arises. It is suggested that as many organisms as possible should be studied by different groups in the class.
   The procedure is detailed on the worksheet. This section may be related to the work on human reproduction and contraception in Chapter **B**20.

Worksheet B23B   Investigating the value of camouflage

REQUIREMENTS

Each group of pupils will need:
Clipboard, paper and pencil
Straws, 100 green and 100 red, cut to about 10 cm lengths
Watch with seconds hand

Access to:
Patch of grass about 15 metres square
Patch of dirt or bare ground about 15 metres square

The procedure is detailed on the worksheet.

Worksheet B23C   Comparing vertebrate limbs

REQUIREMENTS

Each group of pupils will need:
Paper glue
Photocopy of the worksheet plan of vertebrate forelimbs
Scissors
Table, arranged as in worksheet, but large enough to accommodate cut-out "bones"

The procedure is detailed on the worksheet. It is important that pupils appreciate that the original vertebrates developed by moving into a wide variety of niches. As they did so, the appearance of their limbs slowly changed as a result of natural selection over the course of many generations. Although the pattern of bones in the limbs has hardly altered, the final form of the limb has developed markedly.

Worksheet B23D   Changes in humans

REQUIREMENTS

Each group of pupils will need:
Rulers

The procedure is detailed on the worksheet.

Further information

British Museum (Natural History) *Man's place in evolution* 1980.

British Museum (Natural History) *Origin of species* Cambridge University Press, 1981.

CHEMISTRY

Introduction to Chemistry

Topics and contexts

The Chemistry course is designed to introduce girls and boys to the everyday, industrial, and environmental importance of chemistry, while explaining sufficient theory to show them how scientific knowledge can help them to make sense of the world in which they live.

The content is presented in six topics. However, it can also be reviewed in terms of the following themes:

People and chemistry
Chemistry and the environment
Chemistry and living things
Industrial processes
Materials
Structure and bonding
Chemical change
Chemical analysis
Periodic Table.

The main interlinking ideas show how the properties of materials can be explained in terms of structure and bonding. There is much less emphasis on chemical calculations than there was in Stage II of Revised Nuffield Chemistry.

Significance

Two important influences in the development of the Chemistry were Nuffield Secondary Science and the course of Options in Stage III of Revised Nuffield Chemistry.

Many of the chapter titles chosen relate to topics in Theme 7 "Using materials" in Nuffield Secondary Science. The idea has been to start with contexts which can be developed successfully with the majority of children and then to extend the treatment to bring in more of the theory.

The Nuffield Chemistry Stage III options were written to provide opportunities for pupils to apply their knowledge of chemistry and see the practical importance of what they studied. The Options were originally designed as the finale to what was then an O-level course. The treatment of the topics has had to be modified extensively for a programme designed for the GCSE ability-range over two years.

Many of the more advanced concepts which featured in Stage II of Nuffield Chemistry (and other GCE O-level courses) have been omitted. This has been necessary to change the nature of the challenge presented to pupils. There is now more emphasis on skills, processes and problem solving and less on mastering abstract concepts. Examples of theory which have been omitted include: most of the calculations using the concept amount of substance/mol, dynamic equilibrium, the formal treatment of enthalpy changes, and the explanation of acid/base reactions in terms of proton transfer. We have taken the view that these topics are more suited to A-level, but we have tried to provide experiences which will help those who do go on to A-level to master the ideas at that stage.

Nevertheless, there is a place for theory and we have tried to choose important ideas which can be shown to have wide applicability. Teachers may find it helpful to read Chapter C18 in the pupils' book to find a summary of the main theoretical ideas in the course and to see how they can be linked together and co-ordinated with Biology and Physics. It is not expected that all pupils will study and understand this theory; it is included mainly for those aiming for the higher GCSE grades. We believe that the course will still make sense for pupils for whom such a theoretical treatment is inappropriate.

Differentiation

In most chapters of Nuffield Co-ordinated Sciences Chemistry the starting point is a practical activity. In general the suggested experiments and investigations are such that it is worthwhile for all pupils to tackle them. It is the way in which the results are analysed and interpreted which allows differentiated treatments.

Topic C2, for example, is devoted to the study of materials including glasses, ceramics, metals and polymers. After doing the practical work many pupils will be able to think about the relationship between the properties of these materials and the way they are used. A more theoretical treatment seeks an explanation of the properties of the materials in terms of structure and bonding.

There are several theoretical ideas which are only required of those aiming for the higher GCSE grades. Most of these are boxed in the pupils' book so that the main text can be read without referring to them. Examples include the concept of amount of substance, the ionic explanation of precipitation reactions, and the descriptions of bonding in terms of electron transfer and electron sharing.

Differentiation has been allowed for in the worksheets too. For example, the worksheets for Chapter C12 suggest a series of titration experiments to investigate antacids. Alternative methods of working out an answer from the results are given. The simpler method is based on a conversion scale. The more advanced method uses the equation for the reaction and the concept of amount of substance.

Experimental work

The three main purposes of experimental work are discussed in Chapter 3 of the General introduction to this *Guide*. Here they are illustrated with examples from the Chemistry component of the course.

● To give pupils first-hand experience of phenomena.

In Chemistry we have tried to include a variety of activities which will help pupils to appreciate the significance of the theory while not losing sight of the practical importance of the applications of the subject. (See the table on the next page.)

For example, Topic C2 of the Chemistry course concentrates on the study of materials. There are two main themes: one is the relationship between the uses of materials and their properties; the other is the explanation of the properties of materials in terms of structure. The pupils must have first-hand experience of materials if they are to make sense of these ideas.

Pupils should come to appreciate the importance of chemistry in providing us with new products such as plastics, drugs, dyes and fertilizers. Synthesis and formulation are both necessary. We want them to have the satisfaction of making things for themselves; the course provides opportunities for this, as shown in the table on the next page.

● To teach practical skills.

In Chemistry the pupils have the chance to practise manipulative skills to which they are likely to have been introduced in earlier years. They also have the opportunity to use skills which they are likely to meet first in Physics, involving the use of measuring instruments to determine masses, volumes and temperatures. Skills particular to Chemistry include the handling, testing and measurement of gases as well as the accurate measurement of liquid volumes. A

	Topic C1	Topic C2	Topic C3	Topic C4	Topic C5
Experiments and other activities related to the theory of chemistry	**C2A** Making models of molecules: part 1 **C2B** Cracking hydrocarbons **C2C** Making models of molecules: part 2 **C3B** Investigating carbohydrate molecules **C3C** Models of carbohydrate molecules **C4C** Investigating the electrolysis of a solution of sodium chloride	**C5A** Molecules or giant structures? **C5B** Ions on the move **C5C** Ions and electrolysis	**C9A** Investigating colloids **C9B** Surface tension **C11C** Dyeing with a reactive dye	**C14A** Investigating cells	**C15A** Particle size and the rate of reaction of a rock with an acid **C15B** Concentration and the rate of reaction of a rock with an acid **C15C** Temperature and the rate of reaction of a rock with an acid **C15D** Investigating the effect of pH on the solubility of soil minerals
Experiments and other activities in an applied context ● **Making things – purification, synthesis, formulation**	**C4A** Making alum from shale	**C6A** Making glass **C6B** Glass working **C8A** Polymerization	**C9C** Making a cosmetic cream **C11A** Dyeing with indigo **C11B** Mordant dyeing		**C16B** Making a fertilizer
● **Quantitative analysis**	**C4** problem: How can malachite be analysed?		**C10B** Which is the best way of softening water? **C12A** How much gastric juice does 'bicarb' neutralize? **C12B** Analysis of a magnesia tablet **C12C** Analysis of aspirin tablets	**C13D** Measuring the energy released by burning fuels	
● **Qualitative analysis**	**C3** problem: Are all sugars equally sweet?	**C7B** Analysing an alloy **C7** problem: Which is the best way to stop rusting? **C8D** A key to identify plastics	**C10** Problems : Which is the best descaler? Does descaling kettles save energy?	**C13B** What makes a good fuel? **C13C** Choosing a good fuel **C13** Problem: How effective are flameproofing agents?	**C16A** The catalyst crisis

An analysis of the practical activities in NCS Chemistry. The table does not include the Teacher Demonstrations suggested in this *Guide*. Entries of the form: '**C2A**' refer to Worksheets. Entries of the form: '**C4** problem' refer to the pupils' book. There is no practical work in Topic **C6**.

series of experiments in Chapter **C12** gives pupils some familiarity with the use of burettes and titration techniques. In this way pupils should come to appreciate the importance of chemical analysis. (See the table above.)

● To provide opportunities for pupils to plan and carry out scientific investigations.

Chapter 3 of the General introduction to this *Guide* lists the four types of problem solving which feature in the course. In Chemistry there are examples of two of the types.

Suggested investigations are included as problems in the pupils' book. Time has been allowed for the pupils to tackle some, but not all, of them. Worksheet **C0** is designed to encourage pupils to set out their plans in a form which teachers can check before they start work in the laboratory.

Factual knowledge of the suggested investigations will not be required. This means that pupils and teachers can choose alternative problems to study according to their interests.

Type I: Laboratory investigations designed and carried out by the pupils using equipment supplied

There is an example of a type I problem in Chapter **C7**. The text explains how "corrosion indicator" can be used to detect where iron is rusting. Then a number of possible investigations are suggested.

In a few cases, type I problems in the text deal with experiments covered by the pack of structured worksheets. With some pupils it may be more appropriate to allow them to plan the experiments and do the investigation their own way. Other pupils may need the help of the worksheets. Examples include the problems in Chapter **C2** (How can you crack hydrocarbons in the laboratory?), Chapter **C4** (Can you make alum from shale?) and Chapter **C15** (Investigating the rate of reaction of an acid with a rock).

Type II: Laboratory investigations designed and carried out by the pupils using equipment selected by themselves

There is a variety of type II problems in the Chemistry book. Most of them are included in the table on the previous page. Some are extensions to the worksheets, such as the fastness testing in Chapter **C11**.

Teachers may prefer to tackle these type II problems as they arise in the course of normal teaching and time has been allowed for this. Alternatively a period of time might be set aside later in the course when pupils could be given the chance to choose to investigate one or more of them. Some pupils may come up with ideas for investigations of their own. They do not have to tackle the particular problems specified in the pupils' book.

Worksheet **C0** is suggested for use in connection with these problems. Use of this worksheet will give teachers an opportunity to check that what the pupils are proposing to do is both practicable and safe.

Worksheets

There are three types of chemistry worksheets. Most of the worksheets are designed to help pupils tackle the experiments and learn practical skills.

Other worksheets are based on SATIS units intended to promote thought and discussion of issues arising from the impact of science and technology on society. We have used worksheets for some of these issues so that the topics chosen for discussion can be changed and be kept up to date and topical throughout the lifetime of the course.

The third category of worksheets has been included to help pupils to learn by studying the text. These sheets are designed to promote active reading as suggested in *Reading for learning in the sciences* by Florence Davies and Terry Greene (Oliver and Boyd, 1984). This book is based on the premise that effective reading has to be an active process. It explains why pupils have difficulties with reading science textbooks, and suggests strategies for helping boys and girls to become more reflective as they read so that they will learn to study technical books.

The suggested reading activities are designed to help pupils master the various types of text found in science books. The activities are of two types. There are reconstruction activities which are essentially problem solving and have game like characteristics. They make use of modified text. Examples of this type are Worksheets **C4D**, **C4F**, **C6C**, and **C13A**.

There are also analysis activities. These use straight text and are an introduction to study methods and note-taking. It is essential that the pupils should be able to mark a copy of the text by underlining or labelling selected words, sentences and paragraphs. Hence the need for worksheets to use alongside the main text. Examples of this type are: **C3D**, **C4B**, **C5D**, and **C17B**.

The effectiveness of these worksheets can only be judged when they are used alongside the book they are designed to accompany so they cannot be tested realistically in advance of publication. They are included as an experiment and will be modified in the light of experience.

Safety

Hazard symbols on the worksheets alert pupils to the dangers associated with the chemicals. When pupils are planning their own investigations they might be given access to the CLEAPSE/SSERC Hazcards so that they can check safety aspects for themselves.

Teachers have a responsibility to ensure that their pupils are clearly briefed about safety and are working carefully. The following publications are useful:

Safety in science laboratories (DES, 4th edition, 1987)
Safeguards in the school laboratory (ASE, 1988)
Topics in safety (ASE, 1988)

Teachers can keep up to date with current practice by reading ASE publications including *Education in science* and *The school science review*.

Topic C1   **Raw materials**

Chapter C1   The elements of chemistry

Purposes

Knowledge and understanding

At the end of this chapter all pupils should:

1 understand the meaning of these terms: element, compound, atom, molecule

2 appreciate the distinction between metal and non-metal elements on the basis of their more obvious physical properties

3 appreciate that in the Periodic Table the elements are arranged in order of atomic mass, and understand the terms group and period.

In addition, those pupils aiming for higher grades should:

4 understand that atomic masses can be measured in atomic mass units, symbol u.

Processes and problem solving

Graphical and symbolic representation
This chapter introduces pupils to the symbols for atoms and molecules which they can look up in the Data section at the end of the Chemistry pupils' book. All pupils are expected to be able to understand word equations with state symbols.

The rules for writing balanced symbol equations are given in this chapter. The ability to understand and write equations is a skill which pupils will acquire gradually during the rest of the course.

Timing

We assume that most pupils will already be familiar with the ideas in this chapter. Clearly many pupils will need to revise their knowledge. The skills involved in using chemical symbols will be practised in later chapters. No teaching time is allocated to this chapter at the start of the course.

Suggested routes

We suggest that the course should begin with Chapter C2 so that the pupils have the sense of making a fresh start. This chapter can be used for reference and revision at appropriate times during the study of later chapters.

Opportunities for co-ordination

The particulate nature of matter and kinetic theory are introduced in Chapter P2.

Later Biology chapters dealing with digestion, respiration and plant nutrition assume that pupils understand the difference between elements and compounds.

Notes and answers

This chapter has been included mainly for reference and revision, so that the pupils have access to an account of the main ideas they are meant to have gathered from their work in years 1 to 3. The questions are available for use at any time for homework and revision during the two years of the course.

C1.1   What are raw materials made of?

There are no class experiments to find chemical formulae in this course. The policy is to allow pupils to have access to tables of data which give the formulae. So the Data section at the back of the Chemistry book is used from the start. The questions in this chapter provide plenty of opportunities for the pupils to use the tables of data.

C1.2   When were the elements discovered?

We have decided that it is simpler to talk about **atomic mass** than **relative atomic mass**. Hence the decision to use atomic mass units (symbol u). This has the advantage that every physical quantity in the course is seen to have a number and a unit.

C1.3   How do we write chemical equations?

In this chapter the examples are all molecular. This complements the study of molecular compounds in Chapters **C2** and **C3**. The choice of symbols to represent giant structures in equations is not dealt with until Chapter **C5**.

This section includes one of a number of cartoons in which a girl and a boy are seen to be trying to work out the answer to a theoretical problem. This may appear artificial, but we believe that these cartoons can show pupils how they should try to work out answers to difficult questions. So the cartoons can be seen as a way of exposing the thinking needed to solve problems. We hope that teachers will work through other examples with their classes while studying later chapters in the course. Pupils may be helped by opportunities to work in groups to explore the use of symbols and equations.

Many pupils find it difficult to come to terms with symbol equations. The advantage of starting with molecular examples in Chapters **C2** and **C3** is that it allows pupils to use models to give a picture of what the equations mean.

Practical work

Worksheet C1A   Reacting molecules

REQUIREMENTS

Each group of pupils will need:
Copy of Worksheet C1A
Scissors

Access to:
Stapler

The idea of this flick book is to give pupils an animated picture of what happens during a reaction. This may help to counteract the static impression given by equations. The worksheet is also included as an example because we think that it is a useful exercise for pupils to try and make their own flick books. Pupils have to understand an idea thoroughly before they can make a flick book to illustrate it. Making flick books can be used as a homework activity. In addition to the examples suggested here, they might be asked to make flick books to show a solid melting, a liquid evaporating, or one gas diffusing into another.

Chapter C2   Petrochemicals

Purposes

Knowledge and understanding

At the end of this chapter all pupils should:

1 know that crude oil is a mixture of hydrocarbons

2 appreciate the ability of carbon atoms to join up in chains, branched chains and rings

3 understand that the physical properties of a hydrocarbon depend on the size of its molecules

4 know the meaning of the terms fractional distillation, cracking, polymerization, polymer, monomer and exothermic reaction

5 appreciate some of the issues involved in the location of industry.

In addition, those pupils aiming for higher grades should:

6 understand the meaning of the terms saturated hydrocarbon and unsaturated hydrocarbon and know that bromine solution can be used to distinguish between them

7 understand the meaning of the terms molecular formula and graphical formula

8 appreciate the importance of ethene in the petrochemical industry.

Processes and problem solving

Graphical and symbolic representation
Pupils are not expected to remember chemical names and formulae, but they should be able to look them up in tables of data. Given the molecular formula and a table showing how many bonds the atoms form, they should also be able to work out a possible graphical formula for simple hydrocarbons.
   Question 10 asks pupils to plot a graph to examine the way in which the boiling points of alkanes vary with chain length.
   Worksheets **C2A** and **C2C** provide opportunities for using molecular models to represent the molecules and chemical changes mentioned in the chapter.

Using apparatus and measuring instruments
The cracking of a hydrocarbon oil described on Worksheet **C3B** requires controlled heating and mastery of the technique of collecting a gas over water. Pupils also have to use a liquid reagent to test for a gas.

Observation
When carrying out the experiment on Worksheet **C2B**, pupils are asked to observe the differences between the reactant and the main product.

Interpretation and application
Pupils are asked to use their knowledge of hydrocarbons to explain some of the operating conditions in industry; see for example questions 16–21 and 28–34.

Planning and carrying out investigations
In advance of the cracking experiment on Worksheet **C2B**, pupils can be asked to plan how they would do the experiment, prompted by the information in box 1 on page 17 of their Chemistry book.

Timing   8 periods.

Suggested routes   The flow diagram in figure C1 shows a possible route through this chapter.

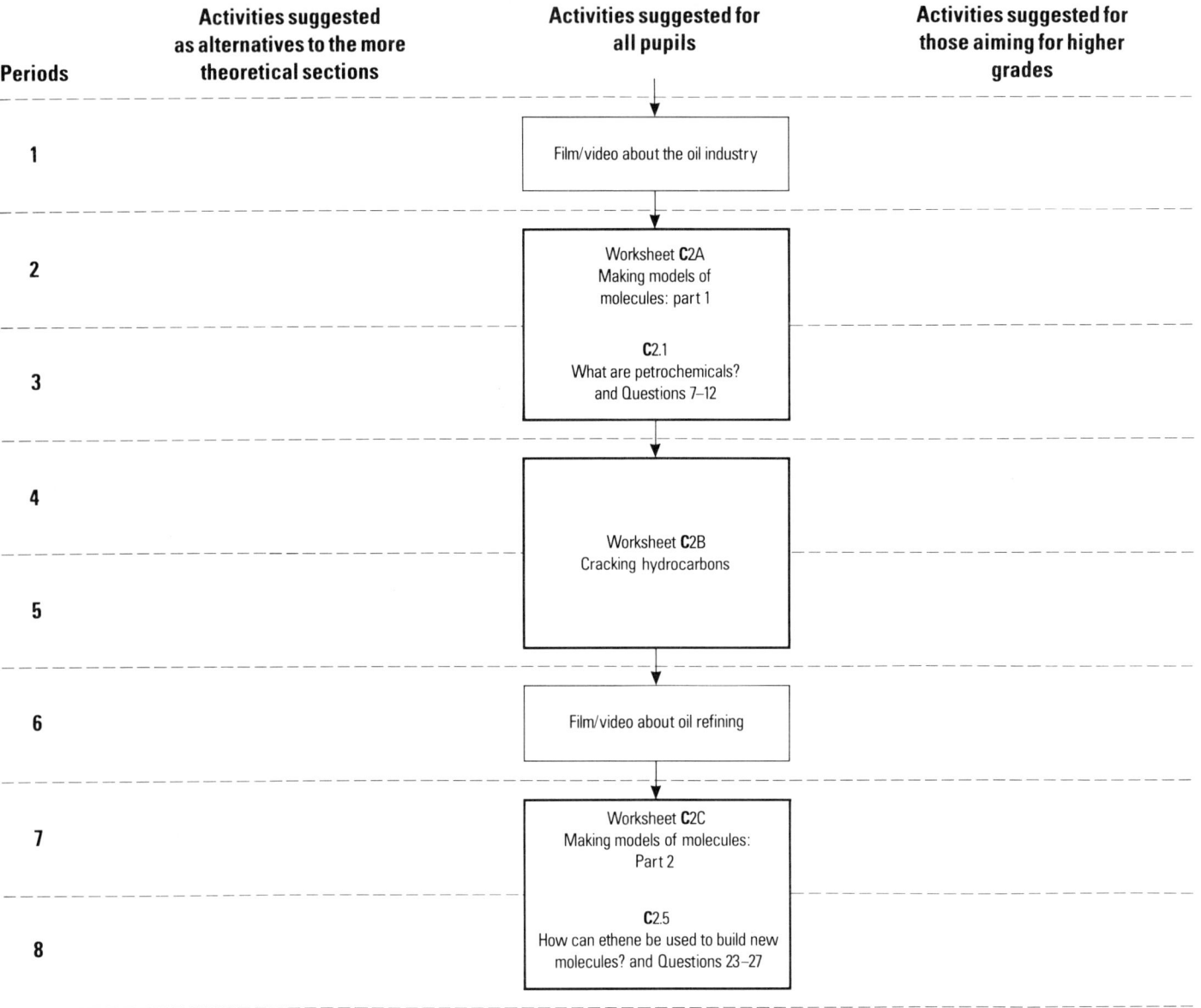

	Activities suggested as alternatives to the more theoretical sections	Activities suggested for all pupils	Activities suggested for those aiming for higher grades
Periods			
1		Film/video about the oil industry	
2		Worksheet **C**2A Making models of molecules: part 1	
3		**C**2.1 What are petrochemicals? and Questions 7–12	
4		Worksheet **C**2B Cracking hydrocarbons	
5			
6		Film/video about oil refining	
7		Worksheet **C**2C Making models of molecules: Part 2	
8		**C**2.5 How can ethene be used to build new molecules? and Questions 23–27	

Figure **C**1

Opportunities for co-ordination   This chapter and Chapter C3 have been placed early in the course so that pupils are introduced to the idea of thinking in terms of atoms and molecules before they meet explanations of photosynthesis, digestion and respiration in Biology.

This chapter touches on some of the civil engineering problems involved in the discovery and exploration of North Sea gas, and so it might be useful to refer to some of the ideas about structures and forces in Chapter **P**1. This Chemistry chapter also deals with liquids and gases, as well as changes of state, so there are links with Chapter **P**2.

Notes and answers

C2.1 What are petrochemicals?

Sections C2.1 and C2.3 are designed to give pupils an image of what happens in an oil refinery. Broadly the processes can be divided into three:

- separation by fractional distillation
- conversion by cracking, reforming or polymerization
- purification by removing sulphur and arenes from fuels, and waxes from lubricants.

The focus in this chapter is on distillation, cracking and polymerization. The purification steps are dealt with in Chapter C13, which also includes more detail about the products of fractional distillation.

A film or video will help pupils to gain an idea of the scale of operations in the oil industry. Most of the major oil companies have produced suitable films for the purpose. Sources of films and videos are listed in the Appendix in this *Guide*.

Questions 2–6 revise the distinctions between elements, compounds and mixtures, and introduce some rather more complex molecules than those in Chapter C1.

C2.2 What are the rules for making molecules?

This section gives pupils an opportunity to use tables of data, and to note both that pure compounds have a particular boiling-point (under given conditions) and that there is a correlation between boiling-point and molecular size. The family name for the alkanes is introduced, but there is no need to use the term "homologous series".

Question 9 asks pupils to explore the possibility of isomerism, but a formal treatment of the concept is not required for examination purposes. This is one of many examples in the course where a topic is introduced as an opportunity for the pupils to exercise skills and processes. It should not to be taken to mean that knowledge of the idea will be assumed as an examination requirement.

This section is complemented by Worksheet C2A.

C2.3 How can the molecules in oil be sorted out?

Pupils are not expected to remember the details of this section. The idea is that they should have some impression of the scale of the industry and be aware of some of the problems involved.

Answers to selected questions

15a 500 tankers; **b** 1000 times.

16a To prevent corrosion.
b Near villages and towns for safety.
c Under roads and railways to protect the pipe.
d To make sure that it is not damaged by ploughing and other farming activities.
e To cut off part of the pipeline in case of accident.
f By checking that the flow past each point is the same.

C2.4 How can molecules be broken into smaller pieces?

This section shows that North Sea gas and oil are not just sources of fuel but are also the basis of the petrochemical industry in Britain.

This section points out the importance of people in industry. It also mentions some of the factors which determine the location of industry and the issues which have to be faced in relation to those who live nearby. These points may mean more to the pupils if they can see a film or video about the petrochemical industry.

The problem at the end of the section (page 39) is a planning exercise. Some may come up with a workable solution with the help of table 7 in the Data section. If not they can be given Worksheet **C2B**. Attempting the planning exercise may help pupils to appreciate the design of the apparatus on the worksheet.

C2.5   How can ethene be used to build new molecules?

The terms *saturated* and *unsaturated* are introduced because they appear on household products and crop up in the debate about diet and health. (See Chapter **B6**.)

Ethene is shown to be able to add to other molecules and to itself, but the term addition reaction is **not** used. The model equations provide an opportunity for pupils to practise the use of symbols and to see why chemical equations balance.

Worksheet **C2C** complements sections **C2.4** and **C2.5**.

C2.6   Why did the chickens stop laying eggs?

A chemical plant does not run simply according to the simple chemical description of the process. This section is included to give pupils some impression of the challenging problems which can face those responsible for operating an industrial plant.

Practical work

Worksheet C2A   Making models of molecules: part 1

REQUIREMENTS

Each group of pupils will need:
Copy of Worksheet **C2A** (see note 1)
Set of ball-and-spring models (see note 2):
    4 black atoms, four hole
    4 red atoms, two hole
    10 white atoms, one hole
    4 long bonds
    10 short bonds

Access to:
Book of data or textbook giving the formulae of alkanes

Note:
1 The worksheet is designed for ball-and-spring/stick models and will have to be revised if alternative models are used.
2 The models are conveniently supplied in a plastic bag with a checklist on a card inside.

It is very important that pupils should have the opportunity to make their own models, here and elsewhere during the course. We think that it is well worth while buying enough models for a class of pupils working in groups.

The worksheet is largely self-explanatory, but some pupils will need help to see that double bonds are needed in oxygen, carbon dioxide and ethene molecules so that their formulae are consistent with the bonding rules. There are no detailed instructions on the worksheet to show pupils how much they are expected to write down. It is left to teachers to decide how much drawing and writing is appropriate.

Pupils who work rapidly can go on to the text and questions of section **C2.2** in the Chemistry book.

Worksheet C2B Cracking hydrocarbons

REQUIREMENTS

Each group of pupils will need:
Copy of Worksheet **C2B**
Hard-glass test-tube
Glass rod
3 test-tube with bungs, to collect gas
Delivery tube with bung to fit the hard-
    glass test-tube (see worksheet)
Bunsen valve to fit delivery tube (see
    note 1)
Trough, or large crystallizing dish (see
    note 2)
Stand, with boss and clamp
Burner and mat
Eye protection

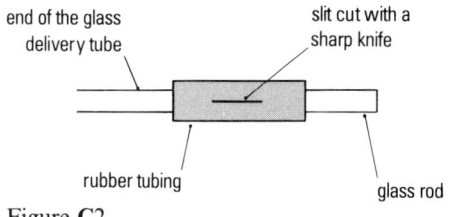

end of the glass
delivery tube

slit cut with a
sharp knife

rubber tubing

glass rod

Figure **C2**
A Bunsen valve.

Access to:
Mineral wool
Liquid paraffin, medicinal, in bottle with
    dropper; allow 5 ml per group
Broken chips of porcelain
Strips of copper gauze, 10 cm × 3 cm
    (optional)
Iron wool (optional)
Aqueous potassium manganate(VII),
    0.001 mol/L in bottle with dropper
Dilute sulphuric acid in bottle with
    dropper

The teacher will need access to:
Aqueous bromine in bottle with dropper
    (see note 3)
Fume cupboard

Notes:
1 The design of a Bunsen valve is shown
in figure **C2**. It is made from glass rod and
rubber tubing. Use a sharp blade to cut
the slit in the rubber tube. This allows gas
to escape but makes it difficult for water
to suck back. Do not use old or perished
rubber, as it may not be flexible enough.
2 Large plastic margarine tubs can be
used as cheap troughs.
3 1,2-dibromoethane is dangerous, but
very little will form if aqueous bromine is
used for the test. The products should
preferably be disposed of in a fume
cupboard.

This practical exercise provides an opportunity for pupils to make observations
and interpret them. Some skill is needed to carry out the experiment successfully.
In experiments like this, the biggest problems are blocked apparatus (such as
molten bungs) and suck back.

Pupils know that small molecules boil at a lower temperature than larger
molecules, so the conversion of a liquid to a gas suggests that cracking has taken
place. The reactions of the product with potassium manganate(VII) and aqueous
bromine show that the product is more reactive than the oil which has been
cracked.

Pupils who get on quickly can try the further investigations to compare
alternative catalysts.

Worksheet C2C Making models of molecules: part 2

REQUIREMENTS

Each group of pupils will need:
Copy of Worksheet **C2C** (see note 1)
Set of ball and spring models (see note 2):
    4 black atoms, four hole
    1 red atom, two hole
    2 green atoms, one hole
    8 white atoms, one hole
    4 long bonds
    8 short bonds

Note:
1 The worksheet is designed for ball and
spring/stick models and will have to be
revised if alternative models are used.
2 The models are conveniently supplied in
a plastic bag with a checklist on a card
inside.

This follows on from Worksheet **C2A**. It is designed for use alongside sections
C2.4 and **C2.5**. Pupils who work more rapidly can be asked to attempt the
questions in those sections after they have finished the model-making.

Further information

Petrochemicals
The Education Service Departments of the main oil companies provide a variety
of materials which can be used to complement this topic including: films/videos,
worksheets, booklets and wallcharts. (See the Appendix for addresses.)

Science and Technology in Society
The SATIS unit 105 "The Bigger the Better" is a data analysis exercise about
crackers; it covers economic aspects of the industry and illustrates the
importance of ethene.

Unit 1002 "Quintonal: an industrial hazard" is a simulation exercise
concerning industrial safety.

University of York Science Education Group

The unit *Transporting chemicals* in Salters' Chemistry includes a consideration of the issues involved in the location of the chemical industry. The hazard warnings used when chemicals are transported are described.

The Chemistry in Action series includes a unit called *Cracking the problem* which puts pupils in the position of a technician employed in a petrochemical plant. The problem is to discover the source of an unpleasant "gassy" smell which is annoying local residents.

Chapter C3   Chemicals from plants

Purposes

Knowledge and understanding

At the end of this chapter all pupils should:

1 appreciate the wide range of useful products from plant sources

2 know that sugars, starch and cellulose are carbohydrates

3 know that carbohydrates are compounds of carbon, hydrogen and oxygen

4 know that starch and cellulose are polymers of glucose

5 appreciate that protein molecules consist of long chains of amino acids.

In addition, those pupils aiming for higher grades should:

6 understand that large molecules can be separated from smaller ones by a selectively permeable membrane

7 appreciate that the bonding in carbohydrate and protein molecules is essentially the same as in simpler carbon compounds

8 know that amino acids are compounds of carbon, hydrogen, oxygen, nitrogen and (sometimes) sulphur.

Processes and problem solving

Graphical and symbolic representation
For most pupils it will be enough to describe carbohydrate and protein polymers as monomer "beads" on a polymer "string". However Worksheet **C3C** provides an opportunity for some pupils to make models of these more complex molecules to see that in principle they are the same as simpler molecules and that the same bonding rules apply. Questions 10, 11, 14, 17, 25, and 27 give further practice in the use of molecular and graphical formulae.

Observation
Worksheet **C3B** provides an opportunity to make observations while carrying out test-tube tests on carbohydrate solutions.

Interpretation and application
Questions 18–24 ask pupils to use their knowledge of carbohydrates to interpret the results of the experiment described in box 2 on page 52 of the pupils' book. Similarly, question 34 asks for an explanation of a problem which can spoil jam.

Planning and carrying out investigations
The problem posed in box 1 on page 48 is included as a possible practical problem for the pupils to investigate.

Timing   4–7 periods, depending on the route taken.

Suggested routes   Alternative routes through this chapter are suggested in figure C3.

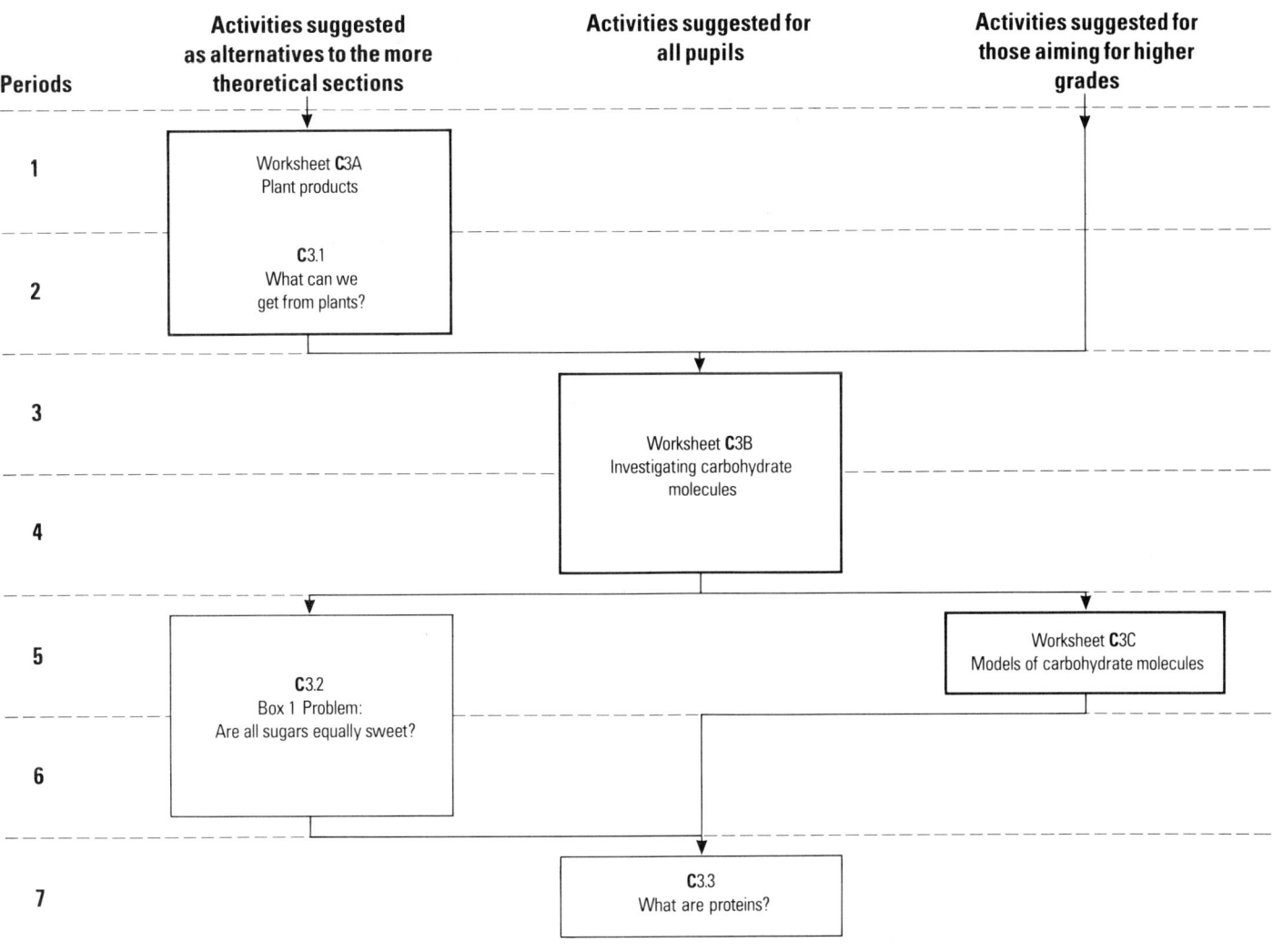

Figure C3

Opportunities for co-ordination

This chapter provides the chemical background needed for Chapters B3 to B6 and B8. Section C3.4 might be omitted at a first reading of the chapter and then returned to later as a revision topic once the pupils have met enzymes in Biology. Careful co-ordination with Biology is needed at the beginning because this chapter may be taught in parallel with Chapter B3. The later Biology chapters should help to give pupils more confidence in their knowledge of the ideas in this chapter.

Notes and answers

C3.1   What can we get from plants?

This section is designed to emphasize the extent to which we depend on plants. The pictures speak for themselves. The pupils might be asked to make a collection of pictures from magazines and other sources, and to produce their own illustrated introduction to this topic in their notes.

    Worksheet C3A is designed to be used in conjunction with this section.

C3.2   What are carbohydrates?

This can be developed in parallel with the introduction to photosynthesis in Chapter **B**3. There are only three elements in carbohydrates, but the molecules are much more complex than the hydrocarbons studied in Chapter **C**2. Pupils will need time to relate to the models and representations of molecules used in this chapter; hence the importance of Worksheet **C**3C.

The problem in box 1 "Are all sugars equally sweet?" could be used simply as a planning exercise. However, it raises problems of experimental design which will become much more apparent if the pupils are able to try out their plans. (See under Practical work.)

The experiment in box 2 on page 52 is designed to show pupils that they can use their knowledge of carbohydrates to interpret results. It is worth trying this as a group activity in class. The ideas raised will be important in Biology Chapter **B**5 where pupils investigate digestion. It may help to set up the experiment as a demonstration (see under Practical work). For those pupils who may go on to A-level, this experiment provides a possible introduction to the concept of dynamic equilibrium. There is no need to mention the term at this stage, but discussion of the experiment can lead to the idea that the smaller molecules continue to move freely in and out of the tubing in both directions until the concentrations are the same inside and outside the tube. Thereafter the rates of movement into and out of the tube are the same and there is no apparent change.

Questions 6–9 revise photosynthesis, first introduced in Chapter **B**3.

Questions 10–15 can be answered in conjunction with Worksheet **C**3C. The method of polymerizing glucose to make starch is different from that used to make poly(ethene). The difference is noted but the terms "condensation polymerization" and "addition polymerization" are not used here.

C3.3   What are proteins?

In Biology, the pupils need to know that proteins consist of long chains of amino acids. It also helps if they know that the five main elements in amino acids are carbon, hydrogen, and oxygen, together with nitrogen and sulphur.

The questions in this section reinforce the point that biological molecules can be understood in the same terms as simpler molecules.

C3.4   How does all this clever chemistry happen in living things?

It may seem odd to mention the process of inversion and not to use the more general and chemically useful word "hydrolysis". It is no part of this course to explain inversion in terms of the effect of sugar solutions on polarized light. Here the word is just a name for the reaction which splits sucrose into glucose and fructose. The justification for mentioning it is that it crops up regularly on food labels. The importance of inversion in the manufacture of confectionery is discussed in Chapter 9 of Nuffield Home Economics *Food science*. (Note that the formula of sucrose is incorrect in the first edition of that book.)

Worksheet **C**3D is one of a number which have been designed to help pupils to study the text. This type of worksheet is discussed in the Introduction to Chemistry in this *Guide*. The worksheets can be reused if they are protected by plastic covers or envelopes. The marking of the text can then be done with washable pens and later removed. However, where possible the pupils should be allowed to keep the sheets they have worked on as models to remind them of how they studied the information.

Practical work

Worksheet C3A   Plant products

REQUIREMENTS

Each group of pupils will need:
Copy of Worksheet C3A

The teacher will need:
Set of slides (see note 1)
Slide projector

Note:
1 The idea is to have a set of slides showing local examples of plant products familiar to the pupils and in a context they recognize. The cheapest way of getting a suitable set is to ask a senior pupil, members of a photography club, or a member of staff to take them. Pupils are likely to be much more interested in examples in and around the school. They will also enjoy seeing people they know in the pictures. The captions to figures 3.1 to 3.9 in section C3.1 of the Chemistry book include ideas for possible pictures. (See also Worksheet C8C.)

Worksheet C3B   Investigating carbohydrate molecules

REQUIREMENTS

Each group of pupils will need (see note 1):
Copy of Worksheet C3B (printed on two sides)
Copy of the planning sheet (Worksheet C0)
3 test-tubes in rack
Beaker, 250 ml
Tripod and gauze
Burner and mat
Measuring cylinder, 10 ml
Dropping pipette
Thermometer, 0–100 °C
Stopwatch or stopclock
Eye protection

Access to:
Iodine solution (12.7 g iodine and 20 g potassium iodide in 40 ml water, diluted to 1000 ml) in a dropper bottle
Benedict's solution (see note 2) in a dropper bottle
Glucose solution (10 g in 100 ml); allow 10 ml per group
Fructose solution (10 g in 100 ml); allow 10 ml per group
Fresh sucrose solution (10 g in 100 ml); allow 20 ml per group
Starch solution (see note 3); allow 10 ml per group
Samples of glucose, fructose, sucrose and starch as solids
0.1 mol/L dilute hydrochloric acid (see note 4) labelled "stomach acid"; allow 25 ml per group
1 mol/L sodium carbonate solution (10.6 g of the anhydrous compound in 100 ml water) in dropper bottle
Indicator paper
Distilled water
Balance

Notes:
1 The pupils are asked to make their own plans for the investigation on side 2 of the worksheet, and so some modification of this list may be necessary.
2 Benedict's solution is made by dissolving 17.3 g of sodium citrate and 10 g of anhydrous sodium carbonate in 85 ml of water. Then 1.73 g $CuSO_4 \cdot 5H_2O$ is dissolved in 15 ml water and added to the citrate/carbonate solution with constant stirring.
3 The starch solution must be fresh. Make a cream of 1 g soluble starch in a little cold water. Pour this into 100 ml boiling water and continue to boil until the solution is clear.
4 The stomach acid does not have to be accurately 0.1 mol/L. Dilute 25 ml of 2 mol/L hydrochloric acid with water to make 500 ml.

For the initial tests it is convenient to supply the carbohydrates already in solution, but samples of the solids are required for the investigation on side 2 of the worksheet. This activity covers all the main carbohydrates mentioned in Chapter C3. Benedict's solution distinguishes glucose and fructose from sucrose and starch. There seems no advantage, at this level, in introducing the term "reducing sugar".

It will save time if each working group only tackles two of the carbohydrates for their investigation on side 2. They should then be advised to try one compound which is demonstrably affected by acid (starch or sucrose) and one which will not seem to change according to the tests used (either glucose or fructose).

Worksheet C3C   Models of carbohydrate molecules

REQUIREMENTS

Each group of pupils will need:
Copy of Worksheet **C3C** (see note 1)
Set of ball and spring/stick models (see
note 2):
  6 black atoms, four hole
  6 red atoms, two hole
  12 white atoms, one hole
  12 short springs
  12 long springs

Notes:
1 The worksheet is designed for ball and
spring/stick models and will have to be
revised if alternative models are used.
2 The models are conveniently supplied in
a plastic bag with a checklist on a card
inside.

There are no questions on the worksheet. Questions 10–15 and 28–32 can be
answered in conjunction with these model-building activities.

Some pupils may be puzzled by the different representations of glucose
molecules in figures 3.14 and 3.15. Starch is a polymer of the alpha form of
glucose, while cellulose is a polymer of the beta form. With models it is easy to
show the difference between these two forms and this should be enough to satisfy
the curiosity of those interested. Pupils are not expected to remember the details of
these differences.

Box 1 Problem: Are all sugars equally sweet?

REQUIREMENTS

*The precise requirements will depend on the
plans made by the pupils. For reasons of
safety it will be sensible to provide:*
Copy of the planning sheet
  (Worksheet **C0**)
Drinking straws
Disposable cups

Access to:
Selection of sugars (in bottles or packets
  which are new, or reserved for use in
  this investigation)
Balance
Plastic spoons (to be used as spatulas)
Measuring jugs (or some method of
  measuring volumes of water not using
  laboratory measuring cylinders)

Safety:
Ideally this experiment should not be done in a chemistry laboratory.

The main purpose of this experiment is to explore the problems of designing an
experiment which will give meaningful results. Different groups can try alternative
approaches and then compare the results. Some of the aspects of the design of the
experiment which pupils have to consider are hinted at in box 1 on page 48.

As a result of doing this investigation, the pupils will become more familiar with
the nature of carbohydrates and be aware of sugars as a class of compounds.

This is one of a number of practical investigations suggested during the course.
No pupil is expected to tackle all of them (see Chapter 3 "Skills and processes").

Teacher demonstration: Molecules and membranes

REQUIREMENTS

The teacher will need:
Visking tubing, 15 cm length soaked in
  distilled water
Strong, fine thread to tie the tubing
Boiling-tube
Test-tube rack
Plastic syringe, 25 ml
Burner and mat
Eye protection

Access to:
Glucose solution (see the notes on
  Worksheet **C3B**)
Starch solution (as above)
Distilled water
Iodine solution (as above)
Benedict's solution (as above)

This demonstration might be set up when the pupils are asked to think about the
experiment in box 2 on page 52.

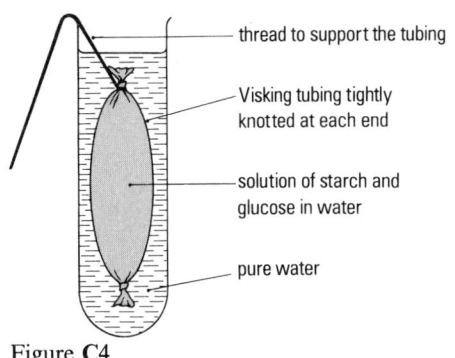

- thread to support the tubing
- Visking tubing tightly knotted at each end
- solution of starch and glucose in water
- pure water

Figure **C4**

Further information

Procedure

1 Close one end of a 15-cm length of Visking tubing by tying it tightly. Wet the other end so that you can open it up.

2 Use a syringe (without a needle) to fill the tube nearly to the top with a mixture of glucose and starch solutions.

3 Tie a tight knot at the top of the tube, leaving a length of thread which you can use to hold the tubing.

4 Rinse the outside of the tubing thoroughly under the tap.

5 Put the tubing in a boiling-tube and then fill the tube with distilled water.

Nuffield Home Economics

The publications of this course include a variety of activities relevant to this chapter including experiments. The worksheets are also useful. Among the relevant sections are:

The Basic Course pages 72–7.
Food science pages 20–1, 60–7, 106–9.
Nutrition pages 31–3.
Worksheets for the Basic Course: M1, M19b and c.
Worksheets for Food science: FSM3a and b, FSM4, FSM6, FSM7, FSM8a and b.

Nuffield Science 13 to 16

The module *Meddling with molecules* provides an alternative approach to parts of this topic. Experiments include the use of chromatography to identify the products when starch is hydrolysed with acid or with an enzyme. This chromatography experiment could be done here to show how complex biological molecules can be investigated. It might replace the experiment to analyse an alloy in Chapter **C7** because it involves the same range of techniques. (The chromatography experiment is also described in Revised Nuffield Chemistry *Teachers' guide II*, page 270–3.)

Science and Technology in Society

Unit 1004 "Lavender" includes a demonstration of the use of steam distillation to extract a perfume.

Chapter **C4**   **Chemicals and rocks**

Purposes

Knowledge and understanding

At the end of this chapter all pupils should:

1 appreciate that rocks are an important source of chemicals including metals

2 understand that some minerals are relatively pure chemical compounds

3 appreciate that geological timescales are very long compared with human life-times

4 understand the names and formulae of minerals given in tables of data

5 appreciate the economic importance of salt and limestone and be aware of the need for alkali made from these raw materials

6 know that heating and electrolysis are methods used to split up compounds

7 appreciate that economic, social and environmental issues may be involved when minerals are mined.

In addition, those pupils aiming for higher grades should:

8 know the meaning of the terms electrode, electrolyte, anode and cathode

9 be aware that there are patterns in the results of electrolysis experiments which can be used to predict the likely products at the electrodes

10 understand the terms oxidation and reduction in terms of the addition and removal of oxygen.

Processes and problem solving

Graphical and symbolic representation
The description of common minerals and the interpretation of the account of the alum industry provides more practice in the use of chemical formulae. See questions 3, 8, 12, and 14.

Using apparatus and measuring instruments
Worksheet **C4A** involves techniques of heating, filtering, neutralizing, evaporating and crystallizing. Worksheet **C4C** involves setting up a circuit and testing gases.

Observation
During the electrolysis of brine (Worksheet **C4C**) pupils have to observe the changes at the electrodes.

Interpretation and application
The experiments described in boxes 3 and 4 on pages 72–3 ask pupils to look for patterns in the results and make predictions.

The pupils' book provides opportunities for pupils to show that they can use their knowledge to interpret the accounts of industrial processes including the alum industry, the production of chemicals from salt and limestone and the extraction of aluminium. Questions 25 and 26 are based on aspects of the work of Humphry Davy.

Planning and carrying out investigations
Pupils are asked to devise a method for finding out how much copper there is in malachite. They may also be asked to devise their own method for making alum from shale given the information in the text and the prompting in box 2 on page 65.

Communication skills
The Limestone Inquiry provides an opportunity for pupils to take part in discussion, and then to argue a case based on technical information.

Problem solving
Those aiming for higher grades should be able to work out the percentage composition of a compound, given its formula and a table of atomic masses.

Timing

12–13 periods, depending on the route taken.

Suggested routes

A common route is suggested for most of this chapter. Routes diverge to allow time for some pupils to be introduced to calculations based on formulae.

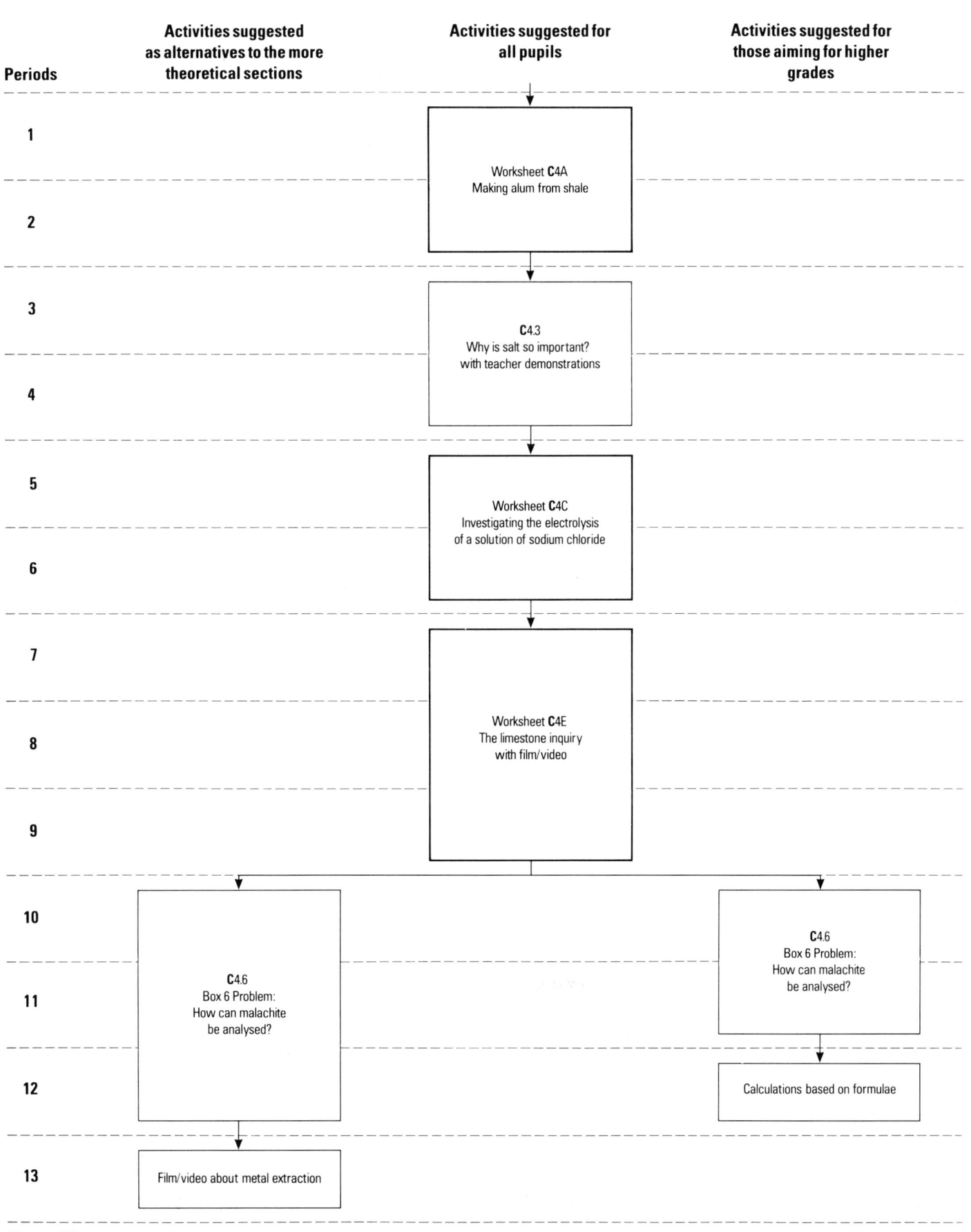

Figure **C**5

Opportunities for co-ordination

Section **C**4.1 gives an indication of the geological timescale which is also useful background for Chapter **B**23. Sections **C**4.3 and **C**4.4 can be used to provide examples to illustrate Chapter **B**17.

Section **C**4.3 gives pupils experience of electrolytes as a class of electrical conductors and this is useful background for Chapter **P**16.

Notes and answers

C4.1   What is the difference between a rock and a mineral?

This section provides links with work which pupils may have done previously in science or during a geography course. It provides a context for the rest of the chapter. Pupils are not required to have detailed knowledge of this section for examination purposes.

If possible the pupils might be shown specimens of rocks and minerals. The pupils can be asked to discuss answers to some of the questions 2–5. (See Further information for details of a key which can be used to identify a limited range of rocks.)

Box 1 and questions 2 and 3 remind pupils of the basic rules for naming simple inorganic compounds.

C4.2   How was alum made from rocks?

The main purpose of Worksheet **C**4A is to give pupils the satisfaction of getting a good yield of an attractive product from a raw material which looks very unpromising. The emphasis is on manipulative skills. The Problem: "Can you make alum from shale?" in box 2 on page 65 is included as an optional planning exercise. It is designed to help pupils to use two-dimensional line diagrams to draw apparatus.

Pupils will not be required to remember the history of the alum industry. Worksheet **C**4B is included to help pupils focus on the main points in the passage. Questions 5–17 are also designed to encourage pupils to reflect on what they are reading and relate it to other knowledge.

For example, question 5 sets political and social events alongside some of the key developments in science and technology from 1500 to 1900.

Question 13 raises some of the issues to do with the location of industry.

Question 14 includes some daunting formulae but the questions only require a recognition of symbols and are intended to illustrate the fact that chemical changes involve the rearrangement of elements.

Questions 16 and 17 are numerical problems in an unusual context.

Answers to selected questions

16 Mass of potash produced = 377 tonnes.

17a Mass of ammonia = 11 kg = 0.011 tonnes per person per year.
b Number of people required = 341.

C4.3   Why is salt so important?

Pupils are likely to have studied rock salt previously and purified it in the laboratory. The section starts with text, diagrams and questions (18–21) which revise these topics.

Electrolysis is introduced as a process which decomposes compounds and so rearranges elements. There is no need, at this stage, to attempt to explain the changes in terms of ions and electron transfer. Ions are first introduced in Chapter **C**5. Many pupils find it hard to understand the theory of electrolysis;

the detailed treatment of electrode processes is delayed in the text until Chapter C18. By this time atomic structure will have been described in Physics.

Pupils will not be required to remember the details of the work of Humphry Davy. The account of his work is included to show that science is the result of human activity and imagination. The first, optional, demonstration repeats Davy's "capital experiment" and is worth doing if there is time. Alternatively pupils might be shown the electrolysis of lead(II) bromide as an example of the decomposition of a molten salt. Worksheet **C4C** gives pupils some practical experience of electrolysis. They are told what to do and the emphasis is on careful investigation, accurate observations, and discussion of the results.

Box 3 Experiment: The electrolysis of molten compounds
Box 4 Experiment: The electrolysis of compounds in solution

Two experiments are described on pages 72–3 to give pupils the opportunity to look for patterns in the results. The emphasis should be on the activity of seeking the patterns, **not** on remembering them. Discussion of questions 27–41 can follow the experiment on Worksheet **C4C**. This will not be suitable for all classes.

Questions 27–32 suggest this pattern:

- metals are deposited at the negative electrode;
- non-metals are released at the positive electrode.

Questions 33–41 explore what happens when water is also present. The results show that water must get involved in electrolysis.

- Metals low in the activity series are deposited at the negative electrode.
- Hydrogen is formed at the negative electrode if the metal is high in the activity series.
- Oxygen is usually formed at the positive electrode unless the salt is a chloride, bromide or iodide.
- If the salt is a chloride, bromide or iodide, then the halogen is formed at the positive electrode.

Note that there is no need to mention the complication of active electrodes which get involved in electrolysis, but this may be raised by pupils who have had experience of electroplating.

Worksheet **C4D** is included to help pupils to study and make sense of the description of the manufacture of sodium hydroxide and chlorine from salt. In this course pupils are not expected to remember details of manufacturing operations for examination purposes. They are expected to show that they have experience of using their knowledge of chemistry to make sense of accounts of related industrial processes.

C4.4   Why is limestone important?

Worksheet **C4E** is a role-play exercise about the quarrying of limestone. It highlights the importance of limestone as a raw material and raises many of the environmental and social issues involved when mineral resources are exploited on a large scale. If the pupils are unfamiliar with limestone scenery it is very desirable to show the ICI video "Limestone", which gives a picture of a large quarry at work and describes the chemistry and uses of limestone, as well as discussing the problem of what to do with a quarry when it has been worked out.

The text of section **C4.4** summarizes much of the information involved in Worksheet **C4E**.

C4.5   Where do metals come from?

The extraction of aluminium is included here as another example of the importance of electrolysis. A film, video, or set of slides will help pupils to gain some impression of the scale of the process. Suitable visual aids are included under Further information.

Worksheet **C4F** is designed to help the pupils study this section.

Questions 47–53 cover the extraction and uses of aluminium.

Answers to selected questions

48 About 70 years.

51 The bulb will run for 150 hours.

C4.6   How much?

The question "How much?" is very important in chemistry, and so quantitative chemistry has been covered at several levels in this course. The concept "amount of substance" (measured in moles) is introduced in Chapter **C5** for the benefit of those who are likely to go on to more advanced study of the subject. In this section a simpler treatment uses atomic masses to work out the percentage of metals in metal ores.

Box 6 Problem: How can malachite be analysed?

An important planning exercise is given in box 6 on page 82. This example has been included to illustrate the importance of quantitative chemical analysis and the difficulties involved. It has been chosen because pupils are expected to have had experience of a qualitative investigation of malachite in previous years. So they are in a position to think about the problem.

Pupils should be allowed to attempt any procedure which is safe even if it will not lead to a satisfactory result. In this context they will learn as much from failure as from success. The planning is best carried out in small groups in class, and questions 54–8 are included to guide the discussions.

Answers to selected questions

59a 39.3 % sodium
b 70 % iron
c 77.5 % lead
d 78.8 % tin
e 34.8 % copper

Practical work

Worksheet C4A   Making alum from shale

REQUIREMENTS

Each group of pupils will need:
Copy of Worksheet **C4A** (see note 1)
Tin lid
Beaker, 250 ml
Watchglass to cover the beaker
Conical flask, 250 ml
Funnel
Evaporating basin
Burner, tripod, gauze and mat
Tongs
Eye protection

Access to:
High alumina shale, 10 g per group, in container with spatula (see note 2)
Dilute sulphuric acid (2 mol/L), 20 ml per group, with measuring cylinder
Potassium hydroxide solution (2 mol/L), allow 20 ml per group, with measuring cylinder (see note 3)
Full range, or Universal, indicator paper
Filter paper
Balance to weigh 20 g

Notes:

1 The worksheet will not be needed if the pupils have made their own plans based on the problem in box 2.

2 The high alumina shale is available from: Mineral Industry Manpower and Careers Unit, Prince Consort Road, London SW7 2BP. It should preferably be broken up into small pieces in advance.

3 Stress to pupils that alkali (potassium hydroxide) in the eye is **more** dangerous than acid of comparable strength.

The main point of this experiment is to give the pupils the satisfaction of getting a good yield of attractive alum crystals. Good results are achieved using the high alumina shale described in note 2. The shale should be broken into pieces about 0.25–0.5 cm across.

A variety of types of fired clay may be used instead of shale, and scrap unglazed pottery from the art department can be crushed and investigated as a possible source of alum.

Trials have shown that the main part of this experiment can be completed in a double period. Filtering takes time but is quicker with fluted filter papers. The filtrate may be greenish due to impurities, but this does not affect the appearance of the crystals at the end.

During step **d** the contents of the flask should be swirled vigorously while adding the potassium hydroxide solution. This limits precipitation due to local excesses of alkali. Sometimes an orange-brown precipitate appears, so filtering may be necessary at the end of step **d** before the solution is evaporated and allowed to crystallize.

Worksheet C4C   Investigating the electrolysis of a solution of sodium chloride

REQUIREMENTS

Each group of pupils will need:
Copy of Worksheet **C4C**
Electrolysis cell (see note 1)
Glass rod
2 test-tubes, to collect the gases over the electrodes
2 connecting wires, each fitted with a crocodile clip at one end and a plug at the other
d.c. supply, 6 V (see note 2)
Stand, boss and clamp
Eye protection

Access to:
Sodium chloride solution (30 g/L), allow 80–100 ml per group
Indicator paper
Splints

Notes:
1 The cell must be large enough to allow the pupils to investigate what is happening around the electrodes. A home-made cell is easily made by cutting the top off a plastic chemical bottle and fitting it with a large bung and carbon electrodes as shown in the diagram on the worksheet.
2 Make sure that the lab pack cannot give more than 20 volts.

The worksheet tells the pupils what to do: the activity is an exercise in observation and interpretation. They should be able to identify hydrogen by showing that it burns with a pop, and chlorine by its smell and bleaching action. The experiment illustrates the fact that the water has to be taken into account when aqueous solutions are electrolysed. This point is explored further in the Experiments described in boxes 3 and 4 on pages 72–3.

Worksheet C4E   The Limestone Inquiry

REQUIREMENTS

Each student will need:
Copies of the General briefing sheets and a copy of one of the Briefing sheets (1 to 7).
For a class of thirty, 30 copies of the General briefing sheets and 5 copies of each of the Briefing sheets will be needed.

Procedure

1 Preliminary

Tell the class that in the next lesson they will be taking part in a Public Inquiry about a proposed extension of a limestone quarry.

Divide them into seven groups. One group will play the role of Inspectors and organize the Inquiry. They should elect a chairperson to do the talking. Members of this group need copies of Briefing sheet 1. The Inspectors play a key role because they control the Inquiry. It is important to have pupils with appropriate personal qualities in these roles, particularly the Chairperson.

Three groups will be in favour of the quarry extension. They will represent Limeco, the quarry operators (2), the industrial users of limestone (3) and the trades unions (4).

Three groups will oppose the extension. They will represent the National Park Authority (5), local residents (6) and the local conservation group (7).

Issue each member of the class with copies of the General briefing sheets, and their Briefing sheets (1 to 7) according to the group they are in. They should study these sheets in class or for homework (or both).

In school trials it has been found necessary to allow plenty of time for pupils to assimilate the information and discuss it together. This can be a good point to show a film/video to give pupils a picture of a quarry and the surrounding landscape.

2 On the day of the Inquiry

Each group should spend some time together using the Briefing sheets, their notes and other sources of information to plan how they are going to present their arguments.

The Public Inquiry should as far as possible be organized by the team of Inspectors. It may be better to do this in a classroom, or laboratory where there is movable furniture, so that the Inspectors can arrange the seating suitably. The Inspectors should be encouraged to take firm control of the Inquiry to ensure that everyone gets a fair hearing.

A suggested sequence for the Inquiry is given on Briefing sheet 1.

Box 6 Problem: How can malachite be analysed?

REQUIREMENTS

These will depend on the plans made by the pupils, but each group is likely to need:
Beaker, 100 ml
Boiling-tube
Glass rod
Tongs
Burner, tripod, gauze and mat
Funnel
Eye protection

Some groups may also need some of the following:
Hard-glass test-tube with a small hole blown near the closed end
Bung and short delivery tube to fit the test-tube
Rubber tubing to connect the delivery tube to the gas supply
Low voltage, d.c. supply
2 copper electrodes, 4×6 cm or bigger
Connecting wires with crocodile clips
Stand with clamp

Access to:
"Malachite" (i.e. powdered copper(II) carbonate), allow 2–3 g per group
Dilute sulphuric acid, 2 mol/L
Zinc metal, foil or powder
Filter paper
Balance

Safety
Care may need to be taken over what pupils think of doing – some procedures might be hazardous.

At the start, pupils may be shown samples of rock which contain the mineral malachite but for their own experiments they should be provided with pure "malachite" (i.e. copper(II) carbonate) on the assumption that the mineral processing stages have been completed.

The main purpose of the activity is to give pupils a chance to explore the problems involved in carrying out a quantitative analysis. Some pupils will respond to the idea that their group is competing for the contract to be awarded to an analytical firm by a mining company.

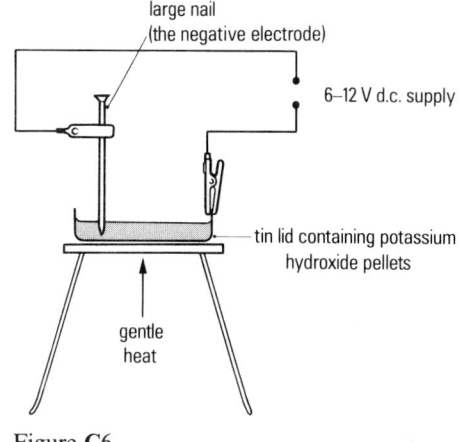

large nail
(the negative electrode)

6–12 V d.c. supply

tin lid containing potassium
hydroxide pellets

gentle
heat

Figure C6

Teacher demonstration: Davy's capital experiment

REQUIREMENTS

The teacher will need:
d.c. supply, 6–12 V
Iron nail, 5–10 cm long
Small tin lid (about 1.5 cm deep)
Burner, tripod and mat
Stand with boss and clamp
Spatula
2 connecting wires, with crocodile clips at
   one end and plugs at the other
Beaker, 100 ml
Eye protection and protective gloves
Safety screens to protect teacher and pupils

Access to:
Hexane, or naphtha
Potassium hydroxide pellets
Desiccator

Figure C6 shows the arrangement for this experiment. The apparatus gives small pellets of potassium at the point of the nail, quite safely and reliably, provided that the conditions below are observed. The goggles and gloves are to protect against any spray from the molten alkali. The pellets may even be skimmed off, using a small spatula, and placed quickly under a hydrocarbon solvent.

Procedure

Before the lesson. Fill a small tin lid, which should be about 1–1.5 cm deep, with pellets of potassium hydroxide and warm until molten. If necessary add more pellets until a depth of at least 0.5 cm is obtained. Cool in a desiccator. It is essential that the potash should be really dry before starting the electrolysis. Set up the rest of the apparatus but do not put the tin lid with the electrolyte in position until you are absolutely ready to begin the demonstration.

The demonstration. Adjust the nail so that its point penetrates the surface of the potash, but does not touch the base of the tin lid. Heat gently, just below the nail, and switch on the power pack at 6 V. It is only necessary to heat until electrolysis has started. After that the less heating the better. (Davy achieved fusion by using a higher voltage with slightly damp terminals.) Small silvery globules appear. Their size can be about 2 mm; optimum conditions are best found by trial and error, adjusting the voltage and rate of heating to get the desired results. Use a spatula to lift out some of the globules and put them under a hydrocarbon solvent in a small beaker. It is possible to make the potassium burn at the cathode by raising the voltage. However, this should only be attempted with a safety screen in place or in a fume cupboard, and if you are confident about doing it after preliminary practice.

The next demonstration is more familiar but is also optional. Pupils should have seen at least one example of the electrolysis of a molten compound before studying the results of the experiments in box 3 on page 72.

Teacher demonstration: The electrolysis of lead(II) bromide

REQUIREMENTS

The teacher will need:
d.c. supply, 10–12 V
Demonstration ammeter, 3A
4 connecting wires, crocodile clips and plugs
Rheostat
2 carbon electrodes
U-tube
Stand, with boss and clamp
Burner and mat
Pestle and mortar
Eye protection

Access to:
Lead(II) bromide
Fume cupboard

This demonstration must be carried out in a fume cupboard because poisonous vapours are given off if the apparatus is overheated.

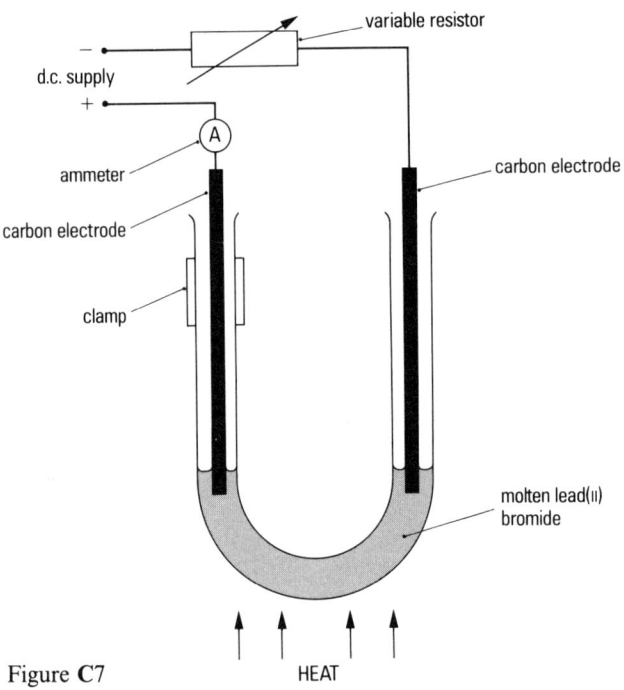

Figure **C7**

HEAT

Procedure

1 Set up the apparatus as shown in figure **C7** and heat the bottom of the U-tube with a small flame. You may have to add more lead(II) bromide when it starts to melt to provide an adequate depth of liquid, but this can be a tricky operation and is best avoided if possible.

2 Adjust the rheostat to give a current of about 1 A; bromine vapour will then be seen almost at once around the positive electrode.

3 Allow electrolysis to continue for about five minutes, then pour the molten contents of the U-tube into a mortar. If you gently crush the solid lead(II) bromide you should discover a small bead of metallic lead.

Further information

Nuffield Science 13 to 16
Section 4 and Worksheet C in the *Keys and detection* module show how a limited range of rock types can be identified using a key.

Nuffield Secondary Science
Theme 7, *Using materials*, page 185 describes a method for using electrolysis to make chlorine and bleach.

Science and Technology in Society
There are three SATIS units, published by the ASE, which can be used as alternatives to the Limestone Inquiry:

Unit 307 "Chemicals from salt" places more emphasis on economic and technical problems but also includes social issues. This exercise requires the pupils to work in groups to answer a series of questions. There is no need for a debate involving the whole class.

Unit 502 "The Coal Mine Project" is more like the Limestone Inquiry, but the imaginary situation supposes that major coal deposits have been found near the school, so the pupils are thoroughly familiar with the locality which may be affected by major industrial developments.

Unit 1001 "Chocolate chip mining" is a practical, problem-solving activity linked to an analysis of data about copper mining.

University of York Science Education Group

The following units in the Salters' Chemistry course can be used as a source of alternative activities and questions: *Buildings*, *Minerals*, and *Making and using electricity*.

The unit *Salt solution* in the Chemistry in Action series deals with the mining of salt and the environmental aspects of potash mining.

ICI

The ICI Video "Limestone" is very useful and can be purchased from the Argus Film and Video library. (See Appendix.)

ICI Mond Division have some useful resource material about limestone and salt. (See Appendix.)

National Parks

The Council for the National Parks distribute a kit, *Know your National Parks*, which includes factsheets on many aspects of the parks including geology and mineral resources. (See Appendix.)

Topic C2   Materials in use

Chapter C5   Materials and structures

Purposes

Knowledge and understanding

At the end of this chapter all pupils should:

1 understand some of the vocabulary used to describe the properties of materials, including words such as: strong, weak, stiff, flexible, hard, elastic, transparent, opaque, porous, impermeable, conductor, insulator, biodegradable and rotproof

2 appreciate that there is a connection between the properties of materials and their chemical structure

3 understand the distinction between a molecular structure and a giant structure, with the help of a limited range of simple examples such as: water, oxygen, carbon dioxide, diamond, graphite, and silicon dioxide

4 know that an ion is a charged particle and that the compounds of metals with non-metals are ionic.

In addition, those pupils aiming for higher grades should:

5 appreciate that the forces holding atoms together within molecules are much stronger than the forces between molecules

6 understand why ionic compounds only conduct when molten or when in solution

7 know that the quantity "amount of substance" has a precise meaning in chemistry and that amounts are measured in moles.

Processes and problem solving

Graphical and symbolic representation
The chapter is based on the extensive use of models to describe structures. Symbols for ions are introduced, and pupils aiming for higher grades should be able to work out the formulae of salts if given a table of ions with their charges.

Observation
There are opportunities to observe changes during heating and electrolysis experiments (Worksheets **C5A** and **C5B**).

Interpretation and application
Pupils are asked to look for patterns in the properties of substances and relate the patterns to the known structure of substances (see questions 12 and 24 to 26).

When doing the experiments described on Worksheets C5A and C5B, pupils try to interpret their observations in terms of atoms, molecules and ions.

Problem solving

Problems such as question 8 ask pupils to determine the physical state of substances under stated conditions with the help of tables of data. Question 23 is based on a key for determining the structure of substances with the help of data tables.

Questions 28 to 37 are quantitative problems based on formulae and equations. The reactions chosen for the examples have been met in previous chapters.

Timing

9–11 periods, depending on the route taken.

Suggested routes

Those aiming for higher grades spend more time on this chapter to gain an introduction to the idea of measuring amounts in moles. (See over.)

Opportunities for co-ordination

In Chapter **P1** the pupils will have considered the use of materials to build bridges. In that chapter they meet words such as strong, stiff, plastic, elastic and ductile. This can provide a useful lead into this chapter and Topic **C2** in general.

In Chapter **P2** states of matter are discussed in terms of particles. A model is used to discuss in general terms what happens to the atoms in a solid as the temperature is raised.

In Chemistry it is almost always necessary to be precise about the meaning of the term "particle" and to specify whether they are atoms, molecules or ions. In Physics we have tried to be specific where possible but there are times when it is more helpful to use the general term. Unfortunately there is evidence that pupils easily confuse the use of the term "particle" to mean atoms, molecules or ions, with its everyday meaning which refers to small specks of stuff such as sugar crystals and dust. For this reason we have avoided the word when possible.

This chapter introduces the idea of ions. Ions are mentioned in the context of plant growth in Chapter **B15** and in the context of ionizing radiation in Chapter **P3**.

If pupils are taking courses in CDT or Home Economics it will be worth building on their experience of materials in those contexts.

Notes and answers

C5.1   What are materials?

This section introduces pupils to some of the vocabulary used to talk about materials. Questions 1–4 are included to reinforce the ideas in the text.

C5.2   Why use models?

The treatment of structure in this course is heavily dependent on the use of models. At some point it is likely to be appropriate to discuss the advantages and limitations of chemical models. This section can be used as a basis for the discussion.

The PEEL model of ethanol is included in figure 5.10 simply to show that there are several ways of representing the same molecule. There is no intention that pupils should have any knowledge or understanding of the use of these models.

Periods	Activities suggested as alternatives to the more theoretical sections	Activities suggested for all pupils	Activities suggested for those aiming for higher grades

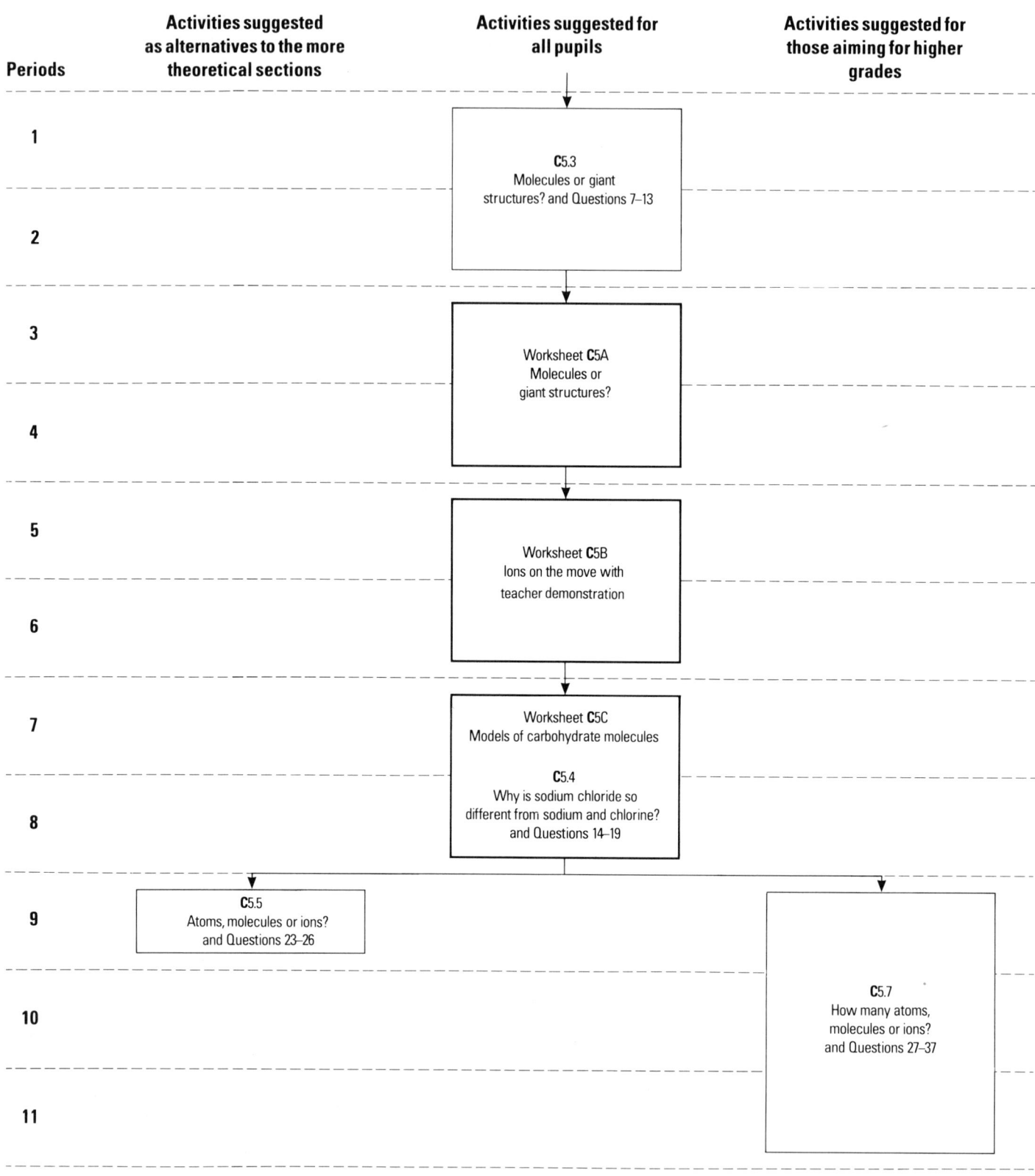

Figure C8

C5.3 Molecules or giant structures?

It may be helpful to start by exploring some of the meanings of the word "structure" which has different levels of meaning in science. The word is used in its engineering sense in Chapter **P1**. Microscopes reveal the microstructure of materials. X-ray diffraction reveals the crystal structure which describes how the atoms are arranged. But we are also interested in the atomic structure in terms of electrons, neutrons and protons.

The important thing is to be aware of the difficulties which pupils may have with the word "structure" and not to confuse them by going into all the meanings in detail. Here it is sufficient to discuss "engineering structures" and "crystal structures".

The suggested treatment makes a clear distinction between giant structures and molecules. The term *giant molecule* is deliberately avoided because it has two meanings. Some texts refer to diamond as a giant molecule on the grounds that the bonding in both small molecules and diamond is covalent. Other texts call polymers giant molecules.

For clarity, in an introductory course, it seems better to separate the words *giant* and *molecule*. In a giant structure there is a continuous two- or three-dimensional network of strong bonds. In a molecular structure there is strong bonding within the molecules but weak bonding between the molecules. Thus metals, diamond, silica, graphite, mica, and salts all have giant structures. Organic compounds, liquids and gases, and thermoplastic polymers are all molecular.

As a general rule the metal elements and compounds of metals with non-metals have giant structures. Non-metals and compounds consisting only of non-metals are normally molecular, but there are exceptions; principally diamond, graphite, silicon and silicon dioxide. These generalizations are illustrated by the summary at the end of the chapter in the Chemistry pupils' book; the information for completing the summary is in the Data section.

There is no substitute for making and handling models of structures. Time and cost are, unfortunately, limiting factors. Most models of the diamond structure are too small to bring out the idea of a giant structure, which is why figure 5.20 is so important. Worksheet J in the teachers' guide for the Nuffield 13 to 16 module *Chemical giants* is a copy of this diagram which can be duplicated for the pupils. Worksheet D in the same teachers' guide gives instructions for making a diamond model from polystyrene spheres. A diamond structure can also be built up using the carbon atoms from a set of ball-and-spring/stick models as used in Chapters C2 and C3.

C5.4   Why is sodium chloride so different from sodium and chlorine?

In Chapter C4 the pupils investigate electrolysis and look for patterns in the results. At that stage there is no attempt to explain the observations. This section starts the introduction to ionic theory.

Faraday invented the idea and the name "ion" long before electrons were discovered. In the publications for this course, the idea of ions is introduced and used in Biology, Chemistry and Physics before pupils are asked to think about how it is that atoms can turn into ions.

However, some teachers may wish to explain how ions are formed here, using parts of Chapter C18. If so they will have to do some introductory work on atomic structure. This requires co-ordination with the treatment in Physics, but there is no fundamental problem. The approach to atomic structure in Nuffield Co-ordinated Sciences does not involve a survey of the evidence leading to the picture of a nuclear atom with electrons. We have decided to present the model and then to show that it is plausible by demonstrating the range of problems which the model helps to solve.

Worksheet C5B and the associated teacher demonstration give evidence that there are particles on the move during electroysis. The ionic explanation for electrolysis can then be explored with the help of Worksheet **C5C**. Worksheet **C5C** is designed to help pupils with questions 17–19.

C5.5 Atoms, molecules or ions?

This section could be developed into a laboratory activity. Pupils might be asked to use the key in figure 5.36 to work out the structures of a selection of substances, given appropriate data and apparatus for testing conductivity. Note that it may be necessary to make sure that pupils do not have access to the Data section in their Chemistry book which includes the structures of most common elements and compounds.

C5.6 How can we discover the structure of substances?

Some pupils will want to know the answer to the question in the heading to this section. The section does not answer it in detail, and pupils will only be expected to be aware of the fact that modern methods for determining structure are based on X-ray diffraction and other instrumental methods.

The importance of this section is that it shows the personal involvement of scientists in their work. It demonstrates that much scientific research is a collaborative venture which may take years to develop.

Worksheet **C5D** is designed to help pupils study this section.

C5.7 How many atoms, molecules or ions?

This section starts by extending the rules for writing equations in Chapter **C1** to cover giant structures. The data tables should help here because they show the symbols normally used in equations.

The treatment of amounts of substance, here and later in the course, is designed to emphasize the usefulness of the idea as a means of making fair comparison between equal numbers of particles. Worked examples show how measuring amounts in moles can be used to interpret equations quantitatively. The examples are highly structured. The hope is that most of those pupils who tackle this section will be able to experience some success with the questions by following the examples step by step.

Note that we have deliberately avoided the term "mole concept" which does not fit with normal usage. We do not talk about the "gram concept" or the "joule concept" either! We have also been careful to use the word "amount" in Chemistry only when referring to quantities measured in moles.

Chemical formulae are taken as given. No experiments to determine formulae are included, on the grounds that it is difficult to get good results under school conditions. Also, the interpretation of the results can make the mole seem a difficult idea from the start.

We think that it helps to work in terms of molar masses with the units g/mol. This makes it possible to include the units in every stage of calculations, leading to the correct units for the final answer as shown in box 6 on page 110. This is consistent with the use of units in Physics and Biology. It is very important that those pupils who may go on to more advanced studies in science should learn to use units in a correct and consistent way from the start.

It is better to omit the work on "amount of substance" altogether, rather than to try to find pedagogical devices to allow pupils to get the right answer without really understanding what is happening. So this topic is only required of those aiming for top grades in public examinations. We have also limited the number of types of calculations.

Questions 27 and 34 to 37 refer back to a number of important reactions introduced in earlier chapters.

Answers to selected questions

28a 1 mol
b 2 mol
c 0.01 mol
d 0.1038 mol.

29a 39 g
b 216 g
c 140 g
d 32 g
e 5.6 g.

30a 40 g
b 32 g
c 414 g
d 3 g.

31a 28 g
b 71 g
c 64 g
d 63 g.

32a 1 g
b 2 g
c 88 g
d 43 g.

33a 58.3 g
b 200 g
c 78 g
d 102 g.

34 90 g

35 11.5 g

36 1.6 g

37 560 g

Practical work

Worksheet C5A   Molecules or giant structures?

REQUIREMENTS

Each group of pupils will need:
Copy of Worksheet C5A
Tin lid
Tongs
Burner, tripod and mat
Eye protection

Access to:
Small samples of the following solids
(preferably in lumps rather than as
powders): copper, iron, zinc, graphite,
silicon, sand, sodium chloride,
magnesium oxide, calcium carbonate,
candle wax, glucose, polythene, ice

Restricted access to:
Polystyrene
Small lumps, or crystals, of sulphur and
iodine

The action of heat on sulphur and iodine should only be carried out in a fume-cupboard. Teachers may prefer to demonstrate what happens to sulphur and iodine. It is also important to restrict the amounts of wax and plastics which are heated.

Worksheet C5B   Ions on the move

REQUIREMENTS

Each group of pupils will need:
Copy of Worksheet **C5B**
Microscope slide
2 crocodile clips with connecting wires
Power supply, 20 V d.c. (see note 1)
Pencil
Eye protection

Access to:
Filter paper and scissors
Tap water
Crystals of potassium manganate(VII), with
  tweezers

Note:
1 Make sure that the lab pack cannot give
more than 20 volts.

This is a reliable experiment and pupils should have no difficulty in observing the
movement of the purple colour towards the positive electrode.

The colour of other salts is likely to be too pale to give clear results. One
possibility is to moisten the filter paper with ammonia solution and then put a
crystal of copper(II) sulphate on the pencil line.

Teacher demonstration: Watching coloured ions move

REQUIREMENTS

The teacher will need:
U-tube
Stand and clamp to support U-tube
2 carbon (or preferably platinum)
  electrodes
2 long leads
Power supply, 20 V d.c.
Pipette, 25 ml
Beaker, 500 ml
Eye protection

Access to:
2 mol/L sulphuric acid
Concentrated solution of copper(II)
  chromate(VI) in 2 mol/L sulphuric
  acid and saturated with urea, allow
  40 ml (see note 1)

Note:
1 Dissolve solid copper(II) chromate(VI) in
the minimum volume of 2 mol/L sulphuric
acid, and then saturate the solution with
urea to increase its density.

The arrangement for the experiment is shown in figure **C9**. The demonstration
needs to be started early in a double period to allow time for the results to
become obvious. The class can do Worksheet **C5B** while the demonstration is
running and then come to the front in groups to look at the results.

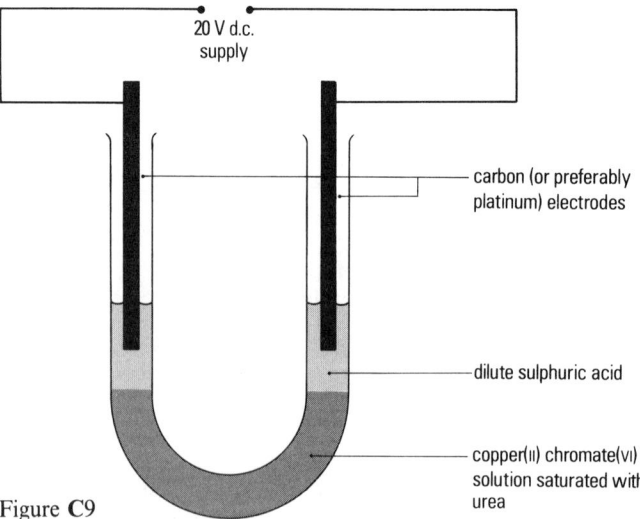

20 V d.c.
supply

carbon (or preferably
platinum) electrodes

dilute sulphuric acid

copper(II) chromate(VI)
solution saturated with
urea

Figure **C9**

Procedure
Fill the U-tube with dilute sulphuric acid to about one-third of its depth. Run in
the copper(II) chromate(VI) solution very slowly from a pipette, delivering it to
the bottom of the U-tube so that it forms a separate layer and has a clear layer

of sulphuric acid above it on both sides. Withdraw the pipette carefully to avoid mixing. (An alternative arrangement using a W-tube is described in the teachers' guide for the Nuffield Science 13 to 16 module *Charged particles*.)

Insert an electrode into each arm of the U-tube to dip into the acid layer. Connect up to a source of 20 V d.c. Results should be visible after about 10 minutes and will be clear after half an hour. If the contents of the U-tube start to get hot, cool with a large beaker of cold water.

There is an interesting series of suggestions for discussing this demonstration with a class on pages 88–94 in *Visual communication in science* (Barlex and Carré, Cambridge Science Education Series, 1985).

Worksheet C5C   Ions and electrolysis

REQUIREMENTS

Each group of pupils will need:
Copy of Worksheet C5C
Scissors
Glue, or Sellotape

Pupils can use this model in conjunction with section C5.4 in the text. They can represent the chemical change at the electrodes by turning the ion circles over and writing the atom symbols on the back. The chlorine atoms can then be joined in pairs (with glue or Sellotape).

Unless they have already studied atomic structure in Physics, pupils cannot explain how ions lose their charges and turn back into atoms at the electrodes. This idea is developed further in Chapter C18.

Further information

Nuffield Science 13 to 16
Two modules contain ideas and worksheets which can be used in conjunction with this chapter. They are: *Charged particles* and *Chemical giants*.

Unfortunately *Chemical giants* refers to polymers as "giant molecules" which introduces a confusion which we are trying to avoid.

Science and Technology in Society
The following SATIS units might be used in conjunction with this chapter:

Unit 101 "Sulphurcrete"
Unit 506 "Materials for Life – new parts for old"

Chapter C6   Glasses and ceramics

Purposes

Knowledge and understanding

At the end of this chapter all pupils should:

1 know some of the characteristic properties of common glass and ceramic articles

2 know that glass is made from silicon dioxide combined with other metal oxides

3 understand that a glass has a giant structure with a disordered arrangement of atoms

4 know that common ceramic objects are made from fired clay

5 appreciate the industrial importance of refractories

6 appreciate arguments for and against recycling materials such as glass.

Processes and problem solving

Graphical and symbolic representation
Questions 1, 4, and 5 provide further practice in the use of chemical symbols.

Using apparatus and measuring instruments
Worksheets **C6A** and **C6B** are designed to encourage pupils to take a pride in developing their practical skills.

Interpretation and application
Some pupils may concentrate on understanding the accounts of the manufacture and use of glasses and ceramics in terms of their properties.

Others will attempt to interpret the properties of glasses in terms of their structure. This may include the use of ionic theory to provide an explanation of the observation that some glasses conduct electricity when molten.

Planning and carrying out investigations
Questions 24–7 could well be the basis of a survey planned and carried out by the pupils for homework.

Problem solving
Question 6 provides further practice in the measurement of amounts in moles.

Timing

5–8 periods, depending on the route taken.

Suggested routes

This is one of the chapters for which the suggested routes soon diverge. Those who are giving attention to the theoretical aspects will need more time for the details of structure and the introduction to the idea of "amount of substance" in Chapter **C5**. They may only be able to spend 5 periods on this topic, covering just one of the worksheets. Others will spend less time on Chapter **C5** and be able to investigate ceramics and glass in greater detail. The programme allows up to 8 periods for this chapter, but there are many possible ways of extending it.

Opportunities for co-ordination

Chapter **P1** covers the use of concrete in bridges and shows that it is weak in tension. The insulating properties of brick, concrete and glass are relevant to the investigation of strategies to prevent energy loss from houses in Chapter **P9**. Sections **C6.5** and **C6.6** in this chapter show that there is an energy cost involved in the manufacture of materials. This can be taken up during the discussion of energy resources in Chapter **P12**.

The effects of quarrying and the problems of waste disposal are relevant to the whole question of the impact of industry on the environment. This is an important part of Chapter **B17**.

If there is a pottery department in the school, this chapter can provide an excellent opportunity for links between the science and art departments. All the experimental work could be based on clay and glazes. The effects of drying and firing clay to different temperatures can be investigated with small samples extruded from cork borers. The length and strength of the samples can be measured at each stage. There are also many possible investigations into the texture and colour of glazes. This work can serve to illustrate the need for accurate methods for measuring mass when making up glaze mixtures and for measuring temperature when controlling the kiln if results are to be repeatable. Other possibilities are included in the unit on *Pottery* in the Nuffield Working with Science project; this is designed for the first-year sixth and students in colleges of further education, but can be modified for use with younger pupils.

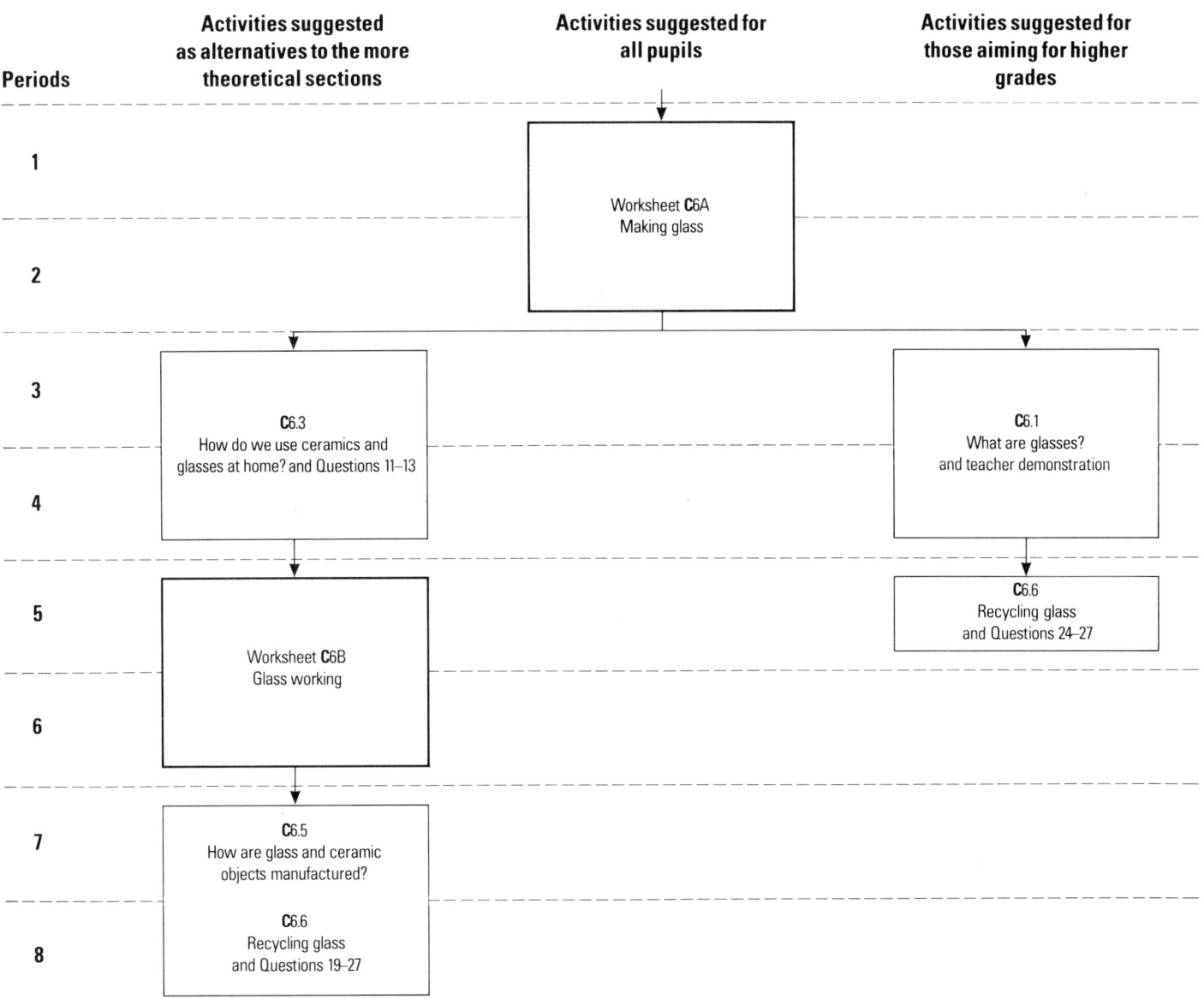

Periods	Activities suggested as alternatives to the more theoretical sections	Activities suggested for all pupils	Activities suggested for those aiming for higher grades
1		Worksheet **C6A** Making glass	
2			
3	**C6.3** How do we use ceramics and glasses at home? and Questions 11–13		**C6.1** What are glasses? and teacher demonstration
4			
5	Worksheet **C6B** Glass working		**C6.6** Recycling glass and Questions 24–27
6			
7	**C6.5** How are glass and ceramic objects manufactured?		
8	**C6.6** Recycling glass and Questions 19–27		

Figure **C10**

Notes and answers

C6.1 What are glasses?

Some pupils will not be aware that there is a great variety of glasses. A small exhibition of objects made from different types of glass might help to put across the idea (see also the notes on section C6.2).

A glass may be regarded as a supercooled liquid with such a high viscosity that it is effectively a rigid solid. It does not have the regular arrangement of atoms found in crystals. One of the most obvious similarities between glasses and liquids is the fact that they are transparent, unlike polycrystalline materials in which the many internal surfaces scatter and reflect light.

Silicon dioxide glass is difficult to melt and shape, so other oxides are added to lower the viscosity and hence the working temperature. Alkali and alkaline earth metal carbonates are included in the mixture fed to the furnace. The carbonates decompose to oxides which modify the glass giant structure by reacting to break up the network of strong and directional covalent bonds, as shown in figure **C11**.

Doubly charged calcium ions produce stronger lattice forces than singly charged sodium ions. Calcium ions also act as a bridge between two negatively

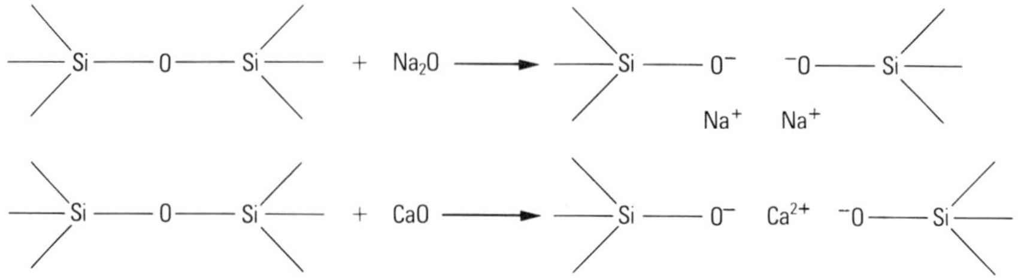

Figure **C11**

charged oxygen atoms, so they have a smaller effect on the viscosity but help to prevent a complete breakdown of the glass network.

A teacher demonstration described under Practical work provides evidence for the existence of ions in glass and helps to revise some of the ideas met in Chapter **C5**.

Answers to selected questions

6a Si:Ca ratio is 7:1
b 73.8 % SiO_2, 16.3 % Na_2O, 9.8 % CaO.

C6.2　What are ceramics?

An exhibition of ceramic objects might help to draw attention to this group of materials which we take very much for granted (see also the notes on section **C6.1**). This chapter concentrates on traditional ceramics based on clay. Lack of time prevents a review of the many new ceramic materials which are important for their electronic, magnetic, abrasive, refractory or piezo-electric properties.

There is some argument about the classification of ceramics and glasses. An American ceramicist, W.D. Kingery wrote as follows in his *Introduction to ceramics*:

> "We define ceramics as the art and science of making and using solid articles which have as their essential component, and are composed in large part of, **inorganic, non-metallic materials**. This definition includes not only materials such as pottery, porcelain, refractories, structural clay products, abrasives, porcelain enamels, cements and glass, but also non-metallic magnetic materials, ferroelectrics, manufactured single crystals, and a variety of other products which were not in existence a few years ago – and many of which do not exist today."

In this course we are using a more limited definition of ceramics and we distinguish ceramics from glasses. Attention is directed mainly to traditional ceramics based on clay.

Answers to selected questions

7 A kaolinite crystal about 15 mm across would actually be 0.0005 mm or 500 nm across.

8 5000 silicon atoms across the crystal.

C6.3　How do we use glasses and ceramics at home?

C6.4　How are glasses and ceramics used in industry?

There is an opportunity here for groups of pupils to make wall charts illustrating the many uses of ceramics and glasses as well as their advantages and disadvantages as materials. Leaflets, booklets, magazines and catalogues contain many pictures of materials in use.

Ceramics and glasses have giant structures and so they have high melting-points. They are made from oxides and cannot burn because they have already been oxidized. This is the basis of their refractory properties. These two aspects of their chemistry should be accessible to pupils and should be emphasized.

C6.5   How are glass and ceramic objects manufactured?

If time permits, this section might be illustrated with a film, video or a visit. If there is a pottery department in the school then a demonstration of the stages in making a glazed pot from raw clay will add interest to this section.

Worksheet **C6C** is designed to help pupils think about the Float Process. This can be a group activity in school. Clearly the pupils should not have access to their Chemistry book while doing it.

C6.6   Recycling glass

A more detailed treatment of this topic is given in Science Unit 2: *Glass*, published by the Keep Britain Tidy Group Schools Research Project (see Further information).

The Glass Manufacturers' Federation publishes a number of booklets, magazines and leaflets about Bottle Banks and the campaign to increase the amount of glass recycled (see Appendix).

Answers to selected questions

25 Non-return bottle – one trip 7.1 MJ
   Re-usable bottle   – one trip 9.7 MJ
                  – two trips 6.1 MJ
                  – five trips 3.9 MJ

26a Overall saving per tonne = 5552 MJ
b Volume of fuel oil saved   = 135 L

Practical work

Worksheet C6A   Making glass

REQUIREMENTS

Each group of pupils will need:
Copy of Worksheet **C6A**
Sample tube or test-tube with stopper
Crucible (see note 1)
Tongs
Burner, tripod and mat
Pipe-clay triangle
Eye protection

Access to:
Lead(II) oxide with spatula, allow 4 g per group
Boric acid with spatula, allow 2 g per group
Zinc oxide with spatula, allow 0.5 g per group
Balance

Further investigations

The chemical resistance of glass

Each group will need:
4 test-tubes in rack
Eye protection

Access to:
Dilute nitric acid
Dilute hydrochloric acid
Dilute sodium hydroxide solution
Bleach

Colouring glass

(See note 2)

Each group will need access to:
Further quantities of the glass-making
   chemicals listed above
A few grains of selected metal oxides:
   iron(III) oxide, manganese(IV) oxide,
   copper(II) oxide and cobalt(II) oxide

Notes:
1 After use the crucibles can be cleaned
by soaking overnight in dilute nitric acid.
This treatment may have to be repeated
two or three times.
2 Only minute amounts of the metal oxide
are needed. The teachers' notes for the
Keep Britain Tidy Group unit on Glass
give more details; they suggest that simple
jewellery can be made by using epoxy
resin to fix coloured beads of lead borate
glass to metal ring mounts. The unit also
includes a worksheet showing that the
colouring of glass can be investigated
using borax beads. (See Further
information.)

This experiment shows clearly how a mixture of powdered oxides can be converted
into glass. It is also fun to do, and another example of making something useful
from chemicals. The practical application of glass making can be emphasized if
there is time to go on and make ornamental coloured glass beads.

Lead borate glass is not resistant to attack by aqueous reagents. The glass
dissolves in dilute nitric acid overnight. Treatment with dilute hydrochloric acid
results in a white, powdery surface. Dilute sulphuric acid has little effect. Bleach
has no effect, but the surface of the glass is pitted after treatment with dilute
sodium hydroxide.

Worksheet C6B   Glass working

REQUIREMENTS

Each pupil will need:
Copy of Worksheet **C6B**
Length of glass rod, to make a stirring
   rod (see note 1)
2 lengths of glass tubing, for making a
   dropping pipette and a right-angle bend
   (see note 1)
One longer length of glass rod for glass
   blowing
Burner, tripod and mat
Tongs
Eye protection

Access to:
Glass-cutting knife or file (see note 1)
Flame spreader or batswing burner (one
   between four pupils)

Note:
1 The glass rod should be cut in advance.
Cutting tubing is easier and safer than
cutting glass rods, so teachers may prefer
the pupils to cut their own lengths. On the
other hand, cutting the tubing in advance
is likely to be more economical.

This experiment will give pupils experience of the behaviour of hot glass so that
they can contrast it with the melting of crystalline solids. They will also come to
appreciate the skill involved in glass blowing when they find how difficult it can be
to make quite simple items. In a double period the majority of the pupils will
develop some ability to manipulate glass.

The worksheet has been prepared on the assumption that the teacher or
technician will demonstrate the techniques first. If the technician has been trained
in simple glass working, this activity is a good opportunity to remind pupils of the
technical skill needed in science prep. rooms. Three of the items to be made are
useful, and so the glass is not wasted. The dropping pipette is easier to make and
more robust than ones made by drawing a jet.

The instructions on the worksheet suggest that the wider end of the dropping
pipette is spread out by pressing it down onto a heatproof mat when hot. Better
results are achieved using a moulding cone, or simply a length of graphite rod
sharpened into a pencil shape. (See figure C12.)

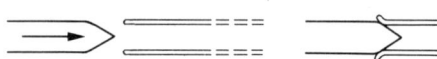

Figure **C12**

The pupils are likely to be most interested in glass blowing. **It is vital that they wear eye-protection.** If they blow too hard and burst the bulb there may be fine fragments of glass in the air.

Glass blowing can be extended by asking the pupils to make a thermometer. After blowing a thick-walled bulb and letting it cool, they half-fill the tube with coloured water. Warming near the surface of the water produces steam which drives out the air. The open end is then sealed by rotating it in a flame. After cooling, the thermometer is calibrated in the usual way. This is a challenging test of manipulative skills.

The suggested tasks on the worksheet are functional and some pupils may respond to a more creative approach. It can be fun to make glass ornaments as shown in figure **C**13. Thin coloured rods for ornamentation can be made by drawing out coloured rod from suppliers.

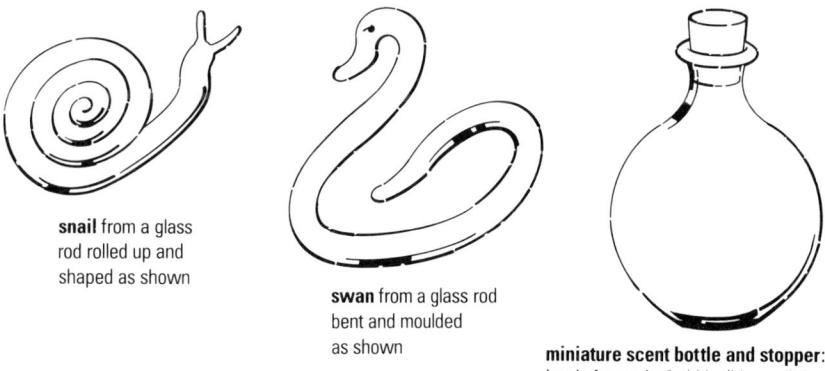

snail from a glass rod rolled up and shaped as shown

swan from a glass rod bent and moulded as shown

miniature scent bottle and stopper: bottle from tube/bubble, (blow a little glass bubble and flatten the end to form the base of the bottle) stopper from rod: a glass rod is formed in a stopper shape

coloured bubble:

glass tube

sealed end

thin coloured glass rod (made by drawing out coloured rod) is wrapped around the **sealed** end – then the bubble is blown

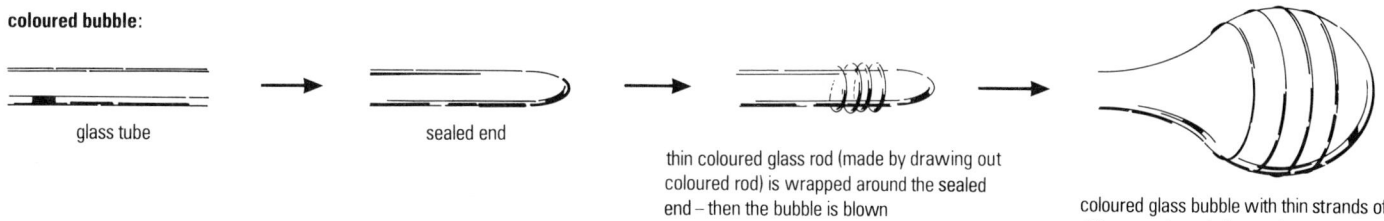

coloured glass bubble with thin strands of different-coloured glass rod

funny faces from bubble and coloured blobs and rod: make a glass bubble, stick on coloured blobs for eyes, nose, mouth, attach fine coloured rod with blobs on ends for antennae

Figure **C**13
Some simple glass ornaments which pupils can make.

Teacher demonstration: Evidence for ions in soda-lime glass

Safety note
This demonstration is potentially hazardous. Teachers should check that they are permitted to do practical work with exposed mains voltages by their LEA. At the time of publication the Health and Safety Executive does permit such practical work (GS32 "Electrical safety in schools").

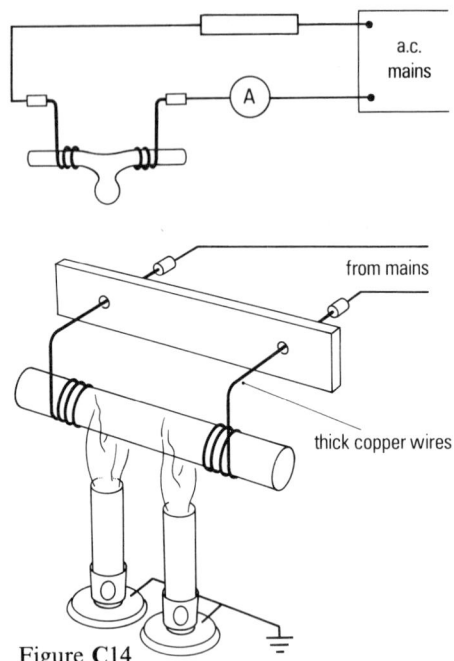

Figure C14

It is a wise precaution to prepare the demonstration before the class arrives; to switch off and unplug immediately the demonstration is finished; and to avoid trying to reassemble the apparatus for a repeat demonstration in the presence of pupils.

A further precaution is to use a plug with protection from a Residual Current Device (RCD).

Despite all these warnings, if the suggested procedure is followed the demonstration is effective and worthwhile and it is easier to set up than the detailed instructions below may suggest. It is a remarkable sight when the glass becomes soft enough to let the ions in it carry current; the current then maintains the heating which increases until the glass melts and drips.

REQUIREMENTS

The teacher will need:

Demonstration meter with a.c. dial, 5 A (optional)
2 lengths bare copper wire, 20 cm, s.w.g. about 14, each fitted with a 4-mm plug
Mains lead ending in two 4-mm sockets
Length of soft glass rod (soda glass, 6–8 cm long, 7–12 mm diameter)

1 or 2 stands with bosses and clamps with earthing leads
Limiting resistor (e.g. a radiant heater or 100 W mains lamp)
2 burners, with earthing leads
Strip, or two tubes, of insulator
Heatproof mat
Safety screen or wire-mesh barrier

Procedure

1 Wind two tight coils, each of three or four turns, of thick, bare copper wire, on the soda-glass rod at places 3 to 5 cm apart.

2 Support the wires by a strip of insulating material which is held by a clamp on an earthed stand. The wires should end in 4-mm plugs while the mains lead terminates in 4-mm sockets.

3 Arrange the glass rod at such a height above the bench that a burner flame can reach it and heat it strongly.

4 Cover the bench below the rod with a heat-resistant mat.

5 Connect the two thick wires in series with a limiting resistor (e.g. a radiant heater or a 100 W bulb) and with the 240-volt a.c. mains. An a.c. ammeter may be included.

6 Before switching on, make sure that safety screens are in place to prevent the teacher or pupils accidently touching the live wires. Ideally the bare wires should be surrounded by an earthed wire cage (of 2 or 3 cm mesh).

7 Also make sure that the burners are earthed.

8 Switch on.

9 Heat the glass rod strongly with two burner flames for 2 or 3 minutes. There may be tiny sparks at the contacts between the wire coils and the glass. Soon after that the glass will start to glow dull red; it is conducting and the heating effect of the current will then suffice. Turn off the burners. Watch the rod slowly redden and melt.

10 Switch off and unplug.

Further information

The Mineral Industries Manpower and Careers Unit

Let's look at china clay is a set of curriculum materials available from the Unit (MIMCU – see Appendix). The pack includes a teachers' guide, worksheets which teachers are free to copy, a resource book for pupils and samples of rocks and minerals. A modest fee is charged. The use of this material would introduce more Earth Science into the course. Topics covered include the origins, mining, processing and uses of china clay as well as economic and environmental issues.

Keep Britain Tidy Group

Science Unit 2: *Glass* is a kit of curriculum materials which includes teachers' notes, a set of booklets for the pupils, practical worksheets and a film strip which can be made into slides. The practical cards include experiments to investigate the toughening and colouring of glass. The text of the pupils' book covers the reuse and recycling of glass in some detail and also revises some basic optics by showing how discarded and broken bottles might start fires in dry summers. (See Appendix.)

University of York Science Education Group

The unit *Buildings* in the Salters' Chemistry course includes investigations of glass and clay.

Science and Technology in Society

Unit 410 "Glass"

This unit includes reading, questions and practical work on the manufacture, uses and recycling of glass.

Science at Work

Section 1 of *Building science* includes experiments to investigate mortar and concrete. There is also a description of how bricks are made from clay.

Chapter C7   Metals and alloys

Purposes

Knowledge and understanding

At the end of this chapter all pupils should:

1 know some of the properties of common metals and alloys

2 understand that metals have giant structures

3 know that alloys are mixtures of metals

4 know that rusting involves a reaction of iron with air and water

5 appreciate the advantages and disadvantages of alternative methods of preventing rusting.

In addition, those pupils aiming for higher grades should:

6 understand that metals are polycrystalline and that the atoms are arranged in close packed layers in metal crystals

7 appreciate that the bonding in metals must be somehow different from that in the giant structures in glasses to account for the fact that metals can be bent and stretched

8 appreciate that alloying can modify the properties of metals because the atoms of metals differ in size.

Processes and problem solving

Graphical and symbolic representation

In question 5 the pupils are presented with the problem of studying a model of a copper crystal, working out what can be explained in terms of the model, and examining the limitations of the model. Further aspects of this problem are covered by questions 6 and 8.

Using apparatus and measuring instruments
Worksheet **C7B** revises the techniques of chromatography and introduces pupils to the use of a locating agent. (Some may prefer to introduce these methods in the context of Chapter **C3** as suggested on page 175 in this *Guide*.)

Observation
The investigation of rusting requires accurate observations of the changes in the corrosion indicator.

Interpretation and application
Questions 3 and 4 ask pupils to look for patterns in the properties of metals. Questions 7 and 14 relate to the connection between the properties of materials and their uses.

Planning and carrying out investigations
The study of corrosion is developed from a practical investigation to be designed by the pupils based on a given procedure and using equipment supplied. This is prompted by box 1 in section **C7.4**.

Question 11 asks pupils to revise work they have done in earlier years involving the design of a control experiment to investigate rusting.

Problem solving
The following questions are to some extent open-ended and allow for a variety of responses: 1, 2, 10, and 12.

Question 9 asks those who have been introduced to the concept of amount of substance to use it to investigate the amounts of two metals in an alloy.

Timing

8–9 periods, depending on the route taken.

Suggested routes

All pupils are expected to undertake two practical activities. One might be an investigation of alloys and the other a study of corrosion. Other possibilities are given under Further information.

Sections **C7.1** and **C7.3** give an illustrated account of the properties and uses of metals and alloys and are designed to be accessible to all pupils.

Section **C7.2** is more difficult and develops ideas of structure and bonding. Those aiming for the higher grades will give more attention to this section.

Opportunities for co-ordination

There are links to be developed with Chapter **P1**.

There are opportunities for co-ordination with CDT. The subject of heat treatment is not covered in this chapter, nor are the effects of hot and cold working discussed. Those who do any metalwork will have some knowledge of these topics.

Chromatography as a method of analysis is used in Worksheet **B3A**.

Notes and answers

C7.1   Why are metals so useful?

Questions 1 and 2 provide alternative ways of making pupils more aware of the importance of metals. These can be class activities or they can be set for homework. Copies of Worksheet **C7A** will be needed if pupils are asked to answer question 1.

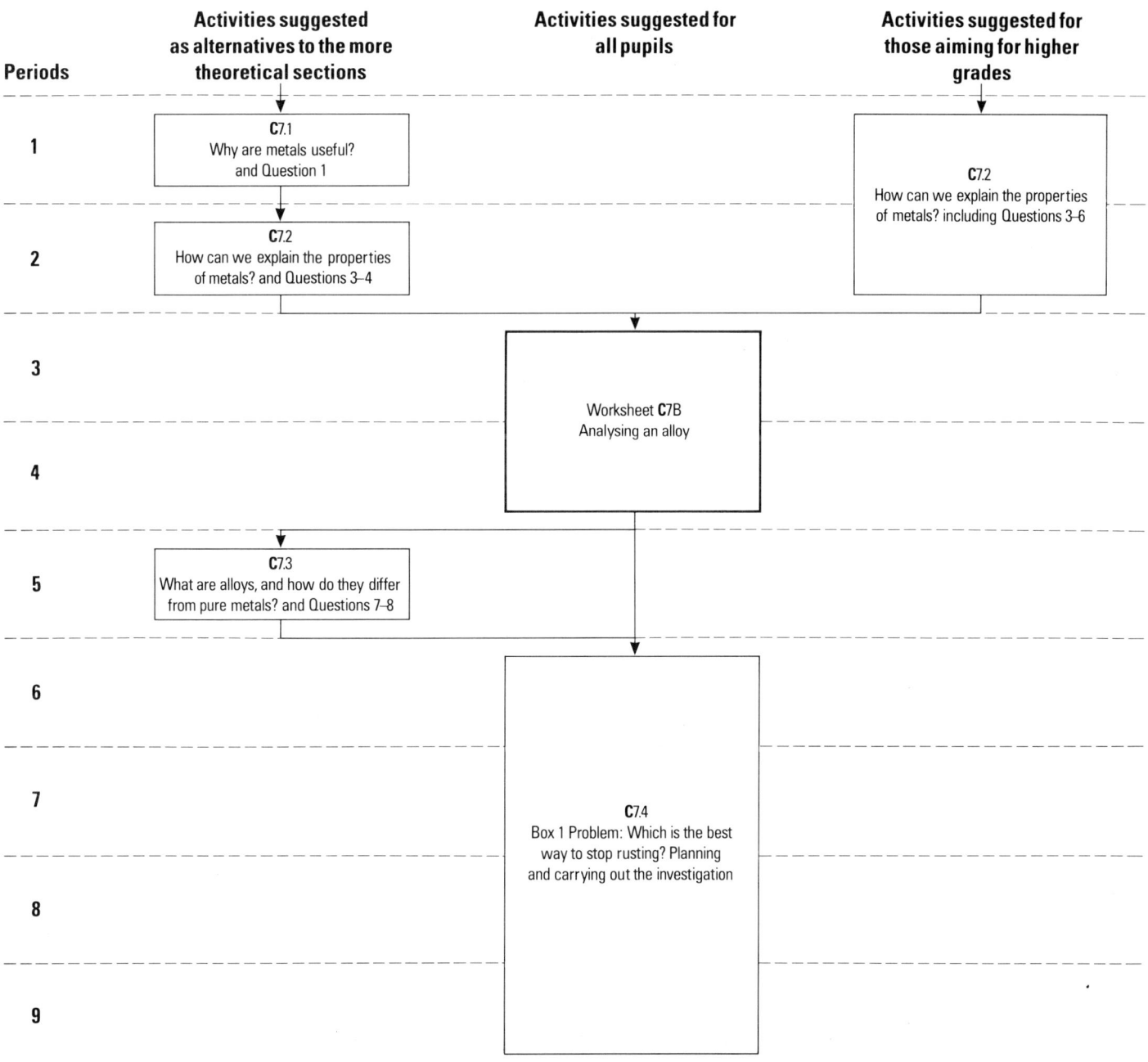

Periods	Activities suggested as alternatives to the more theoretical sections	Activities suggested for all pupils	Activities suggested for those aiming for higher grades
1	**C7.1** Why are metals useful? and Question 1		**C7.2** How can we explain the properties of metals? including Questions 3–6
2	**C7.2** How can we explain the properties of metals? and Questions 3–4		
3		Worksheet **C7B** Analysing an alloy	
4			
5	**C7.3** What are alloys, and how do they differ from pure metals? and Questions 7–8		
6		**C7.4** Box 1 Problem: Which is the best way to stop rusting? Planning and carrying out the investigation	
7			
8			
9			

Figure **C**15

C7.2   How can we explain the properties of metals?

If possible, pupils should be shown examples of the grain structure of metals. This can be demonstrated quickly and easily by the lead-pancake experiment (see under Practical work). In schools which study a metallurgy option at A-level it may be possible to show pupils samples of polished and etched specimens of metals which have been preserved in plastic.

The lead-pancake experiment can be difficult to interpret on an atomic scale. Pupils might use a stencil to add "atoms" to a diagram such as figure C16. They add atoms two at a time to each "grain" and see what happens when they meet.

There is no intention to distinguish the three main types of metal structure. Metallic bonding is named to distinguish it from the bonding in other giant structures such as diamond, and to point out that the forces holding metal atoms together must differ from those between non-metal atoms to account for the fact

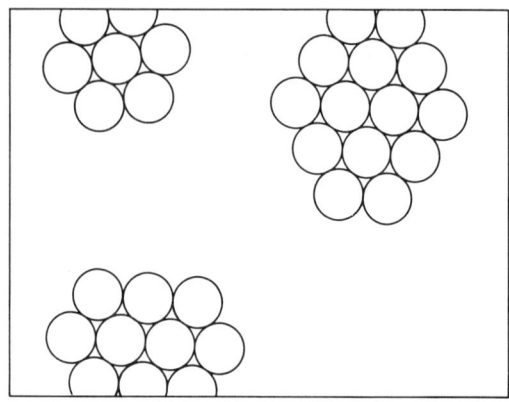

In the diagram opposite you can see that three crystals have started to grow. Copy the diagram using a stencil or a coin to draw the circles – they do not have to be the same size as the ones drawn here.

Now make your three crystals grow by adding more and more atoms until there is no room for any more.

Figure C16

that metals can be bent and stretched without breaking. There is no attempt to explain metallic bonding.

Question 5 asks the pupils to reflect on their understanding of the structure of solids. Some of the suggested false deductions from the model have been shown to be common misconceptions by the Children's Learning in Science Project (see for example CLIS "Aspects of secondary students' understanding of the particulate nature of matter", January 1984).

The behaviour of layers of atoms in a metal structure can be demonstrated on an overhead projector with a bubble raft, with ball bearings in a Petri dish, or with marbles (see Further information).

Figure 7.24 gives another opportunity for pupils to reflect on the difference between a giant structure and a molecular structure.

C7.3   What are alloys, and how do they differ from pure metals?

Pupils who are doing metalwork in a craft and design course should be able to contribute a good deal to this section of the course. Pupils are not expected to remember the details of the compositions of alloys.

The suggested practical work involves the analysis of an alloy by chromatography. A different method of analysis is given in the *Metals* unit of the Salters' Chemistry course. Instead of analysing alloys it is possible to make and test alloys as described in the *Metals* module of Nuffield Science 13 to 16 or in the *Building materials* booklet of Science at Work. (See Further information.)

Answer to selected question

9 The ratio by amounts is 3 mol Fe: 0.5 mol Cr.
So the atomic ratio for Fe:Cr is 6:1.

C7.4   How can we stop corrosion?

It is assumed that the pupils have done an experiment to show that air and water are needed to make iron go rusty. In this section, the pupils should focus their attention on designing an experiment to investigate the available methods for preventing corrosion. Different groups in the class can tackle different questions. Finally, representatives of each group can be asked to give a brief report on their findings to the rest of the class.

Practical work

Teacher demonstration: How do crystals form from molten lead?

REQUIREMENTS

The teacher will need:
Crucible
Pipe-clay triangle
Burner, tripod and mat
Tongs
Smooth metal plate
Beaker, 250 ml
Spatula
Eye protection

Access to:
Lead metal, 30–40 g (see note 1)
Powdered charcoal
Dilute nitric acid, 2 mol/L, about 50 ml

Note:
1 Avoid lead shot. Lead foil can be used, but if it is thin it may oxidize rather quickly during melting. Thick lead sheet or lead piping is better.

Procedure

1 Melt the lead in the crucible, but do not overheat. If the metal is dirty, a scum will collect on the surface. This can be removed using a spatula, preferably after adding a little powdered charcoal.

2 Pour the molten lead onto the flat surface so that it forms a pool some 30 to 50 mm in diameter. Use the spatula to hold back any remaining scum, or charcoal, as you pour.

3 Immerse the cold lead "pancake" in dilute nitric acid. Remove the specimen after 15–30 seconds when the metal crystals reflect light and sparkle. Wash with distilled water and dry. A typical etched pancake is shown in figure C17.

Figure C17

Worksheet C7B   Analysing an alloy

REQUIREMENTS

Each group of pupils will need:
Gas jar and lid, or large beaker with aluminium foil cover
Chromatography paper, Whatman No. 1 (see note 1)
2 or 3 plastic paper clips
Tweezers
Eye protection

Access to:
Solvent (90 % propanone,
    5 % concentrated hydrochloric acid,
    5 % water), allow 20–50 ml per group
Solutions containing the following metal ions, each at about 0.1 mol/L: Ag^+, Cu^{2+}, Fe^{3+}, and Ni^{2+}, a few drops per group
Fine glass tubes provided with each of the metal ion solutions (see note 2)
Large watchglass or dish, with 0.1% dithio-oxamide in ethanol, in fume cupboard
Trough in fume cupboard with concentrated ammonia solution
String and plastic clips to act as a "washing line" for chromatograms, in the fume cupboard

The teacher will need:
Evaporating basin(s), one per sample to be investigated
Tongs
Eye protection

Access to:
Aqua regia, a mixture of 3 parts by volume of concentrated hydrochloric acid with one part by volume of concentrated nitric acid
Alloy sample(s) for analysis (see note 3)
Distilled water
Measuring cylinder, 10 ml

Notes:
1 The chromatography paper should be cut to size so that it will stand inside the gas jar provided without touching the sides. Excellent results can be achieved using slotted chromatography paper; this is available from the usual suppliers. The slots prevent the spots from running into each other.
2 If there is time, the pupils may enjoy drawing their own fine glass tubes from soda-glass tubing. The technique will have to be demonstrated and pupils should be reminded of safety precautions required when glass working (see under Practical work for Chapter C6).
3 Suitable samples include pre-decimal coins and foreign coins.

R_f values for the metal ions under these conditions are as follows: Cu^{2+}: 0.09;

Ni^{2+}: 0.05; Fe^{3+}: 0.73; and Ag: close to zero. So copper or nickel can be separated from iron. Silver can be distinguished from copper but not very well from nickel. The spots on the developed chromatogram have different colours, and this helps to identify the ions.

The teacher must demonstrate the preparation of the solution of the unknown sample by dissolving a very small amount of the alloy in about 0.5 ml of aqua regia, which is highly corrosive. This can be done by immersing a coin in the reagent for about 30 seconds. The solution formed is diluted with about 5 ml of distilled water. The pupils can spot the diluted solution onto the paper.

This is an interesting experiment, but pupils should perhaps be told that nowadays an analyst would be unlikely to use chromatography to analyse alloys. The modern techniques include solvent extraction, spot tests, and atomic absorption spectroscopy.

Box 1 Problem: What is the best way to stop rusting?

REQUIREMENTS

Each group of pupils will need:
Copy of Worksheet **C0**
Petri dishes or test-tubes
Eye protection

Access to:
Warm solution of corrosion indicator (see note 1), 30–60 ml per group depending on the containers used for the samples
Metal samples (see note 2)
Cleaning agent for metal samples (see note 3)
Derusting agent for metal samples (see note 4)
Zinc foil, magnesium ribbon and copper foil
Various tools including snips, a file, hammer and pliers
Commercial corrosion inhibitors (see note 5)
Various types of paint, with brushes
Oil and vaseline

Notes:
1 Prepare the corrosion indicator shortly before the lesson. Make a warm solution of 5 g gelatine in 100 ml water and then dissolve 0.2 g of potassium hexacyanoferrate(III) in it. Keep the solution warm.
2 Scraps of mild steel are likely to be available from the craft department. Clout nails from a hardware store are a convenient source of galvanized steel. Tin-plated steel can be cut from tinned fruit cans. Stainless steel screws or bolts can be obtained from a hardware store or from a boat chandler.
3 Dirt, grease and finger marks will interfere with the results. A suitable cleaning agent is a solution containing 5 % sodium carbonate and 0.5 % household detergent.
4 Existing rust must be removed from samples before the experiment. Rust can be removed with dilute hydrochloric acid followed by thorough rinsing in cold water.
5 Pupils should be advised to note the safety warnings on the packs of commercial inhibitors and to handle them with care.

This investigation is suggested in box 1 on page 143 of the Chemistry pupils' book. It may be helpful to demonstrate the use of the indicator with unprotected iron nails before the groups of pupils start to think about their plans.

The suggested indicator is only designed to detect iron(II) ions. With the suggested concentration of potassium hexacyanoferrate(III) it will take up to half an hour before obvious signs of corrosion appear. This allows time for the solution to gel. It also gives a clearer distinction between treated and untreated specimens. The results are more rapid if sodium chloride is added to the reagent (5 g in 100 ml).

In warm weather it may be helpful to increase the concentration of gelatine, using about 8 g in 100 ml of the solution. The standard ferroxyl indicator also includes phenolphthalein to show the regions where hydroxide ions are being formed. For most pupils it will be simpler to omit this complication, but if desired add 1 ml of phenolphthalein solution to 100 ml of the reagent.

In studies to see what happens when iron is linked with other metals, it is important to make sure that the second metal is tightly gripped to the iron to ensure good contact.

Further information

Nuffield Science 13 to 16
Three modules contain ideas and worksheets which can be used with this chapter. Section 2 of *Chemical giants* covers the structure of metals and alloys including bubble rafts. Sections 6 and 7 of *Metals* include an experiment to make and test an alloy as well as a series of investigations into the mechanical properties of metals. Section 8 of *The Periodic Table* deals with corrosion and its prevention.

Science at Work
Science of the motor car includes a section on corrosion with an experiment to study the effectiveness of corrosion inhibitors. *Building science* includes an experiment to make and test solder with information and diagrams to explain the use of solder to join metals.

University of York Science Education Group
Chemistry in Action includes a unit called *Aluminium can. . .* Pupils are asked to compare the advantages and disadvantages of aluminium and steel as packaging materials for food.

The unit about *Metals* in Salters' Chemistry has a section about the analysis of the alloy used to make drawing pins. Another section covers the effect of alloying on the properties of metals. Three sections deal with the causes and prevention of corrosion.

Keep Britain Tidy Group Research Project
Science Unit 3, *Metals*, covers alloys, the shaping of metals, the conservation of metals and the effects of lead in the environment. The kit includes booklets for the pupils together with slides and practical worksheets dealing with alloys, heat treatment, corrosion, anodizing and air pollution.

Science and Technology in Society
The following SATIS units might be used in conjunction with the work in this chapter:

Unit 310 "Recycling aluminium"
Unit 103 "Controlling rust"
Unit 604 "Metals as resources"

Chapter C8   Polymers

Purposes

Knowledge and understanding

At the end of this chapter all pupils should:

1 know some of the properties and uses of polymeric materials

2 appreciate that there are both synthetic and natural polymers

3 know the meaning of the term "plastic", and know how thermoplastics and thermosets behave on heating

4 understand the basis of some of the methods of fabricating useful objects from plastics.

In addition, those pupils aiming for higher grades should:

5 understand the difference between addition and condensation polymerization using simplified models

6 understand the difference between thermoplastics and thermosets in terms of weak "between molecule" forces and cross-linking.

Processes and problem solving

Graphical and symbolic representation
Long chain molecules are represented with simplified models. Questions 1 and 2 test the pupils' ability to use these models. Some pupils will appreciate the link between these models and the more detailed structures studied in Chapters **C2** and **C3**.

Using apparatus and measuring instruments
The nylon experiment on Worksheet **C8A** requires practical skill and an awareness of safe working methods when handling toxic chemicals.

Observation
Accurate observations are needed when attempting to identify plastics according to Worksheet **C8D**.

Interpretation and application
The scheme for identifying plastics involves the use of a key to interpret the results from Worksheet **C8D**.

Planning and carrying out investigations
Box 2 in section **C8.2** suggests an investigation which might be planned and carried out by the pupils as an alternative to other experimental work which involves planning.

Communication skills
Worksheet **C8B** provides opportunities to practise skills in the collection and presentation of data, and the retrieval of information.

Timing

7–8 periods, depending on the route taken.

Suggested routes

Alternative activities are suggested to emphasize the everyday importance of polymers. One possibility is for the pupils to do part 1 of Worksheet **C8B** for homework and then follow it up by starting part 2 in class. The other possibility is to show a series of slides showing polymeric materials in use in the locality of the school as described for Worksheet **C8C**.

All pupils can attempt Worksheet **C8D** which is based on a key for identifying common plastics. Simpler schemes for identifying a more limited range of plastics, or fibres, are given under Further information at the end of this chapter.

With some pupils it may be preferable to concentrate on the connection between the properties of polymers and how they are used as described in section **C8.2**. With other pupils it may be appropriate to give more attention to the connection between structure and properties covered in section **C8.3**.

There are several films and videos which can be used to illustrate this chapter (see Further information and the Appendix).

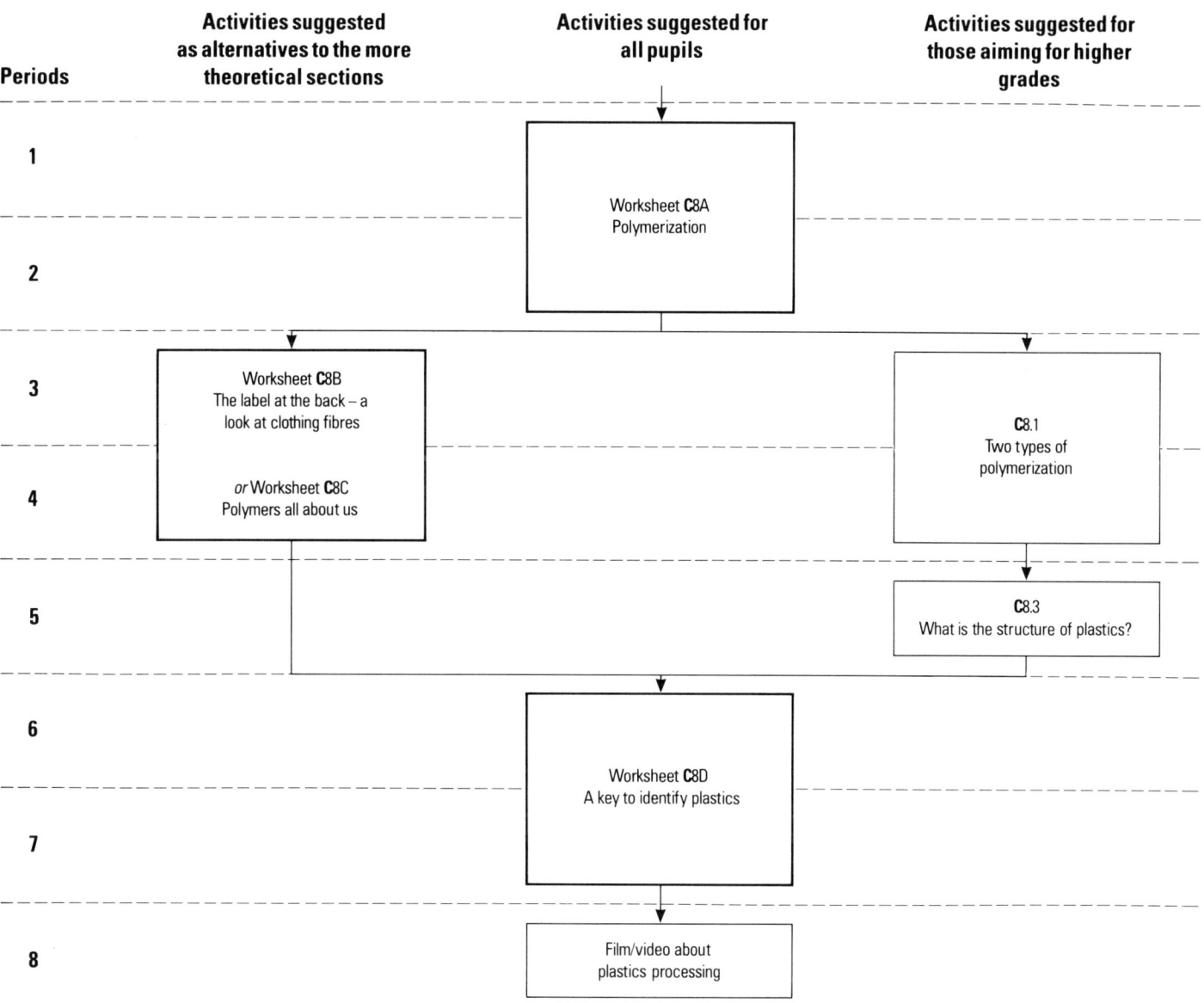

Figure **C**18

Opportunities for co-ordination

The skill of using keys for identification is introduced in Chapter **B**1. There are links with the study of protein and carbohydrate polymers in Chapters **B**6 and **B**10.

Plastic and elastic materials are mentioned in Chapter **P**1. The strength of synthetic fibres and fabrics is referred to in connection with seat belts in Chapter **P**6. Chapter **P**9 features the use of plastics in home insulation.

There are plenty of opportunities to develop links with work done in CDT and Home Economics. Many school workshops now have strip heaters for bending acrylic sheet, ovens for heating plastic sheet before plug moulding, and small vacuum formers. The links with Home Economics are illustrated by some of the entries under Further information at the end of this chapter.

Notes and answers

C8.1 What are polymers?

Teachers may like to take the opportunity to revise the work on polymerization in Chapters **C**2 and **C**3 with the help of molecular models. Use of models will help pupils to see the difference between addition and condensation polymerization.

Box 1 uses simple C_2 compounds to point out the advantages of the newer chemical names. However, a knowledge of formal chemical nomenclature is not an examinable part of this course. Where necessary alternative names will be given and pupils will have access to data tables giving names and formulae.

Figure 8.12 is included to help pupils to think through the idea of condensation polymerization.

C8.2 How do we use polymers?

The modification of cellulose can be demonstrated in two ways. Part 4 of the Science at Work booklet *Fibres and fabrics* describes a procedure for making rayon. Details of a method for making cellulose acetate are given in the section on Practical work below.

C8.3 What is the structure of plastics?

Teachers will know that the majority of pupils have difficulty in grasping the distinction between the bonding within molecules and the bonding between molecules. An appreciation of this distinction is crucial if pupils are ever to understand the contrast between molecules and giant structures. This section provides a good opportunity to develop the idea after they have used the key in Worksheet **C8D**. The first test distinguishes thermosoftening plastics which only have weak forces between the molecules and thermosetting plastics which are cross-linked. Molecular models can be used to explain the difference effectively.

Some pupils may appreciate the application of the same ideas in hair-dressing. When hair is washed in hot water, set and dried, only weak "between molecule forces" are broken and reformed. The result does not last. However a "perm" involves breaking and reforming strong bonds cross-linking the protein molecules, and the result is permanent until the hair has grown out.

In Chapter **C11** the difference in fastness between natural dyes and modern reactive dyes is also explained in terms of "within molecule" and "between molecule" forces.

More able pupils may appreciate the ICI video *Polymers* (see Appendix). The section on the mechanism of polymerization is at A-level standard; however there is an interesting sequence which illustrates the uses of a number of thermosoftening plastics and explains how their properties can be controlled. The final part shows the variety of plastics used in a modern refrigerator. The film uses systematic names.

C8.4 Who does what in the plastics industry?

This will make more impact if the pupils can see a film or video. The ICI video *Working with thermoplastics* is suitable (see Appendix).

Practical work

Worksheet C8A Polymerization

Part 1

REQUIREMENTS

Each group of pupils will need:
2 beakers, 10 ml
Tweezers
Glass rod
Measuring cylinder, 10 ml
Protective gloves
Eye protection

nylon

Access to:
Fume cupboard
Solution 1: hexanedioyl dichloride (adipyl chloride) in 1,1,1-trichloroethane (5 g in 100 ml solvent), 5 ml per group (see note 1), with 10-ml measuring cylinder
Solution 2: diaminohexane in water (5 g in 100 ml water), 5 ml per group

Note:
1 Solution 1 must be freshly made. Decanedioyl dichloride (sebacoyl chloride) can be used as a cheaper alternative.

Part 2

REQUIREMENTS

Each group of pupils will need:
Disposable container (see note 2)
Glass rod
10-ml measuring cylinder
Protective gloves
Eye protection

Access to:
Fume cupboard
Methanal (40 % formalin), 10 ml per group (see note 3)
Urea, 5 g per group
Dilute sulphuric acid, 1 mol/L, 5 ml per group
Balance

Notes:
2 A section cut from a plastic egg carton is suitable for this experiment.
3 Methanal vapour is poisonous and so this experiment must be done in a fume cupboard. Methanal may form a powerful carcinogen if allowed to mix with hydrochloric acid. Methanal should be stored separately from concentrated hydrochloric acid.

These preparations should be demonstrated if there is any doubt about the competence of the pupils to handle hazardous chemicals.

One possibility is for the teacher to demonstrate a larger scale version of the nylon "rope-trick" and then allow the pupils to do part 2 (working in fume cupboards).

Other polymerization reactions which can be demonstrated are given in the references listed under Further information at the end of this chapter.

Worksheet C8B The label at the back: a look at clothing fibres

REQUIREMENTS

Each pupil will need:
Copy of Worksheet C8B
In case some pupils are unable to carry out the survey at home it would be useful to have a range of garments available in the lesson.

This is based on the SATIS unit 405 and is in three linked parts.

Part 1 Looking at clothing labels
The survey of clothing labels is best done for homework, though it would be possible to bring a range of garments to the class.

Part 2 Which are the most popular fibres?
The class results are combined and summarized in a table.

Part 3 Questions and activities
Questions 10–14 and Factsheet 3 are intended for use only with more able students.

Worksheet C8C   Polymers all about us

REQUIREMENTS

Each pupil will need:
Copy of Worksheet C8C

The teacher will need:
Set of slides (see note 1)
Slide projector and screen

Note:
1 The easiest and cheapest way of getting a suitable set of slides is to ask a senior pupil, members of a photography club, or a member of staff to take them. Pupils are likely to be much more interested if they are having a fresh look at familiar scenes in and around the school. They will enjoy seeing staff and pupils in the pictures. As far as possible the pictures should cover the advantages and disadvantages of plastics listed in figure **C**19. A range of natural and synthetic polymers should be included covering plastics, elastomers and fibres. Some possibilities are included in figure **C**20 (opposite).

Advantages of plastics	Disadvantages of plastics
<ul><li>Easily moulded</li><li>Strong in relation to their weight</li><li>Hardwearing</li><li>Waterproof</li><li>Weather resistant</li><li>Chemically resistant</li><li>Rot resistant</li><li>Fairly cheap</li><li>Clear, or translucent, but can be easily coloured</li><li>Electrical insulators</li><li>Thermal insulators</li></ul>	<ul><li>Many soften and melt at low temperatures</li><li>Flammable – and when they burn some give off poisonous fumes</li><li>May gradually change shape if heavily loaded</li><li>Some slowly break down in sunlight</li><li>Easily scratched</li><li>Not biodegradable</li></ul>

Figure **C**19
Advantages and disadvantages of plastics.

The idea here is that the pupils are shown the slides and fill in the worksheet after discussion in class.

Teacher demonstration: Making cellulose acetate

REQUIREMENTS

The teacher will need:
Beaker, 100 ml
Beaker, 250 ml
Measuring cylinder, 25 ml
Measuring cylinder, 10 ml
Watchglass
Glass rod
2 dropping pipettes
Filter funnel
Eye protection for the teacher and pupils

Access to:
Cotton wool, 0.5 g (see note 1)
Glacial acetic (ethanoic) acid, 20 ml
Acetic (ethanoic) anhydride, 5 ml
Concentrated sulphuric acid, 2 drops
Distilled water, 150 ml
Muslin cloth
Blotting-paper or paper towels

Note:
1 This experiment only works satisfactorily using pure cotton wool.

Picture/s	Useful properties of polymers shown in the picture	Limitations of polymers shown in the picture	Type of polymer (if known)
Plastic drain pipe/ Rusty iron pipe	No corrosion. Strong in relation to weight	May slowly become brittle in sunlight	Unplasticized pvc
Insulated wires in science lab	Electrical insulator Flexible. Easily coloured	Insulation melts if over-heated	Plasticized pvc
Table tennis balls – in action	Light and strong	Easily crushed. Highly flammable	Cellulose nitrate
Overloaded carrier bag with stretched handles	Cheap. Strong in relation to weight	May stretch if overloaded	Low density polythene
Melamine camping mug with enamel and ceramic mugs	Poor heat conductor. Tough. Easily coloured	Can be scratched. May stain	Melamine
Handle of iron or of a saucepan in DS room	Poor heat conductor. Thermosets do not melt	May char if overheated	Phenol-formaldehyde (Bakelite)
White electrical sockets and plugs	Electrical insulator	Brittle, may chip	Urea-formaldehyde
Stacking chairs in classroom – perhaps one damaged	Light in proportion to strength. Easily moulded	May crack or break if grossly misused	Polypropylene
Plastic litter in or near the school	Cheap and easily formed. Moisture proof. Easily coloured	Not biodegradable	Various – polythene, polypropylene
Car rear light in staff car-park	Transparent non-brittle substitute for glass. Easily coloured	Easily scratched	Acrylic
Clothing, e.g. school tie or blazer	Can be spun into fibres. Rotproof. Hardwearing	May be less absorbent than natural fibres	Polyester fibres
Resin used for fibre glass repairs or canoe building	Strong but light. Easily formed	Dangerous fumes during mixing and setting	Polyester resin
Bottle for fizzy drinks	Strong but light		Polyester film
Plastic casing of food mixer	Tough and strong. Can be formed into intricate shapes		ABS
Foam filled crash mat in gym	Light, flexible, durable, elastic	Can be a hazard in case of fire in the home. Fumes are very poisonous	Polyurethane covered with pvc
Foam plastic packaging or ceiling tiles or drinking cups	Good heat insulation. Absorbs shocks	Flammable	Expanded polystyrene
Model kit	Can be accurately moulded into intricate shapes	Dissolved by some solvents	Polystyrene
Photographic film	Transparent. Not attacked by chemicals		Cellulose acetate

Figure **C20**
Some possible slides.

Procedure

1 Place 20 ml of glacial acetic acid, 5 ml of acetic anhydride and 2 drops of concentrated sulphuric acid in a 100-ml beaker. Stir the reagents then add 0.5 g of cotton wool. Use a glass rod to make sure that all the cotton is immersed in the liquid mixture.

2 Cover the beaker with a watchglass and set aside in a fume cupboard for 24 hours, or until all the cotton wool has dissolved. (The viscosity of the polymer solution can be a discussion point with some pupils.)

3 Pour the mixture into a 250-ml beaker containing 150 ml of water. The cellulose acetate will now precipitate.

4 Filter the product using a cloth in a funnel. Press out as much moisture as possible and then blot dry. Complete the drying process by putting the product in an oven set at 50 °C.

Commercially this plastic is made from wood cellulose, not cotton. Fibres of cellulose acetate are produced by dry spinning using a solution of cellulose acetate in acetone (propanone).

Worksheet C8D   A key to identify plastics

REQUIREMENTS

Each group of pupils will need:
Tongs
Eye protection

Access to:
Samples of plastics (see note 1) with scissors, or snips
Fume cupboard suitably equipped (see note 2)
Trough or large margarine tub for the float test
Washing up detergent, a few drops per group
Blue litmus paper

Notes:
1 Sources of the plastic samples are suggested in figure **C21**. As far as possible the plastics should be free of fillers and pigments, but this is impossible for urea-formaldehye and phenol-formaldehyde plastics. The pieces provided for the heating tests must be very small. If pupils prepare their own samples, this should be carefully supervised to ensure that they do not heat and burn large quantities.
2 Each fume cupboard will need: one or two medium-sized nails; tongs; burner; heat proof mat covered with large tin-lid to catch any drips; source of a small flame (such as a supply of wood splints or a candle).

Name of plastic	Sources of suitable samples
Urea-formaldehyde	light coloured domestic plugs and light fittings
Phenol-formaldehyde	dark coloured electric fittings, some screw caps for reagent bottles.
Nylon	curtain rail fittings, some plastic hinges
pvc	cling film, many transparent cooking oil or shampoo bottles
Polythene (ldpe)	sliced bread bags, bin liners, carrier bags
Polythene (hdpe)	some carrier bags and food bags (thinner, whiter and 'noisier' than ldpe)
Polypropylene	transparent film for crisps and other snack foods
Acrylic	'Perspex sheet', motor vehicle rear light covers
Polyester film	carbonated drink bottles (but not the base)
Polystyrene	disposable cups (not the expanded ones), translucent egg boxes, yoghurt pots (may be co-polymerized with butadiene)

Figure **C21**

The key is only designed to work for the range of plastics listed in figure **C21**. It is dangerous to allow pupils to heat any unknown plastics they may collect and bring to the laboratory.

The Keep Britain Tidy Group worksheets include a key for identifying an even more limited range of packaging plastics. Some pupils may find this simpler to follow.

Worksheet **C8D** should only be used in a laboratory with fume cupboards. Otherwise it is much safer to use a key to identify fibres. Possible keys are included in the Nuffield Science 13 to 16 module *Keys and detection* and in the Science at Work booklet *Fibres and fabrics*.

Further information

Nuffield Science 13 to 16
Chemical giants section 6 deals with the chemistry of Perspex and nylon. Section 7 distinguishes thermoplastics and thermosets. Section 8 covers elastomers including an experiment to make thiokol.

Keys and detection describes a scheme for identifying a limited range of natural and synthetic fibres. The scheme is presented as a key. This is suggested as an alternative to Worksheet **C8D** if there is limited access to fume cupboards in the lab.

Nuffield Home Economics
Chapters 16 and 19 of *The Basic Course* and Chapters 4, 5, 6, and 7 of *Fibres and Fabrics* give information and ideas for investigations which can be used in association with this chapter. In particular section 7.5 on page 43–4 of *The Basic Course* describes a method for investigating wrapping films as suggested in box 1 on page 154 of the pupils' book.

Science at Work
Fibres and fabrics includes sections on paper, a key for the identification of fibres, as well as the nylon experiment and experiments to investigate the strength, wear resistance and the heat insulation properties of fabrics.

Building Science has a section on plastics including an investigation of stress in plastics using polarized light and information about the moulding of plastics.

University of York Science Education Group
The unit on *Plastics* in Salters' Chemistry is particularly relevant to this chapter. The unit on *Clothing* has some helpful ideas dealing with fibres and fabrics including an investigation involving the use of a key.

Keep Britain Tidy Group Research Project
Science Unit 4 *Plastics* could be used as an alternative but parallel approach to the one in this chapter. The unit includes booklets for the pupils, slides, worksheets and teachers' notes. A particular feature of the approach is the work on recycling plastics. Science Unit 5 *Waste management and resources* deals with plastic rubbish alongside other forms of waste. It is supported with booklets for the pupils, slides, worksheets and notes for teachers.

The Education Services of major oil companies
There is a wealth of material available which can be used to support or extend the work in this chapter (see Appendix).

The Education Service of the Plastics and Rubber Institute (ESPRI)
ESPRI publish a book called *A foundation course for science teachers* which covers all the ideas in this chapter and gives ideas for practical work. A variety of other resources is available from this source too (see Appendix).

Topic C3

Chemicals in our homes

Chapter C9   Foams, emulsions, sols and gels

Purposes

Knowledge and understanding

At the end of this chapter all pupils should:

1 know that a colloid consists of one substance finely dispersed in another and know the meaning of the words foam, emulsion, sol and gel

2 appreciate the everyday importance of colloidal systems

3 appreciate that colloidal systems scatter light

4 understand that dialysis is a method for separating colloidal particles from smaller molecules and ions

5 appreciate the purpose of emulsifiers.

In addition, those pupils aiming for higher grades should:

6 understand the molecular explanation of Brownian motion

7 appreciate that surface tension can be explained in terms of weak forces between molecules

8 understand, in simple terms, the action of emulsifiers

9 appreciate some of the conditions which can cause colloidal particles to coagulate

10 understand that the stability of some colloidal systems depends on the presence of electric charges on the particles.

Processes and problem solving

Using apparatus and measuring instruments
Worksheet **C9C** introduces the practical techniques involved in making a cosmetic emulsion.

Observation
The main purpose of Worksheets **C9A** and **C9B** is to give pupils the chance to observe the behaviour of colloids during various tests.

Interpretation and application
Questions 16–19 ask pupils to interpret the results of an experiment. Questions 5, 6, 12, 13, 14, 20, 21 and 22 ask them to apply their knowledge to explain everyday situations.

Planning and carrying out investigations
Box 1 on page 169 provides an opportunity to plan an investigation.

Timing

7–8 periods.

Suggested routes

The flow diagram in figure **C22** describes possible routes through this chapter.

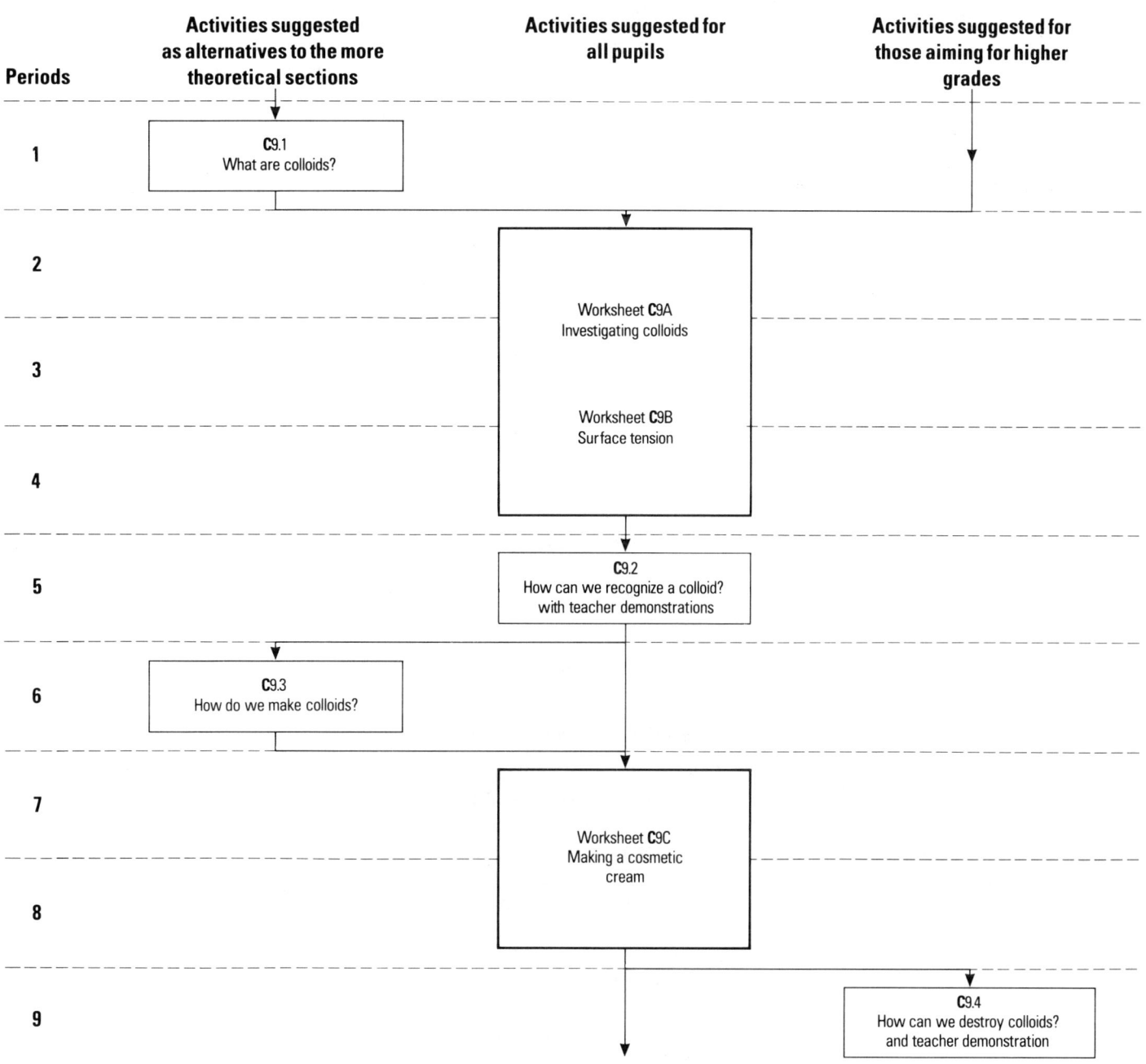

Figure **C22**

Worksheet **C9A** outlines a series of investigations to introduce the general properties of colloids. This will need about three periods for the practical work and follow up. Teachers may choose to demonstrate some parts. Worksheet **C9B** may be included in the series of experiments if there is time.

Worksheet **C9C** will need a double period. This could be extended with groups more interested in the applications rather than the theory. Additional experiments are given in the material referred to under Further information.

One period might be used to show the Unilever film which is now quite old but nevertheless relevant to this chapter (see Appendix).

At least one period will be needed to give help with some of the more theoretical sections. This could be supported by one or two demonstrations (see under Practical work).

Opportunities for co-ordination

Links with Biology: food additives (Chapter **B6**), emulsifying action of bile salts in the digestion of fats (**B5**), blood plasma as a colloidal system (**B8**), enzyme chemistry (**B5**), dialysis and kidney machines (**B12**).

Links with Physics: aerosols and Brownian motion (Chapter **P2**); forces between electrically charged particles (Chapter **P16**).

Notes and answers

C9.1   What are colloids?

The illustrations in this section are designed to emphasize the picture of a colloidal system consisting of one material finely dispersed in another. As far as possible familiar examples are used. There is some new vocabulary; pupils will need help with it, especially where the everyday use of words differs from the technical use. Question 4 may help pupils to understand the use of the terms "continuous" and "disperse".

Colloquially the term "aerosol" is often taken to refer to a spray container and its contents rather than to the dispersion of liquid droplets in air formed when the product is in use. The difference between the everyday meaning as used in Chapter **P2** and the scientific meaning may have to be discussed with the pupils.

The use of the word "particle" may also need discussion. In this chapter it is used to mean a little bit of a solid, or a small droplet of a liquid. Elsewhere the word is sometimes used as a general term for an atom, molecule or ion. We have avoided the latter usage where possible, but in some cases it is difficult to do so without replacing it with the formally correct but difficult word: entity.

Box 1 can be used as a planning exercise. It is also an opportunity to revise work done on enzymes and proteins.

Answers to selected questions

2 Example	Type of colloid
meringue	solid foam
fog	aerosol
salad cream	emulsion
clouds	aerosol
head on beer	foam
jelly baby	gel
muddy water	sol
whipped cream	foam
insecticide spray	aerosol
sponge	solid foam
crunchy bar	solid foam
bread	solid foam
chocolate mousse	gel/foam
hand cream	emulsion
lipstick	solid sol
mascara	sol or emulsion
rubber pillow	solid foam

toothpaste	sol stabilized by a gel
bubble bath	foam
cold custard	gel
non-drip paint	sol/gel

3 Figure 9.8:
a about 0.25 to 0.5 μm (2500 to 5000 atoms across);
b about 0.5 μm (5000 atoms across);
c of the order of 3 μm (30 000 atoms across).
Figure 9.9: about 1.4 μm (14 000 atoms across).

C9.2   How can we recognize a colloid?

This section is designed to be read in the light of the experience of Worksheet C9A.

C9.3   How do we make colloids?

The treatment of surface tension is deliberately simplified. The main thing is to show yet another application of the idea that there are weak attractive forces between molecules.

The treatment of emulsifying agents is extended in Chapter C10 where the action of detergents is explained.

Answers to selected questions

9a 6 cm^2
b 10^{12} cubes
c 6×10^{-8} cm^2
d 6×10^4 cm^2

C9.4   How can we destroy colloids?

Teachers may like to demonstrate the electrophoresis experiment. It is also possible to demonstrate the action of an electrostatic precipitator. These demonstrations are described under Practical work.

Note that the terms "lyophobic" and "lyophilic" have been avoided deliberately.

A more detailed treatment of the stabilization of colloidal systems is given in the Nuffield Advanced Chemistry Special Study *Surface chemistry*. All that is required here is summed up as follows:

● Some colloids are stabilized by the repulsive forces between the particles which all carry the same charge.
● Ions of opposite charge to the colloidal particles can bring about coagulation.
● Ions with a larger charge are more effective at coagulating colloidal particles than those with a smaller charge.

This section provides an opportunity to revise the idea that compounds of metals with non-metals are generally ionic.

Practical work

Worksheet C9A   Investigating colloids

The five investigations on this worksheet can be set out as a series of stations in a circus. Some of the experiments, especially "Dialysis" and "The effect of ions on a colloid", take longer than others and this will have to be allowed for when setting up the circus. Worksheet C9B can be used as a "buffer activity".

Light scattering

Requirements for one station
Copy of Worksheet **C9A** (side 1)
Bright light source, or projector (see
note 1)
Stoppered test-tubes in rack containing the
following and labelled accordingly:
gelatine gel labelled "gelatine" (see note 2)
starch solution labelled "starch" (see
note 3)
glucose solution labelled "glucose"
salt solution labelled "salt"

Notes:
1 This needs to be set up in a darkened
area of the laboratory. One possibility is
to line the inside of a cardboard box with
black paper and lie it on one side. The
bright light source can then be shone
through a hole cut in one of the vertical
sides of the box.
2 Prepare the gel by sprinkling the
required amount of gelatine into hot water
in a beaker. Stir well. Use at the rate of
11 g gelatine to 500 ml water.
3 Make a cream of 2 g soluble starch in
cold water. Pour into 100 ml of nearly
boiling water and then boil for a minute
or two.

Milk under the microscope

Requirements for each station:
Copy of Worksheet **C9A** (side 1)
Several microscope slides and coverslips
Seeker
Microscope with high and medium powers
Milk (fresh or UHT)
Glass rod

Types of emulsion

Requirements for each station:
Copy of Worksheet **C9A** (side 2)
Selection of emulsions which have been
lightly sprinkled with a dye mixture on
labelled watchglasses (see notes). Do not
stir after adding the dyes.

Notes:
1 Suitable emulsions include mayonnaise,
salad cream, milk, cream, butter, hand
cream and other cosmetic or medical
creams.
2 The dye contains equal amounts of
powdered methylene blue and sudan III
well mixed. These dyes stain skin strongly
and so protective gloves should be used
when mixing and using them. There is no
need for the pupils to handle the dyes.

The effect of ions on a colloid

Requirements for each station:
Copy of Worksheet **C9A** (side 2)
Boiling-tube with stopper
Four test-tubes, with stoppers, in rack
Spatula
Distilled water, with 25-ml measuring
cylinder
Labels
Titanium dioxide (a few grams) – see note
Sodium chloride solution, 2 g in 100 ml
water, with 10-ml measuring cylinder
Magnesium sulphate solution,
8 g $MgSO_4 \cdot 7H_2O$ in 100 ml water, with
10-ml measuring cylinder
Potassium alum solution, 15 g in 100 ml,
with 10-ml measuring cylinder
Eye protection

Note:
1 A suitable grade of titanium dioxide is
supplied by Griffin & George for use with
the Nuffield Advanced Chemistry Special
Study *Surface chemistry.*

Dialysis

Requirements for each station:
Copy of Worksheet **C9A** (side 3)
Dialysis apparatus which has been set up
   for at least an hour (see note 1)
Dropping pipette
Measuring cylinder, 10 ml
2 test-tubes and 2 boiling-tubes in rack
Burner and mat
Test-tube holder
Dropper bottle containing fresh or UHT
   milk
Benedict's solution in dropper bottle (see
   note for Worksheet **C3B** on page 173 of
   this *Guide*)
Sodium hydroxide solution, 2 mol/L, in
   dropper bottle
Copper(II) sulphate solution, 0.1 mol/L, in
   dropper bottle
Eye protection
Filter funnel
Filter papers

Note:
1 Set up the dialysis apparatus as follows:
Soak a 30 cm length of Visking tubing in
water until soft. Tie a double knot at one
end. With the help of a funnel pour milk
into the tube until it is a little over half
full. Tie the open end with thread. Rinse
the outside of the tube with distilled water
and then place it in a 250-ml beaker as
shown in the diagram on Worksheet **C9A**.
Add distilled water to the beaker until the
liquid levels are the same inside and
outside the tube.

Worksheet C9B   Surface tension

This is suggested as an optional but enjoyable extension to the circus.

Requirements for each station:
Copy of Worksheet **C9B**
Wire frames as shown on the worksheet
   (see note 1)
Trough
Thread
Soap solution (see note 2)

Notes:
1 The wire frames should be rigid and not
too irregular.
2 Make the soap solution by dissolving
30 g sucrose in 30 ml warm water. Cool,
then add 30 g propane-1,2,3-triol
(glycerol) followed by 2 g of washing-up
liquid. Stir well. This mixture produces very
stable films.

Worksheet C9C   Making a cosmetic cream

Requirements for each group:
Copy of Worksheet **C9C**
2 beakers, 100 ml or 150 ml
2 stirring thermometers, 0–100 °C
Burner, tripod, gauze and mat
Jar, or other container, for the product
Protective gloves (see note 1)
Eye protection

Access to:
Balance
Stearic acid, 15 g per group
Glycerol (propane-1,2,3-triol), 8 g per
   group
Distilled water, with measuring cylinder
Potassium hydroxide pellets, 0.7 g per
   group (see note 1)
Perfume (see note 2)
Preservative (see note 2)
Grease paint
Cotton wool

Notes:
1 It may be safer to provide preweighed
samples of the potassium hydroxide to
avoid any danger that the product will
contain a dangerous excess of alkali.
Protective gloves should be provided if the
pupils are going to weigh out the
potassium hydroxide themselves.
2 The perfume and preservative are
optional. A suitable preservative for the
emulsion is nipagin M. If no preservative
is added the emulsion must be used in a
short time.

The emulsifier is potassium stearate which is formed when the two phases are mixed.

Pupils might be asked to cost this and other cosmetic preparations with the help of catalogues and then compare their answers with the price of commercial products.

Additional cosmetic formulations can be found in the materials listed under Further information.

Teacher demonstration: Colloidal particles and electric charges

REQUIREMENTS

The teacher will need:
U-tube
Pipette, 20 or 25 ml, with filler
Two electrodes, platinum or carbon (see note)
Connecting wires with crocodile clips
Power pack, 25 V d.c.
Stand with boss and clamp
Gummed paper or grease pencil

Access to:
0.1 mol/L sodium chloride solution (1.5 g in 250 ml water)
1 % dispersion of TiO_2 in 0.1 mol/L NaCl solution containing 3 % sucrose to increase its density, 100 ml

Note:
1 The electrodes can be held in place with extra stands and clamps. Alternatively, corks can be used if vertical grooves are cut in their sides to allow any gases formed to escape.

This experiment is described in the pupils' book (in box 2 on page 176) and teachers may well decide not to demonstrate it. The apparatus is shown in figure 9.35.

Procedure

1 Support the U-tube with the stand and clamp. Fill the bottom half of the tube with sodium chloride solution. Now fill a pipette with the TiO_2 dispersion. Carefully lower the tip of the pipette to the bottom of the U-tube and allow the dense dispersion to run in slowly. Withdraw the pipette carefully so as not to disturb the boundary between the two layers. Wait for a few minutes while the boundaries become clearer then mark their positions with gummed paper or a grease-pencil.

2 Insert the two electrodes and connect to a 25 V d.c. supply. Movement of the boundaries will only become obvious in the course of a double period so it is essential to start the demonstration early in the session.

Teacher demonstration: A model electrostatic smoke precipitator

REQUIREMENTS

The teacher will need:
Van der Graaff generator (or induction coil and low voltage d.c. supply)
Drying tower adapted as shown in figure C23
Filter pump
Connecting wires with clips

Access to:
Cigarette, or other source of smoke

This demonstration is only worth trying on days which are dry enough for the Van der Graaff generator to work. (An induction coil can be used in place of a Van der Graaff generator and may be more reliable in humid conditions.) A simpler version of the experiment is described on Worksheet C in the Nuffield Science 13 to 16 module, *Charged particles.*

Safety notes

1 Induction coils made in the last twenty years should be used as they cannot produce a current of more than 3 mA; older ones may do so and must not be used.

2 The two terminals and the related parts of the apparatus constitute a

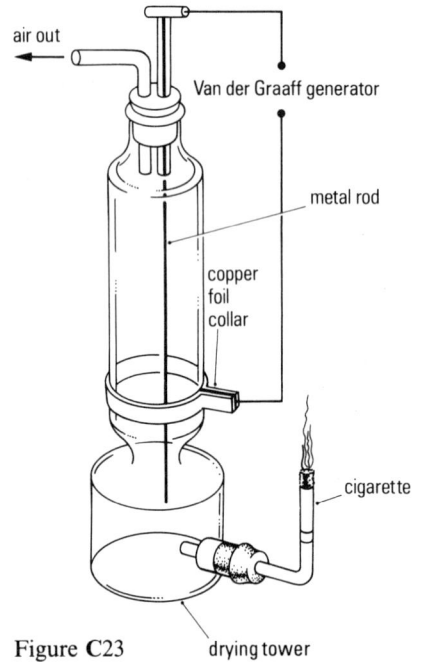

air out

Van der Graaff generator

metal rod

copper foil collar

cigarette

Figure C23   drying tower

capacitor. The terminals should be shorted out across each other at the end of the experiment to remove any residual charge.

Procedure

1 The drying tower is arranged as shown in figure **C23**. The copper foil is folded to form a collar. The inner metal rod should not touch the sides of the drying tower.

2 A filter pump is connected so that air can be drawn through the apparatus. A cigarette is inserted into some rubber tubing and connected to the lower end of the tower.

3 Once the drying tower is filled with smoke, switch on the Van der Graaff generator. The smoke is cleared rapidly and deposits of tar appear on the glass sides.

Further information

Nuffield Science 13 to 16
Making molecules work for us includes a section on cosmetics including a formulation for a cold cream and a barrier cream. One of the cold cream ingredients raises the issue of the use of whale products in cosmetics.

Nuffield Home Economics
Food science Chapters 10, 11 and 12 are particularly relevant to the work in this chapter. Worksheets FSM 10, 11a and b, 12 and 13, as well as *Fibres and fabrics* Worksheet FM18 could all be the basis of good homework exercises.

Nuffield Working with Science
Cosmetics

Science at work
Cosmetics includes several sections about emulsions and cosmetics which could be used to extend the treatment in this chapter.
Photography includes a simplified account of the manufacture of a photographic emulsion.

University of York Science Education Group
In the Salters' Chemistry course the unit *Keeping clean* includes an experiment to make a cosmetic cream. The unit *Food processing* investigates the use of emulsifiers in salad dressing and mayonnaise as well as studying milk and butter.

Chapter **C10**   **Keeping clean**

Purposes

Knowledge and understanding

At the end of this chapter all pupils should:

1 appreciate why detergents are needed to help get things clean when washing with water

2 understand the processes involved in supplying pure water

3 appreciate that the oxides of non-metals such as sulphur and nitrogen are acidic and may cause pollution

4 know some of the domestic, industrial and agricultural sources of water pollution

5 know that hardness is caused by the presence of dissolved calcium or magnesium compounds and be familiar with the behaviour of soap in hard and soft water

6 know that a scale of calcium carbonate may form when hard water is boiled and understand that scale removers are acids which dissolve calcium carbonate

7 know one method for softening water.

In addition, those pupils aiming for higher grades should:

8 understand a simple molecular explanation of the action of detergents

9 know that it is hydrogen ions which make water acidic

10 appreciate that many precipitation reactions involve ions

11 understand the measurement of concentrations in mol/L

12 understand the equations which describe the formation of hard water, scale formation and water softening processes

13 understand how the process of ion exchange can be used to soften water.

Processes and problem solving

Graphical and symbolic representation
Questions 2, 3, 17, 22, 23, 25, 38, and 43 provide practice in the use of chemical symbols and equations. Those aiming for higher grades should be able to use symbols for ions to explain what is happening during precipitation reactions.

Using apparatus and measuring instruments
Worksheets C10A and C10B give practice in the measurement of mass, volume, temperature and time.

Observation
Pupils have to make a series of observations while carrying out the experiments suggested on Worksheet C10A and C10B.

Interpretation and application
Questions 4, 11, 14, 15 and 40 ask pupils to reflect on patterns in the behaviour of substances. Questions 32 to 36 ask pupils to interpret results of an experiment. Questions 5, 6, 7, 8, 10, 20, and 42 depend on pupils being able to apply their knowledge of chemical ideas.

Planning and carrying out investigations
The problems in the boxes in section C10.4 are included as the basis of possible investigations to be planned and carried out by the pupils. The experiment to compare detergents might be planned by the pupils who could then follow their own suggestions instead of using Worksheet C10A.

Problem solving
Questions 24 to 27 and 28 to 31 are examples of problems based on the concept of amount of substance. In this chapter this is extended to cover the measurement of concentration in mol/L.

Timing 11–13 periods, depending on the route taken.

Suggested routes Possible routes are shown in figure C24.

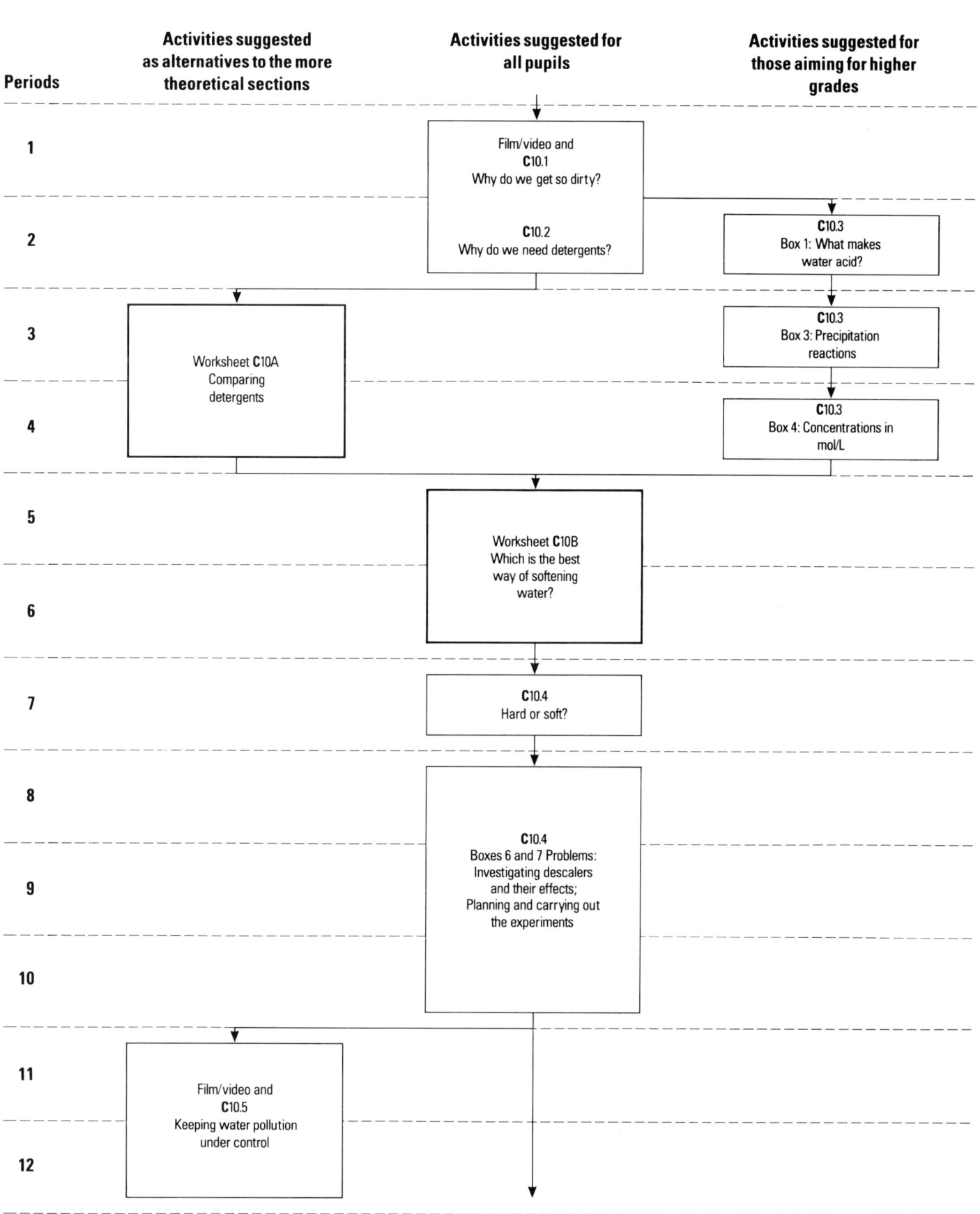

Figure C24

This chapter will have to be interpreted by teachers to suit the ability of the class. Routes for those aiming for higher grades should include the theory of ionic reactions and the measurement of concentration in terms of amount of substance. More descriptive accounts of the chapter are possible which do not incorporate these ideas.

A double period will be needed for sections C10.1 and C10.2. In this time a film or video might be shown to give an animated picture of detergency.

A single period will be needed to introduce water treatment.

A period will be needed to introduce concentrations in terms of moles per litre to those who are tackling the more theoretical aspects of the course. Another period will be needed to explain ionic precipitation reactions.

The formation, properties and softening of hard water might usefully be illustrated by showing a film.

Worksheet C10B will need a double period for practical work. Investigating descaling as suggested in the boxes in section C10.4 will take three periods, allowing one for planning and a double one for practical work. This could be developed more fully with groups spending less time on the theoretical parts of the chapter.

The section on pollution can be read for homework.

Opportunities for co-ordination

There are a number of links with Biology: the water cycle (Chapter B15), enzymes (B5), and eutrophication (B17).

The action of fluorescers in washing powders has links with Physics Chapter P15. The measurement of energy transfer by immersion heaters/hot-plates in one of the problems about kettle descalers has links with Chapter P9.

There are also opportunities for co-ordination with geography in the section on the water cycle/water supply and with home economics in the sections about dry cleaning and washing.

Notes and answers

C10.1 Why do we get so dirty?

Coming before section C10.2, this introduction serves as a reminder of the difference between a true solution and a colloidal dispersion. Questions 2 and 3 revise the structures of ethane and ethene.

C10.2 Why do we need detergents?

This part of the chapter follows on from section C9.3 and shows the importance of the ideas developed in the earlier chapter. The Unilever film, "Outline of detergency" gives an animated picture of the theory. (See Appendix.)

Worksheet C10A is related to this section.

C10.3 How do we get pure water?

Pupils are likely to be familiar with the water cycle from work in biology and geography. This section concentrates on the specifically chemical aspects of water treatment.

Several of the stages can be demonstrated. Worksheets included in the Keep Britain Tidy Group unit 5, *Waste management and resources* describe experiments on the removal of suspended solids and the effect of chlorinating water. (See Further information.) A suspension of calcium hydroxide can be shown to neutralize acids with the help of a coloured indicator such as litmus. The adsorbing properties of charcoal can be demonstrated by shaking a large spatula measure of charcoal with a dilute solution of a dye such as methyl violet (Gentian violet) and then filtering.

The ionic theory of acids, alkalis and neutralization reactions is introduced step by step in this chapter and in Chapters C11 and C12. Questions 11 to 14 in box 1 on page 185 lead to the suggestion that it is hydrogen ions which make water acidic.

This section also includes the first mention of ionic precipitation reactions. Pupils are not expected to be able to write formal ionic equations which are notoriously difficult at this level. However they should be able to appreciate the meaning of diagrams such as figure 10.19. When introducing this topic teachers may wish to demonstrate a number of precipitation reactions and show that knowledge of the solubility of salts can be used to predict whether or not a precipitate will form.

The sample calculation in box 4 on page 191 shows the advantage of using units consistently. The pupils who study the working in this box will be helped if they can come to see the value of checking the consistency of units in every step.

Answers to selected questions

25b 0.64 g of sulphur dioxide

26 0.000 02 mol/L

27 1 mol/L sodium carbonate
2 mol/L potassium hydroxide
0.5 mol/L copper(II) sulphate
0.1 mol/L silver nitrate

28 188 u

29 60.6 %

30 2.65 mg

31 5.3×10^{-5} mol/L.

C10.4   Hard or soft?

Pupils can deduce that calcium and magnesium ions make water hard from the evidence given in the experiment described in box 5 on page 193. The formation of an insoluble scum with soap and calcium ions is the most familiar example of precipitation for those who live in hard water areas.

Worksheet C10B is related to this section. The problems posed in boxes 6 and 7 on pages 196–7 can be the basis of practical investigations planned and executed by the pupils.

Videos from ICI can be used to illustrate the importance of this section (see Appendix).

C10.5   Keeping water pollution under control

Study of this section should be co-ordinated with the treatment of pollution in Chapters B17 and B18. There are possibilities for practical work to illustrate this section as suggested under Further information.

Practical work

REQUIREMENTS

Each group of pupils will need:
4 pieces of white fabric, 15 cm × 15 cm
  (see note 1)
Bowl or trough large enough for washing
  the fabric samples
Wooden stick, or other suitable agitator
Thermometer
Eye protection

Worksheet C10A   Comparing detergents

Access to:
Marking pen
Measuring cylinder, 500 ml
Stains: motor oil, moist clay, powdered
  charcoal, lipstick, cooking fat, dust
Hot water, from a tap, kettle or water
  heater
"Lolly sticks" or spatulas to apply the
  stains to the cloth samples
Soap powder, in its packet
Soapless detergent powder, in its packet
Wall clock or wrist watch
Washing line for drying the washed
  samples
Balance

Note:
1 Pupils may be able to provide their own remnant samples for washing. Each group should have four pieces of fabric made of the same material. If the different groups use a variety of natural and synthetic fabrics this will add interest to the investigation.

Pupils will have to scale down the quantities given on the detergent packets. They will need to know the approximate capacity of a washing machine and weigh a measure full of powder so that they can work out how much powder to use in the containers provided.

Worksheet C10B   Which is the best way of softening water?

REQUIREMENTS

Each group of pupils will need:
Test-tube with bung
Test-tube rack
Measuring cylinder, 10 ml
Dropping pipette
Beaker, 250 ml
Glass rod
Thermometer, 0–100 °C
Burner, tripod, gauze and mat
Eye protection

Access to:
Hard water (see note 1)
Soap solution in dropper bottle (see
  note 2), allow 25 ml per group
Calgon, allow 1 g per group
Bath salts (sodium sesquicarbonate), allow
  1 g per group
Ion exchange column (see note 3)
Balance, to measure 0.5 g

Notes:
1 If local tap water is not very hard, a sample of hard water can be made before the lesson. Bubble carbon dioxide through 100 ml limewater until the precipitate redissolves. Dilute with 900 ml tap water, then add 0.25 g of magnesium sulphate.
2 Soap solution can be made by dissolving 10 g of soap flakes (or soft soap) in 250 ml of ethanol and then adding 250 ml of water.
3 A suitable resin is Zeo-carb 225 (sodium form). Any cation exchange resin in its sodium form will do. A suitable mesh size is BSS 52/100.

The column shown in figure **C25** has the advantage that it cannot run dry. An old burette can be used if shortened to about 15 cm. The burette tap replaces the clip. The plastic plug can be cut from foam plastic with a cork borer several sizes greater than the column diameter.

It is **most important** that the resin should be made into a slurry with distilled water in a beaker or flask before being added to the column. The resin beads swell and can crack the column as they expand.

Setting up the column:

Fill the empty column with distilled water. Displace any trapped air bubbles by squeezing the rubber tubing.

Saturate the foam plastic plug with water and gently push it into position with a glass rod. Do not force the plug into the tapered part of the tube.

Pour the resin slurry into the column through the burette funnel.

Adjust the glass tube so that the level of the outlet is about 5 mm above the top of the resin bed.

The column can be reused if regenerated with a concentrated solution of sodium chloride. After regeneration it should be washed through several times with distilled water.

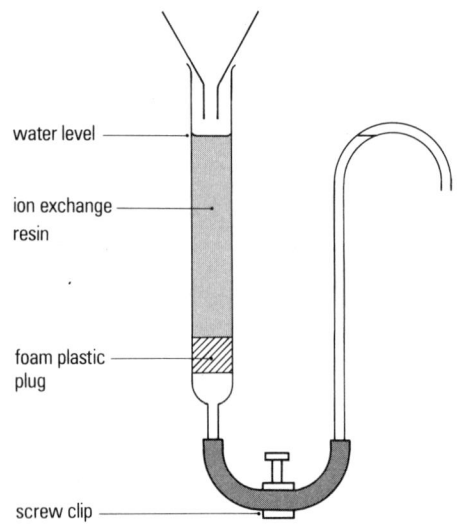

water level

ion exchange
resin

foam plastic
plug

screw clip

Figure **C25**

Box 6 Problem: Which is the best descaler?

Box 7 Problem: Does descaling kettles save energy?

REQUIREMENTS

Each group of pupils will define their own requirements on the planning sheet (Worksheet **C0**).

The teacher will need:
Samples of commercial descalers in their original packs (see note 1)
Kettle(s) with scale

Notes:
1 Some of these commercial descalers are quite dangerous acids, and pupils should be encouraged to make safety a major consideration when planning their experiments.
2 The problems will seem more important to pupils living in hard water areas. However, hardness is widespread in Britain.

Pupils can choose to investigate one or other of the practical problems outlined in section **C10.4** of their book.

Which is the best descaler?

Manufacturers of products affected by scale have to deal with the problem whatever the nature of their own – or the school's – local water supply.

The problem of descaling might be put to the pupils some weeks before the laboratory session. This will allow time for planning and research. They can be encouraged to find out which descalers are on sale locally. They may be able to review test reports in magazines such as *Which?* in their local public library. They can find out something about the chemical properties of known descalers from textbooks.

Each group might take on one aspect of the problem so that the class as a whole can combine the findings to produce a final recommendation. The chemical principles involved include the chemistry of acids, metals and carbonates, and a knowledge of the effects of temperature and concentration on reaction rates. Pupils who have been introduced to the concept "amount of substance/mol" might calculate the amount of descaler needed in theory to remove a given quantity of scale.

In a hard water area the class could follow up its recommendations by packaging agreed quantities of the chosen descaler with appropriate labelling for use at home. The exercise can be costed to determine an appropriate pack price.

Does descaling kettles save energy?

Which? reports suggest that the effect of descaling is much more marked with kettles heated on an electric hotplate or gas ring than with electric kettles.

This problem provides some useful links with Chapter **P9**. It is only possible as a quantitative exercise using gas rings if some method of metering the gas used is available.

Further information

Nuffield Science 13 to 16

Six of the seven sections in *Making molecules work for us* are related to this chapter and include experiments covering the manufacture and use of soaps and detergents, hardness of water and pollution.

Section 4 of *Earth, air and water* deals with the chemical weathering of limestone rocks.

The water cycle and pollution problems are included in *Is the environment changing?*

Revised Nuffield Chemistry

Section 6 of Option 1 *Water* in Stage III of Revised Nuffield Chemistry includes a series of experiments to investigate water pollution.

Science at Work

Cosmetics includes sections dealing with soap and hard water.

Pollution has several sections dealing with water. Experimental work covers the identification of pollutants as well as biological monitoring. Water treatment is dealt with and so is the problem of oil pollution.

Dyes and dyeing includes experiments to investigate the use of solvents to remove stains and to find out whether solvents can damage fabrics.

University of York Science Education Group

In Salters' Chemistry:

Drinks deals with water treatment, fluoridation, and sewage treatment.
Keeping clean deals with hardness of water, and detergency.

Chemistry in Action

The *Invergrog reservoir project* requires pupils to use their knowledge of chemistry to choose the site for a new reservoir which will supply a whisky distillery. The *Eboclean* unit requires pupils to take on the role of a scientist employed to analyse samples of the product which appear to be inferior and which are being marketed by a rival, unscrupulous manufacturer.

Keep Britain Tidy Group Research Project

Science unit 5 *Waste management and resources* includes worksheets for experiments to do with soaps, detergents and water pollution. The text covers sewage treatment and the use of water at home and in industry. Domestic, industrial and agricultural pollution problems are covered.

Science and Technology in Society

Unit 607 "Scale and scum" examines the claims made for a commercial water softening unit and thus covers much of the chemistry of hard water.

Unit 801 "The water pollution mystery" is a data analysis exercise about solving the problem of death of fish in a river.

Chapter C11   Dyes and dyeing

Purposes

Knowledge and understanding

At the end of this chapter all pupils should:

1 know the meaning of these terms: mordant, vat dye

2 understand that a good dye must be fast to washing and light

3 appreciate that the discovery of synthetic dyes made a dramatic change in the range of colours of fabrics

4 appreciate some of the problems involved in discovering and marketing a new chemical product

5 appreciate the relative merits of natural and synthetic dyes.

In addition, those pupils aiming for higher grades should:

6 know that it is hydroxide ions which make water alkaline

7 understand that dyes which react with cloth fibres are faster than dyes which are held by "between molecule" forces.

Processes and problem solving

Using apparatus and measuring instruments
The practical work for this chapter gives a chance for pupils to improve their ability to follow instructions carefully. They will be able to see from their results whether or not they have been successful.

Observation
Worksheets C11A, C11B and C11C and the associated fastness testing provide opportunities for pupils to make observations.

Interpretation and application
This chapter may be used to show that chemical theory can make sense of practical situations. The theory of ionic precipitation applies to the formation of mordants. Ideas about oxidation and reduction can be used to interpret the changes seen when indigo is dyed. The fastness of reactive dyes can be interpreted in terms of chemical bonding. Many pupils will need much help with this but they can all be encouraged to make sense of the ideas for themselves.

Planning and carrying out investigations
As an extension to each of the Worksheets C11A, C11B and C11C, the pupils are asked to devise and carry out experiments to test the fastness of their dyed samples.

Timing

6–7 periods, depending on the route taken.

Suggested routes

Suggested routes are given in figure C26 (over the page).

Each of the three worksheets will need a double period. Fastness testing can be the basis of a practical homework, but this might have to be planned during a period of school time. Most of the text is designed to be read for homework. Some time will be needed to explain points of chemical theory including oxidation/reduction, precipitation of mordants, and the reaction of Procion dyes with cellulose.

Opportunities for co-ordination

There are links with the work in Biology on the treatment of diseases (Chapter B14). The development of modern drugs was closely linked to the study of dyes. Robert Koch (1843–1910) and his co-workers developed the use of dyes to stain cells and so discovered the bacteria which cause eleven diseases including anthrax (1863), tuberculosis (1882) and cholera (1883). One of Koch's co-workers was Paul Ehrlich (1854–1915) who was fascinated by the new synthetic dyes. He was interested in selective dyeing and thus arrived at the idea that it might be possible to find chemicals which would selectively kill bacteria in the body without harming healthy cells. After a long period of research he discovered Salvarsan which was the first effective treatment for syphilis. Later the study of dyes lead to the discovery of Prontosil in the 1930s and hence the sulphonamide drugs.

The topic of colour is discussed in Chapter P15.

There are considerable opportunities for co-ordination with art, CDT and home economics. This chapter is designed to focus on the more chemical aspects of the subject.

There are also opportunities for co-ordination with history. Many syllabuses are now based on the twentieth century including World War I, so the strength of German industry up to the outbreak of the war is of interest. Pupils who have made a study of dress over a period of time may be able to comment on the range of colours available to the mass of the population, and to the nobility,

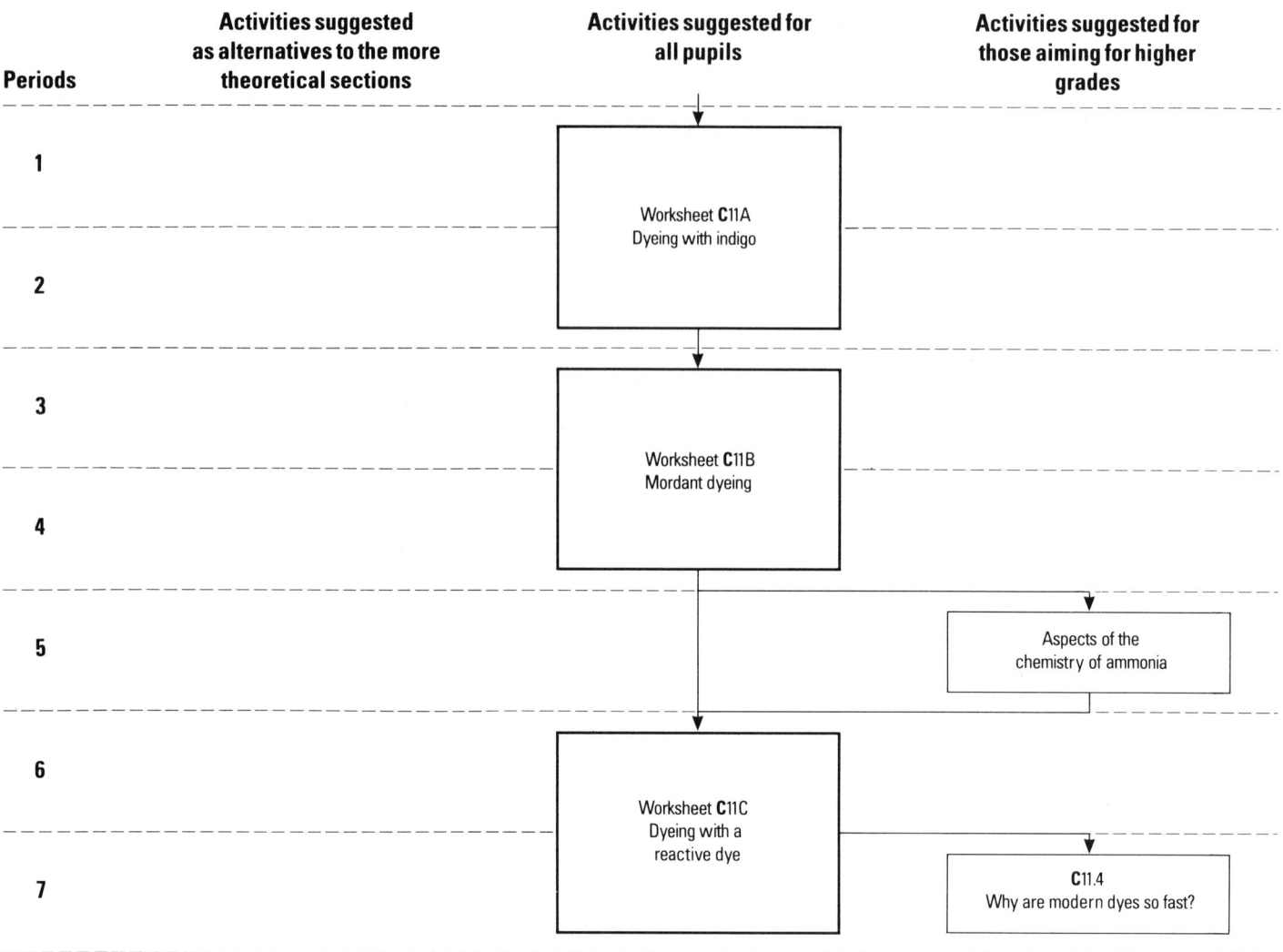

Periods	Activities suggested as alternatives to the more theoretical sections	Activities suggested for all pupils	Activities suggested for those aiming for higher grades
1		Worksheet **C**11A Dyeing with indigo	
2			
3		Worksheet **C**11B Mordant dyeing	
4			
5			Aspects of the chemistry of ammonia
6		Worksheet **C**11C Dyeing with a reactive dye	
7			**C**11.4 Why are modern dyes so fast?

Figure C26

before the mid nineteenth century. If there is time to extend the practical work with natural dyes to a variety of fabrics, it is possible to show why silk was (and is) so highly valued. The dye from onion skins is a dull yellow on cotton. On silk it has a golden sheen. (Remnants of silk are often available remarkably cheaply in department stores and fabric shops.)

Notes and answers

C11.1   What is a dye?

Pupils are not expected to remember the details about the dyes. The information is included for those who may be interested.

When they tackle Worksheet C11A pupils should notice that the surface of the dye bath stays blue however much they stir. Those interested might be asked to suggest ways of demonstrating that it is oxygen in the air which is responsible for restoring the blue colour. This provides an opportunity to mention oxidation reactions and to review examples which they have met previously. Reduction is defined as the opposite of oxidation (see question 2).

The pupils should keep careful records of the results of all three dyeing experiments. Then they have to plan and organize tests to see if the dyes are fast to washing and light.

This can be linked to a home survey of the coloured textiles in their homes: looking for patterns in the extent to which different coloured fabrics suffer from fading in use.

C11.2   What is a mordant?

Recommended methods for mordanting cloth are based on longer treatments in hot solutions of salts. Worksheet C11B suggests the use of ammonia to precipitate metal hydroxides as a quicker way of depositing the mordant in the fabric. The text explains this in terms of ionic precipitation as a further example of these reactions which were introduced in Chapter C10. Ionic equations are used in box 1 on page 205. Pupils are not expected to be able to write their own ionic equations under examination conditions, but they should be able to show some understanding of simple examples.

C11.3   How were synthetic dyes discovered?

See Further information for details of an experiment to repeat Perkin's discovery. Pupils are not required to remember the historical details. It is more important that they should reflect on what Perkin achieved by the age of twenty, and think about the problems of exploiting scientific discoveries. A keen stamp collector may be able to produce a penny mauve stamp.

C11.4   Why are modern dyes so fast?

The superior fastness of reactive dyes over direct dyes provides an interesting demonstration of the greater strength of the bonds within molecules compared to the weak attractive forces between molecules.

The reaction between the dyes and cellulose can be explained in the same terms as one step of a condensation polymerization process. Here there is an opportunity to revise the structure of cellulose described in Chapter C3.

When pupils have completed their own series of dyeing experiments they might evaluate the dyes they have used according to the criteria in figure 11.14.

Practical work

Worksheet C11A   Dyeing with indigo

REQUIREMENTS

Each working group will need:
Copy of Worksheet C11A
Beaker, 400 ml
Glass rod
Tongs
Burner, tripod, gauze and mat
5 boiling-tubes in rack
Protective gloves
Eye protection

Access to:
Indigo, allow 0.4 g per group, with spatula
Sodium hydroxide, allow 1 g per group, with spatula
Sodium dithionite, allow 2 g per group, with spatula
Cotton cloth for dyed samples (see note 1)
Extra cotton cloth for part 2 of the worksheet, 5 small squares per group
Balance
Absorbent paper (e.g. paper towels)
Distilled water with cylinder to measure 200 ml
Bench reagents: dilute hydrochloric acid, hydrogen peroxide (1 volume strength), and acidified potassium dichromate(VI), 0.02 mol/L, allow about 15 ml of each per group
Solution of sulphur dioxide in water, about 15 ml per group

Note:
1 Rolls of plain cotton bandage are excellent because they have not been treated with surface dressings which confuse the results. It is also easy to cut suitable lengths of fabric for these experiments. **Each pupil** needs enough cotton to be able to have three samples to keep (see worksheet). Each **group** needs five further pieces for part 2.

Part 1 of this worksheet is accessible to all pupils. Part 2 introduces the idea that there are chemicals which "do the same thing as oxygen" and so can be classified as oxidants. Examples are hydrogen peroxide and acidified potassium dichromate(VI) solutions which rapidly turn the cloth blue. They must not be too concentrated or they will then bleach the indigo. There is no colour change in sulphur dioxide which is a reductant. It is impossible to exclude oxygen completely and so water is included as a control.

For the less academic, an alternative to part 2 would be to try tie-dyeing; this can work well with indigo (see Further information).

Pupils are expected to prepare one dyed sample for display under "results" and to keep two other samples for fastness testing.

Worksheet C11B   Mordant dyeing

REQUIREMENTS

Each group of pupils will need:
Beaker, 250 ml, for the dyebath
2 beakers, 100 ml
Glass rod
Tongs
Measuring cylinder, 100 ml
Burner, tripod, gauze and mat
Cotton fabric (see note 1 under Worksheet C11A)
Protective gloves
Eye protection

Access to:
Alizarin, allow 0.2 g per group, with spatula
Alum solution (25 g potassium alum in 1 L water), allow 50 ml per group, with 50-ml measuring cylinder (see note 1)
Dilute ammonia solution (50 ml 0.88 ammonia made up to 1 L with water), allow 50 ml per group, with 50-ml measuring cylinder
Absorbent paper (e.g. paper towels)
Balance
Fume cupboard

Note:
1 Pupils may have time to try other mordants such as iron(II) sulphate, magnesium sulphate and tin(II) chloride. These should be made up in similar concentrations to the alum solution. Tin(II) chloride and iron(II) sulphate will have to be prepared immediately before the lesson to avoid oxidation by the air.

Pupils must be reminded that they will have to keep their samples in an orderly way so that they know which is which when it comes to fastness testing (see below). They can be encouraged to make an attractive display of the dyed samples in their notes. The specimens look much better if they are cut neatly and ironed.

Worksheet C11C   Dyeing with a reactive dye

REQUIREMENTS

Each working group will need:
Beaker, 400 ml
Beaker, 100 ml
Glass rod
Tongs
Burner, tripod, gauze and mat
Thermometer
Test-tube
Measuring cylinder, 100 ml
Protective gloves
Eye protection

Access to:
Procion yellow M-R, allow 1.2 g per group, with spatula
Sodium chloride, allow 15 g per group, with spatula
Hydrated sodium carbonate, allow 4 g per group, with spatula
Cotton cloth (see note 1 for Worksheet C11A)
Balance
Sink or bowl with cold water to speed up the cooling in step **c**
Absorbent paper (e.g. paper towels)

Pupils must be reminded to keep samples of the dyed cotton, both for their results and for fastness testing.

For some pupils this will simply be an opportunity to use a modern dye and to compare it with natural dyes for depth of colour, brightness, and fastness. With more academic pupils it provides an opportunity to explain observations in terms of structure and bonding.

Further investigations: Fastness testing

This investigation lends itself to being done as a home experiment. For light fastness the pupils only need opaque paper or card, scissors, staples or sticky tape and access to a window. For washing fastness they need a basin, a source of hot water and some soap or detergent.

Some pupils can be given minimal instructions and asked to plan, execute and report on their investigations largely unaided.

Others will need more help and they can do the planning in school. If there is time the experiment can be done in school too.

Light fastness is conveniently tested by attaching the pieces of dyed cotton to thin card and then covering them with a second piece of card with windows cut in it. The samples can then be exposed to sunlight in a (south-facing) window. Significant results will be seen after three or four weeks with some dyes (depending on the weather and the time of year). The exposed parts of some pieces of cotton will be noticeably paler than the parts hidden under card.

Washing fastness can be tested following the instructions for coloured cotton on the packet of washing powder. (Pupils should perhaps be warned not to put the samples in with the family wash!) Wash fastness is sometimes tested by stitching the sample to a piece of undyed cotton to see if any colour transfers to it from the dyed specimen. (See Nuffield Home Economics under Further information for more details.)

Pupils might be asked to set up a five-point rating scale for fastness testing ranging from 5 (no change) to 1 (very great loss of colour).

Further information

Nuffield Home Economics
The Basic Course, Chapter 20 covers fabrics and colour. Several experiments are suggested covering natural dyes, mordant dyeing, the selection of dyes suited to particular fabrics and fastness testing. Worksheets M32 and M33 are also relevant.

Fibres and fabrics, Chapter 10 covers the origin of colour and the dyeing of cotton/polyester fabrics. Worksheets FM10, FM11 and FM12 investigate the effectiveness of different dyes and how well they withstand light, washing and dry cleaning.

Science at Work
Dyes and dyeing includes practical work dealing with natural dyes, mordant dyeing, and fastness testing as well as tie-dyeing and Batik. There is also an experiment to make two brown dyes which involves the use of ammonia to precipitate iron(II) and chromium(III) hydroxides in the fibres of cotton. Chlorine is then used to oxidize the iron(II) to iron(III). If there is time this experiment could provide further experience of precipitation and oxidation reactions.

Science and Technology in Society (SATIS)
Unit 510 "Perkin's Mauve" includes details of an experiment to make a sample of mauveine.

Chapter **C12**   **Chemicals in the medicine cupboard**

Purposes

Knowledge and understanding

At the end of this chapter all pupils should:

1 know the meaning of these terms: drug, analgesic, antacid, chemotherapy

2 appreciate that drugs are often discovered as a result of studying chemicals from plants

3 know that salts are formed when acids are neutralized by alkalis.

In addition, those pupils aiming for higher grades should:

4 understand that during neutralization reactions hydrogen ions combine with hydroxide ions to form water molecules.

Processes and problem solving

Graphical and symbolic representation
Questions 6, 7, and 9 provide further practice in the use of symbols and equations.

Using apparatus and measuring instruments
The practical work associated with this chapter introduces titration techniques; it also provides opportunities for pupils to learn to measure masses and liquid volumes accurately in contexts in which they can check the accuracy of their results.

Problem solving
Box 2 in section **C12.4** suggests that pupils should explore patterns in the solubility of ionic and molecular substances.

The main problems in this chapter involve working out the results of the titration experiments. Two methods are suggested as explained in the notes below. Only pupils aiming for higher grades are expected to work in terms of amounts of substances.

Timing

6–8 periods, depending on the route taken.

Suggested routes

Figure **C27** shows possible routes through this topic.

Opportunities for co-ordination

This chapter can be linked to Chapters **B4** and **B6** which deal with health and hygiene. The problem of drug abuse is not raised in this chapter but is covered in Chapter **B11** of Biology.

The work on acids, alkalis and neutralization should be related to the study of pH, and acids in the mouth and stomach which are covered in Chapters **B4** and **B5**.

Notes and answers

C12.1   What is the difference between a drug and a medicine?

The extraction of caffeine from tea might be demonstrated here. The details are given in the pupils' book for Option 3 of Revised Nuffield Chemistry (see under Further information).

C12.3   How was aspirin discovered?

The story of aspirin illustrates the importance of plants as sources of drugs. Sometimes it is possible to make the drug synthetically, sometimes not. Once the chemical structure is known it is possible to make modifications to the drug in the hope of improving its properties.

The conversion of salicylic acid to aspirin is easily demonstrated. (See under Practical work.)

Our dependence on plants for new drugs is one of the arguments in favour of retaining the genetic diversity of wild species of plants and for protecting the tropical rain forests.

	Activities suggested as alternatives to the more theoretical sections	Activities suggested for all pupils	Activities suggested for those aiming for higher grades
Periods			

1

2

Introduction to the use of burettes

3

4

Worksheet **C**12A
How much gastric juice does "bicarb" neutralize?

5

6

Worksheet **C**12B
Analysis of a magnesia tablet

7

8

Worksheet **C**12C
Analysis of aspirin tablets

9

Ionic theory of neutralization

10

Calculations based on equations

Figure **C**27

Some pupils will want to discuss the ethical problems raised by the testing of new drugs on animals. Animal tests include measuring the pharmacological activities of the drug while a watch is kept for side-effects. The toxicity of the drug is determined. The short-term toxicity is normally given by the LD 50 (lethal dose 50) test which determines the dose which causes immediate death in 50 % of the group of animals to which it is administered. Long term toxicity is investigated by administering smaller doses to a group of animals for about two years. At the end of this time the animals are killed and their organs examined for evidence of damage.

Animal species vary considerably in their tolerance to drugs. It is therefore considered essential that these animal studies be carried out on a representative range of different mammals before treatment of human patients is considered.

Once a drug has been passed for general use, animal testing continues as part of quality control. It is estimated that between 1955 and 1976 some 1.5 million monkeys were killed worldwide during the production and testing of polio vaccine. An alternative based on cultured human cells has since been developed.

Scientists are now responding to public pressure to reduce the scale of animal testing. Cell cultures are being used to replace tests on whole organisms. Alternatives for the assay of the potency of drug products are also being developed.

It may take from three to twenty years to discover a new drug. A further two to three years is needed to carry out and evaluate animal tests. Clinical trials of the efficacy and safety of the drug with human patients may require three to five more years before the drug can be marketed.

All this contrasts markedly with Felix Hofmann treating his father with acetylsalicylic acid.

The text shows that the traditional English and German names for salicylic acid and its derivatives are different. This provides an opportunity to point out to those who may go on with their study of chemistry that newer IUPAC names are becoming standardized internationally.

C12.4   What is an antacid?

The term *indigestion* often appears in inverted commas in medical reference books. Dyspepsia is merely an old-fashioned term for indigestion. Heartburn is a burning sensation below the breastbone which arises when some of the acid contents of the stomach are regurgitated into the oesophagus.

There is a clearly a big market for products which treat the symptoms of "indigestion". Most of the products are formulated with hydroxides or carbonates. Apart from neutralizing hydrochloric acid, the compounds used may have other side-effects.

Sodium hydrogencarbonate (bicarbonate) works fastest but is absorbed into the bloodstream and in large quantities can upset the chemical balance of the body. It must be avoided by those on a low sodium diet.

Calcium and aluminium compounds tend to constipate. Magnesium compounds are mildly laxative. Thus many branded products are mixtures designed to avoid upsetting bowel habits.

Answers to selected questions

10a 100 ml
b 15 ml
c 7.5 ml
d 122.5 ml

C12.5   What is chemotherapy?

The work of Paul Ehrlich is referred to in Chapter **C**11 of this *Guide* under "Opportunities for co-ordination". There is an account of his work in Option 3 of Revised Nuffield Chemistry. This can be related to the subsequent development of sulphonamide drugs, antibiotics, monoclonal antibodies and cancer treatments.

Practical work

Volumetric analysis

REQUIREMENTS

Each group of pupils will need:
Burette and stand
Burette funnel
Beaker, 100 ml
Bottle of distilled water
Graduated pipette, 25 ml, with safety filler
  (see note 1)

Access to:
Balance

Note:
1 Pupils will only need to learn how to use a pipette if they are going to tackle Worksheet C12C.

This is an introductory exercise to train pupils in the correct use of volumetric glassware. They can practise delivering volumes of water into a weighed beaker and then reweighing to find the mass (and hence volume) of water measured out. In this way they can check the consistency and accuracy with which they use a burette. Those who will do the aspirin analysis can also practise the use of a graduated pipette.

Worksheet C12A   How much gastric juice does "bicarb" neutralize?

REQUIREMENTS

Each group of pupils will need:
Flask, 100 ml
Burette and stand
Burette funnel
Beaker, 100 ml
White tile, or piece of white paper
Eye protection

Access to:
Balance, to weigh to 0.01 g
Sodium hydrogencarbonate with spatula
"Gastric juice" (0.1 mol/L hydrochloric acid), allow 75 ml per group
Screened methyl orange indicator in dropper bottle
Distilled water with 25-ml measuring cylinder

This experiment provides an opportunity for pupils to do a quantitative experiment without having to do any calculations.

The worksheet shows the "bicarb" being weighed in the titration flask; this is simple, but not the best practice. Some teachers may prefer to use weighing bottles.

Worksheet C12B   Analysis of a magnesia tablet

REQUIREMENTS

Each group of pupils will need:
Conical flask, 100 ml
Burette and stand
Burette funnel
Glass rod with flattened end
Distilled water wash-bottle
White tile, or piece of white paper
Eye protection
Balance

Access to:
Milk of magnesia tablets, 2 per group
Dilute hydrochloric acid, 75 ml per group
  (see note 1)
Screened methyl orange indicator in a
  dropper bottle (see note 2)

Notes:
1 If the concentration of the hydrochloric acid is 0.517 mol/L, then 1 ml of the acid neutralizes 15 mg of magnesium hydroxide. The acid concentration must be known accurately.

The easiest way of preparing for the experiment is to make an approximately 0.5 mol/L solution by diluting 100 ml concentrated hydrochloric acid to 2 L. This can be standardized by titration against a milk of magnesia tablet as described on the worksheet.

Suppose the average titre is x ml. The tablets contain 300 mg of magnesium hydroxide.

Calculation (alternative one):

1 ml of the acid reacts with $\dfrac{300}{x}$ mg magnesium hydroxide

Calculation (alternative two):

The concentration of the acid $= \dfrac{10.34}{x}$ mol/L

2 Bromothymol blue is an alternative indicator with a colour change from blue to yellow, which some pupils may find easier to see.

The tablet does not dissolve completely because of the inert material used to bind the magnesium hydroxide together. This means that the solution is cloudy during the titration. The magnesium hydroxide gradually dissolves as the titration proceeds. The contents of the flask must be mixed well during the titration. In the later stages of the titration, adding a drop of liquid from the burette may temporarily turn the indicator to its acid colour, because the reaction is relatively slow. The titration should continue until the indicator shows its acid colour for some time even after thorough mixing.

An alternative procedure for doing the experiment is described in SATIS unit 709 (see under Further information).

Magnesium hydroxide tablets have been chosen because they contain only one chemical. Other antacid tablets with mixtures of chemicals may have a marked buffering action which leads to confusing titration results. Some antacid ingredients react very slowly with hydrochloric acid, and the apparent end-point continues to change for a long time.

The worksheet is designed so that there are two ways of working out the results of the analysis. Alternative one is relatively simple. Alternative two involves a calculation based on the equation for the reaction.

Worksheet C12C   Analysis of aspirin tablets

REQUIREMENTS

Each group of pupils will need:
2 beakers, 100 ml
Graduated flask, 250 ml
Funnel and glass rod
Graduated pipette with safety filler, 25 ml
Conical flask, 250 ml
Burette, 25 or 50 ml
White tile, or piece of white paper
Distilled water wash-bottle
Burner, tripod, mat and gauze
Eye protection
Balance

Access to:
Commercial aspirin tablets, 5 per group
1.00 mol/L sodium hydroxide, allow 30 ml per group (see note 1)
One or more communal burettes to dispense the sodium hydroxide
Screened methyl orange indicator in dropper bottle
0.100 mol/L hydrochloric acid, allow 60 ml per group (see note 1)

Note:
1 The solutions must be accurate and are conveniently prepared from volumetric concentrates. This is only justified if pupils adopt correct titration procedures and read the burettes to at least the nearest 0.1 ml.

This is a demanding practical exercise which is likely to be suited to only a minority of pupils.

Teacher demonstration: Making aspirin from salicylic acid

REQUIREMENTS

The teacher will need:
Beaker, 100 ml
Beaker, 250 ml
Glass rod
Measuring cylinder, 25 ml
Measuring cylinder, 100 ml
Buchner funnel and flask
Water pump
Filter paper to fit funnel
Eye protection for the teacher and the pupils

Access to:
Salicylic acid, 5 g
Concentrated sulphuric acid in dropper bottle
Ethanoic (acetic) anhydride, 10 ml
Balance

Procedure

1 Weigh out 5 g salicylic acid in a 100-ml beaker.

2 Add 10 ml ethanoic anhydride.

3 Stir with a glass rod until the solid has dissolved, then add 12 drops of concentrated sulphuric acid, while continuing to stir.

4 Cool the mixture to room temperature (this will be quicker if an ice-bath is used) and then pour it into a beaker containing 150 ml distilled water. The aspirin is insoluble in the mixed solvent of water and ethanoic acid so it precipitates as a fine white powder.

5 Separate the solid using a Buchner filtration apparatus. Wash the solid well with about 50 ml distilled water. Suck dry.

Further information

Revised Nuffield Chemistry
Option 3, *Drugs and medicines*, in Stage III of Revised Nuffield Chemistry includes further experimental work as well as sections covering anaesthesia, chemotherapy, the development of new drugs and the misuse of drugs.

Science and Technology in Society
The following units are related to this chapter:

Units 304 and 305 "A medicine to control bilharzia" – parts 1 and 2
Unit 609 "Hitting the target – with monoclonal antibodies"
Unit 709 "Which anti-acid?"
Unit 710 "What is biotechnology?"
Unit 805 "The search for the magic bullet".

Topic C4

Energy changes in chemistry

Purposes

Chapter C13 Fuels and fires

Knowledge and understanding

At the end of this chapter all pupils should:

1 understand burning in terms of the fire triangle, and know that carbon dioxide and water are among the products of burning hydrocarbon fuels

2 know some examples of solid, liquid and gaseous fuels and their uses

3 understand what is meant by the term fossil fuel

4 appreciate the environmental issues which arise from the use of fossil fuels

5 appreciate that there are different classes of fires and different methods for controlling them.

In addition, those pupils aiming for higher grades should:

6 appreciate the need for the separation, conversion and purification stages in an oil refinery.

Processes and problem solving

Graphical and symbolic representation
Worksheet **C13E** gives practice in the skills involved in interpreting information presented in the form of graphs and tables.

Using apparatus and measuring instruments
The experiment on Worksheet **C13D** uses skills first introduced in physics to measure energy transferred when a fuel is burned.

Observation
When doing the experiment on Worksheet **C13C**, the pupils make observations in the light of the criteria they have chosen for judging a good fuel.

Interpretation and application
Worksheet **C13B** suggests that pupils draw up a list of criteria for judging fuels; they then have to evaluate their experimental results in the light of the checklist.

The boxes in sections **C13.1** and **C13.2** describe the results of experiments for the pupils to interpret.

Worksheet **C13E** is a data analysis exercise about air pollution.

Section **C13.6** poses a series of questions which ask pupils to apply their knowledge to problems which have arisen during the control of fires in an oil refinery.

Planning and carrying out investigations
The problem in the box in section C13.5 can be the basis of an investigation planned and carried out by the pupils.

Timing

11–13 periods, depending on the route taken.

Suggested routes

Figure C28 (over the page) describes possible routes through this chapter.

Opportunities for co-ordination

Ideas about energy pervade this course as explained in Chapter 2 of the General introduction. The development of energy concepts is set out in figure 2 on page 10.

By the time pupils start on this topic they will have studied photosynthesis and respiration in Biology (Chapters **B**3 and **B**7). They will have used the analogy between food and fuels (**B**9). They will also have met the carbon cycle and looked at energy transfers in food webs (**B**14).

In Physics they will have been introduced to energy transfer by heating and by working. They will have used the concept of specific heating capacity to measure energy transfer in the home (Chapter **P**9). They will also have studied machines and engines including internal combustion engines (Chapter **P**8).

Questions of energy cost crop up in both the Physics and the Chemistry courses (Chapters **P**8, **P**10, **C**4, **C**6, and **C**17).

This chapter provides a lead into Chapter **P**12 which reviews the various energy sources and the problem of saving energy.

Notes and answers

C13.1   What is burning?

Air and burning are investigated in most introductory science courses, but for many pupils it will be necessary to revise the chemistry involved. It may help to demonstrate the experiment in box 1 on page 225. Pupils can then attempt questions 1–10 (see under Practical work).

The fire triangle can be a focus for much of the work in this chapter. Note that in this course we have avoided using the word "heat" as a noun, for the reasons explained in Chapter 2 of the General introduction.

C13.2   What is a good fuel?

Worksheet **C**13A is designed to help pupils study this section. This can be a group activity: the pupils can work out the meaning of the passage among themselves, and discuss the possible words which might fill the blanks. They should not have access to the text while using the worksheet.

Worksheets **C**13B and **C**13C are also designed to be used alongside this section. Brainstorms and rounds are ways of encouraging all members of a class to contribute ideas.

During a brainstorm, no idea should be rejected however odd it may seem at first sight. This encourages the less confident pupils to join in. All ideas should be recorded. They can be displayed on the blackboard, on a large chart, or with the help of an overhead projector.

Following a brainstorm, a round gives everyone a chance to say what they think of the ideas which have been suggested, but no-one should be forced to do so. Each time someone refers to a particular idea during the round, make a mark against that statement in the summary list from the brainstorm.

Tests of a good fuel might cover its burning characteristics (how easy it is to light, how much smoke it produces, how much ash it leaves); its convenience (how safe and easy it is to transport, store and use); and economic aspects (how

CHEMISTRY CHEMISTRY CHEMISTRY CHEMISTRY CHEMISTRY

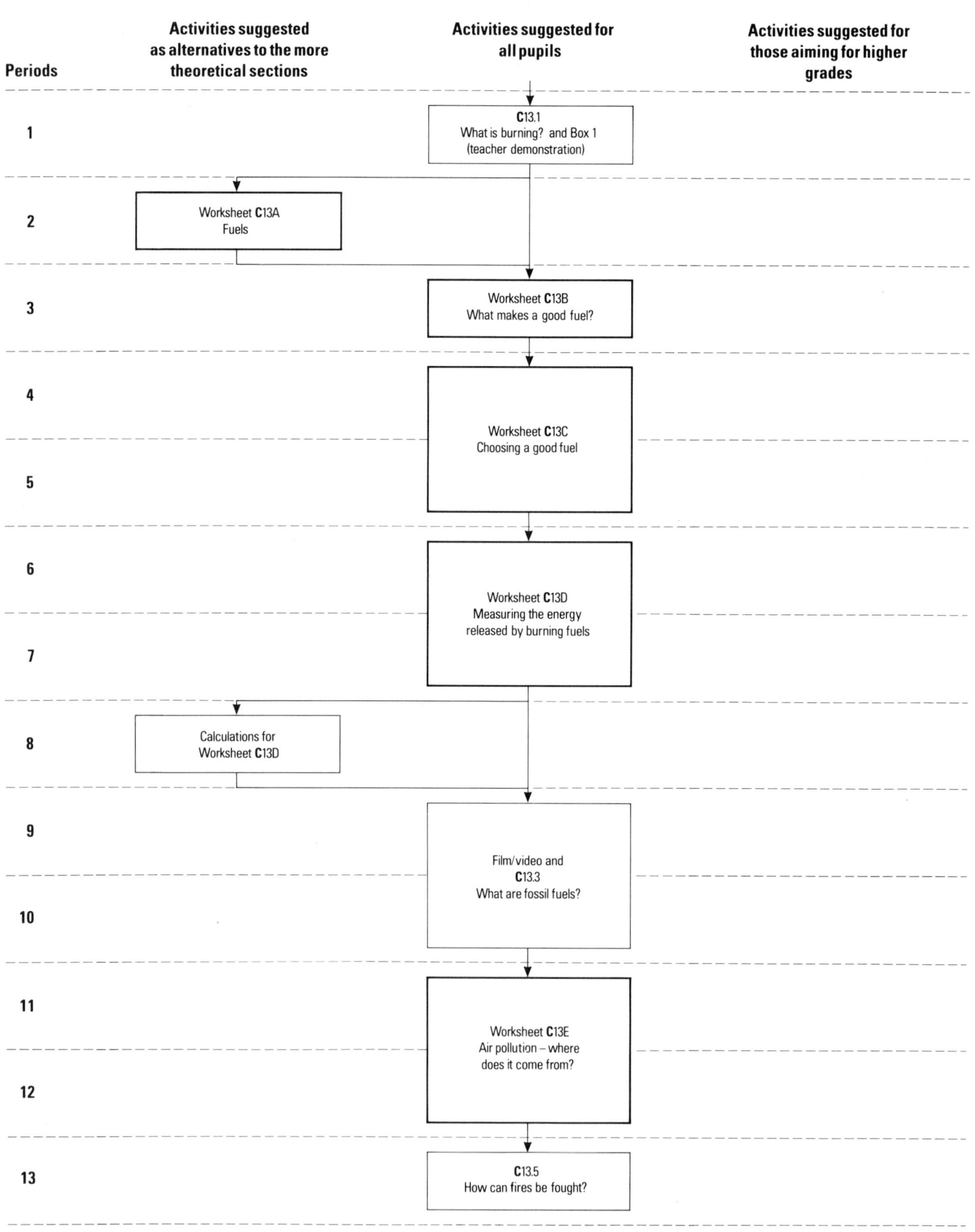

Figure **C28**

cheap or expensive it is in relation to the amount of energy released on burning, and whether it is renewable). A suitable checklist is needed as a result of discussions such as those suggested on Worksheet C13B, so that pupils can go on to Worksheet C13C.

The experiment described in box 2 on page 228 is probably better considered after the pupils have done the experiments described on Worksheet C13D. It is included to give pupils more practice with the methods of calculation and interpretation which are introduced in Chapters P8, P16 and P17 and used in connection with the worksheet.

Answers to selected questions

18a Energy transferred $= 25$ J/s $\times 600$ s
$$= 15\ 000\ \text{J}$$
b 15 000 J
c Energy released $= 15\ 000$ J/0.5 g
$$= 30\ 000\ \text{J/g}$$
$$= 30\ \text{kJ/g}$$

C13.3   What are fossil fuels?

There are several films available free from the libraries of major companies which can be used to illustrate this section (see Appendix). This should be co-ordinated with the work to be done in Chapter P12 on energy resources.

C13.4   Fossil fuels and the environment

Worksheet C13E "Air Pollution – where does it come from?" might be set for homework and followed by reading and discussion of this section in class. Some pupils may have difficulty with the graph on the worksheet; they can be helped by being given a copy of the graph sheet with the axes already marked on it. Others may manage without this assistance.

The main pollutants discussed are carbon dioxide (greenhouse effect), carbon monoxide, sulphur dioxide and nitrogen dioxide. It should be appreciated that there is usually a trade-off between reducing pollution and extra expense, and that many aspects of pollution are complex and incompletely understood (such as the acid rain problem and global warming).

These issues should be discussed in co-ordination with Chapter B17. The SATIS unit 502 "The Coal Mine Project" might also be used to involve pupils in more of the issues raised.

The problems mentioned in this section are likely to remain topical and controversial for many years. It is important to show that it can take a long time to reach definite answers when investigating the effects of chemicals on the environment. Newspaper articles and cuttings from magazines can be used to supplement the information in the pupils' book.

C13.5   How can fires be fought?

The local fire brigade may be able to help with this section, either by allowing a visit or by sending a speaker to talk to the class and answer questions.

No time has been allowed in the "Suggested routes" for the problem in box 3 on page 245. However, this investigation might be carried out in place of one suggested in another chapter. Pupils can make their own plans and state their requirements on Worksheet C0. Possible procedures for experiments are given in several of the publications listed under Further information.

C13.6 Fire on the farm

Questions 47 to 52 are based on a serious refinery fire in Europe which resulted in the death of fourteen fire fighters when a burning tank of oil "boiled over." After the accident, the investigators decided that water sprayed onto the tank had sunk below the oil. The oil at the surface became increasingly dense as the lighter fractions burned away until the hot oil sank and came in contact with the water underneath. The water rapidly turned to steam so that the tank seemed to "boil over". One possible modification is to fit pipework and valves so that liquids can be drained from the bottom of the tank in an emergency.

Practical work

Teacher demonstration: What are the products of burning fuels?

REQUIREMENTS

The teacher will need:
2 test-tubes with side-arms and bungs
Beaker, 400 ml
Filter pump
Glass tubing including thistle funnel (see figure 13.2 in the Chemistry pupils' book)
Thermometer
Anhydrous copper(II) sulphate, or cobalt(II) chloride paper
Limewater
Ethanol in a dropper bottle
Crucible
Mineral wool
Heatproof mat
Eye protection for teacher and pupils

It will only take approximately 10 seconds to see evidence of water and carbon dioxide. The water collected can be boiled, but it takes 20 minutes or so to collect enough to boil. Anhydrous copper(II) sulphate or blue cobalt(II) chloride paper can also be used as tests for the presence of water. Carbon will be seen round the thistle funnel – evidence of incomplete combustion. Thoughtful pupils might point out that the limewater would eventually go cloudy anyway because of carbon dioxide from the air. They may be able to suggest a modification to the apparatus.

The questions in the box in section C13.1 can be used as a basis for pupil activity during the demonstration.

Worksheet C13C Choosing a good fuel

REQUIREMENTS

Each group of pupils will need:
Copy of Worksheet **C13C**
Tin lid
Tongs
Burner, tripod and mat
Dropping pipette
Eye protection

Access to:
Variety of solids in very small pieces:
  wood, coke, coal, wax, paper, straw
Variety of liquids in small reagent bottles
  with droppers: methylated spirits,
  paraffin, petrol
Mineral wool
Wood splints
Waste container for hot residues
Spatula or knife to scrape the tin lid clean

This worksheet is designed for use after the pupils have drawn up a list of criteria for judging a good fuel. One approach to this is suggested by Worksheet **C13A**.

Safety

It is very important to control the issue of materials to be burned – especially the liquids. Some pupils will be tempted to burn far too much. It will generally be safer if the teacher dispenses the liquid fuels.

Testing liquid fuels needs to be organized particularly carefully. The liquid must be dispensed well away from flames. The liquid must not be put onto hot mineral wool or a hot tin lid. The tin lid must be cool enough to pick up with fingers before a liquid fuel is added to the mineral wool.

Worksheet C13D Measuring the energy released by burning fuels

REQUIREMENTS

Each group of pupils will need:
Crucible
Tin lid
Metal can (see note 1)
Measuring cylinder, 100 ml
Thermometer, 0–100 °C
Stand with boss and clamp
Heatproof mat
Eye protection

Access to:
Ethanol in a dropper bottle (see safety notes on Worksheet C13C above)
Meta fuel
Gas fuel burner (e.g. cigarette lighter – supervision by teacher is necessary if this is used)
Balance weighing to 0.01 g

Note:
1 An empty ring pull can with a domed bottom makes a cheap, disposable calorimeter.

If time is short, each group can do the experiment with one fuel and then compare results with other groups.

The calculation can be simplified if 100 ml of water is used. Then the pupils can be told that a rise in temperaure of one degree corresponds to a transfer of 420 J of energy to the water.

Further information

Nuffield Science 13 to 16
The module *Fuels* covers fires and fire extinguishers, good and bad fuels, air pollution, fossil fuels and their origins as well as the changing patterns in the consumption of fuels in recent times.

Science at Work
Section 1 of *Energy* includes experiments and information about fuels. (Note that section 2 is written in terms which we have deliberately excluded from Nuffield Co-ordinated Sciences.)

Science and the motor car includes experiments and information about crude oil, oil refining and lubricants.

Section 8 of *Pollution* investigates the effects of sulphur dioxide on plants and includes information about air pollution.

Fibres and fabrics describes an experiment to study the effectiveness of flame-proofing fabrics.

Science and Technology in Society
The following units can be used in conjunction with this chapter:

Unit 205 "Looking at motor oil"
Unit 403 "Britain's energy sources"
Unit 502 "The coal mine project"
Unit 702 "The gas supply problem"
Unit 902 "Acid rain"
Unit 1003 "A big bang"

University of York Science Education Group
The unit *Warmth* in Salters' Chemistry includes sections about the choice of fuels and the effects of air pollution. The unit called *Burning and bonding* studies fires and fire prevention fund includes a quantitative comparison of fuels.

Nuffield Working with Science
Fire

Keep Britain Tidy Group
Waste management and resources includes an experiment to investigate whether a fuel can be made from solid waste. The booklet includes methods for doing this on an industrial scale. Air pollution problems are also described and investigated.

Nuffield Home Economics
The Basic Course includes an experiment to investigate the flammability of fibres (see pages 116–17).

Chapter C14   Batteries

Purposes

Knowledge and understanding

At the end of this chapter all pupils should:

1 know that a cell consists of two different electrodes dipping into an electrolyte solution

2 know that changing the electrodes changes the cell voltage

3 understand that there is a limit to the life of a simple cell because one or more of the reactants is eventually used up

4 appreciate some of the cost and convenience factors which dictate the choice of cells for particular purposes.

In addition, those pupils aiming for higher grades should:

5 appreciate that the voltage of a cell with two metal electrodes can be related to the position of the metals in the activity series

6 understand, in principle, the differences between simple cells, rechargeable cells, and fuel cells.

Processes and problem solving

Using apparatus and measuring instruments
Worksheet **C14A** involves setting up circuits and the use of voltmeters so it provides a chance to practise skills first met in Physics.

Interpretation and application
Questions 1, 4 to 7, 8, and 9 ask pupils to interpret the information given in the text.

Planning and carrying out investigations
Worksheet **C14A** is relatively unstructured and suggests a variety of problems for the pupils to investigate.

Timing

5 periods.

Suggested routes

Figure **C29** suggests a route through this chapter.

Periods	Activities suggested as alternatives to the more theoretical sections	Activities suggested for all pupils	Activities suggested for those aiming for higher grades

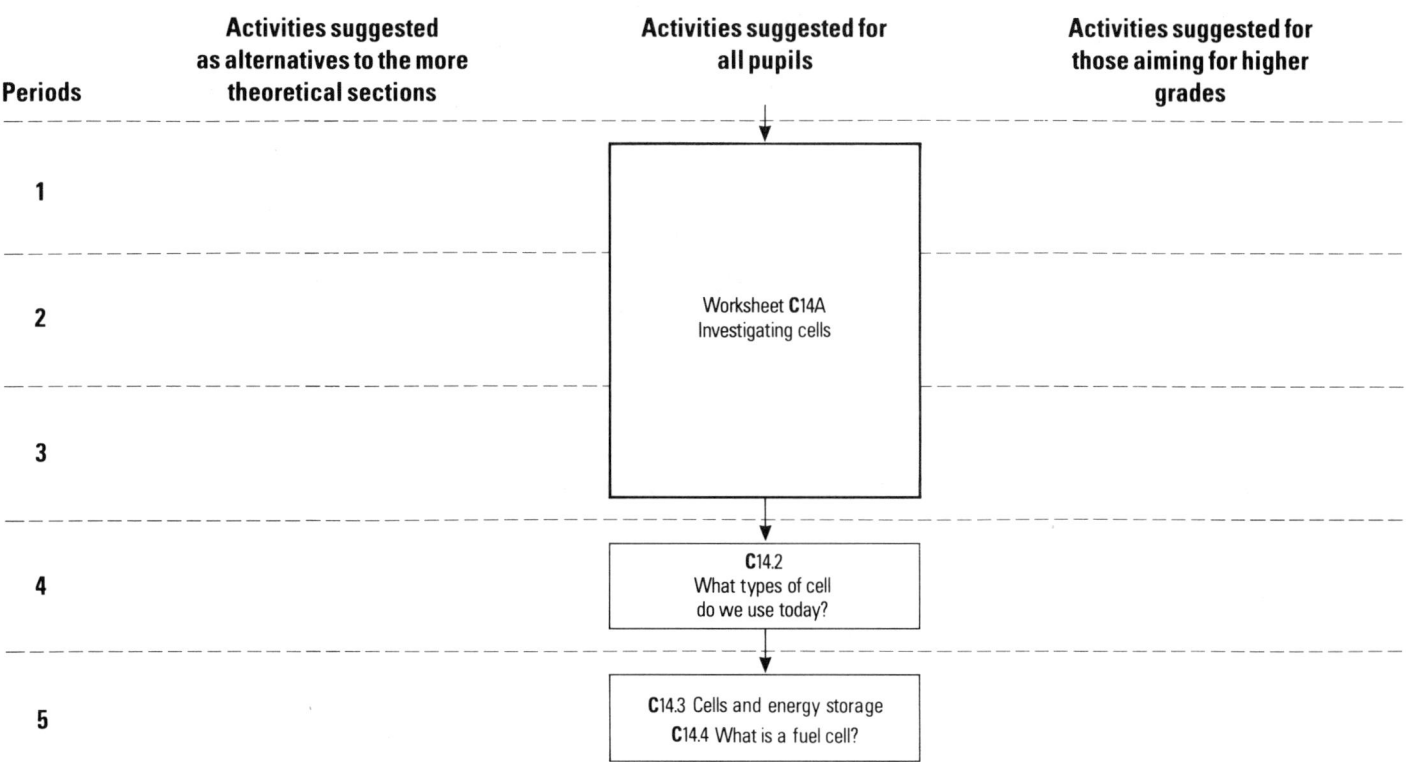

Figure C29

Opportunities for co-ordination

The pupils have used cells in Physics (Chapters **P**17 and **P**18) but they have not investigated their construction. Worksheet **P**18A deals with the use of rechargeable cells in electric vehicles.

The theoretical advantages of fuel cells can be contrasted with the relative inefficiency of power stations which burn fuels to raise steam to drive turbines.

Notes and answers

C14.1   How were batteries invented?

There are various versions of the story of the discovery made by Luigi and Lucia Galvani which give differing degrees of credit to husband and wife depending on the sympathies of the author.

In this chapter it is necessary to distinguish clearly between cells and batteries, but elsewhere in the course we have generally used the word "battery" in its everyday sense.

C14.2   What types of cell do we use today?

Pupils are not expected to remember the technical details of the cells described. The SATIS unit 706 "Dry cells" includes a practical investigation of a dry cell but it depends on a chemical test which the pupils will not have met before. It is very important to warn pupils of the dangers of opening cells other than dry cells.

C14.3   How can cells be used to store energy?

The sodium-sulphur cell is described here partly because it is new, and partly because it is relatively easy to describe the chemistry of the cell as an example to illustrate the ideas in Chapter **C**18. Another new type of cell which is becoming available commercially is the aluminium-oxygen cell.

A battery of sodium-sulphur cells is surrounded by a double-walled container filled with glass fibre so that it stays at its operating temperature. If the cell is discharged and recharged by 80 % of its capacity every 24 hours, it stays at its working temperature because the energy lost to the surroundings is replaced by the heating effect of the current in the cell.

C14.4   What is a fuel cell?

A fuel cell can be demonstrated as suggested under Practical work. Fuel cells are still "exotic" but research continues in the quest for a reliable and safe cell for commercial use. Reports appear in newspapers and magazines from time to time about the progress of this development work.

Practical work

Worksheet C14A   Investigating cells

REQUIREMENTS

Each group of pupils will need:
2 beakers, 100 ml
White tile
2 connecting wires with crocodile clips
Voltmeter, 0–5 V (see note 1)
2 lead electrodes, 3 cm × 5 cm
Power supply, 2–6 V d.c.
Bulb in holder, 1.25 V/0.25 A
Eye protection

Access to:
Metal electrodes: copper, iron, magnesium, nickel, zinc, and others if available
0.1 mol/L solutions of metal salts: copper(II) sulphate, iron(II) ammonium sulphate, magnesium nitrate, zinc sulphate, 50 ml per group (see note 2)
Potassium nitrate solution, 0.5 mol/L, about 50 ml per group
Dilute sulphuric acid, 1 mol/L, 50 ml per group
Filter paper
Scissors
Snips

Notes:
1 For good results a high impedance voltmeter should be used. These are likely to be in short supply. If a limited number of meters is placed at convenient access points, groups can make their cells on a mat or tray, then take them to a meter to measure the voltage.
2 The solutions might be labelled: copper salt solution, iron(II) salt solution etc.

The pupils should have read section **C14.2** before starting on this worksheet. They are not expected to cover all the suggested investigations. The various groups might tackle different parts and then report their findings to the class.

Teacher demonstration: A fuel cell

REQUIREMENTS

The teacher will need:
Beaker, 400 ml
2 hydrogen electrodes, platinized
Connecting wires
High resistance voltmeter
Hydrogen cylinder

Oxygen cylinder
Connecting tubing
Sodium hydroxide solution, 2 mol/L, 200 ml
Eye protection for the teacher and pupils

The apparatus is illustrated in figure **C30**. The voltage rises and steadies at a value just under 1 volt.

The advantage of this apparatus is that it is clear that the cell is continuously supplied with the fuel and the oxidant which is the essential feature of a fuel cell. A much simpler apparatus is described in section A23.5 of Revised Nuffield Chemistry *Teachers' guide II*, but it suffers from the disadvantage that pupils might believe that the process of using electrolysis to generate the oxygen and hydrogen might be akin to charging up a lead-acid cell.

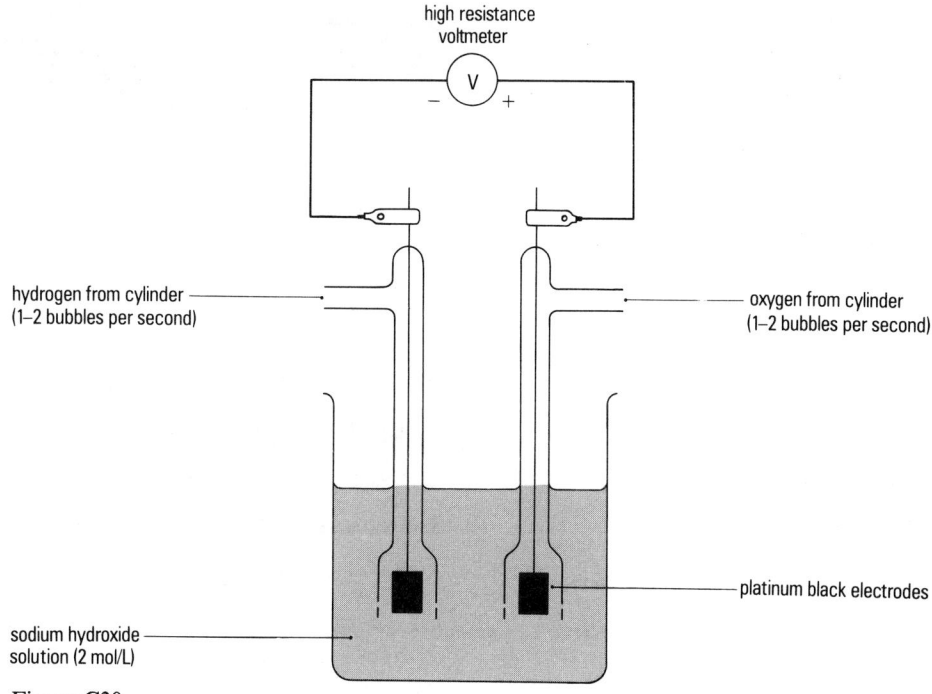

high resistance voltmeter

hydrogen from cylinder (1–2 bubbles per second)

oxygen from cylinder (1–2 bubbles per second)

platinum black electrodes

sodium hydroxide solution (2 mol/L)

Figure **C**30

The disadvantage of the suggested apparatus is that it is only schools running A-level courses which are likely to have hydrogen electrodes. So this should be regarded as an optional demonstration.

Further information

Nuffield Science 13 to 16
Cells, including rechargeable cells, are studied in section 7 of the *Periodic Table* module.

Science at Work
The booklet called *Science and the motor car* includes a section about car batteries including an experiment, pictures and information.

Science and Technology in Society
Unit 706 "Dry cells" might be used in conjunction with this chapter.

University of York Science Education Group
In Salters' Chemistry there is a topic called *Making and using electricity* which includes a series of sections relevant to this chapter.

Soil and agriculture

Chapter **C15**   **Soil**

Purposes

Knowledge and understanding

At the end of this chapter all pupils should:

1 appreciate that weathering of rocks is the result of both physical and chemical changes

2 know that weathering of rocks releases the salts into the soil which plants need for growth

3 understand that concentration, temperature, and surface area are factors which affect the rates of chemical reactions.

In addition, those pupils aiming for higher grades should:

4 understand that soil pH affects plant growth partly because it affects the solubility of the salts which plants need.

Processes and problem solving

Graphical and symbolic representation
The practical work provides plenty of opportunities to display results graphically.

Using apparatus and measuring instruments
The practical programme introduces the techniques for studying reaction rates quantitatively.

Observation
Worksheet **C15D** requires careful observations of the effects of pH on precipitation reactions.

Interpretation and application
Those aiming for higher grades can apply their ability to carry out calculations based on equations to compare the neutralizing power of lime products.

Planning and carrying out investigations
Pupils may be asked to plan their own investigations into the factors affecting the rate of the reaction of marble with acid.

Problem solving
There is an opportunity to devise a simple soil test kit and then to make a survey of local soil using the kit.

| **Timing** | 10–12 periods, depending on the route taken. |

Suggested routes

Figure C31 (over the page) shows two suggested routes through this chapter. One route puts a greater emphasis on pupils planning their own investigations, based on the problem in the box in section C15.2. This route leads to Worksheet C15D which is only for those who have studied the ionic theory of precipitation reactions in earlier chapters. The route ends with calculations to compare the neutralizing power of lime products.

The other route follows the worksheets and is more concerned with manipulative skills; it allows more time to help pupils with graphs and the interpretation of the results. As shown here, this route ends with the design and testing of a kit to test soil pH.

Opportunities for co-ordination

Pupils have studied some aspects of soil biology in year 3. Some of the living organisms found in the soil are described in Chapters B2 and B15. In Chapter B15 there is also an account of the mineral salts which plants need for growth.

Pupils will already have some knowledge of the factors which affect the rates of chemical (and biochemical) reactions from their work in connection with Chapters B3 and B5.

Pupils have already used graphs in Chapter P4 to describe moving objects, so they should be familiar with the idea that the rate of a change can be represented by the gradient of a graph.

There are opportunities for links with geography in connection with land forms, weathering and soil erosion.

Notes and answers

C15.1 Why study soil?

Some books about environmental chemistry emphasize pollution, others concentrate on chemical changes in the natural environment. In this course it is not possible to go into these matters in any depth, but it is important to relate the impact of industry, farming and other activities on the environment to the scale of natural processes. This was hinted at in Worksheet C13E.

C15.2 How is soil formed?

The power of frost to shatter rocks can be emphasized by means of the demonstration suggested under Practical work.

Two alternative approaches to the practical work in this section are given under Suggested routes. Further details are given under Practical work.

C15.3 What is in soil?

This section shows that ion exchange is not just a process used to soften water. Ion exchange is an example of a reversible process.

C15.4 Why does soil pH matter?

There is a diagram of the pH scale in the Biology pupils' book (Chapter B5). The practical work in connection with this section either involves a study of the effect of pH on solubility or the design of a kit to measure soil pH.

C15.5 How can the pH of soil be controlled?

This section provides an opportunity to revise the chemistry of limestone as

CHEMISTRY CHEMISTRY CHEMISTRY CHEMISTRY CHEMISTRY

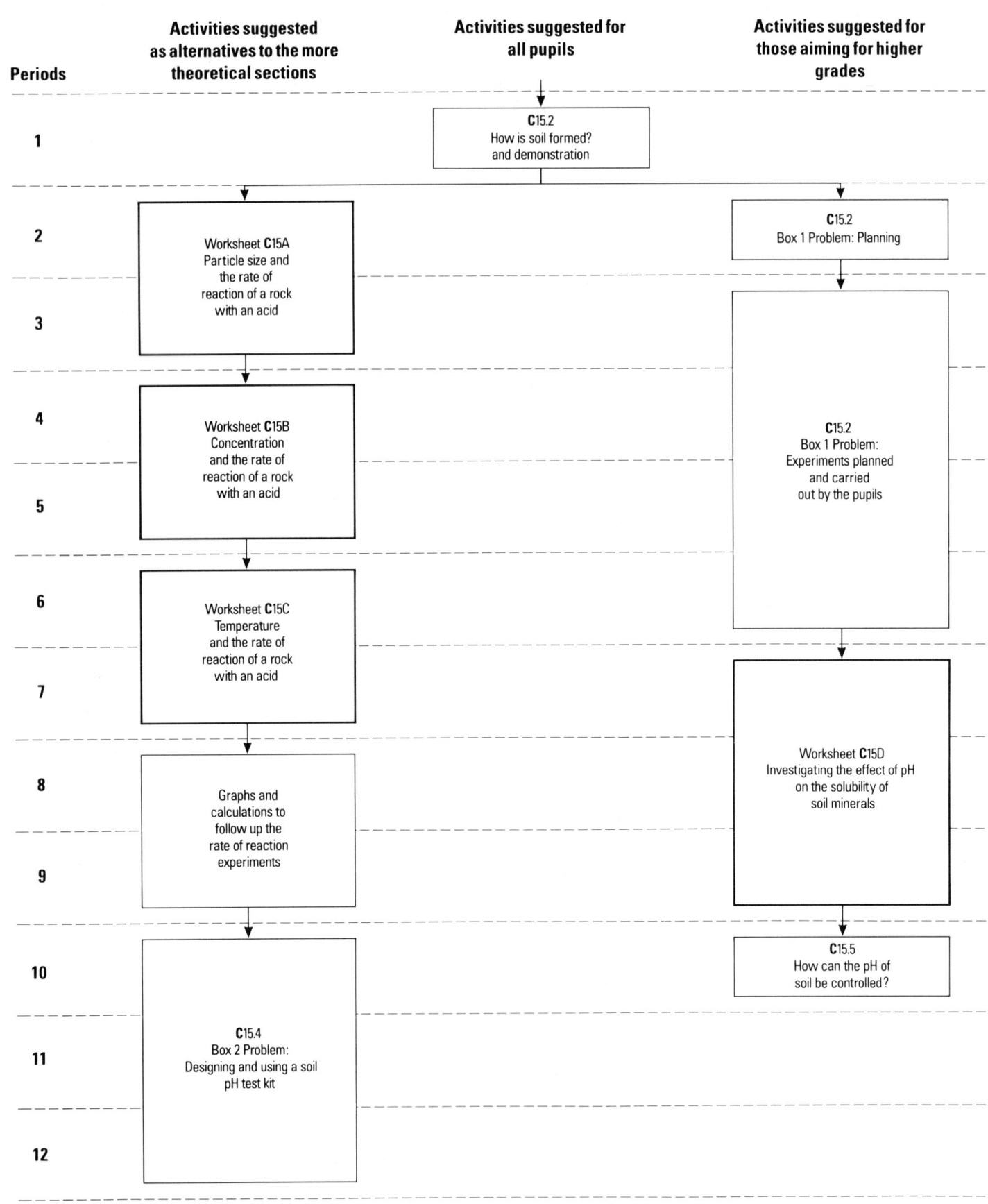

Figure **C**31

described in Chapter **C4**. It also shows that the formulae and equations for the reactions of calcium carbonate and calcium oxide with acids can explain their neutralizing power, as described on garden and agricultural products.

Practical work

Teacher demonstration: Freezing water

REQUIREMENTS

The teacher will need:
Either:
Small screw-cap glass bottle, such as a
　medicine bottle
Plastic ice-cream tub

Access to:
Freshly boiled and cooled water
Refrigerator with deep freeze compartment

Or:
Cast iron bursting bottle (available from
　suppliers of apparatus)
Plastic ice-cream tub with lid
Ice
Crushed rock salt
Freshly boiled, cooled water

Procedure

Either:
Carefully fill a screw-cap bottle to the rim with water which has been boiled and then allowed to cool. Screw on the lid, making sure that no air remains in the bottle. Stand the bottle in a plastic container and put it in the deep freeze section of a refrigerator. Leave overnight.

Or:
In advance cool the iron bursting bottle in ice. At the start of the demonstration fill the bottle completely with boiled, cooled water and screw the plug in tightly with a spanner. Submerge the bottle in an ice-salt freezing mixture. Cover with the lid. After about fifteen minutes a sharp crack will be heard – the bottle will split open.

Planning lesson: Investigating reaction rates

If pupils are asked to make their own plans for the experiments to investigate rates of reaction, the teacher may wish to demonstrate the reaction first and then show the pupils a range of the apparatus which they might choose to use. For this purpose the teacher will need one example of each type of apparatus listed below for Worksheets **C15A**, **C15B** and **C15C**. The pupils' plans are prompted by box 1 on page 260. They can set out their requirements on Worksheet **C0**.

Worksheet C15A　Particle size and the rate of reaction of a rock with an acid

REQUIREMENTS

The teacher (or each group of pupils) will need:
Copy of Worksheet **C15A**
Conical flask, 100 ml
Measuring cylinder, 100 ml
Stopclock, or watch
Top pan balance, reading to 0.01 g,
　preferably with a tare button
Eye protection

Access to:
Large marble chips, 20 g (see note 1)
Small marble chips, 20 g (see note 1)
Scrap paper
Dilute hydrochloric acid, 2 mol/L
Cotton wool
Graph paper, 1 piece per pupil

Note:
1 The marble chips should be washed beforehand in dilute hydrochloric acid and then in water to remove surface powder. They should then be allowed to dry in air.

This experiment can be organized as a demonstration carried out by a group of pupils while the rest of the class records the results and plots the graph. If the balance does not have a tare button, then one member of the demonstration group can use a calculator to work out the values for the loss in mass as the balance readings are read out. One group can do the experiment with large chips, then a second group can take over for the small chips.

Alternatively this experiment can be set up as part of a circus with Worksheet C15B and C15C.

Worksheet C15B Concentration and the rate of reaction of a rock with an acid

REQUIREMENTS

Each group of pupils will need:
Copy of Worksheet C15B
Conical flask, 100 ml, with a wide neck
Bung to fit flask, with delivery tubes as
    shown on the worksheet
Trough
Measuring cylinder, 50 ml
Stopclock or watch
Eye protection

Access to:
Large marble chips,
    about 1 cm × 1.5 cm × 1.5 cm, 1 per
    group (see note 1 for Worksheet C15A)
2 mol/L hydrochloric acid, 100 ml per
    group, with 50 ml measuring cylinder
Graph paper, 1 piece per pupil

One large marble chip can be reused in each part of the experiment on the assumption that its surface area does not change significantly. If single large chips are not available use several chips of equivalent bulk.

Questions 5–8 on side 2 of the worksheet ask pupils to calculate values for the rate of reaction and plot a second graph. This should be omitted if it will confuse rather than help the pupils.

Worksheet C15C Temperature and the rate of reaction of a rock with an acid

REQUIREMENTS

Each group of pupils will need:
Copy of Worksheet C15C
Test-tube in a rack
Stirring thermometer, 0–100 °C
Burner, tripod, gauze and mat
Beaker, 100 ml
Stopclock or watch
Eye protection

Access to:
Balance, reading to 0.01 g
Small marble chips, about 3 mm across
    (see note 1 for Worksheet C15A)
4 mol/L hydrochloric acid, 30 ml per
    group, with 10 ml measuring cylinder
Graph paper, 1 sheet per pupil

This experiment gives good results if the marble chips are carefully matched for size.

Questions 7–9 on side 2 of the worksheet should only be set to those who will not be confused by them.

Box 2 Problem: Measuring the pH of soil

Here the requirements will depend on the pupils' plans. The information for this exercise is given in box 2 in section C15.4 of the pupils' book. Two possible procedures are as follows:

Method A

1 Take 5 g of dry soil or compost.

2 Grind in a pestle and mortar.

3 Transfer to a boiling-tube and add 40 ml of tap water.

4 Add 3 drops of Universal Indicator solution.

5 Shake and leave for 2 minutes.

6 Filter into a test-tube.

7 Read off the pH from a colour chart.

Method B

1 Take a 2-ml plastic syringe, remove the plunger, and seal the jet with a cap (or small bung which has been partially drilled).

2 Use a cork borer to cut a disc of filter paper and then push the disc down to cover the bottom of the barrel of the syringe.

3 Fill the syringe to the 0.5-ml mark with dry soil or compost.

4 Add water to the 2-ml mark, followed by 2 drops of Universal Indicator solution.

5 Insert the plunger just inside the barrel of the syringe, and shake the soil and Indicator together for 30 seconds.

6 Remove the cap or bung, and press in the plunger to force the solution through the filter paper into a test-tube.

7 Read off the pH from a colour chart.

Pupils can be asked to bring in soil samples from a range of localities. The pH of compost in pots for house plants can also be tested.

An important part of this problem for the pupils is the preparation of a clear set of instructions for the assembly and use of the kit.

Worksheet C15D   Investigating the effect of pH on the solubility of soil minerals

REQUIREMENTS

Each group of pupils will need:
Copy of Worksheet C15D
Beaker, 100 ml
Glass rod
Measuring cylinder, 10 ml
Eye protection
1 mol/L aqueous ammonia in a dropper bottle
1 mol/L nitric acid in a dropper bottle

Access to:
The following aqueous solutions (approximately 0.5 mol/L) in reagent bottles:
sodium sulphate (7 g/100 ml of the anhydrous salt, or 16 g/100 ml of the hydrated salt)
potassium chloride (4 g/100 ml)
calcium chloride (11 g/100 ml of the hydrated salt)
ammonium nitrate (4 g/100 ml)
ammonium sulphate (6.5 g/100 ml)
disodium hydrogenphosphate (18 g/100ml of the hydrated salt)
iron(III) nitrate (20 g/100 ml of the hydrated salt)
magnesium nitrate (13 g/100 ml of the hydrated salt)
manganese(II) chloride (10 g/L of the hydrated salt)
Small pieces of Universal Indicator paper

This experiment provides an opportunity for students to extend their knowledge of precipitation reactions.

It may be necessary for the pupils to measure the pH of the distilled water used to make the solutions first so that they can see whether the dissolved salts have made any difference. The pH of distilled water is often below 7, and this might lead to misleading interpretations if not noted.

Further information

Revised Nuffield Chemistry, Stage II
Topics A18, B13 and B22 in *Teachers' guide II* include alternative experiments for studying the factors which affect the rates of chemical reactions.

Science at work
Two booklets include experiments to investigate soil. *Forensic science* describes an investigation to compare soil samples by measuring their pH. The suggested procedure suffers from the disadvantage that the indicator is added after the clay and humus have been filtered off. *Plant science* includes a series of experiments to analyse soil based on a commercial soil testing kit.

Nuffield Science 13 to 16
Experiments to investigate factors affecting the rates of reactions are included in *Changes in acidity*.
   Earth, air and water includes sections dealing with weathering, the formation of soil and soil pH.

University of York Science Education Group
The unit in Chemistry in Action called *Gardeners' question time* is a practical exercise in which pupils are asked to apply their knowledge of chemistry to advise a market gardener to decide how to treat an acidic soil.

Chapter C16 Fertilizers

Purposes

Knowledge and understanding

At the end of this chapter all pupils should:

1 know that fertilizers are inorganic salts which supply plants with the elements they need, including nitrogen, phosphorus and potassium

2 know the meaning of the term "nitrogen fixation" and appreciate that the chemical basis of the nitrogen problem is the inertness of nitrogen gas

3 appreciate the role of the chemical industry in manufacturing fertilizers and appreciate the need for catalysts.

In addition, those pupils aiming for higher grades should:

4 understand equations which describe the chemical changes involved in the manufacture of ammonia and nitric acid

5 appreciate the difference between ammonia and ammonium salts

6 appreciate that leaching of nitrates from the soil is a problem while leaching of phosphates and potassium salts is not.

Processes and problem solving

Graphical and symbolic representation
In section C16.1 pupils have the opportunity to interpret information presented in the form of tables and charts. The chapter provides further experience of the use of formulae and equations, including the symbols for ions.

Using apparatus and measuring instruments
The preparation of a fertilizer on Worksheet **C16B** involves measurement and a variety of preparative techniques including filtration, evaporation and crystallization.

Observation
Pupils will need to make careful observations when doing the investigations suggested by Worksheet **C16A**.

Planning and carrying out investigations
Worksheet **C16A** is a structured investigation into the choice of catalysts for the oxidation of ammonia.

Interpretation and application
Questions 1, 2, 10, 11, 29, and 36–38 ask pupils to interpret the information in the text.

Problem solving
Worksheet **C16B**, sides 2 and 3, present pupils with the problem of costing the process of manufacturing a fertilizer.

There are further opportunities in this chapter to solve quantitative problems based on formulae and equations (see questions 21, 32, 35, 36 and 37).

Timing

8–9 periods, depending on the route taken.

Suggested routes

Figure **C32** (over the page) shows possible routes through this chapter.

The study of industrial processes in this chapter can be made more interesting with the help of films and videos. ICI videos cover the manufacture of ammonia, the manufacture and use of fertilizers as well as industrial catalysts (see Appendix).

Opportunities for co-ordination

This chapter concentrates on the chemistry of the manufacture and use of fertilizers. This complements the references to the impact of fertilizers in the environment in Chapter **B17**. The chapter also looks at chemical aspects of the nitrogen cycle described in Chapter **B15**.

Chapter **B17** deals with the advantages and disadvantages of pesticides from the biological point of view. The chemistry of agrochemicals is not accessible at this level.

There is a substantial energy cost in the manufacture of fertilizers so there are links between this chapter and Chapters **P8** and **P10**.

There are also opportunities for co-ordination with the study of World War I in history. New methods of making ammonia and nitric acid were needed for the manufacture of explosives at the beginning of the war (see below under section **C16.4**).

Notes and answers

C16.1   Why do we need fertilizers?

Plant breeding coupled with the use of fertilizers and agrochemicals has dramatically increased crop yields in recent years. Figure 16.2 attempts to show diagrammatically the contributions made by the various changes in farming practice.

As well as science and technology, the other big influences on agriculture are economics and politics. For the last forty years the main aim of agricultural policy has been to increase output. This may be changing now that we have

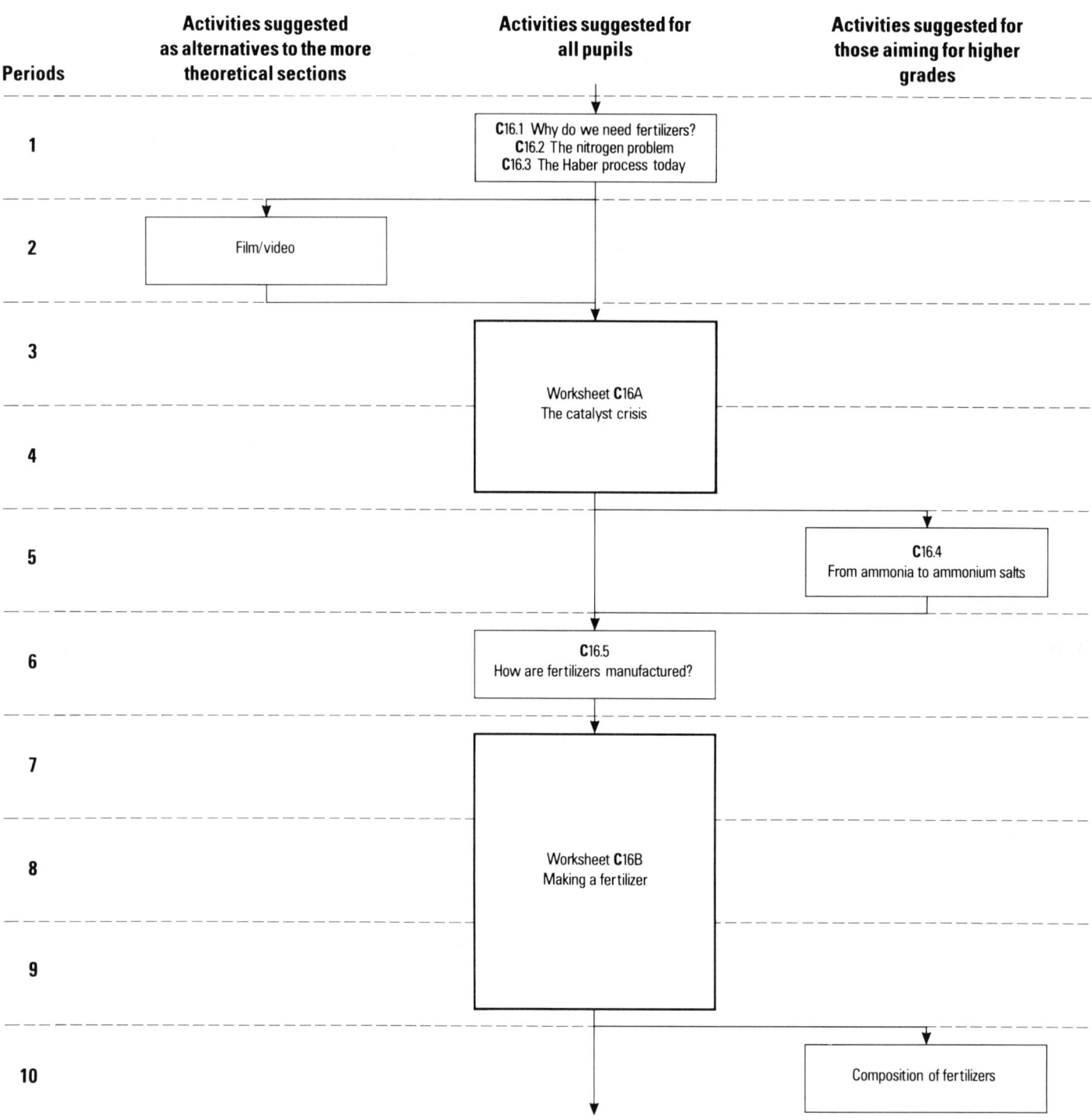

Figure C32

over-production in Europe with the notorious grain mountains, as well as increasing public concern about the effects of fertilizers and farm chemicals on the environment.

C16.2   How has chemistry helped to solve the nitrogen problem?

Chemistry and Biology textbooks often give a different emphasis to the treatment of the nitrogen problem and nitrogen fixation. In Chemistry nitrogen fixation is any method, natural or industrial, for producing nitrogen compounds from nitrogen gas in a form suitable for plants. The nitrogen problem is seen to arise from the chemical inertness of nitrogen.

In Biology the focus is on nitrogen fixation by bacteria. The nitrogen problem is seen to arise from the existence of other, denitrifying bacteria which result in losses of nitrogen from compounds in the soil to the atmosphere.

In this course we have tried to co-ordinate these two view-points, in this chapter and in Chapter **B**15.

C16.3   The Haber process today

Pupils are not required to remember the details of the Haber process, but they should be able to show that they can understand an account of the process and interpret data about it. The effects of pressure and temperature on the yield are presented graphically and without reference to equilibrium ideas.

C16.4   From ammonia to ammonium salts

The study of gases has had an important place in chemistry ever since Jan van Helmont (1577–1644) coined the word "gas" from the Greek for "chaos" and Stephen Hales (1677–1761) developed techniques for collecting and handling gases. The chemistry of ammonia provides a good opportunity for teachers who enjoy demonstrations to show pupils a variety of interesting reactions. Some suggestions are included under Practical work.

The reaction of ammonia with water is described in box 1 on page 205 in Chapter **C**11. The box in this section explains the difference between an ammonia molecule and an ammonium ion.

Factual recall of the process for the manufacture of nitric acid is not required, but pupils should be able to answer questions about this, and other similar processes, given appropriate information.

Worksheet **C**16A is a problem solving exercise based on events which faced German chemists at the start of World War I. The Royal Navy cut off supplies of Chilean nitrates to Germany. So chemists had to find a replacement for the traditional process of making nitric acid by distilling a mixture of sodium nitrate and concentrated sulphuric acid. They had the difficulty of developing and scaling up the recently discovered, and little-used, catalytic conversion of ammonia to nitric acid.

Copper can be used as the catalyst, but the yield is low. The German chemists used iron-bismuth catalysts which were replaced by platinum after the war. Successful large-scale production of concentrated nitric acid from ammonia began in the spring of 1915, and may have added as much as twelve months to the fighting capability of the German High Command.

Haber's involvement in the preparations for the use of chlorine gas at this time is the basis of questions and discussion in the SATIS unit listed under Further information.

C16.5   How are fertilizers manufactured?

The ions taken in by plants from the soil are described in Chapter **B**15. This section describes the production of fertilizers to supply nitrate, phosphate and potassium ions.

The text points out the two uses of the word "compound" in this context.

Worksheet **C**16B provides an opportunity for pupils to carry out an industrial process on a small scale and then cost their product.

C16.6   What happens to fertilizers in the soil?

This section is based on ideas introduced by sections **C15.3**, **C15.4** and Worksheet **C15D**.

C16.7   Are fertilizers a good thing?

The use of fertilizers and farm chemicals has become controversial; there are regular articles in newspapers and magazines which can be used to supplement the information in this section.

Practical work

Teacher demonstration: The properties of ammonia

Possible demonstrations include the fountain experiment, the catalytic oxidation of ammonia and the reaction of ammonia with hydrogen chloride.

The fountain experiment

REQUIREMENTS

The teacher will need:
Apparatus for filling a flask with dry ammonia gas (see figure **C33**)
Apparatus for the fountain experiment (see figure **C34**)
Spare dry flask to allow a repeat performance
Concentrated ammonia solution
Potassium hydroxide pellets
Mineral wool
Red litmus solution in dropper bottle
Red litmus paper
Eye protection for the teacher and the pupils

Access to:
Fume cupboard

Procedure
With many pupils it will be sufficient just to concentrate on this demonstration

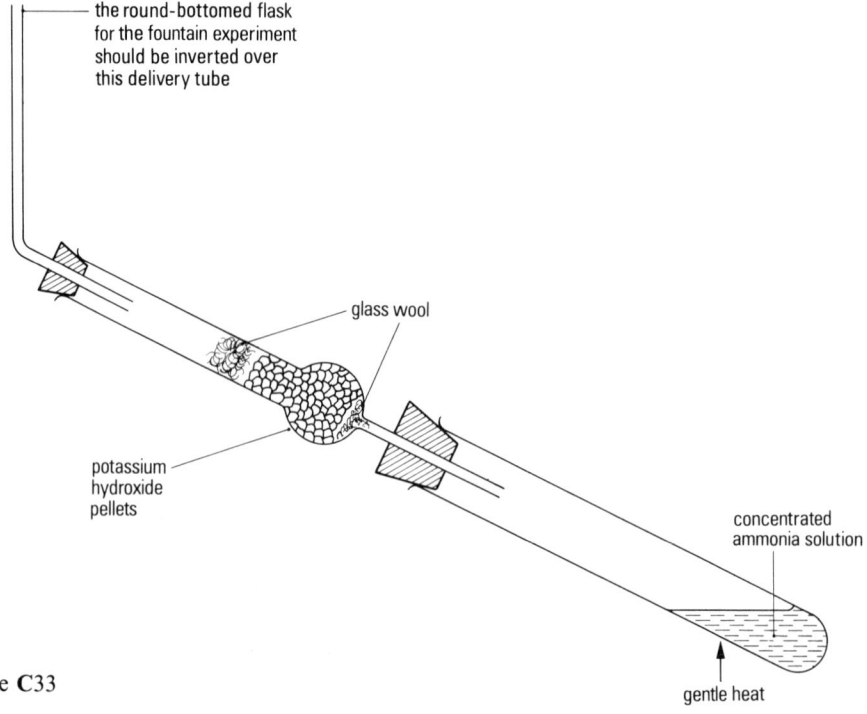

the round-bottomed flask
for the fountain experiment
should be inverted over
this delivery tube

glass wool

potassium
hydroxide
pellets

concentrated
ammonia solution

gentle heat

Figure **C33**

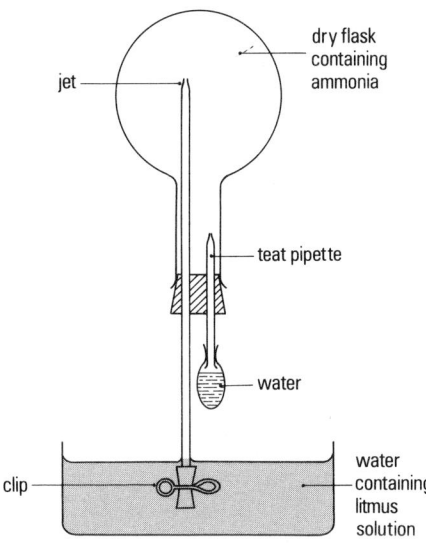

Figure C34

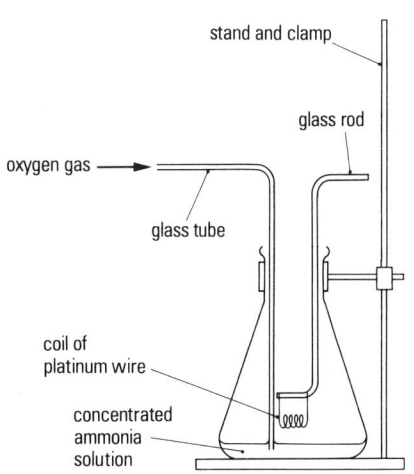

Figure C35

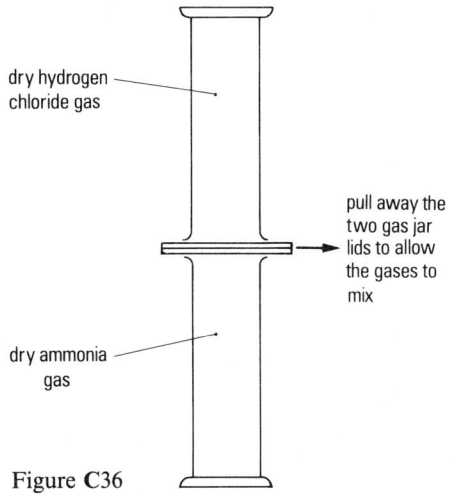

Figure C36

which illustrates several important properties of ammonia. One good demonstration will allow pupils time to work out for themselves how the fountain is created and what it shows about the properties of ammonia.

Fill the flask in a fume cupboard by upward delivery as shown in figure C33. Take some time over this because it is important to displace all the air. Moist red litmus paper held at the mouth of the flask will show when the flask is full.

Filling the flask with ammonia is part of the experiment – it is an opportunity to show that ammonia is a colourless gas which is less dense than air.

Assemble the apparatus as shown in figure C34. First do the experiment just with water in the trough to show that the presence of litmus is not necessary for the fountain effect. Repeat with litmus in the water for a more colourful demonstration and to show that ammonia solution is alkaline.

Start the fountain by squeezing the bulb of the teat pipette to inject a little water into the flask. The advantage of the apparatus in figure C34 is that it is simple, so that it is easier to visualize what is happening than with alternative arrangements with two flasks and more tubes.

The catalytic oxidation of ammonia

In addition to the apparatus for the fountain experiment, the teacher will need:
Apparatus shown in figure C35
Oxygen cylinder (see note 1)
Connecting tubing
Burner and mat
Safety screens
Eye protection for the teacher and the
   pupils

Note:
1 If no oxygen cylinder is available a gas generator is needed, together with hydrogen peroxide solution and manganese(IV) oxide.

This demonstration provides a lead into Worksheet C16A. It uses the same apparatus.

Adjust the oxygen supply to deliver a steady stream of gas. This will produce a mixture of ammonia and oxygen above the liquid surface. Lower the coil of platinum wire into the flask. The catalyst should start to glow. If nothing happens, heat the wire to red heat in a Bunsen flame and then lower it into the flask. Once the reaction starts, the wire should continue to glow for a long time.

The reaction produces nitrogen dioxide which reacts with water vapour and ammonia to form ammonium salts so white fumes appear in the flask.

If the oxygen flow is too rapid there may be minor explosions; these do no damage, but it is important to use a safety screen for the demonstration and to insist that the class wear eye protection.

The reaction of ammonia with hydrogen chloride

In addition, the teacher will need:
Gas generator, with tap funnel, and right-angle delivery tube
Crushed rock salt
Concentrated sulphuric acid
2 gas jars with cover-glasses

Fill one gas jar with ammonia by upward delivery. Fill a second jar with hydrogen chloride by downward delivery. Place the jar of hydrogen chloride upside down over the jar of ammonia, then pull out the two cover-glasses (see figure C36).

Thick white clouds of ammonium chloride appear. The formation of a solid from two gases can be explained in terms of the theory in box 1 in section C16.4. Once the white powder has settled, point out the small volume of solid compared with the original volume of the gases. Pupils can be asked to use their knowledge of states of matter and structure to explain the difference.

Worksheet C16A   The catalyst crisis

REQUIREMENTS

The teacher will need (see note 1):
Flask, 100 ml or 250 ml
Cork or bung with delivery tubes, as on the worksheet
Water pump
Eye protection for teacher and pupils

Access to:
Fume cupboard
Concentrated ammonia solution, 0.880 g/ml
Water tap and sink

Each working group will need:
Copy of Worksheet C16A
Bent glass rod to support the metal wires (as on the worksheet)
Eye protection

Access to:
Selection of metal wires, e.g. nickel, iron/steel, constantan, brass, nichrome, copper (preferably a range of samples of copper with different thicknesses)
Emery cloth to clean the surface of the wires

Note:
1 The worksheet is based on the assumption that pupils will plan their own investigations but that the testing will be done under the immediate supervision of the teacher.

The situation presented by this problem was real in Germany during World War I. The German chemical industry was cut off from supplies of Chilean nitrate by the British blockade. Attempts to beat the blockade failed when the German navy was defeated in the battle of the Falklands in 1914. Research chemists had little more than six months to develop the ammonia oxidation process using a catalyst other than platinum which was not readily available.

This experiment must be done in a fume cupboard. It may be more convenient to organize it as a class demonstration, with different groups preparing the various wires, and then helping the teacher to demonstrate their effect (if any) to the rest of the class.

Pupils should have some success with copper wire, and they can then go on to investigate whether the thickness of the wire or the way in which the wire is coiled has any effect on the efficiency of the process.

Discussion of this experiment can be related to the information in section C16.2 about the way in which Bosch and his team found a suitable catalyst for the Haber process.

Worksheet C16B   Making a fertilizer

REQUIREMENTS

Each group of pupils will need:
Copy of Worksheet C16B
Beaker, 100 ml
Beaker, 250 ml
Glass rod
Measuring cylinders, 10 ml and 50 ml
Filter funnel
Evaporating basin
Petri dish (see note 1)
Burner, tripod, gauze and mat
Eye protection

Access to:
Calcium phosphate, 6 g per group
Sulphuric acid, 2 mol/L, allow 40 ml per group
Dilute ammonia solution, 2 mol/L, allow 40 ml per group
Distilled water
Balance
Filter paper
Labels
Chemical and apparatus catalogues with prices

Note:
1 The ammonium phosphate can be left to crystallize in the evaporating basin. However, the basins may be required by other classes, in which case Petri dishes can be used as crytallizing dishes.

This experiment is based on Experiment B in *Chemicals for Agriculture* which is number 5 in the *Experimenting with industry* series (see Further information).

For some groups it will be enough to make a sample of fertilizer. However, some pupils will enjoy the challenge of costing their product as described on sides

2 and 3 of the worksheet. Side 3 is based on an actual sheet for a production process in the chemical industry.

A: Materials
The materials used include the chemicals and filter paper. Prices can be looked up in catalogues. Capital costs may be ignored, but it should be pointed out that they are very important and a matter of great concern to industry.

B: Labour
Labour costs can be based on earnings from part-time work such as a paper round or a Saturday job. Companies often add a percentage to the labour rate (between 10 and 15 per cent) to cover administration.

C: Overheads such as fuel costs
The worksheet suggests that the fuel costs can be estimated given a value of the flow rate of the burner (typically of the order of 0.15 m^3/h).

The SATIS unit *Making fertilizers* gives details of a procedure for testing fertilizers using cress seedlings.

Further information

Experimenting with industry
Booklet 5 of this series is called *Chemicals for agriculture*. The experiments include investigations into the caking of fertilizers, the production of ammonium phosphate and the manufacture of protein by fermentation.

Science and Technology in Society
Unit 505 "Making fertilizers" could usefully be used for revision and homework. The first suggested experiment presents pupils with the problem of devising a procedure for making ammonium sulphate. The second experiment shows how to test fertilizers using cress seedlings.

Unit 207 "The story of Fritz Haber" raises the issue of the responsibility of scientists and the potential of science for good and bad. The unit includes an account of Haber's work in the development of chemical warfare.

Unit 810 "High pressure chemistry" includes reading and questions about the work of Carl Bosch and his ingenious design of a high pressure reactor for the Haber process.

Keep Britain Tidy Group
The unit *Waste management and resources* includes a section about farming wastes and pollution by fertilizers.

University of York Science Education Group
The unit *Growing food* in Salters' Chemistry includes a series of sections which are relevant to this chapter.

Lab Tech's copy Prep Rm. (BCGS).

Topic C6

The Periodic Table, atoms and bonding

Chapter C17   The Periodic Table

Purposes

Knowledge and understanding

At the end of this chapter all pupils should:

1 know that there is a group of unreactive gases called the noble gases

2 know that calcium and magnesium are similar metals which form compounds with similar properties

3 know that chlorine, bromine and iodine belong to a group of similar non-metals called the halogens

4 know that the soluble oxides of metals are alkaline while the soluble oxides of non-metals are generally acidic.

In addition, those pupils aiming for higher grades should:

5 understand what is meant by a periodic pattern.

Processes and problem solving

Graphical and symbolic representation
The questions in this chapter require pupils to use chemical symbols and conventions, to read information from graphs, tables and charts and also to represent information in various forms.

Interpretation and application
Pupils are asked to look for patterns in chemical data and to make predictions based on the Periodic Table.

Timing

4 periods and the associated time for private study and homework will be needed.

Suggested routes

There are two main strategies for covering the ideas in this chapter. One is to use the chapter as a basis for revision at the end of the course. Section C17.3 in the pupils' book assumes that Topics C1 to C5 have been studied and that this chapter will be used to review and revise the chemistry of some of the elements in groups 2 and 7.

Alternatively, the introduction to periodicity could be used to develop third year work much earlier in the course, perhaps at the beginning of the fourth year.

Figure C37 shows routes through the chapter.

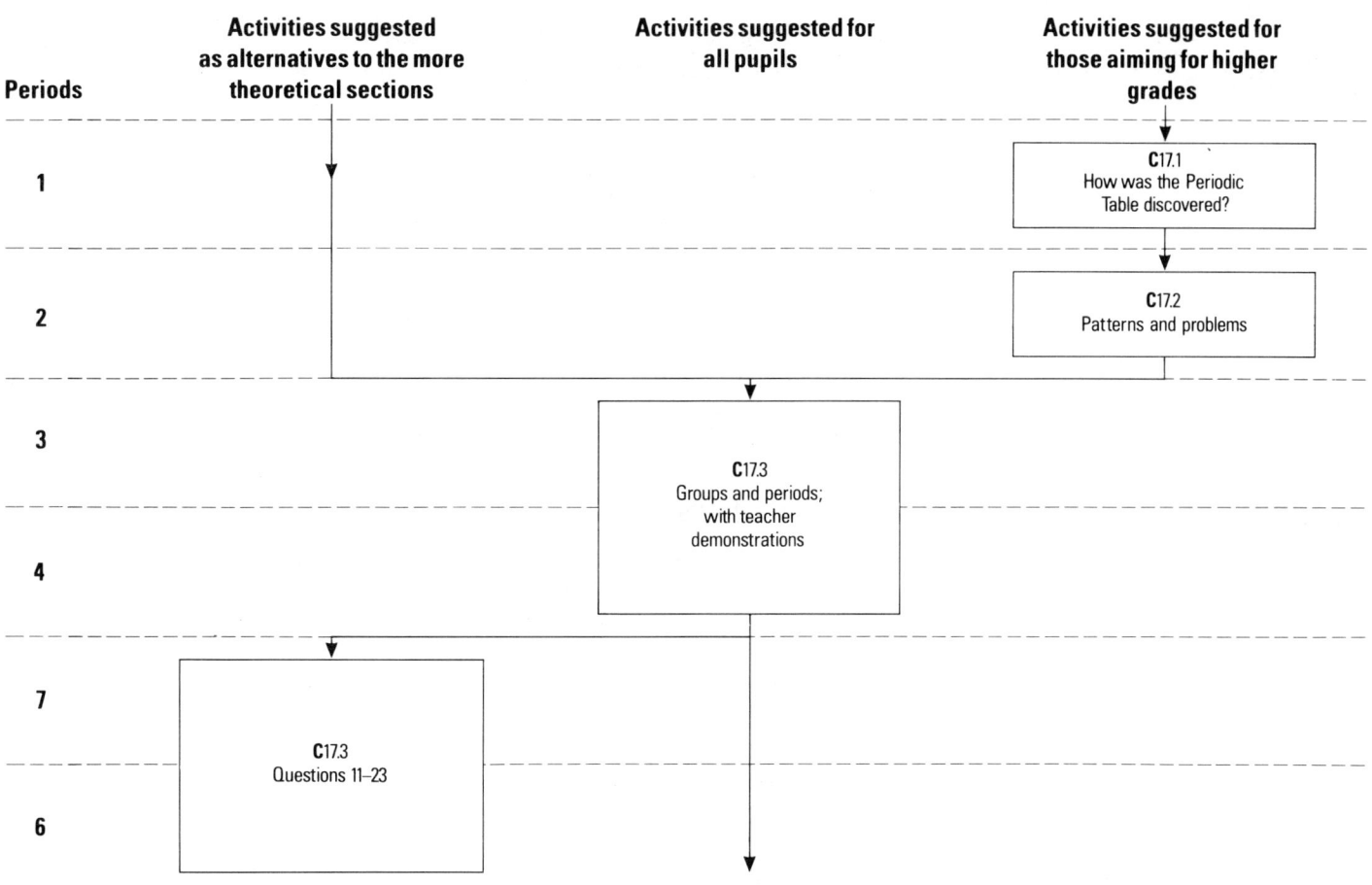

Figure **C37**

Opportunities for co-ordination

This chapter is primarily designed to review ideas which have been met in other chapters. There are limited opportunities for co-ordination with Physics and Biology.

Section **C17.3** compares the properties of metal oxides and non-metal oxides. During Biology practical work the pupils are likely to have used alkaline metal hydroxides to absorb carbon dioxide which is acidic.

Notes and answers

This topic differs in character from the other five. Most of the course is designed to illustrate the importance of chemistry by placing it in its applied, social and historical contexts. This topic is intended to draw together many of the theoretical ideas which have arisen in other chapters and to show that it is possible to make sense of them in terms of atomic structure. Clearly this is of importance for those who are likely to continue to study sciences at a more advanced level.

There is no practical work for the pupils in this topic. The two chapters review the chemistry that has arisen in the rest of the course; they have been written on the assumption that ideas about atomic structure have already been covered in the Physics Chapters **P3** and **P19**. This means that they can be used for revision at the end of the course. However, some teachers will want to introduce ideas about atomic structure and bonding earlier, perhaps during the work on Chapter **C5**. There is no reason why they should not do so, but this will have to be carefully co-ordinated with the treatment in Physics. In both the Physics and the Chemistry books, the approach is to describe the model of atomic structure and then show what it can explain. On this basis, the picture of a nuclear atom made up of protons, neutrons and electrons can be described first in either Physics or Chemistry.

C17.1   How was the Periodic Table discovered?

The notion of periodicity is difficult, and pupils will need help with the idea. The historical background helps to emphasize the nature of the problem, which is to find some pattern in the properties of all the elements. The idea that there is a connection between chemical properties and atomic mass at first seemed ridiculous to many chemists, but was justified when explained in terms of atomic structure as described in Chapter C18.

Worksheet C17A is designed to make clear the repeating patterns of properties in the main groups of the Periodic Table.

Worksheet C17B is intended to help pupils with their study of this section.

C17.2   Patterns and problems

Pupils can appreciate the striking nature of the predictions based on Mendeléev's table. Some may be interested to know more about the discovery of the family of noble gases; there is a suitable account in the chapter on the Periodic Table in *A short history of chemistry* by Isaac Asimov. (See under Further information.)

C17.3   Groups and periods

Questions 11–21 are designed as revision exercises, reviewing many of the topics in the course.

It may help pupils if they see demonstrations of the properties of magnesium, calcium and their compounds. This might concentrate on the information tabulated in figure 17.11 (see under Practical work).

The aspects of halogen chemistry featured in figure 17.13 might also be demonstrated (see under Practical work).

Practical work

Teacher demonstration: The properties of magnesium and calcium

REQUIREMENTS

The teacher will need:	*Access to:*
Tongs	Magnesium ribbon
Burner and mat	Calcium turnings
6 boiling-tubes in rack	Samples of the oxide, hydroxide,
Eye protection	carbonate and sulphate of magnesium
	Samples of the oxide, hydroxide,
	carbonate and chloride of calcium
	Indicator paper
	Distilled water
	Soap solution in a dropper bottle

The idea is to emphasize the similarities between the elements. The properties in the table in figure 17.11 can be demonstrated and discussed. If strontium or barium and their compounds are available this could be extended to making and testing predictions about their properties based on the Periodic Table.

Teacher demonstration: The properties of the halogens

REQUIREMENTS

The teacher will need:
Gas generator with tap funnel and right-
 angle delivery tube
2 gas jars with lids
6 boiling-tubes in rack
3 conical flasks, 100 ml, with bungs
Tongs
Burner and mat
Eye protection

Access to:
Bleaching powder, or sodium chlorate(I)
 solution (see note 1)
Dilute hydrochloric acid
Bromine
Iodine
Solid samples of the chloride, bromide and
 iodide of sodium
Silver nitrate solution (about 0.5 g in
 50 ml water) in a dropper bottle
Blue litmus paper
Distilled water
Fume cupboard

Note:
1 It is safer to make chlorine by adding
dilute hydrochloric acid to bleaching
powder, or to a solution of sodium
chlorate(I). If potassium manganate(VII)
and concentrated hydrochloric acid are
used it is very important to check carefully
that the correct acid is added. (The fumes
of concentrated hydrochloric acid are very
obvious.) It is highly dangerous if
concentrated sulphuric acid is used by
mistake, and so there must be no
possibility of adding the wrong acid.

The purpose of this demonstration is to review the properties of the halogens and
show their similarities as indicated in the table in figure 17.13.

Further information

Nuffield Science 13 to 16
The Periodic Table module includes a section about the halogens and includes
exercises and worksheets to explore the patterns of ion charges and sizes in the
table.

Revised Nuffield Chemistry
Teachers guide II includes ideas for experiments in Topics A13, B16 and B24.

A short history of chemistry
This book by Isaac Asimov (Heinemann Educational Books, 1972) is a readable
account of the history of chemistry.

Chapter C18   Atoms and bonding

Purposes

Knowledge and understanding

Those pupils aiming for higher grades should:

1 know that the electrons in an atom are arranged in a series of shells around
the nucleus

2 know the meaning of the terms atomic number and mass number

3 know that the elements are arranged in order of atomic number in the modern
Periodic Table

4 understand how the arrangement of elements in the Periodic Table can be
explained in terms of atomic structure for the first twenty elements

5 understand the meaning of the term isotope in terms of atomic structure

6 understand how atoms turn into ions and ions into atoms in cells and during
electrolysis (but only with reference to simple examples)

7 appreciate that the number of bonds formed by an atom in a molecule can be
explained in terms of atomic structure.

Processes and problem solving

Graphical and symbolic representation
The pupils practise representing atomic structure with symbols which show the mass number and atomic number. They meet "dot-and-cross" diagrams for describing what happens as atoms bond together.

Interpretation and application
The theory of this chapter is applied to explain the problems faced by Mendeléev. Questions ask pupils to use the theory to interpret ideas met earlier in the Biology, Chemistry and Physics books.

Timing

About 8 periods will be needed to cover the ideas in this chapter with those aiming for higher grades in examinations.

Suggested routes

Figure C38 describes a route through this chapter.

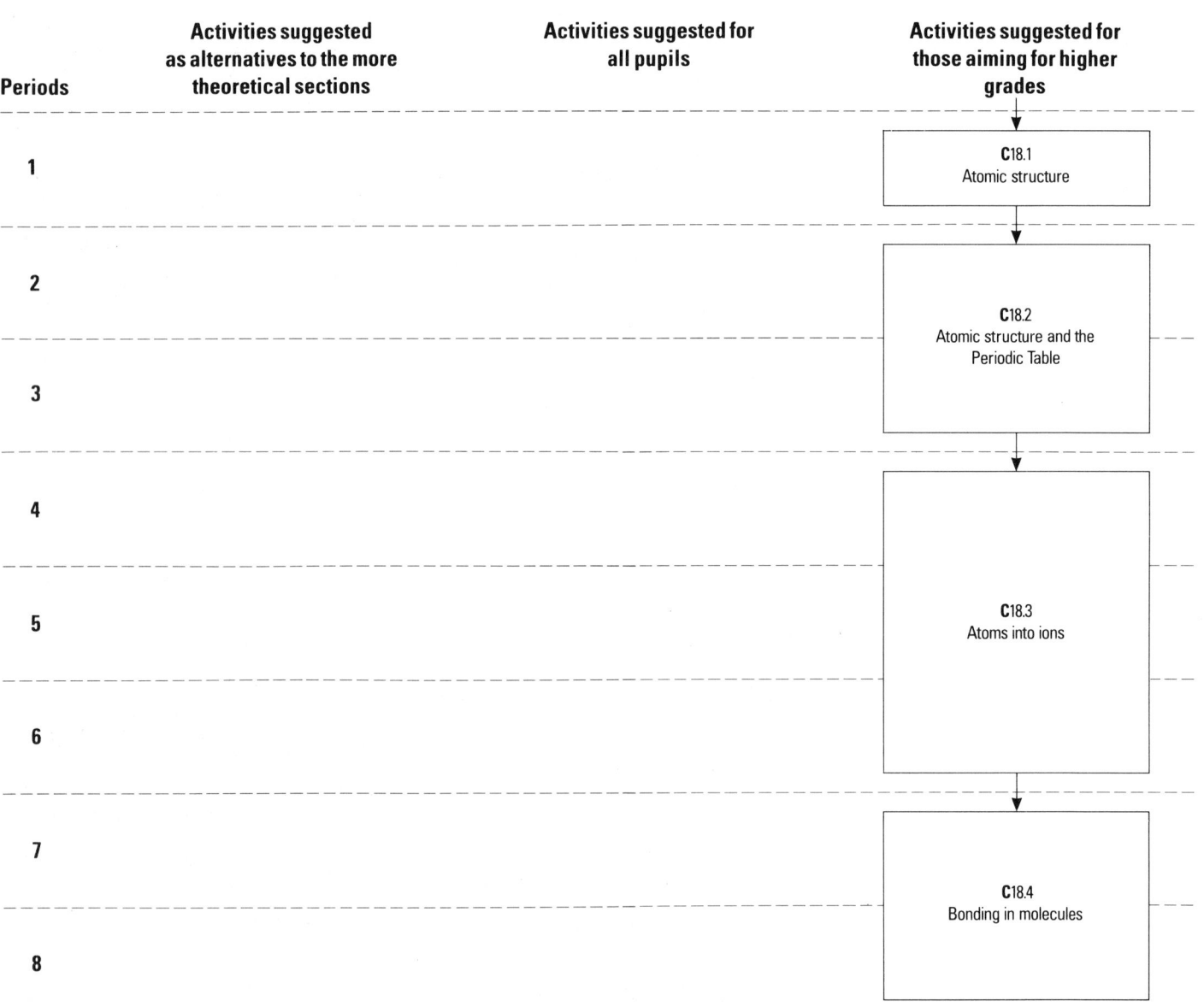

Periods	Activities suggested as alternatives to the more theoretical sections	Activities suggested for all pupils	Activities suggested for those aiming for higher grades
1			**C18.1** Atomic structure
2			**C18.2** Atomic structure and the Periodic Table
3			
4			**C18.3** Atoms into ions
5			
6			
7			**C18.4** Bonding in molecules
8			

Figure C38

The work in this chapter is only required of those aiming for the higher GCSE grades.

Opportunities for co-ordination

This chapter assumes that the pupils have some knowledge of atomic structure from Chapters **P3** and **P19** and that they have studied radioactivity. It explains how one element changes into another as a result of alpha or beta decay. Isotopes and their uses are mentioned in both the Biology and Physics books (see Chapters **B8**, **B9** (worksheets), and **P3**) but the explanation of the nature of isotopes is given here.

In this Chemistry course ions are first mentioned in Chapter **C5**. Ionic theory is then used to explain the changes during electrolysis, the formulae of salts, precipitation reactions, and neutralization, as well as ion exchange processes for water softening and in the soil. The effects of ionizing radiations are described in **P3**. In Chapter **B15** the mineral salts needed by plants from the soil are described in terms of ions. Section **C18.3** gives pupils an opportunity to review these ideas and it then goes on to explain how atoms turn into ions by gaining or losing electrons.

The review of molecular theory in section **C18.4** emphasizes the importance of the idea that the forces within molecules are strong while the forces between molecules are weak. This idea is clearly important and underlies the study of the properties of molecular liquids and gases in Chapter **P2**, the study of digestion in Chapter **B5** and the investigation of diffusion in the lungs in Chapter **B7**.

Notes and answers

C18.1   Atomic structure

Probably the most convincing evidence for the model of electrons in shells is the way it can account for the Periodic Table and the similarities between the elements in a group. However figure 18.3 is included to show that there is other evidence to support the theory. Similar diagrams can be drawn for other elements given a table of ionization energies.

Answers to selected questions

2	p	n	e
carbon	6	6	6
neon	10	10	10
protactinium	91	143	91
iodine	53	74	53
hydrogen ion	1	0	0
chloride ion	17	18	18

C18.2   Atomic structure and the Periodic Table

This section provides an opportunity to build on work which the pupils have done in Biology and Physics (see "Opportunities for co-ordination"). The explanation of the existence of isotopes should be related to examples from other parts of the course.

Answers to selected questions

5 Average atomic mass = 63.6 u

C18.3   Atoms into ions

It is important to stress that this section is a simplified introduction to the theory and that it only accounts for the formation of ions by a limited number of elements.

The word "stable" has been deliberately omitted because it is a thermodynamic idea which is too advanced for this course. Pupils likely to go further with their study of chemistry might be told that at advanced level they will study the reasons for the stability of compounds with noble gas electron arrangements in the ions. (See for example, Revised Nuffield Advanced Chemistry, Topic C6, section C6.5.)

Explanations in terms of ions crop up frequently in Nuffield Co-ordinated Sciences. Most of the examples are reviewed in this section, and so the chapter can be used as a summarizing and revision topic towards the end of the course.

This section includes the final stage of the development of ideas about electrolysis. In Chapter C4 pupils look for patterns in the observations made when liquids and solutions are electrolysed. In Chapter C5 they are introduced to the idea that the changes during electrolysis can be explained in terms of ions. In this chapter they are shown how the changes at the electrodes can be described using ionic equations. Electrolysis is seen to reverse the process of electron transfer which takes place when an ionic compound is formed from its elements.

Figure 18.9 is designed to expose the thinking involved in working out what happens at the electrodes during electrolysis. Worksheet C18A can be cut up to make a flick book which gives a moving picture of ions turning into molecules at the anode. If pupils are able to make their own flick books to show other electrode processes it will demonstrate that they have an understanding of what is happening during electrolysis.

The section ends with an explanation of what happens at the electrodes during the discharge of a sodium-sulphur cell. The advantage of choosing this example is that it involves a reaction of a metal with a non-metal. So it has a close parallel with the reaction of sodium with chlorine, which has been used to explain how atoms turn into ions during reactions.

C18.4   Bonding in molecules

Here too the theory is limited in its application, but it does account for the numbers of covalent bonds formed in many of the molecules met in previous chapters. However, pupils should be warned that they will find that there is much more to the study of bonding than this chapter suggests, as they will discover if they continue with the subject at higher levels.

The misconception that covalent bonds are weak is remarkably common and persistent. As this course shows, it is essential that pupils should distinguish between the strong bonds **within** molecules as compared to the weak attractive forces **between** molecules. Covalent bonds are roughly one hundred times stronger than intermolecular forces.

There is no attempt to explain the nature of intermolecular forces. The existence of molecular liquids and solids is evidence for these forces.

Explanations in terms of molecules are common in Nuffield Co-ordinated Sciences. They are reviewed in this section which is designed for revision.

Further information

Revised Nuffield Chemistry
The supplementary units S1, S2 and S3 in *Teachers' guide II* deal with atomic structure, electrons in atoms and chemical bonding. These ideas are extended in relation to the Periodic Table in Option 7 of Stage III: *Periodicity, atomic structure, and bonding.*

PHYSICS

Introduction to Physics

Topics and contexts

The content of the Physics course has been divided up into five topics:

Topic **P1** Matter
Topic **P2** Force and motion
Topic **P3** Energy
Topic **P4** Waves
Topic **P5** Electricity

However, the content of any one topic is never independent of work in the others. For example, an understanding of radioactivity in Topic **P1** cannot be achieved without some prior understanding of electric charge, dealt with in Topic **P5**. The transmission of energy using electricity, which is a part of Topic **P3**, also requires a prior understanding of electrical ideas.

Physics cannot be presented as a "linear" subject in which one topic leads inexorably to the next. A better representation of the subject is as a web of interconnecting ideas. The ideas in one topic are developed around a common theme, but they are related to ideas developed in the other topics as well. Every point in this web of interconnected ideas is supported by strands which may come from many directions.

A web can be traversed by many different routes. One of the ideas underlying the Physics component of Nuffield Co-ordinated Sciences is that this sense of a self-supporting web of ideas is best appreciated by seeing that they connect together in many different ways. However, as pupils are told in the introduction to the pupils' book, there is one route through the book's content that **cannot** be followed first time through – and that is the order of the chapters themselves! This is the deliberate policy of the authors. It encourages pupils to learn to read selectively, looking in the book for what they need, rather than reading it as one would a novel – from beginning to end. It will also help them to appreciate the different ways in which ideas may be linked together.

Year 4			Year 5		
Chapter	Title	Number of periods	Chapter	Title	Number of periods
	Introduction	1	P6	Crashes and bangs	9
P1	Building bridges successfully	6	P7	Rising and falling	4
P2	Cooking food quickly	6	P18	Making use of electricity	9
P4	Motion	6	P3	Radioactivity	9
P5	Controlling motion	6	P11	Energy where it is needed	6
P8	Machines and engines	6	P12	Waste not, want not?	6
P9	Keeping yourself warm	6	P19	Making pictures with electricity	4
P10	Ideas in Physics	6	P20	Control	6
P16	Using electricity	6	P21	Communication	6
P17	Energy and electricity	9			
P13	Fibre optics and noise	6			
P14	Making waves	5			
P15	Making use of waves	7			
		76			59

A possible route through the Physics pupils' book

One possible route through the pupils' book is shown in the table above. Teachers will find other routes themselves. In devising new routes based on this material, two things have to be borne in mind:

- There is an overriding need to co-ordinate any approach with that of the other sciences — work in Biology and Chemistry will often depend on the prior development of ideas in Physics, and Physics will often need ideas from Biology and Chemistry. The charts shown in Chapter 2 of the General introduction may help in showing how the major themes of Nuffield Co-ordinated Sciences are cross-linked.
- At the end of the course, all pupils will benefit from revising Physics in the order in which it is presented in the book. In this way they will see new links between ideas and gain a better appreciation of the fabric of Physics.

Significance

Both Revised Nuffield Physics and Nuffield Secondary Science have influenced the scope and presentation of the Physics in Nuffield Co-ordinated Sciences. Teachers familiar with the former course will recognize many of the strategies used to develop an understanding of concepts. However, the need to make Physics relevant in the day-to-day world in which pupils live has also been of paramount importance. The pupils' book does this wherever possible by putting applications before general principles. Thus force and equilibrium are introduced by considering the design of bridges, the kinetic theory is introduced by way of pressure cookers, and the magnetic effect of electric currrents is introduced in a study of the working of electric motors. Radioactivity is introduced through people's commonest reaction to the word – "Radioactivity is dangerous!"

In developing such an approach, the choice of application or point of social interest is to some extent arbitrary. No doubt more interesting applications will occur to teachers using the course. If this is so, it is hoped that they will develop their own "points of departure", treating the material in the pupils' book as an example of what **may** be done, rather than something that **must** be followed.

To help with this, the chapters of teaching notes which follow list the main areas of knowledge and understanding dealt with in each chapter. The appropriateness of any alternative applications for the purpose in hand will be dictated by this list of aims.

Differentiation

The course materials – both the pupils' book and the worksheets – have been designed to be used by pupils of a wide range of ability and previous experience in science. No one pupil will find it appropriate to cover the entire content of the Physics book and the worksheets.

The commentary text in the pupils' book is intended to encourage pupils to make their own decisions about what is essential, seeking guidance from their teachers where this is needed.

Each chapter in the pupils' book can be divided up into three parts:

- core material which conveys the essential "message" of the chapter
- supporting material to provide more background and experience for pupils who need it
- extensions to take the work further – often in the form of exploratory investigations.

For example, in Chapter **P16** "Using electricity", the core material (developed in sections **P16.1**, **P16.2**, **P16.3**, **P16.5** and **P16.6**) is concerned with electric current. Pupils who are uncertain of their command of basic electric circuit ideas can gain additional experience in Worksheet **P16B**. Other pupils, who grasp these ideas readily, might find such work tiresome. For them there is a more detailed consideration of electric current as a flow of charge in section **P16.4**, and the more advanced Worksheet **P16C**.

Experimental work

There are no instructions for experimental work in the pupils' book. This policy has been adopted so that pupils have a continuous text they can read without the constant interruption of practical instructions. It also enables teachers to use the published worksheets in a flexible manner, substituting their own if this seems appropriate.

The policy of separating text from experimental work can have its dangers. The commentary text in the pupils' book frequently offers advice as to where practical work could be useful. At times they are advised not to read further until a certain amount of practical observation and experiment has been undertaken. Even so, the provision of worksheets separated from the text may give the impression of a retreat to the days of Physics teaching when "practical work" was divorced from "Physics lessons". This is not the intention. Teachers may wish to integrate the work outlined on the worksheets with other work more fully than might at first be suggested by the existence of the worksheets themselves. They will of course adopt whatever strategy seems appropriate to their own classes and philosophy.

We have included a wide variety of experiments so that pupils are helped to appreciate the significance of theory without losing sight of the practical importance of its applications. The table opposite illustrates the range of different experimental activities included in the Physics course.

The experimental work has three main aims:

● To give pupils first-hand experience of phenomena.

Examples of this are the worksheets on wave motion accompanying Chapter **P14** of the pupils' book and the worksheet on electromagnetic induction (Worksheet **P18F**).

● To teach practical skills.

In general we have tried to avoid introducing pupils to difficult practical skills at the same time as expecting them to make important measurements designed to improve their understanding of certain concepts. So Worksheet **P4B** gives experience in timing **before** the techniques acquired have to be used to measure speeds or accelerations. Worksheets **P16A** and **P17A** give experience in using ammeters and voltmeters **before** these are put to use to measure, for example, resistance in Worksheet **P17D**.

● To provide opportunities for pupils to plan and carry out scientific investigations.

Several of the worksheets are designed to involve pupils in planning and carrying out open-ended investigations. To help pupils do this, Worksheet **P0** is a planning worksheet that can be used in conjunction with all other worksheets in which pupils have to plan work for themselves.

Chapter 3 of the General introduction to this *Guide* lists four types of practical problem solving that come under this heading:

Type I: Laboratory investigations designed and carried out by the pupils using equipment supplied

Investigations of this type figure prominently in material designed as extension work for the more able. These investigations frequently take the form of experimental work which can increase the level of understanding of a concept. However, since pupils are not required to apply the ideas emerging from the experiments there is no pressure to obtain a particular answer (as there often is in "guided discovery experiments"). Their investigations thus gain a flavour of open-endedness which might otherwise be lacking.

	Topic **P1**	Topic **P2**	Topic **P3**	Topic **P4**	Topic **P5**
Experiments and other activities related to the theory of Physics	**P2A** Kinetic theory model **P2.2** Boyle's Law **P2C** The effect of temperature on gas pressure **P3.5** Radiations from radioactive materials **P3.6** The half-life of protactinium **P3.8** Randomness and radioactive decay	**P4B** Measuring time intervals and speed **P4E** Measuring acceleration **P5A** Force and motion **P5B** Friction **P5C** Frictionless motion **P5D** Effects of unbalanced forces **P5E** Inertia **P6A** Kinetic energy **P6B** Recoil **P6C** Collisions **P7A** Free fall **P7.4** Mass and weight	**P8A** Power **P9C** Heating water **P10.2** Rival theories of heating **P10A** Internal energy **P10B** Specific heating capacity of lead **P10C** Conservation of energy	**P14A** Waves on a spring **P14B** Waves on water **P15A** Colour	**P16A** Simple circuits **P16B** Using electricity **P16C** Electric currents **P17A** Voltage **P17B** Power in electric circuits **P17D** The size of an electric current **P17F** Electrical resistance **P17G** Ohm's Law **P18B** Electric currents in a magnetic field **P18D** Magnetism and electricity **P18F** Induced currents **P19A** The diode
Experiments and other activities in an applied context ● **Investigating**	**P1B** Cantilevers	**P7.3** Air resistance and parachuting	**P8B** The efficiency of a ramp **P9A** Investigating warm things **P9D** How efficient is your electric kettle? **P11.4** Power lines **P11A** Transformers	**P13A** Optical fibres **P15B** Colour filters **P15C** Colour vision **P15D** Secondary colours	**P17C** Efficiency of an electric motor **P17E** Resistance of a lamp **P18E** Electromagnets **P19B** The cathode ray oscilloscope **P20A** Switches **P20B** NAND control units **P20C** Bistable units **P20D** Computers in control **P21A** Sending messages using electricity
● **Building**	**P1A** Building a model bridge	**P4A** Inventing a timing device			**P18C** Building a model electric motor **P21B** Building a simple radio

An analysis of practical work in Physics. The table includes demonstration experiments where these involve the collection of data which is then analysed by the class. Entries such as **P2A** refer to worksheets; entries such as **P11.4** refer to sections in the Physics pupils' book.

Examples of such investigations occur in the study of the relationship between force, mass and acceleration (Worksheet **P5D**), and in the study of momentum (Worksheet **P6C**). The degree of help given to pupils in the worksheets varies with the difficulty of the experiments. All share a common policy of leaving the pupil to his or her own devices once the investigation is under way.

Type II: Laboratory investigations designed and carried out by the pupils using equipment selected by themselves

Investigations of this type cover a wider ability range. Examples will be found in Worksheet **P9A** "Investigating warm materials", Worksheet **P5A** "What keeps things moving?" and Worksheet **P18E** "Electromagnets". Similar problem-solving investigations are suggested in the pupils' book, without the benefit of accompanying worksheets. Particular examples in electronics will be found in Chapter **P20**.

Type III: The design of a piece of equipment, or other artefact, to perform a particular task

Worksheet **P4A** is one of a few investigations of this type. In this example pupils are challenged to invent their own timing device in order to measure an agreed time interval as accurately as possible.

Type IV: Investigations outside the laboratory, including field work

There are a number of investigations involving work outside the laboratory. Often the work involves the collection of data, rather than making measurements (as in Worksheet **P13C** "Noise"). Not all such investigations are presented as worksheets. An investigation into road safety, which is described in Chapter **P6**, could involve the practical measurement of vehicle speeds. The extended home heating project described in Chapter **P9** also involves measurement – this time by way of gas or electricity meter readings.

Worksheets

Most, but not all, of the Physics worksheets are designed to accompany experimental work. Those designed to introduce pupils to practical skills or advance their understanding are generally presented as detailed guides to what should be done. Others, designed to accompany investigations, do no more than start pupils working in a profitable direction.

For some of the investigational worksheets, Help sheets have been produced. It is intended that these should only be a guide to pupils who ask for them.

Finally there is another type of worksheet designed to encourage pupils to take a broader view of Physics in its social context, or its relationship to other sciences and technology. (See, for example, Worksheet **P15F** "Earthquakes".) Many of these worksheets have been based on Science and Technology in Society (SATIS) units. Teachers may want to make more use of SATIS (perhaps by replacing some of these worksheets with SATIS-derived worksheets or others of their own). In this way the social context of Physics will remain relevant as "live" issues change.

Safety

Safe conduct of work in the laboratory is an important consideration in all experimental work. But where there are particular issues of safety involved, such as in the handling of radioactive materials, detailed warnings are given in the notes on worksheets in this *Guide*.

Teaching difficult concepts

Some issues, such as the teaching of energy, or the teaching of electricity, demand detailed discussion. Such discussions will be found in the Physics topics introductions in this *Guide*.

The Physics pupils' book introduction

Purposes

1 To explain what it means to "do science".

2 To outline the skills and processes involved in carrying out a scientific investigation, and introduce symbols used throughout the pupils' book which draw attention to the use of these skills and processes.

3 To give some idea about the underlying nature of Physics, and its applications.

4 To describe how best to use the Physics pupils' book.

Timing

A single class period should be sufficient – perhaps combined with a reading assignment for homework.

Notes

Investigating the behaviour of springs

A discussion of the skills and processes involved in doing an investigation in Physics is related to an investigation into the behaviour of a spring under a stretching force. It is important that all pupils should have undertaken such an experiment in the past. Ideally they should have carried out the experiment as an "investigation" in which the pupil has some freedom of operation, rather than just following a set of written instructions. The outline in the pupils' book will need some discussion, as pupils will be expected to refer back to this piece of work later when planning their own investigation.

The symbols introduced on page 6 of the pupils' book are used throughout the book to highlight particular skills and processes in other contexts.

More about Physics

This section tries to relate Physics, as a connected fabric of ideas, to its particular applications, which will have much more meaning to the pupils. The pupils' book is based upon applications of physical ideas; by treating the applications as problems to be solved the book draws out the ideas which underlie them. One major theme which tends to reappear in all the work is that of energy and the transfer of energy.

Co-ordinated Sciences

The strategy used by the science department in presenting co-ordinated sciences will determine in part the order in which the pupils' books are used, and the particular parts which are relevant to individual pupils. However, an attempt has been made to make the pupils masters or mistresses of their own progress by providing some chapters with alternative sets of pathways from which they can choose. Thus to some extent the pupil can "negotiate" his or her own curriculum.

Summary

The summary refers to words which have been highlighted in the text. It encourages the pupils to read the text by asking them to write a sentence or two about each word. Alternative or additional words and phrases could be used here.

Topic **P1**   **Matter**

Introduction

This topic is about the particulate nature of matter. Chapter **P1** shows how we can understand the strength and stiffness of solids in terms of the forces which act between the particles of matter. Chapter **P2** is concerned with the kinetic theory of matter. It looks at the differences between solids, liquids and gases, and relates changes of state to changes in the kinetic energies of the particles. Chapter **P3** is about radioactivity, and thus about the nature of the particles (atoms) which make up matter.

These three chapters cannot be taught in sequence. Chapter **P1** is intended to be the opening chapter in the course. It builds on the example of Hooke's Law, taken to exemplify processes in science in the Introduction to the pupils' book. Chapter **P2** must come early in the course because the ideas about moving particles, which are the essence of the kinetic theory, are essential to work in Biology and Chemistry. Chapter **P3**, on the other hand, requires some knowledge of electricity which will only have been gained by pupils who have completed work on Chapters **P16**, **P17** and **P18**. This inevitably means that work on Chapter **P3** must be postponed until the fifth year (the second year of the course).

The Introduction to Topic **P1** revises the work of the third and previous years, which is essential to this topic. It can be used as a preparatory homework exercise prior to the first lesson. The questions are of the same standard as the original work – not harder questions on earlier themes. Ideas about energy are used in Chapter **P2**. A revision of what pupils should already know about energy is included in the Introduction to Topic **P3** "Energy".

The introduction also explains to pupils the use of the word "particle" in this topic and its relationship to the words "atom", "molecule" and "ion", which are used in Chemistry. This may require some more discussion in class.

Timing

21 periods, as follows:

Chapter **P1** Building bridges successfully	6 periods
Chapter **P2** Cooking food quickly	6 periods
Chapter **P3** Radioactivity	9 periods

Chapter P1   Building bridges successfully
The strength of solids

Purposes

Knowledge and understanding

At the end of this chapter all pupils should:

1 understand that the strength of solids derives from the forces between their constituent atoms and molecules

2 appreciate that a stable structure needs to be able to provide forces that counterbalance the external forces to which it is subject (including its own weight)

3 appreciate the spring-like nature of these forces by comparing the behaviour of materials under tension and compression with the behaviour of springs

4 appreciate that the design of a structure must take account of the use to which it is put and the materials from which it is made

5 appreciate the interplay of use and material by making a short study of a wide variety of bridge designs.

In addition, those pupils aiming for higher grades should:

6 understand that quantities such as force are only specified in full by their size and the direction in which they act, and that they have a reduced effect in other directions.

Processes and problem solving

Graphical and symbolic representation
The analysis of readings which leads to Hooke's Law in section **P1**.3 gives some attention to proportionality. Worksheet **P1B** and questions 7 and 13 give further opportunities for plotting and interpreting graphs and proportionality.

Using apparatus and measuring instruments
Worksheet **P1B** requires the careful measurement of displacements.

Observation
Worksheet **P1C** requires observations of bridge structures to be linked to what has been learned about forces in equilibrium.

Interpretation and application
The majority of the questions in this chapter are concerned with the application of ideas about strength and stiffness to structures.

Planning and carrying out investigations
Both Worksheets **P1A** and **P1B** give opportunities for planning investigations and carrying them out. Question 4 is a pencil-and-paper exercise in experiment design.

Problem solving
Opportunities for problem solving occur throughout the chapter. In particular questions 6, 7, 9, 10, 11, and 13 are problem-solving questions. Worksheets **P1A** and **P1B** both ask for problem-solving skills.

Timing   6 periods.

Suggested routes   The flow diagram in figure **P**1 divides the material in the pupils' book into three levels of difficulty. (All pupils follow the unlabelled route. Where differentiation is intended, alternative routes are labelled "faster" or "slower".)

Periods

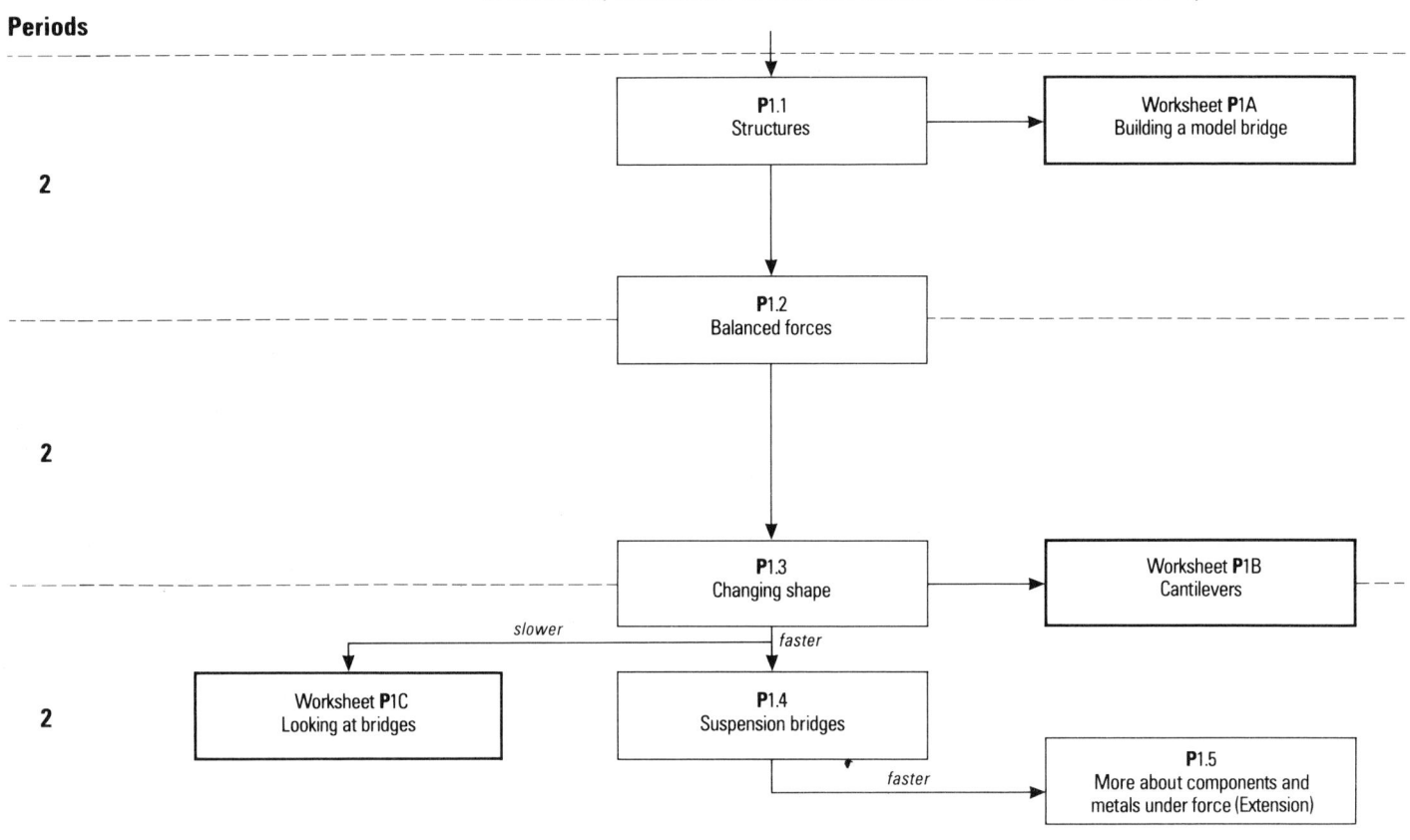

Figure **P**1

Opportunities for co-ordination   The study of materials is taken up in Chapter **C**5 "Materials and structures". Chapter **C**6 "Glasses and ceramics" looks at brittle materials. The reasons why metals are strong are dealt with in Chapter **C**7 "Metals and alloys".

Plants and animals rely on the stiffness of tubular structures. This is referred to in Chapter **B**10 "Skeletons and muscles". The elastic properties of muscles are also referred to in that chapter.

Notes and answers   ### P1.1   Structures

The exercise in building a model bridge to a given specification follows a brief introduction to structures. This is a popular activity and gives point to issues raised later in this topic. Not much over a period should be allowed for the model-building work with most pupils.

P1.2   Balanced forces

The idea that forces must balance if something is in equilibrium is introduced here at an intuitive level – something that will be returned to in Chapter **P**5. It is hard to justify experimentally, as many things like spring balances may well have been calibrated on the assumption that the spring pulls up with a force equal to the weight of any load on it acting downwards. In describing the counterbalancing force, the word "reaction" has been avoided deliberately. Considerable confusion is often caused by the different meanings which are attached to the word "reaction".

Answers to selected questions

Question 4 may seem trivial to many pupils – and if so is best left as such. To an interested group it can prove a good arguing point about assumptions made. In fact the balancing out of the forces is a special case of Newton's second law, since a net force will produce a change in motion – this has to be left until the work of Chapter P5.

P1.3   Changing shape

This section poses the problem of how structures provide the counterbalancing force. By comparing the behaviour of solids with springs it is clear that structures must distort (if ever so slightly) in order to provide that force. The section picks up the results of the investigation into springs discussed in the pupils' book Introduction. Pupils who reach this point quickly (say within two periods including the bridge building) can go on to Worksheet P1B. Two periods should be allowed for this investigation to give time for thorough work with minimum help.

The investigation into the behaviour of springs is used as an opportunity to think about proportionality. This is an important concept in Physics as it leads to easily expressed relationships between quantities. Three features of proportionality are emphasized. The first is the link between the straight-line graph and the algebraic representation. The second is the constant of proportionality and its dependence on the units of measurement. The third feature, developed in question 7, is the realization that there may be limits to proportionality in practical cases.

Answers to selected questions

7a 2 cm; **b** 9 N;
c i $36 = 3 \times 12$, so the extension might be expected to be 3×4 cm $= 12$ cm;
c ii But such a force might well take the spring past its elastic limit.
d i 8 cm; **d ii** 2 cm.

8 Aircraft are an obvious example to give, where weight is important. Similar considerations can apply to boats. Keeping down mass (different from weight) is important in cars, rowing "eights", poles for pole-vaulters, etc.

P1.4   Suspension bridges

Much of this section is for pupils who have coped quickly and easily with the first three sections. Such pupils will have two more periods in which to look at vectors and possibly do some of section P1.5. Worksheet P1C can be cut down to a homework exercise. For others, a longer time can be spent profitably on Worksheet P1C.

The distinction between physical quantities which have only size and those which have direction as well as size is an important one. In this course, not much more is expected than an appreciation that the distinction exists. The vector nature of velocity comes into Chapter P4, where it is contrasted with speed.

Answers to selected questions

11c The keel provides that force, as do yachtsmen leaning over the sides. The closer the boat sails into the wind, the more the component of the wind's force on the sail is directed sideways onto the boat.

12 At right angles to the direction of the force.

P1.5 More about components and metals under force

Definitely extension work for the more able. The ideas are not difficult, but pupils will need to have covered the earlier work quickly if they are to do this section.

Answer to selected question

13d At the maximum force the cable will "run" and snap, as it can do this at a lower force than the maximum.

Practical work

Worksheet P1A   Building a model bridge

REQUIREMENTS

Access to:
Assorted paper and card
Scissors
Tape, adhesive
Blocks to act as piers
Metre rules
Assorted masses to act as test loads
Balance to check mass of bridge

The procedure to be followed is detailed in the worksheet.

Warning
Bench tops, the laboratory floor and pupils' feet should be protected from possible damage due to falling test loads. Ideally bridges should be constructed on benches and not across gaps between benches. If bridges are constructed across gaps, something (such as a carton containing foam offcuts) should be placed under them to catch any falling test loads.

Worksheet P1B   Cantilevers

REQUIREMENTS

Each group of pupils will need:
Two metre rules
G-clamp
Slotted masses, 100 g set
Graph paper

The procedure to be followed is given in the worksheet. Pupils have to devise their own way of carrying out this investigation.

Demonstration experiments

Section P1.2:   Balanced forces

REQUIREMENTS

Some arrangement whereby a large mass can be suspended by a string.

Section P1.3:   Hooke's Law

REQUIREMENTS

It may be useful during the discussion to have a spring set up on a stand so that Hooke's Law can be demonstrated quickly.

Section P1.4:   Force as a vector quantity

REQUIREMENTS

A 2 kg mass supported by strings at an angle. (See figure **P1.21a** in the pupils' book.) The exact arrangement is not important, but it should be possible to use force meters to measure the tension in the strings. (The "traditional" arrangement of pulleys and strings is best avoided – it makes for too many difficulties in interpretation.)

Further information

Science and Technology in Society
Worksheets **P1A** and **P1C** draw heavily on SATIS unit 501 "Bridges". While not really an alternative approach to this work (the two approaches are very similar) some teachers may care to refer to the original publication and perhaps develop the material more closely along its lines. Less emphasis will then be placed on the basic physics of balancing forces and vectors as these are **assumed** by the unit rather than **taught** by it.

Supplementary material

A set of slides or pictures illustrating the wide variety of bridges will be useful.

Chapter P2   Cooking food quickly
Molecules in motion

Purposes

Knowledge and understanding

At the end of this chapter all pupils should:

1 understand the meaning of the term "kinetic theory of matter"

2 appreciate that the three states of matter can be understood in terms of a competition between intermolecular and interatomic forces on the one hand and the kinetic energy of the atoms and molecules on the other

3 appreciate how evaporation and boiling result from that competition

4 know the relationship between the pressure and volume of a gas and understand how the relationship may be predicted by the kinetic theory.

In addition, those pupils aiming for higher grades should:

5 know the relationship between pressure and temperature for a gas and understand how this leads to the Kelvin scale of temperature.

Processes and problem solving

Graphical and symbolic representation
Opportunities for the graphical analysis of data come in section **P2.2** "Pressure and volume" and section **P2.4** "Pressure and temperature". Data is provided for pupils who may not be able to see or do the experiments. The end of section **P2.4** deals briefly with the dangers of extrapolation.

Using apparatus and measuring instruments
Experiments to demonstrate Boyle's Law and to produce a graph of pressure against temperature both involve the reading of thermometers and Bourdon gauges (for pressure).

Observation
Observation is the keynote of Worksheet **P2A** where an analogy between the behaviour of solids, liquids and gases and the behaviour of moving marbles (particles) is drawn.

Interpretation and application
Together, the kinetic theory and the assumption that there are forces between atoms and molecules present a theory which enables many of the properties of liquids and gases to be understood as well as the operation of things like pressure cookers, aerosol sprays and refrigerators.

Problem solving
As in other chapters, the basic theoretical work is presented as a solution to a perceived problem. In this case, the operation of the pressure cooker is taken as the problem, to which an understanding of the kinetic theory provides a solution. Once the theory has been developed, other applications arise, such as the refrigerator, aerosols and the diesel engine.

Timing

6 periods.

Suggested routes

The flow diagram in figure **P2** divides the material in the pupils' book into three levels of difficulty. The work on pressure and temperature is intended for more

Periods

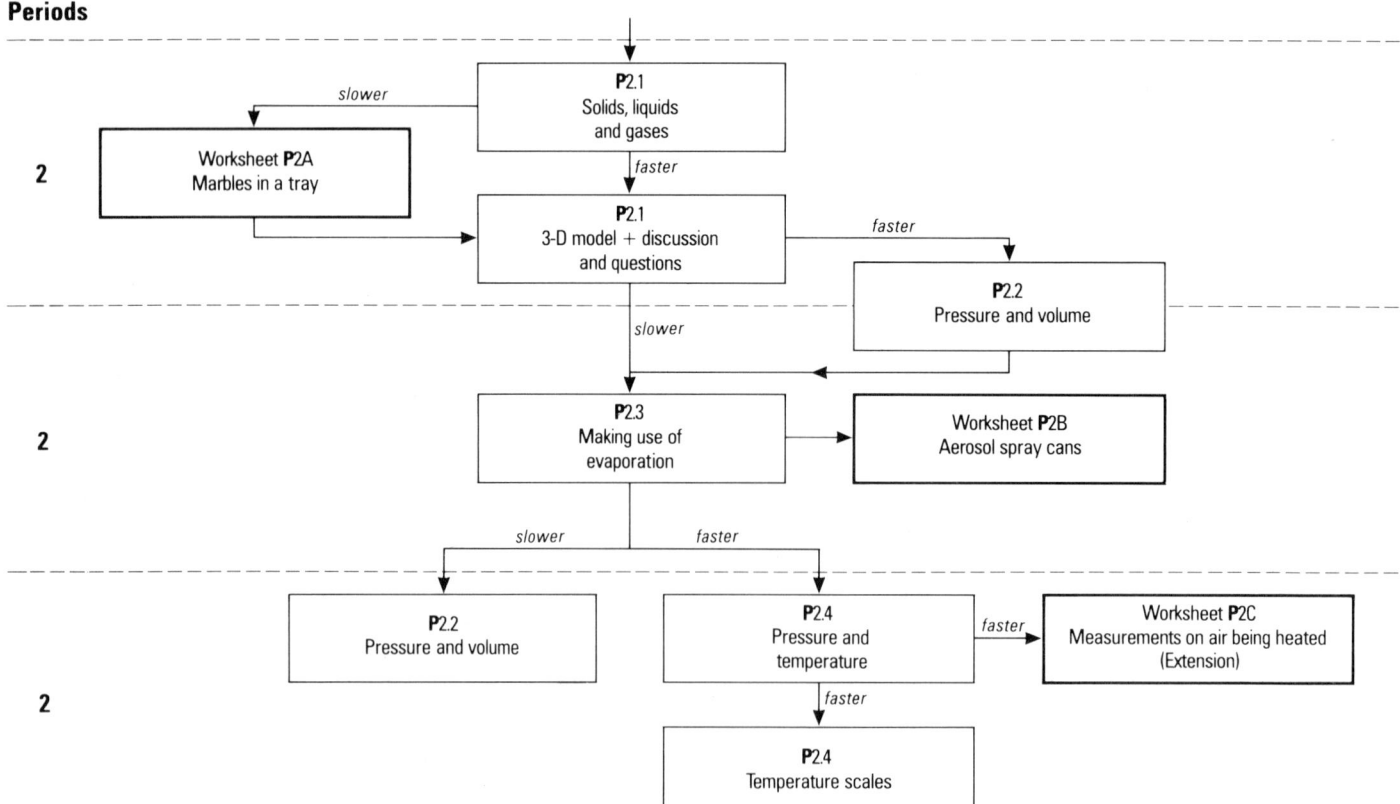

Figure **P2**

able pupils who spend less time on the 2-D kinetic model of Worksheet **P2A**. For these pupils, a demonstration of Boyle's Law will come within the first half of the unit. For less able pupils it is suggested that the work on evaporation (section **P2.3**) follows the completion of the work on section **P2.1** "Solids, liquids and gases". They can then return to section **P2.2** "Pressure and volume" to complete the unit.

Opportunities for co-ordination

The treatment of atoms and molecules in this chapter has been closely co-ordinated with work in Chemistry. The distinction between atoms and molecules is important in Chemistry; this distinction is made in Chapter **C1** "The elements of chemistry". However, the properties of solids, liquids and gases do not often require such a distinction to be made. A term covering both "atom" and "molecule" is needed, and for this reason the commonly-used word "particle" has been retained both in this chapter and in Chapter **P10** "Ideas in physics". It is easy for pupils to be confused by the use of the word "particle" in this context. The same word is also used to mean a "speck of matter" as in the phrase "smoke particles". It is also used in Chemistry in the same sense when dealing with colloids (see Chapter **C9**).

The use of the word "particle" in place of "atom" or "molecule" is explained in the pupils' book, and is from time to time reinforced by putting "atom or molecule" in brackets after it. It may well be necessary to reinforce this when discussing the kinetic theory of matter in class.

A good understanding of the kinetic theory is of importance to work in Biology and Chemistry and for this reason this chapter should come early in the Physics course.

Other areas of co-ordination are:

- The properties of **mists** and **foams** – Chemistry Chapter **C9** "Foams, emulsions, sols and gels".
- **Evaporation** and **cooling** – Biology Chapter **B**12 "Keeping things under control".

Notes and answers

The kinetic theory is intimately bound up with the concept of energy. We interpret the changes in temperature which are associated with energy transfers with changes in the kinetic energy of atoms and molecules. Heating, as a mode of energy transfer, is considered in Chapters **P9** and **P10**. A case could be made for establishing the connection between temperature change and energy transfer before looking in detail at the kinetic theory. In this course we have chosen not to do that. First, many of the details of the kinetic theory are useful in establishing a complete picture of matter as made up of particles (atoms and molecules) – a picture needed at an early stage in Chemistry. Secondly, the connection between energy transfer and temperature change is more easily grasped in terms of the kinetic theory than in terms of the more abstract notion of energy on its own. So the relationship between energy transfer and rise in temperature is assumed in this chapter and its justification awaits the work of Chapter **P10**.

It is assumed that pupils will have gained some ideas about energy and its involvement in change in earlier work. They will also already have gained some insight into the association of "getting warm" with energy transfer. These ideas are used in this chapter when talking about the increasing kinetic energy of the molecules in a liquid and a gas as the temperature rises. Detailed enquiry into energy transfers starts with the work of Chapter **P8**. This will come after the present chapter. However, two important features of the way the concept of energy is developed in this course are also relevant to this chapter.

First of all, the concept of **forms of energy** as exemplified by such phrases as "electrical energy", "mechanical energy", "thermal energy", has been dropped. Secondly the word "heat" is **not** used as a noun, but as a verb. Heating is a process – a way of transferring energy. Both of these matters are discussed at greater length in Chapter 2 of the General introduction to this *Guide*. To be consistent with later work it will be necessary when talking about the ideas in this chapter to avoid using such terms as "heat energy" (which is meaningless in the context of this course), and to avoid talk of energy changing from one **form** to another.

P2.1   Solids, liquids and gases

Introductory work on the kinetic theory is assumed to have taken place in year 3. In particular, pupils should have seen some evidence why matter is considered to be built from atoms and molecules and why we consider these atoms and molecules to be in a continual state of motion. Our work starts with a common piece of domestic equipment – the pressure cooker – and considers, in the light of the kinetic theory, how it works. This will lead to some revision of earlier ideas, but their inclusion at this point seems justifiable. The 2-D model is worth exploring in some detail. It is in fact much more fruitful than the more impressive 3-D model. Even so, more able pupils may not wish to spend very long on the associated worksheet (**P2A**).

We return to the pressure cooker, considering now the change in state from liquid to gas and the effect of pressure on boiling point. This involves some quite difficult ideas. In certain circumstances the change from liquid to gas can be described as *evaporation* (a surface phenomenon); in other circumstances, it is described as *boiling* (a bulk phenomenon). Evaporation can take place at all temperatures, its rate increasing with temperature. Boiling takes place at a fixed temperature which is determined by the external pressure. (Solids also evaporate, changing state from solid to gas. This does not concern us here.)

In both evaporation and boiling, energy has to be transferred to the molecules of a liquid as work is done against the intermolecular attractive forces. This process is referred to in the text as *vaporization*. To vaporize a liquid (whether by evaporation or boiling) energy has to be supplied. This is drawn from the surroundings. Normally liquids boil at temperatures well above normal room temperature, so the energy required is supplied by another hot object such as an electric heater, or a flame. In a refrigerator the liquid can be made to boil at a temperature below normal room temperature. In this case the necessary energy is drawn from the inside of the refrigerator.

Answers to selected questions

4a The kinetic theory explains gas pressure in terms of the collisions of the gas molecules with the walls of the container.
b The same number of particles will collide with the walls at a greater rate than before.

5a The rate of evaporation will increase because at any one time there will be a greater number of molecules with sufficient energy to break free from the attraction of the other molecules.
b The net rate of evaporation will increase because there will be fewer molecules returning to the liquid from the vapour state.

6a The number of people in the supermarket remains roughly constant because as many enter it as leave at any one time.
b See Biology pupils' book, Chapter **B3**.

7 130 kN/m^2; 170 kN/m^2; 200 kN/m^2.

P2.2 Pressure and volume

The pressure cooker directs attention to two features of liquids and gases which can now be followed up. The first, followed up in this section, is that the pressure rises in a pressure cooker as more molecules crowd into the space above the liquid. This suggests a relationship between pressure and number of particles, and leads on to Boyle's Law, where the increased crowding of molecules is achieved by a reduction in the volume they occupy. The relationship between pressure and particle impact is a necessary preliminary to this work and the demonstration illustrated in the pupils' book is a good one to show.

An experimental justification of Boyle's Law can be undertaken as a demonstration. Equipment to do this which is commonly found in many school laboratories is illustrated in figure 2.17b of the pupils' book. Question 10 gives some results for analysis which are typical of those obtained with such equipment. There is no necessity to use this particular equipment to illustrate Boyle's Law. Alternative equipment may do the job just as well. (However, you are advised against using the traditional equipment which involves an open reservoir of mercury. Apart from the safety aspect, pupils do not find it easy to understand what is happening.)

Answers to selected questions

10 Testing for Boyle's Law is not easy because of the reciprocal relationship between P and V. Pupils can easily be told to plot P against $1/V$ and will do so. This does not necessarily imply they understand the relationship between the two quantities. This question tries to take them step by step through the testing process. If the experiment has been done as a demonstration, then experimentally obtained values should replace those of figure 2.18. If a value for V has been obtained at a pressure of 10 units, then only the value of V in part **a** will need altering.

The matter of units is a difficult one here. Volume is often marked out in "arbitrary units" on the equipment illustrated in figure 2.17b. To make the "arithmetic" straightforward and yet give values close to those recorded by such equipment, the volume is given in cm^3. This is very nearly equal to the length of the gas column.

For similar reasons, the pressure is given in kN/m^2.

The graph plotting suggested in question 10f may be beyond some pupils at this stage. It can be omitted from the question without affecting an analysis of the results. Straightforward graph plotting, such as that involved in the stretching of a spring (Chapter **P1**) is assumed to be something all pupils will have done by this stage. A further development of graph-plotting skills is provided by Worksheet **P4C** in Chapter **P4**.

P2.3 Making use of evaporation

The second aspect of the behaviour of matter arising from the pressure cooker has much more direct application in the everyday world – the change of state from liquid to gas. Two particular applications are considered – the aerosol spray (which is the subject of Worksheet **P2B**) and the refrigerator. The relationship between evaporation and temperature is important both for its applications and the way the kinetic theory is able to deal with it.

The energy transfers involved in vaporization are further discussed in this section.

Answers to selected questions

11a Since evaporated water molecules are no longer returning to the pond, not only is the net evaporation more rapid but also energy is being removed from the pond water more rapidly. Hence the pond's temperature falls more quickly and the pond freezes over.
b The evaporating water molecules remove energy from the liquid water which consequently cools.

12a The temperature will fall.
b This will also fall.
c Its temperature will rise.
d The temperature of the pipes will rise.
e The temperature of the room also rises.

P2.4 Pressure and temperature

Only more able groups will have the time to do this section which relates the pressure in a gas to its temperature and introduces the idea of an absolute zero of temperature. The experiment described in Worksheet **P2C** is discussed below and the comments on the necessity to have an experiment not plagued by leaks apply equally to such an experiment performed as a demonstration. Since it is difficult to have several sets of reliable equipment, it may be preferred to do this experiment relating pressure to temperature as a demonstration. The final section in the pupils' book makes a useful general point about the processes of extrapolation and interpolation.

Answers to selected questions

14i The gas molecules make more collisions per second with the walls of the container.
ii Each collision is harder as the particles are moving more swiftly.

15a From work done in compressing the gas.
b Less opportunity for the extra energy to be transferred to the surroundings. (In fact such compressions can take place under a wide range of conditions, extending from those that take place so slowly that all energy is transferred to the surroundings and the temperature of the gas does not rise at all – *isothermal* compressions – to those in which there is no transfer of energy to the surroundings – *adiabatic* compressions.)

16a The temperature of the gas rises.
b Due to the rise in temperature the oil reacts explosively with the air.
c This reaction transfers energy to the gas, raising its temperature and pressure. This excess pressure drives the piston downwards.

18 This question leads into the absolute zero of temperature. The value obtained will depend on the readings used and the line drawn through them. In an ideal situation, pupils should use results obtained experimentally in class – either from their own experiments or from a demonstration.

19a 373 K; **b** 310 K; **c** 90 K.

Practical work

Worksheet P2A   Marbles in a tray

REQUIREMENTS

Each group of pupils will need:
Tray with cork-lined base and ruler or
  piece of wood to reduce "volume"
25 marbles (about 15 mm diameter), one
  a different colour from the rest
Marble (about 25 mm diameter)

Notes:
This 2-D kinetic theory model is one of
the best for gaining an insight into the
kinetic model of matter. The questions
have largely been drawn from Revised
Nuffield Physics. The worksheet will need
some introduction – particularly in
explaining why the tray has to be shaken
continually, while the walls of any
container **seem** to be stationary. Useful
background reading to the worksheet will
be found on pages 142–3 of Revised
Nuffield Physics *Pupils' text Year 3* and
on pages 162–3 of the corresponding
Teachers' guide.

Worksheet P2B   Aerosol spray cans

REQUIREMENTS

No particular equipment is needed, but it will be advantageous to have some or all of the
following:
● An exhibition of a range of aerosol products.
● Any references to the use and mis-use of aerosols, for pupils' research.

This piece of work is designed to give pupils the opportunity to explore the
application of a physical principle to a now common form of packaging. The
range of products now packaged as aerosols and the criteria which govern the use
of a material as a propellant are considered. There is some concern about the
increasing use of aerosols and pupils are encouraged to see that the application is
not without its disadvantages as well as its advantages.

Warning
Aerosols, misused, can be dangerous. It would be unwise to encourage pupils to
bring aerosols to school for the exhibition.

Worksheet P2C   Measurements on air being heated

REQUIREMENTS

Each group of pupils will need:
Pressure gauge, 200 kPa
Round-bottomed, 250 cm^3 flask
  (**not** 500 cm^3)
Bung with hole through it
Glass tube, short length to fit in bung
Rubber tubing
Container (aluminium), large enough to
  hold the flask fully immersed in the
  water
Bunsen burner and tubing
Tripod
Thermometer
Stand, boss and clamp
Stirrer
(Ice is an optional but valuable extra.)

Notes:
The flask must be firmly clamped to hold
it under water. The water level must reach
the top of the neck of the flask, which
may have to be tilted to achieve this. It
may be best to have this set up for the
pupils beforehand.
  A supply of hot water from a tap or
electric kettle is useful, and will speed up
the experiment.

It is likely that only a minority of pupils will do this as a class experiment.
However, the experiment itself is not difficult to perform, **given the right equipment**.
It is essential that the flask used is airtight and that connections to the pressure
gauge are as short as possible, commensurate with safety. The only way to test the

equipment is to do the experiment and examine the results. Experiments which give invalid results due to air leakage or an insufficient proportion of the air being raised to the temperature of the surrounding water are worse than useless. They will undermine any teaching of the relationship between temperature and pressure either now or in the future. It would be much better not to do the experiment at all and rely if necessary on the sample readings in the pupils' book. However, given good equipment (and pupils should receive the flask already connected to the pressure gauge), there is everything to be said for able pupils arriving at the concept of an absolute zero of temperature on the basis of measurements they themselves have made.

(See also Revised Nuffield Physics *Teachers' guide Year 3* pages 170–3.)

Demonstration experiments

Section P2.1: Solids to liquids and liquids to gases

REQUIREMENTS

Kinetic theory 3-D model with driving motor
Power supply for the motor
Stand, boss and clamp, if required for the model

The procedure for using the model varies from one design to another. For the procedure relating to one model commonly available, see Revised Nuffield Physics *Teachers' guide Year 3*, pages 160–1.

Rise in boiling-point of water with increased pressure

REQUIREMENTS

Measuring cylinder, 500 cm^3
Pressure gauge, 200 kPa
Bunsen burner and tubing
Round-bottomed flask, 250 cm^3
Bung with hole through it
Glass tube to fit bung
Rubber tubing
2 stands, bosses and clamps
Safety screens

The apparatus is set up as shown in figure 2.8 of the pupils' book. The pressure on the water boiling in the flask is increased by the depth of immersion of the tube in the cylinder of water.

Section P2.2: Model to show bombardment making pressure

REQUIREMENTS

Balance, 1 kg
Lead shot, or steel balls
Tray, large

The top of the balance is arranged as shown in figure 2.12 in the pupils' book. The balance is placed on a large tray, or inside a transparent container (plastic aquaria are a useful size). The balls are poured in a steady stream from a height of 25 to 50 cm onto the inverted scale pan. As the balls hit the pan and bounce off they exert small impulsive forces – like those due to gas molecules hitting a wall. The comparatively great mass of the pan, etc. smears out these forces into a steady reading on the balance.

Boyle's Law

REQUIREMENTS

Boyle's Law apparatus with pump to provide pressure

Apply pressure to the fluid in the reservoir. Read the pressure gauge and the corresponding length of the air column and record them.

Further information

Revised Nuffield Physics
Pupils' text and *Teachers' guide Year 3:* Chapter 5 "Gases".
Pupils' text and *Teachers' guide Year 4:* Chapter 6 "Gases I".
All the work on the behaviour of gases has been drawn from the Revised Nuffield Physics course. Not all the material in the chapters referred to will be relevant to the present course. However, it will provide more details of experimental procedures and additional questions, if these are needed.

Nuffield Science 13 to 16
Particles and *Energy.* The work in these two units provides information on the sort of background it is expected pupils will bring to the work of this chapter.

Chapter P3   Radioactivity
The structure of atoms

Purposes

Knowledge and understanding

At the end of this chapter all pupils should:

1 appreciate that radiations from radioactive materials are capable of breaking up other atoms and molecules

2 appreciate how radioactivity may be detected and measured

3 understand why radioactivity can be dangerous to living things, and be able to put these hazards into perspective

4 appreciate that the term "ionizing radiation" describes a range of radiations, which differ from each other in their properties

5 appreciate how radioactivity changes with time and understand the concept of half-life

6 appreciate the uses to which radioactivity has been put.

In addition, those pupils aiming for higher grades should:

7 appreciate the link between ionization and electric charge

8 be able to relate radioactivity to the structure of an atom

9 appreciate the idea of randomness in the decay process and relate this to half-life.

Processes and problem solving

Graphical and symbolic representation
An opportunity to make use of graphs occurs in section **P3.6** dealing with radioactive decay (question 13). More able pupils also use graphs to analyse the dice-throwing experiment in section **P3.8**.

Using apparatus and measuring instruments

The main measuring instrument used in the work of this chapter is the scaler counter.

Observation

Careful observation of a qualitative nature is required in assessing the properties of the different radiations.

Interpretation and application

Worksheet **P3B** is concerned with the applications of radioactivity in industry, medicine etc. Radioactive half-life is related to the possibilities of radioactive dating.

Planning and carrying out investigations

There is little opportunity for investigative work in this chapter as pupils below the age of sixteen are not permitted to handle the radioactive sources used in this work. However, question 4 gives them the opportunity to plan an experiment, if not perform it.

Problem solving

As previously, the important ideas should be developed as solutions to perceived problems. One of the difficulties with radioactivity is that the problems have to be presented to the pupils. Most of them are not obvious everyday events. This can lead to an element of artificiality. "Radioactivity" cannot be experienced unless an appropriate experiment is set up to do this. Hence it is first necessary to explore ionization before the introductory experiments with radioactive sources are meaningful.

Questions 3, 4, and 8 are all problem-solving questions in which ideas have to be applied to new situations.

Timing

9 periods.

Suggested routes

It is assumed that the work of this chapter will not be undertaken until the second year of the course (see page 274). By this time work on energy and electricity will have been covered.

The flow diagram in figure **P3** (opposite) divides the material in the pupils' book into three levels of difficulty. A detailed consideration of the process of ionization (section **P3.1**) could be omitted for pupils likely to find the work of this chapter difficult. The last section, dealing with random decay and half-life, is for the fastest pupils only.

Opportunities for co-ordination

The concept of ions and ionization is required in this chapter. This need mean no more than that atoms and groups of atoms can carry electrical charge. The idea of ions will first be encountered by pupils in Chapter **C5** "Materials and structures" where Faraday's ionic theory is used to explain how some atoms bond together to form giant structures. The concept of ions recurs throughout chemistry and particularly so in Chapter **C18**.

Section **P3.6**, dealing with half-life, contains a reference to radiocarbon dating. The carbon content of living organisms is also referred to in Chapters **B3** and **B9** of the Biology pupils' book.

Periods

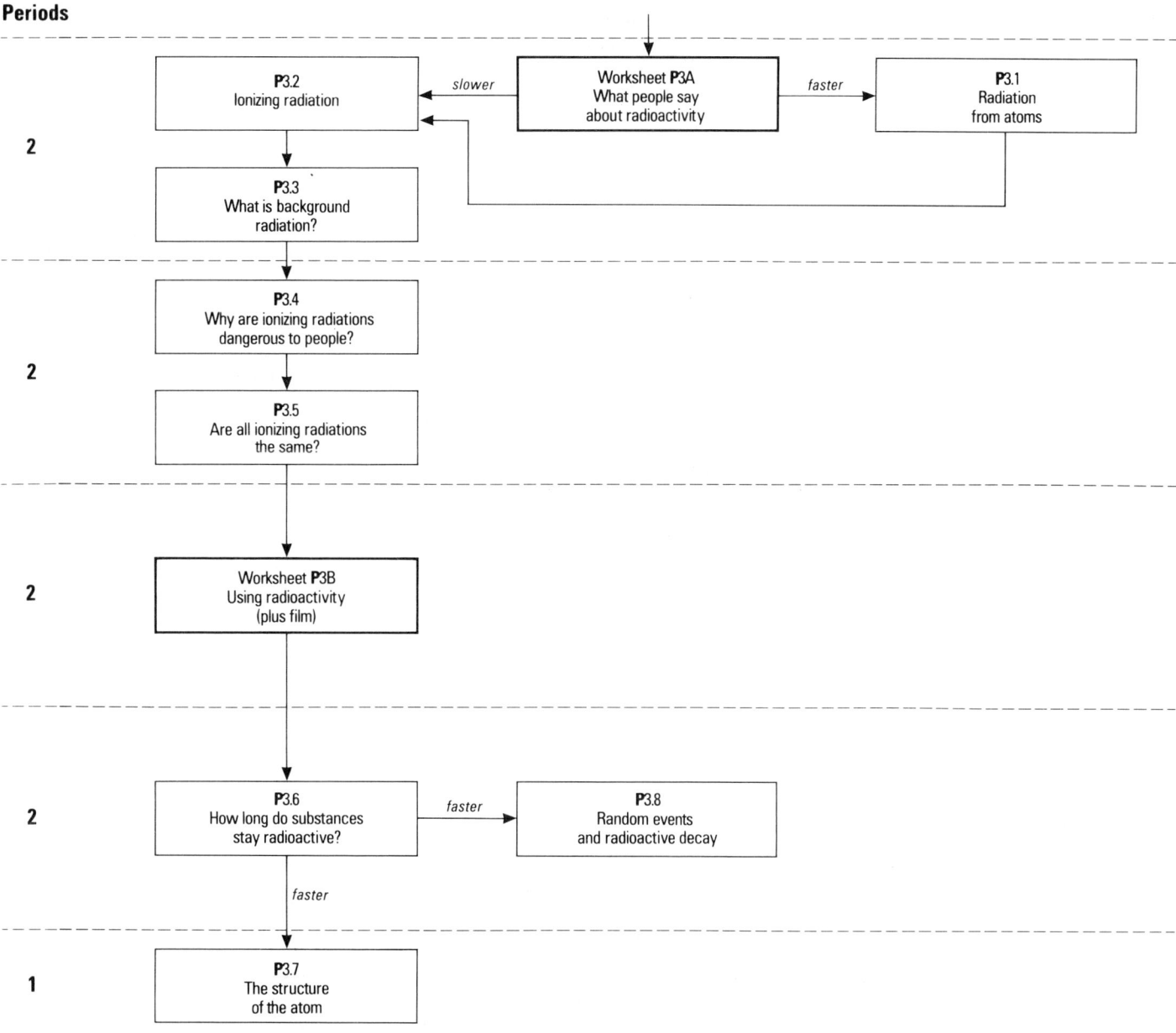

Figure **P3**

Notes and answers

P3.1   Radiation from atoms

This chapter on radioactivity does not start, as other chapters have done, with an obvious application. Instead it takes up the commonly held view that "radioactivity" is to be associated with a "dangerous radiation". While radioactive substances do indeed emit potentially dangerous radiations, there are many popular misconceptions about its powers. Worksheet **P3A** lists some of the things popularly attributed to radioactivity. Pupils are asked to comment on their truth or falsity. At the end of the chapter they are encouraged to review their earlier responses to these statements.

The introduction sets out to show how radiations from radioactive substances can transfer energy to the surroundings. Radiation's ability to break up molecules is given as much attention as the production of charged particles. However, the latter effect leads to the industrial and research term "ionizing radiation" which it seems useful to employ in this context once the capacity of the radiations to ionize has been established.

P3.2   Ionizing radiation

Radiations from a number of radioactive materials are shown to have an ionizing capability, and the spark detector and Geiger tube are introduced. Although a relatively expensive piece of equipment, the spark detector gives a visual and aural impression of the energy associated with ionizing radiations.

The workings of a Geiger tube can be understood as an extension of the spark counter. The experiment shown in figure 3.8 of the pupils' book can be done to form a link between the two detectors, if the appropriate equipment is available. (See the notes on practical work which follow.)

The cloud chamber has been omitted from the work of this chapter. Many may regret this as it is the one class experiment that can be undertaken in radioactivity. However, this mode of particle detection has little relevance to modern work on radioactivity (although of course bubble chambers are a development). Many find diffusion cloud chambers difficult to set up and time-consuming and there is no guarantee of success. They also need a supply of dry ice. Having said all that, there is no reason why they should not be included in the work by a school which has always used them successfully.

Answer to selected question

5 The main advantage of these generators is that their power sources will keep them in operation for many years without attention. Such generators can be used on spacecraft and have been left to power experiments on the Moon's surface.

P3.3   What is background radiation?

No attempt is made at this stage to differentiate between different sorts of radiation. However, the Geiger tube observations lead easily to the observation of "background radiation".

A discussion on background radiation is essential to understanding the work of the next section which returns to the effect ionizing radiations can have on people.

The random nature of radioactive emissions might also emerge from Geiger tube observations. This is a difficult idea and has been omitted from this chapter for all but the fastest pupils. If, however, it is intended that a class works through section **P3.8** "Random events and radioactive decay", now would be the time to introduce the idea of randomness of emission.

P3.4   Why are ionizing radiations dangerous to people?

This section introduces pupils to the units of measurement associated with the ionizing ability of radiations. From a "general knowledge" point of view these units are of as much importance as those of source activity, and it is important that pupils should be able to distinguish between the two. The term "radiation dose" refers to the ionizing capability of an ionizing radiation at a particular place. A high source activity does not necessarily imply a high "radiation dose". The radiation dose depends on the nature of the radiation, distance from the source, and the intervening material, as well as source activity.

No attempt is made to distinguish between ionizing abilities of the radiations in air and in tissue (what used to be referred to in terms of "rads" and "rems"). The correct unit of measurement for a radiation dose received by tissue is now the sievert, and this is used in the pupils' book. It might be useful in discussion to mention the older units of rad and rem as these are still in occasional use, but will soon disappear altogether.

Answers to selected questions

6c Workers exposed to known radiation hazards can be monitored carefully and the level of radiation to which they are exposed is carefully controlled. It is the lack of monitoring or control that necessitates setting low "safety levels" for the population-at-large. It is not (as might sometimes appear!) that risks are being taken with workers exposed to radiation.

7a Any answer to this question may appear to be contentious, but (bearing in mind the word "likely") the answer to this question is "No". There is a body of opinion that **any** level of radiation is harmful, but this involves an extrapolation of current data downwards into a region where the possible effects of radiation are overlaid by other hazards which might have similar effects. "Balance of risks" is not limited to the use and existence of radioactivity. For example, road transport has to balance convenience and necessity against the existence of road accidents. A useful discussion could arise from this question.

P3.5   Are all ionizing radiations the same?

The effect of magnetic fields on radiations leads into a discussion of the nature of the radiations and their differences. This discussion suggests that there is a "family" of ionizing radiations – alpha, beta and gamma. The approach to this is by comparing the behaviour of the radiations from americium, strontium and cobalt, which are respectively alpha, beta and gamma emitters.

This is the approach first introduced by the Nuffield Physics Project and later adopted by other projects such as the Schools Council Integrated Science Project. It is, in many teachers' opinion, much easier to understand than that which uses only radium as a radioactive source. In this alternative approach the ionizing radiation from radium is shown to be of three distinct kinds. It has the advantage of needing only one radioactive source but can lead to teaching difficulties.

The differences between the radiations lead to a more detailed enquiry into the uses of radioactivity. Worksheet **P3B** is based on the SATIS unit 204 "Using radioactivity". Work on the questions in this extensive worksheet will occupy the remainder of the unit. Some of the questions in it use the idea of half-life which pupils will meet in the next section.

Answers to selected questions

8a In a vacuum the particles will travel further.
b Spark detectors rely on the presence of air in order to work.

P3.6   How long do substances stay radioactive?

Radioactive decay as a "clock" forms the basis upon which ideas of half-life are developed. The unit in which source activity is measured is introduced here. This is the becquerel which has now replaced the older unit of the curie. As a unit the becquerel has the tendency to make even very small activities look uncomfortably large. It will be worth spending a little time getting this into perspective. Ordinary laboratory sources with an activity of 5 microcuries in the older unit, have, in the newer unit, an activity of about 200 000 becquerels.

The possibility of radiocarbon dating is used as a good reason for wanting to know the rate at which sources lose their activity. The way in which radioactivity changes with time is investigated by measuring the decay of protactinium – an experiment first introduced by Nuffield Physics. The experiment described in the pupils' book uses a counter (scaler) to collect numbers of decays registered by a Geiger tube. A graph of these results then shows how the radioactivity declines with time, and the concept of half-life can be established.

There are now other and quicker ways of displaying the decay curve. The results can be accumulated by a computer via an appropriate interface and the graph displayed on a video screen. Alternatively, interfacing units such as the VELA enable the decay data to be collected and displayed as a graph on a CRO. Used with care, these newer methods can add greatly to understanding. Graphs obtained in this way are often closer to the expected form than those accumulated "by hand". On the other hand the complexity of the equipment can obscure the nature of the experiment too easily and the rapid production of results reduces "thinking time". Pupils who find the analysis of the results produced by direct counting difficult will benefit most from these "direct display" methods. More able pupils probably benefit most from seeing **both** approaches, if time permits.

Answers to selected questions

15a 256 decays per second; **b** 128 decays per second.

P3.7 The structure of the atom

This section deals briefly with the nuclear model of the atom and its relationship to radioactive decay. No attempt is made to justify this model. Pupils are told it **can** be justified but that doing so is beyond the work of this course.

The model is used to show the nature of ionization as a change in the number of electrons associated with an atom. This idea is taken up again in Chapter **P19** "Making pictures with electricity".

P3.8 Random events and radioactive decay

The chapter ends with a structured analysis of the relationship between randomness of the decay process and half-life. It is intended as an extension to the work of the chapter for more able pupils who complete the remainder of the work in less time than the nine periods allowed.

Answers to selected questions

17a 250 pulses per minute; **b** 250/12 = 21 pulses in five seconds;
c The number of pulses recorded each minute ranges from 230 to 265 – an average range of $\pm 7\%$ of the average value. The number of pulses recorded in five seconds ranges from 10 to 25 – an average range of $\pm 36\%$ of the predicted value.

18a 100/5 (= 20 claims) would be expected.
b No, the numbers are becoming too small for certainty.
c 1 or 2.

19a 20;
b 100;
c 100/6 = 17, to the nearest whole number;
d 83.

21 The theoretical answer is "4.2 throws".

22a, b and **c** The answer should be the same as that to question 21.
e Again, the same answer.

Practical work

(None of the worksheets related to Chapter **P3** are practically-based.)

Demonstration experiments

Warning

In those experiments in which radioactive sources are used, it is essential to follow the guidelines laid down in DES Administrative Memorandum 2/76 "The use of ionizing radiations in Educational Establishments" and the accompanying "Notes for Guidance". All the sources listed here have the approval of the Department of Education and Science for use in schools.

Section P3.1:   Ions in a flame

REQUIREMENTS

2 metal plates with insulating handles
EHT power supply (or Van de Graaff generator)
Compact light source
Power supply for light source
Candle
White screen or wall

Procedure

The arrangement of the equipment is shown in figure 3.1 of the pupils' book.

Place the lighted candle so that its flame is a little below the plates. Place the light source 1 m or more away so that the shadow of the plates and the flame falls on a screen which should be at least a further metre from the plates.

When a high voltage is applied between the plates, the shadow of the flame and the gases above it divides into two parts, one towards the positive plate, the other towards the negative plate.

Sections P3.1 and P3.2:   Spark counter

REQUIREMENTS

Spark counter
EHT power supply
Radioactive source, americium-241
Radioactive source holder

Procedure

Connect the spark detector to the EHT power supply without incorporating the 50 MΩ safety resistor. The terminal connected to the top plate of the spark counter should also be connected to earth.

Turn up the voltage **slowly** until it is just below the point of starting a spark. Usually a p.d. of at least 4500 V is necessary.

Hold the source just in front of the grid. Sparks will be seen and heard.

Section P3.2:   Using a Geiger tube

REQUIREMENTS

Scaler counter
G-M tube, thin window type with holder
Radioactive sources of americium-241, strontium-90, cobalt-60
Radioactive source holder

Procedure

Connect the G-M tube to the scaler counter and apply the proper voltage from the scaler's built-in supply. This voltage can be most easily set by placing a strontium source close to the front of the tube and then raising the voltage until the scaler just starts to record pulses from the G-M tube. The correct operating voltage for the G-M tube is then about 50 V higher than this threshold voltage.

Experiments on the range of the radiations in air and the stopping power of various absorbers can then be demonstrated.

Section P3.5: Magnetic deflection of beta radiation

REQUIREMENTS

Scaler counter
G-M tube, thin window type with holder
Radioactive source of strontium-90
2 magnets, magnadur (slab)
Iron yoke
Stand, boss and clamp
Lead block (or any other material substantial enough to absorb the radiation from the strontium source)
Cork

Procedure

Connect the G-M tube to the scaler counter and hold it in a retort stand so that it is arranged as shown in figure 3.15 of the pupils' book.

Place the strontium source on the other side of the block. Fix it in a cork, pointing upwards as shown in figure 3.15.

The block shields the G-M tube from direct radiation from the source. Only a low count rate will be observed.

Arrange a horseshoe magnet of two slab magnets on an iron yoke. Bring up the magnet above the lead block. Place it so that its field is horizontal, across the path of the beta radiation. If the magnet is the right way round, radiation will reach the G-M tube and the count rate will increase. If the magnet is now reversed, the count rate should fall to its previous low value.

Section P3.6: Radioactive decay of protactinium

REQUIREMENTS

Scaler counter
G-M tube, thin window type with holder
Stopclock
Small polythene bottle (30 to 50 cm³ capacity)
Uranyl nitrate (or uranium oxide dissolved in nitric acid)
Hydrochloric acid, concentrated
Iso-butyl methyl ketone, or amyl acetate
Tray
Absorbent paper

Notes:
Cheap polythene bottles have the advantage of thin walls – but liquids should not be kept in them for more than a few weeks. If the cap of the bottle has a cork lining, screw a small piece of thin polythene under the cap for protection. Do not use **polystyrene** bottles.

The plastic bottle should be nearly full, containing equal volumes of organic reagent and acidified uranyl nitrate solution.

To make up a total volume of 40 cm³ of liquids proceed as follows:
Dissolve 2 g uranyl nitrate in 6 cm³ water in a beaker and add 14 cm³ of concentrated hydrochloric acid. Pour into the plastic bottle. Now add 20 cm³ of iso-butyl methyl ketone or amyl acetate. Screw the cap on the bottle tightly.

Other volumes can be made up by appropriate adjustment of the quantities above.

Procedure

Place the bottle in a tray lined with absorbent paper.

Support the G-M tube with a clamp on the tube holder and tilt it so that it points steeply downwards, slanting towards the neck of the bottle.

Beta radiation comes out to the G-M tube through the thin wall of the plastic bottle.

Shake the bottle vigorously for about 15 s and place it in position. As soon as the two layers of liquid have separated, start the scaler counter and let it count for 10 s. Take counts at 10 s intervals without stopping, or take 10 s counts every half-minute. Record each count.

Also record the "time of day" – that is, the total time from the start of counting to the start (or to the mid-time) of each count. That tells us the "age" of the source.

There is no need to continue counting longer than 5 minutes, when the activity will have dropped to less than 10% of its initial value, apart from background.

Allow for background radiation. Wait for 10 minutes after the start of counting and set the scaler to count for, say, 5 minutes, with the bottle still in position. That count will provide an average value of the background, some of which comes from the lower liquid.

Subtract the background **(reduced to a 10 s rate)** from each of the earlier counts. Discuss the obvious decay and try to find a rough value for the half-life. A graph can be plotted from the results as suggested in question 13 of the pupils' book. But how far the experiment is further analysed will depend on the ability of the class.

Section P3.8:   A game with dice

REQUIREMENTS

Each group of pupils will need:
120 wooden cubes with one marked face (120 dice)

Further information

Revised Nuffield Physics
Teachers' guide Year 5 Chapter 10 "Radioactivity".

The experiments in this chapter have been drawn from Revised Nuffield Physics. Teachers are advised to read the chapter referred to above. This will serve to put the present approach in a wider context and also suggest additional demonstration experiments (especially in connection with ionization) that teachers may care to show, if time permits.

Nuffield Science 13 to 16
Radioactivity. This module also follows a similar approach. Some of the material in the chapter has been drawn from it. Teachers may feel that for some pupils the simpler approach adopted in this unit is more appropriate. It covers very much the same ground as the present chapter.

Supplementary material

A number of films and videos are available which deal with the uses of radioactivity. One of these should be shown in connection with the uses of radioactivity discussed in section **P3.5**, One possibility is a video available from the United Kingdom Atomic Energy Authority (UKAEA), entitled "Using radioactivity".

(It is important at this stage not to show material connected with **nuclear power**. This is a separate issue dealt with in Chapter **P**12.)

Topic P2

Force and motion

Introduction

It is not anticipated that the four chapters in this topic will be taught in sequence, although they are linked together by a common theme. Chapters **P4** and **P5** introduce the basic concepts associated with motion and relate the action of a force to them. Chapter **P4** gives considerable emphasis to the acquisition of skills in plotting and interpreting graphs, but otherwise the content of the chapters is qualitative rather than quantitative. They have been written on the assumption that they will be read and used early in the fourth year.

Chapters **P6** and **P7** are more demanding, and it is anticipated that they will not be covered until early in the fifth year. Chapter **P6** investigates the changes in motion that occur when bodies interact, and looks for laws relating these changes in motion. A simplified approach to the conservation of momentum is introduced for all pupils, called the "Law of Recoil". This can be used to solve several everyday problems. More able pupils are given the opportunity to extend this simple law to the more general pattern of momentum conservation.

Chapter **P7** extends the idea of simple "contact" forces to "action at a distance" and the concept of fields of force. It explores the force of gravity and contrasts the concepts of mass and weight.

As explained in the introduction to this topic in the pupils' book, the work in these chapters tries to do much more than establish ideas about force and motion. Chapter **P4** is used as an opportunity to give practice in very important scientific skills – those of plotting and interpreting graphs. Chapter **P5** uses historical arguments about how bodies move to give pupils an opportunity to test out alternative theories in an investigative manner.

Chapter **P6** shows how ideas of force and motion are important in a wide range of practical situations, from the prevention of road accidents to the launching of space rockets. Chapter **P7** considers the universal nature of gravitation and uses this idea to direct attention to "predictability" in Physics.

Throughout these chapters, experimental work on motion has assumed the use of electronic stopclocks controlled by arrangements of lamps and photodetectors, as these seem easier to understand than the commonly used ticker-timers. However, the work of these chapters will in no way be hindered by the use of ticker-timers for time and distance measurements, if a school or teacher prefers, for reasons of expense and expertise, to use them instead.

Warning
Many of the experiments in this topic use dynamics trolleys on trolley runways. In all these experiments it is essential to have some form of end stop to prevent the trolleys from running off the ends of runways, and thus prevent injury to pupils and damage to the trolleys. It is also important to take due care in moving trolley runways about the laboratory.

Timing

25 periods, as follows:

Chapter **P4**	Motion	6 periods
Chapter **P5**	Controlling motion	6 periods
Chapter **P6**	Crashes and bangs	9 periods
Chapter **P7**	Rising and falling	4 periods

Chapter **P4**   **Motion**
Speed, velocity and acceleration

Purposes

Knowledge and understanding

At the end of this chapter all pupils should:

1 understand the meaning of the terms "speed", "velocity" and "acceleration"

2 appreciate the existence of errors in measurement and understand how they may be reduced by taking the average of a number of readings

3 understand how graphs may be used in displaying relationships between distance, time, speed and acceleration

4 appreciate how the ideas of speed and acceleration can be applied to road transport.

In addition, those pupils aiming for higher grades should:

5 understand how distances travelled can be derived from the area under a speed-time graph.

Processes and problem solving

Graphical and symbolic representation
This chapter gives experience in graph plotting and interpreting graphs. Worksheet **P4C** gives detailed instructions for plotting a distance-time graph and shows how instantaneous speeds can be derived from it. Questions 16 and 22 also contain data from which graphs have to be plotted. Questions 17, 18 and 21 are concerned with interpreting data as a graph.

Using apparatus and measuring instruments
Measurements made in this chapter are those of length and time. Experience is gained in using both manually controlled stopclocks and light-beam controlled clocks.

Observation
The stress in this chapter is on accuracy in observation. Stopclocks have to be started, stopped and read as precisely as possible in view of the small time intervals that have to be measured.

Interpretation and application
The concepts of speed and acceleration are given reality by being related to many events in the world around us. Question 7 looks at the variety of timing devices that have been, or are being, used. Questions 12 and 13 are concerned with a variety of practical speeds. Question 22 and Worksheet **P4D** apply the concept of acceleration to motorcycles and cars.

Planning investigations
More able pupils are encouraged, as part of Worksheet **P4E**, to make their own investigation into the way the acceleration of a trolley is related to the slope of the runway down which it travels. Apart from this, the chapter is largely concerned with acquiring measurement skills that can be put to use in more open-ended investigations in Chapters **P5** to **P7**.

Problem solving
At the beginning of the chapter, pupils are set the task of inventing their own timing device. This home-based project extends throughout their work on Chapter **P4**. There are also a number of "pencil and paper" problems on speed, velocity and acceleration.

Timing

6 periods.

Suggested routes

The flow diagram in figure **P4** divides the material in the pupils' book into three levels of difficulty. All pupils should gain experience in measuring speeds and acceleration and appreciating something of the idea of experimental error. Less able pupils may find it advantageous to spend rather more time on graph plotting and learning to interpret graphs. More able pupils should certainly develop the concept of motion to include the vector nature of velocity and acceleration. Only the fastest pupils will have time to include the work in section **P4.4** on calculating the distance travelled from a speed-time graph.

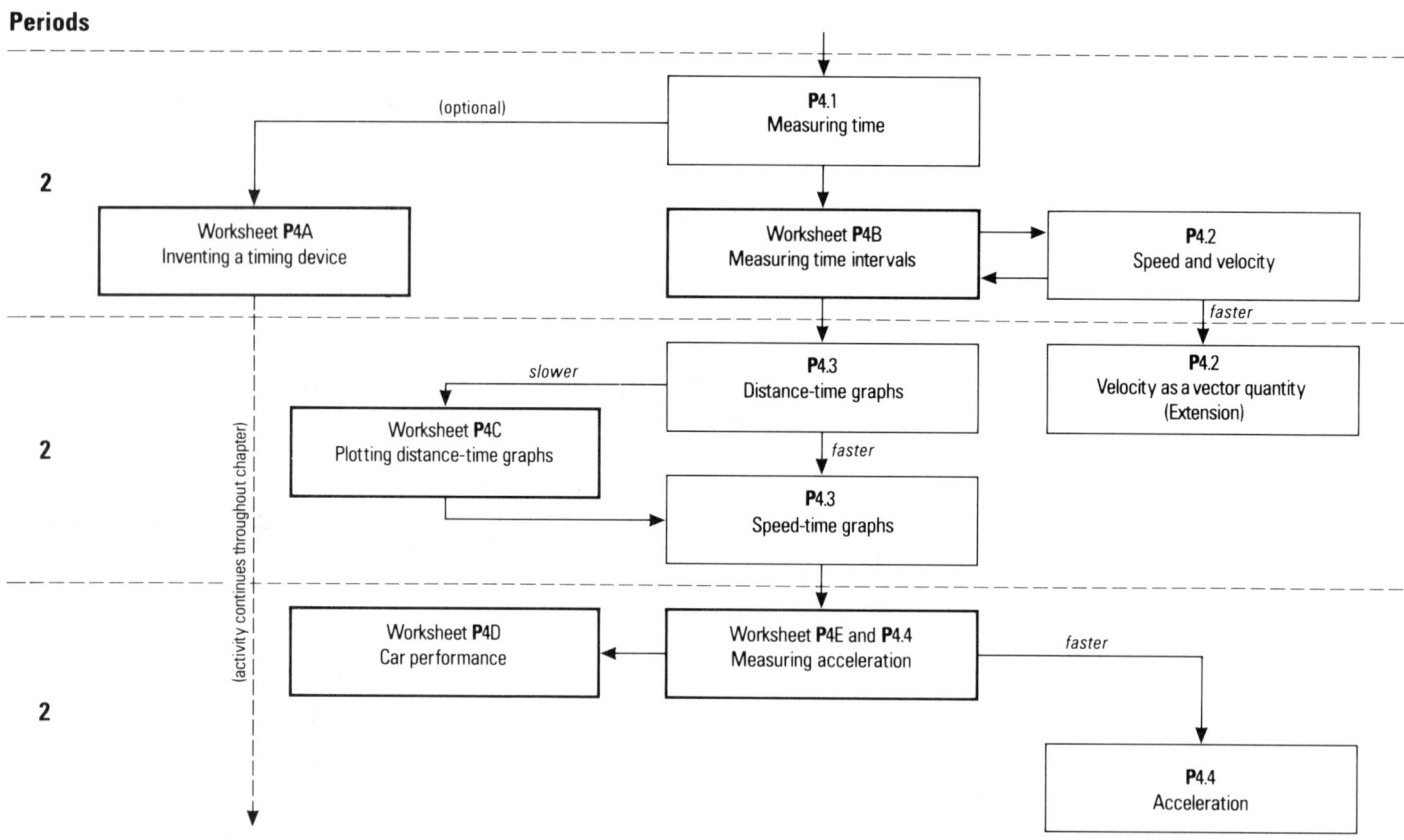

Figure **P4**

Opportunities for co-ordination

There are no specific links between the work of this chapter and pupils' work in Chemistry and Biology. However, two things of importance to work in other sciences are given detailed attention in this chapter. The first is the idea of "experimental error" which arises in connection with the difficulties in measuring small time intervals. The second is the experience gained in plotting and interpreting graphs.

Co-ordination should take place with work in mathematics. Ideas about averaging and the words "mode" and "mean" are introduced, as well as techniques in graph plotting. All of these will also be a part of the pupils' work in mathematics. "Rounding off" to an appropriate number of significant figures is also something that could be co-ordinated between the two departments.

Notes and answers

P4.1 Measuring time

This chapter is about motion and measurement. Measuring the speed of a body in a laboratory presents obvious problems in measuring small time intervals accurately. The chapter thus starts with a brief history of timing devices. This could be expanded in class.

Pupils are challenged to produce a timing device of their own invention and help is given with this in Worksheet **P4A**.

The pendulum is introduced into the discussion and measurements of its period lead to a discussion of errors in measurement. More able pupils might care to discuss whether it is possible to "discover" that a pendulum always takes the same time to complete one oscillation. Against what yard-stick is this measurement made? To some extent adopting a particular "time-scale" is arbitrary. Decisions about atomic clocks being "more accurate" than pendulum clocks are based partly on fundamental laws of physics and partly on the ability of a particular timing device to keep time **with another similar timing device**. Two or three atomic clocks will keep time with each other to far greater precision than any other clock.

Investigations into the time-keeping properties of a pendulum do no more than show that a pendulum "keeps time" with a stopclock. The real importance of the pendulum is that changes in amplitude of (small) swings seem to have no effect on the time taken for each swing – this was Galileo's important discovery.

Along with the discussion of errors in measurement, the process of "averaging" is introduced, as well as the ideas of the "mode" and "mean" of a set of readings. Co-ordination with work in mathematics will be useful here, as suggested in the notes on co-ordination above.

Finally, electronic timing devices are introduced and practice in using them is given in Worksheet **P4B**. It may be much easier for pupils to use and understand an electronic clock controlled by a light beam than to use and understand a ticker-timer. Because simple digital clocks controlled by a light beam are now available at a price which would enable schools to purchase class sets, it was decided to write worksheets using them. Some schools may, for reasons of expense and present equipment, wish to retain the use of the ticker-timer for measuring speeds and accelerations, perhaps confining the use of electronic stopclocks to a demonstration experiment. If this is done, it will be useful for pupils to have gained some experience in the use of ticker-timers in an earlier year, so that their understanding of speed and acceleration is not hampered by learning at the same time to interpret a record from a ticker-timer.

The use of ticker-timers rather than electronic stopclocks will necessitate the re-writing of Worksheets **P4B** and **P4E**. It is hoped, however, that all pupils will at least see a light-beam operated clock in use as well as a demonstration of the use of a microprocessor-based device such as a VELA, GiPSI or similar device, or a microcomputer with an interface. The use of such devices is given more attention in Chapter **P20** "Control".

Answers to selected questions

1b 9.2 s; **c** 4 pupils.

2a The one obtained by pupil F.

4a 9.1 s;
b This result is lower than the mode.
c i 9.1 s; **c ii** 9.2 s.
d This suggests that readings where a mistake seems to have been made should be discarded.

5c 5.3 s (Note the need to correct the answer to one decimal place.)

6a 25/10 = 2.5 s; **b** 25 × 4 = 100 s;
c Her pulse rate was 60 beats per minute.

P4.2 Speed and velocity

The concepts of speed and velocity are introduced in this section. The latter part of the section, which highlights the difference between speed and velocity, depends to some extent on the previous introduction of the idea of vector quantities in Chapter **P1**.

An attempt has been made to maintain the distinction between speed and velocity which is defined in this chapter. Strictly speaking the term "velocity" should not be used unless an associated direction is stated or implied. Thus generally one can only say the **speed** of light is 300 000 km/s since this speed is independent of any direction. On the other hand it would probably be correct to say that the **velocity** of light from the sun to the earth is 300 000 km/s, since here a direction is implied!

Answers to selected questions

8a 6 km/h;
b 0.3 m/s (The data do not really justify an answer to better than one significant figure.)

9 4 km.

10 2 hours 40 minutes.

11 Average speeds for each half hour period are:
15.0 km/h, 12.0 km/h, 10.8 km/h, 9.0 km/h, 13.2 km/h.
i 12.0 km/h; **ii** 12.0 km/h.

12 A with **5**, B with **6**, C with **1**, D with **4**, E with **3**, and F with **2**.

13 500 s (about 8 minutes). The distance from the sun to Earth is 150 000 000 km.

14a 3 m/s; **b** 1 m/s.

15b 3 cm/s due E at A, 3 cm/s due S at B, 3 cm/s due W at C, and 3 cm/s due N at D.

P4.3 Distance-time graphs

Distance-time graphs are introduced and the speed of an object is shown to be given by the slope of the graph line. This is extended to distance-time graphs which are not straight lines. Worksheet **P4C** gives detailed instructions on plotting such a graph and finding instantaneous speeds from it. Such detailed instructions may not be needed by all pupils.

Again it will be useful to co-ordinate this work on gradients of graph lines with work in the mathematics department.

Answers to selected questions

16 See question 11.

17b A: 6 km/h, B: 0 km/h, C: −4.5 km/h.

18a The speed of car P is decreasing, while that of car R is increasing.
b Draw lines at a tangent to the curves at the point corresponding to $t = 2$ s and find the slopes of these tangents.
c Car P: 17 m/s, car R: 11 m/s. (Estimated from a graph.)

P4.4   Acceleration

Several points about the way acceleration has been treated may need explanation. First of all, it seems to be the experience of many teachers that establishing the **concept** of acceleration (as change in speed, or velocity) is very much easier than establishing what **constant** acceleration means.

Since Newton's Second Law of motion is not developed formally in this course, there is no need to stress the idea of **constant** acceleration.

Secondly, problems arise over the fact that the word acceleration can have two meanings. It can mean "change in speed" which is its everyday use. It can also mean "change in velocity" which is its correct scientific usage. In the latter case, the vector nature of acceleration is also emphasized.

That an object can "accelerate" when **only** its direction of motion changes is usually introduced via a study of circular motion. It arises because of previous work on the relationship between force and change in motion. A force is found to be necessary to change the direction of motion even if the speed is not changed. However, Newton's Second Law, established for straight-line motion, relates force directly to rate of change of speed (along the straight line). This law is found to be directly applicable to, say, circular motion if the concept of acceleration is extended to "rate of change of velocity" rather than just rate of change of speed.

These ideas are beyond the scope of the present course, but will be important to pupils who study Physics at a later stage.

In establishing an understanding of any concept we believe it is important to relate it to any ideas the pupil may already have. In the everyday sense, "acceleration" means "change in speed". So for this reason, work on acceleration is confined to straight-line motion and the definition of acceleration is limited to such motion. It is left to later work to extend this definition to include change in direction.

Acceleration in this limited sense can be related to the slope of speed-time graphs. Such graphs are referred to as speed-time graphs since no particular direction is specified. Strictly speaking it could be said to be impossible to plot **velocity**-time graphs, since in general a velocity (which requires three co-ordinates in space as well as a size) cannot be represented on a single graph. But no simple rule can be given. If motion is specified as being in a straight line, some meaning can be given to a **velocity**-time graph. The direction of motion is implied as being either backwards or forwards along the straight line.

Deriving acceleration from a speed- (or velocity-) time graph has no meaning unless it is specified that the motion **is** in a straight line. On the other hand, the area under a **speed**-time graph gives the distance travelled whether or not a constant direction is maintained.

Many of these considerations are beyond all but the very fastest pupils. So this chapter keeps to the policy adopted in Revised Nuffield Physics of referring to all such graphs as speed-time graphs, but specifying that motion is in a straight line where it is necessary to do so.

Worksheet **P4D** applies the concept of acceleration to the performance of cars. This exercise may be more useful for pupils who have difficulty in grasping the concept of acceleration.

Worksheet **P4E** gives experience in measuring accelerations. The extended investigation that forms part of the worksheet (mentioned earlier) could form an alternative to Worksheet **P4D** for some pupils.

Answers to selected questions

20a 9 m/s; **b** It actually has this speed 3 s from the start.

21a i 0 to 1.5 minutes; **ii** 4 to 5 minutes; **iii** 1.5 to 4 minutes;
b i 20 m/s; **ii** 30 m/s; **iii** 30 m/s;
c $30/1.5 = 20$ m/s every minute or 0.3 m/s every second. Both answers are perfectly respectable statements of acceleration, even though the first may be unusual.
d $-30/1 = -30$ m/s every minute or -0.5 m/s every second.
e To work out the distance, all times **must** be in the same units.
Area under the graph $= \frac{1}{2} \times 30$ m/s $\times 90$ s $+ 30$ m/s $\times 210$ s $+ \frac{1}{2} \times 30$ m/s $\times 60$ s
$$= 8550 \text{ m (or 8.55 km)}.$$

22a 0.33 m/s every second; **b** -0.67 m/s every second; **c** 2700 m.

Practical work

Worksheet P4A   Inventing a timing device

REQUIREMENTS

No specific equipment is recommended for this investigation.

This is an investigation intended to be undertaken in the pupils' own time. If time permits it could be undertaken in class. Alternatively it could form part of a science-club activity.

Worksheet P4B   Measuring time intervals

Experiment 1: Using a stopwatch

REQUIREMENTS

Each group of pupils will need:
Box with a set of blocks to fit in it
Stopwatch

This is quite a useful exercise for thinking about errors of measurement and averaging. The exercise is related to "time and motion" studies in industry.

Warning
See the note about trolley runways in the introduction to this topic.

Experiment 2: Using an electric stopclock

REQUIREMENTS

Each group of pupils will need:
Stopclock, electrically controlled
2 connecting wires
Track, grooved, with a 20 cm length of aluminium foil along each edge
Metal ball (ball bearing), about 12 mm diameter to run down track

A detailed procedure is given in the worksheet.

Experiment 3: Using an electronic timer

REQUIREMENTS

Each group of pupils will need:
Electronic timer
Lamp and photodetector, and supports for them
Dynamics trolley
Card: 20 cm × 8 cm

The aim of the experiment is to time the passage of a trolley through a light beam and work out its speed. A detailed procedure is given in the worksheet.

Worksheet P4C   Plotting a distance-time graph

Worksheet P4D   Car performances

REQUIREMENTS

No equipment required.

Worksheet P4E   Measuring acceleration

REQUIREMENTS

Each group of pupils will need:
Dynamics trolley
Card: 20 cm by 8 cm
Runway for trolleys
End stop
Electronic timer
Lamp and photodetector, and supports for them
Stopwatch
Blocks to tilt runway
Sticky tape, or some other means of marking lines on the runway

A detailed procedure is given in the worksheet.

Warning
See the note about trolley runways in the introduction to this topic.

Using a microprocessor

REQUIREMENTS

Timing device (microprocessor-based), or microcomputer and interface
Lamp and photodetector, and supports for them, together with other equipment as needed

The use of microprocessors in a wide range of applications is investigated in Chapter **P20**. The use of a microprocessor-based timing device at this point will eventually assist that work. The procedure adopted will depend on the equipment used. The work can be based around either microprocessor-based timing devices such as VELA or GiPSi, or a microcomputer with an appropriate interface. Interfaces for the BBC microcomputer are available from all the major equipment suppliers. Setting-up details are usually available with instruction manuals packed with all such equipment.

Demonstration experiment

It may be useful to have a pendulum set up for the work of section **P4.1**.

Further information

Revised Nuffield Physics
Teachers' guide Year 3 pages 121–34 and *Pupils' text Year 3* pages 107–18.
Details of an approach to motion using ticker-timers rather than electronic timers will be found in this reference. These pages also contain a helpful discussion on speed, velocity and acceleration. The ground covered in the pupils' text is much the same as the ground covered in Chapter **P4**.

Manuals are provided with microprocessor interfaces. These usually give detailed procedures for carrying out experiments using the equipment.

Chapter P5 Controlling motion
The effect of unbalanced forces

Purposes

Knowledge and understanding

At the end of this chapter all pupils should:

1 understand that unbalanced forces change motion and that in the absence of an unbalanced force an object will either remain at rest or travel with a constant velocity

2 appreciate the place of friction in making sense of **1** above in the everyday world

3 appreciate qualitatively that the acceleration of a body depends both on its mass and on the size of the unbalanced force acting on it.

Processes and problem solving

Graphical and symbolic representation
More able pupils who undertake Worksheet **P5D** may find it useful to display their results graphically. This is optional and depends on pupil initiative.

Using apparatus and measuring instruments
Skills in timing, acquired in Chapter **P4**, will be needed by pupils doing experiments in Worksheets **P5A** and **P5D**.

Observation
Much of this chapter depends on making careful observations and drawing appropriate conclusions from them. Galileo's inclined plane experiments are a particular case in point.

Interpretation and application
Worksheet **P5C** is concerned with interpreting "friction-free" motion in terms of Newton's First Law of Motion. The experiments described in Worksheet **P5E** lead to a number of observations which depend on the inertial properties of matter for their explanation.

Planning investigations
Worksheets **P5A**, **P5B** and **P5D** all require the planning and carrying out of investigations. The pupils are given some help in Worksheet **P5B**; in the other two worksheets little help is given.

Problem solving
This entire chapter is concerned with solving the problem stated in section **P5.1**: "What makes things move?"

Timing	6 periods.

Suggested routes

The flow diagram in figure P5 divides the material in the pupils' book into two levels of difficulty. All pupils take essentially the same route through the material. However, alternative practical investigations are provided at two points in the sequence. At the start, some pupils may benefit more from an investigation into friction which then leads into the possibility of frictionless motion. Others can perform a more open-ended investigation into the theories of motion. Both investigations are to some extent open-ended, but the first sets more limited goals.

At the end of the chapter, the effect of unbalanced forces is investigated. A quantitative statement of Newton's Second Law is not a part of the course. So, following a qualitative discussion and demonstration on the effects of unbalanced forces, pupils have the option of either investigating the inertial properties of matter or of performing an open-ended investigation into the relationship between force, mass and acceleration. They can of course do both, if time permits.

Periods

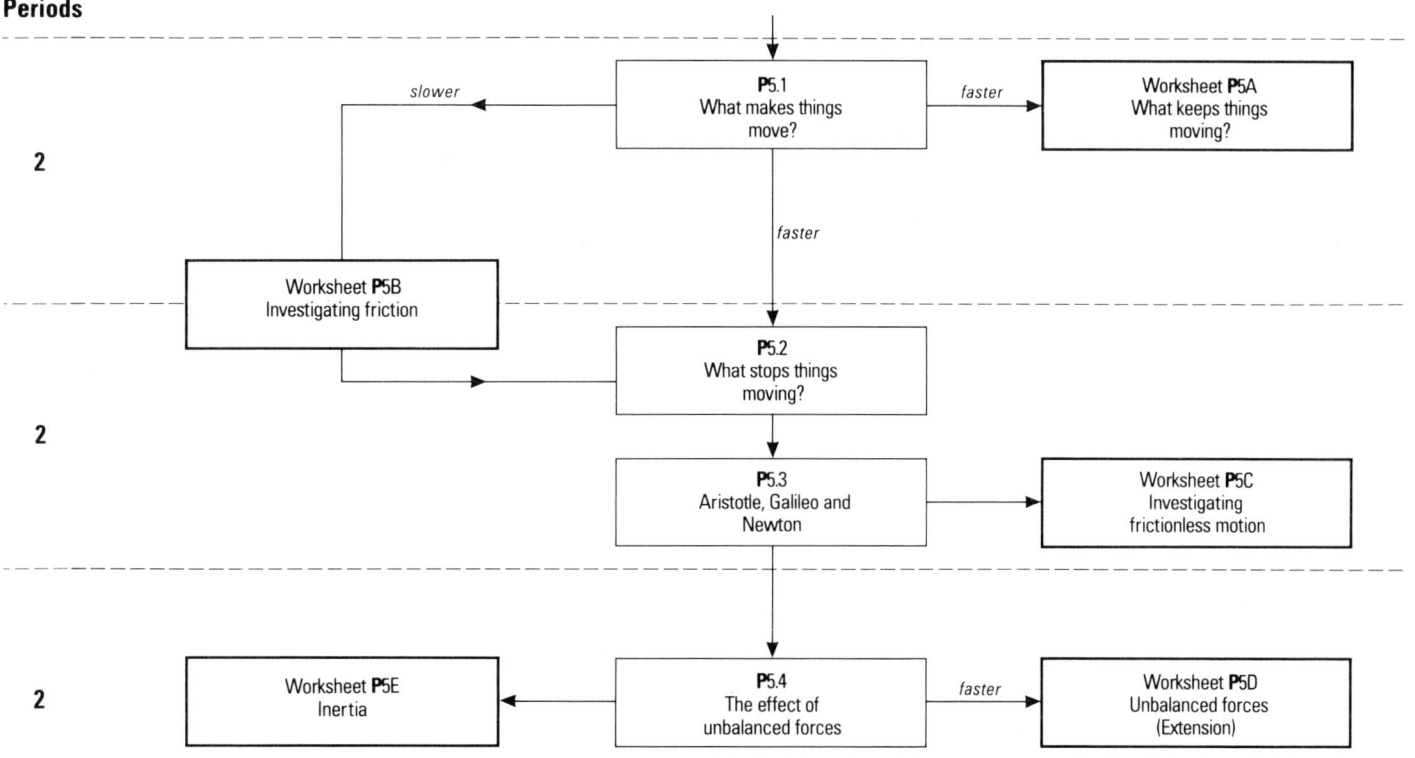

Figure P5

Opportunities for co-ordination

Friction is an important factor when dealing with the joints of the body. Some attention is given to this in Chapter **B**10 "Skeletons and muscles". Also mentioned in the same chapter is the streamlining of fish to reduce the effects of "drag" in water.

Notes and answers

P5.1 What makes things move?

This question leads to two opposing theories of motion. Scientists seeking explanations of events are compared with detectives trying to solve a crime.

In many ways the procedures are similar. In both cases, there are to start with usually too few observations on which to form a judgement. Both scientist and detective look for more facts, usually guided by an expected solution. However, both try to keep as open a mind as possible during the investigation.

This leads to an open-ended investigation by pupils into the effect of forces on objects. Little help is offered to them so they will need as much time as possible to suggest their own experiments that will help them distinguish between the rival theories.

When faced with the two theories, the reaction of many pupils may be "Well, it's friction, isn't it?" They may need to be encouraged to see that such a statement is meaningless as it stands. Discussion may reveal that what they are really trying to say is "Yes, we know a force is needed to keep things moving, but all that force is doing is overcoming friction". Pupils could be asked, "What would happen without friction?" They may suppose that things will then "just keep moving".

Pupils may need to be led to see that they are just "making up stories" about the world without attempting to justify them. They could be asked why such an explanation as they have advanced should be "better" than saying simply (as the first theory says) "A force is needed to keep things moving".

This may stimulate some lines of investigation. Pupils might, for example, measure the force needed to keep a particular object moving. They might ask, "Is that force always the same?" "What if the object is on wheels, or slides on a shiny table, or a rough table?" "What if the object is made to move at a higher constant speed?" Soon it is seen that Theory 1 asks more questions than it answers. If a force is needed to keep a body moving, why is it not always the same force? What patterns of behaviour describe the difference in the forces needed? Why, under some circumstances, is almost no force needed to maintain motion?

However, the alternative theory – that no force is needed to maintain motion – should by now seem equally implausible! But what if it were true? How could one explain the forces which are obviously at work in the "real" world when motion is maintained? Could the earlier observations be explained by assuming that some opposing force is simply being balanced by the push or pull that keeps the object moving? Could the opposing force (which we shall call "friction") be explained in terms of the way objects are built up from atoms and molecules? Can frictional forces be reduced? Or even removed? Are there any examples of motion where there is no friction?

Answers to questions such as these should make it clear that although "friction" is a necessary (contrived) force to overcome the difficulties involved in applying Theory 2 to the "real" world, it nevertheless leads to a much more self-consistent explanation of events.

Instead of tackling such an open-ended investigation, some pupils may benefit more from a class discussion which makes friction an obvious force to be taken into account when dealing with motion. They could then try the alternative investigation outlined in Worksheet P5B.

P5.2 What stops things moving?

This section continues the discussion started in section P5.1. It considers some of the sources of friction and relates friction to the motion of a bicycle. An excellent video on force and motion has been produced by PLON, a Dutch Physics curriculum research group. (See Supplementary material for details.) In this video, the relationship between force and motion is developed by observing children bicycling around the (flat) Netherlands landscape. If available, this would be an excellent time to show the first part, which deals with motion at constant velocity.

P5.3   Aristotle, Galileo and Newton

This section looks at the historical background to the two theories, and Galileo's inclined plane experiments are discussed. The argument which accompanies these experiments is covered in the pupils' book.

This leads on to Newton's work on force and motion, although only his First Law is being considered in detail here.

The acceptance of Newton's First Law of Motion is further encouraged by some examples of nearly friction-free motion. Worksheet **P5C** describes experiments with home-made pucks that float on a cushion of air and with an air-track. While the latter will clearly have to be demonstrated, it should be possible to produce sufficient "air pucks" for pupils to try their own experiments. Alternative or additional demonstrations are also possible, such as air pucks on a glass-surfaced table or pucks on an air-table.

This section continues by considering the bodies which move at a constant velocity in the everyday world – such as a table pushed at a steady speed across the room. If motion at constant velocity requires no force, it follows that the forces on such a moving table must be balanced. This reasoning leads, in fact, to the only way that the force of friction can be measured. When a body subject to friction moves at a steady speed, the size of the frictional force is equal to the size of the force doing the pushing or pulling, if we assume Newton's First Law of Motion to be true.

The section concludes by noticing that forces are required to change direction as well as to change speed. This point is taken up again in question 17c.

Answers to selected questions

12a The forces are those of air resistance (friction) and gravity. Whether or not the forces are balanced will depend on whether the parachutist is falling at a constant speed or not.
b Once the parachute has opened, air resistance will balance the pull of the Earth and the parachutist will fall at a steady speed. (The effect of air resistance on parachutists is explored more fully in Chapter **P7**.)
c Forces of air and water resistance are balanced by the forward push of the engines if the hovercraft is travelling at a steady speed.
d At a steady speed, friction in the wheel bearings and between wheels and floor is balanced by the push of the man. (In this question the man and trolley have to be considered separately. The forces acting on the man involve Newton's Third Law – the reaction of the grocery trolley pushing back on the man. Newton's Third Law is not developed in this chapter, but the idea of action and reaction occurs in Chapter **P6**. More able pupils may care to discuss the point.)
e Again the sledge and the explorers need to be considered separately.
f The answer to this question rather depends on whether the piece of debris comes under the influence of unbalanced gravitational forces or not.
g An answer very similar to that for the hovercraft.

P5.4   What if the forces are unbalanced?

The chapter concludes with a qualitative investigation into the effect of unbalanced forces. The effect of the size of the force and the mass of the body on the acceleration it produces is considered. For the fastest pupils this can lead to a practical investigation into the link between these three quantities. Since there is no need for a precise statement of Newton's Second Law in this course, and no use will be made of it in calculations, such an investigation can be truly open-ended. Some may see a clear pattern in the results – others will get only a qualitative feel for the relationships. Either way, the ground is prepared for quantitative work at a later stage.

All pupils may benefit from seeing the remainder of the video "Force and motion" described above, if this is available.

Different bodies respond differently in the way their motion changes in response to the application of the same force. This is seen to be related to how "big" or "heavy" they are. This property is described as the **inertia** of a body – a property of its mass. No attempt is made to make this concept more than intuitive at this point. A more detailed consideration of the meaning of "mass" is given in Chapter **P7** "Rising and falling".

Worksheet **P5E** gives some experiments that highlight the inertial properties of bodies.

Answers to selected questions

17a A full answer to this question is quite complex and obviously not expected here. The main point is that a passenger jumping from a moving bus is moving with the speed of the bus as he or she touches the ground. A (large) force is needed to bring the passenger to rest, and this is provided by friction between the passenger's feet and the ground. The complicated part is that it is the whole body that has to be brought to rest, but the stopping force is not applied through the person's centre of mass. The consequence of this is that the rotational effects will cause the passenger to fall over.

b If a car is brought suddenly to rest, a force is needed to do the same, harmlessly, to the passengers. A seat belt can do this. Collision between passenger and (say) windscreen may not! This is developed at greater length in Chapter **P6**.

c The change in direction of the car must be matched by a change in the direction of motion of the passengers. A force is needed to make this change, pushing the passengers round in the direction in which the car moves. Without this force, passengers will continue to move in a straight line – which they do until there is sufficient sideways force pushing them round with the car. So passengers in a car **feel** as though they are being thrown outwards.

(Such a discussion is important when dealing with circular motion. It could form a useful background for pupils who intend to continue their studies in Physics beyond GCSE.)

Practical work

Worksheet P5A   What keeps things moving?

REQUIREMENTS

Each group of pupils will need:
Dynamics trolley
Runway for trolley
End stop
3 blocks of wood, different sizes, the largest about the size of a dynamics trolley
Slotted masses, 1 kg set
Force meter, 0–10 N
Electronic timer
Lamp, photodetector and supports
Card: 20 cm by 8 cm

Notes:
This is an open-ended investigation. Hints on how to get pupils under way have already been suggested in the earlier Notes.

Warning
See the note about trolley runways in the introduction to this topic.

Worksheet P5B   Investigating friction

REQUIREMENTS

Each group of pupils will need:
Wooden block, approximately 15 cm × 8 cm × 2 cm (but the precise size is not important),
    with hook to attach thread
Thread
Force meter, 0–10 N
Slotted masses, 1 kg set

A detailed procedure is given in the worksheet.

Worksheet P5C   Investigating frictionless motion

Experiment 1: A model hovercraft

REQUIREMENTS

Each group of pupils will need:
Balloon
Hardboard disc, about 10 cm in diameter, with hole in centre to take a piece of dowel
Dowel, 25 mm length, 10 mm diameter, with 3 mm hole drilled down its centre

Note:
The way these air pucks are made up is detailed in the worksheet.

Experiment 2: An air track

REQUIREMENTS

Air track with accompanying accessories

The only thing demonstrated here is the apparent constancy of motion of the air track vehicles along the track. If pupils are allowed to try the experiment for themselves, they should be told that great care should be taken in launching the vehicles. This should be done using elastic bands at one end of the track as a catapult. There must also be similar elastic bands at the other end. Great damage can be done to vehicles by allowing them to "crash" into the far end of an air track.

Worksheet P5D   Unbalanced forces

REQUIREMENTS

Each group of pupils will need:
3 dynamics trolleys
Dowels to help stack trolleys
Runway for trolleys
Stopclock
Electronic timer
Lamp, photodetector and supports
Force meter, 0–10 N, or dynamics elastics to tow trolleys along the runway.

Details of the procedure are left to the pupils.

Warning
See the note about trolley runways in the introduction to this topic.

Worksheet P5E   Inertia

Experiment 1

REQUIREMENTS

Card, about 10 cm square
Beaker or glass tumbler
Coin
Small piece of dowelling

Experiment 2

REQUIREMENTS

Glass or polystyrene beads, or a tray of glass marbles from the 2D-kinetic model
2 hardboard discs
Masses, 1 kg and 100 g

Experiment 3

REQUIREMENTS

2 identical cans
Sand, to fill one can
String to suspend cans

Experiment 4

REQUIREMENTS

2 identical masses, each about 1 kg, held together by sticky tape
Thread
Thin cotton
Scissors
Stand, boss and clamp
G-clamp

Experiment 5

REQUIREMENTS

Inertial balance kit
G-clamp

These experiments can be set up as an experiment circus. Illustrations of the arrangement of each set of equipment are shown on the worksheet. The two cans in Experiment 3 can be suspended either from the ceiling or from a 1 m long lath resting on two stools.

Warning
For Experiment 4 the bench top will need to be protected in case the masses fall on it. Pupils should also be warned to take care that the masses do not fall on them.

Demonstration experiment

Section P5.3:   Galileo's inclined plane experiment

This experiment can be shown using a pair of "planes" constructed from plastic curtain track.

REQUIREMENTS

Flexible curtain rail, 2 m long, screwed to 2 wooden laths (see Notes)
1 steel ball (or large marble), about 25 mm diameter
2 stands, bosses and clamps
2 G-clamps

Notes:
The rail should be of the symmetrical type with a lip along both edges. A good method of supporting a 2 m rail is to glue or screw a 0.5 m length of wooden lath (1.25 cm × 1.25 cm) to the underside of the rail near each end. Hold each end firmly with a stand clamp, 0.25 to 0.5 m above the bench. (It is not possible to hold the rail steady enough by hand.) If screws are used it is important to make sure the heads do not touch the ball.

Release the ball at the top of one end of the rail so that it rolls down the hill and up the other side. Tilt the rails to various slopes.

Further information

Revised Nuffield Physics
Teachers' guide Year 3: Chapter 4 "Motion and force". Galileo's inclined plane and associated experiments are described and discussed on pages 136–7. Newton's First Law and experiments on frictionless motion are described and discussed on pages 138–40. Further details of the "inertia" experiments in Worksheet **P5E** are to be found on pages 141–2.

Supplementary material

Nuffield Science 13 to 16
Cars on the move. Some teachers may prefer this approach to that adopted in the present chapter. This module develops Newton's Second Law of Motion, using ticker-timers in the same way as Revised Nuffield Physics. Newton's Second Law is not done quantitatively in this course, but sections of the booklet may prove useful.

"Force and motion" – a video
Pupils will greatly benefit from seeing this video produced by PLON, the Dutch Physics curriculum research group. Copies can be purchased from the Audio-Visual Unit of York University. (See Appendix for address.)

Chapter P6   Crashes and bangs
Kinetic energy and momentum

Purposes

Knowledge and understanding

At the end of this chapter all pupils should:

1 understand the meaning of the terms "kinetic energy" and "momentum"

2 be able to find both the kinetic energy and the momentum of an object from a knowledge of its mass and velocity

3 be able to use kinetic energy to solve simple, qualitative problems involving force and motion

4 be able to use momentum in simple, qualitative problems involving recoil

5 appreciate the way the concepts of kinetic energy and momentum can be applied to road safety

6 appreciate how the concept of momentum can be applied to give an understanding of jet and rocket propulsion.

In addition, those pupils aiming for higher grades should:

7 be able to use kinetic energy and momentum to solve simple, quantitative problems involving force, motion and recoil

8 understand the vector nature of momentum and be able to use it in more general cases involving the conservation of momentum.

Processes and problem solving

Using apparatus and measuring instruments
Skills in the use of a light-beam controlled electronic timer, acquired in Chapter P4, will be needed here. Many of the experiments in this chapter will demand more than usual care in setting up if consistent results are to be obtained.

Observation
The experimental work in this chapter places considerable demands on careful measurement.

Interpretation and application
The concepts of kinetic energy and momentum are applied to road safety and to understanding simple recoil phenomena, both of an everyday nature and in jet and rocket propulsion. Those pupils who develop the idea of momentum as far as its conservation in all interactions will need to think carefully about the way both their experiments and everyday interactions fit the conservation law.

Planning investigations
There are two opportunities for investigative work in this chapter. The first, on the factors affecting road accidents, is not experimental; it takes the form of a group project. The second involves an investigation into using momentum to help develop an understanding of collisions. Since the law of momentum conservation is only hinted at at the end of the chapter and not used further, experiments in collisions can take on an open-ended nature.

Problem solving
Both the concept of kinetic energy and the concept of momentum emerge from problem situations. Kinetic energy comes from an observation on the braking distances of cars; the concept of momentum emerges from an experiment and observations on recoil behaviour.

There are also several numerical pencil-and-paper problems designed to develop familiarity with kinetic energy and momentum. Questions 15 to 18 are all concerned with design problems in safety belt manufacture. Questions 26 to 28 set problems arising from some qualitative demonstrations of rocket propulsion.

Timing

9 periods.

Suggested routes

The flow diagram in figure P6 divides the material in the pupils' book into two levels of difficulty. The sections on kinetic energy and recoil are common to all pupils. However, only more able pupils will benefit from a detailed exploration of momentum at the end of the chapter. Pupils for whom a prolonged exploration of momentum would not be appropriate can spend more time on the investigation into road safety which, for them, can extend throughout the nine periods.

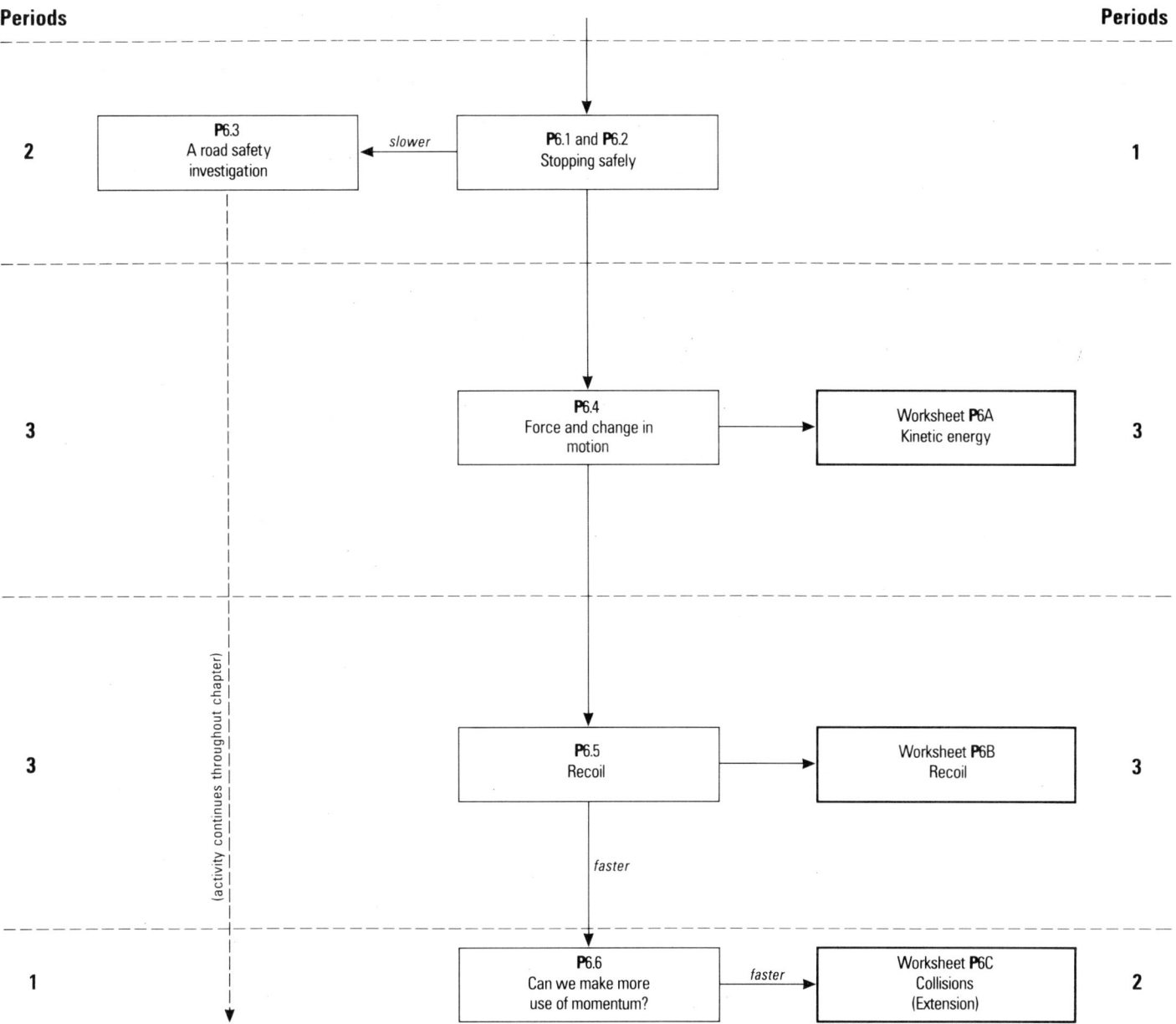

Periods   **Periods**

Figure **P6**

Opportunities for co-ordination

There are no direct links between the work of this chapter and work in Chemistry and Biology. The concept of kinetic energy is important, however, in understanding some of the properties of solids, liquids and gases. Many of these properties are important in Chemistry (such as understanding chemical reactions) and Biology (in diffusion and osmosis).

The effects of alcohol are given greater consideration in Chapter **B**11 of the Biology pupils' book.

Notes and answers

P6.1   Motorway madness

This brief introduction sets some problems about road safety which lead ultimately to ideas about kinetic energy and momentum.

P6.2   Stopping safely

An analysis of data provided by Department of Transport publications suggests a relationship between speed of travel and braking distance. This is extended by questions 5 to 7 to further considerations of road safety. At the time of writing, increasing pressure is being mounted on car manufacturers to advertise the "safe driving" aspects of their cars rather than "aggressive performance" aspects. This pressure may be relevant to answers to question 7.

Answers to selected questions

1a 30 feet. (Units of the foot and miles per hour have been used here as these are the only ones used in Department of Transport publications at the time of writing. Additional data in metres and km/h are given later.)

3a When the speed doubles, the braking distance increases by four times.
b Yes, braking distance again increases by four times when the speed doubles.
c An increase of speed from 40 km/h to 60 km/h is a 1.5 times increase. From the pattern above this should mean a $(1.5)^2$ increase in braking distance: $8 \text{ m} \times (1.5)^2 = 18 \text{ m}$ – just as the table shows.

P6.3   A road safety investigation

The material of this section could form the basis of a discussion for all pupils. But pupils who do not intend to work through section **P6.6** can undertake an extended group project. Each one of a group of five or six pupils can take one or two aspects of road safety. The group can then compile a report. These reports can be presented orally at the end of the work of the chapter. Aspects of kinetic energy and momentum will be important to many of the items. The effects of alcohol are a part of Chapter **B**11 "Detecting changes". Reaction times are also considered in the same chapter.

P6.4   Force and change in motion

The relationship between work and changes in kinetic energy is an alternative to Newton's Second Law as a method of solving problems involving force and motion. This section is based on an experimental investigation into kinetic energy (Worksheet **P6A**). It is difficult to establish the relationship between kinetic energy and the mass and speed of a moving body experimentally. Ideally, such an experiment should be able to measure the energy acquired by a body of known mass and speed. However, the most workable experiments transfer known amounts of energy to a body and then relate this to the body's mass and acquired speed. Such experiments are difficult even for able pupils to interpret without some prior ideas about the relationships expected. Experiments 4 and 5 on Worksheet **P6A** thus assume a relationship between kinetic energy, mass and speed and then test this experimentally.

Quantitative work with kinetic energy is the one area where a knowledge of Newton's Second Law is helpful. More able pupils who have done Worksheet **P5D** in Chapter **P5** may be given the Help sheet "Finding an expression for kinetic energy". This sheet assumes the relationship $F = ma$. This section ends by applying kinetic energy ideas to car safety belts and braking distances.

Answers to selected questions

9 The lorry has 5 times the energy.

10 The faster car will have 9 times the energy of the slower one.

11 The car has $\frac{1}{3}$ the mass of the lorry, but twice the speed. So the energy of the car is $(\frac{1}{3}) \times (2)^2 = 1\frac{1}{3}$ times that of the lorry.

13a 12.5 J; **b** 50 J; **c** 250 J; **d** 125 J; **e** 200 000 J.

15 The actual energy is 3250 J.

20b Speed will have to be reduced to 20 km/h.

P6.5   Recoil

Most of the everyday applications of the conservation of momentum are concerned only with recoil – that is, the change in motion when two objects, initially at rest, push against each other to move apart. This particular aspect of momentum conservation is the one most easily tested. Experiment 2 in Worksheet **P6B** uses two sets of photodetectors and lamps. Clearly most schools will not be able to supply many such sets. For those which cannot, here are some alternatives:

1 Large groups of pupils can work round two or three sets, with individual pupils demonstrating the experiment to others.

2 One set of equipment can be set up and the experiment performed as a class demonstration.

3 The alternative arrangement which has trolleys colliding with end stops, described in Revised Nuffield Physics *Teachers' guide Year 4* (Class Experiment 44, page 80), can be used. While this latter arrangement is cheap to set up, it is more difficult for pupils to understand. Less able pupils, particularly, will benefit from seeing a direct measurement of speed using a timer controlled by light beams.

Similar experiments can be demonstrated using a linear air track. The law of recoil has been deliberately introduced in terms of mass and speed. The importance of "velocity" in considering momentum is developed in the next sub-section "Introducing momentum".

The results are then applied to jets and rockets using a number of demonstration experiments. The carbon dioxide and water "rockets" are popular demonstrations, and both can lead to a number of searching questions. Some of these are given in questions 26–8.

The section ends with a more detailed look at the performance of rockets and jets. This will clearly be enhanced by the availability of appropriate visual material in class. The necessary launch speed of satellites is taken up again in Chapter **P7** "Rising and falling".

Answers to selected questions

22a The "mass × speed" of each vehicle is 600 g m/s.

23 The speed of the boat is 1 m/s.

29 The satellite moves about 20 times faster. (2000 km/h is 556 m/s. The satellite speed is 11 000 m/s.)

P6.6   Can we make more use of the idea of momentum?

This final section extends the use of momentum to collisions generally. Worksheet **P6C** describes investigations that can be undertaken. Again these are "expensive" in electronic timing terms. The alternatives suggested for Experiment 2 of Worksheet **P6B** can also be adopted here. The corresponding experiments in

Revised Nuffield Physics are described in *Teachers' guide Year 4* on pages 75–7. These experiments use a ticker-timer and are harder to carry out as considerable "friction-compensation" is involved in overcoming the drag of the tape.

The chapter ends by giving brief consideration to the law of conservation of momentum and the concept of interaction.

Answers to selected questions

37 Figure **P7** gives a completed table of results.

Before collision

Mass of first vehicle in kg	Speed of first vehicle in ms^{-1}	Mass of second vehicle in kg	Speed of second vehicle in ms^{-1}	Total momentum before collision
0.4	0.29	0.4	0	**1.16**
0.4	0.25	0.2	0	**1.00**
0.4	0.23	0.8	0	**0.92**
0.8	0.17	0.4	0	**1.36**
1.2	0.24	0.4	0	**2.88**

After collision

Mass of first vehicle in kg	Speed of first vehicle in ms^{-1}	Mass of second vehicle in kg	Speed of second vehicle in ms^{-1}	Total momentum after collision
0.4	0.15	0.4	0.15	**1.20**
0.4	0.16	0.2	0.16	**0.96**
0.4	0.077	0.8	0.077	**0.92**
0.8	0.11	0.4	0.11	**1.32**
1.2	0.18	0.4	0.18	**2.88**

Figure **P7**

Differences between the total momentum before the collision and the total momentum after collision are a maximum of 4% of the total momentum. The speeds were measured by timing the passage of a 5 cm length of card through a light beam. Since the clocks read the time to 0.01 s and the cards could not be cut to better accuracy than 1 mm in 50 mm, an error of 4% is within the expected error of the experiment. Thus the results confirm the conservation of momentum for these collisions, to within experimental error.

38a 2 m/s; **b** 8 m/s.

Practical work

Worksheet P6A   Kinetic energy

Warning
Pupils will need to be warned that falling masses can cause injuries. Some form of protection both for them and for the laboratory should be provided.

See the note about trolley runways in the introduction to this topic.

Experiments 1, 2 and 3

REQUIREMENTS

Each group of pupils will need:
2 dynamics trolleys
Runway for trolleys
End stop
Single pulley on clamp
String
Slotted masses, 100 g set
Elastic catapult

A detailed procedure is given in the worksheet.

Experiment 4: Changing the mass

Experiment 5: Changing the speed

REQUIREMENTS

Each group of pupils will need:
2 dynamics trolleys
Runway for trolleys
End stop
Elastic catapult
Electronic timer
Lamp, photodetector and supports
Card: 20 cm by 8 cm

A detailed procedure is given in the worksheet.

Worksheet P6B   Recoil

Warning
See the note about trolley runways in the introduction to this topic.

Experiment 1

REQUIREMENTS

Each group of pupils will need:
Dynamics trolley
Runway for trolleys
End stop
Balloon
Pressure tubing, 50 mm long to fit firmly into neck of balloon
Sticky tape
Slotted masses, 100 g to place on trolley

A detailed procedure is given in the worksheet.

Experiment 2

REQUIREMENTS

Each group of pupils will need:
4 dynamics trolleys (at least one must have a spring-loaded plunger)
Piece of wood (about 20–30 cm long and 50 mm by 25 mm in cross-section)
2 lamps, photodetectors, and stands for them
2 electronic timers
2 cards, both 20 cm by 8 cm

A detailed procedure is given in the worksheet. An alternative to spring-loaded plungers uses slab magnets attached to the front of each of two trolleys. This is detailed in the worksheet.

Worksheet P6C   Collisions

REQUIREMENTS

Each group of pupils will need:
4 dynamics trolleys
Runway for trolleys
Block to support runway
End stop
2 electronic timers
2 lamps, photodetectors, and stands for them
2 cards, both 20 cm by 8 cm
2 corks, one fixed to each of two trolleys
Needle, fixed in one of the corks
Spring

A detailed procedure is given in the worksheet.

Warning

See the note about trolley runways in the introduction to this topic.

Demonstration experiments

Sections P6.4, P6.5, and P6.6:   Linear air track

Experimental work in both kinetic energy and momentum is enhanced by being demonstrated on a linear air track. Detailed procedures for experiments will be found in the manuals supplied with the accessories for the tracks.

Section P6.5:   Carbon dioxide rocket

REQUIREMENTS

Expanded polystyrene block
Wire (minimum diameter 0.5 mm) run along length of laboratory
Carbon dioxide capsule, with mount that will slide along the wire (see figure 6.22 of the pupils' book)

The seal at the end of the carbon dioxide capsule is broken with a round nail given a sharp blow by a hammer. On release it travels at high speed along the wire. A block of polystyrene or similar material should be mounted at the end of the wire to absorb the kinetic energy of the "rocket".

Section P6.5:   Water rocket

REQUIREMENTS

Water rockets can be obtained from toy shops, but can easily be constructed from an old plastic washing-up liquid "squeezy" bottle.

Procedure

The "rocket" is half filled with water and the pressure of the remaining air raised using a pump. In the "home-made" version the end of the "squeezy" bottle is plugged with a bung carrying a small length of rubber tube. This in turn carries a car-tyre valve which is attached to a foot pump. The "rocket" is mounted vertically and the pressure raised by the pump. "Lift-off" occurs when the pressure in the container exceeds that which the bung will withstand. The experiment should be carried out outdoors!

Further information

Revised Nuffield Physics
Pupils' book and *Teachers' guide Year 4*: Chapter 4 "Momentum" and Chapter 5 "Kinetic energy".

Nuffield Science 13 to 16
Rockets.
   All of these books give useful background to the work of this chapter and may suggest alternative experiments. The "Rockets" module gives an alternative approach to some of the material in this chapter which may be helpful to some pupils.

Supplementary material

Any visual material (slides, posters etc) could help the work at the end of this chapter dealing with jet and rocket propulsion.

Chapter P7   Rising and falling
The force of gravity

Purposes

Knowledge and understanding

At the end of this chapter all pupils should:

1 appreciate that gravity is a force even though there is no direct contact between the interacting objects

2 appreciate the meaning of the term "force field"

3 understand the part air resistance plays in the way objects fall when close to the Earth's surface

4 appreciate the distinction between mass and weight.

In addition, those pupils aiming for higher grades should:

5 appreciate why it is possible for objects to orbit the Earth without falling to its surface.

Processes and problem solving

Graphical and symbolic representation
Speed-time graphs are used (question 6) to display the way the speed of a freely falling object varies with time. The graph is analysed to show the constancy of the acceleration under the Earth's gravity. A similar graph is plotted to derive the results of the experiment described in Worksheet **P7A**.

Using apparatus and measuring instruments
In this chapter experience is gained in the technique of multiflash photography.

Observation
Careful observation is called for in the discussion of the effects of air resistance on falling bodies.

Interpretation and application
Parachuting and Earth satellites are two very different applications of the ideas about gravity developed in this chapter.

Problem solving

Parachuting and Earth satellites are presented as problems which can in part be understood from gravitational ideas.

Timing

4 periods.

Suggested routes

The flow diagram in figure **P8** divides the material in the pupils' book into two levels of difficulty. The large majority of this chapter is intended for all pupils. Section **P7.5**, dealing with Earth satellites, is, however, intended for more able pupils only.

Periods

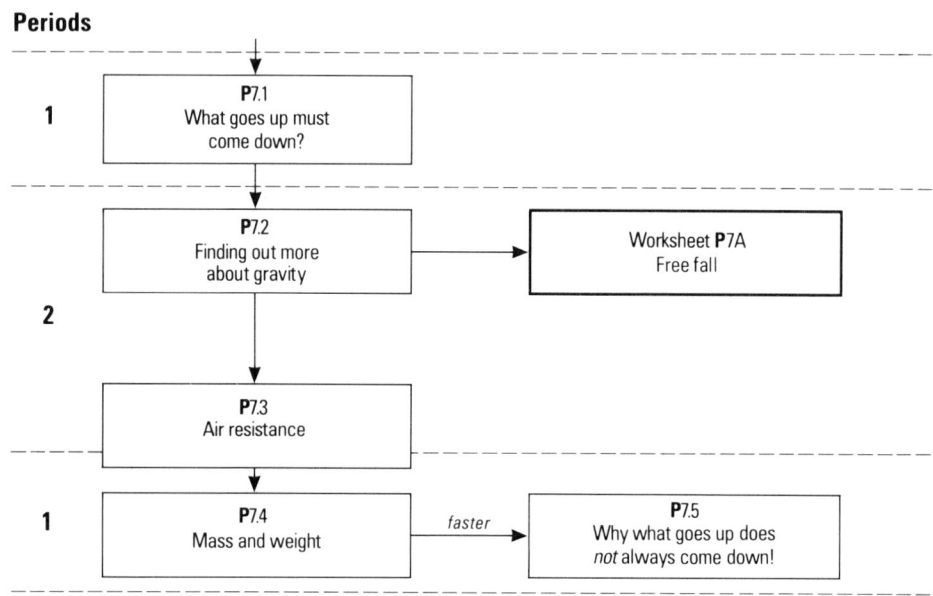

Figure **P8**

Opportunities for co-ordination

There are no direct links between the material of this chapter and work in Chemistry and Biology.

Notes and answers

It is assumed that Chapters **P4** to **P6** have been studied before undertaking this chapter.

P7.1   What goes up must come down?

The first part of this section gives some attention to the fact that Physics is very much concerned with general laws – with **predictability**. But it is asked whether the commonly held view that "What goes up must come down" is universally true.

While the effect of gravity may seem common enough on the surface of the Earth, the force itself is altogether strange. It is not a "contact" force, although our direct experience of it makes it seem so. We are aware of gravity through the counterbalancing force of the Earth pushing up on us to keep us at rest on its surface. Gravity is seen in action when a body falls freely towards the Earth's surface – but if the "body" is **you** the force is not then directly experienced as there is no counterbalancing force acting.

Indeed, in such circumstances a person is said to be "weightless"! Astronauts in orbit round the Earth are falling freely in this way – there is no counterbalancing force acting on them. More able pupils may enjoy discussing this point later on in the chapter where mass and weight are considered.

At this point, however, such discussion would probably not be fruitful. The points above are made to explain why gravity is introduced as a force which "causes things to fall" rather than something which leads to the experience of weight. The force is seen to act because an object, released above the Earth's surface, falls with increasing speed. Earlier work in Chapter **P5** has shown that a change in the speed or velocity of a body means there must be an unbalanced force acting on it.

The final part may be too difficult for some pupils and could be omitted by them. The idea of a "field of force" is developed and extended to electric and magnetic effects. Magnetic fields are introduced again in Chapter **P18**.

P7.2   Finding out more about gravity

This section is entirely concerned with making distance-time and speed-time records of falling bodies.

Familiarity with the way a camera works is assumed to come from third-year work on "Light". (See the Introduction to Topic **P4**.) The technique of multiflash photography is described in the pupils' book, and a photograph is displayed. It is hoped, however, that this will be demonstrated to the class and an analysis made of a photograph produced by them.

Detailed instructions are given in question 6 for plotting a speed-time graph from the data in a photograph. Such a graph, which should be a straight line, can be a little disappointing unless great care is taken in measuring the small distances involved in the photograph given in the text. Much better graphs can be obtained from a negative or transparency taken in class and projected onto a wall.

Worksheet **P7A** gives instructions for obtaining a similar distance-time record using a ticker-timer. This is the only occasion on which experiments described for this course use a ticker-timer. However, its comparison with a multiflash photograph (the timer makes a dot for the position of the falling object every 1/50th of a second) makes its use easy to understand. Results are easy to analyse and usually produce "convincing" graphs! Friction on the tape seems to have a negligible effect on the progress of the mass, and a range of masses from 0.5 kg up to 2 kg can be used, as described below.

P7.3   Air resistance

This section deals with the fact that "real" falling objects do not always move as the results of the experiments done in section **P7.2** suggest! A multiflash photograph of a model parachutist in descent shows that in fact the parachutist falls at a steady speed. Using ideas from Chapter **P5**, this suggests that the forces on the parachutist are balanced.

Pupils who have already studied Chapter **P8** and worked through section **P8.5** "Why do cars have a top speed?" will already be familiar with the idea that air resistance is a force that depends on the speed of the object moving through the air. This idea is also important here.

Also of importance is the fact that air resistance depends on the shape of the object. A piece of paper spread out experiences more air resistance than the same paper crumpled up into a ball, falling at the same speed. A short investigation into this shows why parachutes are effective in reducing the speed of fall.

P7.4   Mass and weight

Mass (or "inertia") was introduced in Chapter **P5** as the property of a body that influences the acceleration it acquires under a particular force. This property is contrasted here with weight, which is related to the everyday word "heaviness".

It is a matter of experience that these two properties seem to be related – big masses have a large weight and small masses have a low weight. The two properties of matter are also compared with a third – how much matter a body contains. This latter property (which is developed in terms of the number of meals different masses of potatoes will serve) is analogous to atom-counting and the mole concept in chemistry.

An investigation into whether heavy objects fall faster than light ones establishes the proportionality between mass and weight.

Answers to selected questions

12a 100 N; **b** 300 N; **c** 1000 N; **d** 1500 N.

13a 16 N; **b** 48 N; **c** 160 N; **d** 240 N.

P7.5   Why what goes up does not always come down!

This (optional) section looks at how objects can go into Earth orbit if they move fast enough. The approach is one first suggested by Isaac Newton and treats orbiting masses as a special case of free fall. The section assumes that the time and speed of fall are unaffected by the horizontal motion. Projectile motion is not studied in this course, but more able pupils may care to note the assumption being made here (and even suggest what tests might be done to verify its truth). The final paragraphs on communications satellites link with the work of Chapter P21 "Communication".

Practical work

Worksheet P7A   Free fall

REQUIREMENTS

Each group of pupils will need:
Ticker-timer and power supply
Tape for ticker-timer
Sticky tape, if self-adhesive paper tape is not used
Several masses in range 0.5 kg – 2 kg.
Clamp

A detailed procedure is given in the worksheet. The range of masses should not extend beyond those given. Friction on the paper tape will markedly affect the fall of masses less than 0.5 kg; the weight of masses larger than 2 kg can too easily break the tape when they are released.

Demonstration experiments

Section P7.2:   Multiflash photography

The experiment described here is the same as that described in the Nuffield Revised Physics *Teachers' guide Year 4*. This experiment uses a rotating strobe disc in front of a camera. The experiment described in the pupils' book uses a strobe lamp. The latter makes multiflash photography easier to understand but harder to do in the laboratory, as the level of illumination is much lower than that in the method described below. Strobe lamps are also expensive and schools may not wish to buy such equipment for this one experiment.

However, if the school has such a lamp it is well worth at least **demonstrating** a ball falling when lit by it, as pupils can see what the camera will "see".

REQUIREMENTS

Steel ball, diameter about 25 mm
Camera with shutter that can be kept open
  ("B" setting)
Stroboscope, motor driven
2 stands and bosses
Support rod for camera
Metre rule
Slotted base for metre rule (or stand and
  clamp)
Black cloth or paper for background
Lamp

Note:
The lamp should be a floodlamp or
photoflood, or, best of all, a small slide
projector pointed horizontally with its
beam reflected down by a mirror at 45°.

Procedure

Set up the motor-driven stroboscope in front of the camera. Illuminate the ball
strongly **from vertically above**. Place a black background behind the path of the
ball. The essence of success here is strong contrast between the bright ball and its
surroundings, so the rest of the room should be three-quarters blacked out.

Include a vertical measuring stick in the picture, so that the photograph may
be used later for an estimate of g. The measuring stick should have alternate
centimetres marked black and white – a plain metre rule is not so good.

Set the camera to "B" and start the motor-driven stroboscope rotating.

Give a countdown. One pupil releases the ball. Another operates the camera
and opens the shutter just before the ball is dropped. The shutter is closed when
the ball reaches the floor.

Record the strobe frequency (motor-driven strobes driving a 5-slot disc usually
give 30 pictures per second).

A general account of multiflash photography and the processing of films in the
laboratory will be found in the Revised Nuffield Physics *Teachers' guide Year 4*
(Appendices 1 and 2).

Section P7.4   The guinea and feather experiment

This experiment can either be demonstrated, or evacuated tubes can be prepared
for groups of pupils to do their own experiments.

REQUIREMENTS

All pupils will need access to:
Vacuum pump
Pressure tubing, 1 metre long
Connecting tube (glass or brass)

Each group of pupils will also need:
Tube (see Note)
Short piece of rubber tube carrying
  Hoffmann clip
Small coin
Scrap of plastic foam

Note:
The tubes are 60 cm long, and 5 cm in
diameter. One end is closed with a plain
rubber bung, the other end with a bung
carrying a tube to take a short rubber
tube with a clip (see page 125 of the
pupils' book). Pressure tubing from the
vacuum pump carries a short connecting
tube to fit the short rubber tube while the
pumping is done.

Procedure

Put a small coin and a scrap of plastic foam in the tube. Close the tube with the
rubber stopper. Pupils should first see what happens to coin and plastic when the
tube is quickly turned upside down a few times.

The tube is now evacuated and sealed. The observations are then repeated.

Finally the air is re-admitted and more observations are made.

Further information

Revised Nuffield Physics
Pupils' book and *Teachers' guide Year 4*: Chapter 1 "Motion". Pages 3–4 and 17
of the teachers' guide will be found especially helpful to the work of this chapter.
Teachers' guide Year 4: Appendices 1 and 2 This gives the details about
multiflash photography referred to previously.

Topic **P3**   **Energy**

Introduction

A uniform treatment of energy has been adopted throughout Nuffield Co-ordinated Sciences. A summary of the main features is as follows:

- When things happen, energy is usually transferred.
- If energy is involved in a change, it will be transferred and re-arranged, but the total amount stays the same.
- We become aware of energy only when it is transferred and there are two important processes of energy transfer: work and heat.
  Heat is the name of a process whereby internal energy is transferred from a hotter to a cooler body.
  Work is the name of a process whereby energy is transferred when a force moves its point of application.
- Many changes involve energy being transferred to the surroundings. But the temperature rise which results is often so small that the energy appears to have vanished.

The concept of energy has two distinct aspects in science. On the one hand it is a **book-keeping** procedure. This is the aspect of energy relevant to the principle of energy conservation. On the other hand energy is something whose transfer is essential in bringing about **useful change**. In this aspect, energy becomes "degraded" or "unavailable" once it has been transferred to the surroundings. Many changes involving the transfer of energy to the surroundings produce a temperature rise so small that it is hardly noticed and the energy may appear to have vanished. It is this latter aspect of energy which is more apparent in everyday experience. The two aspects should be given equal emphasis.

More background to the treatment of energy will be found in Chapter 2 of the General introduction to this *Guide*.

The Energy topic in Physics is divided into three sub-topics:

Transferring energy	Chapters **P8** and **P9**
Internal energy	Chapter **P10**
Energy resources	Chapters **P11** and **P12**

This topic cannot be taught as one uninterrupted sequence. The work on transferring energy will have to come early in the course as the concepts developed here are needed in Chemistry and Biology at an early stage. Work on internal energy (which includes work on the conservation of energy) can come later in the fourth year. Work on energy resources looks at, among other things, the importance of electricity as a means of transporting energy, and at nuclear power. It will thus have to come late on in the course. It might form a good end-point to the work in Physics.

Timing

Suggested timings for the individual chapters are:

Chapter **P8**	Machines and engines	6 periods
Chapter **P9**	Keeping yourself warm	6 periods
Chapter **P10**	Ideas in Physics	6 periods
Chapter **P11**	Energy where it is needed	6 periods
Chapter **P12**	Waste not, want not?	6 periods

Chapter P8   Machines and engines
An investigation into power and efficiency

Purposes

Knowledge and understanding

At the end of this chapter all pupils should:

1 understand that power is the rate at which energy is transferred

2 appreciate that there is an energy cost in making things happen

3 appreciate that machines are devices enabling the transfer of energy, but that the energy cost of doing a job is still at least the same as if the job were to be done without the help of a machine (and will almost certainly be greater than that)

4 understand that engines are devices for transferring energy from fuels to enable force-using jobs to be done

5 appreciate that the use of machines and engines always means some wastage of energy.

In addition, those pupils aiming for higher grades should:

6 appreciate that heat engines cannot function without transferring substantial energy to the surroundings.

Processes and problem solving

Graphical and symbolic representation
Section **P8.5**, intended for abler pupils, gives an opportunity for graph plotting and graph interpretation.

Using apparatus and measuring instruments
Force meters and metre rules are the measuring instruments mainly used in the experimental work.

Interpretation and application
The major concepts in this chapter are developed in terms of their applications. Power is related to the performance of a small lift; the car-jack is used to illustrate the ideas of energy cost and efficiency. The importance of "heat" engines is also emphasized. The ideas of power and efficiency are finally used to answer the question "Why do cars have a top speed?"

Planning investigations
Worksheet **P8B** sets up an open-ended investigation into the factors which affect the efficiency of a ramp, used as a machine.

Problem solving

There are a number of pencil-and-paper problems of a numerical type in this chapter. Together with these, there is an extended problem-solving exercise, "Why do cars have a top speed?", at the end of the chapter.

Timing

6 periods.

Suggested routes

The flow diagram in figure **P9** divides the material in the pupils' book into two levels of difficulty. All pupils should be able to follow all of the work of this chapter up to the summary. The only part which could be omitted by all except the more able pupils is the sub-section dealing with how heat engines work.

After the summary there is an extended problem on why cars have a top speed. This is designed for the fastest pupils, but all may be able to try parts of this problem and gain something from it.

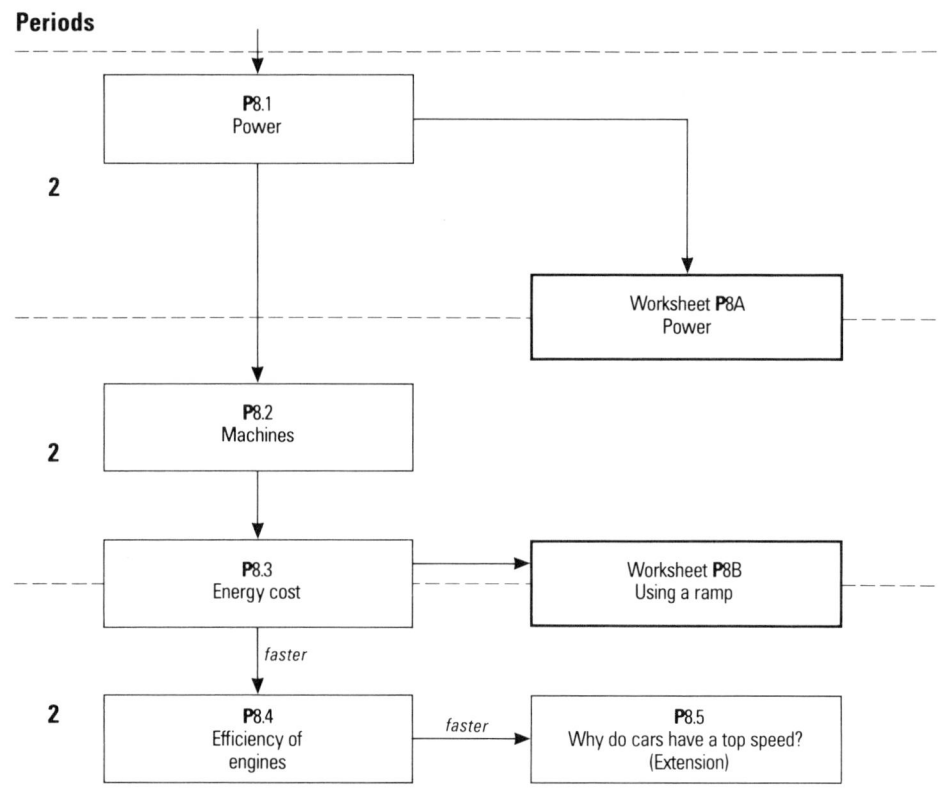

Figure **P9**

Opportunities for co-ordination

There are several major co-ordinating links between the material of this chapter and work in Biology and Chemistry. In the first place, the chapter introduces concepts of power, energy cost and efficiency which are of importance to later work in all three sciences.

The use of fuels as an energy resource is taken up in detail in Chapter **C**13 of the Chemistry pupils' book.

The idea that the human body can in some ways be treated as an engine is developed more fully in Chapter **B**9 "Keeping going".

Notes and answers

P8.1 Power

This is the first chapter which deals with energy, so some time may have to be spent revising earlier ideas. Some questions which cover work assumed to have been done in an earlier year are given in the Introduction to Topic **P3**.

This leads to the concept of power. The main difficulty here may be with the idea of "rate". For this reason, power is introduced as a way of expressing **how quickly** energy can be transferred. This is then related to the more precise word "rate" which pupils may already have met in Biology.

The concept of power is related to the design of a stair-lift in the pupils' book.

Since "force" and "power" are frequently used interchangeably in everyday speech, it seems worthwhile spending a little time explaining the similarities and differences between the two.

This introduction to power is consolidated by a circus of experiments (Worksheet **P8A**) in which pupils measure their own power in different circumstances. An interesting extension to this (easily tested with the arm ergometer) is a comparison between the maximum rate at which someone can transfer energy, and the rate that could be kept up for several minutes (or even an hour or so). Most measurements show that the human body's "continuous power" rating is about 50 per cent of its maximum power rating. There is usually no lack of fit and healthy youngsters prepared to demonstrate this fact!

Answers to selected questions

6a 3000 J; **b** 250 W.

7a 150 J; **b** 25 W.

P8.2 Machines
P8.3 Energy cost

These two sections introduce the idea that all jobs have a minimum energy cost which cannot be avoided. Machines and engines make it much easier to do many jobs, but often at an increase in the energy cost. The extent to which this cost is increased is measured by the efficiency of the machine or engine.

This leads to an open-ended investigation into the use of the ramp as a simple machine, introduced by Worksheet **P8B**. In contrast to the previous circus of experiments, the pupils are this time left largely to use their own initiative in performing the experiment, so most of two periods will be required for it.

Answers to selected questions

8a 80%; **b** 312.5 W.

9a 50 m; **b** 20 000 J; **c** 500 W.

P8.4 The efficiency of engines

This section looks at the possibilities of improving the efficiency of machines and engines. It ends with a brief look at "heat" engines and shows that some energy wastage is unavoidable. More able pupils may be interested to explore in rather more detail why this energy wastage **is** unavoidable.

Answers to selected questions

13a 1000 J; **b** 1250 J; **c** 80%.

14a 1000 J; **b** 1000 J; **c** 200 N.

P8.5   Why do cars have a top speed?

This extended problem uses partly real data and partly computed data. The frictional force data at various speeds has been computed by setting the top speed of a small car with a 37 kW engine at a speed of just over 80 miles/h and assuming the relationship $F = kv^2$, suggested in the text. k has the value of 0.74 N s^2/m^2.

Power output of a car engine can of course be varied at any road speed by using the engine throttle ("accelerator pedal"). The data in this question refers to an engine's maximum power output at particular speeds. It is this maximum power output that will help determine the maximum acceleration of a car. The maximum power output is the power obtained with the throttle fully open.

The second table in the question shows the way the maximum power output of the engine varies with its speed. All engines behave like this and have a highest maximum power. The difference between the maximum power available at each speed and its variation with speed is a difficult one to grasp (two **different** maxima are involved). This is explained in the text but may well require more verbal explanation.

The data for maximum engine power at various speeds is of course "test-bed" data. The question shows that this particular car is in fact incapable of a level road speed of 38.5 m/s! Test-bed data is given in terms of the number of revolutions the crankshaft of the engine makes every second. This has been converted to equivalent top-gear road speed in order that the data can be compared with the friction-power data.

Despite the assumptions made in the question, the fact that the moped turns out to need an engine of 50 cm^3 capacity is remarkable (or very lucky!).

Answers to selected questions

16a

Speed in m/s	5	10	15	20	25	30	35	40
Power in kW	0.1	0.74	2.51	5.92	11.6	20.0	31.7	47.4

c 37 kW.
d It will be travelling at a steady speed.
e 37 m/s; about 84 miles/h.

17a 37 m/s, same as in question 16.

18 The friction power, assuming the same relationship between friction and speed as for the car, is 1.82 kW (calculated). This means the highest power of the engine should be 1.82 kW. This would give an engine capacity of 49 cm^3.

Practical work

Worksheet P8A   Power

The experiments described in this worksheet are best set up as a circus. Experiment 5 takes longer to do and work out than the other experiments. It will be necessary to organize the work so that a queue of pupils does not develop at this point in the circus.

Experiment 1

REQUIREMENTS

3 sandbags, 10 N each
Stopclock (or watch)
Metre rule
Scales, to weigh bags

A detailed procedure is given in the worksheet.

Experiment 2

REQUIREMENTS

"Step" about 30 cm high
Stopclock (or watch)
Metre rule
Personal weighing machine, calibrated in newtons

A detailed procedure is given in the worksheet.

Experiment 3

REQUIREMENTS

Stopclock (or watch)
Metre rule
Personal weighing machine, calibrated in newtons

Access to:
Flight of stairs

A detailed procedure is given in the worksheet.

Experiment 4

REQUIREMENTS

Arm ergometer (joulemeter)
2 sand bags, 10 N each
Force meter, 0–50 N
Stopclock (or watch)

A detailed procedure is given in the worksheet.

Experiment 5

REQUIREMENTS

Cycle ergometer (joulemeter)
Stopclock (or watch)

A detailed procedure is given in the worksheet.

Warning
While these experiments on pupil power are perfectly safe for any normal
healthy pupil to carry out, it is important to watch out for pupils who have
health problems which might be adversely affected by vigorous physical activity.
Colleagues in the PE department should be able to advise teachers. This is
preferable to relying on the pupils themselves to provide such information, even
though they are given the same warning in the worksheets. It might also be
worth advising pupils that these experiments are designed to find **normal** power
capacities – they are not competitions designed to identify the most powerful
person.

Worksheet P8B   Using a ramp

REQUIREMENTS

Access to:
Ramp (see Note)
Metre rule
Pulley on a clamp
Blocks (to give a variable incline)
Tray on which loads can be placed, with hook to attach string
Slotted masses, 2×100 g sets and 2×1 kg sets
String
Force meter, 0–10 N
Dynamics trolley

Note:
A trolley runway would make a suitable ramp. Ramps must be as rigid as possible when supported at each end and will need to be about 2 m long and at least 10 cm wide.

There should be enough equipment not to dictate the method of making measurements. The force needed to pull a load up the ramp can be measured directly with a force meter, but adding masses to a string passing over a pulley is a much more accurate method. In this way the force needed to just move the load on the ramp can be determined.

Investigations can be undertaken using or not using a tray to carry the load, varying the size of the load, varying the slope of the ramp, and perhaps varying the surfaces that slide over each other. Some may want to try the trolley – if possible all suggestions should be met with appropriate equipment.

Warning
Pupils need to be warned that falling masses can cause injuries. Some form of protection both for them and for the laboratory should be provided.

Demonstration experiments

Section P8.2

A car jack will be useful for demonstration purposes. A variety of machines will form useful focal points for discussion. These should be in as realistic a form as possible.

Further information

Nuffield Secondary Science
Theme 3 Biology of Man: pages 8–21 give a detailed account of the experiments used in Worksheet **P8A**.

Nuffield Science 13 to16
Power and *Machines*. Chapters 2, 3, 5 and 8 of the module on power and Chapters 4–6 of the module on machines give an alternative approach to the material in this chapter which some teachers may feel is more suited to less able pupils.

Chapter P9   Keeping yourself warm
Heating: a way of transferring energy

Purposes

Knowledge and understanding

At the end of this chapter all pupils should:

1 understand that "heating" is a mode of energy transfer

2 know the meaning of the terms "conduction" and "convection"

3 appreciate that, unlike work, heating as a mode of energy transfer is not measured directly, but in terms of the rise in temperature it can produce

4 understand the meaning of the term "specific heating capacity"

5 be able to relate the ways in which energy can be transferred by heating to an investigation into "energy efficiency" in home heating.

Processes and problem solving

Graphical and symbolic representation
Opportunities exist for the use of graphs to present the results of the investigation into the heating of water. Gas and electricity meter readings have to be presented as bar charts, as do data on vegetable prices and specific heating capacities.

Using apparatus and measuring instruments
The use of thermometers and stopclocks features in all the laboratory work. Being able to read electricity and gas meters is essential to the home heating project.

Observation
Observational work is involved in making quantitative measurements in all the laboratory work. Careful observation is also needed in linking cause to effect in the investigation into home heating.

Interpretation and application
This chapter is developed around an investigation into "energy efficiency" in relation to home heating. Physical concepts arise from observations made in the investigation. All pupils should have the opportunity of using and applying the equation $E = mcT$ in a practical situation.

Planning and carrying out investigations
Worksheet **P9A** and **P9C** both ask pupils to plan and carry out investigations. Both are provided with Help sheets which should cater for a wide range of abilities. Pupils have to plan their own "home heating" survey and carry it out. Question 11 asks pupils to plan an experiment to find out whether it is cheaper to take a shower or have a bath.

Problem solving
The "home heating" investigation is a long-running problem-solving investigation that takes place throughout this chapter. The problem is simple – "How can we keep our homes warm with the least energy expenditure?" The answers depend on understanding the ways in which hot objects can lose energy and on being able to measure this loss in joules.

Timing

6 periods.

Suggested routes

The flow diagram in figure **P**10 divides the work of this chapter into two levels of difficulty. Whether or not pupils work at the highest level really depends on how much use they make of the Help sheets provided with the investigations.

Periods

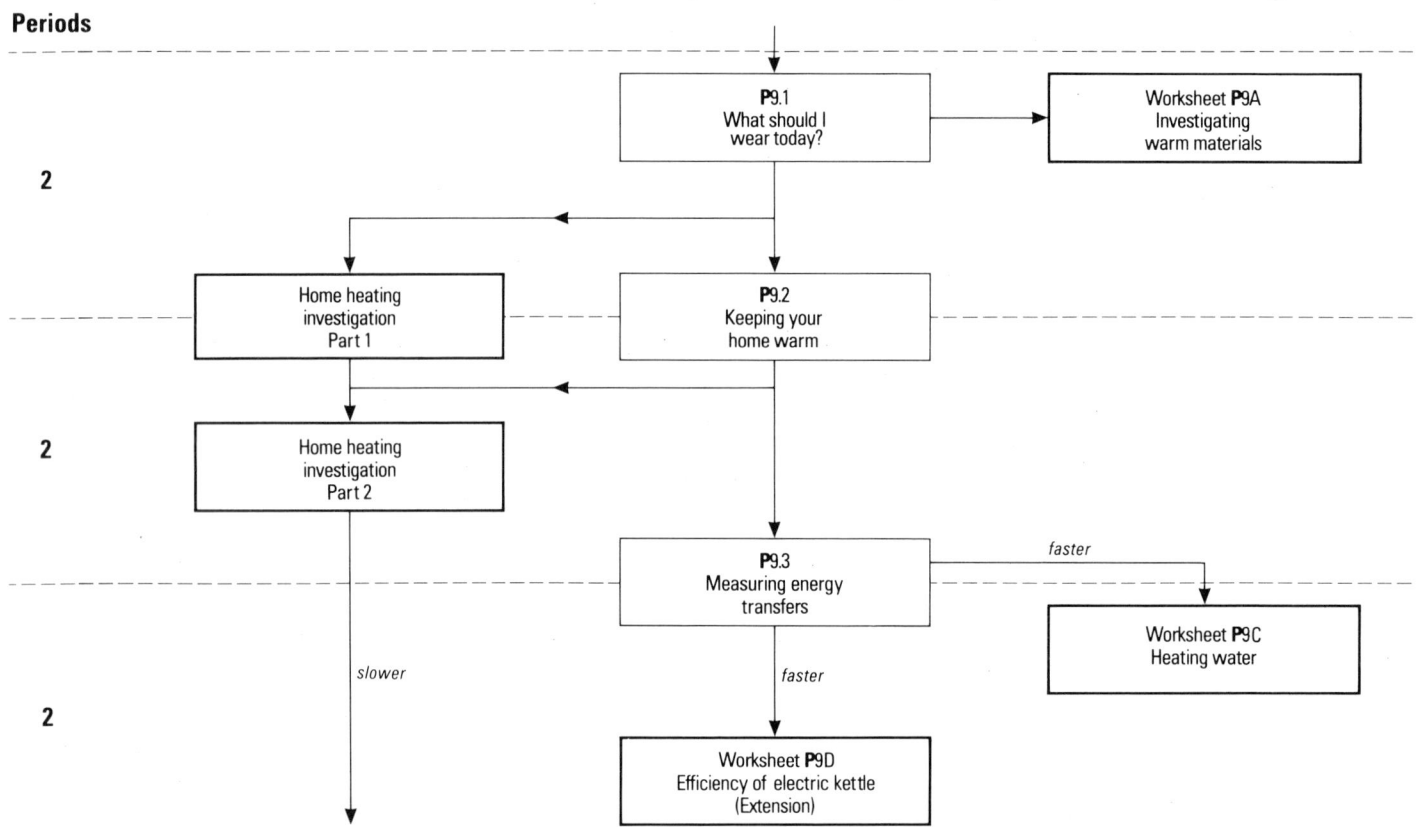

Figure **P**10

Opportunities for co-ordination

Chemistry Chapter **C**13 makes use of the equation $E = mcT$ in order to measure the energy which can be transferred from a measured mass of fuel.

In Biology, rise in temperature as one of the consequences of energy transfer is of more importance than the actual transfer of energy by heating. This subject is discussed in Chapter **P**10.

Notes and answers

This unit of work has been written on the assumption that pupils can carry out, simultaneously with the work in class, an investigation into heating their homes. If this can be done, then probably all work out of school will be devoted to this project. Some pupils will probably need more "class time" support for this project than others. Such pupils could omit Worksheet **P**9D and even Worksheet **P**9C. These alternatives are shown on the flowchart as an extension of part 2 of the "home heating" investigation into the final two periods for some pupils, while others use the time investigating heating experimentally.

Under some circumstances, the "home heating" project may not be feasible. It might be possible to apply the project to a school building or a boarding house – particularly if the project is carried out on a "group" basis with several pupils co-operating. Where circumstances do not permit the project to be undertaken at all, alternative material connected with the use of energy resources for home heating is suggested below. (See the Supplementary material section.) The computer program "CEDRIC", published by British Gas, enables some interesting quantitative work to be undertaken by pupils with access to a computer.

P9.1   What should I wear today?

The work on heating is introduced by an investigation into materials which can be used to keep people warm. Investigations of this sort need not take up a great deal of time in order to be useful. This particular investigation is the same as the one called "Survival" used by the Assessment of Performance Unit in testing investigational skills at age 13+. Pupils who took part in the tests were only given half an hour in which to carry out the investigation. Older pupils should be able, with advantage, to spend rather more time on it, but even so should derive useful experience within the space of a double period.

Although Worksheet **P9A** is written as though for an individual experiment, the work could be organized in a number of different ways. Small groups could co-operate in a single investigation, or a class could be split into groups, with each group undertaking an agreed task. If the latter strategy is adopted, there will need to be time for the class to pool their findings.

The assessment of the investigation "Survival" is given detailed discussion on pages 5–13 of the Assessment of Performance Unit's *Science report for teachers 3: "Science at age 13"*.

P9.2   Keeping your home warm

This section is concerned with settting up the "home heating" investigation. The first task is to collect data on the use of energy for heating the home. The important point being made here is that very little energy indeed has to be used to raise the temperature of a cold home to a comfortable level. Energy is mainly used to replace that being lost from the home to the "outside world".

It will take a week to collect enough data to show the use being made of electricity, gas, oil or coal. The second part of the investigation involves looking at the ways in which energy loss is being limited in any particular home or building. This work can proceed simultaneously with the collection of energy usage data. At the end of a week it should be possible to bring the two parts of the investigation together and suggest how it may be possible to reduce losses in a given home or building.

Some may feel it is worthwhile spreading this investigation over a longer period. In this case, all the laboratory and class work of the chapter can be completed in the suggested time, but the project can be allowed to extend over a longer period.

The class work associated with this section is concerned with a survey of the ways in which energy can be transferred from a room. The emphasis is on conduction and convection as the physical means of energy transfer. Useful material to support this work can be obtained from many manufacturers and also from government agencies concerned with "energy saving". Some examples are given in the Further information section.

P9.3   Measuring energy transfers

The remainder of the chapter is devoted to measuring energy transferred by heating. This will be a sufficient length of time as this mode of measuring energy transfer is taken up again in Chemistry in Topic **C4**.

The transfer of energy from a hot object to a colder one is referred to as "heating". The text emphasizes that energy transferred in this way can bring about the same changes that can come about when work is involved. Both heating and working can raise the temperature of an object. When work is involved we measure the energy transferred from the forces and distances involved. There is no direct way of measuring the energy transferred by heating. We can measure the effect of the energy transfer – namely the rise in temperature it produces. All we can do at this point is see how the rise in temperature of an object might be related to the energy transferred to it.

The concept of specific heating capacity (s.h.c.) is introduced, but cannot be measured until we have some means of relating temperature rise to the transfer of a **known quantity** of energy. This comes in Chapter **P**10. Figures for specific heating capacities are taken "on trust" and likened to the price labels that are put on vegetables. Worksheet **P9C** provides outline details of an experiment to test the relationship between energy transferred, mass and temperature rise. A Help sheet has also been prepared for those pupils who need it.

Finally, Worksheet **P9D** is intended as an extension to the work for the fastest pupils to try.

Answers to selected questions

6 £1.45; £1.22; £0.55; £1.37.

9 Water.

10 Copper.

11a 1800 J; **b** 31 200 J;

12 3350 J.

13 204 000 J.

Practical work

Worksheet P9A   Investigating warm materials

REQUIREMENTS

Each group of pupils will need:
Stopclock (or watch)
Thermometer
Cans to hold warm water
Lagging materials, at least 4 different types, e.g. cotton, wool, plastic, nylon/wool mixture
Scissors
Sticky tape
Rubber bands
Pins

Access to:
Hair-dryer or fan, to blow cold air

This is an open-ended investigation and pupils devise their own experiments.

Worksheet P9C   Heating water

REQUIREMENTS

Each group of pupils will need:
Polystyrene beaker
Thermometer
Measuring cylinder, 250 cm^3
Immersion heater, 12 V
Power supply, 12 V a.c.
Stopclock (or watch)
Joulemeter, electric (if available)

Access to:
Top-pan balance

The normal procedure is to use a clock to time how long an immersion heater has been switched on and to use this time as a measure of the energy transferred. Some pupils – and particularly those who find it more difficult to understand the experiment – benefit by having a joulemeter connected to the immersion heater. The joulemeter gives a direct reading of the energy transferred to the water.

Joulemeters of the pattern used for A-level work are expensive and would only be used here for demonstration purposes. However, simpler (and cheaper) joulemeters are now available. It may well be worth using them in this experiment.

Warning

Some low-voltage immersion heaters of the sealed sort have been known to explode. Do not use any in which the seal is cracked or deficient in any other way.

Worksheet P9D   How efficient is your electric kettle?

REQUIREMENTS

Each group of pupils will need:
Electric kettle
Measuring cylinder, 1000 cm^3
Thermometer
Stopclock or watch

This is an optional experiment.

Further information

Children's Learning in Science Project

"Aspects of secondary students' understanding of heat: summary report"

This report draws upon the results of the Assessment of Performance Unit (APU) testing scheme to show the difficulties many children have with the meaning of "heat" and "temperature". The report is particularly useful in highlighting the different ways in which children will use and come across the word "heat" in everyday conversation. It is for this reason that the policy has been adopted in Nuffield Co-ordinated Sciences of not using "heat" as a noun.

Supplementary material

British Gas

"Domestic gas meters – how to read them"
"Transference of heat"
A short video that surveys ways in which energy can be transferred by heating. (Note that "heat" is used here as a noun for a "form of energy".)

There is a wide range of additional material available to support this work. The following list gives only a few suggestions.

● Advertising material on home insulation and double glazing – many manufacturers will provide material on request.
● *Energy package* – available free of charge from the Energy Efficiency Office.
● "CEDRIC 2" – a computer program available from British Gas, to run on BBC or RML machines. This program enables pupils to put in their own data and find out the consequences for energy usage in home heating.

Chapter **P10**   **Ideas in physics**
Energy and change in temperature

Purposes

Knowledge and understanding

At the end of this chapter all pupils should:

1 appreciate that science depends on ideas as well as facts

2 understand that a scientific theory is one that can be tested experimentally, and from which predictions can be made

3 appreciate that theories are nevertheless not facts, and will be changed if new facts come to light that do not match the theory

4 be able to recall the kinetic theory of matter

5 appreciate the meaning of the phrase "the conservation of energy", and be able to apply it in simple cases

6 appreciate that energy may be transferred to a material in changing it from a solid to a liquid, or a liquid to a gas, without raising its temperature.

In addition, those pupils aiming for higher grades should:

7 be able to recall the kinetic theory and the caloric theory, and to suggest tests that will distinguish between them

8 be able to apply the theory of conservation of energy to more difficult cases.

Processes and problem solving

Using apparatus and measuring instruments
Skill is required in measuring small changes in temperature as accurately as possible.

Observation
Careful observation is needed to distinguish between the predictions made by the two theories of heating in section **P10.2**.

Interpretation and application
Observations of a variety of energy transfers are interpreted in terms of the conservation of energy.

Problem solving
The caloric theory and the kinetic theory are presented as alternative theories. Which is the better of the two is resolved by looking at whether the two theories are able to explain why the temperatures of bodies change in a variety of different circumstances.

Timing

6 periods.

Suggested routes

The flow diagram in figure **P11** divides the work of this chapter into two levels of difficulty.

Periods

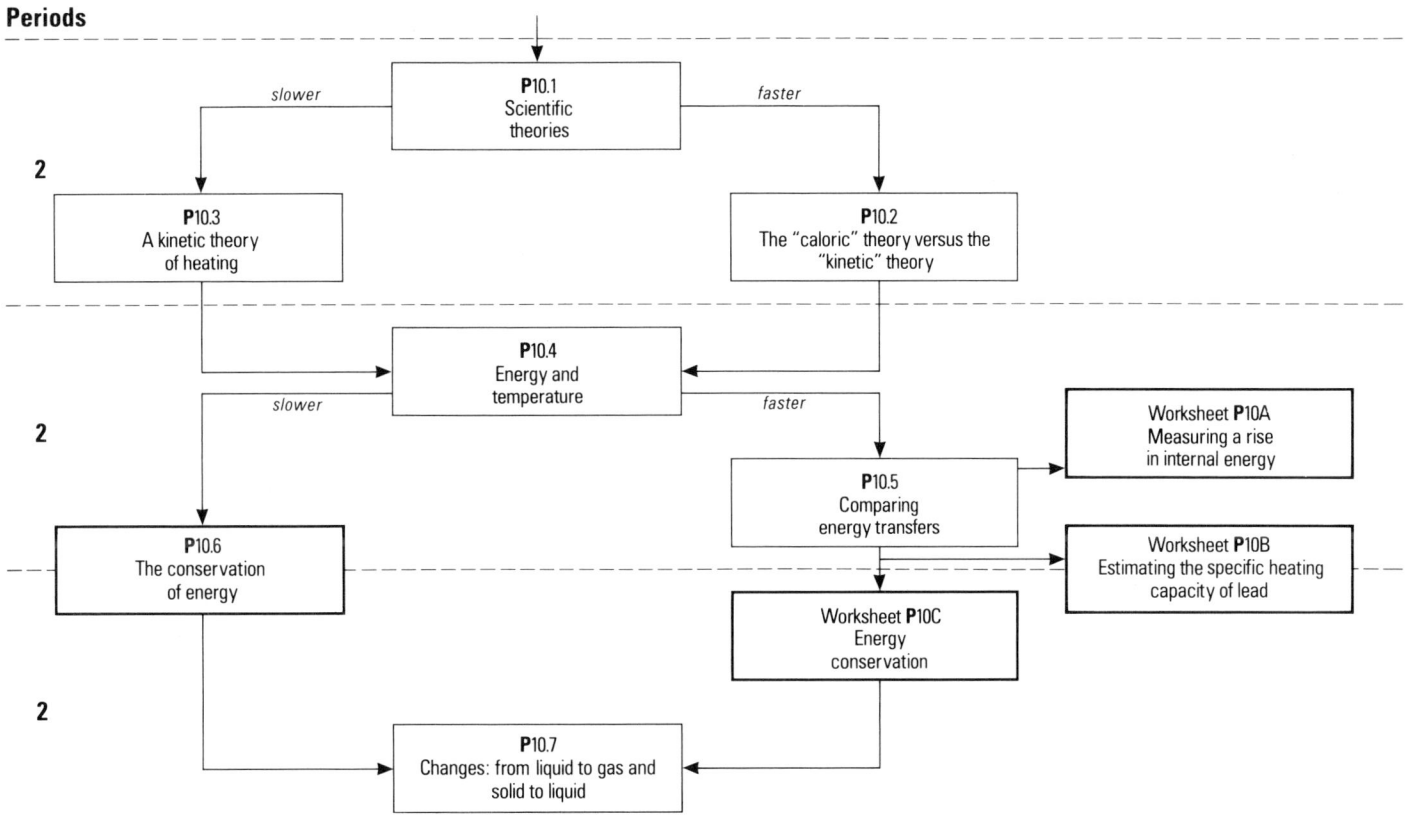

Figure **P11**

Opportunities for co-ordination

The transfer of energy that is involved when the temperature of a living organism is higher than the temperature of its environment is an important feature. References to this will be found in Chapter **B9** "Keeping going", Chapter **B12** "Keeping things under control" and Chapter **B14** "The webs of life". The fact that many organisms are naturally above room temperature is evidence that an energy transfer process is going on inside them.

In the short term some of the energy transferred when changes come about can be re-used. However, in the long term the energy transferred finally ends up in the surroundings where it is spread out and from where it effectively cannot be retrieved. This is paralleled by work in Chemistry where it is shown that the spreading out of materials can make it difficult or impossible to retrieve them for future use. See for example Chapter **C6** "Glasses and ceramics" on the virtues of recycling glass.

Notes and answers

The questions in this chapter ask for qualitative answers only.

This chapter, like Chapter **P5**, is concerned with scientific theories. In Chapter **P5**, pupils were presented with two different explanations of the cause of motion, and they set up experiments of their own to find out which explanation seemed the better. The theory eventually adopted (that in the absence of a force a body's motion cannot be changed) will probably have been new to most pupils and at first sight is by no means an obvious theory to apply to the world around them.

This chapter deals with explanations for changes in temperature. Unlike the work on forces, the theory eventually seen to be the better of two (the kinetic theory) will already be familiar to pupils. A link between temperature change and the kinetic energy of particles is established in Chapter **P2** and pupils may already have met the idea of linking temperature with particle movement in an earlier year.

In the span of time that pupils can spend on Physics as a part of their general education, there is inevitably much that they have to take on trust. However, it seems important that pupils should at least realize that the models and theories presented to them are all based on careful thought and experimentation, and often represent the best (at present) of several conflicting alternatives.

The kinetic theory of matter, by its importance, justifies more than a simple description. So in this chapter it is set against the (historically older) caloric theory. After seeing a series of demonstration experiments in which the temperature of a body changes, pupils are asked to "explain" each set of observations in terms of both theories. At the end of their discussions they should see that the kinetic theory is better at giving an explanation of all the observations than the caloric theory.

Objections can be raised to setting the kinetic theory against the caloric theory in this way. Historically there was no such competition. The caloric theory was first of all replaced by establishing a link between energy transfer and temperature rise, in experiments such as the one in which Rumford drilled out cannons with blunt borers. The caloric theory was unable to explain these observations, but the then newly emerging concept of energy transfer could.

The kinetic theory of matter was established **after** the concepts of energy transfer and energy conservation had been understood. A model for matter based on moving particles gives a further explanation of what happens to the energy that is transferred when the temperature of an object changes.

However, the present approach does not try to suggest that the choice between the caloric theory and the kinetic theory is an historical one. It is felt that pupils may find it easier to grasp the picture of moving particles presented by the kinetic theory than the more abstract concept of "internal energy". So the account moves **from** this particle model **to** a more general interpretation of energy changes within a body, rather than the other way round.

P10.1 Scientific theories

The opening section looks at the important place theories (or "scientific explanations") have in science. More often than not these ideas of how or why things happen determine the direction of a scientist's research. As in Chapter **P5**, no attempt is made to distinguish between "theory" and "hypothesis". It is felt that such a distinction (if one really exists) would be beyond the understanding of pupils at this level.

P10.2 The "caloric" theory versus the "kinetic" theory

At this point in the chapter pupils can proceed by one of two routes. Many pupils will get interest and pleasure from trying to apply two different theories to the same set of experiments. But others may simply find this confusing. For the latter, the alternative section **P10.3** looks simply at the way the kinetic theory can be used to explain changes in temperature without bothering about the caloric theory.

The caloric theory and the kinetic theory are both introduced as simple explanations of what happens when things get hot. The pupils are then presented with four different experiments. For each one they are asked to say what **each** of the two theories will predict. They are then asked to observe what happens and to say which of the two theories seems the best at explaining this particular observation.

Both theories would predict a rise in temperature in Experiment 1 and in Experiment 2. As a rise in temperature is in fact found, there is nothing to distinguish between the two theories. In Experiments 3 and 4, however, only the kinetic theory predicts a change in temperature. So the kinetic theory is more successful than the caloric theory in predicting what will happen in each of these experiments.

The section concludes with a brief account of the historical evolution of the kinetic theory. The theory is seen to result from the atomic theory of John Dalton and others, combined with the relationship between energy and temperature which came from the work of such scientists as James Joule.

P10.3   A kinetic theory of heating

This is an alternative to section **P10.2**. It shows how the kinetic theory is able to explain the link between temperature rise and energy transfer. It limits itself to Experiments 3 and 4 in the last section and gives no consideration to the caloric theory as an alternative explanation.

P10.4   Energy and temperature

This short section links the kinetic theory to a more general relationship between energy transfer and change in temperature. It describes something of the contribution of the work of Joule and Mayer to the development of these ideas. A detailed survey of their work and that of other scientists of the period can be found in Revised Nuffield Physics *Pupils' text Year 4*.

P10.5   Comparing energy transfers

Again, two alternative routes are suggested. This section shows how the relationship between energy and temperature change can be used to measure the specific heating capacity of a material. The way that specific heating capacities could be determined was left as an open question at the end of Chapter **P9**. More able pupils may be able to see that experiments such as these are necessary at some point in the determination of specific heating capacities. But once one specific heating capacity (say that of water) has been established in this way, it can be used as a standard in rather more convenient methods of establishing the specific heating capacity of other substances.

P10.6   The conservation of energy

The idea that energy is conserved (that is, not lost or gained in any interchange) will probably have been a part of the earliest teaching in energy. This is not, however, our everyday experience. Words such as "energy crisis" imply that we are continually using something that cannot be replaced. In pupils' early work on energy they may have learned that in fact energy becomes less useful when used and that this is why we seem to be "running out" of energy.

The relationship between temperature change and energy is a fundamental part of the concept of energy conservation. But the fact that energy is never lost does not solve the problem of the "energy crisis" if in many cases the energy cannot be re-used.

The time spent on this section will depend on the extent to which pupils may find it helpful to repeat energy transfer experiments performed in earlier years, and the time already spent on the work of earlier sections. More able pupils may enjoy the challenge set by Worksheet **P10C** in which they are asked to transfer as much of 10 J of energy to the kinetic energy of a trolley as they can.

P10.7   Changes: from liquid to gas and solid to liquid

The final section extends the idea of energy transfer to the particles of matter to consider what happens when a liquid changes to a gas, or a solid to a liquid.

The idea of "internal energy" – that is, the energy associated with the particles of matter – is extended to include potential as well as kinetic energy. In this way we can understand how it is that heating can lead to a change of state without any change in temperature.

The chapter ends by looking briefly at the role of mathematics in physics. It is suggested that its use is in making predictions from theories and that being able to understand mathematics is not essential to understanding theories. Some hint is offered to the pupils of the way our ideas about energy have now been further extended by Einstein's work.

Practical work

Worksheet P10A   Measuring a rise in internal energy

REQUIREMENTS

Each group of pupils will need:
Mechanical heating apparatus and accessories
Electric heating accessories for the above, if available

Note:
There are a number of alternative versions of this equipment on the market. The actual equipment varies too much from one manufacturer to another to be able to give a detailed list.

The aim of the experiment is to transfer a measured amount of energy to the cylinder and measure the temperature rise which results. There may be a lag between the time when the pupil stops turning the handle and when the temperature stops rising. It is important to read the maximum temperature reached. The results can be used to give an approximate specific heating capacity for the metal of which the cylinder is made.

Accurate results will not be obtained, but the experiment is important as a matter of principle and a very useful vehicle for discussion of the sources of experimental error.

The experiment can be extended to electrical heating. A comparison between the energy transferred by the two methods to produce the same temperature rise in the metal cylinder amounts to a direct "check" on the calibrations on the voltmeter. Pupils may encounter just such an experiment if they continue their study of Physics beyond this course.

Warning
Pupils need to be warned that falling masses can cause injuries. Some form of protection for both them and the laboratory should be provided.

Worksheet P10B   The specific heating capacity of lead

REQUIREMENTS

Each group of pupils will need:
Tube, cardboard or similar, 50 cm long, about 5 cm diameter with bungs or corks for
  both ends
Lead shot, 0.5 kg
Polystyrene beaker
Metre rule
Balance, 0–1 kg

Procedure
A detailed procedure is given in the worksheet. There is of course no need to know the mass of the lead shot in order to work out its specific heating capacity from this experiment. But pupils may find it easier to weigh the shot and use its value, first to find the energy transferred to the lead itself in falling, and then to work out the specific heating capacity.

Worksheet P10C   Energy conservation

REQUIREMENTS

Optional (see figure 10.18 in the pupils' book)

This work involves the pupils in a wide variety of energy transfer demonstrations, set out as a circus. A range of experiments is illustrated in figure 10.18 of the pupils' book. The list of equipment for the experiments shown in figure 10.18 can be found in the Nuffield Science 13 to 16 booklet **Energy** but there is no need to stick to these particular experiments. Pupils may have come across these experiments in their work in year 3, but many will find it helpful to discuss them again in terms of energy conservation and whether the energy is finally reusable.

Warning
Pupils need to be warned that falling masses can cause injuries. Some form of protection for both them and the laboratory should be provided.

Demonstration experiments

Section P10.2

Experiments illustrated in figure 10.7 of the pupils' book:

REQUIREMENTS

Experiment 1
Beaker, glass, 400 cm³
Thermometer
Bunsen burner
Tripod
Gauze
Heatproof mat

Experiment 2
2 beakers, 400 cm³, one containing hot
    water, the other cold water
Thermometer

Experiment 3
The same equipment as for Worksheet
    P10A.

Experiment 4
The same equipment as for Worksheet
    P10B.

Further information

Nuffield Science 13 to 16
Energy. This module is the one recommended for the preceding work in year 3. It is useful to refer to this as the assumed starting point for much of the work of this chapter.

Revised Nuffield Physics
Teachers' guide Year 4: Chapter 9 "Energy and its grand total: Conservation" The approach adopted in this chapter to the relationship between temperature rise and energy is rather different from that adopted in Revised Nuffield Physics. Nevertheless, the approach there also **comes after** a detailed exploration of the kinetic theory. It has points in common with this approach but gives prior attention to the link between energy and temperature rise, which the kinetic theory is seen to support. This is a more fundamental approach to energy and its conservation, and is well suited to able pupils. The approach could be adopted as an alternative to that given in Chapter **P10** – the outcome for the pupils would be (it is hoped) the same.

Children's Learning in Science Project
"Secondary students' ideas about particles" and "Secondary students' understanding of heat". Both these booklets provide helpful information on two ideas that many pupils find difficult. They are based on an analysis of the answers to questions obtained from tests administered by the Assessment of Performance Unit.

Chapter P11   Energy where it is needed
Energy transmission

Purposes

Knowledge and understanding

At the end of this chapter all pupils should:

1 appreciate the need for the transmission of energy

2 understand that energy can be transferred from fuels to electricity by dynamos

3 appreciate the problems involved in the electrical transmission of energy

4 understand the importance of transformers in the electrical transmission of energy and understand how they work

5 appreciate the possible advantages of other methods of transmitting energy.

Processes and problem solving

Graphical and symbolic representation
In this chapter, circuit components are represented by a mixture of conventional symbols and outline drawings. Circuit diagrams for the electricity transmission lines use conventional symbols for everything except transformers. This has been done in the interests of clarity. More able pupils will benefit from being introduced to the conventional symbols for these as well, but they have not been used in the pupils' book.

Using apparatus and measuring instruments
Quantitative investigations into the behaviour of transmission lines and transformers depend on careful reading of ammeters and voltmeters.

Observation
Apart from reading measuring instruments, this process is involved in the interpretation of the way transmission lines lose energy.

Interpretation and application
An understanding of the behaviour of electricity transmission lines depends on prior understanding of current, voltage and resistance, as well as ideas about the conservation and transfer of energy. Transformers are understood in terms of previous ideas on electromagnetic induction. The whole chapter applies these ideas to the transmission of energy.

Problem solving
The work of this chapter centres around a single problem: how can energy be distributed electrically with a minimum of energy loss? Transformers are introduced as one solution to this problem. (The use of local generators called Minichips, introduced in Chapter P12, is another.)

Investigating the behaviour of transformers is a class exercise led by demonstration experiments. The work (described in Worksheet P11A) concludes with a class problem: given a 2 V a.c. power supply, two C-cores and some wire, light a 6 V lamp to full brightness.

Timing

6 periods.

Suggested routes

The flow diagram in figure **P**12 divides the work of this chapter into three levels of difficulty. At the easiest level, pupils who have not worked through the section on electromagnetic induction in Chapter **P**18 are given a simpler approach to the topic in section **P**11.2 of this chapter. They can then look at the behaviour of electricity transmission lines and transformers at a qualitative level. Others who have already investigated electromagnetic induction can work through a feasibility study on the transmission of energy resources by two different methods. They can then continue with the investigation into the transmission of electricity and transformers.

The fastest pupils can make a detailed study of the variations in p.d. along a transmission line and the ways in which these are changed when transformers are used. They can then try to understand these changes in terms of their understanding of current and voltage. This more detailed study is covered in the pupils' book by extension sections at the ends of sections **P**11.4 and **P**11.5.

Periods

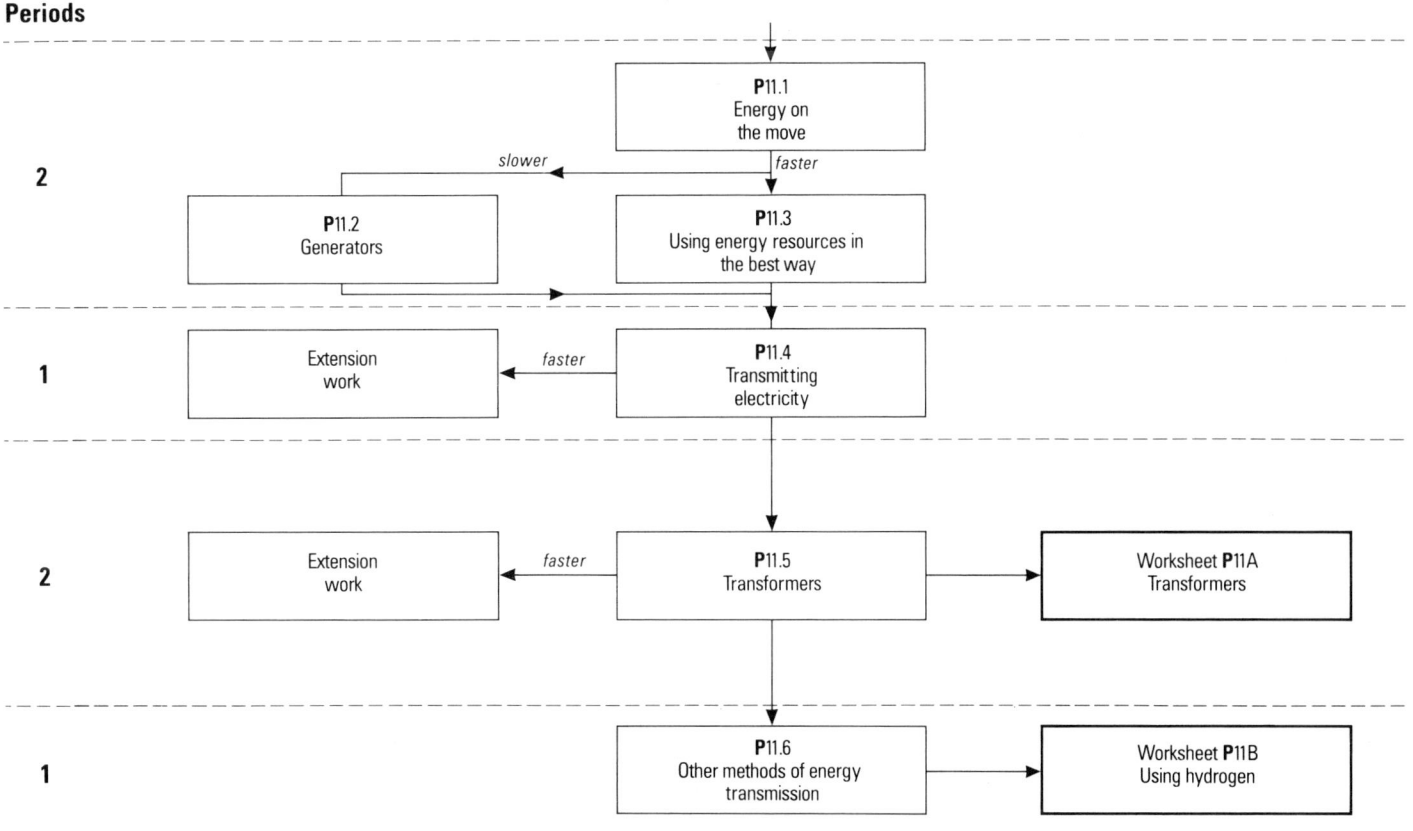

Figure **P**12

Opportunities for co-ordination

There are few direct links between the work of this chapter and work in Biology and Chemistry. Energy from fuels, which is a part of the feasibility study in section **P**11.3, is covered in more detail in Chapter **C**13 "Fuels and fires".

Worksheet **P**11B uses the fact that energy can be released by burning hydrogen in air. This is clearly related to ideas that will be established in the pupils' work in Chemistry.

Notes and answers

The work of this chapter centres around sections **P**11.4 and **P**11.5 in the pupils' book. Both of these sections involve laboratory work, much of which will consist of demonstration experiments.

Demonstration experiments play a large part in this work for two reasons:

- equipment based on transformers may be in too short a supply for individual experiments
- power line experiments using transformers involve dangerously high voltages.

A further benefit conferred by demonstration experiments is the extent to which the class can discuss together the observations made when energy is transmitted along a "power line". Even so, some laboratories may have sufficient equipment to set up several transmission lines. In this case pupils can work in small groups, using the questions in the book as a basis for their own investigations.

It is likely that this central section of the work will take 3 or 4 periods. The time taken will depend on the extent to which pupils pursue the extensions to the work in sections **P11.4** and **P11.5**. One period, with the addition of possible homework, should be left to the last section and Worksheet **P11B**. The introductory section can be covered in a single period by more able pupils, but will need longer if section **P11.2** is to be included.

P11.1 Energy on the move

This introductory section looks at the need to move energy resources to the places where they are needed. The phrase "energy transmission" has been chosen to describe this; "energy transfer", introduced in Chapter **P8**, means something rather different. The delivery of coal and oil to houses by lorry and tanker are both methods of getting energy to places where it is needed. Natural gas is distributed through a network of underground pipes which make up an important method of transmitting energy for heating. However, nowadays the prime method of distributing energy to homes, industry, offices and public buildings is by electricity transmission lines.

To understand how electricity can be used as a means of energy distribution from primary sources such as fossil fuels, pupils will need to understand something about generators and dynamos. They may already have acquired a sufficient understanding from their work with Chapter **P18**. Those who have not are given a simple treatment of the ideas in section **P11.2**.

P11.2 Generators

This approach to the transfer of energy using electricity builds on some previous work pupils will have done in making an electric motor. Electric motors depend on an interaction between an electric current and a magnetic field to produce motion. This result is looked at as an "equation", with electric current and magnetic field on one side and motion on the other. Rearranging the equation suggests that motion (of a wire) in a magnetic field might produce an electric current.

It is ideas such as these that set Michael Faraday on his search for induced currents. Today we have the advantage of much more sensitive measuring instruments than he had, so the possibility of induced currents is easily tested by experiment. An experimental investigation is proposed in question 4 of the pupils' book. This could be undertaken by pupils in the laboratory. Then a mounted bicycle dynamo can be demonstrated. It may be helpful at this point to look at the sort of current this dynamo produces – one that surges backwards and forwards. This can be contrasted with the current from a dry battery, which flows in one direction only.

While the experiments emphasize the production of induced currents, the currents themselves are seen as a means of transferring energy. Generators and dynamos are described in the pupils' book as devices which can transfer energy from fuels to elsewhere, using the flow of electric charge (or simply "electricity" for short) in order to do this. This is a more accurate and more easily understood approach than to say that dynamos transfer energy to electric charge, and that this energy is then used elsewhere. This latter statement seems to imply that electricity can somehow store up energy for future use – and this is not the case.

P11.3   Using energy resources in the best way

This section is for pupils who have already spent some time investigating induced currents during work on Chapter **P18**. It explores two possible schemes for distributing energy on an imaginary island of Pylos, which has a single coal mine.

In investigating the efficiency of both schemes, pupils will need to recognize that energy wastage is more than losing energy to the surroundings by, say, burning coal and passing electric currents through wires, although both of these will be important. Paying people to deliver coal "costs" energy; so does building large power stations, or even small generators.

On the other hand, all members of a community need to be supported by food, energy, buildings and services. It might be preferable for the community to have a "labour-intensive" system for getting energy where it is needed if the alternative is that labour goes unused.

Arguments such as these, which may well appeal to more able pupils, show that decisions over alternatives in any field where technology can be applied are not easily made. The arguments are complex and it is difficult to know whether every factor has been considered.

Whatever conclusions are reached, work in Chapter **P12** will show that the arguments over the best system of energy distribution are far from over.

P11.4   Transmitting electricity

(There is a short discussion about the use of the word "electricity" in the Introduction to Topic **P5**.)

This section is centred around an experiment with a model "power line". The power line is made of "resistance" wire, so that the effects of a real power line can be simulated in the short distances possible in a laboratory.

In the experiment, a 12 V lamp connected directly to a 12 V power pack (representing the power station) is found to be fully lit. Another lamp connected to the far end of the power line is lit only dimly. Measurements with a voltmeter show that in the transfer of the energy from the power pack to the distant lamp, much of it is "lost".

The power line is now rebuilt using transformers. This experiment must be demonstrated, even if the first one is not, as dangerously high voltages are involved. No attempt is made to explain the action of the transformers – they are "black boxes" which connect the power line to the power pack at one end and to the lamp at the other. At once it is seen that the two lamps (one connected to the power pack and the other at the far end of the power line) are equally bright. Voltmeter measurements show there has been little energy loss along the power line. But the voltage across the input and output ends of the power line is found to be 240 V, rather than 12 V. This leads on to the next section, which investigates how transformers work.

P11.5   Transformers

This section includes a simple introduction to induced currents, which can be omitted by pupils who have already covered this in Chapter **P18**. It is assumed that the experiments described in the pupils' book will either be demonstrated, or set out as a circus of experiments. If the latter course is adopted, the questions in the pupils' book will serve as a pointer to the pupils' own investigations.

These experiments lead directly to the transformer and the energy transfers that take place when it is in use. Finally the section ends with an investigation into the way the input and output voltages of a transformer are related to the numbers of turns on the coils.

For some pupils this may be a sufficient treatment of power lines. They will have learned that power lines transmit energy more efficiently if they work at a high voltage rather than a low one. They will have seen that transformers are capable of changing a.c. voltages and that despite the fact that transformers themselves waste some energy, their use can lead to considerable savings in transferring energy electrically.

Other pupils will want to know why there should be a difference in the energy wasted when low and high voltages are used. This section concludes with a more detailed investigation into the voltages and currents along power lines. It shows that transferring power electrically at a high voltage means a lower current in the transmission lines than if the same power is transmitted at a low voltage.

Energy loss comes from heating of the surroundings by the transmission lines through which the current is passing. The smaller the current, the lower the rate at which energy is transferred to the surroundings. So it is more efficient to transfer power at a high voltage than at a low voltage.

The section concludes with a brief reference to the National Grid and then asks some numerical questions about transmitting power electrically.

P11.6 Other methods of energy transmission

The introduction to this chapter showed that electricity is not the only method by which energy can be distributed. This final section looks at two more methods. Belt drives are still important where it is necessary to transmit energy over small distances. Hydraulic transmission of energy was once very important indeed. Over long distances it has largely been replaced by electricity. On a smaller scale, however, it still has a number of advantages.

In the future it may be necessary to replace one major energy resource not previously mentioned in this chapter, namely oil. Because it is a highly concentrated energy resource, it is extensively used for transport. Apart from modern rocket engines, no replacement for fuels extracted from oil has yet been found for use in air travel. Worksheet **P11B** reproduces two articles on possible modes of energy distribution in the future and asks pupils to think about some of their implications.

Practical work

Worksheet P11A   Transformers

Experiment 1 (demonstration)

REQUIREMENTS

Demountable transformer with 1 coil of 3600 turns
Lamp, 2.5 V MES
Lamp holder, MES
Wire, 4 m, flexible, insulated (one of the wires from twin lamp flex is better than solid core insulated wire)

Procedure
Place the 3600-turn coil on one leg of the laminated U-core of the demountable transformer. Connect it to the 240 V a.c. mains supply.

Connect the long flexible lead to the lamp holder with the lamp.

Switch on the 240 V a.c. supply and wind the long wire **turn by turn** round the other leg of the U-core. As more and more turns are wound on, the lamp begins to glow and then gets brighter and brighter. At least 25 turns will be necessary for this.

Provided a spare lamp is available, try placing the I-yoke across the top of the U-core.

Warning

The connections between the mains and the transformer must be made using a mains lead which has two layers of insulation over the conductors, and a proper plug and socket.

Experiment 2

(This experiment may be a demonstration or group work, depending on the available equipment.)

REQUIREMENTS

Demountable transformer with 300, 600 and 1200 turn coils
or
2 C-cores with 60 + 60 turn and 120 + 120 turn coils
2 voltmeters, 10 V a.c. (ideally these should be demonstration instruments if this experiment is demonstrated to the whole class)
Low voltage power supply, 2 V a.c.
Connecting leads

Procedure

The circuit is set up as shown in Worksheet P11A. For use as a step-up transformer, a 2 V a.c. input is convenient. Outputs can range from 2 V to 8 V.

Faster groups can also see what happens if the output is used to light a lamp and the input and output currents are measured as well as the voltages.

Warning

If equipment is provided for pupils to carry out their own experiments it is important that no combination of transformer coils and input supply voltage can produce an output voltage in excess of 25 V. (See Health and Safety Executive Guidance Note 23 *Electrical safety in schools*: 18.) If 60 + 60 and 120 + 120 turn coils are used in conjunction with the low voltage (2 V a.c.) power supplies, as suggested, the maximum output voltage is 8 V.

Problem

REQUIREMENTS

Each group of pupils will need:
2 C-cores
Wire, pvc insulated solid core, 3 m
Lamp, 6 V MES
Lamp holder, MES
Power supply, 2 V a.c.

Pupils are set the challenge of lighting the 6 V lamp fully with the equipment provided.

Other demonstrations and pupil experiments

Section P11.2:   To show that moving a conductor in a magnetic field produces an electric current

REQUIREMENTS

Each group of pupils will need:
Model motor (as constructed in Chapter
  P18)
Galvanometer
Connecting leads

Note:
Centre-zero galvanometers are ideal for
this experiment, but many school meters
allow for the measurement of small
currents in both directions. Choice of a
suitable instrument is best determined by
trial and error beforehand.

The bicycle dynamo (demonstration)

REQUIREMENTS

Bicycle dynamo assembly
Meter, demonstration (or galvanometer), with 2.5–0–2.5 mA scale or similar
Oscilloscope
Lamp, 6 V MES
Holder, MES
Connecting leads

Use the low-speed gearing on the dynamo assembly to demonstrate the output of
the dynamo. The a.c. character can also be shown using the oscilloscope.

Driving the dynamo at a higher speed can light a lamp attached across its
output, thus demonstrating the energy transfer from the operator to the lamp.

This experiment will have to be demonstrated when using a centre-zero
galvanometer. Over-vigorous handle turning will permanently damage the meter
movement.

Section P11.4:   12 V model power line

REQUIREMENTS

Each group of pupils will need:
Pair of power line terminal rods
2 bare Eureka wires, each 1.25 m long, 0.40 mm diameter
2 stands and bosses
2 lamps, 12 V, 24 W
2 lamp holders, SBC
Power supply, 12 V a.c.
Connecting leads

The equipment is set up as shown in figure 11.16 in the pupils' book. Whether the
experiment is done by the pupils or as a demonstration, it will save time and avoid
confusion if the "pylons" and the transmission line are set up beforehand.

For each set, two dowels form the power line terminal rods. They are held
horizontally in bosses at a height of about 30 to 50 cm above the bench and 1 m
or more apart. Two lengths of high resistance (Eureka) wire are stretched between
the terminals to form the power line.

The observations to be made are suggested in the pupils' book.

High voltage model power line (demonstration)

REQUIREMENTS

One set of equipment from the 12 V model power line experiment, plus:
  2 pairs of C-cores with clips
  2 coils, 120 turns, to fit C-cores
  2 coils, 2400 turns, to fit C-cores

Tranformers are now added to one power line, for use as a demonstration. The circuit diagram is shown in figure 11.17 in the pupils' book. It is important to get the transformers the right way round (with the smaller coils connected to the power supply and the distant lamp respectively and the 2400 turn coils connected to the power line).

The observations to be made are suggested in the pupils' book.

Warning
Great care must be taken when demonstrating the high-voltage transmission line. It is very easy to forget that the voltage on the line is 240 V. A card hung on the line warning of the high voltage will serve as a reminder.

Section P11.5:   Experiments demonstrating electromagnetic induction

Experiment 1 (figure 11.19)

REQUIREMENTS

Each group of pupils will need:
Coil, 120 turns (as for use with C-cores)
Magnet, bar
Galvanometer, 3.5–0–3.5 mA
Connecting leads

Experiment 2 (figure 11.20)

REQUIREMENTS

Each group of pupils will need:
C-core
Coil, 120 turns (as for use with C-cores)
Switch
Cell, 1.5 V, in holder
Connecting leads

Experiment 3 (figure 11.21)

REQUIREMENTS

Each group of pupils will need:
2 C-cores
2 coils, 120 turns (as for use with C-cores)
Switch
Galvanometer, 3.5–0–3.5 mA
Cell, 1.5 V, in holder
Connecting leads

Experiment 4 (figure 11.22)

REQUIREMENTS

Each group of pupils will need:
2 C-cores
2 coils, 120 turns (as for use with C-cores)
Power supply, 2 V a.c.
Lamp, 2.5 V MES
Lamp holder, MES
Connecting leads

Circuits for all the experiments are illustrated in the pupils' book (figures 11.19–22).

The meters used must be sufficiently sensitive to give deflections which pupils can easily see.

Further information

Revised Nuffield Physics
Teachers' guide Year 5, Chapter 7 "Alternating currents". This chapter gives useful additional background information on demountable transformers (page 86) as well as comments on the output of the bicycle dynamo (page 83).

Nuffield Science 13 to 16
Why use a.c.? Much of the approach adopted in this chapter has been influenced by Chapters 1 to 5 of this unit, and parts of it may provide additional material if this is needed. The material of Chapters 6 and 7 is more relevant to the electronics topics in this course.Chapter 8 could provide an additional and interesting exercise on the problems of putting transmission lines underground.

Supplementary material

Useful supporting material on the supply and distribution of electricity is available from the Central Electricity Generating Board, or its area offices. Two examples are:
"Your generation" This is a video of the 1985 Faraday lecture.
"Power to the people" This video is about the National Grid.

Chapter P12   Waste not, want not?
Energy resources

Purposes

Knowledge and understanding

At the end of this chapter all pupils should:

1 appreciate the importance of energy in our day-to-day lives

2 appreciate the necessity of finding an alternative to fossil fuels in the near future

3 understand how energy may be released from the nuclei of atoms by both nuclear fission and nuclear fusion

4 appreciate some of the problems involved in the use of nuclear fission as an energy resource

5 understand that there are alternative (renewable) energy resources, but that no single renewable energy source is likely to act as a total replacement for present energy resources

6 appreciate that greater efficiency in the use of energy can be as helpful as finding alternative sources.

Processes and problem solving

Interpretation and application
This unit draws together many ideas that have been developed about energy in earlier chapters and applies them to an understanding of the energy needs of the world. Previous understanding of ideas in radioactivity is also essential to understanding the problems posed by the use of nuclear power.

Planning and carrying out investigations
Investigational work of a new kind is required in this chapter. In work based on

two worksheets, pupils are asked to discuss the use of nuclear power and the use of alternative energy sources. This work will involve all pupils in some research into various aspects of the problems.

Problem solving
Worksheet **P**12B "Ashton Island" sets up a problem-solving situation in which ideas about various alternative energy resources have to be used to find an appropriate solution to the energy needs of a small island.

Timing

6 periods.

Suggested routes

The flow diagram in figure **P**13 divides the work of this chapter into two levels of difficulty.

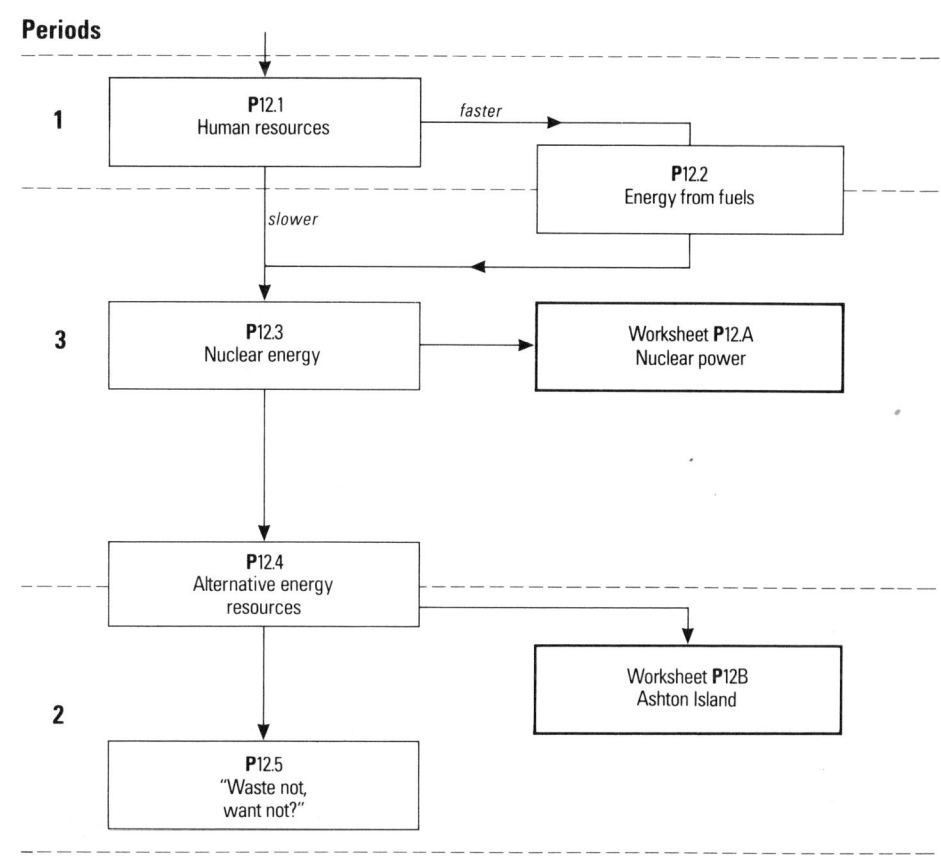

Figure **P**13

Opportunities for co-ordination

The human body, as an engine which needs fuel, is treated in detail in the Biology pupils' book (Chapter **B**9 "Keeping going"). Photosynthesis, as the means by which plants trap energy from the Sun, is covered in detail in Chapter **B**3 "Light means life".

The refining of crude oil to produce fuels is the subject of Chapter **C**2 "Petrochemicals" of the Chemistry pupils' book. Energy from fossil fuels is dealt with in detail in Chapter **C**13 "Fuels and fires". The article on "Sugar: fuel for the future" will be complemented by Chapter **C**3 "Chemicals from plants".

Notes and answers

The theme of the chapter is the world's continuing need for energy resources at a time when fossil fuels are becoming increasingly scarce. All pupils cover essentially the same material. However, section **P**12.2 is optional and intended for pupils who may have the time and interest to study a recent experiment in transferring more energy from the Sun via plants.

The pupils' attention is focussed on two issues. The first is the nuclear fuel alternative to fossil fuels. The second is the availability of sources of energy which are alternatives to both nuclear and fossil fuels. These two issues have been made the subject of two class activities. They are based on two SATIS units: unit 109 "Nuclear power" and unit 107 "Ashton Island – a problem in renewable energy".

These two activities will occupy the majority of the time available for the chapter. Most of the other work can be seen as providing supporting material to these activities.

P12.1 Human resources

This introductory section shows how much energy a human being requires in a day, and how much of this can be transferred as useful work. From these figures it is shown that a day's human labour amounts, in energy terms, to just about 1 kWh – the "unit" in which electricity boards sell energy to the consumer.

The cost of this much energy from an area electricity board was about 5p in 1986. This shows clearly how the scale of human energy compares with that available from fossil fuels. It also demonstrates how a country's prosperity depends on the availability of cheap and plentiful energy resources.

P12.2 Energy from fuels

This is a short optional section for more able pupils. The section compares the time taken to produce fuels based on plant materials with the time taken to use them. It then considers an alternative to the traditional fuels of wood, peat, coal, oil or gas, which nevertheless still captures the Sun's energy through photosynthesis.

P12.3 Nuclear energy

It is necessary for pupils to have studied Chapter **P3** "Radioactivity" before tackling this chapter. The section starts with a review of the most important ideas arising from that chapter.

The section continues with a brief description of the way energy is released from the nucleus of a uranium atom in a nuclear reactor. It then gives a brief pen-portrait of the man who built the world's first nuclear reactor, Enrico Fermi.

The section concludes with an account of nuclear fusion and lists the advantages nuclear reactors based on fusion would have compared with those based on fission. If time permits, the material can be supported by showing one of a number of films that are available. Recommended sources are listed in the supplementary material section.

The entire section provides background for a pupil-based discussion group on the use of nuclear power. Worksheet **P12A** provides pupils with the essential material needed for the discussion groups. The worksheet is based on SATIS unit 109 "Nuclear power". The general briefing sheet in that unit has not been reproduced as the material contained in it is part of the present chapter. Teaching notes to accompany this worksheet are given separately below.

P12.4 Alternative energy resources

This section looks at the possibility of finding energy resources which are neither fossil nor nuclear fuels. Such energy resources are generally referred to as "alternative energy sources".

The material in this section can be supported by a range of display material, posters, and so on, some sources of which are listed in the supplementary material section. Again, if time permits, films are available which illustrate the potential for "alternative energy".

This material should be seen also as background for the second worksheet, Worksheet **P**12B. This worksheet sets pupils the problem of providing energy for a small community on an isolated island which has no fuel reserves and no nuclear power. The worksheet is based on SATIS unit 107 "Ashton Island – a problem in renewable energy". The details about alternative energy resources have been omitted as these are covered in the pupils' book. Detailed teaching notes are given in the notes on worksheets below.

P12.5 "Waste not, want not"

The chapter concludes with some consideration of the effect of greater efficiency in the use of energy on our available resources. The very small amount of energy usefully transferred from fuels is emphasized and examples are given of recent experiments in increasing this efficiency.

Notes on worksheets

Worksheet P12A Nuclear power

The aim of this worksheet is to initiate an **informed** discussion between a group of pupils. To do this, each member of the discussion group becomes an "expert" in some field related to nuclear power. The group then discusses various aspects of nuclear power under the leadership of one member who takes the chair.

The class should be formed into groups of five. Each group should have a group leader, whose task it is to chair the discussions. The group leader will have to be chosen for his or her potential in this respect.

The group leader should be given the Chairperson's briefing sheet. Give the Experts' briefing sheets (1 to 4) to the other members of the group – a different sheet to each person. They should have time to study their briefings before the discussion – this could conveniently be set as a homework assignment.

The running of the discussion is in the hands of the group leader. Avoid intervening, if possible! A time limit will have to be placed on the discussions. The session could conclude with a "report back" to the whole class by each group leader giving the group's views on the "General points for discussion" listed in the Chairperson's briefing.

Worksheet P12B Ashton Island

Pupils tackle the questions on Ashton Island after they have made a brief study of alternative energy sources. They will probably do this best if they work in small groups.

At some time teachers may wish to contrast the problem of providing energy for a limited period of time to a few people (as in "Ashton Island") with the problems involved in using the same resources to replace our day-to-day use of fossil and nuclear fuels. At the time of writing, none of the alternative energy resources discussed in the chapter are viable in economic terms when contrasted with the cost of traditional energy resources. However they may become more attractive as the cost of traditional resources starts to rise, due to depletion of reserves.

Further information

Nuffield Science 13 to 16
Thinking about energy. Chapter **P**12 places considerable demands on pupils' reading abilities. An alternative approach to the material of this chapter is to be

found in this unit from Nuffield Science 13 to 16. It covers much the same ground as the first part of Chapter **P9**. The remaining chapters give an alternative approach to much of Chapter **P12**, but no coverage is given to nuclear power.

Supplementary material

The basic processes of nuclear power:
"Power from the atom"
"Nuclear fusion: Energy for the 21st century"
These videos are available from the United Kingdom Atomic Energy Authority (UKAEA).

"The nuclear reactor simulation"
This is a computer simulation of an advanced gas-cooled reactor developed by the Education Service of the UKAEA and published by Longman.

The cases for and against nuclear power:
Material dealing with the case in favour of the use of nuclear power is available from the UKAEA.
   The case against nuclear power is laid out in a number of publications available from Friends of the Earth.

Other aspects of energy:
"Time for Energy"
This film dealing with alternative energy is available from the Shell Film Library.

"Energy in profile"
A film available from the Shell Film Library.

"A quest for gas"
A film available from British Gas.

British Gas also produce a booklet on the history of gas called *Then and now*.

Topic P4   Waves

Introduction

This topic is about the use that we can make of a wave model to describe a number of energy transfer processes. Particular attention is given to light, but this is extended to include the whole electromagnetic spectrum.

Sound and earthquakes are also included as other examples of energy transfer which can be described by wave ideas.

A wave, as a to-and-fro motion which can be passed "hand-to-hand" through a wave-carrying medium, is something which can only be seen on a medium such as water. To say that light and sound are waves, or that earthquakes travel as waves through the earth is an exercise of the imagination which is both part of the beauty and power of physics and yet at the same time makes it seem "difficult". So in this course the properties of waves on springs and on the surface of water are studied. The behaviour of light and sound is seen in some simple respects to be like the behaviour of the waves observed on springs and water.

This leads to the possibility of light being some sort of wave motion. Further properties of light are explored on the basis of "let's see how far this idea will take us". These further explorations linking waves with light turn out to be very profitable, illustrating the usefulness of using the wave model to describe the behaviour of light. In a similar way, wave motion turns out to be a useful way of describing the behaviour of sound and earthquakes. In these two cases the model is given greater realism as we are able to explain what it is that "waves about" – a question that is very difficult to answer in the case of light and other electromagnetic waves.

Timing

18 periods, as follows:

Chapter **P13**	Fibre optics and noise	6 periods
Chapter **P14**	Making waves	5 periods
Chapter **P15**	Making use of waves	7 periods

Chapter P13   Fibre optics and noise
A revision of light and sound

Purposes

Knowledge and understanding

At the end of this chapter all pupils should:

1 understand the basic properties of reflection and refraction as they apply to light and sound

2 appreciate how these properties can be used to explain the transmission of light down an optical fibre

3 appreciate how noise levels can be measured and appreciate the desirability of reducing noise levels, yet recognize the problems involved in doing this

4 appreciate the importance of communications systems in the modern world.

Processes and problem solving

Graphical and symbolic representation
Ray diagrams for light are revised and used in this chapter.

Using apparatus and measuring instruments
Measurement of angles of rays is a part of an investigation into critical angle.

Observation
Careful observation of the behaviour of light passing along an optical fibre will be required in interpreting the properties of such fibres with respect to the behaviour of light.

Interpretation and application
This chapter is entirely concerned with the application of the properties of light and sound.

Planning investigations
There are no experimental investigations in this chapter, but Worksheets **P**13B on telecommunications and **P**13C on noise will both require research – either by "looking things up" or by asking questions of others.

Problem solving
The way an optical fibre works is presented as a problem which is resolved by a further investigation into the properties of light.

Timing

6 periods.

Suggested routes

The flow diagram in figure **P**14 (opposite) gives a single route through the contents of this chapter. No suggestions are made for treating the contents of this chapter at different levels.

Opportunities for co-ordination

Sound and light are intimately bound up with our senses of hearing and sight. Chapter **B**11 "Detecting changes" in the Biology book deals with sight and hearing.

Optical fibres make use of materials with a very high degree of transparency to light. The fibres may be made of materials such as ordinary glass, or from plastic. Glasses are dealt with in Chapter **C**6 "Glasses and ceramics" in the Chemistry pupils' book. Polymers are the subject of Chapter **C**8.

Notes and answers

Revising work on light

A revision of ideas about light, met in an earlier year, will probably be necessary. The section in the pupils' book entitled "What you should already know about light and sound" reviews the image-forming properties of a lens as well as basic ideas about reflection and refraction. Only the properties of reflection and refraction are essential to the work of this chapter.

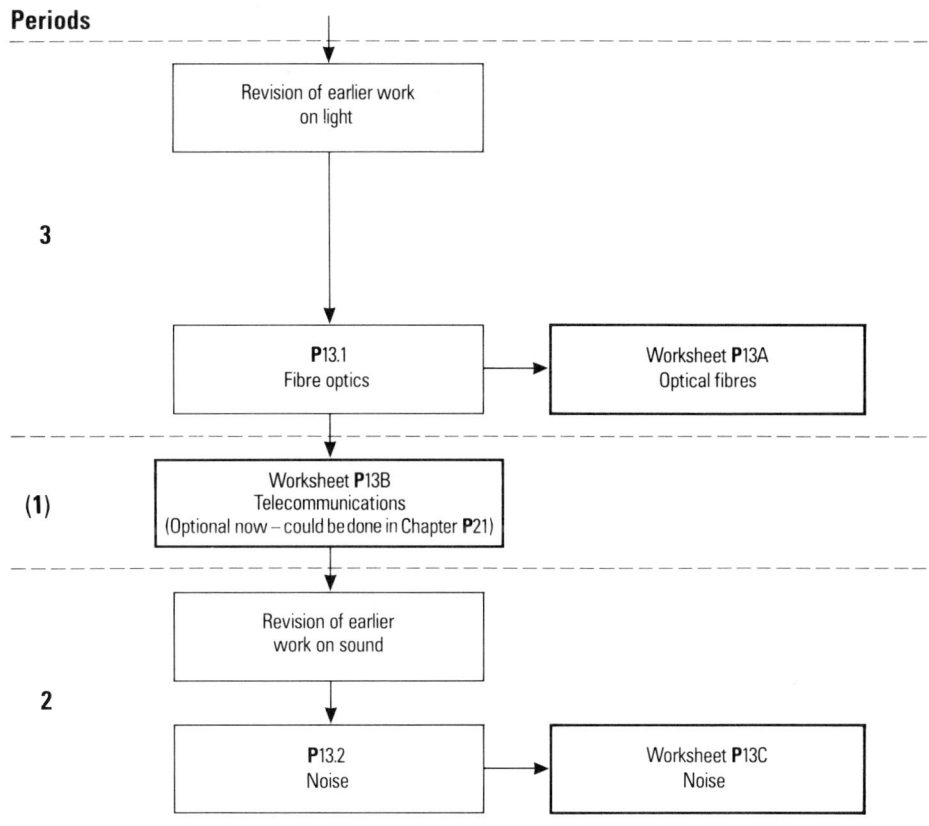

Periods

```
                    Revision of earlier work
                          on light

  3

                    P13.1                 Worksheet P13A
                    Fibre optics          Optical fibres

                    Worksheet P13B
 (1)                Telecommunications
                    (Optional now – could be done in Chapter P21)

                    Revision of earlier
                    work on sound

  2

                    P13.2                 Worksheet P13C
                    Noise                 Noise
```

Figure **P**14

However, work on lenses and optical instruments is also a part of elementary work on light and is included here for the sake of completeness and inherent importance.

Some questions covering these basic ideas have been included in the pupils' book and could be used as the basis for deciding how much revision needs to be done.

P13.1   Fibre optics

The chapter opens by considering the way light has been used for signalling for hundreds of years. It is recognized that there are both advantages and problems in this method of communication. The main problems in using light for communication are hinted at by the questions "How far?" and "How fast?" Speed of communication is not simply a matter of the time taken for a signal to pass over a particular distance – it is also a matter of the length of the message being sent. For example, transmitting a document by morse code would take rather more time than it does to read it. Digital communication systems have greatly reduced the time it takes to transmit messages; such systems have not increased the speed at which the signals cover space (this has been achieved at the speed of light for many years now). How messages can be compressed is dealt with in Chapter **P**21.

Light has great advantages when it comes to "message compression". This is what is really meant when it is said that optical fibres can convey information faster than electrical cables. There is very little gain in actual signal speed.

The use of optical fibres has done much to increase the distances light signals can be sent. Worksheet **P**13A gives pupils a series of experiments that illustrate the way an optical fibre works. It introduces the concept of a critical angle and thus adds to the previous work pupils will have done on refraction.

The section concludes with a brief survey of the advantages of using optical fibres in telecommunications systems. Worksheet **P**13B widens the scope of the enquiry by not only asking questions about the use of optical fibres, but also considering more generally the impact of technology on people's lives. This worksheet is based on one of the same title published for the SATIS project by the Association for Science Education. The worksheet is optional here and could be covered instead at the end of Chapter **P**21 "Communication". Pupils who have had to spend some time on the revision of light will probably not benefit from doing Worksheet **P**21C in that chapter, and Worksheet **P**13B would be a good alternative.

Answers to selected questions

1 This is an "estimates" question for which all but the most able pupils will require some help. The supplementary questions are:
i What is likely to be the average distance between beacons?
ii How long would it take one group of people to sight a lighted beacon and then get their own sufficiently well alight to attract others?
iii How far is it from the south coast of Britain to Newcastle?

The following answers are only personal estimates – others may differ markedly!
i An average distance between beacons might be about 25 km.
ii One might reckon on a time of 20 minutes at least between one beacon being lit and the next being sufficiently alight to pass the "message" on.
iii The distance between Newcastle and the south coast is more certain – it is almost 500 km in a straight line.

An estimate of the time the message would take is:
500/25 beacons × 20 minutes per beacon = 400 minutes.
This is a time of about 7 hours.

P13.2 Noise

Some revision of earlier ideas can take place first of all. Revision questions are given in the introduction to Topic **P**4. Whereas the behaviour of light can easily be treated without any reference to its possible nature, it is common to treat sound as "waves in air" from the first. Thus early work on pitch will probably already have linked this with the idea of wave frequency. Speed of travel may also have been investigated. The companion features of light will probably have received no attention. On the other hand it is much more difficult to demonstrate the reflection and refraction of sound than of light. Since it is important to see later that sound shares many properties with light, and that both can be described as waves, it may be a good idea at this point to demonstrate that sound can at least be reflected. Two experiments are described in the practical work section which demonstrate the reflection and refraction of sound.

Finally pupils can undertake all or part of the investigation into "Noise" described in Worksheet **P**13C. This worksheet is based on one of the same title published in the SATIS series. The final enquiry, "How noisy is your school?", is something that can be undertaken over a longer period than this chapter will take. It introduces another form of data collection – asking questions of others – and encourages a critical attitude to data collected in this way.

Practical work

Worksheet P13A Optical fibres

REQUIREMENTS

Each group of pupils will need:
Transparent plastic block, semicircular
Transparent plastic strip, approximately 3 cm × 30 cm × 0.5 cm
Glass rod, 20 to 30 cm long with smooth-cut ends (neither scratched nor flame polished)
Optical fibre, 0.5–1 m long
Light source (reading or microscope lamp with non-clear lamp bulb)
Ray optics kit: lamp, holder and stand, housing shield, metal plate with slit in it
Power supply, 12 V
Paper, white
Paper, black
Card, white (such as a postcard)
Protractor
Stands, bosses and clamps to hold glass rod, optical fibre and screen

Notes:
The dimensions of the plastic strip are not critical provided it is long compared with its width, and sufficiently thick for a light ray to be seen in it.
   RS Components Ltd supply a suitable fibre optic cable under stock number 368–047. Maplin Electronics also supply a suitable cable in 0.5 m lengths.

Experiment a

The ray of light is directed through the curved surface of the block along a radius. In this way the ray will be undeviated as it passes into the block. One way to achieve this is to mark the middle of the flat edge and then direct the ray at the mark. The angle of incidence of the ray falling on the back, flat surface is increased and it is noted that at first a refracted ray passes out into the air on the other side of the block. At the same time **some** of the light is internally reflected. As the angle of refraction approaches 90° the proportion of light reflected internally increases. At a particular angle of incidence, the critical angle, the angle of refraction is 90°. For angles of incidence greater than this, all the light is reflected internally in the block and the light ray emerges again from the curved face.

Experiment b

A light ray is directed into the short side of a clear plastic strip. By adjusting the angle of entry, a light ray can be made to travel down the strip by total internal reflection.

Experiment c

A piece of white card is flooded with light from the lamp. This acts as the source of light for the glass rod. Light can be seen emerging from the end of the glass rod at all angles. The black paper acts as a background against which the end of the rod can be viewed.

Experiment d

Experiment c is repeated using a length of optical fibre. The end of the fibre can be directly illuminated by the lamp. A small patch of light will be seen to emerge from the far end. This can be seen by directing the end of the fibre at a sheet of white paper. Bending the fibre is seen to have no effect on its ability to pass light along its length.

   Further details of this and other experiments with optical fibres will be found in the ASE/SCSST publication *Optical fibres in school physics*. (See Further information.)

Demonstration experiments

Section P13.2:   Reflection and refraction of sound

REQUIREMENTS

Hard surface (such as a wall)
2 tubes, cardboard (internal diameter not less than 7 cm)
Clock, watch, or metronome with a loud "tick"
Balloon filled with carbon dioxide

The cardboard tubes are used to direct the sound at the hard surface and then to pick up the reflection as shown in figure **P15**.

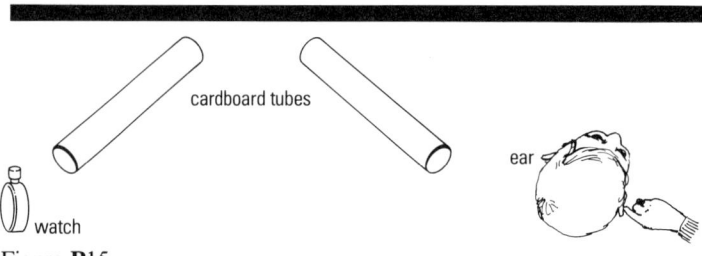

Figure **P15**

A balloon filled with carbon dioxide gas can act as a "sound lens". The arrangement of the equipment is shown in figure **P16**. Careful adjustment of distances is necessary if the demonstration is to be effective. Trial and error will be needed as the precise distances depend on the curvature of the balloon. Try 2 m between clock and ear to start with. Interposing the balloon will make the "tick" seem louder.

Figure **P16**

Further information

Nuffield Science 13 to 16
Seeing and light and *Hearing and sound*. These two modules give an idea of the sort of background expected from the previous year 3 course. Either may provide suitable additional revision material.

Revised Nuffield Physics
Pupils' text and *Teachers' guide Year 3* Chapter 2 "Optics". This material also provides an idea of the background that might be expected to the work in Chapter **P13**.
   Pupils' text and *Teachers' guide Year 3* Chapter 3 "Light and colour". Pages 85–9 of the pupils' text and pages 94–8 of the teachers' guide give details of experiments on the reflection and refraction of light.

Experimenting with Industry
"Optical fibres in school physics". This booklet, number 2 in the Experimenting with Industry series published by the Association for Science Education for the Standing Conference on Schools' Science and Technology, is primarily intended for work with sixth forms but provides interesting background information on optical fibres.

Chapter P14   Making waves
Energy transfer without matter transfer

Purposes

Knowledge and understanding

At the end of this chapter all pupils should:

1 know the meanings of the terms wavelength, frequency, and wave speed

2 understand that a wave transfers energy without transferring matter

3 understand that energy is transferred in the direction in which the wave travels

4 be able to distinguish between transverse and longitudinal waves and appreciate the circumstances in which either or both might occur

5 appreciate that through their behaviour both light and sound are examples of wave motions.

In addition, those pupils aiming for higher grades should:

6 understand some of the properties of waves that distinguish this form of energy transfer from energy transfer accompanying the transfer of matter

7 be able to use the equation:
wave speed = wavelength × frequency
in simple applications.

Processes and problem solving

Graphical and symbolic representation
The representation of waves in two dimensions as a series of lines is used in several places in this chapter. Pupils do not always seem to relate such diagrams directly to the wave behaviour they represent. For example, each line represents the same part of each succeeding wave – perhaps the crest. Thus waves of constant wavelength must be represented as a sequence of equally spaced lines. If the wavelength changes (as when a water wave passes into a shallow region) there is a corresponding change in the separation of these lines.

Using apparatus and measuring instruments
Rulers and protractors will have to be used in assessing the way the direction of a reflected wave is related to the direction of the incident wave.

Observation
To get the most out of this chapter, careful observation of the behaviour of waves on a stretched spring (or rubber tubing) and in a ripple tank will be required.

Interpretation and application
Interpretation of other energy transfer phenomena, such as light, in terms of waves is the main concern of Chapter P15. Nevertheless, pupils are encouraged to see links between wave behaviour and the behaviour of light as they carry out their investigations in this chapter (for example, in Worksheet **P14B** "Waves meet a barrier").

Planning investigations
A quantitative relationship between the directions of the incident and reflected waves is not essential to the rest of the course. Consequently this has been made

the subject of an open-ended investigation for more able pupils only, in Worksheet **P14B**.

A further opportunity for planning an experiment is given by question 11 in the pupils' book.

Problem solving

There are rather fewer problem-solving opportunities in this chapter than in others. The reason for this is that an understanding of waves themselves is required **before** they can be seen to be a possible solution to other problems (such as the behaviour of light). This is one of the very rare occasions in Physics where it seems to be essential to produce a "solution in search of a problem"!

Timing

5 periods.

Suggested routes

Most of the work of this chapter (see figure **P17**) could be tackled by all pupils. The wave equation $v = f\lambda$ could be omitted by those who find the mathematics involved too difficult. The work at the end of section **P14.4**, which looks at what happens to the wavelength and the frequency of waves when the wave speed changes, could also be omitted.

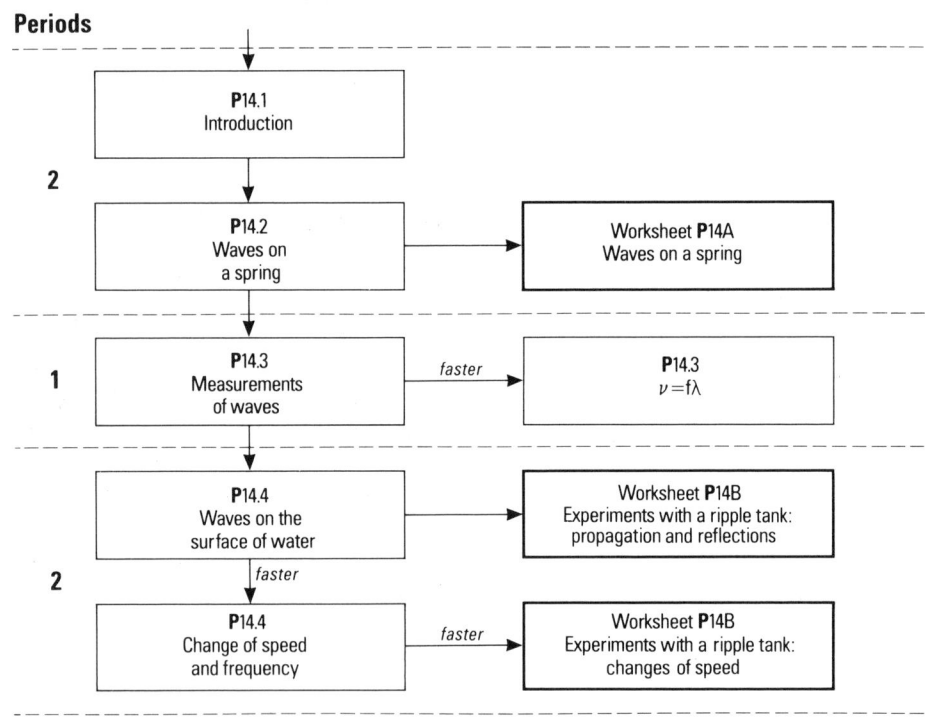

Figure **P17**

Opportunities for co-ordination

In the introduction to "wave pulses" the word "pulse" is likened to the use of the same word in Biology. The flow of blood is described in Chapter **B8** of the Biology pupils' book. It needs to be said, however, that a human pulse is caused by the heart **moving** blood round the body; wave pulses represent a transfer of energy but no transfer of material is involved.

Notes and answers

The study of wave motion is one of the easiest and most practically-based pieces of work found in elementary physics courses. Even so, its appeal to boys and girls is not uniform. Many enjoy the practical work involved, but others find it dull as it does not seem related to any obvious manifestations in their everyday world. By moving work on waves to a point when the use of wave models can be considered it is hoped that this chapter can be given a more universal appeal. It may help to refer back to Chapter **P13** and ask "What **is** light?" and "What **is** sound?", and then to say that an answer to these questions, which we shall find in Chapter **P15**, requires us first to know something about waves.

P14.1   Waves on the sea shore

The introduction relates wave motion to an experience common to many pupils – sea waves. In discussing sea waves it seems worth making the point that their rolling motion makes them untypical. Sea waves have an association with water rushing up the beach – and thus the waves are seen to carry the water forward – but it is just the opposite idea that is important; waves transfer energy without transporting matter.

Questions 1 and 2 encourage pupils to think generally about the nature of wave motion.

P14.2   Waves on a spring

It is worth spending a little while looking at waves on a rope or spring. Such wave motion enables the relationship between the "wave" and the movement of the material carrying it to be studied. If pupils can do their own experiments, they will inevitably set up standing waves. The effect can be simply explained without pursuing it in detail – its complexity makes clear the need to experiment with pulses rather than with continuous waves.

The pupils' book relates waves on a spring to the possibility of waves in solids, liquids and gases, and calls on some work from Chapters **P1** and **P2**. It then describes the meaning to be associated with "wave pulse". The helpfulness and dangers of comparing this with the "pulse" in a human body have already been mentioned.

Not much more than a double period should be spent on sections **P14.1** and **P14.2**.

P14.3   Measurements of waves

A single period can be devoted to the basic wave nomenclature and establishing the relationship between speed, wavelength and frequency. This latter could be omitted by some, to give more time on the first two sections, or on the last one.

Answers to selected questions

5a 400 cm/s; **b** 40 cm.

6 4 Hz.

7 1.5 km.

P14.4   Waves on the surface of water

This section is concerned with waves in a ripple tank. It should not be necessary to spend more than a double period on the work. Those familiar with the ripple tank will note that the continuous wave generator need not be used at all. Much more useful experimenting can be done with the finger or a small water "dropper" to make circular waves, or a rod to produce straight waves. Only the investigation into what happens when waves change speed may benefit from the use of a continuous wave generator. Question 14 refers to such a generator and pupils may be helped in answering it by seeing one in action.

Questions 8–10 and 13–14 should be done at the same time as the ripple tank experiments. No formal record of the ripple tank work is expected – the answers to the questions will provide a suitable record.

Diffraction of waves is introduced – it is an easy effect to see and is as unique to wave motion as wave interference (which is omitted). At this level pupils often confuse the words "refraction" and "diffraction". To avoid this, the word "refraction" is omitted when discussing the change of direction of waves. Diffraction, together with questions 11 and 12, enables some contrast to be made between wave and particle behaviour, without formally setting these up as alternative models of energy transfer.

The behaviour of waves with change of speed can be investigated with roller-generated pulses, but teachers may well feel this is better demonstrated with a continuous wave generator. If so, it is important to avoid spurious diffraction and standing wave effects. This is a case where the only worthwhile demonstration is a good one! This piece of work and the associated questions may be omitted by less able pupils.

Answers to selected questions

9b The reflected part of the wave should "fit into" the circle of the incident wave.

13 Dimensions have been given to encourage careful drawing. It is commonplace to find pupils making "changes" in wavelength in drawings of diffracted waves after they have passed through an aperture.

14 The plate edge is situated between ripple 6 and ripple 7; the plate is to the left of the drawing.

15 The expected phrases or words are, successively, "move up and down", "shallow", "up and down motion", "shallow side of the edge", "deep", "frequency".

16 The ratio of the wavelengths is 3 to 2; the answer is therefore 14 cm/s.

Practical work

Worksheet P14A   Waves on a spring

REQUIREMENTS

Each group of pupils will need:
"Slinky" spring
Sticky tape (to mark coils)

The procedure to be followed is detailed in the worksheet.

Worksheet P14B   Experiments with a ripple tank

REQUIREMENTS

Each group of pupils will need:
Ripple tank kit
Power supply for ripple tank
Sheet of white paper
Ruler, 0.5 m
Protractor

The procedure to be followed is detailed in the worksheet. Failure to use a lamp with the correct filament is a common reason for poor ripple visibility. Any lamp will not do. Special lamps with the correct filament are provided for ripple tank work (item 47 in the Nuffield *Guide to apparatus*).

Demonstration experiments

Sections P14.1 and P14.2:   Watching water waves

It may be helpful to have a rectangular tank half filled with water and a wave "paddle" to show waves travelling over the surface of water. (See Revised Nuffield Physics *Teachers' guide Year 3*, page 8.) Optionally, the experiments in Worksheet **P14A** can be demonstrated.

Section P14.4:   Refraction of ripples

A ripple tank, set up for demonstration with a continuous wave generator, may be useful to show the change of direction of waves as they pass into a shallower region.

Further information

Revised Nuffield Physics
Pupils' text and *Teachers' guide Year 3*: Chapter 1 "Waves".
This chapter covers more ground than the present Chapter **P14**. However, it is full of helpful advice on the use of "Slinky" springs and ripple tanks.

Nuffield Science 13 to16
Vibrations, waves and colour. Chapters 1–4 of this module provide an alternative approach to the work of Chapter **P14**. The first two chapters in the module are about vibrations. Some of this work comes into Chapter **P4** "Motion". These two chapters cannot be entirely omitted, however, as they are used to introduce terms such as "frequency" and "amplitude".

Chapter P15   Making use of waves
Light, sound and earthquakes

Purposes

Knowledge and understanding

At the end of this chapter all pupils should:

1 understand that wave motion is a useful way of describing and explaining phenomena such as light and sound

2 be able to identify wavelength with colour and have some appreciation of the nature of colour vision, including primary and secondary colours

3 appreciate that light is a part of a wide band of wavelengths called the electromagnetic spectrum, and appreciate some of the uses of various parts of that spectrum

4 understand how to interpret the transmission of sound in air as a wave motion.

In addition, those pupils aiming for higher grades should:

5 understand that diffraction and the speed of light in glass, in relation to that in air, are both evidence for the wave nature of light

6 appreciate how energy can be transferred from waves and how it is possible to be selective in making that transfer

7 appreciate why earthquakes involve the passage of waves through the Earth.

Processes and problem solving

Graphical and symbolic representation
Question 15 makes use of graph plotting and extracting data from graphs. Worksheet **P15E** asks for a chart of the electromagnetic spectrum to be drawn.

Using apparatus and measuring instruments
Worksheet **P15A** asks for some care in setting up a good light spectrum.

Observation
Worksheets **P15B**, **P15C** and **P15D** are concerned with careful observation of effects involving colour.

Interpretation and application
Worksheets **P15B**, **P15C** and **P15D** involve the interpretation of observations in terms of some basic rules of colour mixing.

Planning investigations
Worksheet **P15A** asks pupils to plan and carry out their own investigation.

Problem solving
The underlying theme of this chapter is the use of waves to describe the behaviour of several different manifestations of energy transfer. All of these are presented as problems to which the wave model provides a solution. This approach steers a middle course between one which simply **describes** the phenomena in terms of waves and one which sets up **more than one possible solution** and seeks to distinguish between them.

Other more specific problem-solving opportunities are:

● Questions 1 and 18, which require a pencil-and-paper answer to experimental problems.
● Worksheet **P15A**, which sets pupils the task of resolving Newton's problem of whether colour is created by a prism or is a part of white light.
● Questions 15, 16 and 17, which ask pupils to extract data from a given set of experimental results related to the performance of a microwave cooker, and ask a series of questions about its efficiency. These questions are intended for the most able pupils.

Timing

7 periods.

Suggested routes

The flow chart in figure **P18** divides the contents of the chapter into three levels of difficulty. Essentially two different routes through the material of this chapter have been suggested. A third level of difficulty is provided for the fastest pupils by some questions on the transfer of energy from waves.

Even within work intended for all pupils there are options depending on the potential level of understanding of the pupils. For example, investigative, problem-solving opportunities are provided in Worksheet **P15A**. These may not be appropriate for some pupils and may be omitted. Others may find the problem too hard to solve unaided and for them a Help sheet is provided. Similarly, while all pupils can gain some appreciation of the electromagnetic spectrum, the production of a chart using a logarithmic scale will be too difficult for some.

Periods   (The total time spent on this chapter should not exceed 7 periods)   **Periods**

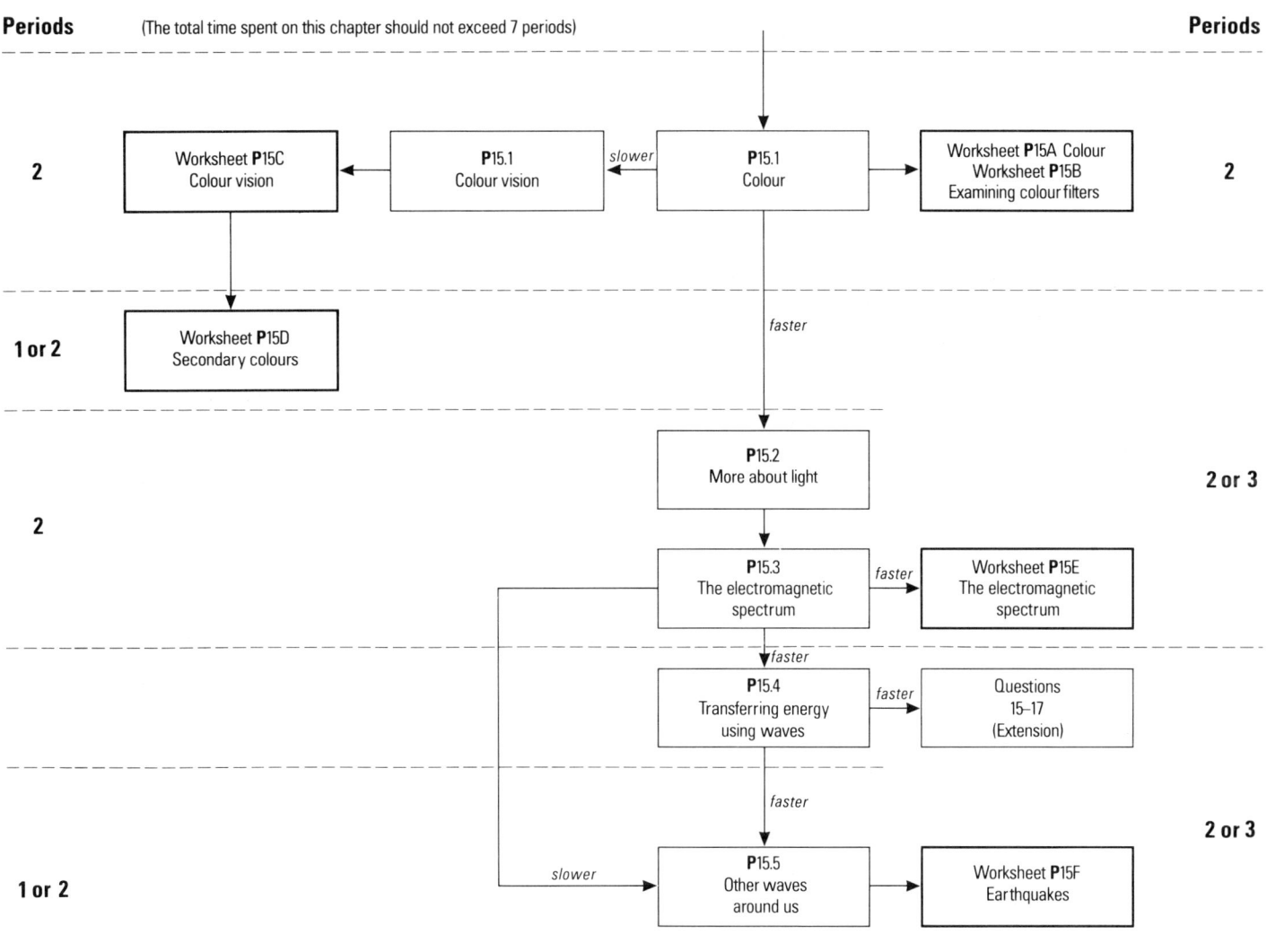

Figure **P**18

Opportunities for co-ordination

Section **P**15.1 "Colour" is complemented by Chapter **C**11 "Dyes and dyeing" in the Chemistry pupils' book. There are other, less direct, links with pupils' work in Chemistry, such as the importance of colour in using indicators to test for acidity and alkalinity. This forms a part of Chapter **C**12 "Chemicals in the medicine cupboard" and Chapter **C**15 "Soil".

The selective absorption of colours is a fundamental part of photosynthesis. Photosynthesis is studied by pupils early in their Biology course (Chapter **B**3 "Light and life"). They will have used the idea that chlorophyll selectively absorbs colours from white light. Against this background an investigation into whether the colours emerging from a prism are a part of the white light falling on it, or are "made" by the prism might appear to lose some weight. This need not be so. The investigation is an important one and it is certainly commonplace in the development of scientific ideas that "logical" gaps are filled in long after a particular conclusion has been accepted. (Millikan's work on the electron is a well-known example.) The important feature here is one of presentation. Pupils have already used the idea that the colours are a part of white light and this has to be acknowledged. It remains a useful exercise to answer the question "Can we **prove** experimentally that this is so?"

X-rays – part of the electromagnetic spectrum – are also studied by the pupils in Chemistry. Chapter C5 "Materials and structures" looks at X-ray crystallography and gives an autobiographical account of Sir Lawrence Bragg's work.

The work on earthquakes will have indirect links with the study of the rocks of the earth which forms a part of several Chemistry chapters – in particular Chapter C4 "Chemicals and rocks" and Chapter C15 "Soil".

Notes and answers

P15.1 Colour

The chapter begins with an investigation into colour. For less able pupils investigations into colour can occupy half the total time available (three or four periods). All pupils should have the opportunity of setting up their own spectrum and doing some colour mixing. However, many of the suggested experiments are more spectacular if carried out in a well-darkened room, using slide projectors carrying colour filters. If this is done, it is well worth spending some time adjusting the intensity of the light from each projector to be nearly the same. The intensity of the "blue" light will be lowest and it may be necessary to cut down the light from the other projectors by adding extra filters or running the lamps on a Variac. Trouble is, however, amply repaid.

Answers to selected questions

1 This requires a prism to analyse the light that has passed through the filter.

2, 3 and **4**. The answers to these questions can all be derived from practical work with colour.

5 This can be demonstrated by overlapping, say, blue and red filters – nothing is transmitted. Many books on photography provide more details of the process of producing colour photographs but the details are very complicated.

P15.2 More about light

There will not be time to spend much more than a single period justifying the fact that we understand light to be a wave motion. No attempt is made to present incontrovertible evidence for this – rather the standpoint adopted is, "Many people understand light to be a wave. Is its behaviour, as we know it, consistent with this idea?"

A discussion of the speed of light is a more advanced option. The experiment measuring the speed of light down an optical fibre uses sophisticated equipment and is, of course, optional. This would seem to be a case where a description on its own can provide some useful experimental data, as the experiment is quite easy, in principle, to understand. However, if it can be set up, so much the better. Details are given in the demonstration experiments section.

Answers to selected questions

6 Red light will have the longest wavelength.

7 Red light is spread out most by a diffraction grating. This is "opposite" to the prism, where blue light is deflected the most.

8 Light must travel slower in glass.

9 Light takes 500 s to travel from the Sun to Earth – about 8 minutes.

10 3.8×10^{13} km.

P15.3   The electromagnetic spectrum

This section deals with the electromagnetic spectrum and centres around Worksheet **P15E**. The worksheet not only asks pupils to prepare their own chart of the electromagnetic spectrum, but also introduces them to the logarithmic scale – seen simply as a device for coping with numbers which occupy a large range. It may be useful to have some additional information on the electromagnetic spectrum available, as pupils may need this in preparing their own chart.

Answers to selected questions

11a 1 000 000 nm to the mm; **b** 500 nm.

P15.4   Transferring energy using waves

This section is an alternative to extended work on colour. It is based around a class experiment designed to show the transfer of energy from a wave to an oscillator. Experimentally it is shown that substantial energy transfer only takes place when the wave frequency matches the natural frequency of the oscillator. This is, of course, part of the whole phenomenon of resonance. However, no terms of this sort are introduced here. The fact of energy transfer is accepted empirically and then applied to such diverse applications as radio reception and microwave cookers.

It is tempting to go further with this work and link it back to colour. However, this involves energy level transitions in which electrons and atoms move from one natural state of vibration to another. Over-simplification could do more harm than good. Even with the microwave cooker there should be no attempt to add unnecessary detail. The "vibration" involved is actually a rotation and it will not be obvious to children that this takes place at some preferred frequency. Despite these difficulties, the fact of resonant energy transfer seems worth including as giving a further important (and commonly observed) aspect of energy transfer.

Questions 15–17 need, for their answers, a knowledge of the relationship between voltage, current and power. This is dealt with in Chapter **P17**, so it might be a good idea to return to these questions later – perhaps as a form of revision.

Answers to selected questions

12 and **14** These questions should be answered after the demonstration experiment has been seen.

15c 33°C; 23°C.
d 260–270 s. The second part of **d** reinforces the comparison between extrapolation and interpolation made in Chapter **P2**.
e 48 300 J.
f 65 000 J.
g No, **f** is bigger – not all the microwave energy is being absorbed by the water.
h 230 V × 5.9 A = 1357 W – yes, it is in good agreement.
i i 48 per cent; ii 36 per cent.
j The experiment could, for example, be repeated for a larger volume of water; different containers could also be used.

16a 155 400 J; **b** 200 000 J; **c** 78 per cent;
d These figures suggest that it is more efficient to heat water in an electric kettle.

17a 3×10^8 m/s; **b** 0.12 m (or 12 cm).

P15.5 Other waves around us

It is not easy to demonstrate the diffraction of sound waves and the variation of their speed in media other than air. It is difficult to separate diffraction effects from other factors leading to the spreading out of sound – such as reflections. On the other hand, it is obvious that sound is associated with a vibrating source and it is easy to see how a "sound" wave could travel through air. If pupils have studied sound in year 3, they may already be familiar with the idea that sound is a "push-pull" wave motion in air.

Worksheet P15F encourages pupils to look at something of the nature and consequences of earthquakes, treated as a wave. Earthquakes and volcanoes feature in many geography courses, where the emphasis tends to be on geographical distribution and with theories of plate tectonics. This worksheet is complementary to that and puts more emphasis on the wave-like nature of earthquakes.

Answers to selected questions

19a 11.3 m; 0.034 m.

b Room dimensions are usually smaller than 11 m. The "bass response" of room and loudspeaker decreases as the size of the room decreases, once room dimensions are less than the wavelength of the sound.

Practical work

Worksheet P15A   Colour

REQUIREMENTS

(The following equipment is part of the Nuffield Physics Ray Optics Kit.)

Each group of pupils will need:
Ray optics kit: lamp, holder and stand, lamp shield, 2 metal plates, each with a single slit in it, plano-cylindrical lens, $+7D$
Power supply, 12 V
2 prisms, each $60°$
Screen

Note:
Examine the filaments of the lamps and replace any whose filaments are not straight and vertical. It will not be possible to produce a pure spectrum of this size from a crooked filament.

The procedure to be followed is detailed in the worksheet.

Worksheet P15B   Examining colour filters

REQUIREMENTS

Each group of pupils will need:
Ray optics kit: lamp, holder and stand, lamp shield, metal plate with single slit in it, plano-cylindrical lens, $+7D$
Power supply, 12 V
Prism, $60°$
Screen
Colour filters, primary blue, green and red, with holder
Coloured objects, various, in the primary colours and some in other colours for more able pupils.

The procedure to be followed is detailed in the Worksheet.

Worksheet P15C   Colour vision

REQUIREMENTS

Each group of pupils will need:
Ray optics kit: lamp, holder and stand, lamp shield, 2 metal plates, each with a single slit
    in it, plano-cylindrical lens, +7D
Power supply, 12 V
2 prisms, each 60°
Screen
Bunsen burner
Stand, boss and clamp
Sodium chloride (common salt)
Wire, steel, about 0.5 mm diameter
2 mirrors, small, plane
Colour filters, yellow, cyan and magenta

The procedure to be followed is detailed in the worksheet. With care and a well-darkened laboratory, surprisingly effective colour mixing can be done on a small scale. However, this is made more impressive if the effect of colour mixing can be demonstrated as well.

Worksheet P15D   Secondary colours

REQUIREMENTS

Each group of pupils will need:
White light source (such as a slide projector)
Colour filters, yellow, cyan and magenta
Coloured objects or brightly coloured paper to make up a picture

The procedure to be followed is detailed in the worksheet. Most of these experiments are best demonstrated to the whole class.

Demonstration experiments

Section P15.1:   Colour mixing

REQUIREMENTS

3 light sources
Colour filters, primary and secondary, for light sources
Screen
Well-darkened laboratory

The three light sources need to project coloured light onto the screen. Ray lamps at the end of cardboard tubes may be used, or three slide projectors if available.

It is necessary to "balance" the intensities of the colours produced by the sources. This can be done by putting more than one filter in, or alternatively by controlling the voltage to each lamp through a Variac or rheostat, if this can be done without damage to the projector.

A great deal more detail about this and all the other experiments described in the worksheets will be found in the Revised Nuffield Physics *Teachers' guide Year 3.*

Section P15.2:   Speed of light in an optical fibre

This is an optional experiment which some schools may care to include in the work of this chapter. The equipment used forms a part of the Revised Nuffield A-level Physics course and a complete set is sold by at least one of the leading equipment manufacturers. Once set up, the experiment works easily and well, and its results are easy to interpret. Nevertheless, the necessary equipment is expensive and schools may not wish to buy it simply to perform this experiment.

REQUIREMENTS

Oscilloscope, double beam
Speed of light apparatus
Metre rule
Leads

The detailed procedure for this experiment will be found in the booklet "Optical fibres in school physics". (See the Further information section.) Equipment manufacturers producing a kit of parts also give detailed instructions.

Section P15.4:   Forced oscillations in a spring-tethered trolley

REQUIREMENTS

Dynamics trolley
Runway for trolley
2 stands
Springs, disposable
Spring, long and heavy, or length of rubber tubing

Note:
A heavy spring is much the best. The mass of the rubber tubing will have to be increased by filling it with sand if this is to be used instead.

The set up is illustrated in figure 15.22 in the pupils' book. This experiment needs setting up beforehand and the number of springs attaching the trolley to the retort stands should be adjusted so that the trolley responds to a wave arriving at 1 or 2 hertz. Attach three springs "in series" to each end of the trolley to give adequate amplitude. To obtain the right frequency it will be necessary to have two or three such sets of springs "in parallel" on each side of the trolley. With a little practice it is possible to demonstrate quite clearly the way in which the trolley will only take up energy at one particular frequency of wave oscillation. The system is quite "sharply tuned" – careful adjustment of the forcing frequency can lead to large amplitude oscillations of the trolley.

Further information

Nuffield Science 13 to 16
Vibrations, waves and colour. Parts of this module cover much the same ground as the present chapter, but in a rather different order. Chapters 1 and 2 (vibrations), Chapters 5 and 6 (colour), Chapter 7 (the electromagnetic spectrum) and Chapter 8 (earthquakes, ocean waves and energy from the Sun) could be used as an alternative and sometimes simpler approach to the work of this section. Worksheet P15E has been based on work in *Vibrations, waves and colour.*

Revised Nuffield Physics
Pupils' text Year 3: Chapter 2 "Optics". The section headed "Spectrum and colour" (pages 98–105) gives a great deal of detail concerning experiments on colour. Most of the experiments described in the worksheets have been drawn from here. In addition, details of different demonstrations, not included in the selection offered here, will be found; schools may like to include these in the work of section **P15.1**.

"Optical fibres in school physics"
This booklet is number 2 in the *Experimenting with Industry* series published by the Association for Science Education for the Standing Conference on Schools' Science and Technology. Pages 17–20 give the details of an experiment designed to measure the speed of light in an optical fibre.

Topic P5 | Electricity

Introduction

The importance of electricity in our lives has led to this being the longest topic in the Physics course. It is also the hardest. Only the effects of "using electricity" can be directly experienced. Matter, force, motion, even waves are things we can either sense or see. Even the transfer of energy (as when we get tired after "working") can be more directly experienced than electricity. It is this intangibility that makes the understanding of electricity especially difficult.

In starting this topic, it is assumed that pupils will all have had some experience of wiring up a simple circuit – to light a lamp, say. They may well have used an ammeter to measure an electric current. However, it is also assumed that many pupils will not have understood many of the things they have already seen. Consequently the first sections of Chapter P16 provide an opportunity for going over what may be for many pupils "old ground". The amount of time spent on this will depend on the pupils' understanding and ability. Certainly there will be no point in sacrificing understanding in order to take in the more advanced ideas in the rest of Chapters P16 and P17. Alternative routes have been provided in both chapters so that emphasis can be given to simple qualitative ideas if this seems more appropriate for some pupils.

Chapter P16 "Using electricity" is concerned with electric current. It seeks to establish the idea that much of what we call "electricity" is to do with electric **charge** moving round closed loops of wires and components – things we refer to as **circuits**. Chapter P17 "Energy and electricity" takes the story further. The flow of an electric current is associated with the transfer of energy – from the electricity supply to elsewhere. This chapter looks at the meaning of "voltage" and its relationship with electric power. Chapter P18 "Making use of electricity" shows how an electric current can produce a magnetic force which can be used to drive motors. Reversing this effect, the chapter goes on to show how dynamos enable the electrical transfer of energy from fuels to other uses.

Chapter P19 "Making pictures with electricity" looks more closely at the nature of electric charge. Chapter P20 "Control" is concerned with the way electricity can be used not only to help us do things by transferring energy where it is needed, but also to control this transfer of energy. This leads, via a discussion of simple switches, to some elementary electronics. Finally, Chapter P21 "Communication" is concerned with the way in which electricity is used in telephone and radio communication systems.

Timing

40 periods, as follows:

Chapter P16 Using electricity	6 periods
Chapter P17 Energy and electricity	9 periods
Chapter P18 Making use of electricity	9 periods
Chapter P19 Making pictures with electricity	4 periods
Chapter P20 Control	6 periods
Chapter P21 Communication	6 periods

Note on use of the word "electricity"

The frequent use of the word "electricity" rather than the more specific phrases "electric charge", "electric current", or even "energy" needs some explanation.

The word "electricity" is in common use. If pupils are to make any sense of the ideas we associate with the study and use of electricity then it is important that they link these with their everyday language and their preconceived ideas. In everyday usage, the word "electricity" may take on several different meanings:

1 It may refer generally to a group of related phenomena, as when we speak of the study of light, or dynamics.

2 It may refer to the energy source that provides the electric current, as in the words "electricity supply".

3 It may refer to the energy we can transfer via an electric current, as when we refer to "using electricity".

4 It may be a loose way of referring to electric charge, as when we say "we depend more and more on electricity to transfer energy from fuels to where we need it."

In the pupils' book, all of these usages will be found where they seem to help clarify the ideas being developed by linking them to everyday experience and usage. However, in view of the fact that the word "electricity" is a loose translation of either "energy associated with electric charge" or "electric charge" itself, phrases such as "electricity generators" or "making electricity" have been avoided where possible, since neither charge, nor energy, can be **made**.

Chapter P16   Using electricity
Electric power and electric currents

Purposes

Knowledge and understanding

At the end of this chapter all pupils should:

1 appreciate the need for a complete circuit when making use of electricity, and recognize that electricity is a means of transferring energy

2 appreciate that energy can be transferred by an electric current, and that the current can be measured by an ammeter

3 be able to apply some of these ideas to the safe use of electricity.

In addition, those pupils aiming for higher grades should:

4 know that an electric current is a flow of electric charge

5 know that electric charge is measured in coulombs, and that a flow rate of one coulomb per second is called one ampere

6 appreciate that electric charge produced by friction is the same in nature as the charge which, moving round a circuit, produces an electric current

7 understand that the readings on ammeters in simple and branching circuits support the idea that the behaviour of electricity in a circuit is analogous to the behaviour of currents of, for instance, liquids in pipes.

Processes and problem solving

Graphical and symbolic representation

The ability to recognize and use an agreed set of symbols to represent circuit components is an important skill. So is the ability to draw and interpret circuit diagrams.

Using apparatus and measuring instruments

This chapter makes use of ammeters, and pupils have to learn both to read ammeter scales accurately and to interpret these scales in terms of the ammeter's inherent range. They also have to be able to wire up circuits from circuit diagrams and make them work.

Observation

Careful reading of ammeters is essential to interpreting the meaning of these readings.

Interpretation and application

Observations of a moving charged ball and of ammeter readings are important in interpreting the moving charge nature of electric current flow. Electric circuit phenomena are interpreted in terms of models of water flow.

Planning investigations

Opportunities for investigations are not suggested in this chapter, which is more concerned with the problems posed by simple electrical behaviour.

Problem solving

The chapter is concerned with the overall problem of interpreting simple electrical circuit behaviour. Representing this as depending on a flow of charge is seen as a possible answer to the problem.

At a simple practical level, a chance to apply elementary ideas is given in an experiment to find out why a torch is not lighting, and to sort some fuses into those that will work and those that will not (Worksheet **P16B**). For more able pupils, taking ammeter readings in a complicated branching circuit provides the opportunity to see that these readings relate to each other in the way expected if the ammeters are measuring a flow of electric charge (Experiment 3 on Worksheet **P16C**).

Timing

6 periods.

Suggested routes

The flow diagram in figure **P19** (over the page) divides the contents of the chapter into two levels of difficulty. In essence, more able pupils ought to be able to cope with all the ideas in this chapter, but may not do all of Worksheets **P16A** and **P16B** if they are to complete the chapter within the allotted time. Less able pupils will need to spend more time on simple circuits. They can omit the work linking electrostatic charge to electric currents, and can also omit Worksheet **P16C** and the associated section in the pupils' book.

Opportunities for co-ordination

Chapter **C14** "Batteries" looks in detail at the way energy is transferred inside an electric cell. Work on this chapter will almost certainly come after pupils have studied Chapters **P16** and **P17**. Their future work on the chemistry of electric cells can usefully be referred to when studying both this chapter and Chapter **P17**.

Periods

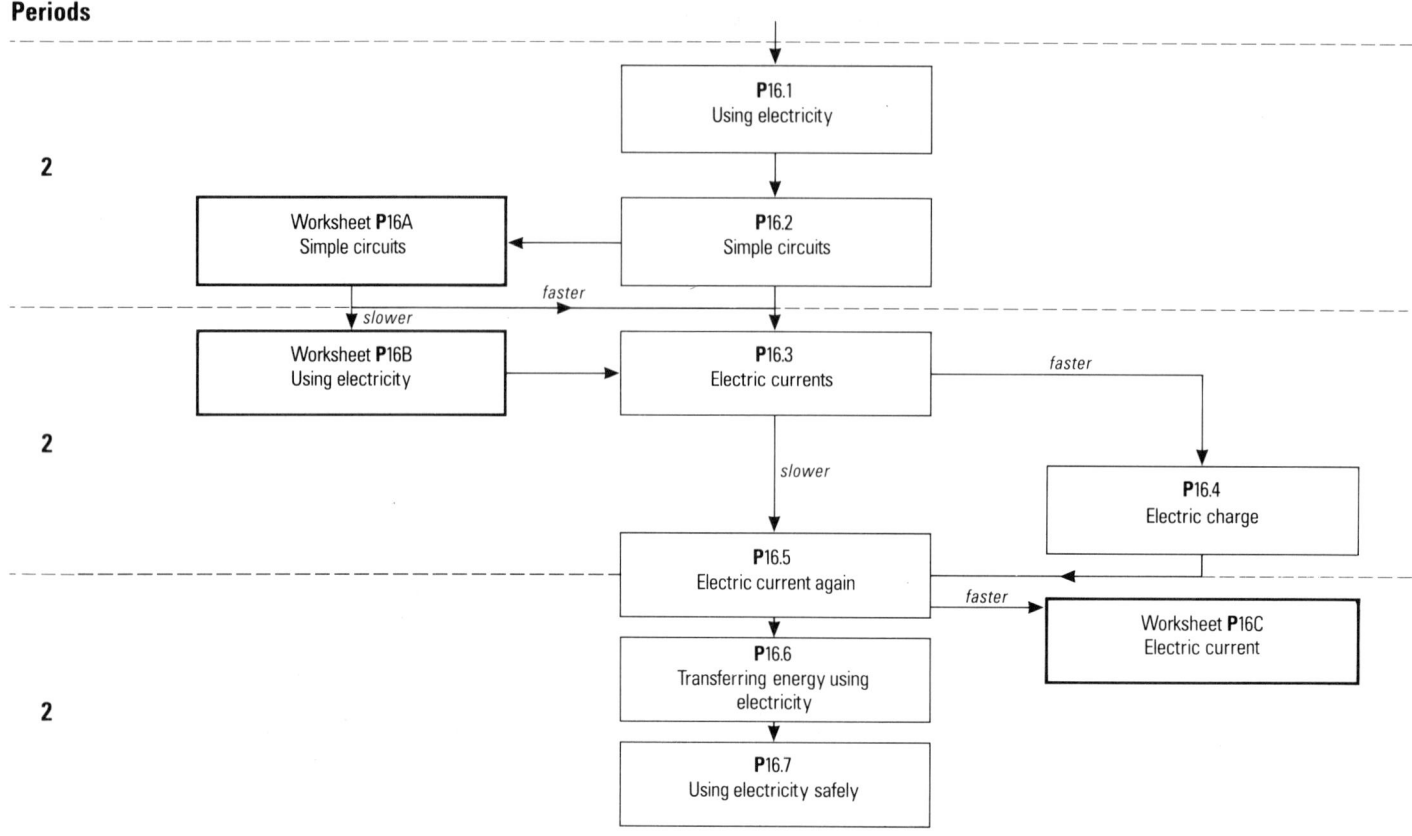

Figure **P**19

Notes and answers

P16.1   Using electricity

The chapter starts by looking at the everyday use of electricity and asking some questions about it. Why is electricity often said to be dangerous? What do the labels found on all electrical appliances mean?

Attention is directed to the "power rating" given on such labels and some questions link this to earlier work on power in Chapter **P**8. The acceptance of power values of electrical appliances as being "what the label reads" is central to the development of electrical ideas in this chapter and in Chapter **P**17. It serves to relate electrical phenomena to other, more readily understood, phenomena involving energy transfer. It also helps the understanding of the meanings of both "amperes" and "volts". No circular argument is involved here, for while it may well be true that manufacturers have calculated these powers from "volts × amperes", they could in principle be measured directly.

Answers to selected questions

4a Electric cookers do not, of course, always work at full power. Even if all the rings and the oven were switched on, the average power used would be much less than the maximum power (11 000 W in this case), due to the operation of temperature control devices.
b The input power is the power actually drawn from the supply; the output power relates to the (maximum) output to the speakers.
c This question revises the link between power and energy. Karen is quite right to suppose that a refrigerator will use much less energy – the refrigeration unit only works intermittently in response to thermostatic controls.

P16.2 Simple circuits

This short section revises ideas about simple circuits which pupils should already have met. However, two worksheets are provided (Worksheets **P16A** and **P16B**) which can provide more extensive practical experience for those who need it.

P16.3 Electric currents

This section introduces the main question posed by this chapter: "What happens in an electric circuit?". Two "mains" devices of different powers are connected to the mains supply via ammeters, and the readings of the ammeters are compared. These are seen to be related in the same way as the "power ratings". The higher power device is transferring energy more quickly. This suggests a simple explanation of energy being transferred from the supply by something that is flowing round the circuit – something we call the electric charge. Ammeters read this flow of charge in units called amperes. For some pupils this may be sufficient explanation. They could go on to section **P16.5** to look more closely at the meaning to be attached to the phrase "electric current". Others will benefit by a closer look, first, at electric charge.

Answer to selected question

8 The circuits may well be demonstrated. Pictures are included here to give pupils practice in drawing circuits and in reading ammeters. Many pupils find this difficult and the question could be supplemented by further examples of (low-voltage) circuits laid out in the laboratory.

P16.4 Electric charge

This section introduces pupils to electrostatic charging, which has obvious direct links with ions and electrons. Both of these are important concepts in later work in Physics and Chemistry. Charging by friction is a process of charge separation. This point is illustrated in figure 16.10a in the pupils' book but is not elaborated.

By using a Van de Graaff generator to produce the charge separation, it can be shown that these charges, when moving, will deflect an ammeter just like the charges from a battery. They are the same in all respects.

If a coulombmeter is available it is well worth using it to measure the charge on a charged polythene rod. The tiny amount of charge on the rod can be contrasted with the amount of charge flowing in a low-voltage circuit containing, say, a 12 V, 5 W lamp.

Answer to selected question

10 It would be necessary to transfer some charge from the black terminal of the battery to, say, an insulated conductor and then see if it repelled a charged polythene rod. This can be demonstrated using an EHT power supply.

P16.5 Electric current again

This section emphasizes that current is rate of flow of charge, not speed of charge. An analogy is drawn between electric currents and the flow of water in rivers and streams.

The section goes on to look at the readings of ammeters in series and branching circuits and investigates whether these readings are consistent with measurements of electric currents. This latter section could be omitted by pupils who have spent some time on the more elementary parts of the chapter. Worksheet **P16C** provides some experiments the pupils can do to test these ideas.

Answers to selected questions

12 2 A.

13 7200 C.

14 50 s.

15 A_1: 9 A; A_2: 5 A; A_3: 3 A.

16a A_2 and A_3 will both read 2 A.
b The lamp will dim; the readings on both A_1 and A_3 will both be 1 A.

P16.6 Transferring energy using electricity

This short section compares the transfer of energy using electric currents with the transfer of energy that can come about by pumping water round a closed circuit. In both cases energy transfer takes place as soon as the pump or battery is switched into the circuit. Energy is transferred **via** the water or the charges; it is not first **given** to the water or charges which **then** carry the energy round the circuit. This point is re-emphasized in Chapter **P**17. It is particularly important in understanding how alternating currents can be used to transfer energy. In an electric circuit work is done by the electric field set up by the battery pushing the charges through whatever circuit component is transferring the energy.

The section concludes by looking at how energy can be transferred to the surroundings by a wire, heated by an electric current. It shows how the temperature of a wire is related to the rate at which this transfer of energy has to take place. This leads to a discussion of one of the dangers associated with the use of electricity – the danger of fire. Fuses are discussed briefly.

Answer to selected question

18 This question compares the gain and loss of energy by a hot wire with the equilibrium of an evaporating liquid. The analogy with shoppers in a supermarket is again relevant. If the rate at which people enter a supermarket increases, the number of shoppers in the supermarket will increase until, once again, they are leaving at the rate at which they are entering.

P16.7 Using electricity safely

The issue of safety (which started this chapter) is continued in this final section by looking at the value of "earthing".

Practical work

Worksheet P16A Simple circuits

REQUIREMENTS

For Experiments 1 and 2 each group of pupils will need:
2 lamps, 1.25 V, 0.25 A MES
2 lamp holders, MES
Cell, 1.5 V, in holder
Ammeter, 1 A d.c.
Connecting wires

Notes:
There is no particular reason why these component values should be adhered to. All that is needed is to match bulbs to batteries and holders, and to supply an ammeter of appropriate full-scale deflection. The main point is that "circuit boards" should not be used, except as cell holders. These would produce more constraints on how the circuit can be wired up than is required in these experiments.

For Experiments 3 and 4 each group of pupils will need:
3 cells, 1.5 V, in holders
2 lamps, 3.5 V, 0.3 A MES
2 lamp holders, MES
Switch
Ammeter, 1 A d.c.
Connecting wires
Resistor, 15 Ω, 10 W wire wound (see Notes)
Resistor, 4.7 Ω, 7 W, labelled "X" (see Notes)
Resistor, 10 Ω, 7 W, labelled "Y" (see Notes)
Rheostat, 15 Ω

Notes:
Any resistors of a rated power suitable for the circuit will do, provided they are 15 Ω or less.

Again the circuits are meant to be wired up with connecting wires, rather than on a circuit board. "Clip component holders" developed for Nuffield A-level Physics are a convenient means of providing small components like resistors with sockets.

All four of these experiments could be set up as "stations" for a circus of experiments. As far as possible, pupils should work individually at setting up the circuits.

Worksheet P16B   Using electricity in the home

REQUIREMENTS

Each group of pupils will need:
Torch, electric, working
Torch, electric, not working
Plug, 13 A mains
Wire, 3-core mains, with one end wrapped in insulating tape
Fuses, a selection, some of which have "blown"
Cell, 1.5 V, in holder
Lamp, 1.25 V, 0.25 A MES
Lamp holder, MES
Screwdriver
Wire strippers

Note:
A Worcester circuit board, with fittings, could be used as an alternative to the cell and lamp arrangement for testing fuses.

The length of 3-core flex should be terminated in some way so that a wired-up plug cannot be pushed into a socket, leaving bare wire exposed at the other end! The connecting cable could be ready wired to a mains component such as a lamp in a battery holder, or terminated as described above. Even so, pupils should be warned not to "try out" the newly wired plug for themselves. It is recommended that the power to the bench sockets is turned off during this work.

Worksheet P16C   Electric currents

REQUIREMENTS

For Experiments 1 and 2 each group of pupils will need:
3 cells, 1.5 V, in holders
Rheostat, 15 Ω
2 lamps, 1.25 V, 0.25 A MES
2 lamp holders, MES
3 ammeters, 1 A d.c.
Connecting wires

For Experiment 3 (optional) each group of pupils will need:
Power supply, 12 V d.c. (or rechargeable cells)
Resistor, 15 Ω, 10 W wire wound
2 rheostats, 15 Ω
2 lamps, 12 V, 5 W SBC
2 lamp holders, SBC
6 ammeters, 1 A d.c.
Connecting wires

These circuits use so many ammeters that it will only be possible for one or two to be set up at a time.

A suitable circuit for Experiment 3 is given in figure **P20** (over the page). Adjust the rheostats so that the readings on A_2 and A_3 are different from each other, and from the reading on A_1. The total of A_1, A_2 and A_3 must not exceed 1 A (the maximum reading on A_6).

There is, of course, no need to stick to these values – an alternative circuit will do, but for the purposes of this exercise all the ammeters should be alike and should have the same full-scale deflection.

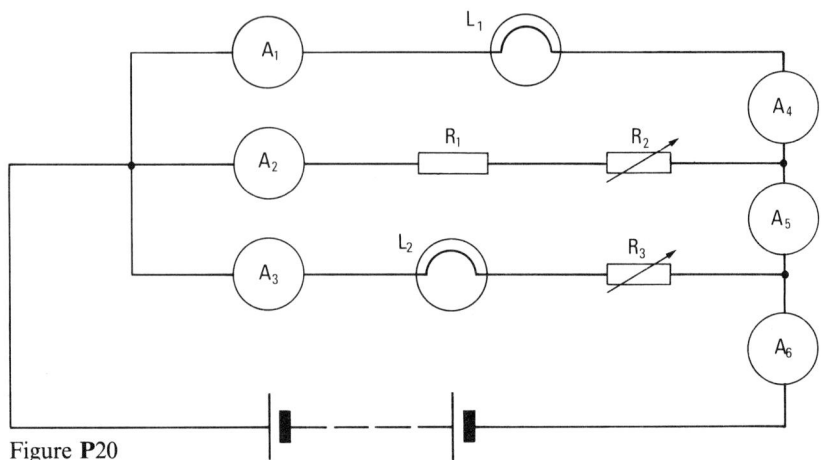

Figure **P20**

Demonstration experiments

Section P16.1:   Electric data plates

REQUIREMENTS

One or more appliances on which the data plate can be seen and read (an electric iron is illustrated in the pupils' book).

Section P16.3:   Comparing electric currents (Optional)

REQUIREMENTS

Mains electric fire, 1000 W
Mains lamp, 100 W
2 ammeters, 5 A a.c.
2 mains connecting blocks

It is best to keep to the same full-scale deflection for each ammeter in order to emphasize the difference in currents.

Section P16.4:   Electric charge

REQUIREMENTS

Experiment A:
2 electrostatics rods, polythene
Duster
Electrostatics rod, acetate
Stirrups to hang up rods
2 stands, bosses and clamps
Thread, nylon

Experiment B:
Van de Graaff generator
Ping-pong ball coated with Aquadag and
  suspended on a nylon thread
2 circular brass plates, 125 mm diameter,
  on insulating handles
3 stands, bosses and clamps
Sensitive ammeter (see Note)
EHT power pack (optional)
Connecting wires

Note:
An ammeter or galvanometer reading currents of a few microamperes is required. Any such meter can be used. A light-beam galvanometer or electronic equivalent can be used.

The equipment is set up as in figure 16.12 in the pupils' book. The plates should be placed about 10 cm apart. When the Van de Graaff generator is started, the conducting ball should move back and forth between the plates, and the ammeter should record a current flowing. It is important to place the ammeter so that one terminal is connected to the "earth" terminal of the Van de Graaff generator. In this way the potential difference between the wire of the galvanometer coil and its surroundings is made as small as possible. Van de Graaff generators produce very high potential differences – higher than the galvanometer coil insulation is designed to withstand.

Changing the plate separation changes the rate at which the conducting ball shuttles between the plates – and consequently the current recorded by the galvanometer changes.

Optionally, the Van de Graaff machine can be replaced by an EHT power pack (giving 5000 V). The experiment can be repeated with the same result. This shows that charges from both sources are the same in nature.

Section P16.6:   Water circuit

REQUIREMENTS

Water circuit board
4 cells, 1.5 V, in holders
Electric motor, 6 V
Connecting wires

If available, this can be demonstrated here. It is an expensive piece of equipment to buy for just this one demonstration.

The behaviour of the water circuit can be compared with a similar circuit consisting of a battery and a motor.

Further information

Revised Nuffield Physics
Teachers' guide and *Pupils' text Year 4:* Chapter 11 "Electric circuits with voltmeters". The treatment in Revised Nuffield Physics is different in many ways from the approach used in this chapter, but on reading it will be clear that many of the ideas here are drawn from the original Nuffield approach. Only the first part of the chapter is relevant to this one. The rest is related more closely to material in Chapter **P17**.

Nuffield Science 13 to 16
Charged particles The experiments in section **P16.4** have been drawn from this module. Other experiments using a Van de Graaff generator are also described in the module and schools might like to use these, given time.

Chapter P17   Energy and electricity
Voltage and electrical resistance

Purposes

Knowledge and understanding

At the end of this chapter all pupils should:

1 understand that the "voltage" of an electrical supply is a measure of the energy it can transfer elsewhere

2 be able to use the relationship: power = voltage × current

3 understand the meaning of the term "electrical resistance", and know that the resistance of a component (in ohms) = voltage across component (in volts)/current through component (in amperes)

4 appreciate some of the factors affecting the resistance of a component.

In addition, those pupils aiming for higher grades should:

5 be able to apply the idea of voltage numerically to circuits containing more than one component, and apply correctly the term "potential difference"

6 know that a potential difference of one volt is equivalent to an energy difference of one joule per coulomb of charge

7 appreciate the experimental evidence leading to Ohm's Law.

Processes and problem solving

Graphical and symbolic representation
This chapter continues the use of circuit symbols and circuit diagrams started in Chapter **P**16.

Using apparatus and measuring instruments
To the use of ammeters introduced in Chapter **P**16 is now added the correct use of a voltmeter.

Observation
Observational work is directed to the correct and careful reading of ammeters and voltmeters.

Interpretation and application
Those pupils who cover the work in the latter part of section **P**17.2 will need to link together previously established ideas about current, charge and power in order to understand the volt as a "joule per coulomb". Ideas about energy and power in electrical circuits are applied to a wide range of devices which "use electricity". For all pupils, the chapter ends by applying all these electrical ideas to the design of a hair drier.

Planning investigations
More able pupils are given the opportunity to apply ideas about power and electricity in planning and carrying out an investigation into the efficiency of a small electric motor (Worksheet **P**17C). A further opportunity for investigation is provided in Worksheet **P**17E, where pupils are asked to explore how the resistance of a small lamp varies with the voltage across it. Problems on electrical resistance form the basis of investigations at two levels. Less able pupils try to see if there is any relationship between a wire's length and its resistance (Worksheet **P**17F); more able pupils are set the task of finding a relationship between current and potential difference (p.d.) (Worksheet **P**17G).

Problem solving
There are a number of problem-solving questions in the pupils' book designed to consolidate their understanding of the volt. More generally, the factors affecting the resistance of a piece of wire emerge as answers to a problem about the power of a light bulb: measurements of current and voltage when the light bulb is cold predict a power output much larger than that found in practice. It is in seeking an answer to this question that Ohm's Law and the conditions under which it can be used emerge.

Timing   9 periods.

Suggested routes

The flow diagram in figure **P**21 divides the contents of this chapter into three levels of difficulty. All pupils cover the same ideas, however. Differentiation is a matter of the depth to which they can develop them. No one pupil will attempt the experiments described in all seven worksheets. Some experiments are meant as alternative treatments of the same idea.

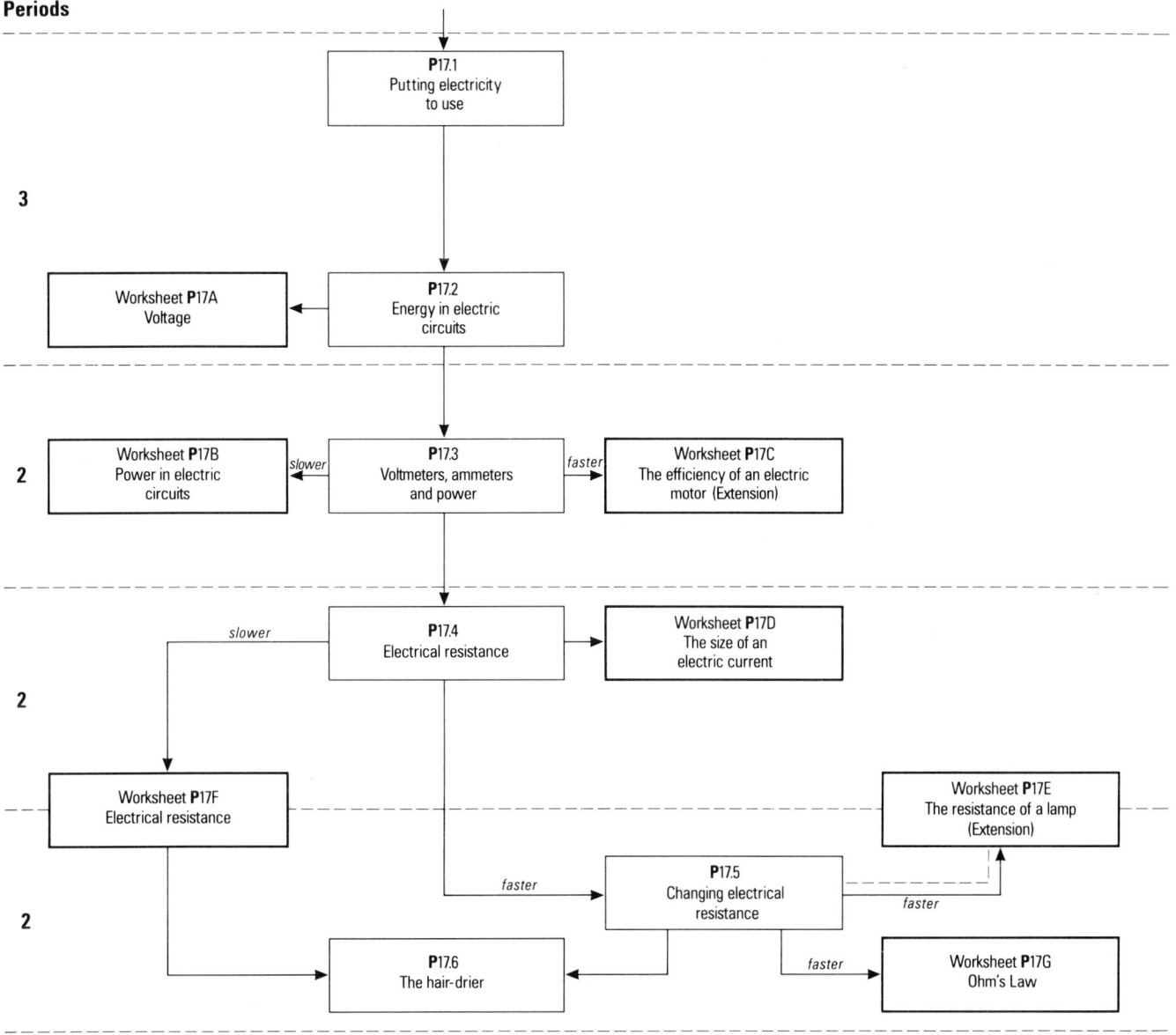

Periods

Figure **P**21

Opportunities for co-ordination

There are no direct links between the work of this chapter and work in Biology and Chemistry.

Notes and answers

This chapter is concerned with energy transfer and electrical resistance. Understanding the process of energy transfer and its measurement in volts is one of the hardest parts of work in electricity at an elementary level. Yet it has to be understood if electric circuits are to be used sensibly and correctly. This introductory note is concerned with the background to the approach to energy transfer adopted in the pupils' book.

In the notes on Chapter **P16** it was stated briefly that every attempt had been made to **avoid** the suggestion that energy was transferred in electrical circuits by a process in which the cell, battery, or power supply delivers this energy to electrical charges, which **then** transfer the energy elsewhere. This is not the mechanism of energy transfer and to suggest that it is can lead to many difficulties. For example, it can be shown that electrons move very slowly indeed round circuits even when there is a large current flowing. If the supply delivers energy to the electrons which then transfer it elsewhere, pupils can legitimately ask why, for example, lights come on as soon as a switch is closed. It is also not at all clear how these moving charges can carry energy.

In fact the transfer of energy in an electrical circuit involves work, in the same way as many other energy transfers. Forces within the conducting wires act on the charges in them and move those charges. Energy is transferred and can in principle be measured (as force on charges × distance moved in the direction of the force). The force comes from an electric field set up by the cell, battery, or power supply in the connecting wires and components in the circuit. The force acts on the charge in the wires and components. If there is a complete circuit, this force can move the charges and energy is transferred.

With this picture in mind it becomes clear how energy can be transferred in a circuit carrying alternating or direct current (a.c. or d.c.). Charges do not have to travel **from the supply** to transfer energy. It is sufficient that there is an electrical force capable of moving the charges in the connecting wires and components. Whether this force continually changes direction (as in a.c.) or is in one direction only (as in d.c.) is immaterial to its ability to transfer energy.

The charges act in some ways like the piston in a steam engine, or the oil in a hydraulic system. They are the mechanism which enables forces to do work.

This description of energy transfer in electrical circuits seemed inappropriate to an elementary course as it depends on some understanding of electric fields. Furthermore, these electric forces cannot be directly measured. Even in more advanced work their size is deduced from measurements of potential difference. So in fact we say nothing about the mechanism of energy transfer in electric circuits in the pupils' book and content ourselves with describing a cell's or power supply's "energy capability".

Unfortunately, just knowing something's energy capability does not give us all the information we need when assessing its usefulness for a particular job. As pupils will have seen in the problem of the stair-lift in Chapter **P8**, having a motor which will transfer the necessary energy is not sufficient to lift a person up the stairs. It has to be able to provide the necessary force as well.

Electric batteries, like many other sources of energy, vary in their "strength" as well as their total energy capability. That is, they vary in the electric force they can apply to charges in circuits. The "voltage" of a battery is a way of describing this "strength". This can be seen by comparing two circuits, like those shown in figure **P22**. The first circuit contains a 60 W mains lamp connected to

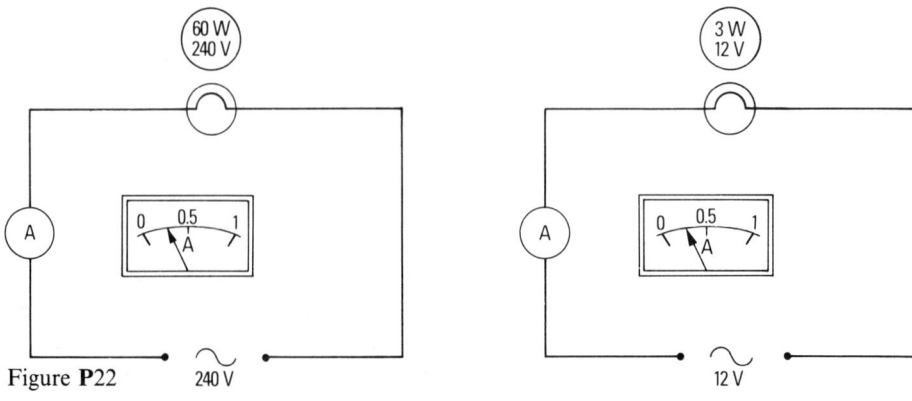

Figure **P22**

the 240 V mains supply. The second circuit contains a 12 V, 3 W lamp connected to a 12 volt battery in an otherwise identical circuit. Identical currents flow in the two circuits. In four seconds, one coulomb of charge will have flowed round both circuits. In terms of electric forces, the force in both circuits will have moved charges the same distance. But in one case 240 J have been transferred and in the other 12 J have been transferred. So the electric force set up by the mains supply is 20 times bigger than that set up by the 12 V supply. Hence a description of the "energy capability" of a supply in terms of the energy it can transfer per coulomb of charge flowing in the circuit gives a measure of the strength of the supply as well as a means of calculating the energy it can transfer.

P17.1 Putting electricity to use

The first section "sets the scene" for the chapter as a whole by surveying a wide range of energy transfers in which electricity is involved. Question 1 is a "comprehension" question which tests understanding of the passage just read.

P17.2 Energy in electric circuits

The first part of this section compares the behaviour of two circuits which carry identical currents. The first contains a 60 W mains lamp connected to the 240 V mains supply. The second contains a 12 V, 3 W lamp connected to a 12 V supply. The energy transferred in the lamps by the time one coulomb of charge has passed through each lamp is calculated on the assumption that the marked powers of the lamps are correct. This leads to numbers identical with those describing the voltages of the supplies from which the lamps are run.

This introduction to the meaning of voltage may be sufficient for some pupils. They can now turn to the section headed "Measuring voltage" on page 267 and do Worksheet P17A.

There is no circularity of argument in this method of using marked power ratings to arrive at voltage. As has been said in the notes on Chapter P16, these powers could in principle be measured directly by transferring energy from the lamp to a known mass of water. More able pupils are given the opportunity in question 8 to devise such an experiment for themselves.

For pupils who will benefit from a closer study of voltage, question 2 gives an opportunity to apply the same arguments to a different pair of light bulbs and question 3 gives some practice in relating energy to voltage and charge.

The next subsection extends the idea of voltage to circuits containing more than one energy-transferring component. The behaviour of lamps in series is compared with that of lamps in parallel. The ideas emerging from this comparison are applied to an investigation of ring main circuits in question 6.

The way the energy transferred from the supply is divided up between components is generalized further in the subsection entitled "Potential difference". This introduces the term "potential difference" because it is particularly appropriate when considering energy transfers in circuits with many components. However, for the rest of the chapter the more colloquial term "voltage" is preferred. While such a policy has the benefit of linking a concept to commonly used terms, it does tend to lead to pupils also talking about "ampage" for current – something that may need to be actively discouraged!

The section concludes with a brief introduction to the use of voltmeters. No attempt is made to explain their working. Worksheet P17A provides a number of experiments in which voltmeters are used and are seen to give the readings that would be expected of such an instrument.

Answers to selected questions

2a 0.05 C/s; **b** 20 s; **c** 2.4 J/s, 0.7 J/s;
d 2.4 J/s × 20 s = 48 J, 0.7 J/s × 20 s = 14 J.

3a 60 s; **b** 180 J; **c** 15 C.

4 The current increases by 3 times (for 3 lamps) and by 4 times (for 4 lamps).

5a 0.25 A; **b** 1.0 A; **c** 10 C, 40 C; **d** 9600 J.

7a 3 J; **b** 4 C; **c** 12 J; **d** 12 J/10 s = 1.2 W.

9 A_1 and A_2: 0.5 A; V: 1 V.

P17.3   Voltmeters, ammeters and power

This section reverses the arguments that lead to the introduction of voltage, and shows how values for power may be derived from the potential difference across a component and the current passing through it.

This work serves to enhance an understanding of the meaning of voltage, so most of the work derives "power" from values of voltage and current by going back to first principles rather than by relying on the equation:
power = voltage × current.

Answers to selected questions

10b 6 J; **c** 2 C; **d** 12 J.

11a 2 J/C; **b** 0.5 C/s; **c** 1 J/s; **d** 1 W; **e** 3 J/C × 0.8 C/s = 2.4 J/s;
f It will be brighter. **g** 2.4 W;
h Power = current × voltage.

12c Maximum power = 240 × 13 = 3120 W;
d i 36 000 W; **ii** 132 MW.

13b 6 V × 0.8 A = 4.8 W.

P17.4   Electrical resistance

This section emphasizes the fact that batteries provide a force which drives a current round a circuit. The factor in a circuit which determines the size of the current is called the electrical resistance of the circuit.

Some of the factors which determine the size of the electrical resistance of pieces of wire are explored using Worksheet **P**17D. After this exploration has been completed, the electrical resistance of a component is defined as being the voltage across the component divided by the current through it. No reference is made at this stage to any relationship between current and voltage. In this way electrical resistance is understood to be a property of any component which passes an electric current. (Those particular components for which the current through them is proportional to the size of the voltage across them have a resistance independent of the current passing through them.)

Answers to selected questions

14a 1 A; **b** 6 A; **c** 3 A.

15 60 Ω.

P17.5 Changing electrical resistance

Sufficient work may already have been done on resistance for some pupils. They can now go on to the final section of the chapter – concerned with the design of an electric hair drier.

The section starts by measuring the electrical resistance of a 60 W mains lamp, using a voltage of only 3 V. The expected output power of the lamp is calculated and found to be over 1000 W. This leads to an exploration of the way the resistance of a light bulb varies with the current passing through it. Data for a 60 W mains lamp is provided in the pupils' book, but pupils themselves are invited to carry out a similar investigation using a 24 W, 12 V lamp.

The results of these investigations show that the resistance of the lamp increases as the current through it increases. This might be due to the wire in the light bulb getting hotter (the obvious explanation). But it might also be that the current through a lamp is not proportional to the voltage across it, even if the temperature remains constant. This latter point is explored experimentally, using Worksheet P17G. The graph plotting necessary in this experiment to show that current is in fact proportional to voltage leads to a further comment about experimental error and the need to draw best straight lines.

The investigation leads to a statement of Ohm's Law, true if the temperature of the wire does not change. That it is the change in the temperature of the wire that leads to the variation in the resistance of a light bulb is confirmed by removing the glass envelope from a 24 W, 12 V lamp and showing that if the filament is kept at a constant temperature (by immersing it in water) then the resistance is the same no matter what current passes through it.

Answers to selected questions

19a 3 A; **b i** 1 A; **ii** 120 A;
c Probably not, in the case of the 240 V supply, as the resistor's temperature would increase.

P17.6 The design of a hair drier

The section concludes by applying ideas of current, voltage, resistance and power to a design problem – that of designing a hair drier. The problem is that of getting the energy transferred to the wire away fast enough, so that neither the air nor the wire gets too hot.

Answers to selected questions

20a 1200 W / 240 V = 5 A, 350 W / 240 V = 1.46 A;
b 48 Ω, 164 Ω.

Practical work

Worksheet P17A   Voltage

REQUIREMENTS

Each group of pupils will need:
2 cells, 1.5 V, in holders
2 lamps, 1.25 V, 0.25 A MES
2 lamp holders, MES
Voltmeter, 5 V d.c.
Connecting wires

The procedure to be followed is detailed in the worksheet. Circuit boards could be used for these introductory experiments.

Worksheet P17B   Power in electric circuits

REQUIREMENTS

Each group of pupils will need:
2 cells, 1.5 V, in holders
Lamp, 2.5 V, 0.2 A MES
Lamp holder, MES
Electric motor, 6 V d.c.
Voltmeter, 5 V d.c.
Ammeter, 1 A d.c.
Connecting wires

The procedure to be followed is detailed in the worksheet. It is not essential to stick to any of the values listed. A larger motor and a more powerful lamp could be used with adjustments to the power supply and meters as necessary. All that is necessary is to give pupils the opportunity to measure electric power in two different circumstances.

Worksheet P17C   The efficiency of an electric motor

REQUIREMENTS

Each group of pupils will need:
Electric motor, 6 V d.c.
Power supply, 6 V d.c.
or
4 cells, 1.5 V, in holders
Ammeter, 5 A d.c.
Voltmeter, 10 V d.c.
Rheostat, 15 Ω
Switch
Slotted masses, 100 g set
Stopclock
Metre ruler
String
Connecting wires
G-clamp, or similar, to anchor the motor to the bench so it can lift a load

The aim of this investigation is to explore the efficiency of a small electric motor. To do this, pupils will have to measure the input power (multiplying voltage by current) and work out the output power by timing how long it takes the motor to raise a known load a measured distance. More than one factor may affect the efficiency. It will vary with the input power and with the load lifted.

Worksheet **P17C** gives pupils a bare minimum of help. Those who need it can ask for a Help sheet which will give them some assistance with the investigation.

Worksheet P17D   The size of an electric current

REQUIREMENTS

*For Experiment **a** each group of pupils will need:*
5 cells, 1.5 V, in holders
Resistor, 10 Ω, 7 W wire wound
Ammeter, 1 A d.c.
Connecting wires

*For Experiment **b** each group of pupils will need:*
3 cells, 1.5 V, in holders
Wire, resistance, fixed to a board (see Note)
Resistor, 4.7 Ω
Ammeter, 1 A d.c.
Connecting wires

Note:
Eureka resistance wire of diameter 0.28 mm (32 s.w.g.) has a resistance of about 10 Ω per metre. 0.5 m of such a wire would have resistance of about 5 Ω and the current recorded by the ammeter would vary from about 1 A to about 0.5 A.

For Experiment c each group of pupils will need:
3 cells, 1.5 V, in holders
2 wires, resistance, each 0.5 m long, one 0.28 mm in diameter and one 0.56 mm in diameter (see Notes)
Wire, copper, 0.5 m long and 0.56 mm in diameter (see Notes)
Ammeter, 1 A d.c.
Resistor, 4.7 Ω
Connecting wires

Notes:
One wire is the same as that used for Experiment **b** (0.28 mm in diameter, 32 s.w.g.). The other wire needs to be about twice the thickness (0.56 mm in diameter, 24 s.w.g.).

Copper wire 0.56 mm in diameter (24 s.w.g.) has a resistance of less than 0.1 Ω per metre. This should have an almost negligible effect on the meter reading, end to end. This is the point that needs to be made.

The procedure to be followed is detailed in the worksheet. Different equipment can be used, depending on the resources available. The outcome of the experiments is largely qualitative. If component values are changed, a check should be made to see that ammeters cannot be damaged by overloading.

Worksheet P17E   The resistance of a lamp

REQUIREMENTS

Each group of pupils will need:
Power supply, 12 V d.c. variable
Ammeter, 1 A d.c.
Voltmeter, 15 V d.c.
Lamp, 12 V, 24 W SBC
Lamp holder, SBC
Switch
Rheostat, 15 Ω
Connecting wires

Note:
It may be necessary to supply a 0–50 V voltmeter, or a dual-range instrument giving 0–10 V and 0–50 V or similar.

This is another investigative practical for those who cope easily with the work. Again the pupils have to design their own circuit and then take appropriate readings. They may have difficulty in adjusting the current and voltage if they do not have a power pack with continuous voltage control. Ideally they should also be left to work this out for themselves – given sufficient time and careful use of the equipment.

Unusually perhaps (and as in the pupils' book) the graph plotted is resistance (defined as V/I for any particular pair of values) against current. This is consistent with the approach adopted to resistance in the pupils' book.

There is no reason to stick to the values given. It may be more convenient to supply a lamp of different power or voltage. Results which are in essence the same will be produced, but suitable changes will have to be made to the other pieces of equipment.

Worksheet P17F   Electrical resistance

REQUIREMENTS

Each group of pupils will need:
2 cells, 1.5 V, in holders
Ammeter, 1 A d.c.
Voltmeter, 5 V d.c.
Wire, resistance, 0.28 mm in diameter (32 s.w.g.), Eureka, wound into a coil (see Notes)
Wire, resistance, 0.28 mm in diameter (32 s.w.g.), Eureka, mounted on board (see Notes)
Connecting wires

Notes:
The coil can be wound on any suitable small tube, but it should be fastened down onto the tube so that the turns of bare wire do not touch each other. Such a resistor will have a resistance of about 5 Ω. It can be fixed in a clip component holder (already referred to in the notes on Worksheet **P**16A).

The board can be made up using four lengths of 0.28 mm Eureka wire: 60 cm, 45 cm, 30 cm, and 15 cm long.

The procedure to be followed is given on the worksheet.

Worksheet P17G   Ohm's Law

REQUIREMENTS

Each group of pupils will need:
3 cells, 1.5 V, in holders
Rheostat, 15 Ω
Wire, resistance, 0.28 mm in diameter,
Eureka, 0.5 m long (see Note)
Ammeter, 1 A d.c.
Voltmeter, 5 V d.c.
Connecting wires

Note:
It is best to leave the wire loose so that its temperature does not change significantly during the experiment.

The procedure to be followed is detailed in the worksheet. This experiment is open to the traditional objection that the use of a voltmeter to establish Ohm's Law involves a circular argument. However, the voltmeter has been introduced empirically. While pupils cannot help but see that it is in some way related to an ammeter, the calibrations can in principle be checked by an energy transfer experiment which itself would involve no appeal to Ohm's Law.

Demonstration experiments

Section P17.2:   Energy in electric circuits

REQUIREMENTS

Lamp, 60 W mains, in holder
Lamp, 12 V, 3 W, line filament, in holder
Power supply, 12 V a.c.
2 ammeters, 1 A a.c.
Mains connecting block
Connecting wires

Notes:
The comparison of a 60 W mains lamp with a 12 V, 3 W lamp can be demonstrated. A suitable 3 W lamp is available from equipment suppliers as a line filament lamp. It is best to run both lamps from an a.c. supply so that the two ammeters are identical in appearance. The fact that a.c. is used rather than d.c. does not invalidate the argument, and the concept of voltage should be well established before pupils come to recognize the difference between a.c. and d.c. supplies.

   Great care should be taken when wiring ammeters into circuits connected to the mains supply. All connections should be shrouded with insulating material; rubber tubing is very useful for this. No adjustment to connections should be made once the supply has been turned on.

   Lamps in parallel and in series can also be demonstrated using 60 W mains lamps. Again, the same precautions need to be taken when wiring up circuits.

Section P17.5:   Variation of the resistance of a mains lamp with current

REQUIREMENTS

Lamp, 60 W mains
Ammeter, 1 A a.c.
Voltmeter, 300 V a.c.
Variac, to vary input voltage
Connecting wires

In addition to the demonstration experiments, any of the circuits shown in the pupils' book could with advantage be set up in the laboratory. This helps in enabling pupils to relate symbolic drawings of circuits to the "real thing".

Further information	*Revised Nuffield Physics* *Teachers' guide* and *Pupils' text Year 4:* Chapter 11 "Electric circuits with voltmeters", Chapter 12 "Ohm's Law and others", Chapter 13 "Power in electric circuits". All of these chapters contain material relevant to Chapter **P**17. Some of it (particularly the work on power) has been directly drawn upon.
	Nuffield Science 13 to 16 *Circuits.* Chapters 4 to 8 of this module cover much the same ground as Chapter **P**17, and may provide useful alternative ideas, particularly for less able pupils.

Chapter P18   Making use of electricity
Electromagnetism

Purposes

Knowledge and understanding

At the end of this chapter all pupils should:

1 know that forces can act on an electric current when it flows through a magnetic field

2 know that the force on an electric current in a magnetic field is at right angles to the directions of the current and the field

3 be able to apply these ideas in understanding how an electric motor works

4 appreciate that an electric current itself has a magnetic field and that this can be applied to the design of electromagnets and relays.

In addition, those pupils aiming for higher grades should:

5 understand that an electric current can be induced to flow in a wire moving relative to a magnetic field

6 be able to apply this idea to understand how dynamos and alternators work.

Processes and problem solving

Graphical and symbolic representation
The symbolic representation of electric circuits, used in Chapters **P**16 and **P**17, is continued in this chapter.

Using apparatus and measuring instruments
Experimental work in Worksheets **P**18B to **P**18F depends on the ability to use power supplies and ammeters and the ability to wire up a simple series circuit.

Observation
Much of this unit depends on careful observation, in particular: Worksheet **P**18B "Electric currents and forces", Worksheet **P**18D "Magnetism and electricity", and Worksheet **P**18F "Induced currents".

Interpretation and application
The relationships between magnetic fields and electric currents, and between the movement of wires in a magnetic field and the current induced, are supported by a careful analysis of what has been seen. In both cases a wide range of observations is reduced, after discussion, to one simple relationship. The relationship between magnetic fields and currents is derived in response to a need

to understand the working of an electric motor. The magnetic field surrounding a current-carrying wire is made the basis of an investigation into electromagnets. Finally, electromagnetic induction leads to an understanding of how dynamos and alternators work, and to an introduction to a.c.

Planning and carrying out investigations

There are two areas in which pupils can plan their own investigations. The investigation into electromagnets is open-ended. Pupils not going on to the work on electromagnetic induction should be able to spend some time on this investigation.

The fastest pupils may have time to plan an investigation on the performance of their model motor, as suggested at the end of Worksheet **P18C**. Apart from those opportunities mentioned here, pupils undertake a guided investigation into the relationship between forces, fields and currents (Worksheet **P18B**), and into induced currents (Worksheet **P18F**).

Problem solving

Apart from the problem-solving exercises implicit in the investigations, finding out how an electric motor works is posed as a problem which this chapter sets out to solve. Building a model motor is itself a construction problem, although pupils are given considerable guidance.

Almost all the written questions are of the problem-solving type, designed to consolidate understanding of the main principles developed in the chapter.

Timing

9 periods.

Suggested routes

The flow diagram in figure **P23** (opposite) divides the contents of this chapter into three levels of difficulty. The main differentiation is between the two lower levels. Pupils having most difficulty with this unit are advised to concentrate on the work up to and including the design of an electromagnet in the first part of section **P18.5**.

Quicker pupils will be able to cover the introduction to electromagnetic induction in sections **P18.6** and **P18.7**. An alternative (and easier) introduction to electromagnetic induction will be found in the first part of Chapter **P11**. Pupils who cover all this chapter are provided with an alternative investigation when the work of Chapter **P11** is covered. All pupils study transformers in Chapter **P11**.

Opportunities for co-ordination

There are no direct links between the work in this chapter and work in Biology and Chemistry.

Notes and answers

Much of this work has been drawn from the Revised Nuffield Physics course. Originally intended for year 3, experience suggests that pupils' understanding of this work more nearly matches their obvious enjoyment if the work is postponed to a later year.

Transformers have been included in Chapter **P11** where they arise naturally in the discussion of problems related to the transmission of electric currents over large distances. This is a part of the topic on Energy, but both Chapters **P11** and **P12** are postponed until late in the course.

P18.1   Electric motors

This unit of work starts with the electric motor as a common mode of utilizing electricity. The advantages and disadvantages of electric motors can be investigated using Worksheet **P18A** "Electric Vehicles". This worksheet is

Periods

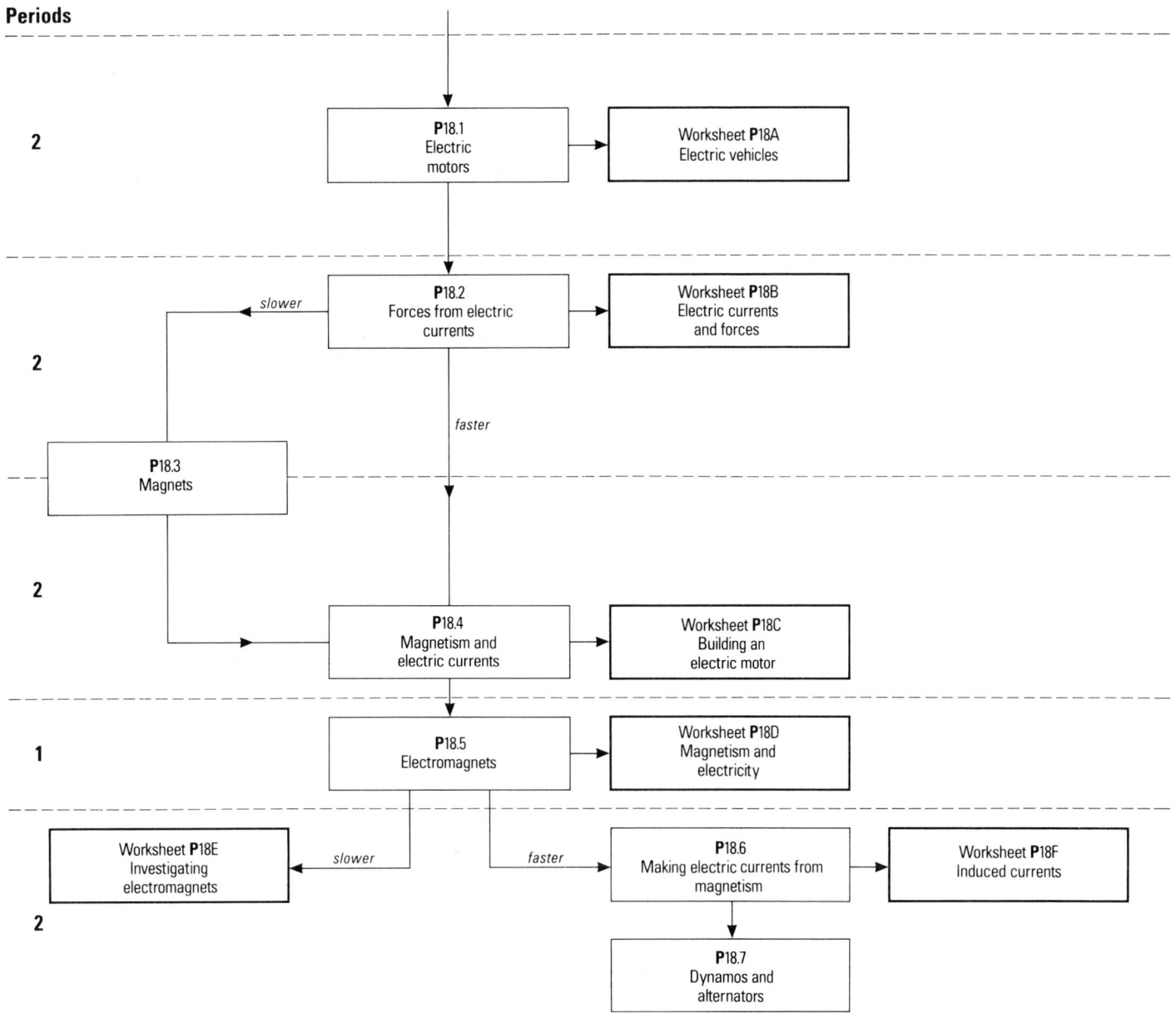

Figure **P23**

designed to occupy a **maximum** time of 2 periods, but can be restricted to a shorter time by appropriate choice of questions. Teaching notes to accompany the worksheet are given in the section on practical work.

Examples of commercial motors quoted in the following work invariably run from a.c. There might seem to be a problem in reconciling this with the treatment of motors adopted here. However, many domestic motors use brushes and commutators, just like d.c. motors. They run in this way because the a.c. passes through both the armature and the field coils of the electromagnet. Thus the a.c. nature of the supply is irrelevant to their operation – the current through the armature reverses fifty times per second, but so does the field direction. To explain their operation, it is best to regard them as d.c. motors. This point is not mentioned in the pupils' book, but a bright pupil may need an answer when he or she realizes that the domestic counterparts are running on a.c.

P18.2   Forces from electric currents

This section is based on Worksheet **P18B** which explores how forces can be produced by an electric current. This in turn introduces the magnetic field, extending the field concept already introduced in Chapter **P7**. While demonstrating the principle behind the working of an electric motor, there remain many design problems, such as getting the current into and out of the rotating coil and arranging that the forces on the coil produce continuous rotation.

Before dealing with these problems pupils are given the opportunity to revise ideas about the magnetic fields of permanent magnets which they will have met in an earlier year.

P18.3 Magnets

This section is a short revision of work on magnets that will have been covered in earlier years. Some pupils may wish to repeat some of the experiments. One way to do this is to use Chapter 2 "Magnets" of the Nuffield Science 13 to 16 unit *Magnetism and electricity* referred to in the Further information section.

P18.4 Magnetism and electric currents

This section is the heart of the chapter. It starts by returning to the results obtained from Worksheet **P18B**. The relationships between the direction of the force, the direction of the magnetic field and the direction of the current when the force is a maximum are summarized. The specific relationships summarized by Fleming's Left Hand Rule are not required in order to understand the working of the motor. It is sufficient to know that the force is at right-angles to the plane containing the field and the current, and that if either (but not both) of these directions is reversed, the direction of the force is reversed. However, many pupils feel more comfortable with an explicit knowledge of Fleming's Left Hand Rule and enjoy using it. They should not be denied this comfort if it helps them to understand what is going on!

The section continues by applying these ideas to the design of a simple electric motor, and the commutator is introduced.

Worksheet **P18C** gives details for the construction of a simple electric motor using components from the Westminster Electromagnetic Kit.

P18.5 Electromagnets

Little attention is given in this chapter to the magnetic field surrounding a current. The behaviour of an electric motor is treated in terms of the interaction between an electric current and a magnetic field, not as the interaction between two magnetic fields, as is often the case. The latter interpretation is too sophisticated for present needs and is appropriate only to abler pupils.

There is thus no need to make a detailed exploration of the patterns of the magnetic field surrounding a current-carrying wire. However, the magnetic field within a motor is commonly produced using an electromagnet. This provides an opportunity for an open-ended investigation into the factors affecting the strength of such a magnet (Worksheet **P18E**). The time spent on such an investigation will depend on the ability of the pupils and how much of the rest of the chapter is to be done by them. If the introduction to electromagnetic induction is left until the beginning of Chapter **P11**, then there should be time during this chapter for a thorough investigation into electromagnets. If, however, the pupils are to complete all of this chapter in the time available, the investigation may have to be brief.

This section concludes with a brief account of Oersted's work and uses it to make an important point about scientific discovery. The point made by Bernal in the extract quoted is that many people may well have observed what Oersted did, but only he was able to recognize its significance. The passage is in language which may be "difficult" for the pupils, but their understanding is encouraged by a "comprehension" question (question 11).

Worksheet **P18D** gives details of experiments pupils can do to repeat Oersted's observations and to see the pattern of a magnetic field around a straight wire.

P18.6   Making electric currents from magnetism

This work on induced currents is introduced by seeing what happens to the electric motor working "in reverse" – in other words, wires from the coil are connected to a sensitive meter and the coil is spun manually. This could be done as a class experiment, since both motors and galvanometers will be available. Worksheet **P18F** follows and its general conclusions are argued out with the help of the subsection headed "Induced currents".

The distinction between d.c. and a.c. can be made at this stage. In fact three types of current output are discussed in the pupils' book: d.c. from a cell is a current flowing in one direction which in the short term is of unvarying size if the circuit is not changed. The output from the model motor, however, is a current of varying size, but always in the same direction. If the commutator is replaced with slip rings, the output continually varies in both size and direction. This is best demonstrated at low speed using a centre-zero galvanometer.

P18.7   Dynamos and alternators

The link between commercial dynamos and alternators on the one hand and electromagnetic induction on the other is made via the cycle dynamo. This will probably be done by demonstration and class participation. (Traces from the cycle dynamo on a CRO seem to be more confusing than helpful and are best avoided.) The cycle dynamo introduces two useful points:

1 the rotation of a magnet rather than a coil, and
2 the fact that a.c. is just as good as d.c. when it comes to things like lighting and heating.

This is a good moment to review, with abler pupils, the nature of the process of energy transfer in electrical circuits as discussed in the notes on Chapter **P17**. If the process is seen to involve a force acting on the charges, then it becomes clear that alternating voltages are just as effective as direct voltages in transferring energy.

The importance of dynamos and alternators lies in the way they can be used in the process of transferring the vast amount of energy needed by an industrial society to the place where it is needed. A calculation is included in the pupils' book that shows how small a contribution the energy stored in a car battery can make even to our everyday domestic needs. This calculation may only be of relevance to the more able pupils, but it is a useful application of ideas developed in Chapters **P16** and **P17**. Even so this would be a good opportunity to stress the dependence of an industrial society on very large energy resources, and so form a link between this chapter and the work of Chapters **P11** and **P12**.

The chapter concludes by looking briefly at power station generators. This topic is returned to in Chapter **P11**.

Answer to selected question

18 14 300 A.

Practical work

Worksheet P18A Electric vehicles

Though this worksheet does not involve experiments, the following notes may be helpful.

Questions 1 to 5 revise work from Chapters **P8** (energy) and **P6** (kinetic energy).

Question 7 reminds pupils that there is an energy loss in power stations which has to be taken into account when comparing the efficiencies of electrically driven vehicles and petrol driven vehicles. The data suggests that there is little to choose between the two methods of propulsion when it comes to overall energy losses.

Question 9 highlights one of the major difficulties electric vehicles have to contend with. Even though batteries used for vehicles can be recharged at much higher rates than normal battery recharging requires, they can never be "re-energized" as quickly as a petrol driven vehicle.

One section of the worksheet deals with pollution. As with efficiency, electric vehicles seem to score heavily over petrol vehicles at first glance. But again the problems are really transferred elsewhere. Power stations can cause considerable pollution. However, it might be said that pollution can be much more easily controlled in a few large power stations than in a large number of separate vehicles.

Worksheet P18B Electric currents and forces

REQUIREMENTS

Each group of pupils will need:
Power supply, low-voltage, Westminster type
Support block (see Notes)
Wire, copper, pvc covered, 0.6 mm in diameter, 0.75 m long
Wire, copper, bare, 0.45 mm in diameter, 0.25 m long
Wire, copper, bare, 0.28 mm in diameter, 0.25 m long
Iron yoke
2 slab magnets, Magnadur
Wire strippers

Notes:
All of the experiments included in Worksheets **P**18B to **P**18F make use of items from the Westminster Electromagnetic Kit. Details concerning the low-voltage power supply and the support block used in conjunction with this kit will be found in Revised Nuffield Physics *Teachers' guide Year 3* pages 184–5.

The diagram on Worksheet **P**18B gives an idea of the support block required. Dimensions are not critical. Some varieties of power pack have their terminals in such a position that a support block may not be needed.

The procedure to be followed is detailed in the worksheet.

Worksheet P18C Building an electric motor

REQUIREMENTS

Each group of pupils will need:
Wire, copper, pvc covered
Iron yoke
2 slab magnets, Magnadur
Motor kit: base, 2 split pins, knitting needle, 4 rivets, armature, valve rubber
Sticky tape
Power supply, low-voltage, Westminster type
Wire strippers

Pupils are provided with construction details, but few motors work first time. The usual fault is poor contact between the brushes and the commutator. Revised Nuffield Physics *Pupils' text Year 3* gives some very detailed instructions about ensuring contact here. These have been omitted from the worksheet to avoid overloading it with verbal description. However, teachers are advised to have *Pupils' text Year 3* to hand.

Pupils should be given time to persevere with making their motors work – they get great satisfaction from it. Those fortunate enough to get theirs working quickly can go on to investigate its performance. Such pupils will need the following apparatus.

REQUIREMENTS

Each group of pupils will need:	*Access to:*
Ammeter, 5 A	Balance, 100 g
Voltmeter, 5 V	
Plasticine, to make loads	
String	
Metre ruler	

The procedure they might adopt is that described in Worksheet **P17C**.

Worksheet P18D   Magnetism and electricity

REQUIREMENTS

Each group of pupils will need:
Power supply, low-voltage, Westminster type
Wire, copper, pvc covered, 1 m long
Card and supporting blocks
Plotting compass
Iron filings
Wire strippers

The procedure to be followed is detailed in the worksheet.

Worksheet P18E   Electromagnets

REQUIREMENTS

Each group of pupils will need:
Power supply, low-voltage, Westminster type
Rheostat, 15 Ω
Ammeter, 5 A d.c.
Wire, copper, pvc insulated, 2 m long
Steel rod pieces, 50 mm long or longer (see Note)

Access to:
Force meters, small masses, string, pieces of iron, small iron nails

Note:
Pieces of steel knitting needle can be used. Pupils may want to bundle several together to form a core.

Pupils are expected to invent their own method of measuring the magnetic force of the electromagnet. They could do this by using a force meter to pull off another piece of iron, or by hanging masses on a piece of metal attracted to the electromagnet.

Worksheet P18F   Induced currents

REQUIREMENTS

Each group of pupils will need:
2 magnets, Ticonal
Wire, copper, pvc covered
Galvanometer (see Note)
Iron yoke
2 slab magnets, Magnadur
2 iron C-cores, and a clip to hold them together
Cell, 1.5 V *or* low voltage power supply

Notes:
The major reason for disappointing results in these experiments is lack of a sufficiently sensitive meter. A suitable meter must be capable of responding to currents of a few microamperes. Centre-zero instruments or meters capable of reading a small negative current are not essential, but highly desirable.

The procedure to be followed is detailed in the worksheet.

Demonstration experiments

The majority of the time spent on this chapter will involve pupils in their own experimental work. However, the following items will be useful for demonstration purposes.

REQUIREMENTS

Model motor already made up
Galvanometer, demonstration
Motor, fractional horse-power
Electric drill that can be taken apart
Bicycle dynamo
Bicycle dynamo that can be taken apart

Further information

Revised Nuffield Physics
Teachers' guide Year 3: Chapter 6 "Electromagnetism". The approach to electromagnetism in this chapter is based on that developed by the Nuffield Physics course, for which the Westminster Electromagnetic Kit is available. Teachers are strongly recommended to read relevant sections of this book as it gives more practical detail than can be included in these notes.

Nuffield Science 13 to 16
Magnetism and electricity. This unit could provide an alternative approach to the material in this chapter if teachers felt it more appropriate for their pupils.

Chapter P19   Making pictures with electricity
Electrons

Purposes

Knowledge and understanding

At the end of this chapter all pupils should:

1 appreciate that the behaviour of the thermionic diode can be interpreted in terms of negatively-charged particles given off from a heated tungsten wire

2 appreciate that the electron, as a basic component of the atom, could be the particle carrying an electric current in a thermionic diode, and could also be the particle responsible for carrying charge round an electric circuit

3 understand how this production of electrons from a heated wire has led to the cathode ray oscilloscope and made television possible.

In addition, those pupils aiming for higher grades should:

4 appreciate that a flow of negatively-charged particles (electrons) is the best explanation of the behaviour of a thermionic diode.

Processes and problem solving

Graphical and symbolic representation
The use of circuit symbols is continued in this chapter.

Using apparatus and measuring instruments
Ammeters are used in Worksheet **P19A**. All pupils gain experience of the use of the cathode ray oscilloscope in Worksheet **P19B**.

Observation

Worksheet **P**19A places considerable emphasis on careful observation.

Interpretation and application

Interpreting observations made with the diode is at the centre of this unit. This leads to the electron concept which is then used to interpret earlier observations in electricity.

Planning and carrying out investigations

For pupils who find they have the time there is an investigation into many of the features associated with sound at the end of Worksheet **P**19B.

Problem solving

At higher levels all of the work in this chapter should be developed as a problem-solving activity. The concept of the electron is seen as one solution to the problems posed by the observations made. At the lowest level it at least answers the question "How does a television work?"

Timing   4 or 5 periods.

Suggested routes   The flow diagram in figure **P**24 divides the contents of this chapter into two levels of difficulty. The central point of differentiation is the diode. At the most elementary level this will be treated as no more than an illustration of how an electric current can flow through a vacuum, carried by moving charges. The electron is introduced empirically as the charge carrier in conducting wires and in the vacuum inside a television or a cathode ray tube. All pupils should get an opportunity to familiarize themselves with the use of the cathode ray oscilloscope (CRO).

At a less elementary level it should be possible to give more justification for this picture of charge flow. Observations made with the diode can lead to the question "What carries the current across the tube?" The electron concept can be seen as providing a satisfactory explanation of this and earlier observations in electricity.

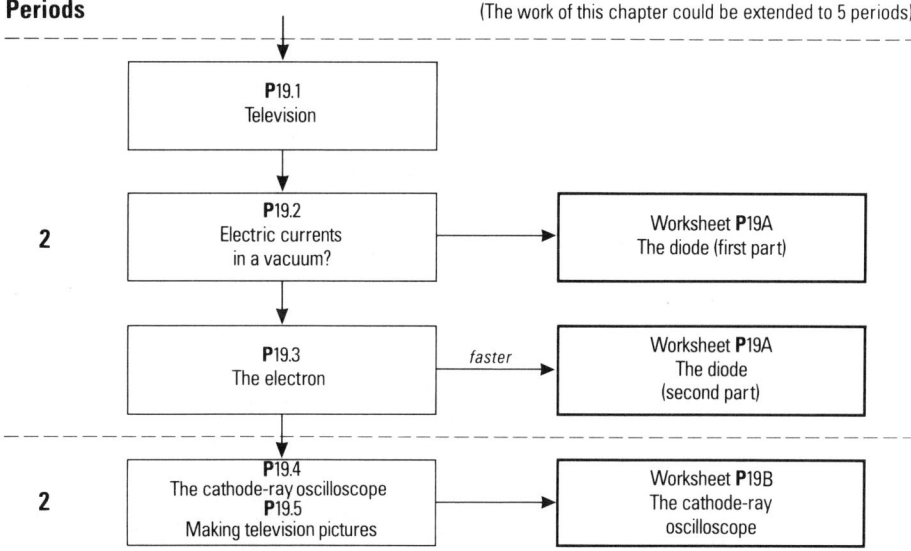

Figure **P**24

Opportunities for co-ordination

The concept of ions as charged atoms is used extensively in Chemistry and in Chapter **P3** of the Physics course. However, the fact that ions are formed by atoms gaining or losing electrons is not taken up in Chemistry until Chapter **C18**, which will be tackled by pupils after they have studied Chapter **P19**.

The work of Chapter **C18** should therefore be seen as a direct development of chemical ideas established in Chapter **C17**, and ideas about the electron established in Chapter **P19**. The work in Physics and Chemistry has been carefully co-ordinated with this progression in mind.

Notes and answers

P19.1   Television

The introduction places the electron within a context which will be familiar to all pupils. Although brief, it is essential to the work and is returned to at the end of the chapter.

P19.2   Electric currents in a vacuum?

The approach to the diode depends very much on the ability of the class. The differentiation between various approaches is detailed in the section on possible routes through this work. No matter what approach is adopted, it is unlikely to take more than a single period. It is anticipated that pupils will see the experiment demonstrated and afterwards read an account of the experiment in their pupils' book. The arguments which relate the observations to an assumed cause are not easy. It is hoped that, by reproducing the observations in this way, pupils will have more opportunity to reflect on their meaning. The description of the results of such an experiment given in the pupils' book is not intended to be a substitute for the pupils seeing the experiment for themselves.

P19.3   The electron

The electron is first introduced into the Physics course in Chapter **P3**, where it forms part of the description of the structure of the nuclear atom. No attempt is made there to justify the description, but it is suggested that ionization could be described in terms of the loss or gain of electrons by an atom. This section shows that the behaviour of the diode valve can be understood in terms of a stream of negatively-charged particles emitted from the hot cathode. The picture of the atom as a positively-charged nucleus surrounded by a cloud of negatively-charged electrons is recalled and it is suggested that the negatively-charged particles in a diode are in fact identical with the electrons surrounding an atom.

If this is so, then some electrons are easily detached from atoms in the formation of ions, as has already been suggested. The existence of these readily detachable electrons can account for the charges that can move freely through metal wires forming an electric current, and for the charging of insulating materials by friction. This short section ends by showing how an "electron gun" is made which provides the electron beam in both cathode ray and television tubes.

P19.4   The cathode ray oscilloscope

A period or maybe more should be allowed for pupils to familiarize themselves with the cathode ray oscilloscope (CRO). The extensive Worksheet **P19B** has been provided in recognition of the fact that some of the more able pupils will in fact find their way round a CRO in a matter of minutes, and will have completed the first three investigations in not much more than fifteen minutes. For them, Investigation 4 provides adequate investigative work. Some schools may not have sufficient class CROs to make this a practical proposition as a class experiment (8 CROs will be required for a class of 32 pupils). Even so, the work should not be omitted. Using a demonstration CRO, pupils can still gain a helpful insight into its use. The Worksheet P19B should still be used as a basis for this (class) investigation.

P19.5   Making television pictures

The chapter closes by showing how an electron beam can be used to make pictures. Particular attention is given to the way the beam can be deflected using magnetic fields. This will give useful revision of the link between electric currents and magnetic fields established in Chapter P18. There is also a link with the use of a magnetic field to deflect beta particles in Chapter P3.

A picture is produced on a television screen by changing the brightness of the spot as the electron beam sweeps over it. This beam modulation can be simulated on some cathode ray oscilloscopes. In such oscilloscopes there is a socket usually labelled "Z modulation" – implying a variation in beam strength perpendicular to the plane of the screen. The application of a suitable alternating voltage to this socket will produce a dotted line on the screen instead of the usual continuous line.

Colour television involves a more complex modulation procedure using a colour mask which produces a screen made up of spots of three primary colours which blend to produce the full colour pictures seen. This can be linked with the earlier work on colour covered in Chapter P15.

Practical work

Worksheet P19A   The diode

This worksheet is for use during a demonstration experiment.

REQUIREMENTS

Diode, hot filament type with stand
Power supply for filament, 6.3 V
Power supply, high tension (HT)
Ammeter, demonstration, 2 mA d.c.
Connecting wires

Notes:
The Teltron demonstration diode on which this description is based has a coil of wire (filament) at one side of the bulb, which is heated by passing a current through it. The other electrode in the glass bulb is a circular disc of metal, about 2 cm in diameter. In the description that follows, this disc of metal is called the "plate", while the coil of wire is called the "filament".

The maximum current from this tube is no more than 1 or 2 mA.

Procedure
Set the diode in the stand and apply 6.3 volts to the filament.

Connect the plate ("anode") in the tube through the demonstration milliammeter to the positive terminal of the power supply. Earth the other terminal of the supply and connect it to one of the filament terminals. The supply should be able to keep the plate at up to a few hundred volts either positive or negative relative to the filament.

Show the action of the tube, first with the filament cold, then with the filament hot.

Whatever the p.d. across the tube, no current flows as long as the filament is not glowing. When the filament is hot, a current flows if the plate is positive. No current flows if the plate is negative.

(More details may be found in Revised Nuffield Physics *Teachers' guide Year 4* from page 243 onwards.)

Warning

Care needs to be taken in handling the high tension power supply. Although the voltage is much lower than that of EHT power supplies, the maximum current of the high tension power supply is much larger. Shrouded 4 mm plugs should be used to make connections. (See also Health and Safety Executive Guidance Note 23 *Electrical safety in schools 18.*)

Worksheet P19B   The cathode ray oscilloscope

REQUIREMENTS

Each group of pupils will need:
Oscilloscope designed for class use
3 cells, 1.5 V, in holders
Power supply, low voltage a.c.
Microphone
Connecting wires

Access to:
Tuning forks and other musical
   instruments for pupils doing
   Investigation 4

Note:
If this work is based on a class demonstration, a larger demonstration CRO should be used. Otherwise, the ancillary equipment will be the same.

The class CRO should be set up so that a bright, focussed spot is formed in the centre of the screen when it is switched on. It should then be switched off before class use. The rest of the details will be found in the worksheet.

Demonstration experiments

Electric and magnetic deflection of electron beams

The precise details of the equipment for the electric and magnetic deflection of an electron beam will depend on the equipment available. The details of equipment given here are for the Teltron fine beam tube. The requirements may differ slightly if other tubes are used (such as the Leybold fine beam tube, or the Teltron *e/m* tube).

Ideally when demonstrating both these experiments and those with the diode, the equipment should be wired up in front of the pupils. Ready-wired experiments that work "at the touch of a switch" are second best and can simply seem a confusing mass of wires to even the brightest pupils.

REQUIREMENTS

Fine beam tube, with stand
Helmholtz coils for the tube
Power supply, high tension (HT)
2 rheostats, 15 Ω
Power supply, 12 V d.c. smoothed, or
   12 V battery
2 slab magnets, Magnadur
Magnet, bar
Ammeter, 1 A a.c.
Ammeter, 1 A d.c.

Notes:
The a.c. and d.c. ammeters are only used when setting up the apparatus. A 5 kΩ, 10 W resistor may be used as a safeguard for the tube anode circuit if the power supply does not have current limited output.

A 200 or 300 V d.c. voltmeter will be needed if one is not included in the power supply.

Procedure

Notes on setting up this and similar tubes are provided by their manufacturers. They should be read and their instructions should be followed carefully.

Set up the tube and connect **both** deflecting plates to the anode.

Switch on the heater of the electron gun which fires a horizontal beam. Adjust the current to 0.3 A. Wait until the cathode has become hot.

Raise the gun voltage (anode voltage) until the beam hits the end of the tube. Use 80 to 120 V for the demonstration.

1 Bring a bar magnet near the tube while the pupils watch.

2 Bring a magnet with face-poles (such as a Magnadur slab magnet) near the tube, taking care not to make sharp contact with the glass.

3 Without installing the coils in the tube base, turn on a current of about 0.2 A in one of them and bring this near to the tube.

The demonstration shows that the beam is bent most where the magnetic field is strongest, and that the deflection is at right-angles to the motion of the electron stream.

Further information

Revised Nuffield Physics
Pupils' text and *Teachers' guide Year 4:* Chapter 14 "Electrons". This chapter gives more details about the use of the diode and the development of the idea of the electron gun from observations with the diode.
Teachers' guide Year 3: Chapter 4 "Measuring electrons". Pages 27–9 give additional details about the setting up and use of fine beam tubes and the deflection of electron beams by magnetic fields.
Teachers' guide Year 3: Appendix 3 "Operating instructions for cathode ray oscilloscopes". These details could usefully be read in conjunction with Worksheet **P19B**.

Chapter P20   Control
An introduction to electronics

Purposes

Knowledge and understanding

At the end of this chapter all pupils should:

1 understand that electronics is an extension of the study of electricity

2 appreciate that a knowledge of changes in resistance can be used to produce detectors which can respond to changes in the environment

3 understand how a reed relay can be used to operate devices which need larger currents than detectors can pass

4 appreciate how electronics can be used to solve simple problems in everyday life.

In addition, those pupils aiming for higher grades should:

5 understand how a bistable unit works, and some simple uses that can be made of it

6 appreciate that integrated circuits, called microprocessors, are the control units of many devices in everyday use.

Processes and problem solving

Graphical and symbolic representation
Appreciating the link between the symbolic representation of circuit elements and the devices used in a practical situation is important in work in electronics.

Using apparatus and measuring instruments
The work of this chapter depends on the ability to wire up circuits, both from circuit diagrams and ones devised by the pupils themselves.

Observation

The behaviour of control circuits has to be related to changes in the inputs. This requires accurate and careful observation.

Interpretation and application

The observations referred to above have to be interpreted in terms of simple patterns of behaviour and then used to generate more applications for the control devices.

Planning and carrying out investigations

Pupils are presented with several open-ended, problem-solving investigations in this chapter.

Problem solving

This chapter, more than others, enables pupils to engage in problem solving using equipment on the bench. Two sorts of problems are presented to pupils in this chapter:

1 Problems which are clearly defined but for which there may be more than one solution. An example of this might be the design of an alarm system that operates when someone passes through a door.
2 Problems which reflect a need and which it may be possible to solve through the application of scientific ideas. An example of this might be the use of a computer to develop an aid for a handicapped person.

Timing

6 periods.

Suggested routes

There is no differentiation in the work of this chapter. All pupils will probably be able to cope with all the material, given sufficient time. Overall time constraints make it necessary to restrict work on this chapter to six periods – enough to show how basic ideas in electricity can be applied to form the area of application that we call electronics. It is hoped that all pupils will complete the work up to and including the NAND control unit. Pupils with more background knowledge, or those who quickly grasp the ideas, may be able to go further. The flowchart in figure **P**25 (opposite) shows how the available time might be used to cover all of the work in the chapter, given pupils who either have some previous background in the topic, or the ability to work quickly through the experiments and problems.

Opportunities for co-ordination

Using sensors for control is an integral part of the behaviour of living organisms. The ear, eye, and sense of touch all rely on transducers that change external stimuli into electrical signals which are processed by the organism. Chapter **B**11 "Detecting changes" is concerned with how an organism responds to its environment, using sensors to do this. Chapter **B**12 "Keeping things under control" also has close links with the ideas developed in the present chapter. The process of control described in Chapter **B**12 is however rather different from that being described here. Chapter **B**12 is concerned with negative feedback, whereby the changes produced by the controlling mechanism (the output) are fed back to the input. This form of control is very important in many electronic circuits but is something that has to be developed after the work of the present chapter has been understood.

Although there is not time to do this in the present course, making the link between control in organisms and control in electronics should be explicitly encouraged, and interested youngsters should be encouraged to explore the essential electronic ideas involved for themselves.

Periods

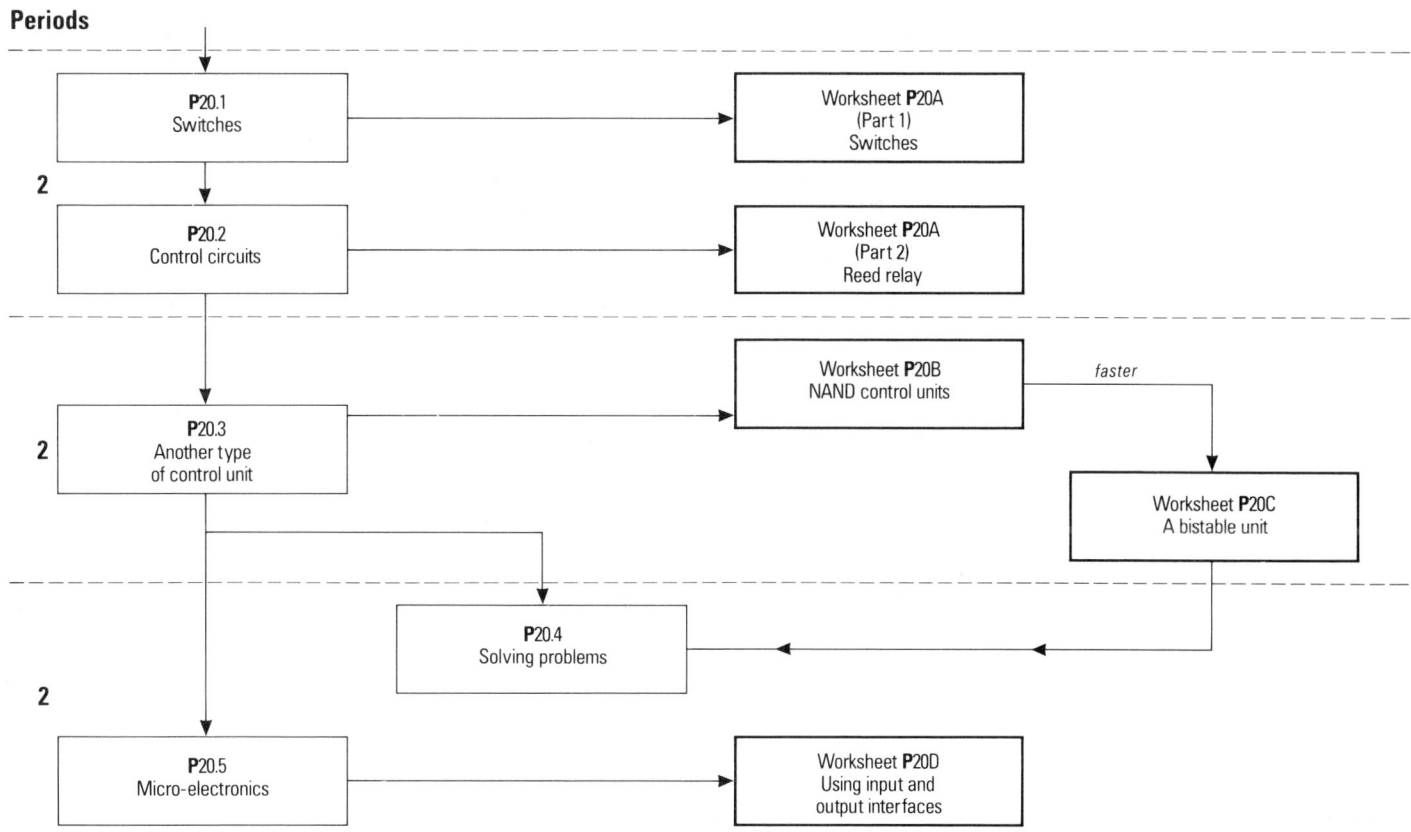

Figure **P25**

Notes and answers

There are many arguments both for and against the inclusion of electronics in a Physics course at this level. Its inclusion in a broadly-based science course in which the constraints of time mean that other more commonly included topics have been discarded might seem to require more justification than usual. Here are some of the arguments for paying some attention to electronics.

1 Electronics is a technology that both draws heavily on scientific ideas and has in turn stimulated scientific research. One way of defining technology is to say that it is the process by which people cope with their environment. It is therefore a problem-solving process which draws on the knowledge and resources available to us, working within the constraints placed on it by scientific knowledge, society and the resources of our planet. Electronics is just such a technology. It is a technology which uses ideas about electricity, and it is in the context of electronics that people mostly deal with electricity. Throughout this course, pupils' attention has been directed towards the use that is made of scientific ideas. Including work from electronics is consistent with the inclusion of technological applications found in other areas of physics.
2 Because electronics is so often developed in isolation its relationship to basic electrical ideas of current and voltage is not always clear. This chapter concentrates on linking the technology to the basic physics.
3 Electronics is an excellent medium for problem solving, using equipment. It can thus contribute to the overall problem-solving aims of the course.

The approach adopted in this chapter owes a great deal to the work of the Independent Schools Microelectronics Centre and in particular the book *Electronics* by Foxcroft, Lewis and Summers.

P20.1   Switches

The first section looks at the way a switch can be thought of as a simple form of circuit control. Simple switches are introduced, as are switches that can be indirectly controlled such as the reed switch (a form of relay).

From make-and-break switching, attention is turned to the way in which a variable resistor can exercise similar control. A variable resistor, whose maximum resistance is so high that the current flowing though it is unable to drive a motor, can be used to turn a motor on and off just as a switch can. In this way the pupil is led to see that light-dependent resistors and thermistors can be used as switches, operated by light and by a change in temperature respectively.

Answer to selected question

2 A magnet could be inserted in the edge of the door. This magnet could be used to close a reed switch, inserted in the door frame, when the door closes.

P20.2   Control circuits

The difficulty in using light-dependent resistors and thermistors to control other devices directly is that the maximum current they can pass is usually low. This section shows how other devices, referred to as "control units", can be used as intermediaries, interfacing the device to be controlled (say a central-heating pump) with the controller (a temperature-dependent switch, say). The simplest control unit for pupils to understand is the relay, already described in Chapter **P**18.

Having shown how the relay can operate as a control unit, pupils are asked to accept that the same job can be done by other electronic devices. No attempt is made to explain how such devices (gates) work – they are simply shown to do the same job as the relay. This "black box" approach to electronics has already proved successful. It is not necessary to know how a device operates in order to make use of it; pupils merely have to understand what it will do.

Answers to selected questions

4 A suitable circuit is shown in figure **P**26.

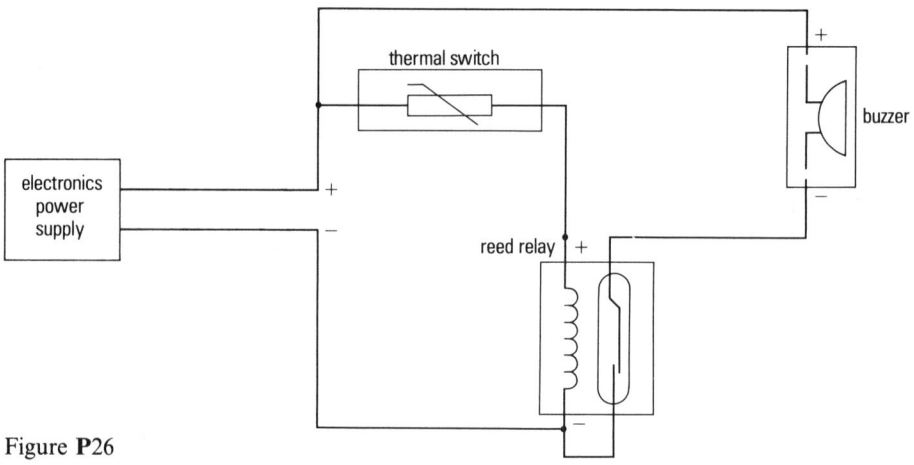

Figure **P**26

5 The circuit diagram in figure **P27** shows one possible solution to the problem.

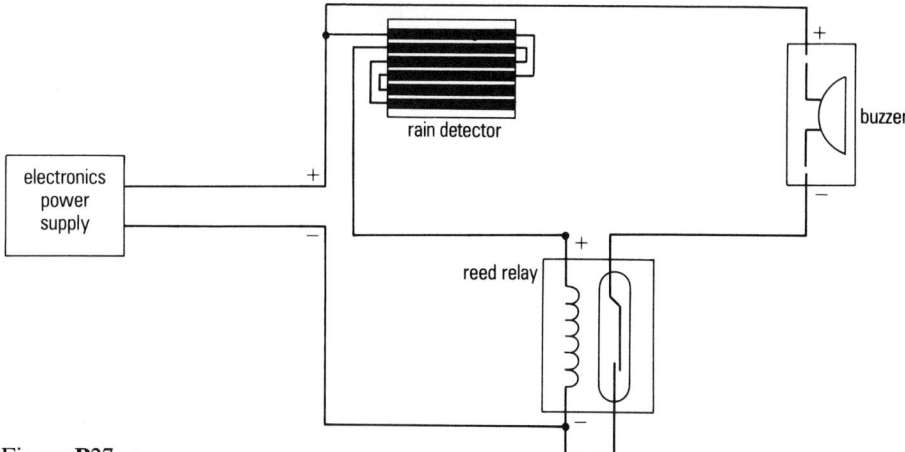

Figure **P27**
The "rain detector" consists of two strips of metal. Water, with a little salt added, will form a conducting bridge between the metal strips.

6 Figure **P28** shows one possible solution to the problem.

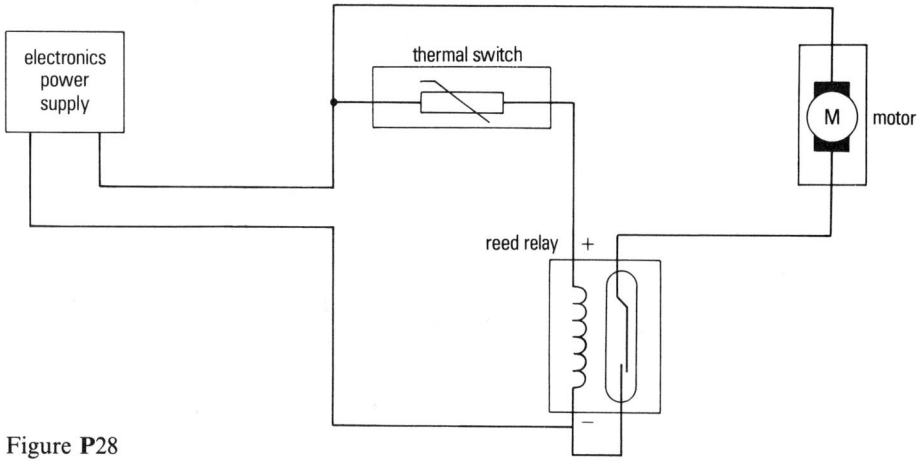

Figure **P28**

P20.3　Another type of control unit

This section shows that control units can be more complex than the sort just described. The NAND unit introduced here is a control unit that responds to particular settings of two inputs. The reason for the name of this control unit may be of interest to some pupils, but it is not intended to use the NAND unit as an introduction to a study of logic gates – as a family of such control units is called. However, pupils with the interest and the time may like to know about similar multi-input control gates – OR gates, AND gates, NOR gates and NOT gates. These, together with the bistable unit introduced next, are the "building blocks" of computers.

NAND gates are available in the form of "plug-in" units which enable circuits to be constructed easily. This aspect of easy circuit building is dealt with in the introduction to the section on practical work.

Once the operation of the NAND unit is understood, pupils are set the challenge of producing a burglar alarm. This leads to the introduction of the bistable unit – constructed from a pair of NAND units.

Answers to selected questions

7 Figure **P29** shows a suitable arrangement that could function as a cooker warning light.

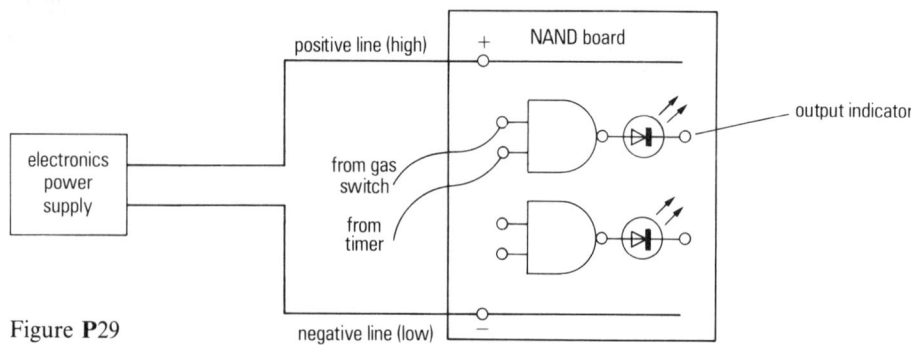

Figure **P29**

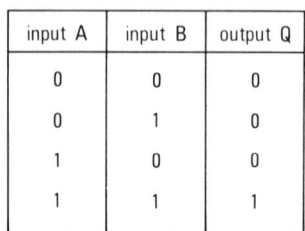

input A	input B	output Q
0	0	0
0	1	0
1	0	0
1	1	1

Figure **P30**

8 Figure **P30** shows the table of inputs and outputs expected from the two NAND gates shown in figure 20.21 of the Physics pupils' book. Such a combination of NAND units forms an AND gate.

P20.4   Solving problems

Provided pupils still have sufficient time, this section encourages them to formulate and solve a problem using the electronics control units they have now met.

P20.5   Microelectronics

This last section asks the pupils to make another step in their imagination and realize that microprocessors, which form the heart of personal computers and many domestic appliances, such as washing machines and sewing machines, are no more than very sophisticated control units.

Such microprocessors operate according to a plan called a *program*. In automatic machines the microprocessors are pre-programmed before installation. Such programs cannot be altered by the users of the machine. Microcomputers allow the user to program the microprocessor so that it can exercise control of external devices, via an *output interface*. They can also be made to respond to external inputs from light-, sound- or temperature-sensitive devices. This requires an *input interface*.

Pupils may be given the opportunity to program a computer to operate a set of lights as traffic lights. Special software is available which allows this programming to be done in "everyday English".

The chapter concludes by inviting pupils to develop ways of using computer-controlled systems to help handicapped people.

Practical work

It is intended that most of the pupils' time during which this chapter is studied should be spent on practical work. The pupils' book itself is meant to do no more than assist this practical work and provide more problems to solve.

The equipment for practical work in electronics uses units that are mounted on boards which readily fit together to provide working circuits. Such circuits ought to be easy to wire up following simple instructions. It is hoped that the instant success that this gives will provide the confidence required to tackle problems using devices which may have been unfamiliar to pupils only minutes before.

There are already a number of units on the market designed to do the jobs suggested in this chapter and many schools may possess such units; the ones needed are listed under Requirements below. Schools requiring complete sets will be able to buy them as a set specifically put together for this course or they can use units developed for other courses, such as those used by ISMEC (the Independent Schools Microelectronics Centre).

Worksheet P20A   Switches

Worksheet P20B   NAND control units

Worksheet P20C   A bistable unit

REQUIREMENTS

Each group of pupils will need:
Power supply for electronics kit
Electronics kit: switch SPST, light-
  dependent resistor, thermistor, reed
  switch, light-emitting diode, reed relay,
  buzzer, motor, 2 NAND units
Connecting wires

Note:
If the NAND units do not have light-emitting diodes connected to the outputs of the NAND gates, an additional light-emitting diode module will be required. Ideally there should be one such set of modules to each pair of pupils in a class.

The wiring up of the modules and the experiments to be carried out are described in the worksheets.

Worksheet P20D   Using input and output interfaces

REQUIREMENTS

Microcomputer, e.g. BBC and monitor
  (see Note)
Computer interface, output
Computer interface, input
Electronics kit
Cassette recorder or disc drive
Computer software to control interfaces

Note:
Other makes of microcomputer can, of course, be used if suitable interfacing units are available.

Full details of how to set up the interfaces and install the software are included with the kit of interfaces and software from the manufacturers.

Further information

Electronics
G. E. Foxcroft, J. L. Lewis and M. K. Summers (Longman Group, 1986). This book is essential background reading for the approach adopted in this chapter. It will also show how work in electronics may be continued outside this immediate science syllabus.

Chapter P21   Communication
Transferring information electrically

Purposes

Knowledge and understanding

At the end of this chapter all pupils should:

1 understand how, historically, the use of light greatly increased the speed of communication, but that this required the use of a code

2 understand how the use of electrical signals has further improved long-distance, high-speed communication

3 be able to describe the operation of the microphone and earpiece and relate their operation to basic physical principles

4 understand something of the operation of the telephone system and of radio.

In addition, those pupils aiming for higher grades should:

5 understand the difference between analogue signals and digital signals, and recognize that the latter require an extension of the idea of a code for transmitting information

6 understand some of the benefits of digital coding for transmitting information

7 understand that a wide range of scientific ideas may be used in any one technology – in this case the improvement of communications.

Processes and problem solving

Graphical and symbolic representation
Digital coding of analogue signals involves another exercise in graphical analysis.

Using apparatus and measuring instruments
Worksheets **P21A** and **P21B** provide further opportunities for the construction of electronic circuits.

Observation
The practical use of the Morse code shows the difficulties involved in coding messages.

Interpretation and application
One of the main outcomes of this chapter is to show how technological developments can call on a whole range of ideas in physics. The final exercise asks pupils to make a survey of the range of physical principles used in the chapter.

Problem solving
The technology of the development of communication systems is seen as a problem to which the development of physical ideas and processes provides solutions.

Timing

6 periods.

Suggested routes

The flow diagram in figure **P31** (opposite) shows the way the work of this chapter could be distributed over six periods of work. No differentiation is suggested except for Worksheet **P21C**. This exercise shows how an analogue signal can be digitally coded, and is probably only suitable for more able pupils. Less able pupils may instead choose to do Worksheet **P13B** at this time (see page 364).

Opportunities for co-ordination

Chapter **B11** "Detecting changes" is partly concerned with the transmission of information within an organism. There are obvious similarities between the human nervous system and a national, or even worldwide, communication system. Section **B11.7** "The faster the better" contains some points which can make for interesting comparisons with national communications networks. Section **B11.8** "Nerves and nerve cells" compares a nerve with a complex telephone cable.

Periods   (The work of this chapter could be reduced to 5 periods)

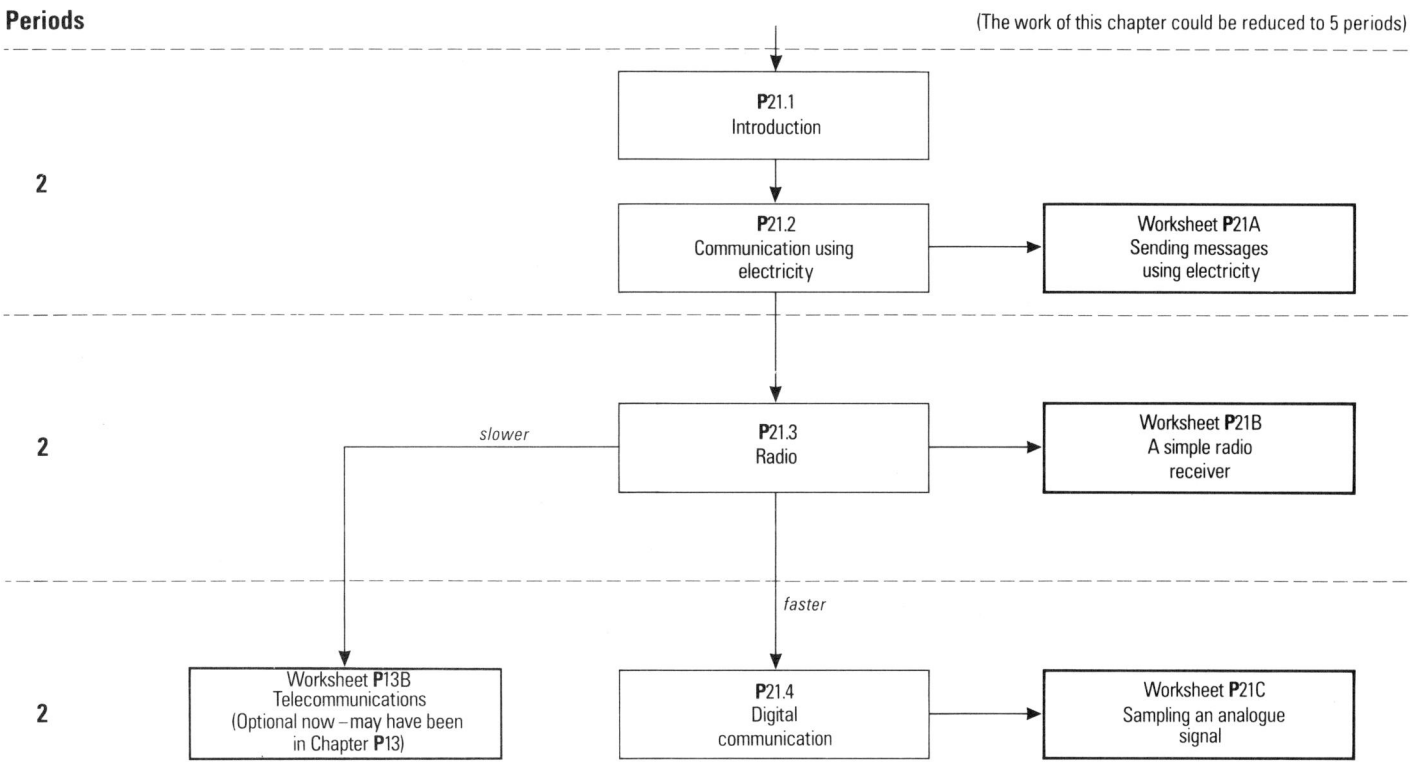

Figure **P31**

Notes and answers

P21.1   Introduction

The aim of this introductory section is to show that increasing the speed of communication has often involved the use of some sort of code. Semaphore uses a complex coding system, but Morse code, introduced in the next section, is simpler, using only long and short sounds. Later in the chapter pupils will be introduced to digital coding which, with its **highs** and **lows**, can be seen to be closely linked to Morse. Just as Morse code represents each letter and number by an agreed sequence of short and long sounds ("dots and dashes") so the ASCII code, commonly used in computers, represents each letter and number by an agreed sequence of high and low voltages. (ASCII stands for American Standard Code for Information Interchange.)

P21.2   Communication using electricity

The invention of the electric telegraph came only a year or two after Oersted's discovery of the magnetic effect of an electric current. It demonstrates how a discovery in physics was used to satisfy an immediate need. The need for a reliable method of fast, long-distance communication arose in this country with the development of the railway system.

Worksheet **P21A** introduces pupils to the way in which messages can be coded in Morse, and at the same time shows that this coding method needs considerable skill to operate it. This worksheet paves the way for digital coding and helps illustrate the need for some automatic way of coding and decoding messages.

A more direct way of sending messages electrically is to use a microphone and an earpiece. The operation of this system depends on the same physical principles as the electric telegraph, but the message is not coded and decoded. It is an analogue system in which variations of electric current follow the variations of air pressure on a microphone produced by a sound wave.

This leads to a short discussion of the telephone system. Some of the problems encountered in the present-day telephone system have already been discussed in Chapter **P13**.

P21.3   Radio

The discovery of radio waves and their use by Marconi to send information from place to place is seen as overcoming one major disadvantage of the telephone system – it dispenses with the need to connect sending and receiving equipment with wires.

Instructions are given in Worksheet **P21B** for the construction of a simple radio receiver. The process of radio transmission by modulating a carrier wave is described briefly. It is recommended that this section is covered only if time permits. There are several methods of wiring up the simple radio. One method which involves no soldering is described in the notes on practical work that follow.

The section ends by considering some of the many uses to which radio communication is now put.

Answers to selected questions

10 i 267 s (almost $4\frac{1}{2}$ minutes);
ii 4270 s (about 1 hour 10 minutes).

P21.4   Digital communication

Digital coding of signals has two major advantages. First, it enables messages in both words and pictures to be sent with great accuracy. The signal is not subject to the same degree of interference that analogue signals are. Secondly, it enables a large amount of information to be sent in a very short time (as well as allowing it to be stored in a very compact form).

Two forms of digital coding are introduced in this section. The first is in many ways like Morse code. Each letter and number is given a code in the form of a decimal number: A = 65, B = 66, C = 67 and so on. This decimal number is then turned into a binary number. (So A = 100 0001; B = 100 0010 and so on.) Turned into electrical voltages, A = high, low, low, low, low, low, high; B = high, low, low, low, low, high, low.

The second form of digital coding is able to transmit electrical signals which are analogues of variations in sound and light. This form of coding is harder to understand and may be omitted for less able pupils. In this form of coding the analogue electrical signal is transmitted as a sequence of numbers which represent the variation in voltage of the signal with time. The numbers are transmitted in digital form and the original signal is reconstituted by the receiver as a time-varying voltage. This is much the same as the way in which someone might pass on information about a graph in the form of a table of numbers to be plotted.

Worksheet **P21C** is a pencil-and-paper exercise along these lines. It shows pupils with what frequency these numbers would have to be sampled for a fairly faithful copy of the original graph to be reproduced.

The chapter concludes by looking at the use being made of digital communication techniques. Digital coding of analogue signals requires that numbers have to be transmitted at a very high rate if a faithful copy of the original signal is to be made by the receiver. To transmit pictures in this way involves very high rates of number transmission – something that can only really be achieved using light itself travelling down optical fibres.

Because optical fibres allow very high rates of information transmission, they are also being used increasingly for telephone communication. As this idea concludes the work of the chapter, this would be a good point at which to do Worksheet **P13B** if it has not been done earlier.

Practical work

Worksheet P21A   Sending messages using electricity

Experiment 1: Using the Morse code

REQUIREMENTS

Each group of pupils will need:
Power supply for electronics kit
Electronics kit: Switch SPST, buzzer
or:
Morse key
Ticker-timer to act as "buzzer"
Power supply for ticker-timer
Connecting wires

The procedure to be followed is detailed in the worksheet. If the design task allowing two people to send and receive a message is undertaken, additional switches etc. will be required.

Experiment 2: Using a microphone and loudspeaker

REQUIREMENTS

Each group of pupils will need:
2 loudspeakers, small, moving coil
Amplifier
Connecting wires

The procedure is detailed in the worksheet.

Worksheet P21B   A simple radio receiver

REQUIREMENTS

Each group of pupils will need:
Battery, to power radio
Radio kit: ZN414 radio integrated circuit, resistor, 100 kΩ, resistor, 500Ω, capacitor,
 0.1 μF, capacitor, 0.01 μF, capacitor, 330 pF
Earpiece, crystal
Coil, copper wire, 0.35 mm in diameter, 2.5 m long
Ferrite rod, 1 cm in diameter, 8 cm long
Cardboard, thin
Sticky tape
75 turn coil made with fine insulated wire with connections already attached to 75th turn
 and centre turn.

Notes:
It may be possible to use one of a number of kits to build a simple radio. Each may use components different from those on this list. The list of components given matches the circuit on the worksheet, and can be used by teachers who wish to put together their own kit of parts.

The detailed procedure for connecting together the components for a simple radio will depend on the source of the components and the ability of the pupils. Schools may devise their own system working with basic components. Some pupils will benefit by being allowed to solder this circuit together, while for others it might be better to have an easier method of connection using either a connection board, or modules with 2 or 4 mm sockets.

If, alternatively, a kit of parts is purchased, the instructions enclosed with the kit should be carefully followed.

Demonstration experiment

Section P21.3: Slow radio

REQUIREMENTS

Oscilloscope, demonstration type
Slow a.c. generator
Signal generator
Diode, any general purpose
Resistor, 1 kΩ
Resistor, 330 Ω, variable
Capacitor, 8 µF

A circuit diagram is shown in figure **P32**. Turning the handle of the "slow a.c." generator will "modulate" the 1 kHz signal from the signal generator. The modulation is displayed on the oscilloscope.

A diode and capacitor can be inserted, as shown in the circuit diagram, to show how the "carrier wave" can be removed, leaving only the modulating voltage.

The slow a.c. generator can be driven by a small electric motor rather than be hand-turned.

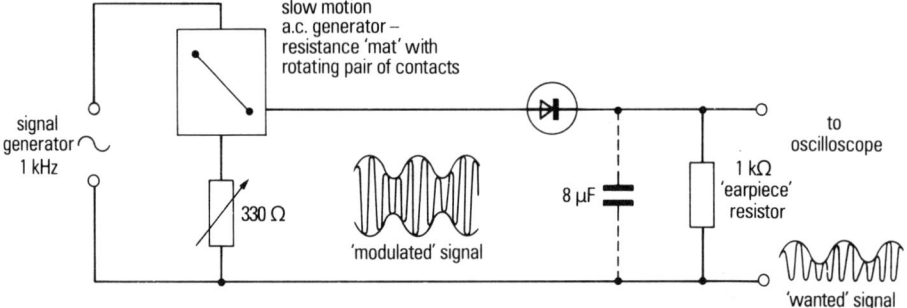

Figure **P32**

This amplitude modulated signal goes to a diode and a resistor to represent the earpiece used in the "real" radio. The modulated signal across this "earpiece" resistor is shown in the middle of the diagram. Its average value rises and falls at the frequency of rotation of the slow motion a.c. generator. If a capacitor is placed across the resistor, the rapid 1 kHz fluctuations are filtered out, leaving only the slow "wanted" signal, which does not pass as easily through the capacitor.

Further information

Communication

This resource pack of slides and workcards is available from the BP Education Service, or the Science Museum, Exhibition Road, London SW7.

About Information Technology

(CRAC Publications, Hobsons Ltd for British Telecom and Rank Xerox.)

Science Museum publications

Telecommunications – a technology for change
Guglielmo Marconi by Keith Geddes. Useful background booklet for pupils.

There is also a permanent exhibition on communications technology in the Science Museum, London.

Physics apparatus list

This alphabetical list contains all the items that might be required for the Physics part of the course. The list is comprehensive in that it contains items needed both for basic experiments and for optional experiments (such as the speed of light along an optical fibre) which will only be carried out by schools who happen to have the equipment for A-level work, or who can borrow it for a one-off demonstration. It is not suggested that schools need to have all the equipment listed here in order to carry out the aims of the course successfully. On the other hand, successful completion does demand that pupils are able to carry out a very large majority of the experiments listed in the worksheets.

The items carry numbers which group the equipment in various sets, as follows:

Nos 1–999. These are the items specified for Revised Nuffield Physics. They carry the same numbers as in the apparatus list for that course.

Nos 1000–1599. These are items specified for the Revised Nuffield A-level Physics course, not found in Revised Nuffield Physics.

Nos 1600 and following. These are items not specified in either of the above lists. Some are new to the course, but others are drawn from the Nuffield Secondary Science course. Many of them will already be available in schools.

"Local purchase" items carry the number 1601.
Miscellaneous small laboratory items carry the number 1602.
Chemicals carry the number 1603.

Many schools will find that they already possess the remaining 43 items specified, or can find a reasonable substitute.

Schools should refer to the published apparatus lists for Nuffield Physics and Nuffield A-level Physics for more detail, where items from these lists are specified.

The descriptions given both below and in the earlier apparatus lists referred to above do not represent rigid specifications. Many pieces of equipment have been, or are being, manufactured which will do the required job just as well, even better, or at a cheaper price than a prescribed piece of equipment. Teachers should always make their own judgment about the appropriate equipment to use. The question that should be asked of any equipment is "Does it do the right job?" rather than "Is it the right piece of apparatus?"

No.	Item	Used mainly in Chapter
1019	Air track and accessories	P5, P6
1020	Air track blower	P5, P6
	Ammeters — see Meters	
1601	Aerosols, various	P2
1604	Amplifier	
	(One which can produce a clearly audible output into a small loudspeaker when a similar loudspeaker is used as a microphone.)	P21
1602	Ball bearings, 15 mm and 25 mm in diameter	
1601	Balloons	P5, P6
1605	Bathroom scales, calibrated in newtons	P8
20	Balances: 5-kg, domestic	
42	Balances: 100-g	
	(Other mechanical and cheap electronic balances are a more than acceptable alternative to the lever-arm pattern specified in the Nuffield Physics list.)	

No.	Item	Used mainly in Chapter
1602	Beads, glass or polystyrene	P5
512/2	Beakers, glass, 400-cm^3	
103	Bicycle dynamo assembly	P11, P18
1606	Bicycle dynamo which can be taken apart	P18
1607	Box with set of about 24 wooden cubes which fit into it – dimensions are not important	P4
109	Boyle's Law apparatus with pump (A simple kit which can be used by pupils is an acceptable alternative to the demonstration apparatus specified in the Nuffield Physics list.)	P2
1602	Bung with hole to fit 250-cm^3 round-bottom flask	P2
508	Bunsen burners	
92G	C-cores with clips	P11, P18
1608	CO_2 capsule with mount that can be suspended to propel itself along a wire stretched across a laboratory	P6
19/1	CO_2 cylinder	
133	Camera with shutter that can be kept open	P7
1601	Candle	P3
1601	Cans, tin	P9
1601	Card	
1601	Cells, 1.5-V in holders (For most experiments, Worcester 1601 circuit boards are an acceptable alternative.)	
65	Circular brass plates on insulating handles	P3
1602	Clip, Hoffmann	
127	Coils for C-cores: 120 turns	P11, P18
128	Coils for C-cores: 2400 turns	P11
1609	Colour filters, set of primary red, blue and green	P15
1610	Colour filters, set of secondary yellow, magenta and cyan	P15
1611	Coloured objects, various, in primary and other colours	P15
21	Compact light source	P3
16/1	Computer, with disc drive or cassette recorder	P4, P20
1612	Computer interface, input	P20
1613	Computer interface, output	P20
1614	Computer software to control interfaces	P20
1000	Connecting leads	
1602	Container, aluminium	P10
1601	Corks	
1512	Coulombmeter	P16
119	Curtain rail, flexible, 2 m long	P5
147	Demountable transformer kit	P11, P18
1601	Dice	P3
135	Diode, hot filament with stand	P19
1601	Dowel, 10 mm diameter	
1615	Electric drill which can be taken apart	P18
	Electric heating accessories for mechanical heating apparatus (q.v.)	
1616	Electric kettle	P9
9A	Electric motor, 6-V	P17
1617	Electronics kit containing:	

Electronics kit containing:

light-dependent resistor	reed relay
thermistor	buzzer
switch SPST	motor
reed switch	2 NAND gates
light-emitting diode	
(A power supply (q.v.) will be required)	P20

No.	Item	Used mainly in Chapter
51G	Electrostatics rod, polythene	P16
51F	Electrostatics rod, acetate	P16
1601	Expanded polystyrene block	

No.	Item	Used mainly in Chapter
1618	Fan or hair-drier to blow cold air	P9
61	Fine beam tube and base	P19
81	Force meters, 10-N	P5, P8
1619	Force meters, 50-N	P8
44/2	G-clamps, 50-mm	
44/1	G-clamps, 100-mm	
	Galvanometers – see Meters	
510	Gauzes	
130/3	Geiger–Müller tube, thin end window type, with holder	P3
1602	Glass rod, 20 to 30 cm long, with smooth cut ends (neither cut nor flame polished)	P13
1602	Glass tubing	
1601	Glue, general purpose	
1601	Hammer	
1601	Hardboard disc with hole in centre to take a piece of dowel	P5
139	Helmholtz coils for fine-beam tube	P19
1603	Hydrochloric acid, concentrated	
146	Inertial balance kit	P5
75	Immersion heater, 12-V	P9, P10
1620	Ionization chamber, simple open type to detect α-particles	P3
92W	Iron filings	P18
92I	Iron yoke for Magnadur magnets	P11, P18
1603	Iso-butyl methyl ketone	P3
1621	Joulemeter, arm – to measure energy transferred by arm	P8
1622	Joulemeter, cycle – to measure energy transferred by legs	P8
1623	Joulemeter, electric – to measure energy delivered by 12 V a.c. supply. (Rewound domestic electricity meters or electronic equivalents are already present in many schools. A simpler version that causes a light to flash for every 100 J transferred is to be preferred for pupils' use.)	P9, P10
11	Kinetic theory model kit (An apparatus with an integral motor is easier to use than those driven via a belt from a separate motor.)	P2
1601	Lagging materials, e.g. strips of cotton cloth, foam rubber, cotton-wool, wool scarf, to lag tin cans	P9
1624	Lamp, e.g. photoflood, for bright illumination	P13
1602	Lamp, 2.5-V, 0.2-A, MES	
52A	Lamp, 1.25-V, 0.25-A, MES	
72	Lamp, 12-V, 24-W, SBC	
1625	Lamp, 12-V, 3-W (e.g. line filament type with holder)	P17
52D	Lampholder, MES	
23	Lampholder, SBC	
1601	Lath, about 25 mm × 50 mm × 1 m	P1
1602	Lead block, about 1.5 cm × 5 cm × 5 cm	P3
1603	Lead shot	P10
130/2	Light gate, any arrangement for timing interruption of light beam	P4, P5, P6, P15
1151	Loudspeakers, small moving coil	P21
92A	Magnets, bar, Ticonal	P18
92B	Magnets, Magnadur, slab	P18
1626	Mains electric fire, 1000 W	P16
1627	Mains electric lamp, 100 W, in holder	P16
1601	Mains electric lamp, 60 W	P17

No.	Item	Used mainly in Chapter
1628	Mains connecting block (A means of connecting equipment safely to the mains supply, and of measuring currents and voltages, is required in some experiments.)	
12B	Marbles, 15 mm in diameter	**P2**
12C	Marbles, 25 mm in diameter	**P2, P5**
32	Masses, 1-kg	
1629	Masses, 100-g	
518/3	Measuring cylinders, 250-cm^3	
518/2	Measuring cylinders, 100-cm^3	
1011	Mechanical heating apparatus with equipment for heating it electrically	
	Meters, electric, for class use:	
79	ammeters, 1 A d.c.	
178	5 A d.c.	
80	voltmeters, 5 V d.c.	
1630	10 V a.c.	
179	15 V d.c.	
180	galvanometers, 3–0–3 mA, or similar	
70/71	Meters, electric, for demonstration use:	
	ammeters, 1 A a.c.	
	5 A a.c.	
	voltmeters, 5 V d.c.	
	10 V d.c.	
	15 V d.c.	
	galvanometer, 3–0–3 mA, or similar	**P11** and **P16–P20**

(The ranges quoted above are a guide to the size of the readings likely to be obtained. The meters can have any ranges that are clear and easy to read, provided a measurably large deflection is obtained in use. 100 µA meters, diode protected, are electrically robust and are conveniently used with plug-in shunts and multipliers. For such meters, those with ranges of 0–3 and 0–10 need fewest shunts and multipliers and should be considered as suitable alternatives to the ranges specified above. It is important that pupils are easily able to interpret the meter scale in terms of the measuring range in use. Less able pupils may benefit from using direct-reading meters.

Low-cost digital meters are becoming more common and are useful in circuits in which the current and voltage are not changing quickly. When a reading is changing rapidly, as in electromagnetic induction experiments, a moving coil (analogue) meter is essential.

The same criteria apply to demonstration meters. Ease of use and clarity of reading are paramount considerations. Demonstration meters based on the same movements as corresponding class meters are convenient as they both use the same set of shunts and multipliers.)

No.	Item	Used mainly in Chapter
501	Metre rules	
157	Microphone	**P19, P21**
116	Mirrors, plane	**P13**
92	Motor kits, electric, containing:	
	base	
	2 split pins	
	spindle	
	4 rivets	
	armature	
	valve rubber	**P11, P18**

No.	Item	Used mainly in Chapter
150	Motor, fractional horsepower	**P**18
1601	Nails	
1601	Needles	
1631	Optical fibre, 0.5–1 m length	**P**13
158, 64	Oscilloscopes, single beam	**P**19, **P**21
1511	Oscilloscopes, double beam	**P**15
1602	Paper, black	**P**13
1601	Paper, white	
1602	Pressure tubing, short length to fit neck of balloon	**P**6
572	Ping-pong ball coated with Aquadag and suspended on nylon thread	**P**16
1601	Pins	
1601	Plasticine	
92D	Plotting compasses	**P**18
1601	Plug, 13-A, mains	**P**16
1602	Polystyrene beaker	**P**9, **P**10
1602	Polythene bottle, 30 to 50 cm³ capacity	**P**3
27/104	Power supplies, 12 V a.c./d.c. (Pupil experiments frequently need low voltage a.c. and d.c. supplies for electromagnetic experiments and 12 V a.c./d.c. supplies for lamps and heaters. It would be convenient to have these combined into a single, economical unit.)	
59	Power supplies, 0–12 V d.c., variable, smoothed	
15	Power supply, HT	
14	Power supply, EHT	
1632	Power supply for electronics kit (Different kits will have different requirements. Many can be supplied from dry cells. Some will need a regulated supply.)	
67	Pressure gauge, 200 kPa (This gauge should read absolute pressure. It should be either stand-mounted or designed to be mounted directly into a bung or tube.)	**P**2
111	Prism, glass or plastic, 60°	**P**15
550	Protractors	**P**1, **P**13
40	Pulley on clamp	**P**10
	Radioactive sources:	
195/3	Americium-241, 5 µCi (0.18 MBq)	**P**3
195/2	Strontium-90, 5 µCi (0.18 MBq)	**P**3
195/1	Cobalt-60, 5 µCi (0.18 MBq)	**P**3
196	Radioactive source holder	**P**3
1633	Radio kit, to allow easy assembly of radio (A DIY kit can be made up from: ZN414 integrated circuit capacitors, 0.1 µF 0.01 µF 330 pF resistors, 100 kΩ 500 kΩ crystal earpiece ferrite rod, 10 cm × 1 cm diameter.)	**P**21
94	Ray optics kit (cylindrical lenses are not required)	**P**13
1634A	Resistors, 15 Ω, 10 W, with sockets	**P**17
1634B	Resistors, 4 Ω, 7 W, labelled X	**P**17
1634C	Resistor, 10 Ω, 7 W, labelled Y	**P**17
90	Ripple tank kit (Any simple arrangement to demonstrate simple wave phenomena; a motorized vibrator is not required.)	

No.	Item	Used mainly in Chapter
548	Round-bottomed flask, 250-cm^3	P2
1601	Rubber bands	
1635	Rules, half-metre	
107	Runway for dynamics trolley (Runways and trolleys based on a pattern published by the Nuffield Secondary Science project make a satisfactory alternative.)	P4, P5, P6, P10
1601	Sand	P8
1636	Sandbags, 10 N and 20 N	P8
130	Scaler counter, for GM tube	P3
529	Scissors	
	Screen, white	
1601	Screwdriver, small	
31/1	Slotted masses, 100-g sets	
31/2	Slotted masses, 1-kg sets	
30	Slotted base	
17	Spark counter	P3
1523	Speed of light apparatus (A cheap DIY version is described in "Experimenting with Industry" No. 2, published by ASE/SCSST.)	P15
1013	Spring, long, heavy	P14
2A	Springs, disposable	
101	Spring, Slinky	P14
503, 504 505, 506	Stands, bosses and clamps	
1601	Steel rod pieces, 50 mm long or greater (Pieces of knitting needle can be used)	
1637	Step (strong box to stand on, about 30 cm high)	P8
1601	Stirrer	
51H	Stirrups to suspend electrostatics rods	P16
507	Stopclock	
163	Stopclock, electrically controlled (for use with light gates)	
1601	String	
	Support block for electromagnetism experiments	P18
1638	Support rod for camera	P7
1639	Switch, on–off, with sockets	
1601	Tape, adhesive	
108/3	Tape for ticker timer	P7
542	Thermometer	P2, P9, P10
1601	Thread	
108/1	Ticker timer (Any reliable mechanism to mark tickertape for dynamics experiments.)	P7 (Optional: P4, P5, P6)
1640	Torches, electric, one working and one not working	P16
1641	Track, grooved, with 20 cm aluminium foil fitted along each side of part of groove	P4
1642	Transparent block, plastic or glass, semi-circular	P13
1643	Transparent strip, plastic, approximately 0.5 cm × 3 cm × 30 cm	P13
1644	Tray, about 20 cm × 30 cm, with hook to attach string	P8
12A	Tray for 2-D kinetic theory model	P2
511	Tripod	
160/1	Trolley, dynamics (See note under Runway.)	P4, P5, P6, P10
1601	Tubes, cardboard, about 50 cm × 5 cm diameter	P10, P13
110	Tube for "guinea and feather" experiment	P7

No.	Item	Used mainly in Chapter
1602	Tube, rubber	**P**19
1645	Tuning forks	
1603	Uranyl nitrate	**P**3
13	Vacuum pump	**P**7
50/1	Van de Graaff generator	**P**3, **P**16
	Voltmeters — see Meters	
89	Water circuit board	**P**16
167	Water rocket	**P**6
	Wire, flexible, insulated, e.g. 16 × 0.5 mm	
	pvc insulated, solid core, e.g. 0.6 mm diameter	
	tinned copper, 0.45 mm (26 s.w.g.)	
	bare Eureka, 0.56 mm (24 s.w.g.)	
	bare Eureka, 0.40 mm (28 s.w.g.)	
	bare Eureka, 0.28 mm (32 s.w.g.)	
	3-core mains	
	steel, about 0.5 mm diameter	
84	Wire strippers	
1646	Wire resistance board with 4 different lengths of 0.28 mm bare Eureka wire	
52	Worcester circuit board	
	(Basic electricity kits which connect with conventional plugs and sockets are an acceptable and sometimes preferable alternative to circuit boards.)	

Appendix

Useful addresses

This list of addresses and telephone numbers covers the suggestions for sources of visual aids and further information that we have made in this *Guide*. It is not an exhaustive list. Some of the smaller organizations, especially the charities and campaigning societies, appreciate it if you enclose a stamped addressed envelope.

Association for Science Education (for Science and Technology in Society – SATIS – units)
College Lane, Hatfield, Hertfordshire AL10 9AA. (Tel. 07072 67411.)

Films, slides and television programmes

Argus Film and Video Library (for ICI videos)
15 Beaconsfield Road, London NW10 2LE. (Tel. 01–451 1127.)

BP Educational Service (for BP tape–slide sets)
PO Box 5, Wetherby, West Yorkshire LS23 7EH. (Tel. 0937 843477.)

BP Film Library (for BP films and videos)
15 Beaconsfield Road, London NW10 2LE. (Tel. 01–451 1129.)

British Broadcasting Corporation (schools broadcasting)
School Broadcasting Council for the United Kingdom,
Portland Place, London W1A 1AA. (Tel. 01–935 2801.)

BBC Enterprises (education and training)
Woodlands, 80 Wood Lane, London W12 0TT.

British Gas Education Service (for British Gas slides)
Room 707A, 326 High Holborn, London WC1V 7PT. (Tel. 01–242 0789.)

British Plastics Federation
5 Belgrave Square, London SW1X 8PH. (Tel. 01–235 9896.)

The Guild Film Library (for Thames Water films and videos)
Guild House, Oundle Road, Peterborough, Cambridgeshire PE2 9PZ.
(Tel. 0733 63122.)

National Coal Board Film Library
Hobart House, Grosvenor Place, London SW1X 7AE. (Tel. 01–235 2020.)

Philip Harris (Biological) Ltd (for Philip Harris slide sets and filmstrips)
Oldmixon, Weston-super-Mare, Avon BS24 9BJ. (Tel. 0934 413063.)

Phillips Petroleum Film Library
15 Beaconsfield Road, London NW10 2LE. (Tel. 01–451 1127.)

Scottish Central Film Library (for Unilever films)
Dowanhill, 74 Victoria Crescent Road, Glasgow G12 9JN. (Tel. 041–334 9314.)

Shell Film Library
Unit 2, Cornwall Works, Cornwall Avenue, Finchley, London N3 1LD.
(Tel. 01–349 0025.)

Viscom Ltd (for British Gas, British Steel, British Sugar Bureau, De Beers,
Esso, RTZ Group, Wiggins Teape and UKAEA films and videos)
Audio–Visual Library, Park Hall Road Trading Estate, London SE21 8EL.
(Tel. 01–761 3035.)

Audio–Visual Unit, University of York (for PLON video "Force and motion")
Heslington, York YO1 5DD.

Booklets, leaflets, wallcharts and other sources of information

Allied Breweries (UK) Ltd
Burton-on-Trent, Staffordshire. (Tel. 0283 45320.)

Aluminium Extruders Association
Integrated Marketing Services, Whitegates, Rudge Heath Road, Claverley,
Wolverhampton WV5 7DJ. (Tel. 074 66310.)

Anglian Water
Ambury Road, Huntingdon, Cambridgeshire PE18 6NZ. (Tel. 0480 56181.)

The Association of Agriculture
Victoria Chambers, 16–20 Strutton Ground, London SW1D 2HP.
(Tel. 01–222 6115.)

The Association of the British Pharmaceutical Industry
12 Whitehall, London SW1A 2DY. (Tel. 01–930 3290.)

Bass Brewing Ltd
137 High Street, Burton-on-Trent, Staffordshire DE14 1JZ. (Tel. 0283 45301.)

The Brewers' Society
Technical Secretary, 42 Portman Square, London W1. (Tel. 01–486 4831.)

BP Educational Service (for enquiries)
Britannic House, Moor Lane, London EC2Y 9BU. (Tel. 01–920 6100.)

BP Educational Service (for ordering materials)
PO Box 5, Wetherby, West Yorkshire LS23 7EH. (Tel. 0937 843477.)

British Agrochemicals Association
93 Albert Embankment, London SE1 7TU. (Tel. 01–735 8471.)

British Ceramics Manufacturers' Federation
Federation House, Station Road, Stoke-on-Trent ST4 2SA. (Tel. 0782 48631.)

British Gas Education Service
Room 707A, 326 High Holborn, London WC1V 7PT. (Tel. 01–242 0789.)

British Museum (Natural History)
Cromwell Road, London SW7 5BD. (Tel. 01–589 6323.)

British Steel Corporation
9 Albert Embankment, London SE1 7SN. (Tel. 01–735 7654.)

British Sugar Bureau
140 Park Lane, London W1Y 3AA. (Tel. 01–493 4546.)

Central Electricity Generating Board
Sudbury House, 15 Newgate Street, London EC1A 7AU. (Tel. 01–248 1202.)

Centre for World Development Education
128 Buckingham Palace Road, London SW1W 9SH. (Tel. 01–730 8332.)

Chloride Motive Power
PO Box 1, Salford Road, Bolton, Lancashire BL5 1DD. (Tel. 0204 64111.)

Copper Development Association
Orchard House, Mutton Lane, Potters Bar, Hertfordshire EN6 3AP.
(Tel. 0707 50711.)

Cystic Fibrosis Research Trust
Department PD 130, Alexandra House, 5 Blyth Road, Bromley, Kent BR1 3RS.
(Tel. 01–464 7211.)

Davis Gelatine Division
Upper Grove Street, Leamington Spa, Warwickshire CV32 5AN.
(Tel. 0926 22795.)

De Beers Diamond Information Office
Saffron House, 11 Saffron Hill, London EC11 8RA. (Tel. 01–404 4444.)

Department of Energy
Information Division, Thames House South, Millbank, London SW1P 4QJ.
(Tel. 01–211 3000.)

The Distillers Co. Ltd
20 St James's Square, London SW1Y 4JF. (Tel. 01–930 1040.)

Duracell UK
Crawley, West Sussex RH11 0ZB. (Tel. 0293 517527.)

Education Productions Ltd.
89 St Fagan's Road, Fairwater, Cardiff CF5 3AE. (Tel. 0222 554760.)

Educational Service of the Plastics and Rubber Institute (ESPRI)
Department of Creative Design, University of Technology, Loughborough,
Leicestershire LE1 13T (Tel. 0509 232065.)

The Electricity Council
30 Millbank, London SW1P 4RD. (Tel. 01–834 2333.)

Esso Petroleum Co. Ltd
Esso House, Victoria Street, London SW1E 5JW. (Tel. 01–834 6677.)

Ever Ready Ltd
1255 High Road, Whetstone, London N20 0EJ. (Tel. 01–446 1313.)

The Farm and Food Society
4 Willifield Way, London NW11 7XT. (Tel. 01–455 0634.)

Fertilizer Manufacturers' Association Ltd
Greenhill House, 90–93 Cowcross Street, London EC1M 6BH.
(Tel. 01–251 6001.)

Friends of the Earth Ltd
377 City Road, London EC1V 1NA. (Tel. 01–837 0731.)

Glass Manufacturers' Federation
19 Portland Place, London W1N 4BH. (Tel. 01–580 6952.)

The Green Party
10 Station Parade, Balham High Road, London SW12. (Tel. 01–673 0045.)

Greenpeace Ltd
36 Graham Street, London N1. (Tel. 01–608 1461.)

Green's of Brighton
Consumer Relations Department, 315 Portland Road, Hove, East Sussex, BN3 5ST. (Tel. 0273 417275.)

Arthur Guinness Son and Co. (Park Royal) Ltd
Park Royal Brewery, London NW10 7RR. (Tel. 01–965 7700.)

Health Education Authority
78 New Oxford Street, London WC1A 1AH. (Tel. 01–631 0930.)

ICI Agricultural Division
PO Box 1, Billingham, Cleveland TS23 1LB. (Tel. 0642 553601.)

ICI Educational Publications
PO Box 96, 1 Hornchurch Close, Coventry, West Midlands CV1 2QZ. (Tel. 0203 57272.)

ICI Education Liaison Officer
PO Box 6, Bessemer Road, Welwyn Garden City, Hertfordshire AL7 1HD. (Tel. 07073 23400.)

ICI Mond Division
PO Box 14, Runcorn, Cheshire. (Tel. 0928 511111.)

ICI Petrochemicals and Plastics Division
PO Box 54, Wilton Works, Middlesbrough, Cleveland TS6 8JE. (Tel. 0642 455522.)

Institute of Biology
20 Queensbury Place, London SW7 2DZ. (Tel. 01–581 8333.)

Institute of Physics
The Education Officer, 47 Belgrave Square, London SW1X 8QX. (Tel. 01–235 6111.)

Institution of Metallurgists
Northway House, High Road, Whetstone, London N20 9LW. (Tel. 01–446 2251.)

JET Joint Undertaking
Abingdon, Oxon OX14 3EA. (Tel. 0235 28822.)

Keep Britain Tidy Group
Bostel House, 37 West Street, Brighton BN1 2RE. (Tel. 0273 23585.)

Kodak Limited
Photo Information Services, PO Box 66, Hemel Hempstead, Hertfordshire, HP1 1JU. (Tel. 0442 61122.)

Lead Development Association
34 Berkeley Square, London W1X 6AJ. (Tel. 01–499 8422.)

London Brick Company Ltd
Public Relations Officer, Stewartby, Bedford, MK43 9LZ. (Tel. 0234 851851.)

Metal Box Ltd
Queens House, Forbury Road, Reading, Berkshire. RG1 3JH. (Tel 0734 581177.)

Mineral Industry Manpower and Careers Unit
Prince Consort Road, London SW7 2BP. (Tel. 01–584 7397.)

National Centre for Alternative Technology
Llwyngwern Quarry, Machynlleth, Powys. (Tel. 0654 2400.)

National Coal Board
Hobart House, Grosvenor Place, London SW1X 7AE. (Tel. 01–235 2020.)

National Dairy Council
National Dairy Centre, John Princes Street, London W1M 0AP.
(Tel. 01–499 7822.)

National Society for Clean Air
136 North Street, Brighton BN1 1RG. (Tel. 0273 26313.)

Oxfam (for "Poverty game")
Oxfam Youth Department, 274 Banbury Road, Oxford.

Pilkington Glass Ltd
Group Public Relations Department, Prescot Road, St Helens, Merseyside
WA10 3TT. (Tel. 0744 28800.)

Reed Group Ltd
Public Relations Department, New Hythe House, New Hythe Lane, Aylesford,
Maidstone, Kent ME20 7PB. (Tel. 0622 77777.)

Royal National Institute for the Blind
For Braille texts: 224 Great Portland Street, London W1N 6AA.
(Tel. 01–388 1266.)
For Moon texts: Moon Branch, Holmesdale Road, Reigate, Surrey RH2 0BA.
(Tel. 0737 246333.)

The Royal Mint
Llantrisant, Pontyclun, Mid Glamorgan. (Tel. 0443 222111.)

The Royal Society of Chemistry (Education Officer)
30 Russell Square, London WC1B 5DT. (Tel. 01–631 1355.)

The Royal Society of Chemistry (Distribution Centre)
Blackhorse Road, Letchworth, Hertfordshire SG6 1HN. (Tel. 04626 72555.)

RTZ Services Ltd
PO Box 133, 6 St James's Square, London SW1Y 4LD. (Tel. 01–930 2399.)

Shell Education Service
Shell UK Ltd, Shell-Mex House, Strand, London WC2R 0DX.
(Tel. 01–257 3000.)

Science Museum
Exhibition Road, South Kensington, London SW7. (Tel. 01–589 3456.)

TEAR Fund
100 Church Road, Teddington, Middlesex TW11 8QE.

Thames Water
Nugent House, Vastern Road, Reading, Berkshire. (Tel. 0734 593704.)

Unilever Educational Publications
PO Box 68, Unilever House, London EC4P 4BQ. (Tel. 01–822 5252.)

United Kingdom Atomic Energy Authority
Information Services Branch, 11 Charles II Street, London SW1Y 4QP.
(Tel. 01–930 5454, extensions 368 and 479.)

The United Yeast Co. Ltd
Collingwood House, 819 London Road, North Cheam, Sutton, Surrey
SM3 9AT. (Tel. 01–337 6633.)

The Wiggins Teape Group Ltd
PO Box 88, Gateway House, Basing View, Basingstoke, Hampshire RG21 2EE.
(Tel. 0256 20262.)

The Zinc Development Association
34 Berkeley Square, London W1X 6AJ. (Tel. 01–499 6636.)

Sources of further addresses

Chemical Industry Education Centre
c/o The Chemistry Department, University of York, York YO1 5DD.

Education in Chemistry
Published bimonthly by The Royal Society of Chemistry, Burlington House, London W1V 0BN. (Tel. 01–437 8656.)

Education in Physics
Published bimonthly by the Institute of Physics, 47 Belgrave Square, London SW1X 8QX.

Education in Science
Published five times a year by the Association for Science Education, College Lane, Hatfield, Hertfordshire AL10 9AA. (Tel. 07072 67411.)

Goldmine
A catalogue of resources for teachers, published by David Brown, 62 Newland Road, Worthing, West Sussex BN11 1JX.

The School Science Review
Published quarterly by the Association for Science Education.

STEAM
Published by ICI Educational Publications, PO Box 96, 1 Hornchurch Close, Coventry, West Midlands CV1 2QZ. (Tel. 0203 57272.)
(*STEAM 8*, autumn 1987, contains a detailed address list.)

Chemistry: practical evaluation

Some of the Chemistry practical work was more widely tested.

A detailed evaluation of the whole programme of practical work was carried out by Roger Norris of Wymondham College.

In addition, useful comment and advice was received from groups of PGCE students who tested selected experiments:

London Institute of Education, working under Brendan Schollum:
Mehboob Ahmed, David Colledge, Terry Gould, Nicky Greenbat, Jennifer Hiew, Jeff Hoadley, Josephine Percival, Kerry Ridpath, Gurdip Sagoo, Alison Spurling, Dawn Webster, Andrew Wooley, Nuei Yu

Sheffield City Polytechnic, working under Bill Harrison:
Ian Campbell, Shamima Ditta, K. J. Garner, Ron Green, Keith Young

St Mary's College, Twickenham, working under Tim Brosnan:
David Horsan, John Mollins, John O'Driscoll, Paul Sexton, Neil Young.

Index